From the Greek Mimes
to Marcel Marceau and Beyond

From the Greek Mimes
to Marcel Marceau and Beyond

Mimes, Actors, Pierrots, and Clowns

A Chronicle of the Many Visages
of Mime in the Theatre

ANNETTE BERCUT LUST

FOREWORD BY MARCEL MARCEAU

The Scarecrow Press, Inc.
Lanham, Maryland, and London
2000

SCARECROW PRESS, INC.

Published in the United States of America
by Scarecrow Press, Inc.
4720 Boston Way, Lanham, Maryland 20706
http://www.scarecrowpress.com

4 Pleydell Gardens, Folkestone
Kent CT20 2DN, England

British Library Cataloguing in Publication Information Available

Library of Congress Cataloging-in-Publication Data

Lust, Annette.
    From the Greek mimes to Marcel Marceau and beyond : mimes, actors,
Pierrots, and clowns : a chronicle of the many visages of mime in
the theatre / Annette Lust ; foreword by Marcel Marceau.
        p.   cm.
    Filmography: p.
    Includes bibliographical references and index.
    ISBN 0-8108-3510-X (cloth : alk. paper)
    1. Mime—History.   I. Title
PN1942.L87   2000
    792.3'09—dc21
                                                                98-37892
                                                                CIP

∞™ The paper used in this publication meets the minimum requirements of American National Standard for Information Sciences—Permanence of Paper for Printed Library Materials, ANSI/NISO Z39.48–1992. Manufactured in the United States of America.

For Jean and My Loving Family

Contents

Appendixes

Foreword

In mime Dionysus, Apollo, and Krishna meet. So do Charlie Chaplin, Buster Keaton, Laurel and Hardy, Harold Lloyd, and Harry Langdon. In vaudeville, silent films, and the circus, actors and clowns such as the Marx Brothers, Red Skelton, Danny Kaye, Jerry Lewis, Grock, Emmett Kelly, Pipo, Rhum, Alex, the Fratellini Brothers, Popov, Dimitri, and the famous Moscow Circus clowns have emerged. We must not forget the nineteenth-century prince of grimaces and clownish attitudes, Grimaldi, as well as the Hanlon-Lees, the Deburau father and son, and their disciples Séverin, Louis Rouffe, and Georges Wague, along with the school of French Pierrots. There are also the Italian Arlequins, such as Marcello Moretti and the contemporary Ferruccio Soleri of the Piccolo Teatro of Milan. In Europe many mime companies have emerged since the 1960s, such as those of Henryk Tomaszewski in Poland and Ladislav Fialka in the Czech Republic, as well as those of the Russian mimes of Moscow and St. Petersburg.

With these mimes and others, we enter the temple of the Theatre of the Marvelous, where mime reveals Eternal and Ephemeral Humanity in its most secret and profound aspirations. Mime throws full light on man alone in an instant of truth, torn among space, silence, and time in an attempt to capture love, life, and beauty before the supreme moment of death. The mime is also one who, after giving brilliance and significance to attitude and action, throws out the inner cry of the soul. It is the mime in this dark world who, having sewn up his mouth and torn out his tongue, has received in exchange the grace of silence; that is why the mime will remain the true witness of the human condition.

This study on the art of mime is a useful one, not only for its documentary value, but also for the impressions of the movement forms and artists that Madame Annette Lust has gathered after analyzing what the latter have in common or what differentiates them.

Marceau's Bip has toured throughout the world since 1955, at first with the faithful Pierre Verry—who seemed to step out of a drawing by Honoré Daumier or Jacques Callot—and then with students drawn from my Ecole Internationale de Mimodrame in Paris, proving mime to be an art that goes beyond the barriers of language because neither laughter nor tears are French, English, Russian, or Japanese. The mime–actor belongs to all people, whatever their religion, race, or nationality. Today in the contemporary theatre mime has gone in many different directions.

Mime has become popular in North American universities and colleges, and different mime companies have emerged, such as the Goldston and Johnson Company in Ohio, called The Invisible People. The public has grown more exacting and critical. The fueds between certain mimes, the differences between styles and schools that create a certain sectarianism, are important, for it is through conflict that mime shows new force and galvanizes its resources. This is also important for our new research. A number of books on mime have been published throughout the world. Annette Lust also has shown a great interest in the life of the mime theatre; as the reader will see, her competence is outstanding and, as she demonstrates, without the contribution of mime, the theatre today would lose much of its power.

Marcel Marceau

Preface

Very few accounts of the diverse forms and aesthetic trends of the art of mime down through the centuries have reached us. Until the motion-picture camera was invented, there was no satisfactory means of recording and preserving this art. Although there are accounts of the skills of the Roman mimes and the commedia dell'-arte actors during the epochs in which they flourished, there are other periods, as in the early Middle Ages, without even the most meager records. At times, too, mime lowered itself to the coarse buffoonery of the late Roman Empire and the facile grimaces of the circus and the music hall. Yet this art often rose to great heights with mimes such as Pylades the Roman and Bathyllus of Alexandria, as well as in the pantomimes of Gaspard Deburau and Marcel Marceau.

Ancient Greek saltation (dance-mime-theatre) itself was born from rhythmical movement that united with expressive gesture to create effects more powerful than either element could produce alone; the pity and the terror of ancient Greek drama were the achievements of actor–dancers whose voices as well as physical expressions could match the genius of a Sophocles or a Euripides. In fact, so close was mime to dramatic art among the Greeks and Romans that the ancient writers described an actor as miming a play rather than acting it out. The very origin of the word theatre, from the Greek *theasthai* (signifying "behold"), suggests that this art was as visual as it was auditory.

Mime gave birth through religious rites and liturgy to the theatre and to dance. These two arts cannot be separated from that essentially dynamic, expressive nature that is a silent yet so vital part of themselves. And, even if mime and pantomime have come to be understood as acting without words, it should not be forgotten that, just as the ancient Greeks viewed it, mime has always been intrinsic to verbal theatre and to dance. In the order of creation, gestures preceded speech, religious dance originated the hymn, and expressive movement was adjoined to dance. Whenever this origin was forgotten and mime died on stage, it still remained a part of everyday expression. Here, no matter how imperceptible, it continued to generate and accompany spoken language. By the same token, it is vital to all veritable theatre, in which, rather than stagnate in lifeless verbalization, the spoken word must continually *be* — that is, give birth to dynamic action.

Because I believe that the forefather of the playwright is the dancer and that theatre was born from gestures, movement, and dance as the body went in search of the idea (Alain 1931, chap. 2), I also recognize the significant role of mime in dance. In Greco–Roman times, mime and dance formed one art and were separated only when form became more important than dramatic content, as in classical ballet from the sixteenth century on. In the late twentieth century, mime and dance began to blend to give birth to dance–mime and dance–theatre, which had little in common with dance at the beginning of the century, with the exception of the research of Mary Wigman and Martha Graham, who reaffirmed the importance of expressive movement in dance. However, for reasons of space, I have not been able to extend my findings on dance or on other forms of world theatre. And, for the same reasons, I have barely touched upon the arts of the circus, music hall, puppetry, and cinema, in which the movement and the gestures of Clown, Punch and Judy, and Charlie Chaplin, who belong to all times, depict the entire scale of human emotions.

I also would have liked to devote more pages to what is referred to as total theatre, where movement is given due importance. I believe that total theatre embraces, in Edward Gordon Craig's words, "gestures which are the soul of acting, words which are the body of the play, lines and colors which comprise the very existence of the scenery, and rhythm which is the essence of dance," each of these elements being of equal importance (1943, 104–5). In this respect, such works as Jacqueline Martin's *Voice in Modern Theatre* (1991) that explore postmodern directorial visions that experiment with integrating voice with gestures and other visual elements are invaluable.

Modern theatre theoreticians, from Jacques Copeau to Antonin Artaud, Jerzy Grotowski, Eugenio Barba, Ariane Mnouchkine, and Peter Brook, recognize that the actor's physical presence on stage cannot be denied and that his movement is a necessary source for the creation of his character. The actor also well knows that the most moving aspects of a characterization are often expressed through a gesture performed in silence or through an inflection of the voice accompanied by expressive movement. As the Jesuit playwright Franz Lang wrote in his manual on acting, *Dissertio de Actione Scenica* (1727), "a profound sadness needs no words and is better expressed by silence, or by a short exclamation, a sigh or a moan" (Evreinoff 1947, 100). Our memory retains far longer those exterior signs that reflect the inner movements of the actor's soul and that charm with their grace—grace that, in the words of Raymond Bayer, "is movement and within movement is ease" (1933, 33).

After the 1950s, a growing interest in the visual arts developed in the United States and Europe. Expressive movement became more and more adjoined to verbal theatre, as well as to dance. The study of mime began to be incorporated into acting, dance, and physical education programs and into the curricula of drama schools and acting companies. An increasing interest in nonverbal communication brought about the expansion of numerous movement training methods and martial arts programs. Research on body movement and language also increased in the fields of psychology, anthropology, and biology. Mime not only had an artistic and educational flourishing, but grew as a form of therapy. Persons with physical and emotional illnesses benefited from the creative self-expression process in miming as well as clowning. The Theatre of the Deaf is a shining example of hearing-impaired persons who since the 1960s have found growth and fulfillment in developing their natural skills through the practice of mime.

As mime forms have multiplied, factions have arisen between the practitioners of so-called mime and pantomime, between the practitioners of abstract and traditional techniques and expressions, between the practitioners of pure mime and those who adjoin mime to text, dance, or other movement forms. And within these factions, differences in the use of the terms mime, pantomime, theatre of gestures, etc., have bred misunderstanding and confusion.

I hope that from awareness of this growing multiplicity of movement forms and confusion of terms will come a solid body of knowledge, clarifications and clearer definitions, and a common vocabulary to describe the artistic values of its practitioners. This, along with the development of qualified mime critics and mime criticism, would expand this art form, which has not had the same exposure or means of growth as, for example, dance and theatre. It is my aspiration that there will be findings beyond my present gropings, along with a keener appreciation of this art — so ancient but never ceasing to be reborn.

In the above respects might my book serve as a reference for scholars of movement theatre, theatre, and dance–theatre and as a tool for critics in theatre arts. Might it also offer a sense of roots to those movement theatre artists who, unlike actors and dancers, work in isolation.

My love affair with mime has spanned a period of nearly fifty years. It began in the late 1940s, when I chose this subject for my doctoral thesis at the University of Paris. After receiving my doctorate in 1950, I continued to observe and record the development of mime styles in Europe and North America by viewing companies and artists in various countries, on stage and screen, at schools and workshops, and at national and international mime and clown festivals, publishing articles, and revised and updating my thesis to convert it into a book. I have witnessed many changes in the field during the nearly five decades I have been documenting my research, from Decroux-, Marceau-, and Lecoq-style mime to Eastern European mimodrama, clown–mime, dance–mime, mime and verbal theatre, and other forms and styles of which I have attempted to give an overview.

It is far beyond my competence to advocate definitions, formulas, or systems. I have merely attempted to understand, record, and clarify some of the existing differences among styles, schools, and the artists utilizing them. I have done so while keeping in mind how difficult it is to describe in words the theatre of movement and images without losing much of its vitality.

The format I have chosen to document my observation of the mime field is mainly that of a chronicle, which is a chronological account of events without analysis or interpretation. In writing this chronicle, I have attempted to reveal the different influences, styles, and contributions of companies and artists without engaging in an in-depth critique of the artistic merit of each. And because the work of most of these artists has undergone and is still rapidly undergoing many changes, it is also difficult to foresee how it will evolve in future years. For this reason, it has not been easy to terminate my recordings to submit them to a publisher. As I write these very pages, the mime field continues to evolve, rendering the constant need to record the development of emanating forms and styles.

If this chronicle seems a disparate one containing much documentation on the many different forms and styles unrelated to central currents, it is because mime is an evasive, ever-changing survivor that has had to take on multiple roles difficult to describe. As it continues to breathe life into the theatre, it oftentimes triumphs as a visible, self-sufficient art able to function in silence alone, while at other times its inherent presence is hardly apparent.

My central thread has been to describe mime's many visages, visible or less so, throughout the centuries to reveal it as an expression that has never died and has always been present, revitalizing the theatre in eclectic and multiple ways and even proving itself essential for the very survival of the theatre as a complete art. In attempting to reveal its more subtle roles, I have tried to show that, although mime as an art form might not have been as perceptible or its function as evident during certain periods and in certain stage forms when it blended so well with other expressions that it appeared to lose its identity, its presence was still all-important. Although its role has not always been as clearly defined in, for example, the mystery and morality plays of the Middle Ages, the commedia dell'arte, Molière's farces, or even postmodern visual theatre as it was in Roman pantomime, nineteenth-century pantomime, and Etienne Decroux's corporeal mime, it has been intrinsic to the life of these and other theatre forms. How easy it is to forget, too, that mime has also been at the heart of speaking theatre, which is incomplete without it because the actor's physical presence is no less important than his vocal delivery.

My aim has thus been to document mime not only as a direct and autonomous art, more powerful than words because it can survive on its own as a non-verbal language, but also as a necessary adjunct to all forms of theatre: without it verbal theatre and great stage genres would not have known the harmony, silent poetry, and power of total dramatic expression that they achieved. Mime as a language inseparable from human communication, firmly rooted in the broader meaning of "imitation" from the Greek *mimos* and the Roman *mimus* and despite its ever-changing role as an art form, remains vital to all theatre that aims to mirror human nature.

It is my hope that the inspired reader will view the works of these and other artists and companies and that some will find it useful to utilize the veins of this chronicle as a springboard for further research. I apologize to all the mime artists and companies that I have not included since I have not had the occasion to see their work or obtain documentation of their art. There are still others who, as I write these pages, are training to become the mime and movement theatre artists of the twenty-first century.

It is also my hope that this book will bring about a deeper understanding and love of this ancient art that, each time it seemed on the verge of dying, has been revived to invent visual poetry in another fashion. In my years of researching the diverse expressions of mime in theatre, dance, and cinema, I have also come to believe that this art is too all-encompassing to be limited to mere dumb show. I do not think that mime need be autonomous from words, dance, clowning, or other forms; nor need it be referred to exclusively as the art of the mime artist rather than that of the actor, dancer, or clown. I have concluded that this art has many visages and roles, each of which is equally significant.

Lastly, I would like to thank my reader for patiently perusing these pages. But because mime must be seen rather than described, I encourage the reader to see many kinds of movement expression and to be aware of its vital role in all of the theatre arts. I would also like to invite any suggestions the reader might have to enhance my understanding of this language and art, which I believe has never ceased to be an intrinsic part of humankind's personal as well as artistic expression.

Acknowledgments

I wish to express my gratitude to all those who generously gave of their knowledge, advice, and support in the preparation of this book. Many artists, teachers, scholars, colleagues, and friends provided interviews, documentation, and aid in the compilation, editing, translation, and updating of what began as a doctoral thesis on the art of mime, submitted to the University of Paris in 1950 and for which I received my *doctorat de l'université.*

I wish, first of all, to thank my parents, grandparents, and sister, who gave me encouragement and financial support to undertake research for my doctoral thesis. I am deeply grateful to Professor Raymond Bayer, who guided me in preparing my thesis, and to Anton Giulio Bragaglia, the author of *Evolutione del Mimo*, who provided me with a wealth of documentation and illustrations on ancient mime and the commedia dell'arte.

I would like to express my special indebtedness to Etienne Decroux, who initiated me into the art of corporeal mime and generously gave of his time and writings, and to Marcel Marceau, who wrote the foreword to this book and continuously provided his enthusiastic support.

To numerous artists such as Jean-Louis Barrault, Louis Jouvet, Georges Wague, Jacques Lecoq, Mamako, and many others who deepened my understanding of theatre and mime, as well as contributed written and oral interviews, I owe my gratitude.

I am thankful to André Veinstein and Madeleine Horn Monval, who made many documents at the Bibliothèque de l'Arsenal available to me. My research would not have been complete without the assistance of the staffs of the Bibliothèque de l'Arsenal and the Bibliothèque Nationale in Paris, as well as the New York and San Francisco Public Libraries, the San Francisco Performing Arts Library and Museum, and the Centre National de la Cinématographie.

I am especially indebted to Robert Fleshman, Professor Emeritus of the Drama Department of Loyola University, New Orleans, whose guidance as consulting editor was invaluable. As editor of *Theatrical Movement: A Bibliographical Anthology*, he also invited me to submit a chapter of my book for the collection and encouraged the publication of my entire work. Thomas Leabhart, editor of the *Mime Journal* and *Mime News*; Marguerite Mathews of the *Movement Theatre Quarterly*; Achille H., Louis M., and Anthony J. Muschi of the *Swiss Journal*; and Phyllis L. Sherman of *The West of Twin Peaks Observer* published my articles on a number of the movement theatre artists in my book.

Thanks are due to Peter Bu, Giuseppe Condello, Wayne Specht, and Michael Pedretti, who invited me to write about the artists at their international mime festivals and gave interviews on mime.

Dominican College, where I have been teaching French and directing theatre productions, generously provided me with the opportunity to pursue a year's research in mime and awarded me faculty grants to attend festivals in Europe.

Madame Adrien Pol, Mona Walston, John Savant, Gregory Woodruff, Mary Adams, Barbara Scrafford, Ken Bullock, Roger Pinatel, Edmond J. Majeski, J. Barry Gurdin, and Stefania Riedl were among the friends who offered their editorial aid or assistance in obtaining information, and Magdalen Ross and Ken Bullock spent innumerable hours proofreading the original manuscript.

My deepest gratitude I owe to my husband, Jean, for his loving patience during the years of this book's preparation and for introducing me to the art of utilizing a computer and devising a format for my book. My thanks also to my three children—Jean-Claude, Eliane, and Evelyne—for their understanding and support when I was buried in my papers.

And to my drama teachers and friends—Madame Darius Milhaud, Henry Schnitzler, and Cyril Clayton, who inspired my love for the theatre—I am very grateful.

Finally, I am thankful to the numerous mimes and authors, living and dead, for their performances and writings, without which this book never would have come into existence. And to countless other mime theatre artists and teachers, whose contributions I might not have acknowledged specifically, I am profoundly indebted.

Introduction: On the Meaning of Mime and Pantomime

Are there real differences between mime and pantomime? If so, what are these differences? And how have their meanings changed throughout the centuries?

As the arts of mime and pantomime have evolved, differences have shifted and sometimes even disappeared. Both mime and pantomime stem from the word *mimesis*, an imitative process by which the primitive dancer or singer interpreted someone or something other than himself, using animal, human, or even superhuman disguises. In antiquity, mime, the ancestor of pantomime, was an imitative art that portrayed life in all of its aspects (Duckworth 1952, 14). This meaning soon became subsidiary or was ignored.

Although among the ancients expressive movement essentially comprised both mime and pantomime, the general distinction was that in mime words combined with movement. Among the Greeks and Romans, mime—from the Greek *mimos* and the Latin *mimus,* meaning "imitator"—was a short comedy written in prose or verse that portrayed life (*mimesis biou*) and consisted of expressive gestures or dances, especially among the Romans, which were more prevalent than the spoken text. It also referred to the mime–actor who performed in such a play, as well as to the buffoon who played in popular entertainments. Among the Greeks it was extended to mean anyone who made grimaces. Historian Margarete Bieber describes this dual meaning: "it was a play without masks imitating real life," but it was also "the performer in this simple drama" (1961, xiii).

Pantomime has not always been clearly distinguished from mime. In *The Dictionary of Latin Literature,* pantomime and mime have the same definition (Mantinband 1956, 208). However, pantomime—from the Greek *pantos,* meaning "all," and *mimos,* meaning "imitator"—was born when recitation and song separated from mimetic art. Among the Romans, with whom pantomime was especially popular, it denoted a performer, with different masks, playing all characters and portraying objects and animals by means of rhythmical movements and gestures while a singer or chorus accompanied him. (The Greeks more commonly called this actor–dancer *orchestes.*)

The ancient pantomime actor's art included both acting and dancing. In his essay on pantomime, Greek author Lucian describes the *pantomimus* as a dancer who is, above all, an actor (1905, 238, 256). Because his movements were expressive and rhythmical, the *saltator* (mime–dancer) among the Romans was, in effect, also a pantomimic performer. The functions of both dancer and actor are also implied by the term *histrio*, the Roman actor of tragedy and comedy, originating from the Etruscan *hister*, meaning "a performer" (Duckworth 1952, 5). The first *histriones* from Etruria were pantomimic dancers who performed to flute music. During the Roman Empire, *histrio*, *mimus*, *pantomimus,* and *ludio* (player) were often used synonymously (*A Dictionary of Greek and Roman Antiquities* 1857, 728). These terms, also allied to *saltator* (dancer) and *joculator,* or jongleur (minstrel–buffoon), were retained until the late Middle Ages (Hunninger 1961, 67–68).

During and after the Middle Ages, mime acquired several meanings. It meant not only the performer or his performance, but also the art of gesture practiced by all sorts of entertainers. By the ninth century, *mimus* implied a singer, dancer, or actor (Hunningher 1961, 72). Like the *ioculatores*, *prestigitators,* and puppeteers of the Middle Ages, they were, broadly speaking, imitators of all human things (Nicoll 1963a, 152). Similarly, the masked commedia dell'arte players of the Renaissance, who mimed, sang, and performed acrobatics, were imitators of life.

Since the sixteenth century, these meanings have expanded. Pantomime alluded (especially from the eighteenth century on) to the all-mute entertainment rather than to the performer. It also referred to the *lazzi,* or short, comic scenes in dumb show (for example, Harlequin catching flies and pulling off their wings) played by the Italian comedians. During the seventeenth and eighteenth centuries, allegorical and mythological, pageant-type ballet–pantomimes were performed at the courts and in the theatres of Europe. Among them were the Duchesse du Maine's ballet–pantomimes at Sceaux and John Weaver's staging of *The Loves of Mars and Venus* at Drury Lane in 1717. The traditional dumb show in the eighteenth- and nineteenth-century French and English melodramas, as well as the Elizabethan dumb shows, were also called pantomimes. In France, after the Italian Comedy was prohibited from playing in the official theatres, and spoken dialogues and monologues were also forbidden, pantomimes with commedia-type characters played at the Théâtres de la Foire. When staged in the English music halls at Christmas, they were called harlequinades. By the end of the nineteenth century, English Christmas pantomimes such as *Cinderella* and *Jack and the Beanstalk* contained spectacular scenic effects and popular music hall interludes with dialogue, acrobatics, singing, and dancing in which Clown had replaced Harlequin and Pierrot. The Christmas pantomime had almost no mime or dumb show. Yet even when dialogue, singing, and dancing were more predominant in such entertainments as these, they were still called pantomimes or dumb shows because they contained some element, however remote, of the technique and art of miming. In nineteenth-century England and America, pantomime was incorporated into circus acts, as in clown George Fox's (1825–77) *Humpty Dumpty* and in the performances of the Hanlon-Lees. Meanwhile, in France, Gaspard Deburau had immortalized the silent Pierrot pantomimes, which we today call *pantomime blanche* because of the whiteface worn by the artist.

Modern Meanings of Mime and Pantomime

As the text in the theatre of the nineteenth century grew more important and the actor's voice and diction were singled out, his movement training was neglected. On the other hand, during that same century mime became a specialized art. And although twentieth-century mimes retained much of the conventional nineteenth-century meaning of pantomime or acting without words, it grew to be a nonliterary, silent entertainment in which the mime artist created his own particular style. The mime, for example, of Marcel Marceau differs considerably from that of the Mummenschanz Theatre or Henryk Tomaszewski's Polish Mime Theatre.

What, then, are the modern meanings of mime and pantomime? On one hand, the terms "mime" and "pantomime" have continued to be used interchangeably. In Walter Bowman and Robert Ball's *Theatre Language Dictionary*, mime is a synonym for pantomime (1961, 248). Yet, because of the impetus of the twentieth-century French school of mime, as traditional nineteenth-century pantomime evolved into modern whiteface pantomime and other mime forms, a keener awareness of movement developed in all the theatre arts, with similarities and differences becoming more apparent. In the lineage of mime forms—from whiteface pantomime to abstract–corporeal mime, for example—the mime used no words, sets, costumes, or props. In the mime–actor's expressive movement, concrete content combined not only with sets, costumes, and props, but also with words. Various codified expressions and techniques developed, and definitions varied according to school, practitioner, and personal style. These definitions became as divergent as the mimes practicing them.

The following descriptions manifest the changing perceptions of the terms mime and pantomime and how their meanings were modified according to different periods, artists, and teachers.

François Delsartre, whose research during the mid-nineteenth century rendered movement more natural and meaningful and had repercussions on twentieth-century mime and dance, broadly describes pantomimic movement as "the conveying realistically of emotions, dramatic episodes, human situations, and activities without the use of words. It also deals with space and direction" (Shawn 1963, 71–72). Although today the principles of Delsartre's system might seem outdated, his definition encompasses much of modern mime and pantomime.

At the turn of the century, French mime Georges Wague rejected nineteenth-century classical pantomime (made popular by Gaspard Deburau and which had grown stereotyped by translating each word or idea literally into gestures) for a more spontaneous form that he developed and called "modern pantomime."

For Jean-Louis Barrault later in the twentieth century, both mime and pantomime refer to a purely silent art that depicts actions through gestures and movements; they are, in Barrault's words, "really the same thing—the art of gesture." Yet he distinguishes between popular, traditional pantomime of the second half of the nineteenth century and twentieth-century mime. Popular, traditional, nineteenth-century pantomime is a "dumb or mute art" in which gestures substitute for words. Twentieth-century mime is a silent art that does not, like the older, conventional pantomime, rely on a limited gesture language—however eloquent. It is lyrical and spontaneous, forever seeking new movements, new gestures, and aspiring to a more intense and poetic expression. Even twentieth-century pantomime often comments on the action through a mute language that renders it naive and antiquated. And while pantomime deals more often with comedy, mime has a noble quality and excels in expressing the tragic (Barrault 1996, 179–80).

Mime and pantomime, for mime master Jacques Lecoq, also belong to the art of gesture. However, while pantomime translates spoken language into movement, as in the Deburau codes of the nineteenth century, and while traditional pantomime belongs to a particular period and today has value mainly as a teaching technique, mime is a silent language that precedes, accompanies, or follows the spoken word when it is present.

Finding more similarities than differences in mime and pantomime, Bob Fleshman of Loyola University in New Orleans compares all theatrical movement to music, of which there are many kinds: serious and playful, commercial and artistic — but all are music. However, "mime, potentially a more serious form than pantomime, can express a greater view of life with more depth and subtlety than pantomime. Pantomime seems more audience-oriented. Just as clowning, it is a popular art form giving much joy but asking little. Some dramatic forms require an audience with a certain knowledge and special sensitivity. Such is the case with mime."[1]

Ronnie Davis, founder of the San Francisco Mime Troupe, compares the pantomimist to the dancer and the mime to the actor. "The pantomimist, usually masked and mute, moves to music and deals with nothing there. The mime, who may even speak or sing, moves to act and uses tangible props, manipulating their symbolism to comment on the story. The pantomimist charms his spectator, who wonders, 'What does he have there?' Even when the mime works with tangible objects, he stimulates his spectator to ask himself, 'What does he have there [and what does it] mean?'" (Passman 1973, 40). For Davis, Marcel Marceau is basically a pantomimist who sometimes engages in mime and Charlie Chaplin is a mime who deals with tangible objects.

Mime and pantomime can be differentiated by a movement form's concrete or abstract, poetic quality. David Alberts, author of *Pantomime: Elements and Exercises,* believes that "pantomime depends upon accurately described objects, action, situations and events to tell a story while mime, even if it tells a story, depicts a theme more implicitly and abstractly. Mime has a greater potential for diversity, for responsive imagination, and a broader range of subject matter" (1971, 54–55). Mime–clown Don Reider adds that pantomime replaces words with gestures similar to signals, while silence in mime, which is on a deeper level and not as "talky," increases its potential to express visual poetry.

For teacher and author Thomas Leabhart, pantomime portrays a specific character in a specific situation (Marceau's *Bip Chases the Butterfly*) in which the face and hands have more importance. It is individualized and charming; the typical posture is crouched, knees bent, the mime moving backward with small movements. Mime depicts universal man in a universal situation or in one that is symbolic of a universal idea, as in Etienne Decroux's *Love Duet, Carpenter* and *Combat.* Thus, while pantomime is personal, mime is impersonal; the face is masked or mask-like and subordinate to the expression of the total body.[2] Leabhart also differentiates between abstract mime and Decroux's corporeal mime. Rather than depict a character or object concretely, the abstract mime artist evokes the dynamics of the body's inner spirit. In corporeal mime, though he expresses a concrete situation with movements of his total body, the artist evokes symbols of broader ideas and conflicts.

Although mime, pantomime, theatre of gestures, movement theatre, and other terms have taken on particular meanings ("pantomime" refers to antic mime and nineteenth-century, Deburau-type pantomime, and "mime" to Decroux-type mime), for mime specialist Peter Bu they are all synonyms. Bu, author of an essay entitled "Mimes, Clowns, and the Twentieth Century?" in *Mime Journal* (1983, 19–58), prefers the term mime theatre rather than *théâtre gestuel* ("gestural" theatre or theatre of gestures), corporeal theatre, movement theatre, or other terms to designate all theatre that incorporates mime, from Deburau to Decroux and beyond, in which the performers express uniquely or principally through their bodies—that is, through gestures, mimicry, and attitudes (1983, 9–11). There should be no frontiers between forms in which mimes make use of no other means except gestures, mimicry, attitudes, and other kinds of gestural theatre. Why must mimes no longer be mimes if at times they speak, sing, dance, or perform with marionettes, provided that their gestures, facial expressions, and attitudes predominate? (The opera does not cease to be opera even if the singers at times speak or if dancers appear.) However, when gestures, words, songs, dance, and/or puppets are incorporated equally, this is no longer mime, spoken, musical, dance, or puppet theatre but total theatre. Bu's definition of mime breaches barriers between mime as a specialized art and multiple kinds of physical theatre.[3]

In addition to these individual distinctions, mime and pantomime are related to acting, dancing, and clowning. Today mime is sometimes used synonymously with acting. In Bowman and Ball's *Theatre Language Dictionary*, mime is defined first as "to act" and then as "especially to act in pantomime" (1961, 220). Pantomime is described as "expressive movement in acting sometimes called stage action or business" (1961, 248). Jacques Lecoq defines a mime as an actor who moves better. Richmond Shepard, author of *Mime: The Technique of Silence*, sees mime as acting in stylized form (1971, 4). For Paul Curtis, while mime is any kind of silent acting, pantomime is the art of creating an illusion of reality through imaginary objects and situations.[4]

Early in the twentieth century, mime–dancer Angna Enters pointed out that for the Greeks there was always a true union among pantomime, mime, and dance and that Greek dance contained expressive movement that one could call mime (1951, 86). In modern dance, the work of François A. Delsartre and Rudolf Laban brought about a growing awareness of the importance of gestures and expressive movement. Laban, the inventor of Labanotation (the method of notation for classical and modern ballet), believed that the stage arts developed from mime and that music in dance and speech in drama are movement forms that have become audible (1971, 99). Artists such as Charles Weidman relate their gifts as dancers to their talents as mimes.

We often forget the role of mime in clowning. The clown is defined as a comic performer who wears an outlandish costume and make-up and entertains by pantomiming common situations or actions in exaggerated or ridiculous fashion, as well as by juggling or tumbling (*Random House Dictionary* 1961, 280–81). Although clown pantomime contains more slapstick and farcical gestures, it is still a form of physical theatre. Even as early as the eighteenth century, Grimaldi, the father of today's circus clown, mimed as well as spoke. Inspired by the commedia dell'arte, mime served to enhance his clown character. In the early twentieth century, Charlie Chaplin and Buster Keaton derived their comic effects from mime–clownery. Clowns today are more aware of the importance of mime in their art, and a number of mime schools, such as that of Jacques Lecoq, have incorporated clowning techniques into mime training. Hovey Burgess, author of *Circus Techniques* (1976), believes that most good clowns are either natural or trained mimes. Lecoq-trained Avner the Eccentric combines miming and clowning in his clown shows. Clown–mime Ronlin Foreman feels that mime training gives the clown more artistic as well as physical strength and a better understanding of how the body speaks.

Although these definitions vary, one could broadly summarize all mime forms, whether stylized and symbolic or natural and spontaneous, as expressive movement brought into play by the mime artist, actor, dancer, or clown. However, whenever mime or pantomime is an autonomous form obeying only its own laws, it is an art belonging to the mime artist rather than to the actor, dancer, or clown who harmonizes it with a spoken text, dance steps, or clowning. How, then, can the various forms within the arts of mime and pantomime be described? While autonomous, concrete, and occupational illusion-type movement characterizes pantomime, non-illusion and nonstylized movement and the use of props and sets typify the actor; universal and figurative or metaphorical movement typify the abstract–corporeal mime performer. In abstract–corporeal mime, as in pantomime, movement is not subsidiary to a spoken text or to any other element, such as dance movement, which depends on a musical score. But abstract–corporeal mime differs from pantomime in that it depicts neither object illusions nor a specific character or anecdote. It also differs from the mime of the actor who plays with real objects and concrete movement, as in the silent films of Buster Keaton or Harold Lloyd. Rather, abstract–corporeal mime expresses universal emotions and ideas by means of nontraditional and figurative or metaphorical movement. Examples of abstract–corporeal mime, in which the total body's movements convey universal emotions and ideas, are Étienne Decroux's *The Factory* and Jean-Louis Barrault's *Maladie, Agonie, Mort.* What, then, are the differences between abstract and corporeal mime, which, though they differ from pantomime, are not always easily distinguishable from one another? When mime conveys inner intention and mood through a transfiguration of universal emotions and ideas rather than by means of concrete objects, specific situations, or specific characters, it is described as abstract or nonrepresentational, as in Marcel Marceau's *The Hands*. And when it expresses emotions and ideas through nontraditional movements of the total body, refusing the conventional use of facial expressions and arm and hand movements, it is called corporeal, as in all of Decroux's pieces. In direct contrast to abstract–corporeal mime, which throughout this chapter and book refers mainly to Decroux-style mime, is the denotative expression of nineteenth-century traditional pantomime, in which familiar pantomimic conventions transferred from father to son or from mime to mime. Modern examples are Marceau's Bip and certain Style Pantomimes, which, though they do not represent the denotative expression of nineteeth-century pantomime, still contain occupational movements and gestures that give the illusion of the presence of concrete, specific, and familiar objects, persons, and action (*Bip at a Society Party*, *The Public Garden*).

Regarding this summary of general distinctions, mime–actor Leonard Pitt offers clear definitions of pantomime, which is based on conventional object illusions; mime, which deals with real objects and specific characters; and abstract–corporeal mime, which is nonrepresentational and universal:

> Pantomime is best defined by its use of the object illusion. This is its essence, the primary element that distinguishes it from mime. Without the object illusion there is no pantomime. The illusions created are of conventional objects we are all familiar with; rope, stairway, or door. Because objects are conventional and characters all have a specific identity, the expression of pantomime is literal rather than abstract. The anecdotes make up the stories which can happen to all of us. These elements are exemplified in Marceau's Bip Pantomimes. The pantomimist ingeniously changes from one role to another, cleverly creating a world out of nothing. The audience delights in seeing some-

thing that isn't there and is more than willing to give itself up to this world of make-believe. This quality of magic and fantasy is pantomime's greatest appeal.

Generally speaking, there are two types of mime, literal and abstract. Two good examples of literal mime are Charlie Chaplin and Dimitri the Clown. Rather than creating the illusion of an object, they use the actual object and relate to it only as long as it serves as a vehicle for the story. The object is never an end in itself. Rather than the spectators focusing on what is not there, they are allowed to focus on what is being communicated.

Abstract mime seeks to express the universals of human experience without referring to the specifics of character, plot, or anecdote. This is true in Decroux's corporeal mime or in the work of Mummenschanz. Although the two differ in many ways, the main thrust of their expression is abstract. In a corporeal mime piece which revolves around the illusion of an object there is no attempt to tell a story, as in Decroux's *The Carpenter*, which explores the movements of the human body as it adapts to the weight and function of the objects. The movements are economized and heightened to reveal the dynamic relationship between the body and the object. In other pieces which do not revolve around an object illusion, a theme is chosen and elaborated upon within the highly stylized movement of corporeal mime. The emotional and psychological states of mind being expressed are real, but do not refer to specific individuals or situations. Whereas in pantomime the focus would be on the specific character and the events which surround his predicament, like losing a job, etc., the corporeal mime would seek to articulate the inner dynamic rhythms of the emotion or state of mind as they are common to all. The abstract expression goes beyond the individual toward the universal, as in the Mummenschanz Company where, although their work has none of the stylization or "esprit classique" of the corporeal mime, it nevertheless emphasizes the universality of human interaction without relying on the specifics of a given situation. In their pieces with animal and insect movements they go beyond abstraction and express the very essence of organic intelligence, perception, and response.

When I see the wide variety of performances which fall under the heading of mime I wonder if there is any such thing as mime. Perhaps fifteen or twenty years ago it would have been easier to render definitions, but today where the boundaries between the various performance types have dissolved to give us mime–ballet, mime–theatre, dance–clowning, clown–theatre, etc., the task of drawing clear cut lines is difficult. What we do have today is physical theatre, a theatre rooted in the body and developed from improvisation rather than one derived from a written script.

If there is a thing called mime, it is really a pool of physical skills from which evolves a vocabulary of expression which can be applied to any type of performance. Possessing this vocabulary consists in being able to tap one's own physical and psychological energy and knowing how to articulate this energy in every part of the body. Although the springboard for the mime is essentially physical, it is not only limited to the body. All the different aspects of theatre can be used, including the spoken word.[5]

We can more concretely understand the differences between mime and pantomime by imagining the same dramatic action in a pantomime, a play or a film, and an abstract–corporeal mime piece. A pantomimist playing a given character and action—for instance, a prisoner desperately pounding on a prison wall—would create the illusion of an imaginary wall existing in space with conventional gestures and facial expressions. In this same scene, the stage or film actor making use of literal mime would pound in despair on a real wall with nonstylized movement. Rather than pound in anguish on a specific, imaginary wall, as would the pantomimist, or on a real wall, as would the actor, the abstract–corporeal mime would utilize stylized movements through the use of all of his body and a neutral facial expression to evoke an inner emotion and a universal image of anguish, such as that of a human being's plight to suffer on earth. In the same way, while a pantomimist would pluck an imaginary flower and create the illusion of smelling it, a mime–actor on stage or screen would pluck a real flower and smell it, and an abstract–corporeal mime would convey a less literal, more universal, inner sensory appreciation with figurative or metaphorical movements of his entire body. Thus the pantomimist, with stylized, conventional movements, creates a specific illusion of objects and portrays a precise idea or emotion. The mime–actor reacts to real objects with nonstylized movements. And the performer of abstract–corporeal mime challenges the spectator's imagination by creating a universal emotion or idea with unconventional movements of his whole body. Otherwise, in corporeal mime master Etienne Decroux's words, the latter would "just be pantomime" (Avital 1973, 21).

Beyond this summary of general distinctions based on the preceding individual descriptions of nineteenth- and twentieth-century pantomime and mime, there are still more subtle and complex differences in technique and expression that are too extensive for the purposes of this chapter but will emerge in the study of mime styles and artists further on in this book.

Besides referring to a specific technique and form of expressive movement the mime, actor, dancer, clown, or theatre artist use, mime has also been regarded as the basis of all art; every creative artist has been regarded as a "specialized mime" who responds to exterior stimuli and channels his responses into some form of artistic expression (Udine 1910, xvii). If, as the ancients believed, the source of all emotion lies in the soul's movements that respond to the outer world, then these inner movements translated into art can be described, broadly speaking, as a form of mime expression. Thus the mime's gestures, though still of the same reality, are a more direct transposition of movement than, for example, the poet's words. Before he created the psalm, David is said to have danced it in front of the altar; the music of his soul was expressed first of all in the rhythms of his body, to which he later suited his psalms (Pepler 1932, 83). A painting also can be a direct and lifelike or a more abstract transposition of movement. Each painter transforms an image drawn from movements in life into color, form, line, and space, releasing his particular vision into his art (Enters 1951, 83).

In his *Anthropologie du Geste,* Marcel Jousse, who influenced mime master Jacques Lecoq, describes "mimism" as a process by which we understand objects and human beings through the body's inner replaying or "gesturizing" of them (1978, 61). Mimism (as opposed to "mimetism," which is the imitation of objects or persons) is grasping the essence of, for example, a tree—its rootings, its vertical direction—or of a human being—his rhythm, his internal space. In this same way, the artist transposes onto his canvas not the forms as they exist, but what he sees as their essence. For Jousse, man's thinking begins with corporeal reactions, and his thoughts are the "intellection" of these reactions. Language Jousse adds that developed when mimism became vocalized or when words made gestures audible. Aristotle believed that man, the most miming of animals, acquires knowledge through the process of mimism (Jousse 1978, 54–55).

After mime, pantomime, abstract–corporeal mime, and other forms of movement theatre regained popularity during the second half of the twentieth century, various styles developed and were taught in actor training, movement education, dance, and physical therapy programs. Mime was no longer a realistic art imitating life but had developed abstract, surrealistic expressions and integrated itself into other art forms. More specific definitions of mime and pantomime differentiated traditional techniques from modern and abstract techniques, and mime used autonomously was distinguished from mime combined with music, dance, verbal theatre, pictorial art, or other art forms. By the end of the twentieth century, mime and pantomime are no more exclusively a silent expression founded upon a grammar of movement. No longer providing the aesthetic definition that the words mime and pantomime evoke, they could hardly be called such. Mime and pantomime have extended themselves beyond silent corporeal expression to incorporate diverse forms of physical theatre, as well as music, song, and even verbal theatre. Conversely, they were also included in dance, clowning, and theatre forms that utilized multiple visual means, such as performance art and image theatre. This incorporation of numerous forms into mime and pantomime, as well as their presence in other kinds of theatre, rendered mime and pantomime even more difficult to identify. They resisted classification, other than such terms as "new mime" or "postmodern mime," which were loosely used and not always clearly defined.

Thus, while the modern school of art had clear definitions and codes that master teachers established, postmodernism defied such limitations. And while the modern artist saw his art as a coherent, aesthetic whole with a given structure, which endowed it with purity of expression, the postmodernist was opposed to endowing his artwork with a preconceived structure, code, or meaning. Postmodernism, which disdained absolutes, left doors open to subjective meanings and hybrid forms. Continuing the antitraditionalist thrust begun in modernism, the characteristics of postmodernism became flagrant in dance and other arts, as well as in movement theatre. And because movement theatre underwent a crossbreeding of forms and styles in a pluralistic ensemble, it was characterized by an impurity of expression. This impurity of expression derived from an unconventional blending of movement theatre with puppets, video, film, dance, performance art, and clown art. Comprised of overlapping forms, mime became an art with no boundaries and difficult to describe.

But why differentiate among mime, pantomime, abstract–corporeal mime, or other kinds of movement theatre? With the expansion of movement theatre and its fusion with other theatre arts, these terms often are loosely interchanged or characterized by ambiguous, subjective meanings. Rather than create systems and formulas that isolate schools and styles, the development of a more precise terminology would serve to more clearly delineate the techniques and expressions particular to each school and style. Clear definitions and a vocabulary of common terms that differentiate the various forms would enable mime artists, teachers, critics, and enthusiasts to better understand and appreciate them. Most importantly, an articulate means to comprehend mime not only as an autonomous art but also as an indispensable adjunct to all the stage arts would offer insight into its significant role in theatre throughout the centuries.

Although it might resist verbal limitations, mime, like other art forms, is governed by laws and principles that should be made articulate. Just as the discoveries of Sigmund Freud, Carl Jung, and Alfred Adler have been embodied in a coherent system to aid contemporary psychoanalysts, the findings of mime masters such as Etienne Decroux, Jean-Louis Barrault, Marcel Marceau, and Jacques Lecoq should be incorporated into a solid body of knowledge to aid mimes, actors, dancers, and all movement artists. Although mime and movement theatre organizations in Europe (the European Mime Federation) and in America (the National Movement Theatre Association) have made attempts to establish archives and information services for new findings in the art of mime, more documented research is needed, as well as descriptions of new styles and expressions. This would identify and stimulate further research in a fast-growing art evolving into many diverse forms and styles.

Further findings may also bring about a realization of the need—not only of each mime artist but also of each actor, clown, and dancer—to comprehend that form cannot exist without expressive content and that acting, clowning, and dancing without expression are "soulless." For only with a keener and deeper understanding of expressive movement can the mime, actor, clown, or dancer fully master his own craft, as well as perpetuate the vital role of mime in all of the theatre arts.[6]

Notes

1. Letter to author, April 1977.
2. Letter to author, September 14, 1973.
3. Letter to author, September 1992.
4. Letter to author, June 1970.
5. Letter to author, July 1981.
6. Lust 1986b, 66–78.

MAJOR DEVELOPMENTS OF THE ART OF MIME IN THE OCCIDENT AND ORIENT

	Antiquity	Middle Ages	16th Century	17th–18th Centuries	19th Century	20th Century
Egypt	Primitive In Religious Dances: Evocations to the Gods, Dancers of Osiris	Karagoz Shadow Play				
Greece	Dancers of Dionysus, Mimed Saltation, Dorian Mime Phlyakes, Mimodramas of Epicharmus, Sophron, Theocritus, Herodas, 5 B.C.–2 B.C.					
Roman Empire	Mimed Saltation, Fabula Atellana 4 B.C.–A.D. 1, Roman Pantomime A.D. 1–5					
Etruria, Italy, Spain	Etruscan Mime Dancers	Fair Buffoons, Mime–Jongleurs in Italy, Religious Plays, Processions, Gracioso (clown) in Spain	Commedia dell'Arte, Italy Farce and Mimed Ballet in Spain, Italian Comedians in Spain	Popular Italian Theatre, Vigano, Gozzi, Italy	Salvatore Petito, Carlo Blasis	Eduardo De Filippo, Toto, Angelo Musco, Leopoldo Fregoli, Dario Fo in Italy, Postmodern Mimes and Clowns

MAJOR DEVELOPMENTS OF THE ART OF MIME IN THE OCCIDENT AND ORIENT (CONTINUED)

	Antiquity	Middle Ages	16th Century	17th–18th Centuries	19th Century	20th Century
France	Mimes of Caesar	Fair Buffoons, Mime–Jongleurs, Feast of Fools, Farce, Mystery Plays 13th–16th Centuries, Soties 15th–16th Centuries	Italian Comedians Polichinelle	Molière, Ballet–pantomime, Théâtre de la Foire, Opéra Comique, Noverre, Arlequinades	Gaspard Deburau, Théâtre des Funambules, Séverin, Clown Footit and Chocolat	Georges Wague, Jacques Copeau, Antonin Artaud, Etienne Decroux, Jean-Louis Barrault, Marcel Marceau, Jacques Lecoq, Postmodern Mimes and Clowns
England	Early Sacred Plays	Gleemen, Farce, Mystery Plays, Fair Buffoons, Mime–Jongleurs	Italian Masque, Italian Comedians	Ben Jonson's Masques, Ballet Pantomime, Harlequinades, Punch, Clown	Fairy Pantomimes, Joseph Grimaldi, Théâtres de la Foire, Dan Leno	Christmas Pantomimes, Grock, Edward Gordon Craig, Sadler's Wells Ballet, Decroux, Marceau, Lecoq Styles Postmodern Mimes and Clowns
Germany, Austria, Switzerland	Germanic and Celtic Festivals B.C.	Scops, Spielmanner, Carnival Farces, Passion Plays, Mystery Plays, Fair Buffoons, Mime–Jongleurs	Hans Sachs	Italian Comedians, Straritsky, Hanswurst	J. Nestroy, F. Raimund, Kasperl	Jacques Dalcroze, Bertolt Brecht, Mary Wigman, Rudolf Von Laban, Ballets Joos, Decroux, Marceau, Lecoq Styles, Postmodern Mimes and Clowns

MAJOR DEVELOPMENTS OF THE ART OF MIME IN THE OCCIDENT AND ORIENT (*CONTINUED*)

	Antiquity	Middle Ages	16th Century	17th–18th Centuries	19th Century	20th Century
Byzantium, Russia, Eastern Europe		Byzantine Pantomime, Greek and Roman Traveling Mimes, Processions and Religious Plays, Skomorokhi, Russia		Italian Comedy in Russia; Smirnov's Interludes, Russia		Meyerhold, Eccentrism, Ballets Russes, Henryk Tomaszewski, Ladislav Fialka, Alfred Jarry Pantomime, Circus Alfred Litsedei Clowns
North America				John Durang, Anna Gardie in "The Black Forest"	George L. Fox, Humpty Dumpty,	Silent Films, Harold Lloyd, Buster Keaton, Charlie Chaplin, Bert Williams Isadora Duncan, Martha Graham, Decroux, Marceau, Lecoq Styles, Postmodern Mimes and Clowns
Orient	Mimed Scenes of the Ramayana, Hindu Pantomime, Vidusaka (buffoon), India, Symbolic Temple Dance, Dwarves, Jugglers, China. 200 B.C.	Tsa-Chü, China 12th–14th Centuries; Shinto and Buddhist Religious Dances, Japan 9th Century; Saragaka, Japan 10th Century Dengaku, Japan 11th Century	Kathakali, India; King-Tiao, 14th–17th Centuries, China; Dance–Pantomime, China			Peking Opera, China; Mei Lan Fang, China; Yan-ko Dance, China; Butoh Dance, Japan

MAJOR DEVELOPMENTS OF THE ART OF MIME IN THE OCCIDENT AND ORIENT (*CONTINUED*)

	Antiquity	Middle Ages	16th Century	17th–18th Centuries	19th Century	20th Century
	Kagura, Sacred Dances, Japan	Noh and Kyogen, Japan, 14th Century	Kabuki, Japan			
Middle East	Religious Saltation, Traveling Mimes from Greece and Rome, God Mardouk Pantomimes of Babylonia	Karagoz Shadow Play, Persia, Turkey, Syria				

EXPONENTS OF TWENTIETH-CENTURY MIME
SCHOOLS AND MOVEMENT STYLES

Decroux School	*Clowns and New Vaudeville*
Desmond Jones	Avner the Eccentric
Dulcinea Langfelder	Yury and Tanya Belov
Thomas Leabhart	Bob Berky
Yves Lebreton	Franz Josef Bogner
Margolis Brown Adaptors	Howard Butten
Christian Mattis	Crazy Mimes Society
Omnibus	Dimitri
Pinok and Matho	Ronlin Foreman
Leonard Pitt	Geoff Hoyle
Pontine Movement Theatre	Gardi Hutter
Pyramide op de Punt	Bill Irwin
Daniel Stein	Lindsay Kemp
Théâtre de l'Ange Fou	Klauniada
Théâtre du Mouvement	Les Macloma
	Litsedei Clown Theatre
	Pickle Family Circus
	New Pickle Family Circus
	Boleslav Polivka
	Ctibor Turba

Lecoq School	*Modern Commedia dell'Arte*
Axis Mime Theatre	I Colombaioni
Bouffon de Bullion	Dario Fo
Pierre Byland	Dell'Arte Players Company
The Moving Picture Mime Show	San Francisco Mime Troupe
Mummenschanz	Ferruccio Soleri
Theatre Beyond Words	
Théâtre de Complicité	

Classical Mime Barrault–Marceau Style	*Mime and Verbal Theatre*
Jean-Louis Barrault	Akademia Ruchu
Justin Case	Jean-Louis Barrault
Ladislav Fialka	Bewth
Marcel Marceau	Carbone 14
Moebius	Derevo
Samy Molcho	Théâtre de Complicité
Pantomimen Ensemble	Theatre of Yugen
Nola Rae	
Rolf Scharre	
Richmond Shepard	
Robert Shields	
Milan Sladek	
United Mime Workers	
Rob Van Reijn	

EXPONENTS OF TWENTIETH-CENTURY MIME
SCHOOLS AND MOVEMENT STYLES *(CONTINUED)*

Mime–Dance	*Mime, Ritual, and Plastic Arts*
Ariadone	Dog Troep
Pina Bausch	Griftheater
Adam Darius	Jerzy Grotowski
Katie Duck	Tadeusz Kantor
Lotte Goslar	Serapion's Theater
Lindsay Kemp	Snake-in-the-Grass Moving Theatre
Mamako Yoneyama	Will Spoor
Maguy Marin	Vancouver Moving Theatre
Ko Murobushi	Alberto Vidal
Josef Nadj	Robert Wilson
Kazuo Ohno	
Pilobolus Dance Theatre	
Annie Stainer	
Shusaku and Dormu Dance Theatre	
Henryk Tomaszewski	
Mary Wigman	

Mime in Film	*Street Mime*
Charlie Chaplin	Bond Street Theatre Coalition
Buster Keaton	Malabar
Harry Langdon	San Francisco Mime Troupe
Laurel and Hardy	Robert Shields
Max Linder	Tender
Harold Lloyd	Turbo Cacahuète
Marx Brothers	
Jacques Tati	

Puppetry and Mask	*Theatre of the Deaf*
Balinese Dance Theatre	The Flying Words Project
Bharata Natyam Indian Dance	International Visual Theatre of the Deaf
Bread and Puppet Theatre	The National Theatre of the Deaf
Eliot Fintushel	Théâtre Visuel des Sourds
Philippe Genty	
Habbe and Meik	
Theatre Beyond Words	

Part One

Mime through the Ages

Although with the passing centuries many new forms of mime and pantomime developed, the Greco–Roman heritage would remain the cornerstone of Western mime. Greece and Rome continued to mold the expression of this art from the Middle Ages through the Renaissance and beyond. Yet, even if the heritage of Greco–Roman mime was not a continuing or direct one and this art no longer knew the glory it had acquired in Greece and Rome, it underwent a rekindling in the theatre of the Middle Ages. Movement, so essential to all theatre among the ancient Greeks, served to liven the austerely religious miracle and mystery plays. And, while Greco–Roman mime revitalized solemn church drama, at the same time it lent a spiritual dimension to the Greco–Roman emphasis on the here and now. Christian chivalry fused with Greco–Roman mime traditions in mimed-out versions of poems such as *Beowulf* and *Aucassin and Nicolette.* The jongleurs' songs and buffoonery also contained the spirit of *mimesis* or imitation of life.

During the Renaissance, the commedia dell'arte integrated movement with text, clowning, dancing, and singing. By the seventeenth century, the commedia had penetrated France, England, and other European countries. It was not until the nineteenth century, particularly in France and England, that pantomime once again would become, as in ancient Rome, a specialized and silent art. In England it enhanced the clown art of such harlequins as Giuseppe Grimaldi and his son, Joseph Grimaldi, who would become the greatest English clown. The romantic period in France would give birth to a sentimental Pierrot with an exotic and adventuresome life. This poetic and revolutionary figure soon traveled to other countries. Now at the height of its glory as an autonomous yet traditional art, pantomime went from generation to generation and from artist to artist.

1

Mime, First Language and Art:
Mime in Greece and Rome

> If we want to understand in what sense art is language, we must take language
> from its roots. And it is clear that the first language is the most powerful.
>
> Alain

The language of gestures is as ancient as the human race. It is as old as Eros, the god
of love (Lucian 1905, 241). Inherent in each of us, it is born every day and is part of
man's need to express himself.

Before the human voice developed and vocal language was limited to guttural
and vocal sounds, gestures served not only to communicate but also to accompany
vocal expression. Primitive man pointed to an object and articulated a sound. As he
began to express more abstract ideas, these sounds grew more removed from their
mimetic origins. Diverse languages developed, and each became distinctive to the
people who spoke it. And as these languages evolved, body movements continued to
help man communicate his ideas. Although vocal sounds gradually replaced body
movements, they have never entirely disappeared. Movement and gestures were also
incorporated into the first forms of written language.[1] Because of the role that movement and gestures played early in the evolution of language, some language specialists believe that vocal expression is an extension or a specialized form of movement and gestures.[2]

Similar physical movements are found among animals. Charles Darwin believed that the muscular reactions of men and animals are identical when they express basic emotions such as fear, anger, and joy. As verbal language developed,
many of these muscular reactions degenerated. Some are presently so subtle that,
when animals respond to muscular reactions in man, the human eye cannot perceive
them.

In ancient times the word *mimesis*, meaning imitation, also implied communication with the gods. Through movements and gestures in religious rituals, man
sought their protection and prayed for an abundant harvest or victory in battle. From
these primitive rituals, which gradually detached themselves from religious cults but
still retained the imaginative power of symbolic gestures, the theatre was born.

Gestures and facial expressions—found early in man and whether spontaneous, consciously studied, or unconsciously imitated—have had functional purposes that were often combined with artistic and religious events.[3] Because of the
multiplicity of tongues among their tribes, some North American Indians employed
a common sign language. Not only did they imitate animals in their religious dances,

but to appease their prey and better make the kill, hunters imitated their movements. Such mimed performances are still found today in many Native American cere-monies; in courtship, fertility, war, hunting, and fishing dances of certain African and Australian tribes; and in Balinese dance dramas, which contain symbolic *mimesis*.[4] Today conventional body movements and symbolic gestures still exist in the rituals of occult sects and religious orders, such as among the Trappist monks, where sign language is the chief means of communication.

In the Orient, the theatre likewise had its beginnings in religious ceremonies composed of dance, song, music, and symbolic movement, to which dialogue was later added. In India the art of the theatre is said to have been born in the person of Bharata (the Hindu word signifying "actor"), who, at the command of Brahma, mimed out scenes depicting the life of Vishnu, the god whose four arms allow him to make many expressive gestures. For centuries in India, during harvest festivities a Brahmin priest played a comic character similar to Arlecchino, while his female companion, Vita, reminds one of Colombine. Today in the provinces of West India, the poems and hymns of the Aryan culture are still mimed.

The Hindu theatre influenced the Chinese theatre, in which mimes, dancers, singers, and musicians have performed since the earliest known spectacles. The Chinese theatre, in turn, influenced the Japanese theatre. In Japan the Kagura ritual dances, inspired by an ancient dance performed to lure the sungoddess out of her cavern, contain pantomime, which was the first step toward the development of the early secular theatre. The Kagura was one of the first forms of theatrical perform-ance in Japan, presented as a dance–prayer to the gods in A.D. 805 to prevent a vol-canic eruption. The ancient dancer Isono Zenji performed dramatic dances called *mima*, still found in the Noh and Kabuki theatres.

In Egypt, where miming in symbolic religious dances and songs existed two thousand years before Christ, mime–dancers imitated the movements of the sun, moon, and stars, in contrast to the Greek and Roman mimes, who played gods and heroes.

From the ancient ceremonies emerged the actor, who was also a dancer, singer, and mime. In Greece the first recorded pantomime actor is the legendary dancer Telestes, who in Aeschylus's *Seven against Thebes* (467 B.C.) detached himself from the chorus to interpret, with rhythmic steps and gestures, the action that the chorus sang or recited. With the addition of text, protagonists, and stage sets, miming and dance remained intrinsic to both tragedy and comedy. As the Greek theatre devel-oped, movement became basic to the actor's art. The French philosopher Alain (Emile Auguste Chartier) describes this close relationship between movement and voice: "What is most important is the human living form and movement, and the voice depends upon movement" (1931, 118). And just as the Greek theatre estab-lished harmony between movement and the spoken word, so Plautus, Shakespeare, and Molière integrated the physical with the verbal. "Shakespeare as actor, Molière as actor, these are not accidents; it is the body once more in search of the idea" (Alain 1931, 119).

Despite the development of spoken language, man has always instinctively ac-companied his speech with spontaneous gestures and facial expressions, which are part of that dynamic, silent thought that anticipates all vocal communication. As so-ciety evolved, movement varied according to region, social class, and period. The conventionalized gestures of the Oriental still differ from those of the Occidental. The inhabitants of some regions—for example, the Mediterraneans—express themselves with many gestures. The working classes use freer movements than the upper classes. In the eighteenth century, gestures were more formal and elaborate than in the twentieth century because of the accelerated pace of modern life and the practice of mass and individual sports.

Yet, mime—no matter how much it has varied from one period, social class, or country to another and under the influence of climate, geography, religious belief, or temperament of the people—remains vital to humans as a language and as an art. Having manifested itself in many forms, styles, and schools throughout the centuries, it still continues to be reborn in everyday life and in varied kinds of theatre—proof of its vitality as a means of communication and as an art. Rooted in man, the use of gestures and facial expressions reveals the first glimmer of his intelligence and his impulse to communicate. Forever alive, no matter how remote his thoughts or words are from their physical expression, their sensory expression is always present. As John J. Engel has indicated, in man no abstract idea can, in effect, be separated from a sensorial one.[5]

The Art of Mime in Greece

Gesture is mute poetry and poetry is dance which speaks.

Plutarch

For the ancient Greeks, the gods were omnipresent. They pervaded all aspects of life, from the most sacred to the most secular. To thank the gods, to appease them and secure their protection, ritual dances were performed. From the desire to disguise oneself and to play a role in these dances, the art of mime was born. Dramatized stories were soon added to tribal customs, such as that of the hunter who returned from the hunt and imitated the animals he had killed. And, though the art of mime developed into several distinct categories, it rarely separated from dance and speaking theatre. Only among the Romans did it disengage from dance and speech to give birth to pantomime.

We have no reliable record of any point of origin of mime in Greece. It was supposedly brought to Greek lands by strolling acrobats and dancers from Sicily. It is also believed that Doric mime originated in dance (Hunningher 1961, 38). According to Aristotle, it played an important role in ancient religious ceremonies. Nymphs were said to have danced and mimed—half-naked and disheveled, screaming and tearing apart wild animals—in the ritual ceremonies of the mountains of Thrace. Under Pisastratus, the annual festival of Dionysus attracted performers from Megara, who depicted the lives of the gods in dance, mime, song, and poetry. In Athens these ceremonies often took place on the Acropolis. In Delos the virgins consecrated to Apollo reenacted the legends of gods and heroes in mimed dances called mysteries.

Mimed dance was not long confined to temples and sacred sites. Legend tells us that a vineyard owner, finding a goat in his fields, sacrificed it in the presence of his neighbors, who danced around the altar miming the event. Professional dancers took up this ceremonial dance, called *tragoidia* or "song of the goat," and added songs and music to portray the culture of the grapevine and other crops. From here it was only a step to develop a dramatic form with a dialogue.

Thespis, the first person in Greece to convert this festival celebration into theatre, set up a stage, organized a traveling company, and replaced the primitive mask with a more human one (the mask allowed an actor to play many parts and to disassociate the audience and himself from the character he played). In 546 B.C., Thespis originated the idea of the actor by having the chorus leader interpret the dithyramb through a dialogue with the chorus. And, because the actor wore heavy costumes and elevated shoes, the chorus performed expressive movements and dances. Dramatic action soon replaced the ceremonial for a dead person or the celebration of a god. As the action and dialogue became more independent of the chorus, characters and episodes were added (Aeschylus added a second and later a third actor), which were combined with movement and dance.

Mime was no less important in comedy than in tragedy. Inspired by the ancient games and songs of the fields, and having originated in the cult of Dionysus in Megara around 581 B.C., the mimic instinct gave birth to one of the first comedic forms, the Doric farce, seen today as the figures of masked performers on Corinthian vases. Greek satyric drama, one of the most ancient dramatic forms, characterized by its jolly Dionysiac and mimic traits, was the first formal example of the spirit of *mimesis* or imitation. Instead of burlesquing a god or a mythological hero, chorus members mimicked, with boisterous and bawdy speech and movements, satyrs—the word comedy originating from the *komos* (feasting) with these satyrs, who were our first known clowns. Still very much alive in the improvised dances performed to the beat of cymbals and tambourines on the public squares, the mimic style continued on in the improvised farces of the Phlyakes, who inhabited the Greek colonies in southern Italy. From here this mimic style carried over into the Atellan farce and later into Roman pantomime.

While mime infused life into tragedy and comedy, mimed sketches were performed as curtain-raisers, entr'actes, or finales. Before finding its way to Rome, this art was present in Greece in burlesque, mythological, or realistic stagings, as well as combined with dance, song, dialogue, acrobatics, and animal disguises.

Mime Forms, Performers, and Authors

In ancient Greece, the dancer, the actor, and even the writer, all imitators of nature, were, broadly speaking, mimes. As we have seen, mime integrated with dance, music, poetry, and dramatic art and was not always, as in Rome, entirely mute. It thrived in Greece and Rome in three distinct forms:

1. Saltation, from *saltare* (to leap), which combined mime, dance, music, poetry, and dramatic art.
2. Mime, a play with a spoken text accompanied by gestures. Popular mimes were destined to be performed, while literary mimes were recited or read.
3. Pantomime, especially known in Magna Graecia and more popular in Roman culture, which subordinated all elements to the solo mime–dancer's movements.

Saltation, believed to have originated from *Saltus*, the name of an Arcadian from Greece who first taught this art to the Romans, was an interpretative or pantomimic dance that could be understood through a conventional system of expressive movement. It was often combined with recitation, music, and song, and the poet who performed in his own work was called a *saltator*.

The mime play was at first a popular, improvised, and crude sketch of every-day events with innovative gestures, jocose dialogue, song, and dance. In one of the earliest known mime plays, *The Quack Doctor*, the doctor examining a sick wife ends up seducing her. A popular theme was *The Mother-in-Law* (*Hecyra*), recorded on a terra-cotta lamp dating from the third century B.C. In other mime plays, mytho-logical subjects, such as Zeus and his loves, were favorite themes (*Leda and the Swan*). While many mime plays were comical and nondidactic, others had a pointed morality. These monologues, dialogues in rhythmic prose, or verse dialogue had two or three characters. The action was simple, often portraying licentious customs. There were two distinct kinds of mimodramas: the Greek *paignion*—a shorter, vul-gar, and less elaborate sketch of Dorian days, improvised and without stage sets—and the *hypothesis* (Nicoll 1963, 128)—a longer, fully developed Roman type, dra-matic or comical with more evolved characterization. While only one player performed in the recitative mime, in the dramatic mime there were several. Even when the mime play took on a more literary character, it still depicted customs in a realistic manner and had a less refined style and language than comedy.

Pantomime, born from mime and saltation, was the name commonly given not only to this mute art form, but also to the masked performer who could express with simple, rhythmic movements all passions, characters, events, animals, and even inanimate objects while an actor or singer in the wings or a chorus recited or sang. Like the performers of realistic farce, mimes were the heirs to comedy, while the performers of pantomime, who interpreted tragic and mythological themes, were the heirs to tragedy.

What do we know about the performances of the Greek mime players? The popular mimes often improvised in public places on crude platforms before a back-drop called by the Romans a *siparium*. Later they played on larger stages with more elaborate theatrical devices and sets. Unlike the Roman pantomime artists, who fre-quently mimed behind masks in large amphitheatres, the Greek mimes wore no masks. Men played the male roles and women played the female roles. Many per-formed in private homes and at weddings, christenings, and banquets. The scenes performed in private homes were often risqué, such as the love scene between Dionysus and Ariadne described by Xenophon, which was mimed at a banquet at which Socrates was the chief guest (1922, 479–81). By the third century B.C., with the decline of tragedy, the mimes acted out vulgarized versions of tragedy with killings and violence.

The art of the Greek mime performer was a highly evolved one. Lucian of Samosata tells us that the mime knew music and had a prodigious memory, sensi-tivity, and a well-proportioned, strong, flexible body. His intricate technique was di-vided into making gestures (*chieronomia*), jumping (*halma*), and kicking or moving the feet (*lactisma*). He was referred to as *endeicticos* (he who shows), *enterptos* (he who varies his gestures), *tachicheiros* (he who has agile hands), *demagoticos* (he who transports the public), and *polyskemos* (he who knows how to portray all atti-tudes) (Bragaglia 1930, 26–27). Because of his talent for depicting life, the Greek mime performer was called a "biologist." Homer describes his art as noble and di-vine, and Seneca calls it a silent language so well "spoken."

Authors of Greek mime plays were numerous. Epicharmus, the father of com-edy, inspired by the improvised plays of Megara, wrote short, realistic sketches based on mythology entitled *The Bacchae, The Sausage,* and *The Sirens.*[6] Sophron of Syracuse (c. 430 B.C.), a Sicilian of Hellenic culture who influenced Theocritus

(310–250 B.C.) and Herodas (third century B.C.), composed short, moral monologues, dialogues, and scenes in rhythmic prose and popular Doric dialect based on
mythology and everyday events (*The Tunny Fisher, The Sempstress*).[7] Theocritus,
who wrote Alexandrian mimes with sophisticated dialogue in a lively burlesque
manner, gave mime a poetic form. His *Andoniazousai* (*Women at the Adonis Festival*) is one of the finest ancient mime plays. In one of his eighty-two opuscules, entitled *Mimes of the Courtesans*, Lucian describes nocturnal life in Athens.[8] In *The
Mimes of Herodas*, such sketches as *The Women at Breakfast* and *The Gossips,* discovered relatively late, are realistic and cynical pieces containing proverbial wisdom
that were often recited or performed in popular Doric tradition by players wearing
grotesque costumes and carrying a phallic symbol.[9] And Sophron of Syracuse was
said to have inspired Plato's semidramatic dialogues.

Playwrights thus drew upon other arts and, in turn, influenced and enriched
them. One of the literary offshoots of the mime was the Syracusan comedy of the
fifth century B.C., first developed by Epicharmus and Sophron. Dance also played an
important role in the comedies of Aristophanes while Aristotle claimed that tragedy
drew its source from the Dionysiac dithyramb. And, like the jongleurs of the Middle
Ages, who sang their own poetic compositions, playwrights, such as Sophocles, performed in their own plays. Some—for example, Aeschylus—introduced costume
changes, such as a new type of shoes to ease the actor's walk.

As dance and drama developed among the Hellenized arts, mime, while evolving as an independent art, contributed to both of these forms, never losing the élan
of its early sources. To fuse movement with rhythmic dance and scanned verse was
the aim of the Greek theatre, a theatre that, through the harmony of all three elements, would become the pillar of Occidental theatre.

Mimes in Rome

It is believed that the art of mime in Rome was the product of native growth blended
with Greek mime from southern Italy, where it had already flourished for several
centuries. It was brought to Rome through several channels. On the one hand, traveling entertainers in Rome played in Greek mimic comedy, which had originated in
ancient Doria. And, according to Livy, this art, which had existed since the beginning of the Republic, was introduced by Lydians from Asia Minor, who were familiar with Greek culture (Boulenger de Rivery 1752, 1–2). Livy adds that during a
plague in 364 B.C., the Romans brought mime–dancers from Etruria to divert the
anger of the gods. The Romans who imitated their mimed dances, later adapting dialogue and gestures, were called *histriones*, from *hister,* meaning "performer" in Etruscan (Duckworth 1952, 5). Like the Greek mimes, who appeared as early as 211
B.C. at the Ludi Apollinares games and in 173 B.C. at the festival of Flora in Rome,
where they were the main attraction, the Roman mimes interpreted scenes of everyday life, gods, and animals to the music of flutes. A story relates that in 211 B.C.,
when Hannibal's approach was announced during a celebration of the games of
Apollo, the spectators left to arm themselves. After they returned, victorious, they
found the elder Pomponius, one of the first mimic actors to perform at the Ludi
Apollinares, still dancing to the flute (Duckworth 1952, 13). Toward A.D. 100, Sci-
pio Africanus brought Hellenized mimodramas back to Rome from the Middle East,
where Greek mimes had introduced them during the Pyrrhic Wars. Thus, once con-

quered, Greece reconquered Rome through the Middle East. In Greece and Rome, this art became so closely interwoven that it was referred to as Greco–Roman mime.

Nature of Roman Mime and Pantomime

Aside from tragedy, three types of comedy flourished in Rome: Greek comedy, Atellan farce, and Greco–Roman mime. Greco–Roman mime, the parent of popular Roman pantomime, developed out of the character dances performed between acts of a play. A light entertainment without a coherent plot or character portrayal, it consisted of short, improvised, burlesque scenes. It differed from popular comedy in that it contained more mimetic action and dancing and, contrary to comedy and tragedy, women played the female roles. It depicted current events; the gods were often mocked, and love and adultery were popular themes. As in Atellan farce, performed as early as the fourth century B.C. in the Oscan city of Atella (near Naples), a favorite subject was that of the fat, stupid husband who returned to find his wife in bed with a lover. Although the mimes were not confined to playing stock characters, the Roman *mimus calvus* resembled Maccus, the clumsy peasant in the Atellan farce with a long nose, shaven head, and patchwork costume (because of the need to mend it while he traveled). The Roman mime was of the same family as the stupid old Pappus; Bucco, the idiot with thick lips; and Dossennus, the pedantic village hunchback, all of the Atellan farce. He was also the harbinger of Pulcinella, the father of the commedia dell'arte stock characters.

During the age of Julius Caesar, mime became more literary but still was impromptu and indecent. Laberius (106–43 B.C.) was the first to give mime a written and literary form in *The Prison, The Gossips, The Wedding, The Soothsayer, The Well of Good Health,* and *The Ghost.* He also employed themes from regular comedy in *Hot Baths, The Ram, The Mistress, The Fisherman,* and *The Sisters.* During this same period, his rival Publilius Syrus, a former slave of Caesar, wrote *The Tree Cutters, The Grumblers,* and mime plays in verse with maxims, which Seneca ranked equal to Roman tragedy. At the age of sixty, Laberius was persuaded by Caesar to perform with Publilius Syrus. But when Laberius mocked Caesar on stage, his rival was given the palm. The humiliated writer left the theatre, having lost his rank of Roman knight.

Among other well-known mimographers was the Roman poet Catullus (first century B.C.), who wrote *Ghost* and *The Fugitive Slave.* The farce mimes of Lentulus and Hostilius were based on mythological subjects. But because Emperor Domitian believed that Helvidius Priscus's piece *Paris and Oenone* alluded to his own divorce, he had the author sentenced to death. Philistion, a Greek mimographer, was highly esteemed in Rome during the reign of Augustus. Tiberius was renowned for his philosophical mimes, and Romanus Marullus was applauded under Marcus Aurelius for his satirical mimes.

The Roman mime performances were staged much like those of the Greeks. Because the mimes were often ambulatory, their stages in theatres, amphitheatres, or private homes were portable and simple. They consisted of a rudimentary construction with a curtain (*siparium*), which also served as a backdrop. When the mimes performed during the interludes or after plays, a crude platform was erected in the orchestra or in front of the stage. Gradually the mimes moved onto the main stage.

Because the buffoon or *stupidus* played and danced on these rudimentary stages without shoes, he was called *planipes* or barefoot actor. (Plautus supposedly derived his name from performing in bare feet in mime plays and in Atellan farce.) He wore a hood or cloak and a peaked cap, like that of the medieval buffoon and the clown in Shakespeare's plays; when uncovered, his deformed head was bald. Because he made use of exaggerated facial expressions, he did not always wear an open-mouthed mask, and his face, with large lips and a big nose and ears, was painted or smeared with soot. While some buffoons wore multicolored, patched dresses and jackets, others appeared in a simple loincloth or in an animal skin wrapped around the hips, with the phallus sometimes showing.

The Romans soon adapted Greco–Roman mime to their own tastes. Once mime separated from dance and text, it took on the characteristics of pantomime. At first performed during the interludes of plays, pantomime grew popular, especially when the role of the chorus diminished and the mime–actors imitated the action of the play being performed. However, legend attributes the birth of pantomime in Rome to an accident. In 240 B.C., the Greek actor–playwright Livius Andronicus, while performing in one of his plays, lost his voice. As one of his students sang the action, he continued to mime it. His movements so charmed the Roman audience that pantomime soon became their favorite entertainment.

Because the same themes were found in both mime and pantomime, the two forms were often confused with one another. What most distinguished pantomime from mime was that in pantomime a single performer played all the roles (only on occasion would the narrator or solo singer play a minor part) and his performance was totally silent. In the mime play, the *mimi* performed realistic, burlesque scenes before the Roman people (Nicoll 1963, 133). In pantomime, the *pantomimi* played more elegantly in serious historical, legendary, and mythological pieces or in scenes from Greek drama before the higher classes and at the courts. Closer to tragedy, pantomime borrowed themes from the plays of Aeschylus, Sophocles, and Euripides; from mythology, as in *Leda and the Swan, The Loves of Venus and Adonis,* and *Hercules in Anger*; and from history, as in *The Death of Anthony and Cleopatra.*

The action of the Roman pantomime was simple. A synopsis was distributed among the audience or related by a narrator, singer, or chorus reciting or singing the libretto on or behind a lavish stage setting. The pantomime actor entered, dressed in a silken tunic and wearing a cloak like that of the tragic actor, which could also be transformed into a beggar's cloak. While a slave held up a sign indicating the place of action, the mime mimed the action and all the characters with conventional rhythmic movements of his hands, arms, and feet. Accompanying the action were a flute, a harplike instrument, and a tapping sound made with iron shoes (*scabella*), which was augmented in tragic scenes. A mask covered his face for each character he played. At a later date he appeared with his face uncovered.

The Roman Mime's Art

The Roman mime was often a street entertainer who had a variety of talents and could juggle and perform acrobatics. If he was a slave, he received a good education. Depending on the type of performance in which he played, he could be well versed in poetry, music, painting, sculpture, philosophy, mythology, history, dance, and *chironomie* (French from the Greek *chieronomia*, codified rhythmic gestures of the arms, hands, and fingers). To portray characters of any age or sex and perform with grace and elegance, especially in pantomime, he underwent rigorous training.

Just as Plutarch had divided the art of saltation into three elements, the Roman mime's art consisted of three parts: namely, the *species*, the technique and style of the mime's immobile attitudes; the *latio,* the art of gestures and movements (Lewis and Short 1933, 1039, 737); and the *ostensio* (Bragaglia 1930, 44), the art of indicating the time, place, and circumstances of the action.

There were stage mimes, music hall mimes, mime–acrobats, mimes who played in private homes, and mimes who performed in aquacades or aquatic shows. They were classified according to their rank: the *archimimus* played heroes or main parts, and the *deuteragonists* played secondary roles. Each mime specialized in a type role, either a god, youth, or fool.

Seneca attributed the development of tragic pantomime to Pylades of Cicilia (born in 22 B.C.), whose disciples were called the Pyladi. In *Dionysus Coming to Thebes*, by changing masks Pylades played Dionysus, Pentheus, Cadmus, and Agaue. Bathyllus of Alexandria and his disciples, the Bathylli, developed comic pantomime. Although the art and style of Pylades predominated during and after this period, the rivalry between the two led to Pylades's banishment, which caused an uproar among the Romans. When Augustus questioned him about his jealousy, Pylades replied that it was to Caesar's advantage that the people were concerned with his performances rather than with Caesar's actions (Kirstein 1935, 49).

Among other famous mimes, many of whom were Greek or Syrian, was the Syrian freedman Agrippus Memphius Apolaustus, executed in A.D. 189. A mime–actor named Paris, who had lived under Nero, was executed in A.D. 67, and another mime called Paris, a favorite of Domitian, was executed by the emperor twenty years later. Philemon, who refused to worship pagan gods, died a saint and a martyr in A.D. 287. Although women mimes were looked down upon (they played mostly in Byzantium), some performed in both mime and pantomime. Famous women mimes were Pelagia, who later became a saint; Cytheris, Marc Anthony's mistress; Valeria Cloppia; Dionysia; the erudite Eucharis; Hermione (a singer); and Antiodemis. Many costly monuments were erected in honor of the mimes; a statue was placed in Tivoli for Agrippus Apolaustus, and a stone was erected in Taormina for Julia Bassila.

Writers such as Cicero and Diogenes praised mimes highly. Luxurious gifts were heaped on them at private banquets; when he died, Roscius left an immense fortune. Their art achieved a high level of subtle expression. For instance, one could tell whether the mime had been served beef, chicken, or hare by the way he carved the imaginary meat. So skilled were the mimes that when they mimed boxing and wrestling, they drew more spectators than the real matches. In Nero's time, after seeing *The Loves of Ares and Aphrodite* performed by a mime, who played all the roles without a chorus or recitation philosopher, Demetrius the Cynic was convinced that the mime's hands were as articulate as his tongue (Kirstein 1935, 52).

The mimes depicted the customs of the period so well that they were often called ethnologues. Memphius, a student of Pythagoras, interpreted different systems of philosophy. Cicero and Roscius engaged in a famous dispute over whether it was the orator with his words or the mime with his gestures who could convey an idea more perfectly.

Roman mime thrived under the protection of the goddess Polymnia. Dictionaries of mimology existed, and a conservatory of mime was established. Here slaves or freedmen of an advantageous physique trained for two years and then performed on stage or at the circus. The children of noblemen learned mime, and statesmen studied it to improve their oratory. Caligula and other Roman emperors performed before their courts.

Mime in Roman Life

The theatre was an important part of life for the pleasure-loving Romans. The imperial policy of bread and circuses fostered a taste for it among the masses. And because the nobility lived in luxury and debauchery, seeking any pretext to enjoy life, the primary appeal of the theatre was not literary but visual.

The popularity of pantomime can be partly attributed to the size of the Roman theatres. Because no human voice could project to fill them, the actor was obliged to use movements and gestures. Spectators left the theatre with their vocabulary of gestures enlarged. Mime was also important in everyday life, at the imperial court, in public affairs, and in relations with foreigners. To impress the conquered, the heroic actions of the conquerors were mimed. Mimes served as interpreters for ambassadors in foreign lands. Lucian tells us that the king of Pontus, a kingdom situated northeast of Asia Minor, sent Nero an ambassador who, when attending the theatre, did not entirely understand the dialogue. When Nero asked the ambassador what he desired as homage, he replied that to communicate with his barbarian neighbors he wished to have the mime he had just seen perform (Lucian 1905, 256).

During the period of imperial Rome, chironomy (*chieronomia*) was familiar to the citizens and served various purposes. The prostitutes who walked the sacred street between the Coliseum and the Temple of Peace used a sign language forbidden in Rome and Athens called *signum infame*. Greek courtesans who did not know Latin also used this language. In one of his letters, the Roman philosopher Seneca describes the gestures of the libertines, who scratched their heads and winked (*oculus limus*). Ovid tells us about a woman *gesticularia*, who said to him one day:

> Read the words on my fingers as if they were written. When the desire for our love kindles your mind, softly touch your rosy cheek with your thumb. If in your heart an echo speaks to you of me, bring your hand to the point of your ear. Light of my soul, when you desire me, play with your ring between your fingers and touch the table with your hand as if playing solemnly. (Bragaglia "Linguaggio del Mimo")

The poet Tibullus describes how his mistress's delicate and rapid gestures reminded him of secret tendernesses (Bragaglia "Linguaggio del Mimo"). Chironomy also served ends that were not so light. For Plutarch the same finger in mathematical calculations at times signified the number 1 and at times the number 10,000. The mathematical positions of the fingers also symbolized people's social conditions. According to Saint Girolamo, "the number 30 reminds one of marriage and the wife. The number 60 of widows; they suffer; the upper finger is bent and folded" (Bragaglia 1930, 78–79).

At funerals mimes imitated the gestures and attitudes of the dead. Scenes from plays, such as Atilius's *Electra* at Julius Caesar's funeral (44 B.C.), were also mimed. Many of the seductive and beautiful women mimes of Asia Minor and Egypt became the courtesans of the rich and attained a high rank through marriage. The libertine mime Theodora shared the throne with the Emperor Justinian in A.D. 527.

Pantomime grew so popular that during the reign of Mark Anthony many Romans neglected their duties to go to the theatre. Mark Anthony allowed mimes to appear only at banquets, where it was the custom to present at least one *mimus calvus*. A law of Augustus forbade them from being whipped. During the fourth century, the emperor Constantine, fearing famine, exiled the philosophers but retained thousands of mimes. Seneca attributed the Roman citizens' indifference to philosophy to their passion for pantomime.

Although the people held them in great esteem, the popularity of the mimes among the Roman emperors was irregular. They lived their best days under Augustus, who used them to divert attention from government affairs. Other emperors had them punished for their audacity. After Hylas, a pupil of Bathyllus, offended a senator during one of his performances, he was publicly whipped. Mimes were also highly criticized for their lives of debauchery. Lentulus was said to have played robbers so well because he himself was worthy of the gallows. Tiberius, who at first had limited their performances to evening appearances because of their arrogant and lewd conduct and because the theatres had become a place for bloody fights, exiled them to his private island. Caligula, whose favorite mime was Mnester, brought them back to Rome. But when he felt that Mnester was becoming a threat to his own talent as a mime, he had him executed. Nero—who himself wanted to play heroes, gods, and goddesses—for a time prohibited mimes from appearing in public, as had the Emperor Vitellius before him. Titus, himself a poet, preferred the tragic mime style. Under Domitian, whose wife fell in love with the mime Paris, they could perform only in private. Fearing that his wife would fall in love with still another young mime, Domitian had Paris killed as an example. Although Trajan enjoyed private pantomime performances, he exiled mimes because of their indecency (Boulanger de Rivery 1752, 29). The emperor Hadrian, a patron of pantomime, wrote critiques of their art. The young Emperor Heliogabalus, who played Venus in *The Judgment of Paris*, encouraged the staging of their lewd practices. He also showered his favorite mimes with political offices. Because mimes were often slaves, the former were all chased out of Rome. The emperor Julian made use of them to ridicule the Christians. And the mimes soon took such daring liberties on stage that the church condemned them for excessive buffoonery and obscenity. Their art was gradually replaced by horse and chariot races.

Centuries later, entertainers who inherited the Greco–Roman mime traditions sang, danced, imitated, and performed acrobatics at the courts and at private banquets throughout Europe. And despite the ups and downs of their fortune, strolling jongleurs and mimes never abandoned the ancient mime traditions. These entertainers and their traditions had played a role in the development of Latin comedy and in the works of authors such as Plautus. And these same traditions and this mimic spirit would be revived when they fused with one of the richest theatre forms in Europe, the commedia dell'arte.

Notes

1. Much of the ideographic and illustrated writings, for example, of the Egyptians and Aztecs, as well as the pictographic writings of the Hebrews, included images of movements and gestures. And, possibly because of the common use of gestures among these different peoples, certain manual signs of the American Indians resembled Egyptian characters.

2. For Max Muller, movement is important in the origin of language because it is sound derived from the consciousness of our acts (Muller 1890, 33).

3. According to Georges Dumas, there are emotional gestures, such as covering the face with the hands in fear; symbolic gestures, such as making the sign of the cross; and descriptive gestures, such as drawing squares and circles (Dumas 1933, 364, my translation).

4. French philosopher Lucien Lévy-Bruhl writes that mime is familiar to Indians throughout all of the Americas. "In South America the Indians of different tribes who do not understand each other in speaking use a language of gestures. In North America the language of gestures is universally employed. Indians from two different tribes, not knowing the oral language of the other, can remain a whole half day speaking and babbling, telling each other all sorts of stories by the movements of their fingers, heads and feet" (Dumas 1933, 364, my translation).

5. According to J. J. Engel, "When one develops his ideas without any obstacle, his walk is freer; when a series of objects present themselves with difficulty to his mind, his step is slower. When an important doubt suddenly arises, he stops short. In the same manner disparate ideas bring on an irregular walk. When one changes ideas, one changes attitudes. If, for example, in searching for intellectual facts, a man looks down and finds nothing, his eyes change direction and he will look up" (Gratiolet 1865, 323, my translation).

6. Other mimodramas by Epicharmus are *The Dionysians, Cyclops, Logos Kai Logina (Masculine and Feminine Reason), The Trojans, Odysseus Shipwrecked, The Visitors to the Temple, Sphinx, The Dancers, Pyrra, The Months,* and *The Women of Megara.* Phormus, a contemporary of Epicharmus, wrote comical mythological mimodramas, such as *Hippos, The Horse; The Sack of Troy;* and *Perseus.*

7. Other works by Sophron are *The Fisherman and the Peasant, The Matchmaker, The Old Men,* and *The Witches.*

8. In *Mimes of the Courtesans of Lucian* (1935), reprint , Pierre Louys translated Lucian of Samosata's mimes, as illustrated by Edgar Degas, including *Lover of the Heart, Maternal Advice, The Pleasure of Being Beaten, Night,* and others that were popular during the nineteenth century.

9. Among the mimes of Herodas are *The Schoolmaster, Zelotypos, The Jealous Woman, The Shoemaker, The Dream,* and *The Matchmaker.*

2

Mimes and Jongleurs of the Middle Ages

Origins and Nature of Medieval Mime

In the first century B.C., when Julius Caesar crossed Gaul, his mime entertainers accompanied him. After the fall of the Roman Empire, mimes traveled beyond the provinces and performed wherever they could. In A.D. 496, Theodoric, king of the Ostrogoths, was said to have sent a mime, who also sang to the accompaniment of instruments, to Clovis in honor of his victory at Tolbiac.

Although the mimes' repertory disappeared after the fall of Rome, elements of their art have been found in the entertainments of the medieval jongleurs or minstrels. It is also believed that they participated in the religious and comic theatre of the period. However, what we do not know is whether their art, which prevailed throughout the Middle Ages, was a direct heritage and whether the mimes themselves were the sole historical link between the theatre of antiquity and the classical theatre of the Renaissance.

From the fall of the Roman Empire until the flourishing of the medieval religious drama there was no established theatre. And although medieval mimes and jongleurs sang, recited, and acted out scenes, there is no recorded evidence that classical mime continued from the fifth through the seventh centuries. Yet, whether the art of the medieval mimes was a continuation of Greco–Roman mime or merely a spontaneous outgrowth of the period is, no doubt, secondary to the fact that it did flourish.

From the accounts found at a later date, we know that during the Middle Ages there were mime performances. During the eighth century, merchants invited mimes to perform in public markets (E. Duncan 1907, 103–4). Like the Roman emperors before him, Charlemagne engaged mimes to help win the people's favor. During the eleventh century, William the Conqueror encouraged mime entertainments at the fairs, as did Saint Louis in the thirteenth century. The historian Jean Froissart relates that at the end of the fourteenth century, a company of traveling minstrels staged a vaudeville play at the court of Gaston Phoebus, earl of Foix (E. Duncan 1907, 75).

The crude and obscene realism in their performances soon induced the Catholic Church to exclude actors and mimes from the benefit of its rites. In the fourth century, ecclesiastical writers such as Saint John Chrysostom already scorned them because they mocked Christianity and diverted the people's attention from religion (Nicoll 1963, 139). Charlemagne, who esteemed the mimes, later condemned them (*Histoire des Spectacles* 1494), and his son, Louis the Pious, proclaimed them licentious. But even when the actors' social position declined, the continuing attacks of the Church proved that their dramatic activity was significant.

To draw crowds, the mimes of the Middle Ages became singers, dancers, bear trainers, acrobats, magicians, charlatans, puppeteers, necromancers, and court fools—in sum, entertainers in a total sense. Because singing was their principal means of entertainment, in France these medieval minstrels were called *jongleurs*, in England minstrels or gleemen, in Denmark *scalds*, and in Germany *scops*, or singers of the adventures of German mythological warriors.[1] We learn from an epitaph on a tomb that a certain Vitalis, probably of the ninth century, aside from playing women's roles, could sing, recite, and dance (Nicoll 1963, 95–96).

If it was not the mime who turned into a jongleur, the jongleur often turned into a mime. According to the historian William Courthope, "Since no word is more frequently used by the Latin writers of the Middle Ages than *mimus* to denote the minstrel class, we may infer that the arts of mime were imitated by some of the gleemen" (1919, 434). How, then, did the art of these singing poets of the Middle Ages relate to that of the ancient mimes? Besides singing and reciting, many of them danced and imitated others' actions, gestures, and words. For the twelfth-century writer Hugutius, the *mimus* (mime), *ioculator* (jester), and *jongleur* (medieval ballad–singer and poet), often used interchangeably, were all "imitators of human things" (Nicoll 1963, 152–53). In his dramatic monologue, a jongleur, by changing his voice and movements, could imitate several characters, like the Roman mime, who in a single performance played all the roles. Some jongleurs were also court jesters and had the long, hooked nose, shaven head, grotesque mask or painted face, clownish aspect, and multicolored cloak of the ancient *stupidus*. And so, along with his talents as singer, dancer, and acrobat, the jongleur continued the ancient art of "imitator."

Mime in the Songs and Poetry of the Middle Ages

Although there appears to be more speculation than evidence regarding the artistic activities of jongleurs and mimes during the Middle Ages, from the Merovingian period on, roving jongleurs throughout the Frankish territory not only sang and recited but, according to some writers, practiced the arts of juggling, magic, and mime. In his poem *Tournois de Chauvenci,* Jacques Bretel describes how, after they had their wine, a group of jongleurs "tried best who could counterfeit the monk, the hermit, the pilgrim, the peasant and roysterer" (Nicoll 1963, 158). Although there is also little evidence that the English minstrel or the fireside teller of folk tales mimed or acted out the feats of heroes such as Siegfried, Charlemagne, and Alexander, portions of these narratives could easily lend themselves to this kind of dramatization. In contrast to the epic poetry of writers such as Virgil, in which literary detail is sacrificed to a more direct tone, in the eighth-century *Beowulf* and the tenth-century *Battle of Brunanburh*, a narrator could very well have illustrated by his movements the manner of combat and the way to win a battle. And, because of its repetitions and highly dramatic quality, parts of the twelfth-century *Chanson de Roland* could easily have been accompanied by the movements and gestures of the jongleur, who sang or recited.

Movements and gestures could have served not only in acting out songs and poems on stage, but also in humanities students' oral readings of classic works, which was a popular pastime during the latter part of the Middle Ages. Gustave Cohen gives as an example the thirteenth-century *chantefable* classic *Aucassin and Nicolette*, which possesses a style so suitable for staging that it could have originally been a play in the comical repertory of jongleurs and mimes that was preserved as a poem (1948, 74). The successful staging of *Aucassin and Nicolette* by the Théophiliens at the Paris Cité Universitaire in 1977 reinforces the notion that other poems, as well as songs, were mimed and acted out during the Middle Ages.

Jongleurs and Mimes in the Religious and Comic Theatre

Opinion differs as to the role jongleurs and mimes played in perpetuating ancient mime traditions in the religious and comic theatre of the Middle Ages. Although similarities have been found between the plots and characters of the ancient mimes and those of the jongleur's repertory and medieval comic theatre (Nicoll 1963, 175), there is no recorded evidence that jongleurs and mimes inherited, over centuries of handing down traditions, elements of the ancient mime's art. We do know that as *histriones* they imitated the actions of men through movements, gestures, and words. Moreover, whenever the jongleur recited a ballad or a dramatic piece and illustrated his narration or song with gestures, he spontaneously used a semidramatic form. If mime is to be understood not only as dumb show but also as an expression that accompanies verbal language and imitates men's actions, then the theatre of the Middle Ages might owe much to the jongleurs and mimes who participated in it. And, even if they merely aided in the "survival of some kind of histrionic instinct within definite limitations" (Sticca 1970, 11), this was a considerable contribution to the theatre of the Middle Ages.

Paradoxically, while the clergy at first drove them from the public squares because of their licentious entertainment, jongleurs and mimes later practiced their art under the maternal eye of the Church. According to the fourth-century writer Saint Jerome, some of the religious even made use of mimicry to reprimand those who had abandoned God and a pious life. Some historians assume that the ninth-century injunction that warned mimes not to put on priestly garments might have been either because some mimes indulged in secular ridicule of the church or because they actually performed in religious plays (Nicoll 1963, 148–49). A long-existing fraternity between England's monks and the minstrels culminated in 1102, during Henry I's reign, with the founding of a Minstrel's Priory. Thomas Warton gives examples of monks paying minstrels to perform on religious occasions and cites entries of priory entertainments during the reign of Henry VI under the general heading *"De Joculatoribus et Mimis"* (1824, 94).

If jongleurs, minstrels, and mimes performed at monasteries and, on occasion, assisted in the divine service's chants and musical accompaniments, they most likely also participated in religious dramas.[2] And, since their art enlivened dull fourteenth- and fifteenth-century mystery, morality, and miracle plays, it matters little whether these religious plays were staged by mimes under the clergy's supervision, or by the clergy under the mimes' talented guidance. As stage directors and technicians, they were also adept at creating the apparition scenes. And when these plays became too elaborate to stage inside the church, the clerics no doubt welcomed the collaboration of these entertainers.

Stories of the Bible and of the lives of saints and common men that these mystery, morality, and miracle plays dramatized required that the stage be filled with kings, prophets, and holy men, which necessitated skills in stage direction and acting. The attitudes, of an austere grandeur, recalled the stone figures in the typanums of Gothic churches. The voice—at times low, at times high, with the words addressed to eternity—had a profound gravity. The face was placid, the eyes raised toward heaven, reminding the spectator that it was not the drama of man being acted out but that of God.

Besides the slow infiltration of the vernacular from the twelfth through the thirteenth century, the progressive transformation of the liturgical drama into the semiliturgical drama brought other changes. The drama was no longer a divine service, nor did it necessarily offer a moral lesson. Soon the laity performed with the clergy, and the public began to judge the actors' competency. Settings and costumes became more elaborate, and stage directions and movements more precise. This is exemplified in the twelfth-century *Jeu d'Adam*, which the Théophiliens at the Sorbonne University in Paris revived in 1935:

> Paradise should be placed on a raised spot encircled with silken draperies, at a height that the characters may be seen from the shoulders up. Fragrant flowers and foliage are interwoven; fruit hangs from a variety of trees. The Saviour should arrive, dressed in a Dalmatic, with Adam and Eve before him, Adam in a red tunic and Eve in a white dress. Both should stand before the Divine Figure, Adam closer, his face calm, Eve a little more humble, and Adam ready to speak his lines, not too promptly nor too slowly. All the characters should speak their lines with assurance and suit their gestures to the action; they should not add nor omit a syllable from their lines and pronounce them all clearly and in the proper sequence. (Cohen 1948, 20)

Through their own forms of entertainment and the curtain-raisers and interludes in the mystery, miracle, and morality plays, jongleurs and mimes perpetuated or revivified the ancient mime spirit. Gustave Cohen describes how such plays as the thirteenth-century *Courtois d'Arras* preserved this spirit. This typical repertory piece, which contains numerous comical scenes, was probably performed as a dramatic monologue, with one jongleur miming all the parts (Cohen 1948, 77). Physical movement was also abundant in thirteenth-century farces, which developed out of the interludes and were a more highly evolved form of comedy than the licentious and grotesque *Sotie*. Through such comical types as the lawyer Pathelin, the cobbler Culbain, and the good peasant Jacquinot, the farce satirized various social classes in true mimic tradition.

As the farce took precedence over all other comic forms, names of professional actors became linked to the character types they played, such as Tabarin, the practical joker in Gilles's costume, who performed on the Place Dauphine platforms in Paris at the beginning of the seventeenth century, and the famous stage-actor trio of Gaultier-Garguille, Gros Guillaume, and Turlupin, directly descended from fifteenth-century farce types. Gaultier-Garguille played the old, pedantic Pantalon type; Gros Guillaume, women's parts and shrews; and Turlupin the valet or deceived husband who, with his floating, colorful trousers, short coat, wide-brimmed hat, and wooden sword, recalled Brighella, the valet in the commedia dell'arte. This same valet, who resembled the ancient *sannio* (buffoon) and made the action in the French farce go round, would inspire Molière in his creation of Sganarelle.

The medieval farce was born of the religious play. Mimes and jongleurs, who collaborated in the staging of religious plays and whose interludes were gradually "stuffed" into them, supposedly played the devil and comic characters. In England the devil's role in religious plays was to inspire the birth of Clown, who amused the public during intermissions or at the end of the performance by improvising, dancing, and playing instruments. Through their stage skills and technical collaboration, jongleurs and mimes who played the French farce stock character Maistre Mimin, later became the main actors in the medieval farce. In turn, the medieval farce, based upon physical action and imitation of human nature, provided the springboard for Molière's theatre.

From the jongleurs' mimed song and dance, through the religious and comic theatre, to the domain of the narrative poem, satire, and realistic novel, mime continued to flourish in the broader sense of "imitation of human nature." And if, as Aristotle stated, imitation of human nature is the basis of all poetry, did not such ancient sages as Socrates, the great teacher of morals and manners, in this sense also incorporate the mime spirit into his works, a spirit that would perpetuate itself in all literature from antiquity on?

Notes

1. The fourteenth-century English *mummers* or actor–dancers wearing masks, the sixteenth-century Spanish imitators called *momos,* and the *momarie* imitators in Italy during the same period all derived their names from the ancient word *mimus* (Nicoll 1963a, 158–59).

2. Edmondstoune Duncan mentions records of minstrels participating in divine services in *The Story of Minstrelsy* (1907, 38). Benjamin Hunningher and Edmond Faral believe that jugglers and mimes performed in religious plays, but Sandro Sticca denies this (Hunningher 1961, 73–84; Faral: see Hunningher 1961, 76; Sticca 1970, 7–8).

3

Origins of the Commedia dell'Arte and the Théâtres de la Foire

Greco–Roman mime found its way back to Europe via the Middle East. Elements of classical mime were preserved in Constantinople, Antioch, and Alexandria (Nicoll 1963a, 138). These same traits, which gradually took on national or regional characteristics in the Middle East, served in the development of the commedia dell'arte in Europe (Nicoll 1963a, 214–15). Later the commedia dell'arte played a role in helping the French Théâtres de la Foire to survive. Mime and similar type characters, among other typical elements, were found throughout Greco–Roman mime, Byzantine pantomime, the commedia dell'arte, and the Théâtres de la Foire.

Traces of ancient classical mime were thus found in Constantinople (Nicoll 1963a, 107–8), the home of Greek and Roman culture, where it flourished from the fourth century until the end of the Middle Ages. Elements of Greco–Roman mime also survived in Turkish Karagoz theatre, which replaced ancient classical mime after the fall of Constantinople (Reich 1903, chap. 7). This influence was so strong that Karagoz theatre did not take on its own national character until the middle of the seventeenth century. The French traveler Thevenot (1633–1667) noted in his journals similarities between Turkish Karagoz theatre and classical Byzantine pantomime.

Karagoz, the leading character who gave his name to this popular theatre of the Turkish Empire and of Arabia, Egypt, and Tunisia, is dressed in his country's costume. He wears the Turkish turban but sometimes appears, like the ancient *mimus calvus*, with his head uncovered. Like the latter, he carries a phallic symbol and is cheerful, vulgar, and, even if he is seemingly innocent, always ready to play tricks on his neighbor. Although Turkish in appearance and more indecent in his manner, he has traits in common with Pulcinella, Polichinelle, Punch, Kasperl, and Pekelhäring, all descendants of the Latin *sannio* or buffoon and of the Greek mime.

Others in Karagoz theatre who resemble classical mime characters are the idiotic pedant who recalls the Latin schoolmaster Dossennus, and the rich farmer Berky Mustapha, returning from his first trip to the city with his pocketbook empty, who resembles the Latin *rusticus*. There are also merchants, robbers, beggars, farmers, fishermen, and the archetypal characters of different ethnicities, such as the Jew, who also appeared in ancient pantomime.

Like Greek and Roman mimodrama, Karagoz opens with a prologue, followed by several acts in dialogue with pantomime, dance, and stock intrigues. A typical plot deals with family life or with social or political events. Similar to the mime plays of Herodas and the Greek mimographs, this popular, realistic theatre depicts in detail intimate love and brothel scenes. Many of these elements are still found in the modern Karagoz shadow play, which is performed by puppets whose shadows are projected on a white linen screen.

Because some historians have discovered a resemblance between Byzantine and Greek theatre and believe that Greek mimes entertained in Byzantine society (Hunningher 1961, 44), it is also possible that these performers traveled to the Middle East, Palestine, Syria, and as far as the courts of India. The Greek actors who accompanied Alexander the Great to India, where they entertained Hindu princes with dances and pantomimes, could have been a considerable influence on Eastern theatre. In turn, Hindu drama, which originated in religious ceremonies and included music, song, and mime, influenced Greco–Roman drama, as well as all dance and theatre in the Orient.

The mimodramas of both the Greco–Roman and Hindu cultures begin with a prologue and have unity of action, as well as comical *lazzi* or inserted bits of comical stage business. Each has type characters with shaven heads who wear masks (the big-bellied buffoon Viduska belongs to the same family as the *mimus calvus* and the *sannio*). In both cultures, stage settings are sparse or at times nonexistent. And, as in Greco–Roman mime and pantomime, the art of miming using mudras (gestural signs) is highly developed among Hindu mime–dancers.

The Commedia dell'Arte

With the conquest of Byzantium in 1453, mimes fled to Venice, where they performed on public squares and in street entertainments. During the sixteenth century, when Italian street mimes were invited to perform at court, they introduced a type of comedy called *dei maschere* with song, dance, and masked characters, which was one of the elements characterizing the commedia dell'arte.

During the Renaissance, these mimes and buffoons animated the solemn works of Lodovico Ariosto and other Italian playwrights with amusing curtain-raisers and entr'actes. Just as the jongleurs and mimes had done in the miracle and mystery plays, they gradually crept into the action of the play itself. Along with the actors of the period, they soon formed professional companies attached to the court of a prince. They played in theatres, for popular audiences, and at the courts of Europe, which competed to have them perform. Authors wrote sketches that provided them with a rough framework, the success of which depended on their ability to improvise. The name commedia dell'arte was given to this theatre, which was not one of playwrights but of comedians with highly perfected skills, implied in the term *dell'arte*, meaning "of the profession."

Some scholars find only thin evidence of the survival of the classical mime tradition in the commedia dell'arte via the period's mime entertainments (Ogilvy 1963, 619). Rather, they believe the commedia's growth was because of a renewed interest in ancient classical plays and because of the satiric tendency of the period (Nicoll 1963a, 215). Yet, elements of Greek and Roman pantomime and of the Atellan farce (satirical themes, stock characters, and a moral lesson) were found earlier in the comedies of Terence and Plautus, which, in turn, inspired the Renaissance playwrights. So, whether the classical mime heritage was preserved by a continued lineage of mime entertainers or by interest in ancient classical plays combined with the satiric tendency of the period, what is ascertained in tracing the evolution of this art is that the sixteenth-century commedia dell'arte, popular Greek mime, Roman pantomime, and Atellan farce have basic elements in common. Among these elements are the presence of mime and universal type characters that satirize human nature.

Like Greco–Roman mime and Atellan farce, the commedia contains stock character types, masks, farcical action, and scenes full of bastinadoes, acrobatics, and amusing stage business. The scenarios are short and simple and the action flexible enough to allow the actor freedom to improvise, mime, and clown. This improvisational element is reinforced by the use of inserted bits of comical stock business, similar to the *tricae* of Atellan farce, called *lazzi*.[1] Along with perfected technique, the actor's art depends upon successfully linking these *lazzi*, often transmitted from generation to generation, to the main action. Each actor specializes in a stock character, which frequently has a counterpart in ancient mimodrama or Atellan farce. Arlecchino with his shaven head and flat feet, his multicolored coat and black mask, recalls the ancient Roman buffoon, who daubed himself with soot.[2] Like the Roman mime, Arlecchino often wears a phallus and resembles a dancer–or clown–acrobat. Pantalone, the old Venetian merchant, and Dottore, the Paduan academic, appear to be descendants of Pappus of the Atellan farce and of ancient mime's foolish old men and pedantic doctors. Pulcinella, the second valet, a hunchback with a hooknose and a nasal voice, recalls Maccus of Atellan farce. Like Maccus and the *mimus albus*, he dresses in white and wears a skullcap, recalling the ancient mime's shaven head. Although a shrewd fool, he could still be a variation of Maccus, the country bumpkin, and the Roman buffoon. A native of Naples, both he and Maccus, the Oscan mask, originate from the region of Campania. A bronze statue from the Roman period that resembles Pulcinella, with his hooknose and hunchback, reinforces these similarities between ancient mime and the commedia dell'arte.

Why did the *commedia* become so popular in Italy? One reason is that Italy never had a unified theatre. At the performance of each play there was a mingling of dialects that were not always equally intelligible in Milan, Rome, or Naples. Because the *commedia* depends not on the literary merit of a text, but on the actor's talent for improvisation, if his acting was lively and ingenious and he could communicate through movement and gestures, it mattered little whether Pantalone spoke only the Venetian dialect or Dottore exclusively Bolognese. Just before he went on stage, the actor was given the *soggetto* or theme of the prearranged synopsis (usually derived from classical drama and resembling those found in classical mime and medieval farce) and the character type he was to play. The Neapolitans excelled in acting out *lazzi,* and the Lombard authors were skilled in constructing plays; the most sure-fire formula was Neapolitan *lazzi* and a Lombardian subject (Mic 1927, 76).

Another reason for the *commedia*'s success was that the actor developed his art to a high level. In addition to studying history, literature, and philosophy, he trained the body and voice and acquired the skill of spontaneously blending words and movement. Just before appearing on stage, he had to innovatively relate the

theme of the synopsis and character type he was assigned to issues of local or topical interest. *Commedia* actor and author Gherardi describes what was required of
these actors:

> The Italian comedians learn nothing by heart; they need but to glance at the subject of
> a play a moment or two before going on stage. It is this very ability to play at a mo-
> ment's notice which makes a good Italian actor so difficult to replace. Anyone can learn
> a part and recite it on stage, but something else is required for Italian Comedy. For a
> good Italian actor is a man of infinite resourcefulness, a man who plays more from
> imagination than from memory; he matches his words and actions so perfectly with
> whatever is required of him, giving the impression that all he does has been pre-
> arranged. (Duchartre 1929, 30–32)

Some of these Italian players developed their mime talent to such a degree that
their mere appearance on stage would set an audience laughing. David Garrick, who
admired the celebrated Arlecchino Carlino Bertinazzi, told his fellow actors to observe above all "the character and expression of the back of Carlino" (Mic 1927,
116). A spectator left us an account of yet another great Italian actor, Gherardi, and
his ingenious performance in *Colombine Avocat Pour et Contre:* "Scaramouche
made everyone split his sides with laughter during a good quarter hour in a scene of
horror during which he did not pronounce a single word" (Mic 1927, 113).

Italian Theatre Abroad

The *commedia* players were very successful abroad. In France they played at the
courts of Henry III, Henry IV, and Louis XIII and in the festivities of Marie de
Medici and Louis XIV.[3] In sixteenth-century Spain, their influence was manifest in
lavish, allegorical carnivals. When the company of Alberto Ganassa visited Spain in
1574, the stages there were influenced by the platform stages constructed by the
commedia players (Nicoll 1946, 295). In England, spectators appreciated the professional technique and art of such Italian comedians as Drusiano Martinelli, who
performed with his company in London in 1577. A main character in one of the oldest English scenarios, *The Dead Man's Fortune,* is Panteloun.

Before the Italian actors performed at the court of Charles I in 1637, Ben Jonson, in collaboration with the stage designer Inigo Jones, presented masques with
Italian stage innovations (*The Masque of Blackness,* 1605) and used stock characters, such as Captain, possibly inspired by the *commedia's* Capitano. Although the
Italian masque, which eventually found its way to England, was a light form of entertainment consisting of pantomime, music, singing, and dancing and an adaptation
of the *fabulae atellana* of ancient Italy (Broadbent 1901/1965, 98), in England the
poetry, set design, and costumes of this genre became lavish and pompous.

In a number of his plays, Shakespeare incorporated *commedia* elements, as
well as dumb show (*The Tempest, A Midsummer Night's Dream, Hamlet*). In the
speech of the seven ages in *As You Like It,* Shakespeare refers to a *commedia* character in his description of the "sixth age shifting into the lean and slipper'd Pantaloon" (2.7.157–158).

The art of the Italian players had a direct influence on such playwrights as
Molière. The French playwright's own acting style was inspired by the Italian actor
Tiberio Fiorilli, who played with him in 1658; Fiorilli specialized in the role of

Scaramuccia and was said to be the finest actor of his time. In his introduction to Molière's *Précieuses Ridicules*, Donneau de Visé describes Molière as an actor: "Everything in his person spoke; with a step, a smile, a wink of the eye and a wag of the head he made us understand more than the greatest speech-maker would have in an hour" (1963, 14). In Molière's theatre, as in the *commedia,* action precedes the spoken word. The French playwright also drew upon the *commedia* for his dramatis personae. His chicken-hearted, knavish valet Pierrot, forever falling in love, appeared in Italian comedy in 1547 as Pedrolino.[4]

The first permanent theatre of the Italian comedians in Paris was at the Hôtel de Bourgogne, from 1658 to 1697 and again in 1716 under the direction of Luigi Riccoboni, where they performed until the French Revolution. With the continued success of such companies as Evaristo Gherardi's, Arlecchino and Pantalone soon learned to speak French. Gherardi's Italian sketches also shared the bill with plays by the French Jean-François Regnard, Jean Palaprat, Germain Boisfranc, and Charles Rivière Dufresny. The French playwright Marivaux wrote plays in his own language for the Comédie Italienne, incorporating *commedia* themes and characters.

During the second half of the eighteenth century, the *commedia* lost much of its popularity. After seeing the Italian comedians perform to empty houses in France, in 1760 Carlo Goldoni replaced their outmoded scenarios with literary scripts, abolished improvisation and slapstick, and modified the character types. About the same time, Carlo Gozzi, who attempted to reform the *commedia*, wrote scenarios for the Italian comedians, counteracting Goldoni's attempts to abolish it. In Germany, the playwright Johann Christoph Gottsched replaced the farces of Hanswurst (the German Arlecchino) with a more literary theatre. In France, Riccoboni's company began to perform in French; other companies followed suit, abandoning improvised comedy.

Despite the gradual death of the *commedia* at home and abroad, it had developed a highly perfected acting art and perpetuated an organization for professional actors. It had influenced such authors as Marivaux, Shakespeare, Molière, and Lope de Vega. For three centuries it also succeeded in inspiring such artists as Mozart in music; Giovanni Tiepolo, Jean Watteau, and Nicolas Lancret in painting; and Paul Verlaine and Jules La Forgue in poetry.

Les Théâtres de la Foire

The most celebrated Paris fairs were La Foire Saint-Germain in the early spring, which noblemen and students patronized, and the people's fair on the Place Saint-Laurent in August and September. At both one could see pantomimes, marionette shows, monologues, acrobats, trained dogs, and monkeys. The art of the Italian players heightened the success of these fairs during the seventeenth and eighteenth centuries.

From 1570 on, a repertory of light, popular plays was successfully performed in the fair theatres. However, all theatre from the fifteenth through the seventeenth centuries was tightly controlled by *La Confrérie de la Passion*, an amateur guild of bourgeois and artisans that organized in 1402 for performances of mystery plays and that penalized companies playing without a permit. Only during brief periods could these companies perform without a permit, as in 1595, when an edict allowed them to play freely at fairs. Most often, fair-goers could see tumblers and trained animals. And in 1650 Pierre Dattelin Brioché began to stage *commedia*-style marionette shows at the fairs.[5] Others, such as those of Jean-Baptiste Archambault, soon grew popular.

A series of circumstances encouraged more performances of acrobatic feats and dumb shows at the fairs. When Maurice Vondrebeck and Charles Allard's company performed for the first time on February 3, 1678, at the Foire Saint-Germain in *Les Forces de l'Amour et de la Magie*, because of a government interdiction, the actors were permitted to speak only with the presence of tumblers on stage. In the cast of characters—besides Zorastre, the magician and lover of Crésinde the shepherdess, and his valet, Merlin—there were several tumblers on pedestals: four as demons, four as shepherds, and four as Polichinelles (Drack 1889, 12–13).

During these periods when actors were forbidden to speak on stage, the improvised art of the Italian comedians helped the fair theatres survive, as well as provided them with a repertory. In 1697, at the Foire Saint-Germain, the three companies of Maurice Vondrebeck, Alexandre Bertrand, and Charles and Pierre Allard improvised sketches with *commedia* characters and themes. And, at the turn of the eighteenth century, when the Italian players were banned from the stage, French fair actors continued to perform fragments of the Italian repertory.

Continually harassed by the Comédie Française and the Opéra, the Théâtres de la Foire were again prohibited in 1707 from using dialogue. Their ingenious solution was to devise scenes in which only one actor had a speaking part. The others mimed the action printed on an explanatory poster over the stage or on synopses or songs passed out and sung. One of the most talented of these fair mimes was Louis Nivellon, who had his own mime company in 1707, 1708, and 1711.

Jealous of the continuing success of the Théâtres de la Foire, the Comédie Française and the Opéra finally succeeded in having even its monologues suppressed. Harassed by the parliament and unprotected by the throne, the fair actors or *forains* sang the dialogue, danced and mimed the action, or had marionettes perform the play. Half-serious, half-comical plays with songs and themes revolving around the adventures of Arlequin (*Arlequin Invisible, Arlequin Mahomet*) were written by Alain-René Lesage, Louis Fuzelier, Alexis Piron, and d'Orneval, who were among the first to give them a definitive form. With the staging in 1714 of an opéra comique by the widow Baron and Saint Edmé, this genre, which includes Italian comedy, elements of fair theatre, and parodies of serious opera, was established.

While marionette shows, rope dancing, tumblers, and trained animals continued at the Théâtres de la Foire, the Comédie Française managed on several occasions to have opéra comique banned, succeeding in suppressing it completely from 1745 to 1752. But in 1752, when Jean-Louis Monnet, director of the Opéra Comique, obtained permission to reopen his theatre, its character had changed. Although the themes and characters were still derived from the Comédie Italienne, the vaudeville elements had disappeared and music had been written especially for the opéra comique genre. In 1762, the once-more restored Comédie Italienne joined forces with the opéra comique to create a light musical, dramatic form similar to the Neapolitan opera buffa. While this new opéra comique, born from the Comédie Italienne and the Théâtres de la Foire, flourished, another theatre, which borrowed elements from the same sources, would achieve its greatest glory in the silent art of Gaspard Deburau. At the beginning of the nineteenth century, at the Théâtre des Funambules, Deburau would transform the Italian Pedrolino, a last vestige of the ancient *stupidus*, into a poetic, essentially French Pierrot.

Notes

1. The word *lazzi* is probably derived from the Italian *lazzo* or *l'azione*, which signifies action of a piece of business and is related to the Latin *actio*. Another possible origin is from the Tuscan *lacci* (ribbon) and refers to stage business that serves to tie the action of the play together. Examples of *lazzi* are Arlecchino, who pulls off and eats wings of flies or butterflies; imagines how he will hang himself; or pretends to be a statue.

2. One of the origins of Arlecchino relates to the city of Arles and another to *Hellequin*, the French word in the Middle Ages for a suffering spirit that made noises at night. Still another is that of the ancient *Zanni* (buffoon), who appeared on stage with his face daubed with soot, his head shaven, and wearing a costume made of small patches of material. It is also possible that Arlecchino originates from Mercury or Hermes, the messenger of the gods who wore sandals with wings.

3. Among the *commedia* companies that performed in France was Alberto Giovanni Ganassa's, which played at the marriage of the king of Navarre to Marguerite de Valois (1572). In 1577, Flaminio Scala's company (I Comici Gelosi) performed at Blois for Henri III. Among others that played in France were I Comici Confidenti (1571) and I Accesi (1599). From 1600–04, I Comici Gelosi played at the Hôtel de Bourgogne. The Comici Fedeli was brought to Paris by Marie de Medici in 1613; it performed alternately with French comedians in Venetian, Genoese, Castilian, French, and German. In 1639, the company of Giuseppe Bianchi was invited by Louis XIII to direct operas and improvise plays. In 1658, Tiberio Fiorilli (the famous Scaramuccia who inspired Molière) played at the Petit Bourbon alternately with Molière's company. Many French words were inserted into the Italian dialogue, and soon whole scenes were performed in French.

4. Molière gave us the first French Pedrolino in the character of Pierrot in *Don Juan*, differing from Gaspard Deburau's Pierrot, who was a dreamer and an ingenuous poet. In 1673, the Italian actor Giuseppe Giratone interpreted the French Pierrot in an imitation of Molière's *Don Juan*.

5. The term marionette denotes a sacred origin because it is the diminutive of Marie and, in effect, the first French marionettes were little statuettes of the Virgin. At the end of the sixteenth century, there were several marionette theatres in France.

4

Gaspard Deburau and the
Pierrots of the Nineteenth Century

The skeleton of every good dramatic play is pantomime, although the bones
which comprise it must be covered with the living skin of poetry.

Théophile Gautier

Le Théâtre des Funambules

Pantomime found a new haven when, in 1816, Nicolas Bertrand, a former butter
merchant from Vincennes, transformed his little booth of dog and acrobatic shows
on the Boulevard du Temple in Paris into the Théâtre des Funambules. Spectators
could now watch the Montrose acrobats in a basement, where an orchestra of three
blind men played while trained dogs performed on a small stage. But only by special permission could these acrobats include mime acts in their shows.

One day, when Bertrand saw a family of Bohemian tightrope walkers and tumblers perform in a Saint-Maur courtyard, he hired them. One of them was Gaspard
Deburau, born in Bohemia on July 31, 1796. Deburau was such a clumsy acrobat
that his father kicked him about on stage and made him the butt of practical jokes.
The exasperated Deburau wanted to take his own life but changed his mind when Jacomo, an old Italian mime at the Théâtre des Chiens Savants, began to teach him
pantomime.

All Paris came to applaud Deburau at the Théâtre des Funambules. His Pierrot, though inspired by the commedia dell'arte's lazy, mischievous valet, Pedrolino,
soon became an essentially French character. Deburau's creation of Pierrot was a
spontaneous one. One night, while making himself up to play a ghost, he whitened
his face and put on lipstick. Retaining Pedrolino's white trousers and large-buttoned
jacket, he discarded the ruffle at the collar and in place of a hat or white head scarf
wore a black skullcap. Abandoning the traditional Italian mask, he combined the facial expressions and gestures that Jacomo had taught him with the stunts he had
learned as a funambulist (tight-rope performer). Deburau's popular entertainment
was called *La Pantomime Sautante* (jumping pantomine).

Deburau had changed Pierrot from a cynical, grotesque rogue into a poetic fellow. He remained a vain, cowardly liar, but he was also kind and sensitive. The
French poet Théodore de Banville contrasts Deburau's sentimental Pierrot with the
clumsy Italian Pulcinella and the boisterous English Clown. Yet, Pierrot belonged to
all peoples. One can still find him in Petroushka, Hanswurst, and Kasparl.

These Théâtre des Funambules pantomimes—with their mime, ballets, acrobatic stunts, and songs—had elaborate transformation scenes, character metamorphoses, lavish decors, costumes, and many set changes and accessories. The prop list, for example, of *Ma Mère l'Oie, ou Arlequin et l'Oeuf d'Or* (*Mother Goose, or Harlequin and the Golden Egg*), in which Deburau performed in 1829, ran to 250 items. Although not always related to the main plot, each scene of the grandiose Pantomimes–Arlequinades was a spectacle in itself. Like all pantomime at this time, these scenes were essentially comical. Even the nightmarish pantomime–melodrama, familiar to the Boulevard du Temple audiences, always turned into comedy.

Deburau brought a highly personal expression to the fantasy, acrobatics, melodrama, and spectacular staging that characterized nineteenth-century pantomimes. Not only did he add extempore bits of business to a given action, but he also invented many of his own scenarios. Just as for several centuries the commedia dell'arte, which depended on the actor's improvisational skills, had influenced all European theatre, nineteenth-century pantomime, because of the inventive genius of Deburau, reached great heights.[1]

Other Nineteenth-Century Mimes

By 1820 the Paris Funambules, the Acrobates, and the Bobino theatres were renowned for pantomime and acrobatics. As Deburau's name was linked with the Funambules, so was that of the Harlequin–acrobat Félix Chiarini's with the Acrobates and the Funambules, and English mime–acrobat Philip Laurent's with the Funambules. Another mime–acrobat–dancer, Charles-François Mazurier, played the lead in *Polichinelle Vampire* (1823) at the Porte St.-Martin.

Paul Legrand, who began in 1839 in vaudeville shows, went on to play small comic roles in Deburau's company and became his understudy. But Legrand was coldly received in London in 1847; instead of jumping about and boxing like the English clown, he played a dreamy and poetic Pierrot. A victim of his own credulity, his Pierrot was also ingenuous, cheerful, and fanciful. Legrand left the Funambules in 1853 to join the Folies Concertantes across the street.

Alexandre Guyon (1830–1905), who continued the Pierrot of Gaspard Deburau, joined Deburau's company as a stagehand and went on to play with Paul Legrand and Charles Deburau. Sarah Bernhardt, who herself had played Pierrot in *Pierrot Assassin,* noticed his clever mimicry of actors.

Following in his father's footsteps, Charles Deburau (1829–1873) continued to perform in pantomime, differing from Gaspard through his use of spoken prologues and epilogues. The mime–dancer Derudder performed in Deburau's company in 1856, playing Polichinelle in *Arlequin Barbier*. Michel Vautier was one of the period's last Polichinelles.

Mimes in the south of France continued the tradition of Gaspard Deburau. Marseilles was soon second only to Paris. Louis Rouffe and Séverin played at the Café Vivaux, the Variétés, the Concert Parisien, and the Palais de Cristal. At the Alcazar one could see Charles Placide, Brunet, and the Italian Chiarinis. Full-scale pantomimes, such as *L'Armée Française en Russie,* with battle scenes in the Kremlin, military marches, and the burning of Moscow, were a house specialty.

Among the last Pierrots of the Marseilles school, Louis Rouffe (1849–1885) influenced Séverin, one of France's greatest mimes. Born in Ajaccio on May 19,

1863, Séverin studied gymnastics, boxing, fencing, and Rouffe's art with Théodore Thales, a member of Rouffe's company, at sixteen. Séverin, who wore the traditional white Pierrot make-up, soon became known as *l'Homme Blanc* in Montpellier, Nimes, Marseilles, and Bordeaux. In 1891 he played *Pauvre Pierrot* at l'Eldorado in Paris, and in 1896 his *Chand d'Habits* at the Folies Bergères was a brilliant success. When the new school of "intuitives" attempted to abolish traditional pantomime, Séverin defended it. After the First World War, when pantomime vanished from the theatre, this great mime of the classical school, the "Prince of Attitudes," interpreted silent roles on stage and screen.

Although at the end of Séverin's life there were too few Pierrots to inspire a following, pantomime was still alive in the circus and in music hall and vaudeville acts. The clown Jean-Baptiste Auriol mimed, as well as performed acrobatics, at the Cirque Olympique. One could see realistic, melodramatic, or fairy pantomimes on the stages of the Galerie Vivienne, Le Théâtre Moderne, and Le Théâtre d'Application and at the Folies Bergères, l'Hippodrome, l'Eldorado, Les Bouffes Parisiens, and many other famous music halls.

Already, the poet Paul Verlaine had described a fast-changing Pierrot:

> He is no longer the lunar dreamer of the ancient air
> Who laughed at his forefathers in the panel friezes
> His gaity like his candle, alas, is dead
> And his ghost today haunts us, thin and clear. (1939, 190)

In 1888, after pantomime had declined, a group of writers and actors (Champfleury, the younger Coquelin, J. K. Huysman, Paul Legrand, Jules Lemaître, and Jean Richepin) founded the Cercle des Funambules. The Cercle's first staging, *L'Enfant Prodigue*, appeared at the Bouffes Parisiens in 1890, with music especially composed for each movement and gesture. But with the advent of the First World War, the Cercle des Funambules disappeared.

Still, Pierrot had gained a powerful hold on the imaginations of French writers and artists. Adolphe Wilette continued to paint him as a naive dreamer. In Jules Chéret's paintings, he is no longer in white but in a black costume, calling to mind Charles Baudelaire's vision of the world as a curious procession of undertakers mourning some sort of funeral (Hugounet 1889, 224). In Verlaine's verses, Pierrot is decadent and carefree; for the poet Georges Lorin,

> He is the flower of melancholy
> Taking the moon for his mirror
> He is a flight of admirable folly
> Who goes out to combat darkness. (Hugounet 1889, 232)

If by the end of the century Pierrot's nostalgic image had faded away, it lived on still more vividly in the poems of Champfleury, Théodore de Banville, Charles Nodier, and Jules Janin. Théodore Gautier describes Pierrot as

> Fluttering with his sleeve
> Like a penguin on a rock
> The white Pierrot, through a half-note
> Passes his head and winks his eye. (1969, 268)

Notes

1. Gaspard Deburau made his début in 1819 with *Arlequin Médecin.* Next he played in *Arlequin Dogue, Père Barbare,* and *Arlequin Statue*, after which he was called Baptiste. He was at the height of his success in *Le Boeuf Enragé* (1826), a pantomime harlequinade in twelve tableaux, and in *Ma Mère l'Oie, ou Arlequin et l'Oeuf d'Or* (1829). When Deburau died from asthma on June 16, 1846, Paul Legrand succeeded him, playing in Champfleury's *Pierrot Pendu.* When Legrand left, Charles Deburau replaced him, performing in *Les Trois Planètes ou la Vie d'une Rose*. After Charles Deburau's departure with the Arlequin Derudder, the owner of the Funambules, Billion, hired English mimes. Meanwhile, Charles Deburau performed at the Délassements Comiques, returning to the Funambules in 1862 to play in *Le Rameau d'Or*, a harlequinade fairy play with song and dance. That year, the Théâtre des Funambules closed with *Les Mémoires de Pierrot*, a pantomime in two acts and twenty-two tableaux in which Charles Deburau interpreted his father's most memorable creations. The theatre was demolished on July 18, 1862. (For descriptions of Deburau's pantomimes, see F. W. Warner, *Enter Pierrot* [Chapel Hill: University of North Carolina Press, 1963].)

5

English Pantomime

Greco–Roman pantomime did not spread throughout Europe until after the fall of the Roman Empire, when mimes wandered across the continent and possibly as far as England. Although pantomime took on very different forms in England, to this day the Christmas pantomimes retain the names of Greek and Roman characters, such as Momus, the god of comedy, and Charon, the ferryman of the river Styx (Mawer 1986, 33–34).

Like the jongleurs and mimes in France and Italy, the English jester amused nobles at court, played the roles of "vice" or the "fool," and performed in play interludes in the Middle Ages. The spirit of ancient mime was kept alive, too, in the classical tragedies of the Elizabethan theatre, where a dumb show introduced each act and later appeared within the act itself. Shakespeare enlivened many of his scenes with jesters, fools, and clowns.[1] And Ben Jonson incorporated elements of Greek and Roman pantomime and antique comedy into his *Masque of Blackness* (1605), *Masque of Beauty* (1608), and *Masque of Queens* (1609).

Companies and actors from France and Italy also favored the development of pantomime in seventeenth-century England. The *forains* or French fair players performed in traditional English harlequinades. Italian actors, such as Tiberio Fiorilli, who came to London in 1673 to play *Scaramuccia*, inspired English clowns. In 1660, the actor Robert Cox directed scenes called *Humours or Drolleries* in the Italian manner.

In 1702, when John Weaver composed *The Tavern Bilkers* with dances and pantomimes in the Italian manner, it was a failure. But he went on to stage successful ballet–pantomimes in which he imitated Roman pantomime with mythological characters and employed *commedia* masks. From 1716 on, Weaver staged *The Loves of Mars and Venus*—the first entertainment on the English stage to be called a pantomime—*Perseus and Andromeda, Cupid and Bacchus,* and *Harlequin Turn'd Judge.*[2]

About the same time, because of a speech impediment and a poor memory, harlequin John Rich (known as Lun) became a mime and engaged the German mime–dancer Schwartz and his trained dogs to perform in his company. In 1717, Rich staged *The Execution of Harlequin,* a pantomime in the Italian manner, followed by *Harlequin the Sorcerer, Harlequin Chasing the Butterfly,* and *The Necromancer, or the History of Doctor Faustus.* The latter, performed in 1724, marked the height of pantomime as a favorite entertainment. This combination of pantomime, opera, masque, commedia dell'arte, folk dance, song, and magic was highly popular in England. Under Rich's influence, stage effects and costumes became more lavish, dances more elaborate, and transformation scenes more spectacular, all harbingers of the Christmas pantomime.

Pantomime had now become so popular in England that even actors such as David Garrick performed it. Edmund Kean appeared from time to time in harlequinades, which served as curtain-raisers. Among the famous Harlequins of the period were Harry Woodward (Lun, Jr.), who succeeded Rich, the acrobatic mimes Vandemere the Harlequin and William Rufus Chetwood, and James Byrne, who transformed Harlequin's costume into that of a fairy, with a wand and Mercury's wings on the feet to indicate swiftness.

Until this time, English pantomime did not always differ significantly from traditional pantomime on the continent. English pantomime performers and French fair players made use of commedia dell'arte and mythological characters in flexibly structured plots adding songs and dances, elaborate scenery, and mechanical devices. A pantomimist who brought these elements to England was Francisque Molin and his French Fair troupe, whom John Rich engaged to perform in London during the 1718–19 season. The French pantomimist Louis Nivellon appeared as Punch in *Harlequin Necromancer* in 1723 and as Harlequin in *The Robbers, or Harlequin Trapped by Colombine* in 1724 at Lincoln's Inn Fields Theatre. The Italian clown Delpini (1740–1828) moved to London in 1780, where he became a popular Pantaloon and Pierrot.

The Clown

Differences soon developed between the English clown and his continental counterpart. England's major contribution to pantomime was the introduction of the clown, who, though much inspired by the exalted Italian buffoon Arlecchino, created his own comical style. The English clown indulged mostly in acrobactics and slapstick; instead of a half-mask, he wore heavy make-up and, like the ancient mimes, had an enormous nose, large mouth, exaggerated hips, and thin legs. Today, with his red wig and his smile stretching from ear to ear, he is one of the few survivors of pantomime in England.

Grimaldi (born in 1778), the son of the harlequin Giuseppe Grimaldi, first appeared at the age of two, playing a monkey with his father in the Sadler's Wells Company. Later he performed at French and Italian fairs and in ballet–pantomimes at Drury Lane as Harlequin and Pantaloon. The English public took him instantly to their hearts; they preferred this practical joker, with his enormous mouth and nose, his fat hips and spindly legs, his pratfalls and somersaults, to the French and Italian mimes, who jumped little and performed few somersaults. For this reason, when the French Pierrot, Paul Legrand, played in London at the beginning of the nineteenth century, the English gave him a cold reception. Yet, the English Harlequin was much appreciated in France. When Philip Laurent, son of the acrobat Jean-Baptiste Laurent, returned from England to play at the Théâtre des Funambules, he was applauded by the Parisians.

Among the famous nineteenth-century mime–clowns who continued the Grimaldi tradition in England were Grimaldi's pupil Tom Matthews, who trained the one-legged clown Jefferini; Harry Boleno, the grave-looking clown; Harry Richard Flexmore, the dancing clown; Harry Payne, the children's favorite; Whimsical Walker, the last of the Drury Lane clowns; and Leigh Hunt, the last English Harlequin, who died in 1842. The Hanlon-Lees were a family of burlesque acrobats who created pantomimes with perilous stunts and violent horror scenes, as in *Do Mi Sol Do,* in which an orchestra musician attacks his conductor, who, lost in the music, continues to conduct amid the ensuing violence. But as the nineteenth century drew to its end, Clown abandoned the theatre for the circus. So, while in France Deburau left tumbling and acrobatics to become a pantomimist, in England, Clown gave up the art of gesture to become a tumbler and an acrobat.

Twentieth-Century Pantomime

By the end of the nineteenth century, English pantomime was neither a short performance in dumb show played between the acts of a Shakespearean drama nor a vehicle for satire and social comment. It was absorbed into such stagings as *The Tales of Mother Goose,* in which Clown played along with Harlequin, Colombine, and other commedia dell'arte characters. Technical advances in stagecraft made it possible to achieve more elaborate effects; the public could not have enough of pumpkins turning into coaches and slaves becoming princesses. As dumb show gave way to fairy and folk scenes with dialogue and music hall numbers, mime began to die. The great mime–clowns also disappeared. The lovable mime–clown Dan Leno passed on in 1904, and "Little Tich," who influenced the creation of Charlie Chaplin's Little Tramp, died in 1928. Grock (Adrien Wettach), the Swiss-born clown so well known to English audiences, left the circus for the music hall and seldom appeared in London after 1924.

Throughout the twentieth-century harlequinades such as *Babe in the Woods* and the children's Christmas pantomime *Dick Whittington* continued to appear, although they grew more remote from traditional pantomime. The Christmas pantomime, performed since the 1820s, portrays one of fifty or more favorite fairy tales, such as *Sleeping Beauty, Jack and the Beanstalk, Cinderella, Bluebeard,* and *Aladdin.* Staged with fanciful costumes and glittering decors, these have moved from the world of *commedia* into the kingdom of fairies and are far-removed from Harlequin's adventures and Pierrot's daydreams. In these spectacles, filled with tradition and fantasy, while an enchanting fairy enters from stage right, the villain enters from stage left; next, a dainty "spirit" in red velvet and gold spangles appears, singing and dancing, to deliver a message from the queen of fairies. Rarely do Pierrot or Harlequin appear; if they do, they are transformed into graceful, shadowy figures.

By the twentieth century, the English Christmas pantomime, a bustling combination of *commedia*, fairy tales, musical comedy, vaudeville, acrobatics, magic, and slapstick, had become a technical marvel. In the *Cinderella* pantomime, for example, mice and a pumpkin disappear in a flash and are replaced by splendid horses harnessed to a real carriage, ready to drive a magnificently gowned Cinderella to the ball. Between acts, while the audience and the company sing popular songs, Master Clown jokes and performs tumbling feats. In short, the Christmas pantomime contains everything from Harlequin to Mother Goose except the art of mime. Yet, it is this heterogenous "everything" that has rendered the Christmas pantomime, invented in England, unique (Beerbohm 1965, 52).

This spectacular entertainment—first silent and then a speaking harlequinade that turned into a burlesque extravaganza with fantastic themes, elaborate sets, and clown and acrobatic acts—was not the only kind of pantomime found in England. Toward the middle of the twentieth-century, French-style pantomime and commedia dell'arte became popular. Irene Mawer's classical pantomime style in Ruby Ginner's *Et Puis Bonsoir* (1910), performed for more than ten years, and in the popular *L'Enfant Prodigue* (1928), prepared the ground for this revival. In 1947, Clifford Williams founded the Mime Theatre Company, which staged Elizabethan dumb show, traditional French pantomime, farce, and commedia dell'arte. *Commedia* characters also appeared in the ballet *Carnaval* (1934, 1935, 1944) with Robert Helpmann; in *Harlequin in the Street* (1938), choreographed by Frederick Ashton; in *Harlequinade* (1950) with the Markova Dolin Company; and in *Harlequin in April* (1951), choreographed by John Cranko. Pulcinella continued to be applauded in the traditional Punch and Judy puppet shows, popular during the eighteenth century. Stemming from Pulcinella, the mischievous servant with the hooked nose and hunchback, Punch grew still more popular for his grotesque appearance and clever tricks.

By the mid-twentieth century, even though Clown appeared less often in traditional pantomime shows and the Christmas pantomime had little in common with mime, this art had not vanished from the English stage. Pierrot and Harlequin mimed a number in the Christmas pantomime or performed occasionally in a village theatre. And while Punch beat his wife, Judy, and Pierrot still pursued Colombine in ballet slippers, the sprightly and devilish Harlequin was enlivening the modern dance–drama.

Notes

1. In *Der Mimus* (1903), Hermann Reich describes Falstaff as the incarnation of the ancient buffoon and the king of all clowns. Reich also finds Shakespeare as much a mimograph as Philistion or any of the ethnological writers.

2. During a period when dancers stressed technique and virtuosity, John Weaver, in his *Essay toward a History of Dancing* (1712) and *Anatomical and Mechanical Lectures on Dancing* (1721), encourages the use of gesture.

6

Mime and Movement in
German, Russian, and Italian Theatre

German Theatre

While street mimes played at inns, at public festivals, and on church steps, the German heirs to Roman mimes, called *spielmänner,* played in castles. Their performances of Greek and Roman legends and ballads of heroic adventures, such as *Beowulf,* are said to have inspired literary epics such as the *Niebelungenlied* and the *Gudrunlied.* The threads of these heroic narratives, which mimes and jongleurs performed, were later taken up by the church in Austria and southern Germany. The nun Hrosvitha of Gandersheim's (925–1002) highly theatrical, dramatic dialogues, for example, are believed to have been inspired by the entertainments of mimes and jongleurs.

In Germany, as in France and England, the mystery and miracle plays reenacted Bible stories and legends of the saints in elaborate, mimed tableaux. This tradition continues today in Austria, Switzerland, Germany, France, Italy, and Mexico. In Oberammergau, Germany, for example, villagers still stage the *Passion of Christ* every ten years.

The carnival dances and farces of the Middle Ages were filled with gaiety and burlesque. The fifteenth-century farces of Hans Rosenblüt frequently ended with lively songs and drinking bouts. The barber Hans Folz was the author of farcical *Fastnachtsspiele* or Shrovetide plays, and the Nuremberg cobbler, Hans Sachs, wrote spirited comedies for sixteenth-century carnivals that have since been performed in Bavaria, Hungary, and Silesia.

Arlecchino and Hanswurst

At the end of the sixteenth century, English actors brought the buffooneries of Clown, the Dutch Pekelhäring (later known as Hanswurst), and the Italian Arlecchino to Germany. After Arlecchino died, he was reborn in Hanswurst. The Silesian playwright Joseph Anton Stranitsky, who founded the first public theatre in Vienna in 1710, himself played Hanswurst dressed as a Salzburg peasant who moved with Arlecchino's grace. Rechristened Kasperl during the nineteenth century, Hanswurst played a leading role in the Austrian popular theatre. The *commedia* spirit was also revived in the works of German playwrights such as Franz Castelli, who incorporated *commedia*-type characters.

Max Reinhardt

The German theatre in the eighteenth century had become a battleground between the physical and the verbal. While Johann Goethe, Johann Schiller, and Fredrich Gottleib Klopstock defended the popularity of Hanswurst, Johann Christoph Gottsched replaced this genre with a pseudo-classical, literary theatre. Banished from the city theatres, Hanswurst continued to flourish in the suburbs.

In the late nineteenth century, after Otto Brahm founded the Freie Volksbühne in Berlin, where he introduced the naturalistic plays of Hermann Sudermann and Gerhart Hauptmann, Max Reinhardt counteracted this movement through his use of stage design, lighting, costume, text, music, voice, gesture, and movement. The presence of stairs and bridges, lighting effects to conquer space and accentuate movement, vertical lines to make an actor seem smaller, and horizontal lines to magnify him, as well as the use of rhythmic mass movement, all heightened the shades of a play's central meaning. Rebelling against the so-called tyranny of literature, which had dominated the theatre of his time for more than a century, Reinhardt harmonized the actor's art with that of the playwright, stage designer, and musician.

In his production of *Jedermann* (*Everyman*), first performed before the cathedral of Salzburg in 1920, and in *The Miracle*, a pantomime based on the medieval legend of Sister Beatrice, Reinhardt utilized chanting, incense, Gothic vaulting, and light filtering down through rose windows. He also staged the pantomime *Sumurun* (1915), which had an Oriental setting, and the ballet pantomime *Die Gruene Floete* (*The Green Flute,* 1916) by Hugo Von Hofmannsthal.

Bertolt Brecht

Bertolt Brecht (1898–1956), Reinhardt's assistant director in 1923, believed that rather than support the action, the movement, music, choreography, and lighting should serve to destroy the spectator's emotional involvement. Pantomime, dance, films, signs, slides: any contrivance could be utilized to keep the spectator from viewing the play in terms of a conventional plot and dramatic conflicts. Through these theatrical devices, the spectator was not to leave his *Threepenny Opera* remembering what happened or sighing over poor Polly and MacHeath, but rather having gained an awareness of our human condition.

Brecht called the actor's alienation from the spectator *Verfremdung*. The ideal actor did not lose himself in his part; he demonstrated the action with his voice, face, and body, much like the Chinese actor uses conventional signs to communicate the action. To prevent the audience from becoming involved, Brecht would have one actor mime the action while another read the lines or would interrupt the dialogue with mimed action and vice versa. To break the continuity of the dramatic action, Brecht employed songs and sketches. For example, in *The Exception and the Rule* (1930) and in *The Didactic Play of Baden; On Consent*, an oratorio written in 1929, the dramatic action alternates with interludes of miming, clowning, and asides.

Each of Brecht's plays revolves around a basic *gestus* or symbolic gesture, which summarizes the theme of the play and its social import and is served by other gestures, movements, attitudes, groupings, voices, and intonations. In *The Caucasian Chalk Circle* (1948), the basic *gestus* is the drawing of the circle. In *Mother Courage* (1941), it is the wagon dragged by the mother and her children, who disappear one by one until she is left alone, symbolizing the futility of sacrificing her children to war. Aside from using these basic symbolic gestures, Brecht had whole scenes mimed out and engaged mimes such as Benno Besson to train his company.

Brecht's sources were the commedia dell'arte, Chinese theatre (*The Good Woman of Setzuan*, 1940), the comedy of manners, the Greek chorus, the theatre of the fairs, circus art (*The Baby Elephant,* 1924), folklore (*Puntila,* 1940, based on a Finnish tale), the theatres of Vsevolod Meyerhold and Alexander Tairoff, the pantomimes of Max Reinhardt, and the political and epic theatre of Irwin Piscator.

Russian Theatre

Among the earliest Russian rituals were the hunting and peasant tribes' primitive songs, dances, disguises, pantomimes, and dialogues. In the ancient *New Year Play*, still performed at the turn of the twentieth century, a group of peasants enters a nobleman's house—playing instruments, singing, and dancing—with a mime wearing a goatskin and a rudimentary wooden mask and carrying a horn. The *skomorokhi* (buffoons similar to the German *spielmänner*, who, from the tenth to the sixteenth centuries, came from Byzantium to dance, play the flute, and stage bear and marionette shows) mimed, danced, and sang a young couple's engagement and marriage in the *Ukrainian Wedding Play*. Much of religious drama was born from the symbolic movements of the officiating priests in the orthodox church of Byzantium. Precise stage directions for movement, attitudes, and gestures are given in religious plays, such as *The Washing of the Feet on Holy Thursday*.

Italian comedy early influenced Russian theatre. In 1658, Vassili Likhatchov, delegate to the court of Ferdinand de Medici, brought back a detailed account of a performance he had seen there. About this time, Simeon Smirnov's interludes in the Italian style enhanced his comedies. During the reign of Empress Anna (1730–1740), the composer Francesco Araia staged *commedia* scenes with actors, singers, and Italian mimes in St. Petersburg. *Commedia* also reappeared in the stagings of St. Petersburg's Old Theatre during the nineteenth and twentieth centuries.

Although by the end of the seventeenth century Russian dance was known throughout Europe, it was not until the second half of the nineteenth century that the theatre, guided by Konstantin Stanislavsky, emerged as a fully evolved art.

Konstantin Stanislavsky

Konstantin Stanislavsky's name (1863–1938) is identified with realism. For him, the object of theatre, as of any art, was to express inner truth. The actor did not merely appear in his role; he had to become it. He needed not only to develop his imagination and creative powers through the study of history, political science, music, art, and psychology; he also had to acquire control of his body and his voice by mastering dance, pantomime, gymnastics, fencing, and singing. Only with this preparation and a highly tuned instrument at his disposal was the actor ready to use a text. Unforgettable effects were achieved with a minimum of vocal and corporeal expression. Not only would the actor renounce the ringing voice and the declamatory gesture, he might best convey a truth by remaining silent and absolutely still. The dramatist and theorist Nicolas Evreinoff cites Z. Borovski on the use of silence at the Moscow Art Theatre, which Stanislavsky co-founded, as "holding more meaning than thousands of words and which causes the drama to resound and burst forth in a thousand colors" (1947, 317). Stanislavsky influenced stage directors such as Jacques Copeau, who also trained the body and the senses to express dramatic emotion based on inner truth.

Vsevolod Meyerhold

Stanislavksy's student Vsevolod Meyerhold (1874–1943) reacted against realist theatre in order to restore the actor's function to that which he had held in primitive ritual and to reintroduce the theatrical quality of ancient theatre. In Meyerhold's view, the text was secondary. "The word," he said, "is only the design on the material of movement" (Slonim 1961, 184). He viewed theatre as an art of space and time and provided the actor with every means—ramps, stairways, platforms—to extend himself physically. The actor's entire body should be utilized as an expressive instrument. Through what he called biomechanics (a method that researched the body as a living machine and originated from the scientific study of American assembly-line workers using conveyer-belts to eliminate superfluous movement), the actor developed the physical virtuosity of a mime, jongleur, comedian, and acrobat; he became, in Edward Gordon Craig's words, a kind of "supermarionette." With exaggerated gestures and with the aid of designers and technicians, he could tansform himself on stage into a being larger than life. Here again we see the commedia dell'arte's influence at work, where the actor is not concerned with creating an individualized character but with realizing a type character, as exemplified by Meyerhold's staging of Nikolai Gogol's *The Inspector General*. Ideally, each actor, with his own corporeal style and his particular rhythm, should blend into a production, much like the individual timbres of musical instruments blend into an orchestral composition. Although Meyerhold was the first to direct Russian plays by playwrights such as Vladimir V. Mayakovsky, he and his disciples also engaged in nonverbal productions. Inspired by the theatre of the Middle Ages, the Orient, and ancient Greece, his art contained color, rhythm, symbolism, allegory, grotesquery, fantasy, and mystery—all of which had a special appeal for the Russian temperament.

Eugene Vakhtangov

Among his productions, Eugene Vakhtangov (1883–1922), second studio director of the Moscow Art Theatre, staged Carlo Gozzi's *Turandot* with masks and in *commedia* form, stylized productions of Alexander Pushkin's works, and an expressionistic rendering of Ben Jonson's *Volpone*. Trained by Stanislavsky, he aimed to express inner truth, but like Meyerhold, used decorative elements that included carefully choreographed movement.

Alexander Tairoff

Alexander Tairoff (1892–1923), believed that the theatre should return to its origins, with the actor functioning as singer, acrobat, dancer, and mime. Inspired by the non-realistic theatre of the dramatist and stage director Nicolas Evreinoff, Tairoff felt that "words play a subordinate role on the stage and we hear better with our eyes than with our ears" (Slonim 1961, 214). Pantomime was, for Tairoff, superior to other theatrical forms. The Kamerny Theatre opened in 1914 with his staging of Arthur Schnitzler's *The Veil of Pierrette*, a *commedia* pantomime, followed by the Sanskrit poet Kâlidâsa's ballet pantomime, *Sakuntala*. For Tairoff, the dramatic text was a pretext for the actor to unfurl a technique consisting of stylized movements. But rather than draw upon each actor's particular expression, Tairoff blended in a rhythmic ensemble gesture, grandiose movement, dance, music, and masks, excelling in productions with themes of antiquity that called for mass movement.

The Moscow Art Theatre combined Stanislavsky's realism and Meyerhold's style consciousness. Stage directors, such as Iouri Zavadski during the first half of the twentieth century, successfully allied Stanislavsky's psychological truth with Meyerhold's stylization, in which costumes, sets, and plastic effects played important roles. In its varied dramatic forms, the modern Russian theatre strived to combine inner truth with exterior expression. Once the actor attained a psychological inner truth, he communicated this by voice as well as a kind of rhythmic plasticity, with which he not only played the action but actually danced it (Kirstein 1935, 319).

Italian Theatre

> The real Italian Theatre does not have its vital essence in poetry and in literature, but in plastic figuration and mime.
>
> Benedetto Croce

Movement in the Italian theatre—free, spontaneous, instinctive—has always been poles apart from that based on a vocabulary of elaborate gestures, as in the Greco–Roman theatre. The Italian actor's chief instrument has not been his voice but his body. Dialogue, largely improvised, flows from his movement.

The chief reason for this richness of movement is the Italian's—particularly the southern Italian's—inborn expressiveness. In Naples and Sicily, for example, the language of gestures—derived, no doubt, from the Greco–Roman chironomy handed down through the centuries and adapted to its own spontaneous expression—functions at its fullest.[1] Comte de Borch writes of Sicily's language of gestures:

> Another particularity, not less singular, is the common use of gestures and signs here, language so expressive for its citizens that at a considerable distance, in the middle of a group, two people without opening their mouths, understand and communicate their thoughts to one another. A woman uses them in a different fashion, some destined to her husband, others to her lover, still others to her friends; this alphabetic difference produces three languages, each of which the same person uses with as much ease. From a very young age children begin to compose with their comrades signs which are fitting to them. This is a result of the tendency this nation has to make use of gesture. (Borch 1782, 236–37)[2]

Because Italy did not become a unified nation until late in the nineteenth century, there was no uniformity of speech; the dialect spoken in one village might be unintelligible a few miles away, and the Italian player often was forced to use gestures. Also, while in the Greek and Roman amphitheatres a gesture had to be larger than life, in the small, intimate Italian theatres, a single wink or turn of the wrist could be meaningful.

Because long rehearsal periods are today uncommon in the Italian theatre, the actor does not always memorize his part in full. Instead, he allows the character and situation to inspire him, to set up vibrations in his face and body, much like a tuning fork sets up sympathetic vibrations in a stringed instrument. At times, he abandons the text to comment in words or gestures to the audience, recalling the commedia dell'arte actor who gives full vent to his improvisational talent.

Up through the twentieth century in Italy, actors in regional companies called *con maschera*, wearing the masks of Harlequin, Pantaloon, and other *commedia* characters, staged plays in which movement was important because each of the players spoke a different dialect. These same *commedia* types still reappear in village *pupi* or *pupazzi* shows, in which, for example, the Sicilian *pupi*, three feet high, resembles the satirical ancient *sannio or buffoon*. These performances recall the Polichinelle puppet shows in France and Spain, Punch and Judy in England, Hanswurst in Germany and Austria, Toneelgek in Holland, and Karagoz in Turkey. Yet, Harlequin and Colombine are not merely charming and obsolete survivals. Today, Pulcinella mimes the effects of an atomic bomb as naturally and easily as, two hundred years ago, he mimed his aches and pains after a beating from his master.

Italian Actors and Mimes

Among the famous Italian mime–actors of the eighteenth and early nineteenth centuries, such as Francesco Barese (1710–1777) and the Neapolitan playwright–actor Cammarano Vincenzo (1720–1802), one of the most popular was Salvatore Petito, the father of a family of mimes. Petito, born in Naples in 1795, danced at the San Carlo and played Pulcinella. His wife, Donna Peppa, also a San Carlo dancer, directed a small theatre in Naples, where her children performed. Gaetano later played at the San Carlo; Davide and Adelaide specialized in young lovers and servants; Pasquale interpreted children; and Antonio, like his father, played Pulcinella in the plays he wrote.

During the nineteenth century, Pasquale Altavilla (1806–1872) of Naples acted and improvised in his own plays. Edoardo Ferravilla (1846–1915) of Milan portrayed the imbecilic lover, the handsome baritone, the idiotic student, and the naive country uncle. Emilio Zago (1852–1929) of Venice, a leading interpreter of Carlo Goldoni, was a talented playwright. Eduardo Scarpetta (1853–1925), a student of Antonio Petito, was for fifty-six years the idol of Naples and Rome. At the age of fifteen, he performed at the San Carlino and later at the Parthenope theatres in Naples as Don Felice, the role with which he became identified. A famous interpreter of women's and children's roles, he discarded the *commedia* mask. "The face," he wrote, "particularly the eye, is the mirror of the soul. Cover a man's face with a piece of cardboard, leather or soot, and that face will remain in the dark; it is as if you had cut off the head" (Lyonnet 1901, 271).

For fifty years the Sicilian actor Angelo Musco (1872–1937) dominated the Italian stage. Heir to improvisational theatre's traditions, his power of observation and his talent for mimicry enabled him to portray many types. Grabriele D'Annunzio called him "Maestro del Riso," and Paul Hazard wrote:

> I wager there is nothing which Musco cannot translate into gestures, a very superior language to that of words, which are effaced, worn out, at everyone's reach, and banal, while gestures remain personal, original, and alive. A study of these would not furnish the secret. To possess this gift one must be born in the happy countries where, at the invitation of the sun, all is exteriorized, even souls (1917, 379).

Leopoldo Fregoli (1867–1936), one of Italy's last true *pantomimi*, in the space of an hour could portray thirty sharply differentiated male or female characters.[3.]

For Ettore Petrolini (1886–1936), the Roman mime–actor and playwright, the text remained only the skeleton of the dramatic performance. Of his acting and his plays, Anton Giulio Bragaglia wrote: "The art of using a text as a point of departure, that is, as a pretext, triumphs in Petrolini, even if his own plays suffer from it" (Petrolini 1945, 5).

At the turn of the century, the de Filippo family, Eduardo Scarpetta's children, were among the most talented Italian mime–actors. Titina, born in 1898, was a subtle comedian. Eduardo, born in 1900, who interpreted both comical and pathetic roles, was famous for his expressive eyes and shoulders; Eric Bentley calls Eduardo de Filippo the son of Pulcinella and the true heir to the commedia dell'arte (1959, 265–78). Pepino, born in 1903, excelled in the *lazzi* of Antonio Petito and was known for his comical leg movements. During the 1960s, he revived the commedia dell'arte with a Neapolitan company.

Toto, born in 1898, was the idol of the Neapolitan music halls. He had a long head, an austere mouth, enormous, sad eyes, and a neck that he could stretch like a giraffe or shorten like a turtle. A true *mamo* (Italian mime–clown), he created sharp caricatures of his fellow man. He performed with Marcario, a popular Piedmontese music hall mime. Other talented mimes of this period were Alfredo Bambi, born in Rome in 1878, who directed tableaux with mimes moving like white statues; Peppino Villani (1877–1942), a Neapolitan who created ridiculous characters; Nicola Maldacea (1870–1945), a Neapolitan mime–singer who specialized in caricatures; and Gilberto Govi, a Genoese born in 1885 who performed traditional mime.

Although most of the names in this brief survey belong to comic mime–actors, many Italian tragedians did not use their bodies expressively enough. Eleanora Duse (1859–1924) is remembered for her facial expressions during her poetic interpretations of *La Locandièra, A Doll's House,* and *La Dame aux Camélias.* Ermete Zacconi, born in 1857 in Montecchio, played a starkly realistic Nero in Pietro Cossa's *Nerone* and a moving Lindor in Carlo Goldoni's *La Gelosia di Lindoro.* Francisque Scarcey said of Zacconi's interpretation of Hamlet that "he comes on, and before he utters a word we understand his profound sadness, his discouragement, his despair" (Lyonnet 1900, 101–2). And, after beginning in the music halls, Raffaele Viviani (1888–1950) became a great actor and author of tragedy.

Commedia dell'arte in the traditional Italian manner has been performed in Copenhagen for several centuries. It originated there in 1749 with Pietro Mingotti and his opera singers, who played Harlequin, Pierrot, and Colombine scenes during the entr'actes. In 1800, Pasquale Casorti staged a *commedia* pantomime with his company in Dyrehavsbakken, an amusement park outside of Copenhagen. His *Harlequin the Statue* was continued by his son, Giuseppe Casorti (Pierrot), and the Price family. Since 1843, *commedia* pantomimes have played at the Pantomimeteatret in the Tivoli Gardens, where during the summer season one still can watch a twenty-minute performance on an open-air stage with Father Kassander (Pantalon); his daughter, Colombine; Colombine's suitor, Harlequin; and the amusing valet, Pierrot. *Harlequin the Skeleton, Harlequin the Furious Lover, Harlequin the Mechanical Statue, Harlequin the Cook,* and *Pierrot Metamorphosed* are interpreted by well-known actors, such as Lisa Kaergaard (Colombine), Erik Bidsted (Harlequin), Axel Schultz (Kassander), Carl Johan Huid (Pierrot), and Elsebeth Rex (Colombine). The favorite character is Pierrot, who, after the audience applauds and to their enchantment, says several words. The first Pierrot to speak was Volkersen, who, when an actress's dress caught fire, explained that it was because she loved him so. After he played Pierrot for fifty years, a statue was erected in his honor.

If this quick glance at Italian mime seems disparate, ranging from Zacconi as Hamlet to Toto as a giraffe and from commedia dell'arte in Venice to Copenhagen, it is largely because Italy never had a national theatre like the Comédie Française to train actors in a distinctive style. Styles varied as much from Milan to Naples as the Milanese dialect varied from the Neapolitan. Yet mime and *commedia* traditions have remained unbroken. Fixed character types, performed by certain actors, have been transmitted from generation to generation and adapted to each play. Similar to the Renaissance *commedia* players, the mimes and actors who played these types launched into their own improvisations and corporeal creations. Like their sixteenth-century ancestors, their bodies, lively imaginations, and inborn aptitudes for expression all combined to create mime, theatre, dance, opera, and music hall that have never ceased to fascinate the eyes.

Notes

1. In a letter to the author, Anton Giulio Bragaglia—stage director, theatre historian, and author of *Evolutione del Mimo*—wrote:

> I am a Roman, or better still, a Latin from Latium, and it is evident that the Sicilian dialect mixed with Greek, Arabic, and Spanish is not comprehensible for me. Well, I directed a company of mime actors from Palermo in a seventeenth-century Sicilian *commedia* sketch entirely by means of gesticulation and movement. There were voices and actors reciting all at once and I caught only several words in flight. It was a true tower of Babel. (December 20, 1949)

2. The Sicilians claim that these gestures and signs date from the time of Dionysius the Tyrant of Syracuse, who imprisoned his victims in underground vaults, from which the smallest sound could be heard. The prisoners were thus compelled to invent a sign language so that they could communicate among themselves.

3. In the fifth century, Cassidorus, the Roman historian, wrote that the same mime–actor personified Hercules and Venus, a king and a soldier, and an old man and a young man so rapidly that one had the illusion of seeing several characters at once. During the third century, Lucian of Samosata wrote of the astonishment of a barbarian priest at a Roman mime, whose body seemed to possess so many souls.

7

Exit Pierrot. Enter Georges Wague

It is the face which is incontestably the essential part of man's head. It is the mirror or rather the summary of the expression of his movements.

Lavater, *Sur la Physionomie*

After Gertrude Stein said, "Since the twentieth century inevitably was not to know what to do about its artists," she added that "Paris was the place to be." At the turn of the century Paris was not only the place for artists to be, it was the place for mimes to be: it was here that Séverin still performed the traditional Pierrot of Deburau. However, Parisian audiences soon began to applaud the mime Farina's nontraditional Pierrot and Georges Wague's less conventional Pierrot, played in a more spontaneous style that he called modern pantomine.

At the turn of the century, classical pantomime in France had become stereotyped. After Gaspard Deburau and his successors, for lack of talented Pierrots to revitalize the art of gesture, it was reduced to mere formula. Movement no longer expressed emotions but became word-to-word translations that explained and advanced the action. To convey, for instance, "speak more softly," the mime first would point to his mouth and then lower his hand; to express "my mother," he would encircle his face with his right hand and cross his arms over his chest; to portray a "king," he would trace a crown above his head. Soon this code of gestures no longer moved the spectator.

When Gertrude Stein said, "The nineteenth century knew just what to do with each artist but the twentieth century inevitably was not to know," little did she know how well this statement would apply to the world of mime. In literature as well as in all art, the nineteenth century had defined and categorized its artistic movements clearly. The stir of liberal thought that the French Revolution incited brought with it that lyrical literature we call romantic. Both Pierrot and Clown portrayed their century's romantic spirit. The Pierrot of Gaspard Deburau also perpetuated commedia dell'arte traditions in France. In England, Joseph Grimaldi, whom the Italian Pedrolino inspired, introduced the art of the clown. No matter what the traditional differences were between Pierrot, the poetic tragicomic figure, and Clown, the apathetic joker, both Deburau and his successors, like Grimaldi and the clowns after him, had clearly defined pantomime styles. In his classical pantomimes, Deburau communicated the action of a short comedy or drama by using a conventional mime vocabulary to translate each word into gestures. Grimaldi also performed this kind of pantomime, combining it with speech, juggling, tumbling, practical jokes, magical transformations, and dance. By the end of the nineteenth century, though Pierrot appeared less on the stage, he continued to live on in the works of writers and painters.

Early in the next century, as Pierrot passed into the world of classical ballet, brought from Russia by Michel Fokine, and appeared in works such as *Petrushka* and *Carnaval*, Georges Wague was in Paris, training artists and students in his company and school and reanimating Pierrot's silent art by transforming classical pantomime into twentieth-century pantomime.

Around 1910, two artists would breathe new life into this dying form. They were Georges Wague and Felicia Mallet, the French comedian and singer (1863–1928) who played a prominent role, along with the Pierrots of the Cercle Funambulesque, in renewing the art of pantomime. For Wague and Mallet, pantomime was not a specialized branch of acting. Gestures were not translations of words into movement but expressions of concepts that had no verbal parallels; in short, pantomime became essentially the art of expressing feelings. The mask-like face behind which Deburau and his successors played was rejected, and special exercises were created to render the mime's face expressive and alive. Wague and Mallet introduced a natural form of pantomime, with less stereotyped movements and more-human characters. Moreover, Pierrot was no longer the main character in a number of Wague's pantomimes. Just as Clown had appeared in all English pantomimes, few French classical pantomimes had existed without Pierrot. In Wague's pantomimes, Pierrot was incarnated as Scaramouche, Herod, or Cleopatra's lover.

Born on February 14, 1874, in Paris, Georges Wague, after completing his studies as an electrical engineer, entered the Conservatory of Dramatic Art as an auditor and played small roles in the provinces and in Paris. In 1893, he made his debut in Xavier Privas's *Cantomimes* at the Café Procope. In these cantomimes depicting the fortunes of Pierrot, Wague performed with a singer and a piano in the wings in such pieces as *Noël de Pierrot* (1894), in which Pierrot courts and serenades Colombine; *Le Testament de Pierrot* (1895), in which Pierrot dies, leaving his debts to his creditors; *Pierrot Chante* (1899), in which Pierrot sings to the moon; and *Sommeil Blanc* (1899), in which Pierrot drinks to bury his misery. In 1895, at the Théâtre Montparnasse, Wague created his first pantomime (*Le Voeu de Musette*) depicting Pierrot, who joins his dead girlfriend in her tomb. Among the pantomimes that followed were *La Première Faute de Pierrette* (1899), which revolved around Pierrot and Harlequin both vying for Pierrette. Wague also played Pierrot in the provinces and abroad, with Christine Mendelys (later Mme. Wague) as Colombine. His performance of *L'Enfant Prodigue* was acclaimed in 1906, and that same year he played in *Rêves d'Egypte* with author Colette Willy (1873–1954). In 1907, he performed in *La Main, l'Age d'Or,* on female avarice, and in a ballet–mimodrama, *Giska la Bohemienne,* with Caroline Otéro and Christine Kerf. In 1908, he appeared in *La Chair* with Colette. When she made her début at the Mathurins in *L'Amour, le Dieu, la Chimère*, Colette had already published *Dialogues de Bêtes* and *La Retraite Sentimentale*. She then played in *Romanichelle* at the Olympic, the Oeuvre, and the Marigny theatres and in 1911 appeared in Wague's mimodrama *Bat d'Af.* Colette recounts her life as a music hall performer in her books *La Vagabonde* and *L'Envers du Music Hall.* In the following article, she describes the public's reaction to a performance with Georges Wague:

> Saturday and Sunday it turns to a riot. The entrance of W. behind our embracing lovers' heads makes an anguished "Good!" gush forth from all the upper galleries. In one sec-

ond this admirable public has taken sides with the lover against the deceived husband. At W. they yell, "Hide your mutt!" and their indignation mounts when he throws me on the floor. He had better be careful at the exit. (1909, 48)

From 1912 on, Wague played mute roles in films; among the pantomimes he performed on stage were *Scaramouche, Pauvre Pierrot, Barbe Bluette, La Nuit de Noël,* and *L'Homme aux Poupées.* In 1913, he created *Montmartre*, a celebration of Pierrot and bohemian life. From 1916 on, he taught mime at the Conservatoire de Musique et de Déclamation in Paris and played mute roles at the Opéra, including the buffoon in *Jeanne d'Arc* and Hérode in *Salomé.* In 1920, he appeared in his mimodrama *Le Coeur de la Rose* and in *Chand d'Habits* and *L'Enfant Prodigue.* In 1922, he performed in *Faust* as Mephisto and in *Rêve d'Opium.* He also interpreted silent roles at the Opéra and, in 1925, danced with Argentina in *L'Amour Sorcier,* later playing a small role in Fernand Crommelynck's *Le Cocu Magnifique.*

Wague not only revitalized traditional pantomime, prepared the ground for modern mime, and discovered and trained many mimes—such as Colette, Christine Kerf, Caroline Otéro, Angèle Héraud, and Charlotte Wiehé—but he also made pantomime an important choreographic addition to the lyric and dramatic theatres. Convinced that the study of voice and diction alone did not suffice to interpret their roles, singers such as Jean-Paul Cabanal, Paul Franz, Gaston Micheletti, Marguerite Soyer, and Marie-Jeanne Doyen and actors such as Hélène Bouvier began to study movement with Wague.

Author Colette, a mime in Wague's company, gives us a vivid account of how the actor's training neglected this art at the turn of the century. One day, when she attended a class at the Conservatory of Dramatic Art in Paris, Colette closed her eyes while listening to the students interpret Chimène, Lorenzaccio, Chérubin, and Werther and was frequently moved. But when she opened her eyes, she saw only "harsh sales girls, awkward high school students and tall boarders stiffened with timidity" (Wague 1930).

Wague trained actors and singers to acquire strong, flexible bodies and to develop movement that exteriorized their thoughts and feelings. This contribution was greatly felt in the lyric theatre, where a singer's physical appearance did not always correspond to the part he played. The tenor most often played the young lover or hero; the baritone, husbands and confidants; the bass, old men and gods; the soprano, heroines; and the mezzo-soprano, queens and mature women. On the legitimate stage, an actress was cast as Juliet because of her physical presence and acting ability, as well as her voice; in the lyric theatre, she was cast simply because she sounded more like Juliet. For Wague, the illusion of a character could be created in the lyric theatre if a singer possessed a power of dramatic concentration and physical expression that made us see Juliet. Besides helping dramatic theatre actors express fully with their bodies, Georges Wague made the lyric theatre of his time a theatre of actors who could sing rather than one of singers who could not act.

Part Two

Twentieth-Century Mime

Although during the first half of the twentieth century the French literary and artistic trends moved from dadaism to surrealism, which had served mime less than the romantic, naturalist, and symbolist movements, mime still did not cease to flourish. It returned to the fore in 1923, when Jacques Copeau founded an acting school at the Théâtre du Vieux Colombier where miming with a mask and doing exercises that recalled those of Japanese Noh drama helped the actor discover greater corporeal expressivity. Convinced that the human body alone suffices to dress a bare stage, Copeau's student, Etienne Decroux, would endlessly research and perfect these exercises, developing them into a codified form he called corporeal mime. His movement style was a far cry from the *commedia* figure from which Pierrot took his model. Unlike classical pantomime, corporeal mime was also no longer an anecdotal art that used a conventional language of gestures to create illusions of objects or persons. The impetus Decroux's findings gave to twentieth-century mime had repercussions throughout the world, opening dimensions in technique and expression unheard of since ancient Greek mime and Roman pantomime.

By the mid-twentieth century, Paris was still the place for mimes to be. It was here that several great masters gave rebirth to mime as an autonomous art, as well as merged it with other forms. Etienne Decroux, Marcel Marceau, and Jacques Lecoq developed schools of mime that no longer represented traditional, nineteenth-century pantomime. Their schools differed from one another, as much as they differed from Eastern European pantomime. It was in Paris that, after studying and performing with Decroux and creating his own mimodramas, Jean-Louis Barrault brought Pierrot back to the stage in a Baptiste pantomime at the Marigny Theatre in 1946 and in the role of Deburau in the film *Children of Paradise*. It was also in Paris that Barrault integrated expressive movement with speaking theatre. Meanwhile, Marcel Marceau, who had trained with Decroux, would convert corporeal mime into an art that could be more readily communicated. He developed his Bip and style pantomimes, making this art known to the world. While Decroux trained corporeal mimes in Paris and New York, Jacques Lecoq taught mime not as a separate art but as a research tool to further dramatic creativity as well as one which could be combined with other arts. Lecoq's global training method fused the art of the clown and the buffoon, juggling, acrobatics, spoken text, dance, plastic arts, and all of life with body movement. His movement expression, based on the observation of natural movement, opened up new directions for physical theatre. In 1978, Marceau opened his Ecole Internationale de Mimodrame de Paris and taught workshops in America. Decroux, Barrault, Marceau, and Lecoq inspired many mimes and theatre artists to discover multiple styles of twentieth-century movement theatre that, in turn, enriched other stage arts.

8

Etienne Decroux,
Father of Corporeal Mime

Heard melodies are sweet, but those unheard
Are sweeter

Keats

Etienne Decroux[1]—mime, actor, philosopher, and orator—established his own school in Paris, where he taught from 1940 to 1985. Through his teaching, writing, and lecturing, he reinstated mime as a major art form. His reevaluation of acting altered the face of modern European and American theatre. He made actors and directors aware that vitality can be regained in a theatre where corporeal expression is profoundly understood.

Like his mentors Jacques Copeau and Charles Dullin, Decroux waged a war against the suppression of the actor's creative contribution. The actor had to be liberated from the tyranny of directors, composers, playwrights, and designers, as well as released from his role of mere text illustrator. The reign of realism had obliged him to abandon the formalized techiques of earlier periods, and, though he spoke his lines clearly and well, the expressive use of his body remained not fully accomplished and sometimes even untapped. Decroux set out to explore this use. His interest in the potential of the body's expressivity had already been awakened by the mime numbers he saw at the "Café Concert," as well as by his admiration for the boxer Georges Charpentier. His interest in politics and his gift for oratory led him, in 1923, to enroll in a night course at the Théâtre du Vieux Colombier, a little Paris theatre in the shadow of Saint-Sulpice.

Chez Jacques Copeau

In protest against the tide of realism he believed hampered the actor's creative potential, drama critic Jacques Copeau founded his company at the Vieux Colombier in 1913. He aimed to strip the theatre of all the elements that stifled the actor's poetic contribution. He set out to bring the theatrical event back to its original form, as in the Greek theatre, where speech, dance, and music were interwoven in a harmonious ensemble. He cultivated the actor's imagination, as well as his body, in a program of classes that ranged from gymnastics, ballet, and mime to voice, diction and chorus, Noh drama, clay modeling, literature, poetry, philosophy, history of music, and costume. By introducing exercises with a mask to help the actor rediscover the expressiveness of his total body and by staging productions that achieved dramatic poetry through the use of movement, Copeau instilled a new vitality in twentieth-century theatre. For his student Decroux, Copeau's mask exercises would become an end in themselves and the seed of his lifelong work, the theatre of the autonomous mime–actor and of pure mime.

In Copeau's theatre, the actor's art was highly developed and his body well trained; the stage director, even when most respectful of the text, employed all the visual means and physical resources of acting enriched by new uses of design, light, and color. Although Copeau's theatre did not survive, its spirit lived on in the avant-garde theatre of the Cartel in France (Gaston Baty, Charles Dullin, Louis Jouvet, and Georges Pitoëff), in the productions of Michel Saint-Denis and his Compagnie des Quinze, and in those of Jean Dasté and Léon Chancerel. Copeau's concept of the actor's troupe as a human community and theatre, as well as a means of spiritual growth, influenced such European stage directors as Jerzy Grotowski, Peter Brook, Jean-Louis Barrault, and Ariane Mnouchkine. They, too, made use of mime and masks, revived the *commedia* and Greek chorus, and created innovative stagings of the classics and Oriental theatre.

After Decroux enrolled in Copeau's school in 1924, he followed Copeau and his troupe to a village in Burgundy, where, while training and performing, he was the company butcher. Later, in the classes he taught at Dullin's Théâtre de l'Atelier, Decroux continued Copeau's idea of building a technique for the body, which for him was the key to creating an authentic art for the actor. Decroux believed that the actor's so-called art, until it really became an art, could not be a better one (1963, 46). Through mime, he could utilize his own body like an instrument. Possessing a full range of technique, this ideal actor could play any melody he wanted. Working unsupported, with nothing but air and silence around him, he could learn to create in a medium that was complete, containing in its essence all the arts (Gelabert 1959, 66). Only after attaining mastery of bodily expression could he join forces with other theatre artists, designers, composers, and playwrights, firmly subordinating their contributions to his own. But until then, because the actor did not possess any such technique or the freedom to create, he would remain suppressed by these other arts.

At Dullin's school, where Decroux taught and Jean-Louis Barrault, Jean Vilar, and Marcel Marceau studied, mime improvisation, based on analysis of the text, became the key to the actor's creative contribution.

Early Creations and the Ecole Etienne Decroux

As Decroux acted on stage and in films and radio plays, he slowly gained recognition as a mime and a teacher. More concerned with developing a method of mastering movement, he created his pieces with slow and labored effort and most often with his students. Before beginning his school in 1940, in 1931 he staged *La Vie Primitive* (*Primitive Life*) at the Théâtre Lancry with his wife and a sequel entitled *La Vie Médiévale* (*Life in the Middle Ages*) at the Atelier with Jean-Louis Barrault. In *La Vie Primitive*, inspired by Jean-Jacques Rousseau's works, the savage, unrestrained by clothes and social conventions, rejoices as he climbs a tree, picks a coconut, throws it to his mate, shins down the tree, and rows down a river. In 1940, *Le Menuisier* (*The Carpenter*), *La Machine*, *L'Halterophile*, *Le Professeur de Boxe*, and *Les Marches de Personnages sur Place* were performed at Decroux's school. *Le*

Menuisier, in which the carpenter labors away, echoed Decroux's socialist temperament; the carpenter's wife is also a worker in *La Lessive* (*The Washing*). *La Machine*, which with detailed and articulate movements captures a machine at work, began as a solo work and later was adapted for three mimes. In 1941, Decroux created his first mimodrama with his students, *Camping*, which played at the Comédie des Champs Élysées. The following year, he repeatedly performed *Chirurgie Esthétique*, *Dernière Conquête*, *Passage des Hommes sur la Terre*, and *Le Feu* in his dining room with his students, each time before a handful of spectators. In 1945, Decroux and Barrault depicted combat with rich, corporeal movement in a scene from Shakespeare's *Anthony and Cleopatra,* entitled *Le Combat Antique*, at the Comédie Française.

After visiting Decroux's school and seeing his students perform, Edward Gordon Craig wrote an article entitled "Finally a Creator in the Theatre." In it he compared European and English theatre, still under the influence of the realism of André Antoine and Constantin Stanislavsky, with the metaphoric expression of Decroux's art. Although Decroux began by teaching illusion pantomime, his training methods developed into corporeal mime. For Decroux mime was no longer an imitation of the seen world but a revelation of the unseen one. While the pantomimist starts from the particular and works toward caricature, the mime starts from the particular and works toward the universal.

The mime–actor's function was thus not merely to imitate actions of everyday life or to tell a story and establish a dramatic conflict through plot and explanatory gestures, as Gaspard Deburau had done; rather, he had to discover within himself, and with his technique, the poetic sources of his art and express them as such. More intransigent than Marceau or Barrault, for whom the mime and the actor poetize their art with movement, Decroux required that the mime create poetry anew. His object was to find, through the body's movement alone, a pure, autonomous expression of a complete dramatic form—light-hearted, rhythmic, and charming (Decroux 1963, 141)—that could evoke poetic movement images in the spectator's imagination.

As the poet Charles Baudelaire made use of poetic images, the mime–actor, through physical images, could also suggest rather than tell a story. Like the French poet, he could also evoke the "concrete by the abstract and the abstract by the concrete" (Decroux 1963, 46). In *L'Usine,* for instance, the specific movements of one factory machine evoke the mechanical rhythm of all factory machines. The spectator's imagination was challenged to move along a broad range, from the ideal or general to the concrete and specific, or the contrary. And the dramatic conflict was to be created by the mime–actor, not provided by a story line. "The cultivated spectator has need of art, not of stories" (Decroux 1963, 48).

Corporeal Mime

What Decroux called *mime corporel* is mime in the strictest and purest sense. It refers to feelings and ideas depicted uniquely by the body as a whole. Free of sign language and narratives, it aims for a more universally poetic expression. Nor does it rely on any other artistic medium, such as music, decor, costumes, or text. Not since Roman pantomime had mime as an autonomous art reached such a high level of profundity and total body expressivity. Decroux's mime was even more autonomous than that of the ancient Greeks, who combined mime with dance, music, and text. Although nineteenth-century pantomime was, for the most part, a mute form, it was often performed to music, with familiar gestures and conventional movements representing the action. Decroux's conception also differed from that of other mime–actors such as Barrault, who saw mime as "silent" rather than "mute" acting that could be combined with a text, music, or other elements and used to a greater or lesser extent, depending on the importance of the text and other stage elements.

Decroux's aim to perfect the physical expressivity of the total body coincided with Edward Gordon Craig's idea that the actor strive to attain the ideal state of the marionette, an image that inspired Decroux's mime to achieve his body's obedience through a corporeal technique. To this end, he covered his face with a mask, often a veil, as in *Les Arbres*, to offer a neutral quality that allowed for greater expressivity of the total body. When he did not wear the mask, his face remained as impassive as the Oriental actor's, effacing itself behind his creation. Arms and hands were seldom used independently because the gestures that they expressed would be too conventional and literal, even meaningless. Through massive movements of his total body, the mime could achieve a grandiose, noble, less personal, and nonrealistic expression. Emotions originated from the trunk of the body rather than from the arms, hands, and face, which served as a prolongation of the trunk. Facile effects—the bag of tricks—such as a tear in the eye or a finger pointed in scorn, which rob the mime's art of poetry, were no longer available. Gestures and grimaces were abandoned in favor of total body movements. Organic sources were mobilized to reveal inner dramatic emotions; corporeal movement could then engender poetry.

Decroux believed that a truly expressive pose, a meaningful gesture, is an exterior manifestation of inner movement that, rather than depicting the particular, conveys the ideal and the universal in man. Conventionalized gestures and facial expressions are not able to convey the latter. Decroux's love duets were not encounters between specific men and women but represented all male and female attraction and harmony, moving analogies to yin and yang, light and darkness. His piece *Les Arbres* depicts the inner life of all trees. Here, four mimes—clothed in gray, bodies bent, veils over their faces—free themselves from the earth, slowly rising and sprouting branches through the inner life of their trunks.

Such highly perfected and imaginative movements require laborious preparation. For Decroux, the untrained body, like the sculptor's marble, can express nothing but its own limitations. Just as under the sculptor's chisel the marble can surpass its own limitations, so through the mime's precise and highly perfected movements, the body can become a profound expression of his art. In his refusal to reconcile himself with the body's limitations and in his efforts to transcend them by constantly analyzing the means to achieve the purest expression, Decroux entered a never-ending struggle with problems of corporeal expression and style.

Unlike nineteenth-century mimes, Decroux uncovered his mimes' bodies in such pieces as *La Vie Primitive* and *Combat Antique* to reveal the action of the muscles in primitive life and in combat. (He later discovered that the body is more nude when covered by a simple leotard.) Music, too, was used sparingly, and the form was "richer because of its poorer means, being complete only when it is partial" (Decroux 1963, 45).

To his concept of corporeal mime Decroux added that of *mime statuaire*, which he describes as "mobile, nonfigurative sculpture" (Decroux 1963, 9). The mime, "a sculptor of air," becomes a statue when he stops moving. Although he denied any debt to Oriental theatre, Decroux's approach recalls Japanese Noh drama, in which, at the end of a lively dance, the actor's movements freeze like a statue or are arrested as in the Kabakimie. Decroux's art attains similar effects of intense stillness, where the statue is a distillation of the beauty of movement that has gone before and a suggestion of what might follow.

Because *mime statuaire* is composed of a minimum of means, it, too, is a rich art, contrary to that of the music hall, where a maximum of means renders it a poorer form. In this highly structured concretizing of statuary elements, as with the classical artist, the mime abides by a mime vocabulary and rules of movement that deal with curves, angles, and horizontal, vertical, and diagonal lines. The mime's body becomes a keyboard or instrument and the mime the instrumentalist who must know his keyboard to play on it. Like classical art, the movements are disciplined, articulated, and stylized. However, contrary to classic art, which emanates beauty, grace, and ease, the movements appear labored and segmented. Decroux called corporeal mime Promethean in the sense that it defies the limitations of the human body which entail both physical and spiritual suffering. It necessitates a struggle against the body's constant resistance to space, gravity, and itself, an idea that forms the basis of Decroux's theory of counterbalance or muscular compensation. Even when rapid, the movements appear deliberate and slowly rhythmic, eventually reaching a state of petrification, only to burst out again in explosive movement. *Mime statuaire* thus contains within itself an underlying, ever-present tension between immobility and mobility.

Decroux's work is the basis of a new physical theatre, which Barrault called "subjective mime," that depicts the states of the soul and the metaphysical attitude of man in the universe. It is both idealized and corporeal, in contrast to pantomime, which is essentially representational and imitative and relies on the expressive use of the hands and the face to create illusory objects and persons. This slow, intense unfolding of Decroux's statuelike movement, which he described as Promethean and antifatalistic, also contrasts with such improvised and spontaneous theatre as the commedia dell'arte. Rather than tell a story in sign language—as in *pantomime blanche*—or combine movement with dialogue, music, or song in a seemingly improvised and spontaneous art—as in the *commedia*—it depicts arrested, imaginative, significant movement in silence, like an Auguste Rodin statue—motionless, yet bursting with potential movement. Instead of breaking forth into limited, facile movement, *mime statuaire* gradually alternates between movement with varied connotations and a meaningful immobility, stirring the imagination by suggestion. Yet, for Decroux, to suggest significant movement does not mean to render it abstract in the conventional sense. He describes his use of the abstract as the flower of the concrete (as the abstracted essence growing out of concrete movement and themes). Although his subject matter evokes the infinite and the universal in an imaginative manner, it depicts, by means of a precisely codified mime grammar, concrete themes, as the titles of such pieces as *The Carpenter, The Washerwoman, The Machine,* and *Discus Thrower* indicate. The term "abstract" in reference to Decroux's corporeal style was used not by him, but rather by mime teachers and writers to describe the universal, nonanecdotal, and nonpsychological qualities of his work.

A Grammar for Mime

The need for solid technical training for the actor and the mime led Decroux to develop a grammar of corporeal movement. With this grammar, Decroux's mime student could begin to use his body as a keyboard, with which he could create movement in an ordered way and express himself as clearly as in a grammatically logical sentence. For Decroux, the subject of the corporeal sentence was the mime's plastic attitude, represented by the spinal column and the respiratory system. The verb was the mime's trunk moving, and the object of the sentence his arms and legs indicating an action. Beyond this, Decroux's training program, consisting of the spinal column as the center of all movement and the trunk as the source of expression, was based on a geometric analysis of each body part. This was implemented by practicing isolations of the head, neck, chest, waist, pelvis, and legs used in Decroux's exercises of inclinations, rotations, and translations. Precision of movement was acquired by studying the various muscle groups and isolating and contracting each muscle. Exercises to develop the abdominal muscles, strengthen the spinal column, and improve muscle tone rendered the mime's body strong and supple. Exercises in sincerity of feeling joined emotion to movement. Physical and mental concentration and changing points of the latter developed control and focused dynamic energy (Felner 1985, 55–56).

Among other basic findings in the development of Decroux's mime grammar was the notion of *contrepoids* (counterbalance), the key to creating illusion in mime. Through the body's muscular effort in, for example, pulling an imaginary rope, the *contrepoids* created the illusion of that object's presence. By means of the *raccourci* (abridgement in space and time), the mime, while remaining in place, suggested, for example, that he was climbing a mountain or swimming across an ocean. This technique represented a less literal form of movement. The attitude (pose) not only punctuated the movement, but also included the emotion or mental attitude accompanying that action. These and other concepts combined to form a systematized grammar for mime, which served to revive it as an art form (Felner 1985, 57–59).

In his courses and performances, Decroux incorporated what he called *mimo-verbe* or vocal mime, based on a range of voice and breathing sounds that express emotions and feelings. In *mimo-verbe* training, movement and voice sounds are harmonized according to the dramatic and emotional tone of a text or poem. For example, in interpreting Paul Verlaine's poem *Mon Rêve Familier,* the langorous vocal tone expressing the poet's dream is integrated with slow-moving corporeal movement.

Dance and Mime

To distinguish between dance and mime, Decroux described dance as a lyric art and mime as a dramatic art. While the modern dancer might interpret dramatic themes, he does so with predominantly lyrical movements. The mime, on the other hand, works against the pull of gravity, less lyrically and more dramatically than the dancer. His is a continuous struggle, particularly in corporeal mime, which strives to find greater expressivity despite the body's limitations. Dance is an art of exalted expression in which movement is often regular, following slow curves that dissolve into harmonious ensembles; in mime, movement is more at ease with "ill ease" than with grace. Movement in dance is often repeated for its own sake, while in mime it serves a dramatic purpose. Moreover, while in dance a given rhythmic musical score and pattern of timing are the rule, in mime they are the exception. Rhythm might be needed to unify a mime work, but the work itself is based on the unexpected, the surprise, the question mark, the dramatic hesitation. Dance, on the hand, is generally linked to a musical score, and dramatic action, if present, is added afterward. And, while the dancer moves freely in space, the mime is confined dramatically to a more limited area. The dancer soars toward the heavens; the mime, earthbound, struggles with gravity.

Yet, dance does not possess a monopoly on beauty. While the mime portrays essentially labor, why can one not create a beautiful portrait of the ugliness of work without betraying its essence?[2]

Billancourt. 6 décembre.
1966.

Ma chère Ouinette,

J'ai reçu hier votre lettre du 29 novembre.

Faute de mieux, je récapitule ce que vous m'avez demandé et le fais pour que voyiez clairement ma clarté :

1 _ un texte de deux à trois pages ou/ou un rapport avec votre écrit sur mon bastiate et pouvant être incorporé dans votre écrit.

2 _ mon curriculum vitae.

3 _ celui de Maximilien.

Je vais me mettre au travail sur ces trois choses.

J'ai bien reçu votre texte en anglais.

J'ai l'impression, à vous lire, que vous n'êtes pas en possession de mon livre.

Croyez à mon affectueux souvenir.
Mon respectueux salut à Monsieur Leust.
Decroux.

Words on mime by Etienne Decroux.

The Value of Decroux's Work

Through his building of a codified mime grammar, Decroux enabled mime to be re-discovered as an art that could be learned. When he was beginning to formulate his system of mime, not yet known in America, mime–dancer Angna Enters pointed out in her essay "The Dance and Pantomime: Mimesis and Image" that mime needed to be codified in order to be as well-recognized as an art form as dance (1966, 71–72). Without a mime grammar to serve as the basis for a newly created art form, per-formers and teachers such as Marceau and Lecoq and movement-oriented total the-atre actors such as Barrault might never have developed and perfected their art, which, in turn, inspired still another generation of actors, mimes, and teachers throughout the world to develop their own movement forms.

Although Decroux's work has been evaluated as autonomous and highly lim-ited, his initial intention was to free the actor's art from the tyranny of texts, sets, costumes, and lighting that had been dominating the theatrical event. Only after the theatre had undergone a long period of preparation—at least thirty years—could these elements be added under the actor's close supervision. Decroux never intended to separate mime from the spoken word; he meant for one eventually to complete the other. A number of his disciples, described in the following chapters, would prove this truth by going beyond his technique's so-called limitations.

In addition to defining and codifying the art of mime and creating a large body of technique, as well as establishing a universal system of movement that opened up new areas of expressivity, Decroux contributed greatly to the development of the actor's art. Just as manual labor balances intellectual development, endowing thought with common sense and order, so mime training could form the total actor (Decroux 1963, 176). To portray emotions and ideas clearly and to develop their imaginations and creativity, Decroux's acting students worked in mime improvisa-tion grounded on a solid corporeal technique. "The essential part of my art," De-croux said, "is articulation. Thanks to it the body is analogous to the piano keyboard. Our art proceeds like chemistry and music. To succeed at it requires daily study for a period of three to four years. Those who embrace with fervor the formula 'to work from the inside outward' must become aware that that which comes from the inside must have a way of arriving at the outside."[2] For mimes and actors alike, the soul's inner emotions could be revealed through a highly developed technique.

Decroux denied any credit for creating his mime form. Rather, he felt he had contributed to the development of corporeal mime by making analogies to painting, sculpture, music, science, and the theatre and by incorporating the underlying prin-ciples of these arts into the study of mime. Of his contribution to corporeal mime, as inspired by his master, Jacques Copeau, Decroux wrote, "I only invented my belief in it" (1963, 33).

The corporeal mime that Decroux developed aimed, through applied theory and technique, to place the widest range of expression at the student's disposal. Yet, he warned, such technical training did not suffice to furnish the mime or the actor with creative passion, without which there is no art. For creativity could be learned in no school.

In the following passage, Decroux describes what a school cannot give:

> A school teaches technique and the art of the Beautiful, but it does not give the student passion. What I mean by technique is the faculty to do what one wishes and, at least, what

one believes one will do. To acquire it the struggle is long, for the body betrays us. What I mean by the art of the Beautiful is the ensemble of processes which one uses to be understood. I know that such a formula is deceiving. Yet, how far its application may go!

To be understood is the capital object of the art of the Beautiful. To remove one bit without the other being misunderstood, to purify what remains or to aggrandize it, all this is analogous to the art of speaking. It may be taught. As for telling you what must be said, who will tell you this if not your passion?

The value that each person gives to things is known by each and not by the professor.

A school does not teach one to create. It liberates the creative mind, puts it at ease, gives it confidence, but it does not teach creation. For it does not teach passion despite the price of its lessons. There are things which are not acquired with money.

One does not buy one's place in heaven.

One does not buy the education of one's child.

One does not buy love.

One does not buy health.

In paying well one's King one does not obtain Peace or Victory or well-being. Money does not help the issue; one must obtain these oneself.

To pay very dearly for one's lessons costs less than to learn them. The fact alone of signing up already gives the impression that one knows something. Yet, being punctual, attentive and prodigal in muscular effort does not guarantee the power to create. For the essential question is this:

What does the student do outside of school? What is he before entering school? Does he go on foot in the street? Does he stop before building sites? Does he enter a factory? While at the store, does he think only of making his purchases? Does he go about his business or does he look at each passer-by? And as he looks at each passer-by, what does he see if he has no passion? The school is not the provider of what one observes. And since it does not give passion, it does not even give the means to make such observations. The facts which merit reliving on the stage in real life are jumbled pell-mell with the others. What will bring them out? Compassion. In view of our heteroclite life, compassion is the magnet which attracts only those facts worthy of being shown. Is this strange? It is compassion which gives meaning to what is just and unjust. This meaning encompasses a vast domain. Proudhon, who sang of justice, said, "Irony has force only in its own name." And I say: "Justice is compassion for the absent." When one is irritated by disorder and illogical reasoning, the first cause is perhaps compassion which engenders hatred, evil, and even the desire to kill. The wailing clamors of the dog whose belly has just burst under the wheels of an automobile, the shoes of Van Gogh, the description of concentration camps, what does all this do to you? That is the question. So many doctors and so few hearts!

Do you search for cosmic laws in the movements of the body? When looking at objects do you feel reborn in you the religion of Animism? Did you observe that couple of concierges? The woman looks like a queen and the man like a statesman. Did you observe that nobleman with the forehead of a bull and the neck of a ram? Did you note that in that luxurious hotel nothing was provided so that one could read in bed? And if you have observed nothing, if you find that all is well, what would you have to say? And if you have nothing to say, how would the art of speaking serve you?

The mime must have in his head the material of a novelist and in his body the muscles of a gymnast.[2]

Notes

1. Born in Paris in 1898, after working as a hospital attendant, butcher boy, plumber, docker, and bricklayer, Étienne Decroux enrolled in Jacques Copeau's school. After the school

closed in 1925, Decroux played in the companies of Gaston Baty and Louis Jouvet, both of whom Copeau trained. In 1926, Decroux taught at Charles Dullin's Théâtre de l'Atelier and acted in his company for eight years. He performed in more than sixty-five roles in these companies and those of Antonin Artaud, Marcel Herrand, and Sylvain Itkine, among others; he also appeared in a number of film roles, including that of Gaspard Deburau's father in Marcel Carné's *Children of Paradise*.

Decroux opened a school in 1941 and staged *Camping* and other pieces with his students in his dining room for small audiences. Besides the earlier mime pieces that he created from 1931 to 1945 (as mentioned in this chapter), in 1945 and 1946 he staged *La Voiture Embourbée, Le Bureaucrate, L'Esprit Malin, L'Usine,* and *Les Arbres* at the Théâtre de la Chimie and the Théâtre d'Iena. Among other works Decroux and his company created during this period and later were *Jeu de Dames, Relai de Dulcinées et de Petits Soldats, Soirée, Le Toréador, Le Boxeur, Le Lutteur, Quelques Passants,* and *La Statuaire* (*1948*).

From 1947 to 1951, he toured Switzerland, Israel, England, Belgium, and Holland and taught mime throughout Europe, the Middle East, and America. From 1949 to 1952, he taught in Amsterdam and Tel Aviv; in 1952, at the Sorbonne in Paris; the following year at the Piccolo Teatro in Milan; and in 1954, in Stockholm and Innsbruck. From 1957 to 1962, he lectured and taught at New York University, the Actor's Studio, the New School, and the Dramatic Workshop in New York while continuing his own school in Paris.

While in America Decroux formed a company of mimes who performed with him at Carnegie Hall, the Kauffman Concert Hall, and the Cricket Theatre. Many of the pieces already mentioned, such as *Les Arbres, L'Usine, La Lessive, La Statuaire, Le Menuisier,* and *Le Passage des Hommes sur la Terre,* were in the repertory of Decroux's New York company. Among other works performed at New York's Carnegie Hall were *Parade* and *The Museum* (both created from group improvisations), *Lance Thrusts, The Evil Spirit, Envelopment, Street Scenes, The Boxing Match, La Table d'Hôtes, Must One Laugh? Or Cry?, The Lecturer,* and *Love*. Along with several of the above pieces, others performed at New York's Cricket Theatre were *Les Gangsters, Le Matin, Rêve d'Amour, La Glace Prend Feu, L'Homme de Sport* (a demonstration of counterweights), and *Passants* (a demonstration of walks).

In 1963, Decroux published his book *Paroles sur le Mime*. He continued to work actively in his Paris school until 1985. He died in Boulogne Billancourt on March 12, 1991.

Among Decroux's students who went on to teach corporeal mime, several of whom the following chapters mention, were Eliane Guyon in Lausanne; Benno Besson in Berlin; Gianfranco de Bosio, who founded the Teatro Università di Padova; and Soubeyran, who taught mime at the Komische Oper of East Berlin.

2. Letter from Etienne Decroux, November 18, 1967.

9

Jean-Louis Barrault

Our nature is in movement
Complete repose is death

Pascal

It was Jean-Louis Barrault's contribution to the rebirth of mime, an art almost forgotten since Séverin's performance in *Marotte d'Artiste* in 1925, that in 1946 led theatre critic Maurice Delarue to describe Barrault as a rediscovered mime.[1] As a mime artist, Barrault merited this title, but as an actor and stage director he also rediscovered this art as intrinsic to speaking theatre, opening up new vistas in the development of total theatre.

Edward Gordon Craig and Antonin Artaud

The names of André Antoine and Constantin Stanislavsky had been associated with the school of realism, which abolished so-called artificial theatrical conventions in support of a photographic imitation of life. Although Edward Gordon Craig and Antonin Artaud valued Antoine's and Stanislavsky's actor-training methods, they rejected the confines of this kind of realism in favor of restoring poetry to the theatre. Craig and Artaud influenced Barrault early in his efforts to revitalize a theatre that remained captive to the other arts and to an artistic expression fast becoming antiquated.

For Edward Gordon Craig (1872–1966)—stage director, designer, and author of *On the Art of the Theatre*—the theatre is an extension of dance and mime where words are less important than visual elements. He advocated that a supermarionette replace the actor, a symbol he used to abolish the natural tone and gesture in acting. In this way, the actor's body, akin to that of a supermarionette that readily obeys, could develop creative expressivity and thereby give a more poetic rendition. Like a maneuverable part of the scenery, he could also integrate his movements with a stylized ensemble of visual elements that the stage director harmonized.

A pioneer of total theatre, Antonin Artaud (1896–1948)—director, playwright, and author of *The Theatre and Its Double*—would play an important role in the development of Barrault's total theatre. Artaud likewise inspired a whole generation of playwrights, such as Jean Genêt, Eugene Ionesco, Samuel Beckett, Fernando Arrabal, and Harold Pinter, whose plays readily lend themselves to the total theatrical event. Many elements of the theatre of the absurd, the theatre of happenings, guerrilla theatre, and street theatre are also based on Artaud's notions.

Artaud liberated the creative force in the actor and the stage director and incited them to express it totally—that is, through the use of all their senses. His Theatre of Cruelty (cruelty here equivalent to action or creation because all that is alive undergoes pain) was inspired by the Balinese theatre he saw in Paris in 1931, in which movement, gestures, and facial expressions play essential roles. He believed that theatre in the West placed too much emphasis on words and their rational interpretations. Similar to their primitive function, words should be used as concrete sounds to retain the power of their original emotional and poetic content. In sum, theatre should be a ritual with sacramental gestures that become an autonomous poetic language. A theatre with movement could thus be highly metaphysical and reveal inner reality. Artaud rejected bourgeois theatre, traditional plots, partial psychology, and rational characters in order to reintegrate movement (which in itself could enhance the dramatic experience) with lighting, sound effects, music, and other physical stimuli that act on the spectator's sensibilities. For him, passion of every type has an organic base (Artaud 1938, 147). Any actor, even the least gifted, is able to instinctively evoke passion through physical means (Artaud 1938, 145).

Artaud describes how Barrault, as an actor and director, reintegrated dramatic poetry into the theatre through the use of gesture:

> His theatre demonstrates the irresistible expressiveness of gesture; it victoriously proves the importance of gesture and movement in space. He restores to theatrical perspective the significance it should never have lost. He fills the stage with emotions and life. (Knapp 1969, 126)

Influence and Departure from Decroux

Jean-Louis Barrault began his acting and directing career at Charles Dullin's Paris school, where he trained in mime with Étienne Decroux.[2] The teachings and technical training of Decroux, who devoted himself to codifying this long-neglected art, soon marked Barrault's work. For Barrault, too, the mime–actor had lost that noble, tragic quality intrinsic to Greco–Roman theatre. In his stagings of both mime and verbal theatre, he strived for a highly stylized and exalted dramatic expression. He employed movements, gestures, and every possible scenic device to externalize humanity's tragic struggles, the mime–actor's face remaining as inanimate as a mask to express the conflict between inner life and external reality. Yet, Barrault's corporeal expression of that conflict, though highly symbolic, remained less abstruse than his master's.

Decroux stressed the body's weight and the pull of gravity on it, binding man to the earth in fixed movements to symbolize his tragic struggle with reality. In contrast to his master, who remained riveted to the ground like a massive prizefighter turned mime, Barrault, with his light and agile body, was best suited to soaring upward. For Decroux, this body soaring upward, unless carefully directed, could be an impediment to pure corporeal expression. Yet, at times—as in his piece *Maladie, Agonie, Mort*—Barrault excelled in gradual, sustained movements, in progressing with dramatic intensity from one statue-like attitude to another. Like Decroux, he rejected the concept of the mime as an "imitator of life." Rather than incorporating the familiar and trivial into his art, Barrault created physical poems.

While Decroux, like Artaud, believed that mime could be joined to speech, he felt that some texts inherently resist movement and that the spectator should first be reeducated about this process of linking movement and text. Barrault, who earlier had performed in Decroux's *La Vie Primitive* (1931) and in his own mime creations, soon grew convinced that mime should serve speaking theatre. Jean Dorcy describes Barrault's evolution from mime to spoken theatre: "Barrault was born a dancer, made himself a great mime and finally delighted in being a dramatic actor" (1961, 57).

Barrault believed that the most stirring theatre is found in those silences where movement speaks more eloquently than words. Movement can also liven the spoken word, create atmosphere, and lend style. In his 1942 staging of Jean Racine's *Phèdre,* movement heightened the dramatic poetry of the text. *Autour d'une Mère* (1945), based on William Faulkner's *As I Lay Dying*, was performed as a half-spoken mimodrama. In *Hamlet* (1946), corporeal expression animated long verbal passages and intensified dramatic passion. In *Le Procès* (1947), pantomime reinforced a stylized version of actuality. Commedia dell'arte enhanced *Amphitryon* (1947) and *Les Fourberies de Scapin* (1949). Barrault's staging of Pierre de Marivaux's *Les Fausses Confidences* (1946) combined *commedia* techniques with elegant speech. *Rabelais* (1969), an adaptation of François Rabelais's works, resembled a singing, dancing, and mimed happening. When performing in his productions, Barrault the actor remained a mime even when he spoke. In his classical stagings, he and his company made use of the revealing powers of gesture to portray the inner motives of a Hamlet or a Phaedra. His mime piece *Baptiste* (1946), based on his 1943 film *Children of Paradise,* made in collaboration with Georges Wague, depicts the famous nineteenth-century mime Gaspard Deburau. Here, while Barrault incarnated with feline grace Deburau's Pierrot turned assassin, he incited his audience to rediscover the art of mime. In *La Fontaine de Jouvence* (1947) and in Jules Supervielle's *Les Suites d'une Course* (1955), he transported his audience into the world of dance–pantomime.

Mute and Silent Art

Jean-Louis Barrault described traditional pantomime as objective illusion mime that expresses anecdotal action and conventional characters through the movements of the body's extremities and modern mime as a subjective form that communicates the states of the soul through the movements of the body as a whole. While the former is a mute and codified language of gestures superimposed upon an action, the latter is silent acting that, instead of translating words into gestures or being added to an action, becomes the action itself. Pantomime is most often light and comical; mime can better express noble and tragic emotions. During the last half of the nineteenth century, pantomime was a deaf and dumb language aping the spoken word. In the twentieth century, it was replaced by silent mime, which is less concerned with a literal translation of spoken language than with a lyrical interpretation of dramatic action. Silent mime could go beyond traditional pantomime, which comical themes and stock characters limit, to achieve an inner tragic expression. This heightened corporeal interpretation, found in speaking as well as nonspeaking theatre, enriched both the actor's and the mime's poetic contributions. Yet, for Barrault, either traditional pantomime or silent mime, which both spring from the art of gesture, can be incorporated into a play. He employed silent mime in his mimodrama *Autour d'une*

Mère, in his mime piece based on Miguel de Cervantes's *Numance* (1937), and in Knut Hamsun's *La Faim* (1939). He incorporated traditional pantomime into parts of his 1947 staging of Molière's *Amphitryon,* in Molière's *Les Fourberies de Scapin* (1949), and in Paul Claudel's *Soulier de Satin* (1958).

In joining mime to text, which he found lightens dialogue and gives wings to verse, Barrault discovered an intimate relationship between movement and words. Words evoke dramatic emotions related to physical reactions of voice, attitudes, gestures, and movements. Because gestures correspond chronologically to voice transmission, this relationship is all the more rigorous. The movements of the body harmonize simultaneously with the respiratory system and vocal inflection, intensity, and rhythm. Acting involves controlling one's breath, voice, and movement, implying a relationship among all these physical elements. In his stage directions for *Phèdre*, Barrault says, "To act is to know how to direct one's breath, voice and body from head to foot in a determined manner" (Racine 1945, 40). Speech and gestures are, for Barrault, inseparable:

> Speech is the result of oral pantomime and of breathing and muscular contraction. Speech is inseparable from gesture. Speech is dance for the ears and gesture is music for the eyes; they both drink from the same spring, the human body, a marvelous biological mechanism which is placed at our disposal from birth.[3]
>
> This visual language may also reveal secret thoughts which words cannot always render.
>
> Conjointly and simultaneously with the spoken word, one may observe a visible language, reinforcing or contradicting what is said. It may express buried secrets, bad faith, dissimulation, impulses, weaknesses, evasions—all closely observed ways of behavior that make a kind of undercurrent of official behavior. (Racine 1945, 69–70)

Beyond mime's essential role in total theatre, Barrault believed that developing an integrated body connects us to the universe and could even be a means of salvation on a planet endangered by self-destruction:

> I want us all to love each other and to heal the planet which has become a masterpiece in danger. The knowledge of our whole body is salvation. It radiates the respect, the dignity, the tenderness, the religiosity which we should all have for each other.[4]

Barrault and Twentieth-Century French Stage Directors

The total theatre of Jean-Louis Barrault differed from the styles of other twentieth-century French stage directors who had undergone the influence of Jacques Copeau.

Jacques Copeau (1879–1949), the precursor of total theatre in France, had laid the groundwork for the development of the stage director's art. As for the actor, whose problem he felt was essentially a physical one because he stood on the stage (Rudlin 1995, 93), Copeau introduced the use of commedia dell'arte and of miming with masks to broaden his training methods. In his view, the staging of a play comprised an ensemble of decor, words, movement, and silence.

Gaston Baty (1885–1952), also a disciple of Max Reinhardt, opposed the sovereignty of verbal expression, sacrificing the text and even the actor's art to lighting, sets, music, stage movement, and puppetry. He went to greater extremes than Charles Dullin, Georges Pitoëff, and even Barrault to make theatre a pageant for the eyes:

A text cannot say everything. It stops at a certain point where all words stop. Above this point begins another zone, a zone of mystery, silence, what one calls the atmosphere, what you will. The stage director must express this, prolonging the text to render that which words alone cannot render. (Hort 1944, 146–47)

Louis Jouvet (1887–1951), a Copeau disciple, incorporated gestures, movement, and expressive physical attitudes called for by the text, never sacrificing verbal poetry to visual effects. In Jouvet's words, "great theatre is first of all beautiful language" (Surer 1969, 28).

Barrault was greatly influenced by his teacher Charles Dullin (1885–1949), a disciple of Copeau. Dullin harmonized dialogue with movement, music, and decor. He trained actors in mime and *commedia* to exteriorize the inner feelings of their characters. He developed a sense of style in his stagings by introducing gestures and movements that the text required; in scenes without dialogue, as in Richard III's battle scenes, actors mimed and danced to the rhythm of drums.

Georges Pitoëff (1887–1939), an actor in Copeau's theatre, formed his own company in 1924 and—like Jouvet, Dullin, and Copeau—felt that the stage director should respect, above all, the text. Still, he included lighting effects, geometrical stage settings, and movement in his stylized productions of Shakespeare, George Bernard Shaw, and Luigi Pirandello. As an actor, he created "mystery by his walk, doubt by a glance, and anxiety by his gestures" (Surer 1969, 14).

Jean Vilar (1912–1971), a disciple of Copeau and a student of Dullin, organized theatre festivals at Avignon and founded the Théâtre National Populaire in 1951. Vilar stressed clear diction and simple movement and, like Copeau, utilized lighting and costume effects with sobriety in large-scale outdoor productions that brought theatre to the masses.

Like these twentieth-century stage directors, Barrault realized many of Copeau's ideals, such as rediscovering the original source of drama, instilling symbolic poetry in dramatic expression to abolish the limitations of realism in the theatre of the period, and innovatively reviving the classics. But he did so by exploring stage movement more freely than the stage directors of his time, who, with the exception of Baty, made use of movement suggested by the text. For Barrault, "A dramatic text is like the upper visible part of an iceberg which represents one eighth; the other seven eighths are the invisible roots, that part which renders the poetry or the meaning of reality" (Surer 1969, 233).

Barrault adeptly linked gestures to speech, sound, and color and incorporated every available device—stairs, platforms and lighting—to fill space with moving tableaux and physical action. He transformed literary texts into theatrical form, as in his adaptation of Faulkner's *As I Lay Dying* and in his total theatre production of *Rabelais*. By fusing movement with text, he animated such unstageable plays as Claudel's *Tête d'Or*, *Partage de Midi,* and *Le Soulier de Satin,* revealing the playwright's talents as a dramatist.

For Barrault, the theatre, which originally was an art in which the mime–actor–dancer expressed himself through song, dance, and movement, had gradually lost sight of its visual character. By inciting the spectator to respond to the expressive power of the human body and regain a taste for gesture, Barrault infused new life into dramatic art. This "rediscovered mime" not only expanded the expression of modern mime, but also discovered and developed a physical language to enrich acting. By combining verbal art with movement and giving rebirth to total theatre, Barrault revitalized twentieth-century theatre in France and throughout Europe.

Notes

1. Maurice Delarue, "Jean-Louis Barrault, Mime Retrouvé," *Signes*, no. 4 (Winter 1946–47): 68–72.

2. Jean-Louis Barrault was born in 1910 in Vesinet, the son of a Burgundian pharmacist who died in the First World War. He left the College Chaptal in 1930 to study at the École du Louvre in Paris. After entering Charles Dullin's acting school in 1931, he played in Dullin's production of *Volpone* and remained in his company until 1936. In 1931, Barrault and Étienne Decroux performed the pantomime *La Vie Primitive,* and, in 1932, Barrault created his pantomime *Maladie, Agonie, Mort*. In 1935, he staged with Jean Dasté a mimodrama, *Autour d'une Mère,* based on William Faulkner's *As I Lay Dying,* and played in his first film, *Les Beaux Jours*. After performing a number of roles on stage and screen and staging Miguel de Cervantes's *Numance* (1937), a spoken drama with mime insertions and masks, and Knut Hamsun's *La Faim* (1939), he married actress Madeleine Renaud and entered the Comédie Française as a resident actor from 1940 to 1946. In 1945, Barrault and Decroux created the pantomime *Le Combat Antique*. After directing several plays at the Comédie Française and playing in the films *La Symphonie Pastorale* and *Children of Paradise* (1943), based on the life of Gaspard Deburau, his Compagnie Madeleine Renaud–Jean-Louis Barrault opened in 1946 at the Théâtre Marigny with André Gide's translation of *Hamlet*. Among the pantomimes and mimodramas that Barrault then staged were *Baptiste* (1946), *La Fontaine de Jouvence* (1947), *Renard* (1954) (with music by Igor Stravinsky), *Les Suites d'une Course* (1955), *Pantomimes d'un Sou* (1961), and *Les Parapluies* (1963). From 1959 to 1969, Barrault was director of the Théâtre de France. He was reappointed director of the Théâtre des Nations in 1971. He continued staging productions at the Théâtre d'Orsay and at the Théâtre du Rond Point in Paris and toured Europe, North and South America, and the Orient. In 1990, Barrault retired from the theatre. He passed away on January 22, 1994.

3. Jean-Louis Barrault, excerpts from "Le Corps Magnétique," *Cahiers Renaud Barrault* 99 (July 27–August 6, 1979): 71–135.

4. Ibid.

10

Marcel Marceau

Spoken expression is multiple and changes according to nations; gesture is unique and universal.

Marcel Marceau

Although as a child Marcel Marceau was greatly influenced by the movies of Charlie Chaplin, Buster Keaton, and Harry Langdon and imitated people, animals, and objects, his lifelong commitment to mime came only after he studied with actor and stage director Charles Dullin and mime master Etienne Decroux.[1] In his early mimodramas, such as *The Fair* (1949), *The Flute Player* (1949), and *Pierrot of Montmartre* (1952), he portrayed, with his small company of mimes, French street-fair theatres. As in the drawings of Honoré Daumier and Henri de Toulouse-Lautrec, in *Pierrot of Montmartre* Pierrot appeared in black. In *The Three Wigs* (1952) and *A Night at the Funambulists* (1953), Marceau evoked the Théâtre des Funambules. Among the mimodramas he staged in the nineteenth-century romantic style were *Death before Dawn* (1948) and *The Overcoat* (1951), based on Nikolai Gogol's novel. After that, Marceau appeared most often in solo performances wearing a whitened face, a short, tight-fitting jacket, silk pantaloons, dance shoes, and a battered top hat with a flower. This was Bip, the nostalgic hero of Marceau's childhood, inspired by Pip in Charles Dickens's *Great Expectations*. Like Chaplin's Little Tramp and Gaspard Deburau's Pierrot,[2] Bip is misunderstood by the world. And like Pierrot, he is first a soldier, next a street musician, then a tailor, photographer, fireman, or father. He travels, mingles with high society, is invited to mundane parties, attempts to commit suicide, and undergoes the torments of a bumblebee. As a sculptor and a painter, he suffers from an inflamed finger. He is remorseful for having wounded a butterfly and joyful when it recovers. At other times, as in *Walking against the Wind, The Staircase*, and *The Cage*, Marceau deserts Bip for his "style pantomimes," which he performs with codified movements and perfected technique. He portrays an assortment of characters in *The Public Garden*. He introduces us to the world of allegory in *The Hands* and *The Creation of the World*. And he takes us to one of poetic pathos in *The Mask Maker*, in which the hero, at first a prisoner of his social mask, discovers his real self.

Pantomimic Classicism

Marceau's silent art, even when romantic in content, contains classical elements. As in classical masterpieces, he has peopled his sketches with keenly observed human types who possess universal character traits that reflect psychological truths. In *The Pawnbroker* (1956), in a series of scenes recalling Daumier's caricatures, a violinist enters the pawnshop to sacrifice his violin, a boxer his gloves, a young widow her ring, a nearsighted man his glasses, a magician his wand. In *The Public Garden*, Marceau deftly passes from the portrayal of a pert governess gurgling over a baby in a buggy, to a dog walker pulled here and there by his dog's leash, tipping his hat to a passer-by while trying to conceal his dog dropping dung, to a balloon vendor who loses one of his precious balloons to the skies, to a priest who trips over a stone while reading the gospel, to an old woman chatting with an elderly listener as fast as she knits. The caricatures of these character types, as well as Marceau's Bip, differ from the sentimental and romantic nineteenth-century Pierrot. While the melancholic Pierrot in his flowing white gown nostalgically pursuing Colombine moves us, we are amused as Bip is battered about in a real world in which he quickly learns to survive with humor and irony.

A Marceau pantomime is not only a portrait of an exaggerated character type with human hopes and fears; it offers a moral lesson. His mimodrama *The Overcoat* depicts an impoverished clerk who saves for years to buy an overcoat and is robbed of it the first evening he wears it. He dies of pneumonia and, to right his wrong, returns as a ghost to steal other overcoats. *The Seven Deadly Sins* portrays our moments of avarice, gluttony, envy, lust, laziness, anger, and pride. We see our own avarice in the crippled beggar who humbly amasses coins on the street corner and returns home to gloat over them before putting them away in a safe. We watch ourselves abstain before others at a benefit dinner and then slip into the kitchen to stuff ourselves voraciously. We recognize our own envy in the master sculptor's realization that his pupil has surpassed him. We realize our desire to seduce in the artist's flirtation with his model, our indolence in the lazy man's effort to dress himself, and our uncontrolled anger as the chauffeur's car collides with another car. We are aware of our own pride when the general plays one hand against the other and cheats himself to win. The moral element in the satirizing of these character types strengthens the innate classicism of Marceau's art.

Dramatic unity develops according to classic norms. In *The Trial,* the aggressive prosecuting attorney and the imploring defense lawyer argue the case more and more vehemently before a judge who listlessly nods. The piece builds to a tragic climax as the accused, condemned to be hanged, marches off in handcuffs.

As in the classical tradition of a Molière play, form in a Marceau pantomime is well balanced with content. In each piece, a distinctive style and a sense of elegance combine with the meaning. Also basic to this classical art are the elements of clarity and conciseness. Each gesture is drawn clearly and abridged to represent the essence of a feeling or an idea, which Marceau's master Decroux describes as the *raccourci* (shortcut) of gesture. Here, gesture serves meaningful content, an aim that is intrinsic to a classical art enhanced by beauty of form and that moves us as well as elevates us.

The Plastic Style of Marcel Marceau

Early on, Marceau developed a style based on Decroux's technique but combining both pantomime and mime. In his pantomimes, he creates the illusion of a specific character and situation by means of conventional gestures and movements. The mime element in his other pieces consists of expressing inner emotions and ideas not only anecdotally, but also symbolically and universally. On the one hand, the ensemble of Marceau's repertory comprises popular nineteenth-century pantomime, with type characters that are both comical and sentimental; on the other hand, it contains elements of twentieth-century abstract mime, which Marceau simplifies and combines with a poetic lyricism developed and expressed through Decroux's grammar and technique.

Nothing seems labored in Marceau's expression. Ranging from largo to presto (a quality that he attributes to his training with Decroux), Marceau's agile body registers all of life's rhythms, evolving either languidly or with minute, quick, birdlike movements. At first, the trapped prisoner in *The Cage* languorously extends his arms beyond the bars and then frantically accelerates his movements to force his way out of the cage, which grows smaller and smaller until he cannot move.

Through his use of optical illusion, Marceau has enlarged our visual imaginations. At times, he creates a point of support in space, as in *Bip at a Society Party*, in which Bip leans on an imaginary mantelpiece, his head spinning and his forearm dangling listlessly as he feels the effects of the cocktails. In *The Little Café,* Marceau creates an entire set, leading the spectator from the café bar to the dining section, the kitchen, and the area for pool and chess games. In *The Amusement Park,* he is

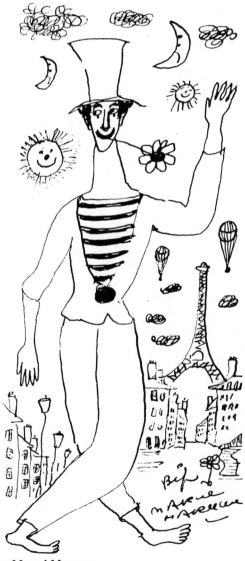

A drawing of Bip by Marcel Marceau.

trapped in a funhouse maze. At other times, he creates the illusion of distance through metaphysical fear. (Watch Bip as a circus performer high in the air, paralyzed with panic.) And once he has made the imaginary real, he makes it disappear. (In *Bip at a Society Party*, after we see him make the imagined meat appear, he cuts it so hard that it vanishes from his plate.)

The sparseness and economy of Marceau's style remind us of the Japanese artists who inspired Toulouse-Lautrec and of Sergei Diaghilev's famous dictum: "Omission is the essence of art." In *Bip as a Soldier*, his back to the audience, he kneels to help an imaginary soldier. As the soldier's right hand slips down along his left shoulder, we understand that he has drawn his last breath. With a single stroke, this master of understatement evokes a dramatic death scene. And in *The Samurai's Sword*, after the samurai has failed to draw his sword from its sheath in time, the bowing of his head to the ground before his ancestors suffices to depict his humiliation.

Contrasting elements rapidly alternate in Marceau's work. In *The Mask Maker*, he switches with lightning speed from a grinning mask to a sorrowful one. This contrast is accentuated when he desperately tries to remove the grinning mask, a symbol of man's social self masking his inner anguish. In *Bip as a Soldier*, Bip, an awkward recruit who carries his rifle on his left shoulder, starts at a gunshot. On the battlefield, he blissfully recalls chirping birds until he suddenly stumbles with horror upon a dying comrade. Throughout these pieces and others, Marceau utilizes sudden change to establish contrast between two or more characters. The comical contrast in *David and Goliath* is based upon his quick transformations from the big, burly Goliath to the small, agile David, giving the illusion that both characters are on stage simultaneously. Marceau provokes laughter in *The Robot* by rapidly shifting from operator to robot. These rapid changes, along with Marceau's keen sense of timing, recall the use of comical contrast in early silent-film gags.

Besides the romantic, nineteenth-century style of such mimodramas as *Death before Dawn* and *The Overcoat* and the more classical manner of *The Seven Deadly Sins* and *The Trial*, a variety of styles, at times mixed, comprises Marceau's art. Melodrama characterizes such pieces as *The Eater of Hearts: A Cruel Tale*, in which the perverted eater of hearts charms his victims and then devours their hearts. Arrested by the face of innocence, after devouring a child's heart, he removes his own to resuscitate the child. In *Pygmalion*, based on the legend of the Cypriot sculptor who fell in love with his own statue, theatrical gestures and movement portray the protagonist's dreams about the statue of a beautiful woman whom he cannot attain come to life. Lyricism characterizes *Bip and the Butterfly*, one of Marceau's most poetic works. Don Juan's romantically flamboyant manner of courting ladies turns to comedy in *Bip Dreams He Is Don Juan*, and comedy turns to tragedy as the protagonist in *The Mask Maker* becomes the prisoner of a smiling mask.

While Marceau's art allies perfected form with content, his virtuosity always remains subordinate to psychological expression. When he plays a magician, the magician's skill is not for a moment divorced from his pride as he appears before his audience. Nor is the acrobat's masterful technique severed from his fear on the tightrope. We admire the butterfly's quick, fluttering movements, but we are also moved by its struggle to survive. In Marceau's words, "A gesture is not sufficient; it needs to be clothed in thought." And "gesture unless lyrically sustained, is but a drawing in space" (Dorcy 1961, 103).

Influence and Departure from Decroux

Marceau is greatly indebted to Decroux for having developed a mime grammar, which gave twentieth-century mime grounding and permitted it to evolve. Like his master, he saw mime as an autonomous art and as a medium more vital than the spoken word. He might have been quoting Decroux when he said, "What I personally see in pantomime is all theatre, dance and sculpture, rhythm, drama—everything but speech, which is unnecessary" (1965, 51). Yet, in regard to the mime as creator, Marceau and Decroux, as well as the Decroux-trained Barrault, differ considerably. While Marceau remains a creator who, like the ancient Roman mime, portrays all things in life, Decroux researched new codes of movement and through mime rendered the theatre a more creative art. Barrault, by adjoining mime to text, enriched the actor's creative contribution to his art. The differences among Marceau, Barrault, and Decroux lay in the direction each took. Marceau performs exclusively as a mime artist, interpreting life lyrically and concretely; through mime, Barrault the actor intensified the performer's dramatic expression in verbal theatre; and the master Decroux sought purity of dramatic expression by teaching and researching solely through the medium of mime.

In their treatment of content, Decroux and Marceau are also far apart. While Decroux's pieces were never directly based on human characterization, we identify Marceau with Bip as immediately as we do Chaplin with the Little Tramp, the silent witness of all men. Never portraying human form for its own sake, Decroux remained resolutely objective; his body became trees in *Les Arbres*, a factory in *L'Usine,* and cleverness incarnate in *L'Esprit Malin.* He stood aloof from his creations, obliterating himself with an impersonal or abstract group of trees or with a factory machine or with cleverness incarnate. Marceau, on the contrary, never separates human feeling from the image he creates. In *The Tree*, the woody protagonist stands firm against nature's vicissitudes, but it also suffers as it witnesses war, bombings, and a soldier's death. After ages of silent torment, it falls to the ground with torn limbs and a broken heart. And when, in *Bip Hunts Butterflies,* Marceau plays the butterfly, he expresses both the wounded insect's pitiful state and Bip's compassion for it. Even in his more abstract creations, Marceau neither forsakes an essentially lyrical quality nor loses his flair for characterization. In *The Dream,* his nightmare incorporates familiar activity, such as walking, running, and climbing stairs. *The Creation of the World* is concretized with specific biblical images, from the appearance of living creatures to that of man. In his autobiographical *Bip Remembers,* love, marriage, war, death, and the romanticized past contrast with an era of discos and space rockets. Through precise human images that evoke universal ideas, Marceau portrays Bip heroically continuing despite life's disparities. Although *Bip in Modern and Future Life* satirizes the futility of technological progress and man as a victim of a mechanical universe, its voice is personal. In his struggle with the modern world, Bip grapples with elevators and escalators that do not function. Sound effects and colored screen projections, which Decroux never employed, here render abstract content more tangible and dramatic.

Master of an art solidly grounded on Decroux's corporeal mime, Marceau nevertheless makes use of conventional body and facial movements that Decroux purists have condemned. Rather than wearing a neutral mask, to exaggerate certain facial traits Marceau employs the white chalk mask, often along with eye and eyebrow expressions. Such pieces as *The Public Garden*, *The Trial*, and particularly *The*

Mask Maker rely on the use of facial expressions. *Bip at a Society Party* could not depict a mundane milieu as effectively without the conventional handshaking, smoking, drinking, and other familiar social gestures. Decroux, on the contrary, insisted that the body as a whole be expressive, no part of it ever independent from the rest. The face should be as immobile as a mask lest it distract from the body's movements as a whole; there was no place in his art for stereotypes or conventionalized gestures and facial expressions. These facile effects, though useful in spoken theatre or dance, have no business with the mime of the mimes. A purist, theorist, and grammarian, Decroux was not concerned with communication through performance; he limited his research to laborious perfection in the classroom. Yet, far from allowing himself to remain a gifted popularizer, Marceau abandoned conventional and literal movements in such pieces as *The Hands,* in which he gives us a whole scale of abstract and universal gestures representing conflict, separation, and peace. In *Youth, Maturity, Old Age, and Death*, where he passes from the fetus through the various stages of a man's life to his shrinking back into a fetus position at death, Marceau shares with Decroux's corporeal mimes a preoccupation with the metaphysical. However, in his treatment of these themes, he freely introduces the story element that Decroux's more austere style rejected.

Marcel Marceau and Charlie Chaplin

Marceau's art and his creation of Bip owe much to Charlie Chaplin's Little Tramp. Beyond the more technical distinctions between mime on the stage and on the screen, how do Chaplin's and Marceau's art differ? Chaplin remained an actor on a movie set, while Marceau is never an actor on stage or on screen. And while Chaplin played with other characters and manipulated props, Marceau, like the ancient Roman *pantomimus*, expresses all characters and objects without props, scenery, or other actors. In *Bip as a Lion Tamer*, as he plays the lion tamer, his hand is also the lion's paw, which strokes his face, as well as the head of the lion that is about to devour him. In *The Creation of the World,* he is a bird, a snake, and Adam and Eve. In *The Bird Catcher,* he is simultaneously the catcher and the birds, as well as the catcher who turns into a bird. While Chaplin animated real objects, as in his "dance of the rolls" scene in *The Gold Rush*, Marceau creates not only the illusion that inanimate objects are present, but also that they come to life. In Marceau's *The Cage,* the imaginary bars become hostile; in *The Kite*, the kite pulls the mime's body here and there, almost into the air, until it escapes from him, leaving his body limp and lifeless. And so, while Chaplin breathed life into real objects, Marceau gives the illusion that these dramatically vital objects created out of the void actually exist. Concerning the differences between mime in the theatre and in the cinema, Marceau says, "Unlike the cinema, which departs from reality to create illusion by hiding artifice, mime in the theatre begins with an illusion of reality by means of an evident artifice" (Verriest-Lefert 1994, 58–59).

Having dispensed with props, scenery, and even other mime–actors, Marceau—unlike Chaplin, who depicts social conflicts realistically—is able to escape all the limitations that realism imposes. For example, time is compressed or expanded for Marceau. Akin to the awkward situations of Chaplin's Little Tramp—with the difference that Chaplin progressed in real time with real characters, sets, and accessories—Bip is invited to a party (*Bip at a Society Party*), where episodes only appear to happen in a span of real time.

Both Chaplin and Marceau base their content upon the satirical portrayal of character types who are victims of societal constraints. Just as with Chaplin's Little Tramp, Bip's efforts to play the gentleman are heartbreaking. He arrives at his host's house, wipes his feet vigorously on an imaginary doormat, and shakes hands with everyone, a forced smile on his lips as one guest crushes his hand. During dinner he cuts his meat with a dull knife, losing it first under the table and then in his neighbor's plate. He helps himself to a drink and, with his fixed party grin, listens to one person's sad tale and another's cheerful story. We laugh wholeheartedly at Bip's awkwardness in society, where, in fleeting episodes and within a limited time span, imaginary characters and props come to life. In *Bip in Modern and Future Life*, while Bip's universe is on the verge of exploding, he still manages to live moments of poetry and humor.

Although Marceau and Chaplin both portray character types who are victims of society, their respective artistic mediums influence their interpretations. Contrary to playing a character in a given situation—as in a full-length movie scenario—in each mimed piece, Marceau synthesizes a dramatic conflict revolving around Bip or another character. And, through his creation of pantomimic illusions within a self-contained work, for instance, we suddenly discover, during the comical climax of *Bip as a Matador,* that the imaginary, ferocious animal Bip is milking is only a cow, not a bull. But when Chaplin awkwardly milks a real cow, this is one in a series of acted-out incidents woven into the movie scenario of a city inhabitant's mishaps on a farm.

In Chaplin's films and Marceau's mimodramas, music accompanies the action. Like Chaplin, Marceau establishes a relationship between real characters and props through the use of music. But in Marceau's pantomimes, though he also uses music as a counterpoint or leitmotif to a theme, he often performs to his own silent music.

Thanks to Chaplin on the screen and Marceau on the stage, the public has regained an interest in mime. And despite this art's decline in France at the beginning of the twentieth century, like Chaplin, whose early appearances on the English stage brought the public to appreciate it, since 1947 Marceau has constantly expanded the range of mime. Besides his talent for poetic invention and embracing all things on a naked stage, he incites his spectator to share his creations' lives. What could be more heart-rending than the Little Tramp's pathetic adventures or gentle, naive Bip's misfortunes told to us in a language that needs no words?

A Universal and Timeless Language of the Heart

For Marceau, mime is the most direct of languages and one that completes spoken words. Everything can be expressed through mime, which shuns deceitful words that raise barriers between men. Words can be misleading, but mime, to be understood by all, must be simple and clear, without ambiguity. Moreover, mime can enhance speaking theatre because it expresses what words cannot. For, paradoxically, without silence the actor could not be heard either.

Of mime's universal appeal, Marceau says, "I have performed before audiences of many nationalities. I have never found it possible to identify laughter or tears that were specifically French, German, American, or Russian."[3]

He has brought his silent art to people all over the world. "It is for the common people it was born, that it was sung. It is for them that it will continue to develop its sources of joy, emotions, struggles, hopes and life."[4] And to communicate this art to the common people, one must first establish love.[5]

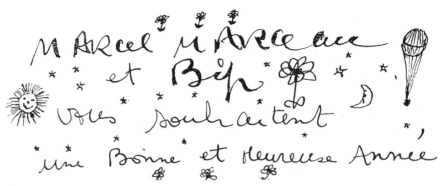

Some thoughts on Bip from Marcel Marceau.

Marceau's classical art defies time. It stands apart from the postmodern exploration of physical theatre styles. More important is the bearing it has had on the expansion of silent expression, which, rooted in nineteenth-century romantic traditions, evolved into a highly lyrical form. In Marceau's hands, the tiny flame rekindled by Decroux and Barrault grew into a glowing torch that by the mid-twentieth century had spread from one end of the globe to the other, giving birth to a new appreciation of the art of mime.

Marceau's art, deepened and matured, has remained an essentially lyrical one. He follows no musical score, no stage directions; he listens to the rhythm of his fancy, creating between himself and his audience that magnetic and indefinable exchange that is theatre's very essence. With a nostalgic air and a daisy between his teeth, this last incarnation of the Théâtre des Funambules vanishes furtively, leaving us with the recollection of a tiny stage in a Boulevard du Temple theatre, crammed with spectators applauding from the first row to the top gallery.

Combining whiteface mask and the ambiance of nineteenth-century pantomime with the techniques and themes of modern mime and mimodrama, Marceau's timeless art has spanned the second half of the twentieth century to broach the threshold of the twenty-first.

Interview with Marcel Marceau

Why did you become a mime during a period when mime was not very appreciated and was hardly known?

Marceau: I became a mime during a period when mime was forgotten by the public. Art does not obey fashion. When a creator has an inventive inspiration, art grows.

Chaplin and Keaton created their styles in mime through the movies. I created mime through the theatre. Because the tradition of mime was lost, it was also necessary to build up a public. The theatre of mime ended with the First World War. Mimes only appeared on stage alone or in one-act plays at the music hall and at the Opéra Comique, as did Georges Wague in Paris and Séverin in Marseilles.

In this respect, I was a pioneer. My theatre of mime in 1947 was the first in France and in Europe. I do not speak of dance, where mime had an important place, as in the Ballets Joos or the dance of Harald Kreutzberg. It is true that Jean-Louis Barrault had staged several mimodramas, such as *Hunger*, *Numance,* and Faulkner's

As I Lay Dying, in the thirties. Alas, he did not continue. He moved into spoken theatre and, as we know, became a great company director.

From 1955 to 1965, I created and staged around twenty-six mimodramas with my company. After I began performing throughout the United States, I was able to produce my company shows in France through the success of my U.S. tours. In 1964, the company was discontinued for lack of funds because I had produced a very expensive show, *Don Juan*, with seventeen mimes and an orchestra. It took me ten years to repay the loss through my world tours. In 1978, I was subsidized by the city of Paris and founded a school, l'Ecole Internationale de Mimodrame de Paris Marcel Marceau. All the disciplines were taught along with mime, such as acrobatics, contemporary dance [jazz], drama, fencing, and the stick art. Among my teachers were Maximilien Decroux, Etienne Decroux's son; my disciple Anne Sicco, who taught in my school until 1985 and then opened her own center for mimodrama, L'Oeil du Silence; Corinne Soum, a disciple of Etienne Decroux for eight years, who taught the Decroux technique at my school; and Gérard Lebreton, who was in my company and also taught mime. When I was not touring, I taught my students the Marcel Marceau technique based on the basic Decroux technique, into which I incorporated my own style, with new aspects in hand movement, different geometrical forms in space, and what I call the *points d'appuis* [points of support] in space. I taught a new dramatic style out of my own creations.

In the seventies, the street mimes started to imitate my style with *The Mechanical Man*, *The Tightrope Walker, Walking against the Wind*, and by putting on whiteface. This might have been normal, but at length it hurt our profession because they copied without learning to deepen the art form. Only our school could teach them our style. Chaplin has also been copied by thousands of artists, but it did not hurt his art because his style and art were so perfect. However, those who saw these Marceau imitations held me responsible for them. There was one exception: Robert Shields, the most extraordinary street mime I have ever seen, who later went into regular theatre and started touring over the world. Even Michael Jackson, a great artist with his own style, admitted that as a kid he saw me perform and that his moonwalk was influenced by my *Walking against the Wind*. In 1988, he saw my show in London at the Sadler's Wells and was impressed by *The Mask Maker* and *The Public Garden.*

From 1967 to 1988, I created eight one-man shows at the Théâtre des Champs Élysées with pieces that caused my style to evolve. In 1982, I began to draw students from my International School of Mimodrama who became my assistants. In 1990, my company performed mimodramas and style pantomimes at the Théâtre de Gymnase in Paris and some of my students played in *Bip, the Museum Keeper*. That same year, we also performed *Obsession*, a mimodrama in the style of *Pygmalion,* in which I played with six mimes. Among the students who have toured with me are Malcolm Scott from Canada, T. L. Galmiche from France, Bogdan Nowak from Poland, Fausco Perinti from Italy, and Blanca del Barrio from Spain. In 1992, Bogdan Nowak and Blanca del Barrio assisted and performed with me in *Pygmalion,* and Bogdan Nowak has assisted me in *Bip, Star of a Wandering Circus.*

In 1993, I revived *The Overcoat*, created in 1951, with ten graduates from my school. The students who enter my new company also learn how to create their own material at my school. The discipline, based on the Decroux and Marceau technique, is strict. My school will be a continuity of the spirit of Marceau and not an imitation. This is my legacy to the dramatic art form of mime.

How was your art received in the United States in 1955, and how did it revive the art of mime?

M: It was extraordinary. I was engaged by the director of the Phoenix Theatre in New York, who had seen me in Stravinsky's *Tale of a Soldier,* based on C. F. Ramuz's text, and in my Bip pantomimes at the Stratford Festival in Ontario. Walter Kerr, the prominent *New York Herald* critic, and Brooks Atkinson reviewed the show three times. Atkinson said that I was of Chaplin's stature. And Walter Kerr said that mime was the essence of theatre and that I should be caught by my butterfly net to play two years rather than two weeks in America.

When I first came to the States, I met all the great stars, such as Frederic March, Gary Cooper, and Charles Laughton. I also met Danny Kaye and the Marx Brothers, who became my friends. In the sixties, Red Skelton invited me to share his show, and we became friends. There were also Danny Kaye and Jerry Lewis, those wonderful actors who also did pantomime in films and on TV and who came from vaudeville and slapstick. In a certain way, they were the successors of Charlie Chaplin and Stan Laurel, who were formed in the English music halls. Buster Keaton, who started in vaudeville, came from a family of acrobats. Many books have been written about their art and on the golden age of silent movies.

Concerning my role in reviving the art of mime, I should mention that the roots of French pantomime have been in the theatre since the Théâtre des Funambules. The Pierrots were influenced by the commedia dell'arte and moved from street performances to the stage. The Théâtre des Funambules blossomed with Pierrot, who was influenced by Pedrolino, an actor of the Italian commedia dell'arte. In the twentieth century, it was in Jacques Copeau's school, where a new form of theatre was created to contradict the naturalism of Antoine's style and where the greatest French directors were formed, that mime was reborn through the teaching of Etienne Decroux, who trained there. Decroux was an actor in Charles Dullin's company and also taught mime at Dullin's school, where I, too, was trained. In re-creating the *statuaire mobile,* Decroux returned to Greek and Roman antiquity, which was the source of mimodrama and mime. Decroux was not against the nineteenth-century Pierrot. He respected the Pierrot school, which had died after the First World War. Séverin, one of the last Pierrots formed by Louis Rouffe in Marseilles, came from the Charles Deburau school. Charles was the son of the great Deburau, who was the subject of J.-P. Prévert's screenplay *Les Enfants du Paradis* [*Children of Paradise*]. The last white-faced Pierrot was Georges Wague, who played at the Opéra Comique throughout the twenties.

When I created Bip, I painted my face in white as an homage to the French school of Pierrot. But my style is definitely contemporary. The essence of an art form is its timeless quality. In France we say, "La mode se démode" ["Fashion becomes old-fashioned"]. But Bip in our dark world is still a romantic figure with a flower in his top hat. Since 1951, when I played my mimodramas with my company, I never used Bip's whiteface.

Do you believe that the public throughout the world has become educated in mime since you made your debut?

M: Certainly the public is educated in mime at present. They know my art, particularly in the countries where I have performed a great deal. Their demands have grown with my evolution. One can now speak of a vast public that likes mime. There are also mime companies and solo mimes all over the world. Their evolution depends on their talent.

Could you speak about the evolution of your art and style since your beginnings?

M: My art has evolved much since my beginnings. I have moved to formal mime. My gestures are purer, my technique more concise. My first numbers were entitled: *Walking against the Wind*; *The Staircase*; *Tug of War*; *The Tightrope Walker*; *The 1,500 Meters*; *Youth, Maturity, Old Age, and Death.* Then came the satirical numbers: *The Bureaucrats, The Tribunal.* Then the lyrical and dramatic pantomimes: *Reminiscences, Contrasts.* Then the symbolical pantomimes: *Creation of the World, The Hands, The Dream, The Eater of Hearts, The Mirror, Combat with Darkness, The Samurai's Sword.* In all of these pieces, my work became more intense and my style grew and developed more power.

The character of Bip has also become more profound; he has matured. At the beginning of my career, Bip was fighting in the metro or he was ice-skating or cruising on the sea. Today, Bip protests against war in *Bip as a Soldier* or is confronted with the machine age and with the future in *Bip in Modern and Future Life* or in *Bip Remembers.*

My conception of life has evolved. My power of suggestion is greater. I feel I am now in full possession of my art. My future creations will project themselves into new dimensions.

I have never separated concrete expression and abstract expression. One cannot express the abstract without presenting it concretely. I have moved away from the anecdotal, toward the elliptic and the symbolic. My art remains very concrete even under its most poetic form. The invisible rendered visible is not abstract. To re-create the world in appealing to the imagination seems to me very concrete.

Could you compare and point out the differences between your art and that of Decroux?

M: Etienne Decroux was first of all a grammarian who based his conception of mime on mobile statuary. He speaks of objective mime and of subjective mime. His grammar is the ABC of our art. But he certainly has directed himself in other channels to follow his personal evolution.

At the beginning of my career, I made much use of the grammar of Decroux to create my own work. With time, my technique has also evolved. I have moved from the identification of man with the elements to that of ideas, combining social satire and symbolic mime. My art has become more elliptical. I condense gestures in time, expressing what is essential with few movements, suggestion playing an important role in my expression. The passage from one movement to another, the revolving characters, the linking of related gesture: all mark the contribution of a style that is my own personal one.

I have therefore created style pantomimes and Bip pantomimes—Bip being a hero, as Pierrot was during the nineteenth century. But Bip is a character of the twentieth century, torn between the tragic and the comic in everyday life. Bip, like Don Quixote, combats windmills.

Decroux, who was the source of my inspiration and for whom I have a great respect, has remained a great grammarian. I am a mime–actor, a man of the theatre who had a company for twelve years, who staged twenty mimodramas and eighty mime numbers, comprising a repertory of more than fifty style pantomimes and more than forty Bip pantomimes.

Although Decroux wanted me to remain at his school to help teach and create a company, I felt that I was not as orthodox as he was, and so I went on to create my

own works and perform elsewhere. I believe that my success reinforced his own
school because many of those who saw my work wanted to return to the source and
study with Decroux.

*How do you feel about the use of facial expression, condemned by certain Decroux
mimes for being too conventional?*

M: I do not think that one can speak of conventional facial expression. The
mime–actor is obliged to adopt a conventional expression when he depicts a sentiment or a character trait, expression that must be recognized by all humans as a part
of the foundation of our existence—that is, of our interior or visual reactions. Conventions are necessary. The mask is conventional because it represents a symbol, of
which the traits reflect expressions and human nuances. One can condemn grimaces
as one can condemn poor actors. But a grimace, which is the ultimate expression of
a sentiment, expresses itself like the traits of a painting or the forms of a sculpture.
The Mask Maker, for example, employs the face like a mask to depict expressions
of joy, astonishment, old age, anger, laughter, tears. Each expression is like a Japanese or Chinese mask because it is in the Oriental theatre that the mask best reflects
human nuances. *The Mask Maker,* influenced by the Kabuki and Noh theatres and
by Chinese opera and Indian Kathak, consists of simulating a real mask by superimposing itself on the mask of the natural face. In other words, the conventions of
the expression of the mask are mimed by the face. The hands, creating the effect of
the superimposing of a mask, cover the face, already in essence a mask. To avoid
grimaces, the face takes on a neutral expression each time a mask is taken off and
replaced by another. The neutral face between two opposite expressions is like a silence between two sentences or tonalities, or like breathing between two pauses. Because mime is a visual art, it is difficult to describe a particular style without adding
the example of an image.

*Do you feel, like Decroux, that the use of face and hand movements is an easy ef-
fect?*

M: Decroux condemned the use of hands when these are employed to make up
for what is missing. Many people use their hands to emphasize a thought when they
feel they are not being convincing. But the hands used in an autonomous manner
(like the trunk or the legs) are necessary in the art of mime, especially if they express
a precise feeling or if they describe either objects, symbols, or signs. The Hindu
mudra is very rich in nuances. Each expression of the fingers represents a sign, an
element, a thought. Etienne Decroux himself has codified the use of the hands. We
have an official term for each, like the orator's hand, the Oriental hand, the geometric hand. I, myself, have added other terms, like the lyrical hand, the butterfly hand,
etc. I have created about two hundred hand positions.

I do not believe that the movements of the face are condemned by Decroux.
Rather, the lack of style is what he certainly condemned. But the necessary training
for the movements of the hands is desirable; it is part of the grammar of mime. Remember the colorful Chinese face masks and those in the Japanese Noh theatre, as
well as the face and eye expressions in the Hindu Mahabharata and in the Kathakali
and Bharata-Natyam.

In the art of mime, conventions are necessary. They are the signs upon which
gestures are based to express men's passions, their rules, their aspirations. Conventions establish a character or a social situation, like, for example, to distinguish a

bourgeois from a student, an accused person from a judge, or a child from an old woman. The mime takes on the physical form of the character he represents in a conventional manner, which does not mean in a banal one but rather in a stereotyped one. One says that an actor has become conventional when his style does not evolve or when his acting lacks brilliance or dramatic intensity.

It is a question, then, of renewing feelings and of giving style, form, and volume to sentiments that create an emotion either by plastic beauty or by dramatic density of the action. One does not speak of the actor as being conventional but rather as being dramatic or melodramatic.

Could you elaborate on the word conventional in regard to movement?

M: I make use of conventional movements to give a definite form to my movements, to situate a character in a precise manner, because conventions are the signs by which men identify themselves. One can speak of conventions of language, conventions of gestures, as of a code that is established on a prearranged basis. The unconventional represents a more abstract research of movement, not routine in the tradition of gesture. In other words, it is an original and renewed transposition of gesture.

Do you believe, as Decroux implies in his book Paroles sur le Mime *[words on mime], that the easier effects of movement do not belong to mime but rather to dance and to spoken theatre?*

M: Dance does not make use of easy movements, or else it is poor dance and not worth speaking of. Any dance having its own style utilizes precise movement, full of virtuosity in order to heighten the dramatic quality of movement. Often that which is truly difficult seems effortless. The public should have the impression that the dancer, the acrobat, or the mime makes sport of the difficulty of weight or of virtuosity and of the equilibrium of movement.

As for the spoken theatre, there are no precise rules concerning gesture. This depends on the *metteur-en-scène*. Great actors make use of few gestures.

In an article I wrote in *Dance Magazine* [1965], I said I could conceive of a performance in which dance, pantomime, sculpture, and rhythm could form an ensemble. Personally, I prefer separating these genres. Dance and mime should have their own autonomy. Both proceed through the use of rhythm in time, and the volumes they create in space inspire sculptors to capture these movements in their art. But dance carries less weight than mime. The dancer escapes weight; the mime seeks it. I call it *l'art du pesanteur ailée* [the art of winged weight].

What about criticism by certain former Decroux students that your work relates to the nineteenth century rather than to the modern or postmodern style?

M: Certain mimes who came out of Decroux's school thought that because I wore the white mask I was only relating to nineteenth-century pantomime. This is not shameful because that was a great Pierrot tradition. However, I don't play like the Pierrots. My style pantomimes opened the door to contemporary mime, which would not have had the same power if my style pantomimes had not existed. One can compare some of my style pantomimes to Etienne Decroux's *The Factory, The Trees,* and other pieces now considered classical. My pieces *The Creation of the World, The Hands, The Tempest, The Eater of Hearts, The Mirror,* and *The Pickpocket's Nightmare* were in the repertory of the Théâtre des Champs Élysées in the seventies and eighties. And *Bip in Modern and Future Life* and *Bip as an Illusionist* used visual techniques and projections, which added another dimension. The development of these works brought much to today's mime visually and dramatically. One cannot say that I am a nineteenth-century mime. And time will decide if I am a timeless mime.

Although some theatre critics understand that my style is a form of pure mime, other mime critics, who have integrated only the Decroux style, in speaking of modern and postmodern mime have made Marceau responsible for a return to the traditional and romantic mime of Pierrot. I only kept the white mask of the nineteenth-century tradition so that the public could understand that there is a mime tradition, just as there are Noh and Kabuki theatre traditions. But my style pantomimes have nothing to do with nineteenth-century pantomime and are totally contemporary. My contemporary work can be transmitted and become part of a repertory, and students can also learn from and interpret my pieces in their own manner. It is as if one said that Chaplin created a world of the twenties and thirties that no longer exists; thus, his art is no longer valid. The technical perfection of Chaplin is a part of the timeless quality of the cinematographic mimodramas. The same is true for classical dance, which is timeless. All creators dream of being timeless. Classicism is the highest form because it shows that art withholds time, even when it is found within a period. This attitude creates confusion among young people because they are taught not to look at the past but only to be preoccupied with present-day mime. Our period must be shown, but we can also return to the Greek period or others, like the movies do and the theatre in general. It is valid in sculpture, painting, literature, and in all forms of art. What is important is the quality and the perfection of the style. What I reproach in the postmodernists is their rejection of the past. It is as if contemporary theatre artists rejected Aristophanes, Shakespeare, and the Elizabethan theatre. In order for theatre to advance, it must evolve with new forms but also respect ancient forms. For me, the past, present, and future comprise one unity in a strong style. I am not inscribed in the past but more than ever in the contemporary period. One day, even what is contemporary will be part of the past. Our future will also be the past. So what will count in the long run is the timelessness that artists have brought to their period, the dramatic force that has made the theatre advance and art and science immortal. And because I believe that the mime is a silent actor of the theatre, for me his art is inscribed in the dramaturgy of timeless theatre.

How has mime changed as an art form?

M: I find that the evolution of mime is taking place now in many directions. There are companies like the Théâtre du Mouvement and many others. All this is very healthy. There are festivals of mime in Périgueux and elsewhere. I was asked by the mayor of Périgueux, Yves Guena, to be the patron of the Périgueux Festival, but I could not accept because I am unable to be there to be responsible for works with which I do not agree. So I have left the festival to its free choice. Instead, I am a member of the Festival Committee of Honor, along with Jean-Louis Barrault, Robert Wilson, Ferruccio Soleri, and Maguy Marin. I accepted this honor because I feel that Yves Guena did well to create a festival and a mime center at Périgueux to allow young mimes to have a home.

What are your future plans for your own mime form?

M: I am more than ever preoccupied with a theatre of mimodrama and with my school in Paris. The latter is the creative élan for future works in mimodrama that will be the continuity of our past and of the twenty-six mimodramas that I staged. With my company of fifteen mimes mostly from my school, I will present a mimodrama that I wrote entitled *Le Chapeau Melon* (The Bowler Hat), along with future creations like *Napoli New York*. However, these new works will not only be a continuation, but also an evolution. When one speaks of the quality of mimodrama, one should differentiate between good and bad. I am not against abstract mime, but I feel that when one organizes a mime company staging mimodramas of a certain period, it is necessary to create a dramatic theatre. And what is important is the creation of a strong style. I also plan to continue developing workshops, such as the one I created in 1984 through 1988 in Ann Arbor, Michigan, with Brian Trim, a former student for three years at my École Internationale de Mimodrame de Paris, and another one in Gambier, Ohio, where I taught since 1991 with the Gregg Goldston Johnson School for Mime. Thus, I will participate in the continuity of contemporary mime and its evolution.

Do you plan to write a book about your ideas on mime?

M: I would love to write a book on mime and theorize about our art form because there are still so many unanswered questions. But I play three hundred nights a year and have little time. However, I am under contract with Random House to write an autobiography. I guess I am a world traveler like Ulysses, only not by sea but in the air. Maybe that is why I am obsessed with angels. The angel has always been a strong metaphor for me, raising questions about life, death, and our timeless vulnerability.

What do you believe is your contribution to mime?

M: I feel that I have succeeded in creating a vast public for mime in the whole world. I believe that I also have opened the doors for possibilities of creation in the theatre of mime to present-day and future creators of strong and poetic works. I hope that each will follow his own evolution. In order for the theatre of mime to live, it is necessary to have creators and mime–actors and–actresses and, above all, schools to train them. Today in America, there are mime–creators like Leonard Pitt and mime–teachers in universities like Thomas Leabhart, who both studied many years with Etienne Decroux. There is also Stephan Niedzialkowski, who was a guest teacher at my school in Paris and who trained and played leading roles in Henryk Tomaszewski's company in Poland. As I have mentioned, in Ohio there is the Goldston Johnson School for Mime and, in Ann Arbor, Brian Trim, who taught there at the Marcel Marceau World Center for Mime.[5]

Notes

1. Marcel Marceau was born in 1923. After studying mime with Decroux at Dullin's school, in 1946, he played Harlequin in the pantomime *Baptiste* and in Noverre's *La Fontaine de Jouvence* with the Barrault-Renaud company. In 1947, he staged his first mimodrama, *Praxitèle et le Poisson d'Or,* at the Théâtre Sarah Bernhardt and performed his first Bip pantomimes, *Bip et la Fille des Rues* and *Bip et le Parapluie* at the Théâtre de Poche in Paris. In 1948 and 1949, with his Compagnie de Mime Marcel Marceau, he staged the mimodramas *Mort avant l'Aube*, for which he won the Deburau prize, *La Foire,* and *Le Joueur de Flute* at the Théâtre de Rochefort in Paris. In 1951, he staged his mimodramas *Le Manteau* and *Moriana et Galvin* in Paris and in 1952, his Bip pantomimes and *Le Duel dans Les Ténèbres* were

performed in London, Germany, Switzerland, and North Africa. That same year *Pierrot de Montmartre* was staged with *Le Duel dans Les Ténèbres* at the Théâtre Sarah Bernhardt. For the next two years Marceau performed in Paris and toured Europe with his Bip pantomimes and with *Le Manteau* and *Les Trois Perruques* (1953). Marceau won first prize at the Berlin Festival of Pantomime in 1954 and in 1955, on his first tour of North America, played in Stravinsky's *A Soldier's Tale* at the Shakespeare Festival in Stratford, Ontario. Marceau created the following mimodramas at the Théâtre de l'Ambigu in Paris: *Un Soir aux Funambules* (1953) and in 1956, *La Parade en Bleu et Noir*, *Le Loup de Tsu-Ku-Mi*, *Le Mont de Piété*, and *Le 14 Juillet*. In 1958, after his second world tour, he returned to the Théâtre de l'Ambigu-Comique with the mimodramas *Le Petit Cirque* and *Les Matadors* and with *Paris Qui Rit, Paris Qui Pleure* in 1959. In 1964, with the revival of his company, his mimodrama *Don Juan* was staged at the Théâtre de la Renaissance in Paris. In 1969, he opened his Ecole Internationale de Mime. In 1971, he was comissioned to create the mimodrama *Candide*, in which he played the title role, for the Hamburg Opera Company in Germany. In 1978, his Ecole Internationale de Mimodrame was opened with a grant from the city of Paris. In 1990, his newly founded company performed in the mimodramas *Le Tragédien un Soir de Générale*, *L'Oiseleur*, and *Obsession* along with his Bip pantomimes [*Bip, Gardien de Musée*] at the Théâtre de Gymnase. In 1993 Marceau and his company staged a new version of Gogol's *Le Manteau* (1951) performed along with his Bip and style pantomimes in Paris and throughout the world. In 1997 Marceau and his company performed *Le Chapeau Melon* in Munich and Paris.

In films Marceau appeared in Roger Vadim's *Barbarella* (1967), portrayed seventeen roles in *First Class* (1970), played a deaf mute puppeteer and a mad scientist in *Shanks* (1973), and played in Mel Brooks's *Silent Movie* (1977) and in Kinski's *Paganini* (1987). Marceau had TV appearances on the Red Skelton show in 1961 and 1965 and interviews on the Mike Douglas, Dick Cavett, David Frost, and Johnny Carson shows.

Among the members of Marceau's first company was Decroux student Pierre Verry who joined in 1951 to perform in his mimodramas and play the presenter of cards, and to direct and teach from 1970 on at Marceau's Ecole Internationale de Mimo-drama. On his world tours in the nineties Marceau was assisted by graduates of his school. Among these former students, who were also performing members in his mimodramas, were J. L. Galmiche, Malcolm Scott, Fausco Periuti, Bogdan Nowak, T. H. Rheinhold, Carlos Agudelo Plata, Judith Nab, Valérie Moinet, Fumihiro Matsuda, Pierrick Malebanche, Etienne Bonduelle, Lionel Ménard, Blanca Del Barrio, who also played with Marceau in *Pygmalion*, Wolfram Von Bodecker, Costantino Raimondi, Stephan Le Forestier, Pierre-Yves Massip, Alexander Neander, Guerassim Dichliev, Laure Myers, Sara Mangano, Elena Serra, and Gyöngyi Biro.

Marceau is the author and artist of *Les Sept Péchés Capitaux* (Paris: Jean Pons, 1965); *Les Reveries de Bip* (Paris: Elmayan, 1966); *La Ballade de Paris et du Monde* Paris: (Elmayan, 1966); *The Story of Bip* (New York: Harper & Row, 1982); *Le Troisième Oeil* (Paris: Lithoprint [Delcourt]); *Pimperello* (Paris: Belford, 1988).

Marceau received Emmy awards in 1955 and 1968, was made commander of arts and letters in 1973 and officier de la Légion d'Honneur in 1986, and was elected a member of the Academy of Beaux Arts in 1991.

2. The painter Auguste Bouquet depicted the various activities of Deburau's Pierrot in his lithographs.

3. Interview with Marcel Marceau, 1966.

4. Program notes of Marcel Marceau's *Pantomimes*, 1966.

5. Interviews with Marcel Marceau, 1980 and 1992.

11

Jacques Lecoq

In Paris in the 1950s—while Etienne Decroux taught mime, Jean-Louis Barrault incorporated expressive movement into speaking theatre, and Marcel Marceau made Bip and his style pantomimes known to the world—Jacques Lecoq began to teach mime as a research tool to further dramatic creativity, as well as combine it with other arts.

At first a physiotherapist and sports teacher, Lecoq turned actor and choreographer when he joined Jean Dasté's Compagnie des Comédiens de Grenoble in 1945 and was introduced by him to mask work.[1] Here, Lecoq absorbed the training spirit of Dasté's father-in-law, Jacques Copeau, and began his research in movement and physical training for the actor. From 1948 on, he taught mime at the University of Padua and at the Piccolo Teatro in Milan. After meeting Ameleto Sartori, Lecoq asked him to make neutral masks for some of his pantomimes. He then went on to direct and choreograph movement for Greek tragedy in Syracuse and for plays, operas, and stage reviews in Rome, Venice, and Milan with animators such as Dario Fo and Franco Parenti. His work in Greek tragedy and *commedia* in Italy greatly influenced his future productions, as well as his teaching. In 1956, he began teaching movement and theatre to mimes, actors, dancers, stage artists, and people of all professions at his École Internationale de Théâtre Jacques Lecoq in Paris. Meanwhile, he lectured and held workshops throughout Europe, Canada, and the United States. By 1960, Lecoq was directing the chorus in Jean Vilar's staging of *Antigone* at the Théâtre National Populaire, teaching mime in Barrault's company at the Théâtre de France, and collaborating in stagings at the Comédie Française, at Berlin's Schiller Theatre, and on the BBC in London, as well as staging his own productions.

Beginning with classical *commedia* pieces such as *Les Disputes*, *La Famille d'Arlequin*, and the romantic, semimystical *Fishing Port*, Lecoq's stage creations evolved toward a less traditional expression in *Passage,* a pantomime with masks; *Le Raid,* a comic sketch in which the mime–actor interprets radar, a vulture, a gasoline pump, and a helicopter; and a piece based on the play of sticks and objects entitled *Les Trois Soldats.* In these works and others, as their art matured, Lecoq's mime–actors developed a rich inner expression, combining movement with text, music, and dance.

Pedagogical Notions

Lecoq believed that mime could no longer tell its own story but had to join forces with other theatre arts. "Mime must leave its anecdote to follow a dramatic road and return to the theatre or to dance."[2] He thus developed a pedagogical method based upon movement as the root of silent, spoken, written, and plastic expression. He added text, decor, costumes, and all other stage elements to movement only after the body's creative potential had been reestablished. And, contrary to Decroux's *mime statuaire*, in which movement is inspired by that which is already contained in a statuary art or a composed aesthetic form, he sought to rediscover the original or natural gesture that precedes all thinking and speaking. He also contrasted this use of gesture with the artificial expression of *pantomime blanche*.

For Lecoq, to develop his creativity, the artist's movement should not be codified in a set aesthetic form. Rather, his use of mime first entails a discovery and analysis of natural movement in everyday life. Based on the notion that physical impressions made on the body are more important than bodily expression, the mime as well as the actor first must learn to look, listen, and observe images and sounds. He must then develop a sensitivity to space, rhythm, and color, as well as a sensory awareness of all animate and inanimate elements. After gathering this knowledge through the body, he may then proceed to the analysis of movement. This comprises the study of the dynamics in nature, animals, man-made substances, and all that moves. After developing physical technique, learning to breathe in relation to emotions and exploring *commedia*, improvisation, and mask work, he is ready to choose his own expression. Technique and expression are then integrated with all forms of spoken, musical, clown, and dance theatre. In short, the Lecoq student not only learns to mime; he also speaks, sings, dances, and clowns.

The program at the Ecole Internationale de Théâtre Jacques Lecoq, an international school for those interested in a theatre of creation, comprises two years of basic training and a third year in the study of Lecoq's pedagogical approach. There is also a one-year course in the Laboratory of Movement Study. During the first two years, the student is exposed to acrobatics, juggling, stage combat, mask work, the creation of characters, *pantomime blanche*, mimed comic strips, storytelling, melodrama, *commedia*, antique and modern chorus, clown and buffoon work, mime and music, mime and text, classic and modern text, and writing for the stage. The training program progresses from a discovery of the body's potential and of movement that revolves around the dynamics in nature, animals, and man-made substances, to an analysis of dramatic gestures and the use of neutral, larval, and expressive masks. Technical and physical exercises are taught, along with related expressive exercises, improvisation, ensemble, and mask work. Expressive exercises evolve from realistic to abstract and stylized forms that eventually incorporate the voice. In Lecoq's words, the student slowly progresses from "mime to theatre to tragedy, from gesture to speech, from gesture to music, and from gesture to its own imitation and the written word is the last stage of this dramatic experience."[3]

Mime well understood, can be the foundation of an actor's training. The latter, when imitation gives way to identification, merges gesture with its own drama and becomes that major mime which holds words in suspense. Thus the spoken word, drawn from a sensitized silence, can be born from and relay with gestures; on this level gestures become sound, thanks to action which becomes drama. Between words and gestures there exists a relationship which is not obvious but profound. Mime and theatre merge on a certain level; the rest are only the rules of the game.[4]

In progressing from his discovery of primary movement or *mime de fond* to secondary movement or *mime de forme,* which is symbolic movement related to spoken language, the student attempts to develop, through a minimum of movement, a maximum of dramatic poetry. This first entails a study of the relationship between the body's dynamics and its expressivity:

> Man manifests himself in his action through gestures, attitudes and movements which themselves are full of meaning and may be characterized as either those of action, indication, or state. For example, I bend over to pick up, to see, or through submission. Our body is linked to certain rules of gravity. The actor must become conscious of these principles.[5]

Improvisation, as in Decroux's corporeal mime, is essential to Lecoq's training method. It begins with an identification with elements in nature, animals, and man-made substances. The student becomes, for example, fire, air, earth, and water and identifies with sounds, colors, shapes, odors, and taste sensations. He takes on such man-made substances as paper, rubber, and plastic, eventually adding corresponding sounds to each element. Groups play out the substances, each reacting to the other's properties. The student then develops character types relating to these physical elements and takes part in individual and group improvisations that dramatize themes based on observations of everyday life.

The use of masks, which Lecoq discovered in Dasté's company and through Copeau's influence as well as while working in Greek tragedy and the *commedia* in Italy, enables the student to employ his body more fully, to ennoble and intensify dramatic interpretation and to express only what is essential. Mask work begins with the neutral mask, which obliterates all one has learned, to rediscover the self and what surrounds us. Working with this mask culminates in the study of Greek chorus, which, for Lecoq, is the neutral state's highest level. Later, in the study of character and grotesque masks, the student learns to portray various characters and to work with stylization. With the counter-mask, the mime–actor's body plays counter to what his mask represents. Work with the larval mask consists of portraying abstract emotional states rather than characterizations. The *commedia* half-mask is used with spoken improvisation to play a type character in *commedia.* The clown's small, red nose-mask develops comical movement and is a tool for searching for one's own clown and humorously playing up one's weaknesses, revealing the true self in relation to others.

After studying clowns, the Lecoq student moves into the world of buffoons, whom he portrays as mocking, one-legged, one-armed beings with hunchbacks, living between gods and devils and bringing to light many truths. The study of clowns and buffoons is important in Lecoq's training program because he believes that the theatre should return to a more tragic dimension. And it is the clown who reflects the human condition's absurdity and alienation:

> The clown has replaced the hero who no longer exists in the theatre. We search for our clown, the one who grew up in us and which society no longer allows us to express. Though it offers an element of great liberty, where the individual finds he can be himself, it also represents an experience with solitude.[6]

The Lecoq student develops poetic invention by observing that which surrounds him. Observation of movement in everyday life is the basis of plastic, sonorous, written, and spoken expression. For example, during his training, the student watches for a three-week period the movements of individuals — in a store, hospital, or factory — so that he can re-create his impressions before a school audience. Through this process, he develops an awareness of the inner dynamics of gestures, words, sounds, colors, and light. He thus divests himself of theatrical devices and preconceived ideas to make himself physically, emotionally, and mentally available to sensations of everyday life. He identifies with the world by allowing himself to "replay" it with all of his being. Face to face with himself, his imagination is challenged. And because no models are imposed on him, he discovers within himself a world based on the observations that he brings to his dramatic creations.

This global training method unites the body's expression with theatre, music, plastic arts, poetry, and all of life. It aims to integrate movement and language with the total being. Words do not translate gestures but are the natural result of basic physical needs, needs expressed by elemental gestures that precede all language and thought. As anthropologist Marcel Jousse, author of *L'Anthropologie du Geste,* whose notions on movement Lecoq encountered in the 1970s and found to coincide with his own, has said, "Man thinks with all of his body" (1974, 17). Jousse based this idea on a process he called mimism, which is an instinctive tendency in the *anthropos* ("man" in Greek) to comprehend the outer world through the entire body. Our use of gestures is therefore a replaying of what has already been absorbed through mimism (1974, 16). For example, when trying to describe the physical form of a spiral staircase, we can more adequately do so by making a spiral-like gesture (grasped through mimism) or a drawing resembling that gesture.

Movement research at Lecoq's school has extended to other arts. In a course he has taught since 1969 to architects at the Beaux Arts School in Paris, Lecoq explores forms, colors, light, constructed space, sound, images, and words in relation to the human body and to the dramatic in everyday life. This research led to the creation of the Laboratoire d'Étude du Mouvement at his school, which explores the use of space and rhythm through plastic representation and relates movement, color, and form to scenography. Summer workshops are also offered to students in language arts, medicine, writing, art, and other fields.

Like Decroux before him, Lecoq rediscovered the human body's expressivity. Continuing the work of his mentors, Dasté and Copeau, he revived the commedia dell'arte and reintroduced the use of the mask to develop corporal expression. He also brought the clown and the buffoon from the circus and the street into the theatre as a means of self-discovery, as well as to enrich their arts. He has found relationships among mime, the plastic arts, and architecture. In his search for broader forms not limited by the boundaries of codified silent mime, Lecoq incited his students to create freely by joining movement to text, music, dance, clown art, and all of theatre art. His contribution to modern mime and theatre has been that of a catalyst. By encouraging the development of many new mime styles, he has played an important role in mime's synthesis with other theatre and art forms, from which it had long been separated, to bring about the revival of total theatre.

Interview with Jacques Lecoq

In the following interview, Lecoq elaborates on his work as a mime–teacher and on movement's role in the theatre arts.

How did you become interested in teaching mime?

Lecoq: At first I was involved in sports, and I also worked with the handicapped. Then I became interested in everything that moves, and I felt a joy in moving. Moving became a vocation for me, a desire to communicate to others and to know more about it. I use the word *movement* because I feel that mime limits itself to the idea of existing as a unique phenomenon that has its own laws. Mime is not one single thing. It is always something else. Usually when we speak of mime, we are alluding to someone who imitates life in his own manner, either loving it, glorifying it, or not caring about it. I believe that in mime there is an element of theatre. I can't conceive of mime removed from the theatre. Mime is more interesting when related to other things. Alone, it ends in sclerotic formalism or mere virtuosity. I believe that mime begins to have a meaning only when it loses its name.

What influences have there been on your work?

L: I mentioned that I began by trying to understand the function of the human body in sports, and I was fascinated by the analysis of how one throws, climbs, and so on. Sports taught me the basis of how the body moves. Secondly, after the war there was a desire to recapture the prewar style and to break down the walls that had been built between people and the arts. For instance, when I was a teacher of physical education, Jean-Louis Barrault was with us in the stadium. We ran together, and we even mimed instinctively. My image of Barrault then was that of a sportsman who gave me another corporal dimension. Another influence was that of Jean Dasté, with whom I performed for two years and discovered acting with a mask. From him I learned Copeau's views on the mask as a means to rediscover the human body. Thus I feel linked to Copeau, even to the Vieux Colombier. Though I was directly influenced by Copeau, I have searched and discovered my own form of mime. In Italy I staged sixty-two productions and collaborated in choreographing many others. There I rediscovered the commedia dell'arte and Italian reality with its human comedy, which I loved in the people and life and could transpose to the theatre. Before working in Italy, I had a more surrealistic imagination. And then when working in Greek tragedy in Syracuse, I had the feeling of the great theatrical dimension that fascinated me. However, after I showed an Italian actor how to walk in place, he said, "It's very good walking in place, but where are you going?" There was another meaning to walking other than simply demonstrating how one walked. This caused me to think about this style of mime.

How important is mime in everyday life?

L: At the basis of mime, there is that human phenomenon that Marcel Jousse in his *Anthropology of Gesture* calls mimism. I don't mean mimetism. Mimism adheres to the meaning of an object or to a person I see when I understand his rhythm and his internal space. It is that knowledge of things we grasp first, through the body and through mimism. I understand what is outside of me because my body recognizes its meaning. Mimism is the common element between people and basically among all arts. Whenever an artist takes up his brush, he begins with an internal impulse and identifies himself with the essence of the object he is painting. For instance, when Picasso drew a bull, he identified not with the form of the bull but with his essence. An artist's talent and art consist in finding in three lines the essence of whatever he is painting. At our school, we try to recognize elements in life that take place before acting them out, a recognition of live things through the body, through mimism. In this manner, we comprehend trees, the rhythm of the sea, colors, space, people—all that is alive and moves, which is infinite.

Could you define the word mimism? Is it an imitation of objects in life?

L: No. In an imitation, one imitates the form of an object. For example, when imitating a tree, I create an image that conforms to its form. In mimism I do not have to recreate the branches and the leaves, but I have to grasp the essence of that tree: its rootings, its vertical direction, whatever belongs to the tree in its essence. And I think that this representation of a tree by any artist has to pass through this phenomenon, or it will be a tree that will not hold up.

Could you distinguish between mime and pantomime?

L: These terms have changed with time. The performer and the art are often confused. The mime means he who interprets, as well as the art of mime itself. Before, we said the mime mimed the pantomime. Among the Romans, the mimes were called buffoon–mimes. Mime was also a short play that was spoken or sung. The word *mime* is cumbersome and limiting. Today the mime is a performer who in silence gives the illusion that things exist with an interpretation that is close to reality. On the other hand, pantomime was a form with scenes that were in part written as if the mimes spoke because there was a code of gestures that replaced words without being a mute art. In France it also referred to a pantomime with a Pierrot character. Today it is called *pantomime blanche* [whiteface pantomime] to identify a certain style. However, for me, pantomime today is still a language of mime that translates spoken language with or without whiteface. Pantomime is also found in the Oriental theatre, where the mime does not always wear white make-up.

How do twentieth-century mime and pantomime differ from Greek mime and Roman pantomime?

L: It is very difficult to know how the Greeks and Romans performed in mime and pantomime. One can only guess that it was very different. There were buffoons and tragic and comic mimes. The Greek mimes were part of the spectacles in the theatre, in a total form of theatre, or during moments of spoken theatre that were mimed, as in the Japanese Noh. In Rome pantomime was an isolated, parasitical, and luxurious art that came after tragedy and that ended in virtuosity. On the other hand, Deburau's pantomimes developed because the Italian comedians were forbidden to perform. So they began to sing, to use posters with words, and to mime. Mime can blossom marvelously in all theatre and dance. There are silent, mimed moments in all great theatre, as well as mime that accompanies the spoken word in the theatre of the Orient and Occident.

Do pantomime and mime have elements in common?

L: Pantomime, for me, is based on the Deburau codes, which characterized the pantomimes of his time. During that period, they also wanted to do Molière in pantomime. Although both forms belong to the art of gesture, pantomime is based on the translation of spoken language and mime is based on a silent language that comes before, beneath, or after the spoken word, a form in which the word does not necessarily have to exist.

Does the term "abstract" apply to certain aspects of your mime art?

L: My art has many aspects. Abstract mime can be found in dance, where it loses its name and we merely call it dance. The imitation of things belongs to mime. When we isolate abstraction from life, the latter is no longer represented but becomes a rhythm, space, and direction that are best expressed by music and dance. The definition of these terms is so difficult, and mime is such an important term today that we do not know where to put it. We know that it exists, but it is ill at ease where we think it should be. Its meaning also continues to change with the different periods.

Why is the art of mime growing today?

L: At the end of the nineteenth century, the human body was rediscovered. The body, which had been imprisoned in corsets and hidden because of religious interdictions, was again made apparent. During the fascist period, the human body and the corporal hero were deified. There was also the development of modern dance based on François Alexandre Delsartre's notions and the Bauhaus movement, with Oskar Schlemmer and the Bauhaus dancers, who danced and mimed with masks. Because words had also become sclerosed, the body reacted and there was a return to movement. Whenever something goes wrong, the body knows more than we do. It manifests itself as a scream or as a sign. So, after the sclerosing of spoken language, there was a return to the source. One should always think of what a form will become in twenty or thirty years. At our school, we can experiment with all forms because we do not have to justify them before the public.

How does mime differ from acting and dancing?

L: For me, the mime performer is first of all an actor, and when the abstract is present, he becomes a dancer. When dance isolates rhythm and space and utilizes music, which is abstract in its nature, then we are in the domain of abstract movement. In mime there is always an imitation of nature and of human beings. Dance needs music, while mime needs theatre. Yet, there still exist many war dances and types of mime–dance.

Why must mime and pantomime eventually be combined with dramatic art?

L: Mime is always better when it is accompanied than in solitude. Otherwise it becomes a fixation. It is an art that begins things and never ends them, as does pantomime, which attempts that dangerous game of not speaking and of using only gestures. Yet, it can be sublime, depending on the talent of the mime interpreter. However, it is better to eat strawberries with cream than to eat strawberries alone or cream alone. When mime is combined with another art, this gives it another dimension and a greater richness. In mime alone, there is a kind of narcissism. One looks at oneself, at one's own image. I find that mime begins to have a meaning when it is related to theatre. I, myself, have explored different regions of mime in relation to the theatre. Mime is present in many forms—among clowns, buffoons; in Italian comedy, Greek tragedy, melodrama—offering a very rich dimension to theatre.

What use can mime training have for an actor, a dancer, or any artist?

L: For me, dancing and acting require mime training because they necessitate a knowledge of life, which one acquires through mimism and which is often lacking in actors and dancers. It is also useful for anyone who creates: for the poet, for instance, because it is at the basis of poetry. Poetry finds its source in that which is not said. It is what comes between words. And each one must find his own style, his own world. The analysis of movement can be taught to everyone, but a transposition is made only through a process of choice on the part of the creator.

In the pedagogical method that you have developed, the student works with masks. What is the use of the neutral mask?

L: In our school, the use of the neutral mask is a means to find that state of balance and nonconflict that is without preconceived ideas and conflicts and that is necessary to better understand the value of drama. Its pedagogical function is that it brings with it no past. It also has a dramatic function because it is a social mask, which is close to the role of the chorus, a collective mask that has a meaning when it becomes a chorus or a collectivity, like a great organism that becomes one true individual.

It also helps us rid ourselves of our tics, grimaces, of commentaries, and of psychology in general. It is like a filter; it allows major intentions to manifest themselves, and it effaces unimportant details. Moreover, it gives a meaning to the body because when the face is hidden, the body shows itself more. The body is discovered when we are masked.

I met a writer who, after training at your school and wearing the neutral mask, said her writing had improved.

L: Yes, because it is like being before an unwritten page. If we write a word on it, it must be an important word. We can no longer write it just like that. Something important has to have happened before writing. The neutral mask filters out little, unimportant dramatic impressions to the profit of something broader and also of only that which is essential.

Could you describe the larval masks and their purpose?

L: Larval masks are a series of masks that are very simple and have indefinite shapes. There are prolonged shapes, pointed shapes, etc. They serve as a sort of elementary tool that can be brought to light in numerous characters but that remain in a state of becoming, as do larvae. They are easy to make and render it possible to isolate simple forms. They also serve to broaden our movements because, in general, if we use more-complicated masks, the movement is hampered by facial expression or those expressions established by other masks, while with these masks it is as if we have rediscovered our childhood. Working with these masks makes us available. They can also be very buffoonesque.

What do you feel you have contributed to the art of mime?

L: I think that if I have done something for mime since the many years that I have been teaching it, it is to have discovered varied expressions that are not isolated in an individual or a given style. I believe that my school has made mime blossom. We were also among the first to experiment with clowns. Now we also experiment with buffoons. We might or might not succeed, but it is important to be open and not to copy the style of someone else because you will never be as good as he is. Each is better in his own style.

What are some of the theatre forms you have revived that include mime?

L: We helped bring back the commedia dell'arte. When I returned from Italy with the Sartori masks, the commedia dell'arte was not that popular. Even in Italy at that time it was quite dormant. But it is a part of mime and corporal expression. That is what urged me to continue in that direction. It is also part of a desire today to rediscover the body, which has taken on quite a few directions. In mime the more directions, the better.

You have trained people who are not going to make a career of mime or theatre. For example, Lawrence Wylie studied at your school and then wrote a book on the differences between American and French gestures, which he also taught in his sociology courses. That leads me to another question. How are gestures related to words, and which are more expressive, gestures or words?

L: I do not believe that one language is more expressive than another. One should not stop at the spoken word itself. One should look for poetry in words. The poet can give a greater dimension to words because in words there is also what is not said. The poets St. Jean Perse and René Char arrive at that kind of dynamics that belong to the body alone. I do not believe that words are limited in the communication of ideas and emotions. But I believe that words and ideas must be related to movement and that they also belong to that which is not expressed, which is poetry. I also believe that fundamentally all the arts resemble one another and that there is no hierarchy or any limits. A great mime can also go very far in his art.

Does an ideal form of mime combine spoken text with mime?

L: Yes, and each period of mime or music and the other arts should take turns in participating in this great dramatic phenomenon. It can be integrated with theatre or dance or belong to a population of mountebanks, that we can no longer call mimes but clowns. For instance, the Czech mime festivals consist mostly of clowns. Dimitri the Clown does not want to be called a mime because it is so limiting. Mimes have killed mime. So today there are mime–actors, mime–buffoons, mime–clowns. There is a whole population that is, for me, buffoonish. There are also individuals who are buffoonish. Rufus, Raymond Devos, and Charlie Chaplin recreate life for us by magnifying and mocking it. They are actor–authors and ambulant poets.

Is this the form of mime that was understood among the Greeks and Romans as an imitation of life?

L: Yes, but on another level and with a transposition that includes or does not include objects and sound effects, with imitations of the sounds of birds, forests, etc.

What are the different forms of mime one studies at your school, and why are these forms explored?

L: What I call *mime de fond* or primary gesture is essential. It differs from *mime de forme* or secondary gesture, which develops later and in relation to a formalized oral language. Our school has explored different domains and styles in mime so that the student can be stimulated in different directions to help him make a choice of a kind of mime that he can integrate with other forms. For instance, there are mime–clowns, mime–buffoons, tragic mimes. And that is how I believe that mime can have a future. One cannot, except from the point of view of technique and analysis, imitate the style of the great mimes, who have their own talent. I would also like to add that the real aim of my school is to have students of different types in order to form creators. I do not wish to impose my art. In my workshop, entitled "Voyages around Mime," I teach basic mime, which is the essential aspect of my school, along with other forms of theatre like clowning or acting, which allows for development in many directions.

What do you predict for the future of the art of mime?

L: I can only hope that that richness that the human body possesses will explode and give rebirth to theatre and dance. And I believe that it is happening today because there is a return to the body to find the basis of things. But this will also evolve toward the incorporation of a text. My hope is that there will also be an evolution toward great tragedy and great chorus, in which everyday man will be linked to universal man. Maybe it is only a utopian dream.[7]

Notes

1. Jacques Lecoq was born on December 15, 1921, in Paris. After joining Jean Dasté's Compagnie des Comédiens de Grenoble in 1945, he taught dramatic art at l'Éducation par le Jeu Dramatique. Two years later, while teaching mime at the University of Padua, he collaborated in Bertolt Brecht's *The Exception and the Rule*, Pedro Calderón's *La Devoción de la Cruz*, Frederico Garcia Lorca's *Don Perlimplin*, a Japanese Noh entitled in French *Les Cent Nuits,* and the pantomimes *L'Usine*, *Port de Mer, La Statue*, and *Fanfan Bar,* among others. In 1951, while teaching mime at the Piccolo Teatro of Milan, he directed the movement in Carlo Goldoni's *L'Amante Militaire*, T. S. Eliot's *Murder in the Cathedral*, Sophocles's *Oedipus Coloneus*, Jean Giraudoux's *Apollon de Bellac,* and Charles Péguy's *Sainte-Jeanne*. He staged his own pantomimes, Plautus's *Pseudolus,* Luciana Berio's opera *Mime Musique Numéro Deux*, Antonio Veretti's *Burlesca* at the Opera in Rome, and the chorus movement for Aristophanes's *The Clouds* in Ostia. In 1956, he staged Eugene Ionesco's *The Chairs* and *The Bald Soprano*.

Lecoq founded his international theatre school in 1956. He also taught at Charles Dullin's school. He collaborated with Léon Chancerel at the Théâtre de l'Enfance, Jacques Fabbri in *La Famille d'Arlequin* and *Sergeant, Je Vous Aime,* Sacha Pitoëff in *Le Roi Serf,* and Jean Vilar in *Ubu Roi*. His company also played on French radio and TV.

In 1960, Lecoq directed the chorus at Vilar's Théâtre National Populaire. In 1961, he staged *The Barker and the Automat* by Gabriel Cousin at the Théâtre Quotidien in Marseilles and choreographed the movement in Brecht's *Sept Péchés Capitaux,* staged by Kurt Weill at the Accademia Filharmonica Romana. The next year, he directed the chorus for Euripides's *Ion and Hecuba* at the Greek Theatre in Syracuse. In 1963, he choreographed Jean Anouilh's *Le Bal des Voleurs* at the Schiller Theatre in Berlin, collaborated with Dasté in Cousin's *Drame du Fukuryer Maru* at the Comédie de Sainte-Etienne, and taught mime at the Théâtre de France. From 1964 on, he lectured and gave demonstrations and workshops throughout Europe and the United States. Lecoq died on January 19, 1999.

2. Letter to author, December 3, 1966.

3. Ibid.

4. Letter to author, May 1, 1968.

5. Ibid.

6. Text from *Théâtre de la Ville,* Program notes, no. 15, January 1972.

7. Interview with Jacques Lecoq, summers 1988 and 1992.

12

Mimes of Twentieth-Century Europe

From the Greek mimes to Pierrot—whether mime–actors danced, acted, sang, or played instruments; performed in Roman pantomime; became jongleurs; participated in medieval miracle and mystery plays; or played Harlequin and Pantalone in the commedia dell'arte—artistic norms regulated their art in a well-defined dramatic expression. And when, from Pierrot in the nineteenth century to Bip in the twentieth century, mimes performed in silence, as did Gaspard Deburau at the Funambules and later Séverin and Marcel Marceau, they did so in the structured movement styles of classical and modern pantomime. And, though mimes still played in silence and with codified or traditional movement in the 1960s and 1970s, this was no longer true in the 1980s. Having exhausted silent physical theatre's expressive capacities, Decroux and Marceau-trained mimes, along with those of the Lecoq school, began to incorporate other genres—such as circus, dance, puppetry, acting, and film—into their art. They danced, played instruments, did clown acts, juggled, tumbled, and even spoke. Their stagings embraced committed theatre, social and political issues, metaphysics, poetry, and folklore. National and international mime and clown festivals included many kinds of physical theatre artists. As in the ancient Greek theatre and the commedia dell'arte, this new physical theatre aimed to synthesize many components. Yet it would differ from ancient Greek theatre and the *commedia*, where mime, dance, song, and circus skills were so well integrated with the spoken text that they were regarded not as a separate art but as part of a total theatre. Many mime styles throughout Europe culminated in movement expressions that broke with modernism's constraints to evolve in postmodernism's uninhibited impurity.

A number of the artists and companies in this chapter are described according to the influences of the aforementioned schools of Etienne Decroux, Marcel Marceau, and Jacques Lecoq. Others represent the commedia dell'arte, classical pantomime, clown–mime, dance–mime, and street theatre and incorporate masks, plastic arts, film, marionettes, and other elements introduced with postmodernism's advent. Many of the postmodern elements contained in these companies' and artists' movement expressions are summarized at the beginning of the chapter, elements that also might apply to the works of those described in further chapters. Also, because of Eastern European mime's significant place and its different movement expression, the artists and companies of this area are placed in a separate section.

Because of their unique contributions and their active roles in the ongoing development of the mime field, twentieth-century European women mimes are discussed later in a chapter dedicated to female mimes. Among them are Pinok and Matho, Ella Jaroszewicz, Nola Rae, Gardi Hutter, and others representing the various schools of mime, clown–mime, physical theatre, and dance–mime.

This chapter offers an overview of mime's many visages that developed among the artists and companies stemming mainly from the Decroux, Lecoq, Marceau, and Eastern European schools. It encompasses a variety of styles and forms that have evolved from these masters' training, from classical and modern schools to postmodern trends, without ranking the artists and companies representing them. In some cases, the documentation has been sparse or unavailable, and there are certainly many who have gone unmentioned.

The Advent of Postmodernism

Through the work and contributions of Etienne Decroux, Marcel Marceau, and Jacques Lecoq, during the second half of the twentieth century three main schools of mime developed in Europe. The more commonly known whiteface, illusion pantomime portrayed concrete emotions and situations by means of conventional gestures, creating the illusion of something there which in reality is not. Corporeal mimes rejected this form to express abstract and universal ideas and emotions through codified movements of the entire body. Those in Lecoq movement theatre combined acting, dance, and clowning with movement. However, in the 1980s, even the whiteface, illusion pantomimists and Decroux's corporeal mimes began expanding in many new directions. Instead of limiting themselves to silent expression and classical pantomime or codified mime technique, they experimented freely with texts and the use of voice. Some mimes wrote their own texts, as did the Greek mime–authors, integrating the mime–actor's art with the author's. They also included props, costumes, masks, lighting effects, and music. Mime in the postmodern era thus incorporated so many new elements that it no longer was referred to exclusively as mime. It was called mime–dance, mime–clowning, mime–puppetry, New Vaudeville, etc. And if it contained other elements along with movement expression, it loosely was alluded to as physical or movement theatre.

While the actor's total expressivity developed through the theories of theatre animators, stage directors, and master teachers such as Jerzy Grotowski and Eugenio Barba, who broadened the actor's physicality by means of new training methods, barriers also began to break down to incorporate other art forms into previously hermetic movement styles. Just as modern mime had revolted against existing artistic forms, so postmodern mime and movement theatre continued the antitraditional wave against a modernism grown too limited. In Europe, as well as in America, postmodernism's tendencies filtered into the works of movement artists, who abandoned the pure forms of modern mime and classical pantomime to search for broader expressions. Because of its open, experimental nature, this new aesthetic is not as easily characterized as the Decroux school's modernist form or that of classical pantomime. The following are among those characteristics found in mime and movement theatre that identify the postmodern aesthetic:

1. Postmodern mime and movement theatre resist the restrictions of preestablished rules or codification found in classical and modern mime and pantomime. There is a new emphasis on the body, no longer determined by a set use of space, rhythm, or codes. If a set space, rhythm, or codified grammar, conventional gestures, and movements are used, they deliberately can be pushed to their expressive limits to deny purity of form and content. Both postmodern mime and movement theatre often are characterized by an aesthetic of impurity.

2. There is no longer the exclusive use of any single expression, such as gestures and movement, in mime theatre, just as there is no longer an exclusive use of verbal expression in verbal theatre. The mime and the movement artist are free to deploy voice, dance, clowning, and other talents.

3. Exchanges between mime and verbal theatre are frequent. While postmodern verbal theatre might contain more movement than, for example, the verbal theatre of the 1950s, postmodern mime also incorporates a broader range of physical and verbal expression, including movement for actors and the use of props and voice. If voice is incorporated, it is not done so traditionally and might consist of only vocal sounds or broken dialogue.

4. There is a recycling or new use of existing forms no longer regarded as separate arts. For example, the frequent crossbreeding with other art forms—such as dance, music, performance art, circus, puppetry, film, and pictorial art—creates an artistic pluralism that is not necessarily integrated but offers a new vitality.

5. Form has precedence over content. The presence of multivisual forms emphasizes the pictorial element and appeals to the spectator's perceptive faculties.

6. The form might represent a collage of mixed and superimposed genres—stylized and nonstylized, romantic, realistic, baroque, mythological, ornamental, decorative, and ritualistic—sometimes employed to the point of excess.

7. The form discovers itself in the piece's development. The aesthetic process, including how the work was created and developed, is revealed. It might be presented as a parody of itself.

8. The content might be at once metaphysical, historical, political, poetic, comic, tragic, and spiritual, offering a cacophony of seemingly unrelated components.

9. The main focus in the mime or movement theatre piece might shift from the dramatic action or narrative to the theatrical means incorporated. The purpose of this shifting is to destroy the theatrical illusion and allow the spectator to reflect on these means. The theatrical illusion might also be broken by the use of excessive theatrical and spectacular means. One way to abolish the fourth wall is through direct contact between performer and audience.

10. The work is more akin to an asssembly of forms and elements rather than to an integrated, unified, or complete aesthetic whole in the traditional sense. Nontraditional theatrical means might be introduced purposely to fragment or deconstruct it. A verbal scene might suddenly arrest and replace a mime scene, or movement and silence suddenly might arrest and replace a verbal scene.

11. There are no given meanings, no central themes, and no development of dramatic action and characters. The characters' or performers' identities, if established, are not necessarily fixed and might undergo change. In this respect, there is little or no communication between characters, performers, or performers and spectators. Provided with few or no references, the spectator creates his own interpretations and meanings.

12. The content could impart a dissatisfaction with our modern world's disarray. It might provoke an irrational consciousness of social, political, spiritual, or other aspects of modern life, as in dadaism and surrealism.

13. Technological and electronic components—such as video, voice-over, synthetic music, and spectacular lighting, among other stage effects—are incorporated into the aesthetic ensemble.

14. The work exudes an international quality and makes use of multicultural and ethnic sources.

15. Time and place are not indicated. Historical periods are intermixed, and antique sources and eras are recycled and intermixed with modern times.

16. Because the work is often created in a spirit of research and experimentation, it does not always have a form that can be categorized easily or a fixed or definitive content.

While some of the following artists' and companies' creations are characteristic of traditional or classical mime, others reflect modern mime's purity and structured codes or postmodern movement theatre's impurity and diversity. Some are actors, clowns, dancers, or street artists; others combine all of these talents. Some engage in traditional *commedia*, others in modern *commedia*. Still others represent the formal mimodramas and dance–dramas of Eastern Europe or incorporate Oriental forms. And, according to the period in which they lived and the influences they have undergone, many of these movement artists and companies slowly have evolved from one form into another. This transition sometimes has been so gradual and complex that it is difficult to know where to draw a clear line between movement styles. A number of these artists' works might incorporate more than one of these twentieth-century movement styles, blending classical, modern, and postmodern aesthetics.

Mid-Twentieth-Century Mime Masters

Even before the French masters of classical, modern, or other mime forms began training their students, and well before the first signs of postmodernism, other stage artists and teachers in France and Europe brought a new interest in movement styles to theatre. One of them, Xavier de Courville, revived the commedia dell'arte. When de Courville appeared at the Paris Cabinet Fantastique in 1942, in the very theatre—formerly called the Théâtre Joli—in which Séverin had played his last pantomimes, he created a new enthusiasm for *commedia*. Playing Harlequin, de Courville and his female partner Pianavia, in *commedia* costumes and half-masks, mimed, danced, and sang the fables of Jean de La Fontaine, old French songs, and opera airs.

In the 1940s and 1950s, Charles Antonetti, a former acting and improvisation student at Charles Dullin's school, and his dancer–choreographer partner Raymonde Lombardin trained actors and dancers in movement at their Paris school and enriched verbal theatre with movement in their productions which ranged from Sophocles's *Antigone* to Nikolai Gogol's *The Inspector General* to John Millington Synge's *Playboy of the Western World*.

It was only a generation later that the students of Decroux, Marceau, and Lecoq began evolving in modern mime and classical pantomime. Among the Decroux students who combined performing and teaching, Maximilien Decroux assisted his father at his mime school before leaving in 1955 to open his own Paris school in 1960, conduct workshops throughout Europe and North America, and teach with Marceau from 1978 to 1988. During the 1961 Festival des Arts d'Avant-Garde in Paris, he performed an experimental piece at the Théâtre de l'Alliance Française. In 1962, he represented France at the Berlin International Festival of Mime with a piece he created. The mime pieces that followed, presented on stage and TV and in cabarets, were closer to total theatre in their use of dance and music. His *Double Faces*, a collection of mime pieces his students performed appeared on European and American television and on *The Ed Sullivan Show* in 1965. He choreographed the mime sections of a number of stage productions, such as *Hamlet* (1971) and Jean-Louis Barrault's staging of Paul Claudel's *Le Soulier de Satin* [*The Satin Slipper*] (1973).

About this time, another Decroux student, Pierre Richy, began a mime company in Morocco and then taught mime in Paris for the government's youth and sports program. His book, *Initiation au Mime*, offers exercises in basic mime training. Meanwhile, Wolfram Mehring taught corporeal mime to actors at the Vieux Colombier and staged his own productions with his Compagnie de la Mandragore, performing a poetic work with masks entitled *Feux Rouges* in 1965. Other mimes of this period who trained and performed with Decroux, Marceau, and Lecoq were Claude Dedieu in Paris, the Belgian mime Marcel Hoste, Gilles Segal and Sabine Lods of Marceau's company, and Eliane Guyon, a former member of Decroux's company and a teacher at his school, who taught and performed corporeal mime in Rome and Lausanne.

Deaf mime Claude Kichky studied mime at Marceau's school and, in 1970, founded his Compagnie de Mime Kichky, comprised of four deaf mimes, which performed throughout France and in Canada. The company's poetic and primarily humorous pantomimes (*The 14th of July Revue, The Automobile, Conflict, The Trap, The Vampire, The Shabby Man, The Chicken*, and *The Encounter*) as well as its serious pieces (*The Three Ages of the Woman* and *The Wall*) were performed without props, music, or text. *Art et Danse* (April 1964) had earlier considered *The Automobile* an example of modern mime.

From the Decroux School

Yves Lebreton

Before training in corporeal mime with Étienne Decroux from 1964 to 1968, Yves Lebreton studied music, painting, and graphic arts in Paris. In 1969, he opened a workshop within the framework of Eugenio Barba's Theater Laboratory in Holstebro, Denmark, to research and teach corporeal mime and vocal techniques. In 1976, he founded his Théâtre de l'Arbre in Paris, which later became the Center and School for International Formation, Research, and Creation in Italy. Lebreton has performed and given workshops throughout Europe and North America.

Lebreton's early corporeal pieces *Obstinacy* (1969) and *Possession* (1972) are abstract in content. In the latter piece, he and corporeal mime Gilles Maheu interact with a large white sheet, which one might imagine begins as the concrete portrayal of two lovers but later becomes an abstract struggle between good and evil. Lebreton's clown pieces *Hein, ou Les Aventures de Mr. Ballon* (1973) and *Bof, ou Les Mésaventures de Mr. Ballon* (1981), based on the clown's futile attempts to manipulate a large balloon along with his dog Bof, recall the sophisticated clown miming that evokes metaphysical stirrings and a sense of alienation in Samuel Beckett's theatre of the absurd. While *Flash* (1991) is a *commedia* piece, Lebreton's clowning in *S.O.S.* (1986) with his doll Lili encompasses the ravages of nuclear war and the vacuum of modern existence. *Exil* (1996) was created and performed by Lebreton to the music of Bach and Gavin Bryars's *Sinking of the Titanic*.

Although Lebreton began as a corporeal mime, his use of movement is not abstract in the conventional sense. Based on corporeal dynamics, with the body as the center of expression, through the extension of the body's movements, objects, costumes, setting, lighting, voice, and other elements are incorporated. In this prolongation of corporeal energy, words are rediscovered in their original sense and with fuller meanings; sounds, cries, and sustained tones evoke emotional and sensory connotations that are vital to the actor's art. Rooted in the body, corporeal energy thus extends itself to establish a dialogue with voice, sounds, sets, props, and costumes, encompassing the spectator. When this corporeal energy and these elements are present, the collective theatre experience is achieved and dramatic art reborn. This rebirth achieved through corporeal energy is at the very core of Lebreton's mime theatre.

Théâtre du Mouvement

Since 1975, former Decroux students Claire Heggen and Yves Marc have performed with their Théâtre du Mouvement Company and taught workshops throughout France and Europe. With a solid technique and artistic expression based on Decroux's mime grammar, they have expanded Decroux's corporeal mime to render the actor aware of other movement forms and enhance his work's theatricality. Their company members have been trained in Decroux's corporeal mime, as well as in classical and modern dance and acrobatics.

The use of masks on various body parts is one of the company's tools to develop creativity. For example, in *Tant Que la Tête Est sur le Cou*, created in 1978, neutral masks attached to different body parts are the principal protagonists that evoke the lives of a man and a woman, from courtship to marriage, sexual relationship, maternity, middle age, old age, and death. An innovative and precise play of masks on a mime's knees, genitals, stomach, chest, and various parts continually interact in harmony or contradiction with other masks on his body or on that of another mime.

Encore une Heure si Courte (1989) is based on the company's objective of discovering movement's musicality. Heightened by a musical text, the piece, which depicts a modern-day quest for the meaning of life, is performed by three actors who, in suits and ties, emerge from boxes. Using mime, movement, and absurdist comedy, they race over crates and planks to compete with a nonstop computer spitting out paper.

Krops and the Magiciel (1987), a piece for a young public, relates the tale of an old servant who finds an ancient keyboard in an attic that animates the stored furniture and the people who live there. The musical and scenographic dramatizations in this fantasy tale are achieved through extravagant corporeal images.

Bearer of the Letter, which won the 1991 Mimos Prize at the Périgueux Mimos Festival, was created by company members Catherine Dubois and Lucas Thiery; its theme is of a last letter that a soldier, who foresees his death in battle, writes to his girlfriend. The work contains an original corporeal technique in which the female protagonist never separates her body from that of the male and never touches the ground. Rigorously precise in its technique, the Théâtre du Mouvement has evolved from a geometric, corporeal movement form into a poetic and humorous mime–dance–theatre.

Desmond Jones

Among the Decroux mimes in Europe who have built reputations as teachers and mime performers is British-born Desmond Jones, who, after returning from a two-year training period with Decroux, from the 1970s on taught and performed corporeal mime in London. His poetic and humorous solo and duo vignettes revolve around such themes as an alcoholic's hallucinations in *Drink*, two mimes reversing the roles of spectator and statue in *Museum Piece*, and abstract movement and content in *White on Grey on Black*. Jones is among the first British mimes to introduce Decroux's mime into Great Britain. His Desmond Jones School of Mime offers intensive training in mime technique and has formed artists such as William Dashwood, a Decroux-trained mime and street theatre performer.

Pyramide op de Punt

Pyramide op de Punt, which Jan Ruts began in 1976 at the Antwerp Mime Studio in Belgium, has remained one of the closest exponents of Decroux's corporeal expression. One of its creations, *Het Zuilenveld* (*The Colony*), performed at festivals throughout Europe and Canada, is a corporeal piece in which bare-bodied mimes interact with five large, metallic, hollow tubes. Climbing in and out of these tubes, the mimes create dramatic tension through austere and technically perfected movement, including the use of voice vibrations and unarticulated cries. Possibly the sole survivors of a global catastrophe, their repeated disappearance into the tubes recalls the alienation that separates the characters in Samuel Beckett's world. This company's creations excite the imagination through their form's aesthetic beauty and their challenging philosophical content.

Christian Mattis

Born in Bern, Switzerland, Christian Mattis began a three-year training period with Decroux in Paris in 1974, studying simultaneously at the National Circus School with Annie Fratellini and Pierre Etaix. After working with Omnibus in Montreal and the International Mime Ensemble of Toronto, he opened his own school in Switzerland. In 1980, Mattis presented his one-man show, entitled *Corporeal Mime*, which he performed at international mime festivals throughout Europe. In 1984, his solo piece *Movimomenti* played at mime festivals in Vancouver and Winnipeg. In this work, Mattis attains a purity and simplicity that recalls the search by Decroux's corporeal mime for an ideal form. Sculpturally graceful, poetic movement—born from a physical attitude, a prop, or the flow of a mime's costume—evolves into corporeal images and silent shapes, such as an Oriental fan, a centipede, or an open-winged bird. To his corporeal skills Mattis brings a freshness of movement in which the physical beauty of form and technique is essential.

Mattis founded Tetra Theatre in 1984, Paradogs in 1989, and the Lynx Company in 1994 in Bern. Under his direction, Tetra Theatre performed his piece *Velcromania* in 1987. Revolving around costume sculptures drawn from the movements of Velcro overalls that four mimes wear, the work offers a multitude of scenarios filled with curious objects, strangely shaped animals, eccentric buffoons, and figures parading in a fashion show with variously styled hats, miniskirts, kimonos, elegant gowns, and furs. Through mime, puppetry, masks, folk dancing, acrobatics, and buffoonery, Mattis satirizes multiple facets of modern life. Mattis's *Alice* (1999) enriches Lewis Carroll's story through innovative movement theatre.

Le Théâtre de l'Ange Fou

While studying and teaching at Decroux's school and collaborating on his creations, Corinne Soum and Steven Wasson began to perform corporeal mime pieces together in 1981. Soum also trained in classical dance and gymnastics, while Wasson studied mime with Thomas Leabhart and performed in his Corporeal Mime Theatre. Soum and Wasson founded their Ecole de Mime Corporel Dramatique de Paris in 1984 with Daniel Stein as their partner, and in 1986 began their Théâtre de l'Ange Fou, engaging their Decroux-trained student Ivan Bacciocchi to perform and to teach at their school. In 1995, they moved their school to London. Soum has also been guest director for other theatre companies, including the direction of an Irish company's *Once Time*, awarded the 1996 play of the year, and Wasson worked with the Royal Shakespeare Company's *Les Enfants du Paradis* in 1996.

In the Théâtre de l'Ange Fou's creations, the corporeal images are dramatically moving, as well as technically perfected. *La Croisade* (1985) revolves around a girl who encounters a timid angel at her birthday party and undertakes a voyage into the realm of memories, illlusions, and the search for identity. *Le Petit Dictateur, Part I* (1986) conveys despotic tyranny and injustice. *Au Delà du Jardin* (1987) portrays childhood fears that prevent us from facing the adult world. The second part of *Le Petit Dictateur* (1990) depicts revolt and the reestablishing of liberty and human dignity. *The Lost Angel* (1993) develops a female artist wrestling with the critics' prejudices, aided by a drunken angel; *The Unknown Familiar* (1996) solo expresses the feminine voice through corporeal mime; *Memories of the Unknown* (1996) interprets the Australian poet Francis Brabazon's *Stay with God*; *The Fall of the House of Usher* (1998) portrays the descent into madness; and *Alice K* (1998) combines Lewis Carroll and Kafka in an absurdist tale of a woman fleeing from home to find love.

Among the few artists who have preserved Decroux's corporeal mime, Soum and Wasson reconstructed pieces of his repertory that span a fifty-year period, entitled *The Man Who Preferred to Stand*, for the Philadelphia Movement Theatre International Tribute to Étienne Decroux conference–festival in August 1992 and in

1993, which also was performed throughout Europe and at the Périgueux Mimos Festival in August 1994.

Résonance, performed at the March 1999 Montreal *Voies du Mime* (*Roads of Mime*) tribute to Étienne Decroux, is based on Decroux's solo work *La Méditation*, along with poetic texts from Robert Desnos, Jean Tardieu, Tristan Tzara, Orson Welles, and Corinne Soum. There are also references to Decroux's *Duos Amoureux* and other Decroux works and new movement compositions that explore masculine and feminine corporeal expression and organic and spiritual completion.

This theatre is based on themes that explore the protagonists' inner lives, aspirations, illusions and disillusions, and thirst for love and acceptance in the face of conflicts and social institutions. Personal conflicts reflect universal ones, as well as serve each work's poetic content. The precision and elegance of Decroux's corporeal mime synchronize with dance, acting, puppetry, and text.

Under the Sign of Lecoq

The mimes who trained with Jacques Lecoq in Paris were among the first to repopularize theatre clowning in Europe. They explored novel techniques and means of expression through movement, mask, *commedia*, Greek chorus, clown art, and *pantomime blanche*, integrating mime with spoken theatre, music, and dance in a variety of new forms.

Pierre Byland

Among Lecoq's students who continued his teaching and performing theories, Pierre Byland began studying at Lecoq's school in 1959, later teaching and touring with his company. In 1971, Byland co-founded the Compagnie Pierre Byland with playwright, poet, performer, and mime teacher Philippe Gaulier. With Gaulier, he created *Les Assiettes, L'Homme à la Valise*, and *Une Belle Journée*. In 1985, he helped establish the French National Circus School. Co-founder of the company Les Fusains, he also participated in the National Center of Circus Arts at Châlons-sur-Marne, where he created the Education of a Circus Actor and Clown Art Program. In collaboration with such clowns and actors as Bolek Polivka and Ctibor Turba, Byland directed and performed in stagings in which he and his clown partners, Mareike Schnitker and Philippe Gaulier, combined clowning, mime, and acting. Schnitker and Byland's piece *Confusion*, performed in Europe and the United States, is a movement–mask demo–performance in which a couple's fusion turns to confusion and everyday characters are created through the use of masks.

Gaulier, a teacher at Jacques Lecoq's International Mime and Theatre School from 1971 to 1980, began a school in Paris with another ex-Lecoq teacher, Monika Pagneux, who trained in the Feldenkrais Method. Together, they taught movement, neutral mask, commedia dell'arte, clowning, tragedy, and melodrama.

Mummenschanz

Based in Lugano, this Swiss theatre company took its name from *mummen* and *schanz* (*mummen* meaning game of dice and *schanz* meaning chance), referring to the medieval mercenaries who wore masks in their dice games to dissimulate their feelings. The company also was inspired by Swiss villagers' traditional use of masks to drive away evil spirits that brought about a cold winter or to celebrate special events. After training at Lecoq's school, clown–acrobat Andrès Bossard and pantomimist Bernie Schürch created their first program in 1969. In 1971, they met Floriana Frassetto, and the trio founded the Mummenschanz company in 1972, performing throughout Europe, North and South America, and the Orient. In 1998, the company created a retrospective of its major works and began a new period of artistic expression, retaining the same identity.

To achieve a highly evolved expression of movement and mask, Mummenschanz, influenced by cubism and dadaist skits in Swiss cabaret shows, reduces content to a given theme or idea's essence. Rather than employ illusion mime and classical pantomime's anecdotal content, the company moves its spectators on a visceral, as well as imaginative, level largely through an innovative use of masks. In place of traditional whiteface, members have devised abstract masks that lend poetry and fantasy to their works. Oversize props that the group creates act as giant masks for the entire body, some covering several mimes. Masks made from household objects (toilet paper rolls for eyes, nose, and mouth), hardware items, or clay (so as to easily reshape them) are transformed from their regular functions into imaginative ones, and puzzles with movable squares serve to change facial features.

The company members develop content, as well as movement patterns and designs, through improvisations with props, such as plastic bags, salad strainers, insulation material, and air hoses found at supermarkets, department stores, factories, and trade shows. Once a pair of gigantic, white-gloved hands has drawn back the bare stage's curtains and signaled for the lights to dim, three figures behind masks dissolve into objects that extend from regular size to several feet high to take on lives of their own. These objects evolve into organisms ranging from amoebas to worms, centipedes, clams, frogs, grasshoppers, monkeys, and primates and to female and male automatons with paper-bag, chessboard, tablet drawings or triangle heads and faces made of ping-pong balls. Beneath fantasy coverings, they transform into a giant octopus whipping its tentacles about, a huge, plastic tissue blob gobbling up a figure and a valise, or a foam-rubber clam opening its huge mouth to devour the stage platform. Two mimes mold clay masks on their own faces, pull them apart, and begin again. Two others draw luminous profiles of faces in the air. Another turns into a moving sculpture made of plastic pipe cleaners. To heighten the visual interplay of elements, these geometrical and abstract forms are presented without the use of words or music. Set off in continuous motion, they float, grapple, and whirl about, forever transforming themselves. The program notes provide drawings of these curious shapes.

Mummenschanz has revitalized the art of masks and developed an original use of mime, acrobatic, and circus techniques. Its art includes mime–clowning, *commedia*, cubist forms, living sculpture, and abstract shapes, which all blend into a rich, visual physical theatre. Based upon the Lecoq mask movement training methods, which encompass dance, circus theatre, and mime, Mummenschanz's theatrical game-playing reveals serious content. It proposes to "show the development of man from the original cell and our kinship to animal forms while ripping away our own masks of pomposity" (Mummenschanz program notes, Berkeley, California, 1979). It also aims to make its viewers aware of the poetry of everyday objects in a world of growing materialism.

Lecoq Mimes Unlimited

British mime–clown and mask and movement teacher Justin Case, who studied for two years with Lecoq, began performing eccentric street shows in Europe that brought him early acclaim. In 1975, Case and comedy actor Peter Wear founded the Two Reel company to develop absurdist improvisational comedy and slapstick clowning.

British mime–clown Mark Furneaux, known as Cheskoo the Clown, captured in his *Raree Show* the old English street entertainment, which he brought to the stage with *The Clerk*, *Big Surgeon, The Baby*, and *Sonatina Bureaucratique* (1972), mimed to Eric Satie's music.

The Lecoq-trained British company Moving Picture Mime Show satirized fast-paced cartoon imagery. After founders Paul Filipiak, David Gaines, and Toby Sedgwick met at Lecoq's school in the mid-1970s, they created a satire on *The Seven Samurai* in which the characters, place, and action are communicated through accelerated gestures, movements, and surprise images, as in animated cartoons. *Handle with Care*, a comical mask piece featuring two geriatrics and their nurse, and *Creatures from the Swamp*, a take-off on horror movies, were performed at the 1993 London International Mime Festival.

From 1990 to 1992, the Oxford-based Bouge-de-là-Theatre founders, Aurelian Koch and Lucy O'Rorke, studied the relationship between body and space at Lecoq's Paris Laboratory of Movement Study. For their first season they staged *Angels on the Head of a Pin* (1993/94), which contained visual images with no narrative. In the following seasons they created *The Man Who Ate His Shoes* (1995/96) with numerous stage effects; *Under Glass* (1996/97); *Time Flying* (1997/98), which emphasized pure images; and the first part of a trilogy *Evolution: Body* (1999), a dance-influenced work based on research into genetics.

Among other Lecoq students, Julian Chagrin performed in music hall and pantomime, and Swiss clowns Pic and Pello developed their own traditional circus-clown shows. Spanish mime–clown Alberto Vidal played at Dario Fo's La Commune Theatre. Matthew Burton, Bryan Divers, and Patrick Iversen founded the Cacofonic Clown Theatre. Parti-Pris, a company that grew out of Lecoq classes in 1990, staged *Hatchet Plan*, based on the world of drills, axes, and odd jobs and the ambience of a hardware store. Maria Sentivany directed and taught *commedia*.

The number of mimes throughout Europe who have based their work on Lecoq's training, which has prepared them to develop their own personal styles, is extensive. Lecoq's influence continues to manifest itself in the creativity of these European movement artists.

More Clowns, Movement Artists, and the Commedia dell'Arte

The clown's art on stage and in the circus also belongs to the broader area of physical theatre. Although a clown might never have formally learned mime and acting techniques, he makes use of expressive gestures and facial expressions. An example is the English-born George Foottit (1864–1921), a popular clown with a wide range of facial expressions who also performed as a comedian on stage and screen. Rhum (Enrico Sprogiani 1904–1953) is remembered for his expressive miming in scenes in which he jabs a knife into a chicken he is about to carve or when, on a date, he dabs his shaving brush in his champagne glass to shave himself. By 1953, the Russian clown Oleg Popov was applauded at the Moscow Circus for mime–clowning and juggling humorously on the slack wire. Leonid Yengibarov (1935–1972) was appreciated for his pantomimic talent and the poetic quality of his movements, as well as for his juggling and his clownish acrobatics in such acts as *Boxing*.

From the 1980s on, clowns and mimes have performed together in clown and movement theatre festivals. Many movement artists trained in clowning have fused their art with that of the clown. Meanwhile, the clown's art has moved from a traditional one that incorporates whiteface pantomime to an intricate one that encompasses several theatre arts and skills as well as a richer clown character. At the end of the twentieth century, clowns are blending mime, magic, dance, *commedia*, silent-film techniques, Chinese acrobatics, political and social comment, video and film, stand-up comedy, verbal clowning, and performance art into their acts. Having moved back onto the stage, their art now belongs to the broader art of physical theatre.

Dimitri

Although marked by his mime training with Decroux and Marceau and regarded as a mime of clownish style, Dimitri considers himself essentially a clown. Born in Ascona, Switzerland, in 1935 of sculptor parents, he began as a potter's apprentice in Bern. After studying with Decroux and Marceau, he played in *The Matadors* and *The Little Circus* in Marceau's company and then became the partner of the clown Louis Maisse. After his first solo show in Ascona in 1959, he toured Europe and North America with such companies as Le Cirque Knie. Winning the Grock Prize for clowning in 1973, he opened his own mime–clown school in Verscio in 1975 and, in 1976, won the Hans Reinhart Ring.

Along with his musical talent, Dimitri's early mime training enriched his clown art with movement, precise timing, whiteface, and dramatic content. In *Porteur*, this meek and gentle little clown moves us with his broad smile, which slowly changes into a pathetic stupor when his pick disappears inside his mandolin or into ecstasy after he opens a valise and discovers a new musical instrument. And when this shy, white faced figure in black knickerbockers, red socks, tennis shoes, and an oversize jacket dances on a prop box supported by a rolling pin, we watch him smile as gleefully as a child after he has mastered this feat. Whether he is spinning plates, playing on four saxophones at the same time, or swallowing and coughing up harmonicas, he is never a virtuoso. He discovers each object with innocent awe, struggles with it, and animates it. Through his wizardry, he turns a rubber hose into a stethoscope and then into a periscope, and finally has it speaking and singing to him. For the most part, he performs in silence except for the sounds of his instruments and his screams of "you-ee" that punctuate his mastery of each feat.

Possessing the corporeal control of Decroux's technique and the agility and poetic fantasy of a Marceau, Dimitri's art belongs not to the circus, the music hall, or to the mime world, but draws elements from each. Although his clown acrobacy and slapstick comedy relate to Grock's art, he moves as lithely as Pierrot and can be as pathetic as this lyrical French figure.

Dimitri believes that while clowning during the twentieth century has been greatly enriched by other arts, mime has undergone transformations that make it difficult to identify as the art form we have known. Yet, he concludes, these changes in both arts might be for the better.[1]

Dario Fo

Dario Fo is among those twentieth-century comedians who have brought the clown's art back to its origins and restored the clown's dignity. Fo's clown is not just an entertainer. Like the ancient Greek mimes, who were the clown's ancestors, he portrays human injustices in his political satires on current issues.

Dario Fo (born in 1926) and his wife, Franca Rame, founded the Nuova Scena theatre collective in 1968 to educate working-class audiences politically and revive popular Italian theatre traditions. The first production of their second collective, La Commune, formed in 1970, was *Accidental Death of an Anarchist*, which revolves around an Italian political figure's interrogation and suicide in the 1960s. They performed throughout Italy and Europe in political satires with clowning, magic, mime, marionettes, dance, folk songs, and music. *The Seventh Commandment, Thou Shalt Steal a Little Less*, a cavalcade of gags, clown sketches, mime scenes, and satirical songs, that appeared at France's Carcassonne Festival in 1971, portrayed modern man as a victim of political propaganda. Fo's *Mistero Buffo* (*Comic Mystery*), consisting of timely monologues based on medieval popular religious theatre, became Italy's favorite political show in the 1970s. *We Can't Pay! We Won't Pay!* (1974), Fo's most popular play outside of Italy, which protests the rise in prices and unemployment; *The Boss's Funeral*, about the plight of factory workers; *About Face* (1981), which focuses on violence and terrorism in politics; and *The Pope and the Witch*, satirizing the Catholic stance on abortion and drugs, all incorporate slapstick and grotesque physical comedy. In Fo's political comedy, directly descended from the commedia dell'arte, which is adapted to modern themes and characters, physical theatre harmonizes with verbal comedy. Fo received the Nobel Prize for Literature in 1997.

Josef Bogner

Born in Germany in 1934, Franz Josef Bogner, at first a civil servant in the German Department of Justice, began studying theatre and mime in 1963. After a summer workshop at Lecoq's school in 1965, he staged one-man cabaret shows for the Cabaret Festival of Essen in 1965, 1966, and 1968, the International Pantomime Festival in 1970, and the Edinburgh Festival in 1973. He also performed throughout Europe and in the United States, South America, Australia, and Southeast Asia. Meanwhile, he wrote and directed radio and stage plays and published a collection of modern fables entitled *Die Maus mit dem Sparbuch*.

Bogner's one-man, clown–mime cabaret shows are not mere slapstick. Their political, philosophical, cerebral, tragic, and humorous content is performed with seemingly spontaneous and nervous movements that are rigorously controlled. Disclaiming any particular mime style, Bogner has freed himself of all modern mime schools. In *Grain, Ballad of Manual Labor*, he satirizes the traditional school's poetry of motion, as well as the pure abstract school's idealization of movement. Styles and definitions are for this artist not an aesthetic but a social, political, and even human issue. Art is not a presentation of artistic skills, illusions, and effects but a representation of the reality of our times.

Bogner's art is best manifested in *Sisyphus, or It's All Too Simple* (1974), which depicts an insecure character reading a newspaper who becomes entwined in the pages, awkwardly attempting to remove his jacket from the back of his chair and struggling to put on a pair of suspenders. At times, Bogner removes his red clown nose to comment to the audience as he endeavors to master the simplest tasks "with childlike conviction against the many, too mighty little things."[2]

Bogner's unconventional clowning style, which combines pantomime, poetry, political satire, cabaret humor, and acting, has enriched the traditional cabaret show's content and technique as well as developed an intellectually challenging clown–mime theatre.

Other Clowns and Mimes

Among other clowns and mimes in Europe, British-born David Glass has created stage clowning composed of a very lucid humor, recalling the best of English music hall and vaudeville, that he first presented in the streets of Paris, Vienna, and Florence. His movement skills are based on modern dance and Decroux's corporeal mime. His early solo work, *Enter Dr. Phillip*, spoofs an eccentric psychiatrist who is the victim of his nervous tics and body contortions. *Pierrot in Love*, performed at the 1993 London International Mime Festival, brings the classical Pierrot into the twentieth century, and *Glass Eye* (1993) is filled with visual puns and haunting images. *Popeye in Exile*, staged in 1990 at the London International Mime Festival, marked the commencement of the David Glass Ensemble company. *Bozo's Head*, which his company performed at the 1991 London International Mime Festival, is a melodramatic mime–clown piece about the nineteenth-century Pierrot's murder of his brother and partner, Auguste, that also incorporates the Grand Guignol's comical and physical violence. *Popeye* (1993), written and directed by Glass, is a production for both children and adults that includes lively audience participation. *Gormenghast* (1994), about good versus evil, relies mostly on atmosphere and imagery, at times resembling a melodramatic opera and at others a *commedia* clown show. *Lucky* (1995) is a sensitive portrayal of an autistic person's inner world, and *The Mosquito Coast* (1995), a visual performance piece based on Paul Theroux's novel, depicts the coastal and jungle peoples of Central America. *La Dolce Vita* (1996) is Glass and writer Paul Sand's musical celebration and reinterpretation of Federico Fellini's film, with multitalented performers in an original approach to musical theatre.

American-born Jango Edwards, who is based in Holland and performs mostly in Europe, founded his Friends Road Show in 1975 with rock-and-roll clowning, which included clown acts, song, parodies, and pantomimes. He created the renowned Festival of Fools in 1976 in Amsterdam. In 1981, he brought his show *Garbage* to New York, where it attracted rock-concert audiences.

Italian clown Leo Bassi, based in France, is a sixth-generation circus eccentric who accompanies his juggling and acrobatics with a bold sense of humor. He has appeared throughout Europe and in North America in nightclubs, cabarets, solo shows, and extravagant theatre events, in which he has included bulldozers, the fire department, and a squadron of airplanes to make a theatrical statement. His *New Neronian* portrays the Roman emperor's madness.

Mime–clowns Abel and Gordon from Belgium and Canada play an awkward couple in love who trap themselves in closets and on ladders and continue their slapstick clowning throughout a wedding ceremony and honeymoon in *Dance of the Chickens*, performed at the Mimos Festival in Périgueux in 1989.

Swiss mime Roy Bosier, who worked with Decroux, Barrault, and Marceau and has resided in Rome since the 1960s, founded the company I Gesti, toured Europe, and appeared on TV with Marceau, as well as taught mime workshops.

The Commedia dell'Arte

Although one of the differences between the clown's art and the commedia dell'arte is that in *commedia* the traditional type characters play more often together than solo, both make use of clownish comedy. The content and style of a number of twentieth-century clowns, clown companies, and regular theatre companies are based upon *commedia,* some in a more traditional manner than others.

The commedia dell'arte had one of its more faithful examplars in Il Teatro de Ca' Foscari, which began as a university company in 1949 in Venice. Its traditional *commedia* players, who staged plays with Atellan and *commedia* character types, performed at the Berlin International Pantomime Festival in 1962. The Teatro a l'Avogaria, established in 1969 by Giovanni Poli as a continuation of the Teatro de Ca' Foscari and to develop research on traditional theatre and commedia dell' arte, performed *commedia* and Venetian drama. Another university company, the Teatro Universita Padova, founded by Gianfranco de Bosio, invited Lecoq to teach mime and *commedia*.

Commedia specialist Carlo Boso began training at the Piccolo Teatro of Milan school in 1964 and worked with actors and directors of the Italian stage, such as Dario Fo, Giovanni Poli, Peppino de Filippo, and Giorgio Strehler. In 1967 and 1968, Boso performed in Strehler's production of *Arlequin, Valet of Two Masters* at the Piccolo Teatro. From 1972 on, he directed for Italian and French theatre companies, utilizing *commedia* techniques in his stagings of *Macbeth* and Jean Racine's *Andromaque*. In 1980, Boso was artistic director of the Milan Teatro di Porta Romana. From 1978 on, he taught *commedia* workshops in Europe and Canada.

The Italian company I Colombaioni has performed modern *commedia* and clowning in the persons of Carlo Colombaioni, who comes from a circus family of several generations, and Alberto Vitali. Inspired by traditional *commedia* and circus, they have renewed this form by playing in modern clothes without make-up or masks and employing mime, pantomime, songs, acrobatics, and whatever is available in shows that consist of five or six realistic clown sketches.

The Tag Teatro from Venice is among the twentieth-century companies that have staged the most authentic productions of commedia dell'arte. The classic *The Madness of Isabella,* which appeared in 1989 and 1990 at the London International Mime Festival, draws upon the theme of a Venetian soldier who brings a fiery Turkish princess back from the wars who confronts his ex-fiancée and goes mad. *Scaramuccia*, performed at the London International Mime Festival in 1991 and filled with action, duels, songs, and slapstick, is rooted in the colorful Scaramuccia's exploits. *La Zincana,* performed at the London International Mime Festival in 1993, mixes farce and melodrama in a *commedia* scenario of a gypsy woman's attempt to enter high society.

Ferruccio Soleri, a teacher at the Piccolo Teatro of Milan, is also an illustrious interpreter of the gamut of commedia dell'arte characters.

Mime Theatre in Eastern Europe

Just as the schools and styles of Decroux, Marceau, and Lecoq differed from one another, so they differed from the stylized and expressionist mimodramas and mime styles of Eastern Europe. In the 1950s in Poland, Henryk Tomaszewski and his Wroclaw (Breslau) Mime Theatre developed full-length mimodramas that blended nineteenth-century pantomime, modern and classical dance, and Pirandello-style theatre.

In Czechoslovakia, Ladislav Fialka revived Gaspard Deburau's themes and literary subjects—along with the use of sets, lights, sounds, props, music, modern dance, and ballet—in his mimodramas at the Theatre on the Balustrade, founded in Prague in 1958. Fialka also choreographed the puppet animation in the films of Jiri Trinka. Meanwhile, Milan Sladek staged monothematic works such as *The Bruise*, revolving around a comic character called Kefka, and founded the Sladek Theatre Kefka of Cologne, Germany, which consisted of drama, mime, marionettes, and black-light techniques. He also founded the Gauklerfest, a major European mime festival, in Cologne in 1976. In 1966, Boris Hybner, an ex-member of Fialka's company, founded the Alfred Jarry Pantomime Company with Ctibor Turba. Their piece *Harakiri*, staged in 1968, began with whiteface pantomime and evolved into silent, realistic acting, along with surrealistic elements, to depict themes of solitude and alienation. In 1974, Turba founded his Circus Alfred, combining circus clowning and street theatre with silent-film comedy. Among the many works that Turba co-authored, directed, and performed, his *Dr. Stivin and Mr. Turba* unites a live performance of wind instruments by flutist–composer Jiri Stivin with stage, screen, and video gags about a clown character's mishaps.

Henryk Tomaszewski's Pantomime Theatre

Henryk Tomaszewski studied drama in 1945 at the Krakow Theatre Studio and ballet at the Polish Parnell Ballet. After becoming a soloist at the Warsaw Ballet and the Wroclaw Opera, in 1956 he founded his mime studio and staged two mimodramas based on Nikolai Gogol's *The Overcoat* and Victor Hugo's *The Hunchback of Notre Dame*. Meanwhile, he choreographed for ballet companies throughout Europe, staged mimodramas, and taught mime workshops. His repertory ranged from ancient myth to modern themes and from biblical and philosophical symbolism to pure space compositions. *The Labyrinth* (1963) is a modern, geometrical composition in space; *The Dress* (1965) is based on Japanese legend; *The Departure of Faust* (1970) stems from Greek mythology and medieval satanism; *A November Night's Dream* (1971) combines expressionism with historical war episodes; *The Menagerie of Empress Phylissa* (1972) is a farce about sex and love; and *Arriving Tomorrow* (1976) moves from ancient legend based on Euripides's *Bacchantes*, to modern times, and back to ancient times.

Commedia dell'arte, traditional nineteenth-century pantomime, German expressionism, Maurice Béjart's ballet, modern dance, and theatre within theatre are all present in Tomaszewski's mimodramas. In his harmonious fusion of mime, dance, and drama, which Marceau has characterized as Polish baroque, elaborate movement and virtuosity are the basis of dynamic choreography in which dramatic tension is derived from individual and group counterpoint. In these visually luxuriant mimodramas, which abound in poetry, philosophy, metaphor, and symbolism, the spectator is reborn in space, along with the mime–actor–dancer, extending himself ad infinitum in sensual movement patterns.

Tomaszewski gives his views on his contribution to mime theatre in the following interview.

How did you become interested in mime and pantomime?

Tomaszewski: While I was a solo dancer, I wanted to find a new expression in theatre, but there was no model for my idea of combining text, voice, music, dance, costumes, and scenery with pantomime. I wanted to fuse dance and pantomime. The basis of my work is prose or pantomime, and for my poetic visions I need dance. Traditional pantomime is realistic, but feelings must be shown by other kinds of movement: for example, poetic movement, which stems from dance. I became interested in full-length mimodrama, which combines varied elements. I feel that I have innovated an interest in mimodrama in our times and even brought it to the level of regular theatre as far as audience appreciation is concerned.

Do you believe that the rebirth of mime in Poland is due to your initiative?

T: Yes. Perhaps I have also brought movement into regular theatre because I have directed plays with much movement. The visual aspect is important in all theatre. But, for example, in French theatre the spoken aspect is more important. French theatre is more rhetorical. In Poland, especially since the nineteenth century, theatre has been more visual.

Why has mime become so important in the twentieth century?

T: Today in our fast-moving, rational world in which such factors as success are so important, this art is an escape. Mime appeals to the child in each of us. It is a return to a simpler form of expression. Today the world is also more visual. One no longer needs to read newspapers to know what is happening. I also believe that the contact between mime and the audience is more direct than words because what is important in mime is what the actor is doing. Movement is not as intellectual as words. It is beyond words, more direct. It can express complex feelings that words cannot express because they are only approximate. Mime is a more total form of expression.[3]

Boleslav Polivka

Born in 1949 in Vizovice, Czechoslovakia, from age five on, Boleslav Polivka played in his father's amateur theatre company. He then began studying acting at the Academy of Arts in 1971. After joining Ctibor Turba's Alfred Jarry Pantomime Company in Prague, he worked with the clown–mime company Theatre on a String in Brno in 1972. After 1972, he performed in Turba's Circus Alfred, which combined street theatre, mime, and circus clowning. His creations *Adam and Eve* (1973), *Pezza versus Chorba* (1976), *The Survivor* (1978), a piece about solitude and the indestructible desire to survive, and *Pepe* (1979) brought recognition. *The Last Hunt* (1981), revolving around a hunter's imaginary hunting trip, was followed by *The Jester and the Queen* (1984), *Therapy* (1985), and *The Seance* (1987), which evokes Gaspard Deburau's life. Polivka also has performed, directed, and written plays for speaking theatre.

Pepe depicts a clown and a child named Joseph facing today's grim, war-threatened world when their chicken, Pepe, dies in an air raid. Their game-playing fantasies end when the child Joseph is killed in a second air raid. This protest against war and human torture unfolds like a fairy tale enriched by miming, clowning, and silent-film gags.

Antitheatre form and content are explored in *The Jester and the Queen*, in which Polivka plays the traditional buffoon who attempts to amuse his bored queen (played by Chantal Poullain). After the buffoon tells the queen stories, flies like a bird, rides a horse, and invents many antics to distract her—at one point exchanging roles with her to end up in the palace dungeon—Polivka throws the script away to comment on the dramatic action and interact directly with the spectators. Much of the work's humor derives from a witty unveiling of the theatrical process, including a satire of Constantin Stanislavsky's acting method and an imaginary lecture by Bertolt Brecht on Brechtian stage techniques. The piece exposes the comedian's plight at the hands of bored and tyrannic spectators, parodied in the queen's role. Polivka's artistic and political commentary—combined with clowning, acting, dancing, puppetry, magic, and vaudeville—place his work in the realm of postmodern theatre. What remains traditional are his use of a central theme—for example, the revolt against a power symbol—and the incorporation of such classical figures as the buffoon and the queen, which stem from comedy of all times. Polivka's ingenuity is in his ability to ally the ancient jester's comic art with that of the avant-garde clown.

Mickey Mouse, Don Quixote and Others (1992) depicts the stage-struck director of a drying-out clinic's attempts to use drama as therapy to cure alcoholics.

Polivka expresses his views on the differences between Eastern European mime and European and American mime in the following interview.

How would you describe your mime style?

Polivka: I like to call my silent art "gestural theatre," not academic pantomime with a white mask and illusion-type movement. Pepe, for instance, is a clownlike character who does not know how to speak. Mime and clowning are, for me, the means to do theatre. I consider myself a man of the theatre, especially of total theatre.

Is there a difference between American and European clowns and particularly Eastern European clowns?

P: For me, this difference is not as important as having something to say that is personal. What is really important is one's own personal style, as in painting, where one can recognize a Degas or a Renoir. However, there are differences between the mime–clowns in Eastern Europe and in America. Our works are more philosophical, and, though they depict tragic events, they are done with humor. They are like Soldier Svejk tales of war, which are tragic but depicted with humor and, like Kafka's stories, are both comical and tragic. In America there are mime and clown styles, such as the Decroux, Marceau, and Lecoq styles, with whom American mimes have studied, which are becoming more personal in their styles and therefore are more interesting. In Czechoslovakia we don't have that many mime styles and mime schools. However, what I feel is more important is to find one's own personal clown.

What do you think about classical pantomime?

P: Marceau is a classical mime, just as the music of Beethoven is classical. Classical pantomime is not dead. It is moving to see Marceau's work. Perhaps there will be more talent and discoveries in classical pantomime in the future.

Has mime changed a lot in the twentieth century?

P: Yes. There is now a tendency to combine mime with dance and dance with mime, theatre with dance and dance with theatre. There are mixtures that for me are good because I like to see a performer use all of his means to express, rather than one who keeps the purity of discipline. But if I see someone do this well, I adore it. Today mime is going in other directions because it is not simple to communicate things. Different means to express them have to be found. I adore Marceau's poetry, but if one wants to speak of other things, one has to utilize other means. Each must find his own.

What do you hope to do with your art?

P: With each show, I learn not only professionally but from humorous and personal points of view. The theatre can make you wise and more balanced. It can also rid one of one's complexes. It can be a form of therapy for the performer, as well as for the spectator. The creative process is also tortuous and renders one's sensitivity more profound. It's like my painter friend, who replied when I asked him why he paints that it is to let others know that he is sensitive and that through his painting he reminds others that one must remain sensitive. I believe it is important for people to remain sensitive.[4]

Litsedei Clown Mime Theatre

Litsedei, meaning "buffoons" in Russian, was born out of the first Russian mime studio, founded in 1957 in Leningrad. Having inherited their art from that of the ancient Russian Empire's buffoons and from the commedia dell'arte, Litsedei's members combine clown and acting techniques with mime. Under Vjacheslav Polunin's direction, from 1969 on, they have staged mime–clown shows such as *The Dreamers* (1976), a game performance; *Assissyai Review* (1984), in which the clowns confront the absurdity of modern life and technology; *Life of Insects* (1985), a black clown show; *Aviation* (1986), a street performance that depicts catastrophe; *Popular Mechanics* (1987), a clown show with Soviet rock stars; and *Catastrophe* (1989), a satire on the nuclear disaster and bureaucratic inefficiency of Chernobyl. The company has performed in international festivals and toured throughout Russia, Europe, the Far East, and Cuba. In 1982, Litsedei organized the "Mime Parade," the first Soviet pantomime festival, and in 1985 initiated the first International Festival of Mimes and Clowns in Moscow. It also has performed on TV, in films, and in variety programs.

Since 1986, Litsedei has revived street theatre in the most remote villages around Leningrad as well as in big cities. The company has participated in the Harvest Festival and in New Year's and other kinds of festivals and carnivals. In 1990, it was part of the Peace Caravan, which brought ten companies from Leningrad to Paris via Warsaw, Prague, and Berlin. It has also brought street theatre to schools on the Baltic Sea coastline.

Playing in its own small theatre and training students in its school, Litsedei offers classes in mime, dramatic art, classical and modern dance, acrobatics, and art history. On the same site, the company established a conservatory with documentation on mime, clowning, and street theatre. It has become a pilgrimage place for those who dedicate their lives to the world of clowns, fools, and comedians and who perpetuate joy and poetry on the stage. Their theatre banner reads "Anima Allegra" (joyful soul) in the spirit of the ancient Russian minstrels and fools, the commedia dell'arte players, and Charlie Chaplin and the Russian clown Leonid Yengibarov.

This company's mime–clown art is unlike ordinary circus clowning or whiteface pantomime. Besides traditional clowning techniques, *commedia*, and miming, its work includes tragedy, comedy, lyrics, parody, grotesque and absurd humor, and spontaneous trickery. The spoofing of topical issues provides an activist humor that is never didactic. For example, in the *Assissyai Review*, in which the clowns wear traditional baggy costumes, floppy shoes, and red noses, much of the satirical humor is based on Soviet inertia and the Russians' attempt to undergo change. One scene satirizes modern technology as an elegantly dressed clown sews on a rubber sewing machine and plays music on a cardboard piano, accordion, and trombone. In *Aviation*, the spectators are warned to arm themselves with bandages, iodine, and stretchers as the sounds of explosions, the howling of sirens, and the screams of humans provoke audience reaction.

Along with reviving the jester's art and the mountebank's art, Litsedei has incorporated the poetic traditions of Russian folklore, which endow the company with its highly personal character. The Litsedei Clown Mime Theatre takes its art beyond the theatre into everyday life, and, like the ancient jesters and the mountebanks of the Middle Ages, the Litsedei performers draw spectators into their antics.

In 1993, three clowns of the original Litsedei Clown Mime Theatre left to form their own company, entitled Litsedei Moins 4 (Litsedei Minus 4), adding to their basic clowning style elements of the theatre of the absurd, Guignol, and silent cinema. Their collective creation *Moumie* was performed in festivals and theatres throughout Europe. In 1996, Litsedei founder Slava Polunin performed his *Snow Show* with Brazilian clown Angela de Castra in London.

Ilkhom Theatre-Studio

Founded in 1976 by Soviet new-wave director Mark Weil under the name Ilkhom, meaning "inspiration," the Ilkhom Theatre Studio of Tashkent, Uzbekistan, is one of the companies which paved the way for *perestroika* in the Soviet theatre. The company, which includes a theatre school, has toured Russia, Europe, and parts of North America with works ranging from the traditional to the avant-garde. *Clomadeus*, performed at the 1991 Movement Theatre International Festival in Philadelphia, manifests an enriched evolution of the clown's art, which has moved into a nontraditional, disengaged, and grotesque kind of buffoonery, at once nonsensical and meaningful, as well as anarchistic and bold, in its portrayal of Russia's changing social climate. The content and style of this absurdist clown theatre, which provokes laughter for no apparent reason, leave much to the imagination.

Raz-Dva-Tri Theatre

Saint Petersburg's Raz-Dva-Tri theatre was begun in 1989 by Alexander Makeev, a movement and pantomime specialist and teacher and author of a movement technique for actors. Beginning with traditional pantomime, the company added various dance genres, clowning, and drama to create a style that appeals to both adults and children. Created during the 1990s, the company's adult pieces include *In That Way*, a lyrical comedy; *Maniminimum*, a fantasy thriller; *Wind of Times*, a plastic composition accompanied by music; and *Sport Mosaic*, a clown–acrobatic–sports piece. Among their children's works are Alexis Tolstoy's *Bouratino's Adventures*; Hans Christian Andersen's *Snow Queen*; and fairy tales by Alexander Pushkin. The company won awards at the international pantomime festival Riga-89 and at the international fairy tale festival Novgorod-94 and has toured and played in festivals abroad.

Theatr Blik

Founded in 1977, Theatr Blik is an eight-member mime and dance company based in Kozalin (Poland) and London. While its movement expression derives from Polish mime, ballet, and acrobatics, the content of the company's pieces satirizes our times. Theatr Blik has toured Eastern and Western Europe with such works as *The Joyous Mystery*, conceived and directed by Jupi Podlaszewski and Ryszard Kotecki. This Kafkaesque portrayal of the political, social, and psychological reality of state control draws its satirical meaning from the protagonist's willingness to be crushed by bureaucracy and undergo a puppet's fate. In one scene, a female authority figure walking two human dogs turns them loose on the willing protagonist to finish him off. Clown humor, exaggerated dance movement, and playful miming with props offer comic relief throughout. The presence of nonsense props to alleviate the bleak void of inertia in a hopeless human condition recalls absurdist theatre. The choreographic precision and the purposely formal, expressionistic movement of Theatr Blik's dance dramas also evoke Tomaszewski's theatre. Avoiding the postmodern pitfall of superimposing one art form upon another, Theatr Blik blends acting, dancing, miming, and music into a meaningful total theatre.

Pal Regos

Pal Regos, who began as a conventional mime in Budapest, researched a new bodily expression in movement and acting in 1974. With a company of actors trained in his conscious body and psychotechnique system, he created six works performed at his Budapest theatre, the Szkene. *Requiem for Joseph K.*, presented at the Gaukler 86 International Pantomime Festival in Cologne, Germany, and at the Winnipeg Mime Festival in 1987, develops a pilgrim's Kafkaesque view of a senseless life that is resolved by acknowledging the need for permanent struggle.

Among the solo artists performing classical pantomime in Eastern Europe is Russian artist Mikhail Vertlin, who parodies classical works such as *Hamlet* and creates humorously themed skits, such as the one about an orchestra conductor who cannot control his orchestra. In *Audience V*, Polish actor Andrzej Grabowski begins a lecture on contemporary music, only to become overwhelmed by his own enthusiasm, which causes physical chaos on stage. Grabowski's piece, which won the Grand Prix at the One Man Theatre Festival in Torun, Poland, was performed at the Philadelphia Movement Theatre International Festival in 1988. Miko [Branislaw Machalski], a deaf mime from eastern Siberia, has performed throughout Eastern and Western Europe, the Near East, and the United States, blending classical pantomime with a style he acquired at Poland's Opera of Wroclaw. Russian actor Ilja Rutberg presented traditional pantomime sketches at the 1977 Gest International Pantomime Workshop in Wroclaw, Poland.

Student Theatre

As early as the 1960s, a number of student groups began mime companies in Eastern Europe. Among these was Poland's Gest Pantomime Theatre, founded at Wroclaw Technical University in 1961 by Andrzej Leparski, the group's artistic director. Besides organizing annual international workshops and festivals since 1974, the company has created mimodramas that break away from whiteface pantomime. *The Dogs*, based on Flemish playwright Michel de Ghelderode's *Escurial* and *School for Buffoons*, abounds with Flemish folklore, masks reminiscent of Bruegel's dwarves and grotesque creatures, and burlesque, sadism, irony, mysticism, and the supernatural. By the 1970s Gest achieved a high level of movement expression. Leparski taught at the Instituto del Teatro in Barcelona, where he created, directed, and choreographed such pieces as *Mimomar* (1993), based on Joan Miró's paintings; *Strip Tease* for the Vol-Ras company; *Amor Amor*, performed in Zurich; and *Who Is Afraid of Kasper Hauser?* (1997), on intolerance.

Another student theatre in Poland that achieved professional recognition was Stu, founded in 1966 in Krakow. Through *commedia,* improvisation, mime, acrobatics, dance, films, political comment, and recitation of literary texts, *The Fall* (1970) and *The Key to Polish Dreams* (1971), performed in Poland and Europe, examine Poland's destiny.

Beginning as a student clown–pantomime company in 1973, the Akademia Ruchu, founded by Wojciech Krukowski, grew into a professional theatre that staged street demonstrations to render spectators conscious of their political responsibilities and choices. The company's movement style incorporates stage acting with that of silent films. *Carthage*, performed at the 1988 Mimos Festival in Périgueux, contrasts Stalinism's constraints with American ideology.

A Spectrum of Styles across Europe

Still other styles—extending from classical mime, to Decroux's corporeal mime, to other movement theatre forms allied with plastic arts, music, dance, clowning, puppetry, magic, and street theatre—comprise the postmodern gamut of movement expression throughout Europe.

Rob Van Reijn

Holland's classical school of pantomime is represented by Dutch pantomimist Rob Van Reijn, who has performed in solo pantomimes since 1949 and from 1968 to 1971 was artistic director of the pantomime theater Carrousel. Among his solo works is *Exegese* (1975), based on his interpretation of the Bible. Van Reijn's group works range from *commedia* to narrative mimodramas derived from classical works and are performed for both adult and children's audiences. The mimodramas *Scrooge and Marley* (1974) and *Oliver Twist* (1987) are adapted from Charles Dickens's tales, which are simultaneously played on tapes or recited. In the eighteenth-century mimodrama *De Harlekinade* (1983), a cast of thirteen interprets the arrival of *commedia* players. In *L'Amfiparnaso* (1986), based on sixteenth-century *commedia*, a madrigal choir sings the action. *De Reiskameraad* (1985) is a children's mimodrama from a Hans Christian Andersen tale. *Lof der Zotheid* (*Ode to Foolishness*) (1990) portrays Erasmus with fools from all segments of society.

Will Spoor and Inccoprodinc Company

After studying with Decroux, violinist Will Spoor returned to Amsterdam in 1963 to teach and begin his Mime Theatre Will Spoor, later renamed Onk Theater Overal, and to pursue his work as a mimographer, mime performer, and director. Inccoprodinc, active since 1977 under Spoor's artistic direction, stages his creations. *Movimenti Cantabili* (1989), which he conceived and directed, develops through corporeal mime and music theatre the theme of a protagonist in a labyrinth who confronts the infinity of time and space. Under Spoor's guidance, the theatre piece *Domus* and the street theatre project *Zebra*, which twenty-five to seventy players of varying talents, ages, styles, and backgrounds perform for seven consecutive days at different hours and places in the city, were staged in 1987 and 1988.

Griftheater

Griftheater has integrated corporeal mime with other art forms and dialogue in its creations. The company grew out of mime classes at Amsterdam's Theatre School, founded in 1968, after former Decroux student Frits Vogels — mime–actor, director, and mimographer — in 1975 staged a visual performance with three students entitled *Grif*, followed by another entitled *Ruit*. The group later adopted the Dutch name *Grif*, signifying strong images engraved in the viewer's retinas. After training in Decroux's corporeal mime, which became the basis of its movement theatre, the company searched for new ideas through the body's play with objects in space and the use of light and color, voice, music, and dramatic interplay. Griftheater engaged actors, dancers, musicians, and other types of artists who brought new kinds of dance and theatre movement into its corporeal mime–based productions.

Since 1975, Griftheater has performed works, which have been created collectively or with a director and the use of a script, in regular theatres and unconventional spaces throughout Europe and in Canada. In close affinity with plastic arts, it developed a theatre of images that primarily addresses the senses. *The Last Meadow* (1984), performed in the stalls and on the bloodstained grounds of an Amsterdam slaughterhouse, is a poetic and provocative group piece that develops, through mime, theatre, dance, and singing, the slaughtering of animals for consumption. In 1986, company member Jan Taks created and performed, in his corporeal piece *Aureool Vitrool*, an alienated male character's fantasies of a night in Paris. With a set composed of materials that provoke dramatic situations and innovative corporeal movement the company in 1987 staged *Caoutchouc,* which derives its title and dramatic tension from two female characters' interactions with various forms of rubber. The protagonists first move through rubber strips that extend horizontally across the stage and later climb a tall, vertical screen of tightened strips, through which they thrust an arm, a leg, a head. This postmodern, living sculpture, with its plurality of dimensions and its physical and vocal elements that resonate with one another, has been presented in museums and on conventional stages.

In 1989, mimographer–director Paul Van Kolck staged a large-scale production of sixteenth-century French author François Rabelais's *Pantagruel* at the Holland Festival in Amsterdam. In 1990, *Unexpressed Desire*, choreographed by guest mimographer–director Wouter Steenbergen, dramatized the attempts of four protagonists to express their desires while a voice constantly interrupts. *La Stanza* (*The Room*, 1990), choreographed by Italian mimographer and stage director Giorgio Rossi, develops a dramatic narrative for three protagonists. In 1991, Griftheater staged a location project based on Richard Foreman's play, *Rhoda in Potatoland. Sa Griffe*, directed by Frits Vogels and presented in 1993 at the Philadelphia Movement Theatre International Festival in an old church gymnasium, contains sensual images from dadaist Man Ray's *Objects of My Affection*.

Inspired by plastic arts, literature, and music, Griftheater remains a corporeal mime theatre. Having exhausted pure abstract mime's expressiveness, the company experiments with other visual art forms, along with narration and drama, creating images that innovatively imprint themselves on the spectator's retinas.

Tender

Dutch street theatre is best represented by a collective group called Tender, founded in 1981 to entertain and provoke onlookers in streets, cafés, post offices, discos, saunas, swimming pools, and other public areas. Winner of the Dutch Mime Award in 1987, Tender balances theatre games with reality, awakening its onlookers to the absurd conventions in everyday life. The performers are mimes, actors, dancers, sculptors, and persons of various professions spontaneously interacting with passers-by. In *Tender Serves*, waitresses create havoc in an outdoor café by combing the hair of embarrassed males, serving raw liver to poodles, and singing opera arias. In *Tender Marries*, a half-dozen weeping brides, grooms flirting with female spectators, and a bride and a groom chewing on each end of the same banana march to city hall, where the brides cast their gowns out the windows to protest the deceptiveness of the marriage ceremony and the institution of marriage. In *Tender Shoots*, the public participates in a photo shoot. In association with the Public Health Department of Amsterdam, the company created a performance about AIDS in which a giant penis is captured and carried away in an ambulance to the sound of sirens. Tender's surprise theatre appears in unexpected places, turning viewers into actors who reenact the ridiculous in everyday life.

Other Mimes and Styles of the 1970s, 1980s, and Beyond

In the 1970s, 1980s, and beyond, a number of European companies and mimes continued to develop styles that ranged from classical pantomime to street, clown, and dance mime. In France, the Théâtre de la Mie de Pain is a popular eight-member group that began in the streets of Paris and performed throughout Europe and Canada. *Séance-Friction,* presented at the Mimos Festival of Périgueux in 1987 and winner of the 1987 Edinburgh Fringe Festival Daily Express Award for Best Comedy, reveals inhibitions in the chamber music world. *Starjob*, performed at the 1989 Philadelphia International Movement Theatre Festival and the 1990 London International Mime Festival, parodies stress, coping, and the pursuit of success in the business world. This company's satirical gags recall the Grand Guignol puppets, Tadeusz Kantor's pictorial theatre, and Eugene Ionesco's anticollectivism all rolled into one.

Le Quatuor from France achieves musical clowning in *Crazy Strings*, performed at the 1992 London International Mime Festival, in which four musicians mix Beethoven and Schubert with the Beatles, along with singing, dancing, mime, and acrobatics.

Argentinian mime–actor–clown Hector Malamud—who is based in Paris and who has performed with Argentinean mime Benito Gutmacher and Argentinean clown–mime Carlos Trafic, a former Living Theatre member—satirizes American cinematic mythologies in *People Love Me*. In this autobiographical work about a candy vendor's infatuation with American cinema and in *The Great Dreamer*, Malamud's silent acting and clowning depict the thin line between cinema and life, illusion and reality.

Japanese choreographer and dancer Ko Murobushi, based in Paris, has created an unconventional dance form drawing upon traditional Japanese dance, Butoh, and contemporary Occidental dance. *Iki* (1983) is an interrogation on the origin of breath as a vital force and its relation to life and death. *En*, performed at the Mimos Festival in 1987, combines traditional Japanese and Occidental dance.

France's Philippe Genty company, which began touring the world in 1961, aside from miming and clowning, animates puppets and objects through movement, magic, and poetry. In *Désirs Parade*, brown wrapping paper and cellophane become spectacular surrealist images of bizarre creatures and elegant dolls, which interact with one another and with their magician puppet masters. Puppets and objects take on lives of their own as they mime and dance, creating visual poetry and vaudevillesque humor.

The Sankai Juku company, which represents the first generation of Butoh sixties dancers in Japan, gave its first full-scale production, *Kinkan Shonen* (*Kumquat Seed*), *A Young Boy's Dream of the Origins of Life and Death*, in Japan in 1978 and was invited to perform at France's Nancy Festival in 1980. For the next four years, the company performed in Europe, its members and director Ushio Amagatsu having been based in Paris since 1980. The Théâtre de la Ville de Paris commissioned two of Sankai Juku's pieces, *Jomon Sho* (1982) and *Unetsu* (1987). *Kinkan Shonen* represents the expressionist Butoh style, in which the body is presented in its primitive form with intensified expressive movement, alternating between slow and rapid changes in facial and bodily postures.

American-born Cary Rick, trained in the expressionist dance style of Mary Wigman and Dore Hoyer, organized and performed in France's Compagnie Les Arts Scéniques. His dance–mime choreography ranged from ritualistic exaltation to Oriental formalism. Rick has taught and published works on his own dance–psychotherapy method in Germany, Austria, and Switzerland.

Although not a mime theatre in the conventional sense, Jerome Deschamps's productions appeal to the eye rather than to the ear. After studying at various drama schools and at the Paris Conservatory of Dramatic Art, Deschamps staged *Baboulifiche and Papavoine*, in which two eccentric professors of a scientific society decide to go to the moon incognito, with a baby carriage and some cooking utensils. *The Deschiens Family* (1979) introduces us to three ragged characters who cook on camping gas while their utensils fly about and who pull their musical instruments from baby buggies and play a canticle. Collaborating with Macha Makeieff from

1978 on, Deschamps began his own company and in 1981 won the Syndicat de la Critique Award for his innovative creations. In 1988, his group received the Molière prize for best musical for its *The Little Steps*, in which elderly ex–music hall performers return to the abandoned Bouffes du Nord to sing and dance *Frou Frou* and past musical hits with fragile voices and faltering steps. In 1989, the company was awarded the Molière prize for best comic production for *Rabbit-Hunter*. And in 1993, it again won the Molière prize for best comic production, for *Feet in the Water*. After staging Jacques Offenbach's opera *Les Brigands* in 1992, Deschamps and Makeieff created *C'est Magnifique* (1994) and *Le Défilé* (1995). In Deschamps's plays, a gesture, an attitude, a look, or a tone of voice reveal the misery and absurdity of people's lives. In this inventive and unorthodox theatre, artifice in acting is abandoned to present real-life characters in situations of comic despair.

Anthony Vienne, who studied with former Marceau student Hervez Luc, has revived classical whiteface pantomime successfully amid the postmodern interweaving of mime with other arts. In his Théâtre du Bimberlot, begun in 1980, he appears in overalls, with or without whiteface, inviting his spectators to participate in his mimed tales, anecdotes, and slices of life, which provoke both laughter and tears. He depicts a whole scale of timeless characters and brings to life familiar, everyday objects. His one-man shows *Ça Tourne*, *Clown-Riz et Mimosa*, and *Le Guerlot*, accompanied by clarinet and percussion artist David Renaux's live music, delight both children and adults throughout France.

Enrique Pardo—former Roy Hart Theatre performer in the 1970s, founder of the Roy Hart International Centre, and co-founder, with Linda Wise, of Pantheatre in 1981—became director of Avignon's Myth and Theatre Festival, which in 1995 was dedicated to the theme of magic, and, in 1999, to Hermes. The festival included performances, master classes, and lectures. Pardo's image theatre, beginning with his solo performance *Calling for Pan* (1981), integrates movement with voice and mythological stories. His workshops combine Roy Hart voice training, Decroux corporeal mime, Dominique Dupuy dance, and Eugenio Barba's gestural research.

Among the many French mimes and mime–clowns whose main object is to entertain their audiences with humorous miming and clowning, Jean-Paul Miroux, who trained in mime at the Carré Sylvia Monfort school, has performed his Jipi Pantomime–Clown show for adults and children throughout Europe and Canada since 1989. Les Turlupins, a French–Flemish, male–female duo, play comical, classical, and modern mime shows in Paris and throughout Europe.

Based in Belgium, Ensemble Leporello was founded in 1986 to create productions that mix text, song, and movement to free the text and take it beyond words. *Twins*, performed in 1994 at the European Mime and Physical Theatre Workshop Symposium in London and based on a novel by Argentinean novelist César Aria Copi, includes slapstick and melodrama in an absurdist underworld comedy. *Monstrueux*, also performed at the symposium in 1994, offers a more movement theatre version of Sophocles' *Antigone*.

In Germany in 1974, the Berlin Pantomime Ensemble of Deutsches Theater evolved from an amateur group into a professional company of ten members. Later adding Das Andere Theater Berlin (The Alternative Theater of Berlin) to its name, it staged more than twenty-four short sketches and mimodramas. Mainly pantomimes using little language, the company's creations range from the collective children's piece, *Clownonade* (1981), to a sophisticated, earthy, and hedonistic comedy entitled *Hanswurst* (1987), with dance, acrobatics, theatrics, and cinema. From 1990 to

1991, it staged *Egotrips, Happy End Station*, and *Mozart, Stimmen aus Papier, Briefzenen* (*Mozart, Voices on Paper, Letter Scenes*).

Elie Levy, an Israeli mime based in Hamburg who studied with Decroux and was a member of Ella Jaroszewicz's Tomaszewski-style Polish Mime Theatre in Paris in 1975, began his career as a mime soloist in 1978. Combining these training styles with his earlier experience in street mime, his character sketches, performed with props, lighting effects, and sound, include caricatures of a professional boxer, surgeon, pianist, politician, and others. In *Rendez Vous* (1985), as the happy protagonist primps for a date, he receives a phone call canceling it. Spectators readily participate in Levy's improvised skits based on familiar themes. Besides teaching mime workshops in Europe, since 1990 he has organized the International Festival of Clowns and Pantomime in Hamburg.

In England, Harold Cheshire, Ernest Berk, and Lindsay Kemp have founded companies and trained mimes. Kemp, a burlesque clown–dancer who studied with Marceau, adapted Jean Genet's *Nôtre Dame des Fleurs* for a movement piece entitled *The Flowers* (1971). Kemp and his company staged *Cinderella* at the 1995 London International Mime Festival.

Self-trained mime–dancer Ben Bennison played in one-man shows and in an improvisation group called the Theatre Machine.

London-based Adam Darius, a dance–mime artist born in North America and a former ballet dancer and choreographer with the Israel National Opera, was formerly a teacher and director of the Mime Center in London.

The Whalley Range All Stars, formed in 1982, is one of Britain's foremost street theatre companies. It performs popular shows resembling cartoon strips, such as *The Headless People*, in which characters carry their heads in bird cages in the style of a Max Ernst painting.

Having met during an advanced course at the Desmond Jones School of Mime, Howard Gayton and Geoff Beale created Ophaboom Theatre Company in 1991. That same year, they staged *The Emigré* and the street pieces *The Mystic* and *Richard III*. In 1992, they toured and performed in festivals with *Harlequin in Disguise, A Woman's Revenge*, and *Il Creduto Morto*, followed by their street show *Orpheus in the Underworld*. Based on both traditional and modern *commedia*, their creations include masks, live music, mime, storytelling, and acrobatics and are played before audiences and in venues of all kinds.

Jon Potter, who trained with Lecoq and Monika Pagneux, founded a company called Talking Pictures.

Macnas, a community-based arts and theatre company, was founded in 1986 in Galway, Ireland. The company stages nonverbal and carnival-style parades with giant masks to celebrate festivities and caricature political trends, such as fascism's resurgence in Europe. Aiming to make historic pageantry and legend come to life, the group staged *Gulliver* on a Dublin beach in 1988 as part of the city's millennium celebrations. *Tain*, a retelling of the eight-century saga of cattle raids and sexual and political intrigues, was presented at the 1992 Expo in Seville, winning a UNESCO nomination for best performance. *Buile Shuibhne/Sweeney,* based on an Irish legend of a king who defies the Christian church's power and is cursed to madness, won the best production award at the Dublin Theatre Festival before touring the United States, France, and Germany in 1995. Director and actor Rod Goodall, who trained at Jacques Lecoq's School and was a member of the Footsbarn Theatre in Europe for twelve years, has acted, choreographed, and trained company members since 1987.

In Switzerland, Jean-Pierre Amiel, who studied with Decroux and Marceau, is among the mimes who did not incorporate clowning, new vaudeville, or verbal theatre into his classical pantomimes. His *Un Jour sur la Terre*, which won first prize at the Edinburgh Festival, depicts man's evolution on earth and the appearance of other planets with a commanding body technique punctuated with humor.

Peter Wyssbrod in Switzerland, in his one-man sketches of daily life—such as *Le Grand Départ*, about a man waiting for a train—has integrated pantomime with his background in applied arts.

Swiss artist René Quellet's mime–clown piece *Le Fauteuil* (*The Armchair*) depicts with absurdist humor solitude and the impossibility of communication.

Patrick Mohr and Michèle Millner began Théâtre Spirale in 1986 after they graduated from the Jacques Lecoq School. In 1987 and 1988, they left Switzerland to work with La Troupe in Sydney, staging the African story *Soundjata* for the Sydney Theatre Festival in 1989. Returning to Switzerland, they created a French version of the piece for the Festival de la Batie Genève in 1990 and the Avignon Festival in 1991 and toured with it throughout Switzerland and West Africa. For the Theatre of Creation Festival at Lehigh University in Bethlehem, Pennsylvania, the company staged a multicultural work entitled *Beginnings*, inspired by the Finnish epic tale the *Kalevala,* which includes stories from Polynesia, Egypt, and the Amazon, performed by artists from diverse cultures.

In Holland, Shusaku and Dormu Dance Theatre, based in Amsterdam, develop theatrical collages with traditional Noh and Kabuki movement in such works as *Angel Core* (1981). Through dance, mime, music, and painting, the piece explores a dream-like ambience with abnormal psychological states. The mime–dancers—their faces painted white, shaved skulls covered with gauze, eyes red-rimmed and wearing weird costumes—create images from a mixture of cultures.

The Flying Dutchmen, Michiel Hesseling from Holland and Jean-Michel Paré from Canada, are internationally known clown–jugglers.

In Spain, Els Comediants, a group of fifteen ambulant comedians who reside and create theatre in a Canet de Mar commune near Barcelona, was founded in 1971. Based on Catalan folklore and culture, their improvised street theatre includes popular music and handmade marionettes, masks, and costumes.

Joan Cuso, Joan Faneca, and Joan Segales formed Vol-Ras Mime Theatre in 1980 out of a Catalonian drama center. In 1981, they performed *El Cas de la Patata Rossa* during International Mime Week in Barcelona. In 1983, they staged their clown–mime show *Flight*, and in 1984 created a grotesque clown–pantomime depicting human follies, entitled *Strip Tease*, directed by Andrzej Liparski, the former artistic director of Gest Pantomime Theatre of Wroclaw, Poland, which was presented at the Tarragona, Valencia, Saragossa, Madrid, and Barcelona Mime Festivals.

Yllana Theatre, a visual comedy company of seven film and theatre artists that began in Madrid in 1991, won the Courge d'Or for best foreign comedy for its creation *Muu* at the 1993 Toulouse Theatre festival. The work also was acclaimed at festivals throughout Europe and in Montreal. *Muu* is a caricature of four matadors who fight an invisible bull with a toothpick, utilizing movement, music, and an exaggerated fashion sense.

Rolf Scharre, who began studying with Decroux in 1957 and toured internationally in 1960, was invited by Ingmar Bergman in 1963 to teach mime in Stockholm and has continued to perform and teach in Europe.

In Austrian mime Walter Bartussek's classical pieces *Don Quixote* and *Plastic*, the artist fuses absurd and surreal elements with music, props, words, mime, and dance to express his joy of life. *Plastomania* reveals the protagonist's obsession with plastic, from which he cannot liberate himself.

Trained in acting, corporeal mime, and singing, Argentina-born Benito Gutmacher toured Europe and North America with *The Cry of the Body*, a multidimensional piece with dynamic social, political, and metaphysical comments on the body's revolt against violence. Gutmacher cries out against the violence found in religion, love, birth, war, and modern life through mime, acting, dance, comical audience interaction, and exclamations in English, French, and Spanish.

Pantomime and puppetry combine in the Italy-based Teatro Hugo and Ines, which Peruvian street artist Hugo Suarez Flores started with Ines Pasic of Bosnia-Herzegovina in 1986. In *The Adventures of Ginocchio*, with their knees, feet, and hands and a few simple props, they create little beings who play on a musical instrument, sing, flirt, and cry. Wearing a clown's ball nose and a plaid shirt, Hugo's knee becomes a musician stringing a ukelele, which Hugo's hands play upon, while a stocking cap placed on Ines's toes and a clown's ball nose on her foot become a long-faced listener. In animating these little figures, Hugo and Ines ally poetry with magic.

Extending the Spectrum in the 1990s

A number of new mime forms containing the postmodern tendencies mentioned earlier in this chapter characterize the works of movement theatre artists and companies presented at European mime festivals. Many of the artists performing at these festivals have broken down barriers between art forms to incorporate dance, clowning, and plastic arts into their particular styles.

At the London International Mime Festival

Since 1979, the London International Mime Festival, under the artistic direction of Joseph Seelig, joined by Helen Lannaghan in 1986, has hosted international companies and artists, many of whom have been mentioned in other sections of this book and have performed at the Périgueux Mimos Festival, among others.

The first London International Mime Festival was held in 1977 at the Cockpit Theatre at the instigation of British mime–clown Nola Rae and the theatre's director, Joseph Seelig. Because at that time mime was a marginal art form that was more traditional in Britain, the first three festivals abounded in illusionary techniques and mime–clowns. Among the performers were Jango Edwards, Moving Picture Mime Show, Milan Sladek, and Nola Rae. In 1979, the festival became more international, hosting new-wave performers such as Bob Berky from the United States, Hector Malamud from Argentina, and the Czech Circus Alfred, with clown–actor Boleslav Polivka. From 1980 to 1982, as the program became increasingly diverse, it included such artists and companies as the Théâtre du Mouvement, Moving Picture Mime Show, Bob Berky, David Glass, Yves Lebreton, Dimitri, Daniel Stein, Jacques Lecoq, Pierre Etaix, Annie Fratellini, and Avner the Eccentric. From 1984 to 1985, the artistic aim changed with the birth of London companies such as the Lecoq-trained

Théâtre de Complicité, Trestle Theatre performing social themes with masks, Trickster combining visual effects with physical skills, and Ra Ra Zoo employing circus skills. These mimes and clowns no longer appeared in traditional whiteface or red noses but introduced a broader approach to mime and clowning. From 1987 to 1990, the festival programs became more language-based and mimes and clowns began to speak on stage. A number of artists also engaged in improvisational theatre. Since 1990, the festival has moved back to visual styles of theatre in which speech plays a secondary role, with such exceptions as the traditional *commedia* Tag Teatro from Venice and Boleslav Polivka's clown theatre.

In 1993 and 1994, the festival included puppetry, dance, theatre, and performance art. Among the companies that appeared at the 1993 London International Mime Festival were the French Cartoon Sardines in *Le Malade Imaginaire*, a clown–cabaret spoof of Molière's *Imaginary Invalid*; Les Cousins deploying their circus skills in *Not So Easy* and *The Boom Room*; and Lecoq teacher Alain Gautré and his comedy trio Brouhaha in a satire of three women's uproarious day, entitled *Whatever the Weather*. Companies from England included Insomniac Productions in *The Lift,* about the New York Mafia; Faulty Optic's theatre of animation and objects in a surrealistic *Darwin's Dead Herring*; the Black Mime Theatre Ensemble in *Heart*, about a male–female relationship; Trestle Theatre with masks in a bittersweet *State of Bewilderment*; Talking Pictures's *Liars, Fakers and People Being Honest* and *Go West*, depicting the post-*perestroika* culture; and Commotion's *No Matter What* on hyper market shopping.

The 1994 festival embraced still more varied styles. In the Mossoux Bonté company's *Twin Houses,* life-size mannequins and live actors created obsessive images. Le Quatuor from France performed musical slapstick in *Devil Strings*. Insomniac Productions staged *Clair de Luz*, a miniature movie fantasy with gestural images. The English Ralf Ralf Company with Bessie Award winners Jonathan and Barnaby Stone satirized TV in *It's Staring You Right in the Face*. The French Jerome Deschamps company's *Feet in the Water* portrayed domestic life's mishaps. Commotion and the Institute of Curiosity and Execution companies adapted *The Quest for Don Quixote* through clowning, puppetry, and physical theatre. English stand-up comedian, cartoonist, and storyteller John Mowat incorporated mime into a historical *Comedy in Error*. In animated cartoon style with dance and song, the Black Mime Theatre Ensemble performed *E.D.R.*, about prison life. Da Da Dumb's rendering of *Da Da Dumb*, about ten mysterious travelers, and of *Chance and Ripeness*, based on scientific discovery's haphazardness, mixed physical theatre with light, sound, and action. The Right Size company's *Moose* blended illusion and eccentric acrobatics with melodrama and humor to depict a Frozen North adventure. The French Moulin Théâtre, an offshoot of the Philippe Genty company, made use of magic and visual imagery in *Alter Ego*. In the John Wright Company's *On the Verge of Exploding*, a mother is unable to guard her daughter from males. Circus performers in Ra Ra Zoo's *Cabinet of Curiosities* uncovered bizarre treasures and a curator in an ancient vault. Reckless Sleepers' performance artwork *Parasite* developed tensions among five people in a crowded space.

Classical and contemporary movement theatre played side by side at the 1995 London International Mime Festival. Among the classical pieces were the Marcel Marceau company's mimodrama of Nikolai Gogol's *The Overcoat* and Marceau in his solo pieces, the Lindsay Kemp company's operetta–dance–pantomime *Cinderella*, and the Théâtre de l'Ange Fou's re-creations of Decroux's solos, duos, and group pieces, entitled *The Man Who Preferred to Stand*. Puppetry, masks, and animation were combined in Spain's Jordi Bertran company's *Visual Poems*; Trestle Theatre and Birmingham Contemporary Music Group's *Goblin Market* and *The Soldier's Tale*, with a score commissioned by American composer Aaron Jay Kernis; German artist Elsa Schonbein's Theatre Meschugge, with human puppetry; and the Swedish Marionetteatren's production of August Strindberg's *Ghost Sonata*, with live actors and puppets in a tale of corruption, decadence, ghosts, and vampires. New pieces also premiered: London's Black Mime Theatre Ensemble explored 1990s male identity in *Forgotten Heroes*; the female clown trio Brouhaha played in *Light at Night*; Mike Ashcroft portrayed a conductor driven mad by his unruly musicians in *Le Baton*; and the People Show 101's postmodern work depicted jazz musician Chet Baker's last days through live and recorded jazz, film, and slides. Among other creations were Backstairs Influence's *She'll Be Coming 'Round the Mountain*, depicting a father and daughter trapped in a surreal civil war; Ernst Fischer's intimate, one-man *A Brief History of (Silence)*; Faulty Optic's eccentric theatre of animated objects and mechanical sets in *Snuffhouse-Dustlouse*; the Glee Club Performance Company in a midwestern tale entitled *Cotton Mather's Wonders of the Invisible World*; Peepolykus in a comical territorial dispute entitled *No Man's Land*; Theatre in Cahoots's *Day of the Dead*, involving two males, a female, and a graveyard picnic on All Soul's Day; the Anglo-Brazilian Teatral Yen in the philosophical *Kao*; and the Told by an Idiot company's Balinese half-mask evening of clowning in *The Bondress*. Yoshi Oida, a member of the Peter Brook company since 1968, presented *Interrogations,* based on questions asked by the performer, who provides answers through music and classical mime. The Australian Umbilical Brothers staged a cartoon–clown show with audio-acrobatics, and a cabaret night featured several new comedy-circus performers.

The 1996 London International Mime Festival offered a wide range of performance styles, opening its nineteenth season with a repeat performance of the Mossoux Bonté company's 1994 staging of *Twin Houses*. In *Le Fou de Bassan* the French Rasposo re-created an eighteenth-century circus theatre evoking baroque opera and Tiepolo tableaux, along with the music of Mozart, Rameau, and Vivaldi. German artist Raimund Hoghe presented *Meinwarts*, a requiem for victims of German fascism and of various forms of nationalism and intolerance, as well as those suffering from new diseases such as AIDS. Sweden's all-female Theatre Manjana staged a clown version of Federico García Lorca's *House of Bernarda Alba*, directed by mime–clown Nola Rae. French juggler Jerome Thomas and his company fused juggling, dance, and Pascal Lloret's piano performance in *Hic Hoc*. British Scarlet Theatre's *Paper Walls* portrayed family life's macabre and absurd aspects. The Belgian street and stage clowns of Wurre Wurre performed their unique vaudeville skits, imitating birds on a rooftop and street cleaners in *Don't Wurre*. Dutch Mister Jones appeared in his street circus show, Stephen Mottram animated little figures to music, Improbable Theatre combined puppetry with storytelling, and Circus Space Cabaret created the bizarre and fantastic in its clown acts. Among the British performances were Reject's Revenge's mime–clown thriller *Peasouper*; the Clod Ensemble in *Musical Scenes*; Ralf Ralf in *The Summit*, a satire of Ronald Reagan and Mikhail Gorbachev's 1987 Cold War negotiations; People Show 101's unique surreal spectacle; Lee and Dawes's sonic illusions performance concert; Academy Productions's staging of Samuel Beckett's *Acts without Words*; the Black Mime Theatre Ensemble in *Dirty Reality II,* depicting black–white relationships; and DNA Cabaret's showcase of puppetry, multimedia, and performance art.

The 1997 festival continued to host a variety of international movement the-atre styles. Among the French stagings were Théâtre du Mouvement's *Retrospectives*, featuring excerpts from the company's most acclaimed works; the Théâtre de l'Ange Fou's student premiere of *Memories of Unknown Ties*, inspired by a Francis Barbazon poem; Les Cousins' clown–acrobat show; the Franco-Russian Théâtre le Ranelagh in a clown version of *Romeo and Juliet*, entitled *Sur la Route de Sienne*; the Pyramide street theatre company in *Photo Roman*; and Ezechiel Garcia-Romeu's miniature animation spectacle, *Le Marotoscope*. Among the English artists and per-formances were physical theatre comedians Gavin Robertson and Andy Taylor in *Fantastical Voyage*; marionettist Stephen Mottram's visual arts, music, and theatre piece, *The Seed Carriers*; Faulty Optic's underwater marionettes and live-video, mi-crotheatre work about a couple's plumbing problems; the Glee Club Performance Company in the surreal comedy *Beatrice on the Frankfurt Express*; Jeremy Robbins in the exotic, performance art–acrobatic *Slippery When Wet* and *Prime Object: Love*; Guy Dartnell in *Bottle*, a sensual choreography moving from joy to despair; Im-probable Theatre's humorous ghost tale *70 Hill Lane* and improvisational *Animo*; Ta Ta Di Di Teatro's *Dr. Zingaro's Secret*; Tantalus's *Seven Ages*; Oddbodies' *True Tragedy of Richard III*; and Ernst Fischer and Helen Spackman in the Butoh-inspired *Love in the Time of Melancholia*. Belgium's Mossoux Bonté company presented *The Last Hallucinations of Lucas Cranach the Elder*; Italy's Teatro del Corretto staged *Snow White*; Circus Space Cabaret performed clown and music-comedy sketches; the solo show of Ireland's popular Barabbas's, *Strokehauling*, depicted Irish mad-ness; and Hungary's The Shamans portrayed a love relationship in *Amine*. A number of the performing artists led mime, mask, *commedia*, and clowning workshops; John Wright gave a lecture–demonstration on masks, as did the Punch and Judy College of Professors on Punch and Judy.

The London International Mime Festival remains one of Europe's most pres-tigious and long-standing movement theatre festivals.

At the Périgueux Mimos Festival

Mimes, dancers, clowns, and actors throughout Europe and from North America and the Orient have brought a variety of movement styles to the Périgueux (France) Mimos Festival, begun in 1983. The festival—hosted by the city of Périgueux under the patronage of Mayor–Senator Yves Guena and Mayor Xavier Darcos and organ-ized by a team of officials that includes Deputy Mayors Jean-Jacques Ratier and Serge Salleron and Mimos president Jacques Canton, with talent selected by artistic director Peter Bu—has broadened movement theatre's frontiers and rejoined ancient theatre, where dance was allied with drama, drama with movement, and movement with music and sound. Each year, Mimos lives up to the highly experimental nature of its programming and continues to be one of Europe's major rendezvous for the discovery of original talent. The following descriptions of companies and artists who performed at the Périgueux festival from 1990 to 1998 (extended to cities in Portu-gal and the Czech Republic in 1991) illustrate the broad range of movement theatre forms and styles.

At the 1990 Mimos Festival, with *In Concert*, staged at the foot of the Gallo-Roman and Byzantine St-Front Cathedral, Spain's prize-winning Semola Teatro par-odied circus acrobats performing daring and buffoonesque feats to classical music.

Fireworks and dramatic lighting effects—along with the music of Beethoven, Mozart, Mahler, and Schubert—set off images of revolt, death, and eroticism in a vivid visual and musical tapestry.

Silence Teatro from Bergamo, Italy, begun at the Lovere School of Theatrical Expression by a group of students who founded the Silent Theatre Association in 1985, won the second prize for itinerant companies for *Figuraazione*, based on Cesare Pavese's *Lavorare Stanca* (*Work Tires*). Throughout the town, the company's tableaux vivants with narration and folk music evoked the beauty and nobility of spinning cotton, weaving, and toiling in the fields. Its 1996 creation, *Your Message until Death*, based on medieval documentation, is designed to be performed in the streets of historic European cities.

The Théâtre de Complicité, begun in London in 1983, is a physical and verbal company of international actors who tour and teach throughout Europe and appear on television. Their collaborative improvisations and humorous adaptations include Friedrich Dürrenmatt's *The Visit*; Shakespeare's *The Winter's Tale*; Lewis Carroll's *Alice in Wonderland*; *The Street of Crocodiles* (1983), an absurdist and minimalist version of Bruno Schultz's short stories; *Out of a House Walked a Man* (1994), based on the plays of Daniil Kharms, who lived in the Soviet Union from 1905 to 1942; and *Foe* (1996), a reworking of Daniel Defoe's *Adventures of Robinson Crusoe*. At the 1990 Mimos Festival, illusion pantomime and burlesque acrobatics enhanced their satire of a son's funeral arrangements for his deceased mother in *A Minute Too Late* (1984). The Théâtre de Complicité's second piece, *Help I'm Alive,* inspired by Italian playwright Angelo Beolco Ruzzante, explored *commedia* techniques in a modern setting, in which the Italian peasant Dina, kidnapped by a rich, older American, is pursued by her husband across land and sea. The company made its American debut at the Lincoln Center Festival for the Performing Arts in August 1996, with *The Three Lives of Lucie Cabrol,* a piece based on a French peasant's continuing love for her beloved after death.

The Théâtre de la Mandragore, founded in Brussels in 1985, staged a cinematic parody of 1920s silent horror films, entitled *The Strange Mr. Knight* in which a scientist turns corpses into monsters through melodramatic thriller and expressionist techniques.

Through clowning, mime, acrobatics, silent acting, and game-playing, the Crazy Mimes—Mila Horacek and Antonin Klepac, from the Czech Republic—created *Crac*, in which two male characters are laid up after an auto crash. Despite their broken legs and arms and the institutional despotism—symbolized by the menacing footsteps of the nurse administering injections—they transform a prosaic hospital sojourn into a lunatic asylum.

In Jean-Paul Cealis's decorative art installation *Jardin à la Française,* objects created of wood, cloth, and plastic in myriad shapes and designs were animated to the accompaniment of sounds derived from blowing on reeds and tubes, vocal cries, and the grating of wood and metal. In Cealis's world, the real protagonists are man's creations, to which he is subjugated.

In *Foam in a Cage,* Ilotopie from Camargue, France, presented mobile human sculptures in outdoor cages exuding foam as they engaged in various activities. A bather in a washtub, a bride reading and a groom watering plants, a laundress washing and ironing, and a male figure drinking as he watches TV gradually buried themselves in their plastic foam to offer a sociological message about man's entombment in routine.

At the 1991 Mimos Festival, the annual Mimos prize was awarded to France's Decroux-trained Théâtre du Mouvement for *Bearer of the Letter*, created by Catherine Dubois and Lucas Thiery. Inspired by *Last Letters from Stalingrad*, written by soldiers in the Second World War, along with letters by Vincent Van Gogh and Thomas Hardy, the work depicts a last letter that a soldier, who foresees his death in battle, writes to his girlfriend. A minimum of narration and a skillful use of corporeal movement reveal the couple's happy and tragic moments of union and separation.

Amsterdam's Dog Troep, comprised of artists and sculptors who spontaneously grouped together in 1975 to create a street theatre, derives its improvised pieces' themes and forms by transforming caves, old factories, churches, and other sites into innovative settings. In *The Ascension of the Mandarin*, performed in an ancient Périgueux convent courtyard, the medieval music and tableaux unveiled a rich, folkloric image theatre, evoking Hieronymus Bosch's paintings, with fire-breathing dinosaurs, grotesque human figures, monsters, and carnivalesque scenes that burst with movement and color. Inanimate objects and strange creatures come to life in visual images abounding with plastic beauty and elemental humor.

Founded in 1977 by Alfredo Corrado, a deaf-mute from New York, the International Visual Theatre of the Deaf began in the Chateau de Vincennes outside of Paris. At first a therapeutic means of communication for the deaf-mute, from 1980 on, the company has staged productions for the hearing public. Employing sign language as a stepping stone to explore nonverbal communication through mime and silence, its members began to work with speaking actors. *The Stones*, created in 1989 and based on Gertrude Stein's *Miss Furr and Miss Skeene*, includes both deaf and hearing actors. Sophocles' *Antigone* was created at the Avignon Festival in 1995 and later performed in Paris at the Cité Internationale. With productions extending from Molière's *The Miser* to Eugène Marin Labiche's farces and Sophocles' tragedies, the company has opened up dialogue channels between deaf actors and the hearing public, integrating deaf actors into the hearing world to give them a sense of accomplishment.

New York performer, novelist, and psychologist Howard Butten's mute, childlike clown is a musician, ventriloquist, mime, magician, and comic dancer called Buffo, who, because of his awkwardness, fails miserably. Butten's creation of a simpleminded character unable to communicate with others evokes the psychologist's work with the autistic, his recent foundation of the Koschise Center for the Autistic in France, and his novel in French, *When I Was Five Years Old I Killed Myself.*

Born in England, Paul Clark has performed solo shows in Holland since 1982. In *Time and the Man*, a satire of the mechanization of time, Clark's hero is immortal because of the 1582 creation of the Gregorian calendar which abolished fourteen days. A talking clock that never sleeps, he builds in his garage a desert island where he can relax, tell time through the sun's rising and setting, and sleep. Witty monologues, contained movement, and a deadpan facial expression reinforce Clark's commentary on man's servitude to his own inventions.

Simone Conein-Gaillard, former member of Luis de Lima's Brazilian company and partner of Marcel Marceau, presented a retrospective of 1960s and 1970s popular illusion pantomime. *Little Animals* is mimed exclusively with hands and fingers; *Tender Dream* is a sentimental portrait of a lady with a parasol rowing a boat; *The Other Self* portrays the outer and inner self's conflicts through mask animation.

The 1991 Mimos Festival included a number of dance programs such as Butoh, which for Peter Bu is one of the twentieth-century forms that has given rebirth to mime ("Mime et Danse" 1994, 81). Japanese Butoh dancer Iwana Masaki, founder of

"The House of Butoh" in Paris, in *Hibernation* portrays the self's tortuous demasking in the face of death. In *A White Day*, Japanese Butoh dancer Carlotta Ikeda, founder of the female Butoh company Ariadone No Kai in 1974, and French dancer Hervé Diasnas contrasted Eastern and Western cultures in a yin–yang search through symbolic dance, clown, and mime images. In Portuguese dancers Francisco Camacho and Monica Lapa's mime–dance–theatre piece *Double Marginal,* sexual desire conflicted with the need for solitude. Adding ballroom dancing to their movement and verbal piece *Trilogy*, Simon Thorne and Philip Mackenzie of the British company Man Act created a provocative rendering of machismo's image in modern society.

The winner of the 1992 Mimos Festival award, Derevo, founded by Antonin Adasinski in Leningrad in 1987 and based in Prague since 1990, staged its piece on the dreams of three soldiers, *Rabbit Skin Drum,* before the Saint-Front Cathedral. *Creation*, played in the former quarries of St-Astier near Périgueux, evoked forceful, visual images in the dimly lit caverns. Challenging conventional staging, Derevo's bold physical performance style integrates everyday life with theatre.

The provocative French Turbo Cacahuète, founded by Pascal Larderet in Grenoble, confronts spectators with the absurdity of such conventions as covering the body and shunning death and sex. In a formal festival inauguration before city officials, performers unveiled a nude female holding a doll. In their daily street shows, they showered outdoors in the nude; utilized open public toilets; lay naked in a pet shop's straw bed, a butcher-shop window, or a marketplace vegetable bin; took part in a nude sculpture exhibit; held a funeral in which family members lugged the casket through the streets; set up a wedding that ended with feathers and foul-smelling fish flying about; and held a demonstration against the obscenity of their own street theatre.

The French company Malabar paraded through the town with colorful costumes and sparkling fireworks. Fusing circus art with street theatre, Malabar presented *Face to Face,* in which science-fiction creatures, appearing on stilts and wearing Oriental masks, confront one another on an open-air battlefield of fire and water.

Among the dance companies that combined dance with mime theatre and clowning, the Sofa Trio from Hungary, founded in 1989, staged *The Divan*, a collaboration among three dancer–acrobat–mime–clowns. Inspired by Hungarian fairy tales and the Christian story of the three wise men, this dadaist hodgepodge integrates the contact dance of Josef Nadj, with whom the trio worked in the late 1980s, with burlesque acrobatics and the use of clownish accessories.

The Hungarian Natural Disaster, created in 1984 by stage director–composer György Arvai, presented a dance–mime entitled *Vital Space*, in which a nude female in a small glass aquarium evolves from a lizard-like creature into a sensuous woman who gives painful birth to a fetus. Her sculptural movements recall Butoh dance's tortuous progressions.

The Belgian Mossoux Bonté company, begun in 1985, brought to life in *The Last Hallucinations of Lucas Cranach the Elder* the bizarre and hallucinatory tableaux of fifteenth-century painter Lucas Cranach. Perverse, ambiguous characters step out of their frames, offering through their sensuality, their costumes' beauty, and each tableau's formal, slow-moving dramatic progression a plastic, theatrical experience that challenges the imagination beyond the painted material.

The 1993 Mimos Festival featured the internationally reputed French dance company Maguy Marin in *May B* (1981), a work based on the destitute atmosphere of Samuel

Beckett's plays. The title—a word play on the name of the writer's mother, May Beckett, and the word "maybe." This work communicates, through theatrical movement, throat sounds, German songs, silence, and repetition of the word "finir" ("to end"), that we live in a doubtful and finite universe among degrading human specimens. In postmodern style, dance, mime, and songs intermix as ten protagonists wearing white nightshirts, bonnets, and pajamas and with pasty white faces fail to reach out to one another. Marin fuses the playwright of the absurd's antitheatre to her own form of antidance.

Inspired by fifteenth-century Italian painting, the French Lartigue-Szerelem in *Portrait of Marjolaine* resorts to expressive dance movement and attitudes with an ultraslow rhythm to portray a seductive, madonna-like female. Choreographer Marceline Lartigue, a student of Merce Cunningham and Lucinda Child before founding her own company in 1989, brings these influences into her synthesis of mime, music, and dance.

La Môme, a dance company created in 1988 by French choreographer Fanny Tirel, conveys in the narrative dance *Pythie* the sexual act and female aggression through sensual movement executed to rapid and vigorous rock rhythms.

Based on Francisco de Goya's *Caprichos*, the Spanish company Danat Danze in *The Sky Is Covered with Bricks* twirls, turns, and dances on and around a giant teeter-totter to capture the vertigo in the painter's works.

The 1993 Mimos Prize was awarded to a group of autodidactic young actor–mimes—the Stoka Company from Bratislava, founded in 1991—for their creation, *Impasse.* With innovative costumes and masks, they incorporate movement, sound effects, and music into their sketches on modern life's disenchanting aspects, which satirize everything from love and sex to politics, opera, medicine, and the American way of life. Their spontaneity and the acuity of their social comment lend a dadaist quality to their iconoclastic creations.

The Temps Fort Théâtre from France, begun in 1971, staged *Middle of the World*, in which characters symbolizing water, earth, fire, and air interact in four Oriental tales. Influenced by the Bread and Puppet Theatre in their use of masks and inspired by the traditional Hindu theatre, the performers evolve with slow, Oriental-style movement and static attitudes.

Passacaille by France's Theatre of Shaman, founded in 1981 by Bruno Meyssat, recalls the stage director's peasant childhood. In slow rhythms evoking the *passacaille* court dance of the seventeenth and eighteenth centuries, two males and a female engage in humdrum farm occupations. Through a predominance of silent nonaction, the rustic ambience and the mystique of inanimate objects challenge the spectator's imagination.

The Russian clown Litsedei Minus 4 Company (three of the Litsedei clowns abandoned the original group to form their own) presented *Moumie*, which drew children and adults into its absurdist clown acts.

The French Cotillard Company, begun by Jean Claude Cotillard in 1980, staged *All Men Are Created Equal*, in which four males apply for the same position in a personnel office. Job-market competition is satirized through chronometrically choreographed slapstick and nonstop gags.

Malasangre, performed outdoors by Chile's Teatro del Silencio, founded in 1989, develops the poet Arthur Rimbaud's struggle with evil and good. Influenced by Ariane Mnouchkine's epic theatre and Étienne Decroux's and Marcel Marceau's corporeal mime, seventeen performers interweave dance, acrobatics, pantomime, Oriental costumes, and rock, jazz, and African music.

Among the street performances, *Immobile Time* by the Hors Strate company, founded by French actress Bernadette Coqueret, portrayed two giant, insectlike creatures on stilts and wearing medieval garments who rub against ancient stone facades and pick at one another. In *The Parade of the Padox,* begun in 1964 by Lecoq-trained French marionettists Dominique Houdart and Jeanne Heuclin, three comic-strip characters wearing friars' attire and with round, animal-like faces and bald heads wreak havoc in the outdoor markets and squares. In *Pesce Crudo*, members of France's Negrabox thrust an arm, a leg, a face, or a mask through the sides of a giant black box amid loud banging and clouds of smoke. The Chantier Theatre, a group of young Périgueux theatre and plastic artists, installed mysterious black eggs of all sizes throughout the city. To close the 1993 Mimos Festival, demons, priests, and medieval figures of the Spanish Xarxa street theatre created a flamboyant fireworks spectacle.

The 1994 Mimos Festival opened with a performance by Marcel Marceau and his company in the city where he grew up during the German occupation. Although organized around the theme of the three mime masters—Etienne Decroux, Marcel Marceau, and Jacques Lecoq—the festival included other artistic expressions.

The main exponent of the Decroux school was the Paris-based Théâtre de l'Ange Fou, with its reconstruction of thirteen of his creations, entitled *The Man Who Preferred to Stand*. Also of the Decroux school, Philippe No of the French Compagnie Trafik depicted in *Fred Fröle* a space scientist who attempts to create life as he moves about in his interstellar laboratory like an astronaut in space.

Marceau's company's performance of Nikolai Gogol's *The Overcoat* offered a nostalgic reminiscence of his beginnings nearly fifty years ago. Blending perfected technique with melodramatic content, the stylized mimodrama in eight scenes was interpreted by nine well-trained mimes, with Marceau performing a moving rendition of the hero.

Among those companies that reflected the Lecoq school's clown–mime and *commedia* was the French Fiat Lux in *Garçon, Un Kir*, in which five waiters preparing a cocktail party wreak havoc whenever the boss disappears. In *Tango*, the Lecoq-trained Vache Libre company staged a comical and poetic rendering of a stormy relationship between a female clown (Meriem Menant) and her boss (Gaetano Lucido).

Festival spectators could also view dance and musical mimodrama. In *Water Lilies*, inspired by Claude Monet's *Nymphéas*, eighty-eight-year-old Kazuo Ohno and his son, Yoshito, danced to classical music and German songs, leaving the viewer with subtle images of nature's harmony in an impressionist homage.

In the musical mimodrama *Charcuterie Nationale*, the Toulouse Manon Troppo conveyed scenes at once naturalistic and melodramatic of war and violence's absurd and barbaric consequences.

The Romanian Teatrul Masca and the Slovak Teatro Tatro revealed rich, ethnic, Eastern European folklore in their mask and puppet animation. Teatrul Masca's version of *The Overcoat* incorporated giant masks in a surrealistic setting to portray society's malefic pressures on the improvised hero, whose dream of a new overcoat symbolizes the human aspiration for beauty and other ideals. Teatro Tatro's *Impromptu*, like a Hieronymus Bosch tableau, flouted death and caricatured knights and young lovers through the use of masks, dance, and choral songs.

In *Désirs Parade*, the Philippe Genty company created spectacular and sophisticated images through clowning, magic, innovative puppetry, and object animation.

The 1994 Mimos Prize was awarded to street artist Ilka Schönbein and her Meschugge Theatre. Dressed as a beggar and utilizing imaginative masks and flea-market objects, Schönbein brought to life original characters and creatures, evoking the suffering of the Jews, birth, death, terrorism, and peace.

The five members of the international Contre Pour, who studied with Lecoq-trained teacher Philippe Gaulier, appeared in the streets hugging metallic objects, like dazzled creatures from another planet, in its absurdist and provocative *Men in Black*. Brazilian street artist Roland Zwicker performed classical clown tricks; American Laura Herts mixed satire with good-hearted fun in her audacious outdoor skits; Hannibal et Ses Eléphants spoofed the future 1998 World Cup in *France-Visiteurs*; and Teatrul Masca's *Medievals* drew bystanders into a satire of medieval times.

The 1995 Mimos Festival, entitled *Le Mime Fait Son Cinéma* (*Mime Creates Its Own Cinema*), explored the affinity between mime and cinema, as well as between mime and dance, theatre, circus, marionettes, and street theatre. The 1995 Mimos Prize was bestowed upon choreographer Josef Nadj and his French-Hungarian company, Theatre Jel, for *Comedia Tempio* (1990), based on opium's influence on the life and works of Hungarian author Géza Csath. While the content exploded with intensity, irony, and Kafkaesque absurdity, a rigorous form harmonized mime with dance.

Hervé Diasnas's *Le Sourire de l'Aube* (*Dawn's Smile*) depicted, through dance, mime, and circus, two young men competing with clownlike virtuosity for the same woman.

In *Les Marmousets* (*The Urchins*), performed by Eddy Del Pino and Christophe Lemoine, Zygom'art from France offered spontaneous mime–clowning that mocked the male ego and the young artists' own attempts to stage a clown show.

American clown Jango Edwards and his company of six clowns, actors, mimes, and musicians performed *Klones*, a tribute to the clown's art that included burlesque cinema, music hall, and audience interaction.

Jazz musician, painter, dancer, actor, and stage director Didier Gary and his Oz Theatreland company from Nancy, France, mixed plastic arts, jazz, rock, dance, mime, film, video, and laser art with images of devils, skeletons, and dragons of the Middle Ages in *La Grande Tuerie* (*The Great Killing*). In an atmosphere of the French street-fair shows, hallucinatory, non traditional images evoke the Apocalypse, the AIDS plague, drug addiction, violence, female abuse, materialistic values, and the 1990s decadent quest for pleasure.

The Lyon-based Cosmos Kolej company presented Wladyslaw Znorko's *Ulysse à l'Envers* (*Ulysses Backwards*), a dramatic tableau of a group of women and a shipwrecked sailor on Blasquet Island off Ireland's misty coast. The work also depicts the longing for one's homeland despite its hardships.

Combining acting, masks, and marionettes, Japanese Dondoro Theatre with artist Hoichi Okamoto's *La Belle et La Moine* (*Beauty and the Monk)* developed a Japanese legend in which a monk seduces and abandons a young girl, who kills him and then commits suicide to join him in heaven. The piece blends Noh, Kabuki, and Butoh movements with those of a human-size marionette.

Among the street performances, Wurre Wurre's Belgian artists Tom Roos and Philippe De Maertelaere staged on a Périgueux street corner *Les Oiseaux* (*The Birds*), in which they played birds perched on a rooftop that chirp at passers-by and swallow salad leaves. In other sketches, they enacted street sweepers, electricians, and plumbers; in their stage piece, *Don't Wurre*, they utilized low-key Flemish humor. Pocheros, a company of jugglers, trapeze artists, and clowns from France, the United States, and Canada, offered stylized circus virtuosity in *Cirque d'Images*. In French company Hors Strate's *Groudeck*, two Gothic gargoyles on stilts returned to Périgueux to rub against ancient stone facades, and in *Aux Détours de la Nuit* (*Detours in the Night*), three mysterious figures on stilts, resembling the buffoons of the Middle Ages, searched for a magic star in the heavens. From Colombia, Palo Q'Sea's *Jeu de Carnaval* (*Carnival Game*) captivated spectators with colorful masked monsters on stilts, fireworks, giant ostriches, and awesome devils. On a tiny outdoor stage, Daniel Raffel's Cinemarionettes re-created the early silent films' art and humor in *The Photographer*. The festival ended with Profil de Face's *L'Attaque du Train Plein de Dollars* (*The Great Dollar-Laden Train Robbery*), a satirical homage to silent films and to the 1903 Hollywood western, *The Great Train Robbery*.

The 1996 Mimos Festival took on an experimental aspect with an evening entitled "Attempts, Temptations, and Appearances," which featured works-in-progress and portions of creations by unknown or lesser-known companies. The remainder of the program ranged from clown and humorous sketches to theatre of images and moving tableaux, theatre of the absurd and traditional pantomime, ritual and mythological performances, sculptural movement, dance and trapeze art, and spectacular street theatre.

In the realm of clown and humorous theatre, the 1996 Mimos Prize was awarded to the British brothers Ralf Ralf, laureates of the Bessie Award in 1989, for *The Summit*, a parody of the 1987 Ronald Reagan–Mikhail Gorbachev talks. The work conveys, through mime, slapstick, clowning, acrobatics, song, and gibberish, verbal communication's limitations in official as well as personal relationships.

First discovered at the 1988 Mimos Festival, Germany's clowns Habbe and Meik in *Nonetheless Noseless* and *My God*, wearing large masks with protruding noses and looking like midgets with gigantic heads and astonished expressions, clumsily cope with material objects and navigate their way through the audience with a compass and map.

In Russian clown Yevgueni Sitokhine's sketch on solitude, the child like protagonist wakes up on a bare stage on his birthday. He extracts poetry and humor from transforming simple objects, such as a shoe into a telephone, toilet paper into a rope with which to hang himself, and a valise into his bed cover. Sitokhine's clown, with neither make-up nor a red nose, is both pathetic and poetic.

In *The Day of the Little Moons*, the French clown quartet Les Nouveaux Nez created more-traditional rather than avant-garde clowning. Its performance as musicians, singers, and puppeteers was more lyrical.

In *The Ex-Hams*, the French Albedo company opened the festival with a parade and a sketch on greediness. Clutching safes full of money collected from taxing passers-by, these histrionic crooks turned their props into a factory, a petroleum well, an airplane, and the moon.

Among the exponents of the theatre of images and moving tableaux, the French Théâtre de la Mezzanine's *Earthenware Dogs* consisted of surrealistic pictures within a gigantic frame—a female in a wide red velvet skirt, a dead antelope shoved into a refrigerator, a clothesline with underwear forever multiplying, and clothes irons hopping about—that all come to life to baroque music and haunting animal cries.

Stoka, a Slovakian company that won the 1993 Mimos Prize for *Impasse,* performed a dark comedy entitled *Vres* (*Heather*) and ironically subtitled *Optimist*, which conveys the anguish and violence that Slovakians underwent in their search for political freedom.

Parodying Eugène Delacroix's *Death of Sardanapalus*, the French Quatre Litre Douze company created in *The Sisters of Sardanapale*, a humorous and erotic portrayal of an impotent tyrant who attempts to make love to three voluptuous women as gunshots and bombings erupt around him and a voice periodically announces the number of minutes he has to live.

Several companies engaged in theatre of the absurd and traditional pantomime. Academy Productions from London, under Andrew Lavender's artistic direction, performed an extract from Samuel Beckett's pantomime *Acts without Words II* and a Beckett-inspired collective creation, entitled *Without a Word*, about a male protagonist who breathes heavily through a mask as he and a second male character build upright triangles with cards that repeatedly collapse. Both works depict Beckett's preoccupation with trivial actions executed with dignity.

Trained at Marcel Marceau's school in Paris, Nguyen Tien Vuong's classically styled pantomimes, entitled *The Tree* and *The Sea*, are nostalgic re-creations of a charming art rarely seen in postmodern movement theatre.

In their street show *Photo Novel*, the Pyramide company from Lyon parodied silent films, mime, and pantomime to enact a couple that meets and marries, a crime scene, and a sculptor chiseling and transforming the actors and spectators into stereotyped burlesque characters.

The French 36ième du Mois company's *The Little Leaks* comprised a collective mimed version of the absurd happenings between two couples recalling Eugene Ionesco's *Bald Soprano*.

Four companies performed ritual and mythological theatre. In their parade *Biogenesis*, the Materia Prima dancers, mimes, and stilt walkers from Nancy created a fantasy in which a male dreams of flying and a female appears pregnant with flowers. Their evening performance of *Sphere* before the Saint-Front Cathedral evoked a tribal world of man's origins amid fire, earth, water, and air in which slow-moving figures confront one another. In *Syllogism of the Crab*, Didier Manuel of Materia Prima developed a ritualistic solo of a protagonist on a spiritual quest.

Enfin le Jour company from Pau adjoined rigorously choreographed Oriental and Occidental dance and mime to rich decors and costumes in *Hostia*, which traces religion from primitive forms to more evolved ones.

In the French L'Arbre à Nomades company's *Soronoume,* movement evoking Butoh dance recounted the origins of man and theatre.

Sculptural movement characterized the work of Maureen Fleming, a resident La Mama artist who performed *Eros*, inspired by the legend of Psyche and Eros. This modern dance piece incorporates Butoh dance's arduous, slow, and controlled contortions, providing for some viewers images of Psyche enraptured by sensual pleasure, while for others evoking universal images of man's quest for the meaning of birth, life, and death.

The French female duo Tournesol combined dance, mime, and trapeze art in *Sea Horses*, which left spectators with poetic reflections of sea creatures dancing and miming above the Saint-Front Cathedral.

In their street piece *The Enraged Fiancées*, the Sol Pico duo from Catalonia enacted to jazz music a vivacious and seductive love–hate combat between a female dancer and a female saxophonist.

The Catalan Liquido Teatro performed an experimental mime–dance/mime–acrobatic work entitled *Ear of Grain* with grace and zest.

The German Theatre Titanick's spectacular street theatre parody of human megalomania and superficiality depicted the *Titanic* luxury liner's demise from the 1912 ship's building to its shipwreck on its maiden voyage. Floods, fires, fireworks, and sensational technological effects accompanied by musicians playing in uniform comprised this gigantic work, which electrified a large crowd of spectators in the shadow of the Saint-Front Cathedral in a striking closure for the 1996 Mimos Festival.

On exhibit at the 1996 Périgueux Mimos Festival were photographs of companies and artists, captured by photographer Guy Charrié in his book *Mimages* and by authors Jean-Marc Lachaud and Martine Maleval in *Mimos, Eclats du Théâtre Gestuel* (see bibliography).

Entitled "Women and Others," the fifteenth annual 1997 Mimos Festival hosted international female, as well as male, stage and street mime, clown, dance, puppet, hearing-impaired, and mentally disabled performers.

Winners of the 1997 Mimos Prize, the Belgian artists Nicole Mossoux and Patrick Bonté blended a puppet with mime–dancer Moussoux in *Twin Houses*.

Inspired by deaf painter Francisco de Goya, the hearing-impaired Czech Brno University students of Studio Marta performed *Caprichos* as a dance–mime with poetic hand and finger miming.

Through drums, rhythmic dance, puppets, cries, and songs, members of Chile's Los de Abayo developed a ritualistic portrayal of their ancestors' struggles to survive in *The Cardinal Points*.

In the French L'Oiseau Mouche and Théâtre du Cristal's collaborative silent theatre staging, mentally impaired patients enacted Samuel Beckett's *Act without Words I* and *Interlude*.

The French Spirili-Deschamps's poetic *Two Times Nothing* discovered a male and female in an airport, silently interacting with baggage objects (electric razors, hair dryers, etc.) that mime on their own.

Among the mime and dance groups, in the Japanese-French, all-female company Ariodone's *Language of the Sphinx*, based on Butoh techniques and modern dance, founder Carlotta Ideda and seven dancers explored the mystery of existence through symbolic dance, mime, theatre, music, lighting, and scenic effects.

The Swiss Compagnie du Revoir's *Ladies Rest Room* blended dance, mime, silent theatrical gestures, and facial expressions with some spoken language in a stylized choreography touching on women's rights.

The French Signes de Vie's *Master of Signs* offered hearing-impaired dancer Claire Bonneton's lyrical rendition of P. Aroneanu's narrated text about a poet's creation of the world.

In thirteen sardonic and burlesque sketches, Spanish dancer Maria José La Ribot began with a striptease, in which she boldly defied her spectators to disrespect her. In ensuing sketches, she expressed abuse of women ravaged by war experiences.

Through Butoh and modern dance, Japanese mime–dancer Mitsuyo Uesugi created in *Elle* (*She*) a requiem for all the women, dead or alive, who spiritually inspire her.

Among the clown–mime companies, the Czech Society of Crazy Mimes staged *Crazy Carmen*, a spoof of George Bizet's *Carmen*, in which supermarionette Carmen is a screaming tyrant who controls her two male rival suitors (Miloslav Horacek and Antonin Klepac) like puppies. In *Crac*, two male victims of a car accident, on crutches and wrapped in bandages, wreaked havoc in a hospital.

From Russia, the Micos clowns engaged in chair-dancing, piano-climbing, and other energetic mime–clownery.

At the close of the festival's indoor performances, renowned Russian clown Slava Polunin appeared in a bright yellow costume to shower spectators with confetti and subject them to his antics.

Along with the outdoor performances were a growing number of off-festival performers playing in the streets and on the public squares.

In the Parisian Décor Sonore's provocative street animation, entitled *Music Box*, a seductive lady (Jany Jérémie) in a white wig invited spectators to crawl under her wide period skirt to see her bare, dancing legs. Nearby, prima donna Annick Hémon, in a nineteenth-century porter's chair, sang erotic songs by Pierre Louys.

In the Uruguayan-French Compagnie d'Ailleurs's *A Man and a Woman*, a middle-aged couple on stilts bought salad and fruit at the marketplace and sauntered down the street, looking for a baguette and a newspaper.

The French Lackaal Dukric's *Totalscope*, nocturnal music hall sketches in a park, featured flamboyant and sexy triptychs of lady fakirs, Provençal virgins, and talking female kitchen objects.

In the French Fenêtre-sur-Rue company's *Malavox*, a half-vegetable, half-animal creature darted in and out of crowds to cling to street windows and doorways.

In *Another World*, the Dordogne (France) company Le Diable par la Queue created mobile sculptures of primitive creatures interacting in a transparent, outdoor vivarium amid rocks, twigs, and minerals.

Périgueux drama students staged an outdoor evening bridal banquet and a day parade with pregnant, abandoned, and male brides.

In *Ostriches*, presented by the A and P company's German Krause Brothers, Sherlock Holmes and Dr. Watson searched for a suspect while atop their tall ostriches, from which they suddenly descended to take their five o'clock tea. In a second sketch, they attempted to walk on stilts and entered a telephone booth.

Among other street spectacles, popular Cuban entertainer Iris combined slow movement with rapid juggling in *The Idiot Runs Fast*. In *Capocomico*, Italian street clown Marco Carolei created lively audience interaction with a whistle, a flag, a red rose, and a flute.

At the 1998 Périgueux Mimos Festival, entitled "The Very Best of Mimos and New Discoveries," new works by former Mimos laureates and other international artists ranged from classical and corporeal mime, image theatre, clowning, dance, and musical theatre to street theatre.

Homage to Etienne Decroux's centennial, *L'Homme Debout* (*The Man Who Is Standing*), was rendered by former Decroux students and teaching assistants Thomas Leabhart, Jean Asselin, and Denise Boulanger of the Omnibus company, and the by Théâtre du Mouvement in Decroux works and their own creations along with videos and personal accounts of Decroux. Mimos laureates for 1991, the French Théâtre du Mouvement reenacted excerpts of their Decroux corporeal-based creations since the 1970s.

Based on their Marceau-Decroux training, along with circus and film elements, the French Commedia Infinita presented a couple hammering out their differences in *Monsieur and Madame O*. They punctuated their meticulously choreographed silent gags with vocal exclamations.

The 1990 Mimos laureates of Semola Theatre from Spain contrasted forceful images of love, marriage, war, and death to portray the tragic absurdism of contemporary life in *Esperanto*.

The Russian collective Derevo, a 1992 Mimos laureate, staged a two part image piece entitled *Zone Rouge*, which began with a ham clown lapping up audience applause followed by Butoh-like performers creating powerful hermetic and solemn movement metaphors.

Awarded the 1998 Mimos prize, Derevo's *Le Cavalier* depicted the male adventurer—suddenly arrested by unbridled buffoonery and clown-like humor—facing delusions of love, faith, and old age.

In *Les Assiettes* (*The Plates*), Ctibor Turba's Theatre Alfred's Czech artists parodied the Czech-Slovak separation through slapstick and plate-breaking. In *L'Homme Suspendu* (*The Hanging Man*), three male protagonists and a female hanging upside down challenged gravitation with abstract and poetic movement images.

In an inventive *Catalogue du Héros*, Groupe Axe satirized the myth of grandeur and the futility of ambition in the group's native Russia through hand-made contraptions, minimalist clowning, and deconstructive game-playing.

In the French Dram Bakus's improvised *Anonymous Company*, house painters encountered unexpected mishaps that evoked modern *commedia*.

The Spanish Teatre Yllana had a vaudeville-like group, *Glub*, which portrayed sailors in mute sketches in which they faced the trials of scrubbing decks and swimming with sharks.

Through dance and expressive movement in *Empreintes* (*Imprints*), France's Théâtre de l'Astrakan created characters leaving behind traces of their personal trauma and disequilibrium.

In *Vertige entre les Oreilles* (*Vertigo between the Ears*), Dutch artist-dancer Barbara Duijfjes interpreted a dwarf who faces a cruel game of seduction in the service of opera singer Marianne Linnenbank.

The German-French Meschugge Theater, with 1994 Mimos laureate Ilka Schönbein and Alexandre Aslé, employed grotesque masks, imaginative and varied sized marionettes, and bawdy humor in their adaptation of the Grimm Brothers' *The Frog Prince*.

Street theatre was never so abundant, rich, and varied as at 1998 Mimos, with many off-festival performers adding to the event. In the French Albedo company's *Bigbrozeurs* (*Big Brothers*), masked 12-foot giants in long yellow raincoats, horn-rimmed glasses, and derby hats nonchalantly emptied their bladders against a wall and poked their retractable heads into people's faces.

While making objects disappear, reappear, and change their form in comic-strip fashion, Sicilian mime-magician Carmelo Cacciato, a 1989 Mimos laureate, walked his invisible dog.

In *Mouth to Mouth*, Great Britain and Australia's Bedlam Oz animated "slinkies," which resembled giant silver stove-pipes flirting on a park bench.

The Dutch Shrikkel Theatre's *Tableau Vivant* brought to life a framed portrait in which the face of a shrouded head progressed from laughter, fright, and surprise to pathos.

In *The Secret of Dr. Zingaro*, the British Ta Ta Di Di Teatro captured the golden age of the expressionist silent horror movies in a melodrama of love, betrayal, and vengeance.

The French Théâtre du Prato's *Mélancolie Burlesque* revealed three males awaiting the ideal female.

In the Polish Biuro Podrozy's *Carmen Funèbre* Theatr, the loss of lives, home, and country during the Bosnian war was reenacted in the shadow of the Saint-Front Cathedral.

Public author Dominique Lemaire read his humorous and lyrical impressions of Mimos 98 at the close of the festival.

At all of the Mimos Festivals, performing artists offered workshops, and there were daily public press meetings with the artists, exhibits, and lectures on movement theatre. Each year, the richness, freedom and versatility of the Mimos Festival's program is a testimony to mime's universality and its intrinsic role in all of the stage arts.

At the Chalon dans la Rue Street Festival

Since 1986, the annual July Chalon dans la Rue national street festival in Chalon-sur-Saône, Burgundy, created by ambulatory marionette artists Pierre Layac and Jacques Quentin, has hosted international companies that perform movement theatre. In 1991, the festival converted L'Abbatoir, a former slaughterhouse, into a residence for companies and artists to create their own works, as well as a space for theatre and musical performances, exhibits, and a photography lab. Among the companies that have obtained residencies for their creations were Lackaal Duckric for *Le Musée d'Histoire Surnaturelle* (1991), a participant at the 1992 Mimos Festival; Daniel Rovai and Friends for *European Cabaret* (1992); and Oz Theatreland for *La Grande Tuerie* (1994). In 1996, Chalon-sur-Saône celebrated ten years of street theatre festivals, featuring artists who have made it successful.

At Gaspard's Kolin Memorial Festival

In 1992, Jiri Turek of Prague organized a biennial festival entitled Gaspard's Kolin Memorial in honor of the legendary mime Gaspard Deburau, born in 1796 in Kolin, in what today is the Czech Republic. Among the featured performers were the Czech artists and companies Ctibor Turba, Michal Nesvadba, and Hamu Praha; the popular German clowns Mahlo and Konig; the American Second Hand Dance Company; and the Russian Derevo and Ilkhom Theatre Studio. A second festival with still more artists and companies participating, which also offered workshops, took place in September 1994. Both festivals hosted high-quality performances and encouraged new trends in theatrical forms related to mime. At the 1994 Kolin Festival, Czech mime Boris Hybner staged a retrospective of his 1976 to 1991 mime sessions. Compagnie Pocheros from France, an international group of graduates and teachers from the École Nationale de Cirque in Chalons-sur-Seine, performed juggling, acrobatics, and trapeze numbers in *Cirque d'Images* (1994) on Kolin Square. The French Compagnie Cealis created a performance art installation entitled *Jardin à la Française*. Former ballet dancer turned pantomime artist Nola Rae, based in England, staged her popular *Elizabeth's Last Stand*. The Swiss company Moira interweaved music, dance, movement, and text in *Gertrud und Wilhelm* (1993), depicting a couple's conflicts and reconciliations. The English mask company Trestle Theatre traced life from early childhood to that of unemployed street adolescents in *Hanging Around*. The Dutch company Warner and Consorten—sculptors, dancers, and musicians whose artistic director founded Dog Troep in 1975—created an experimental outdoor staging. Canadian actor and clown–teacher Daniel Gulko, wearing goggles and holding a whip, improvised clown acts with the public. The Romanian Teatro Tatro staged *Minas Tirith*, a chaotic marionette show on wheels involving spectators.

Among the Czech and Slovak artists and companies, renowned Czech clown Boleslav Polivka's *Shipwrecked Survivor* portrayed the protagonist's loneliness and solitude. Even When, founded in 1993 in Kolin, fused visuals with music and movement in the *Dance of Life*. Klickova-Liska, a new company from the Czech Republic, incorporated video and simple staging in *The Sad Café*. Czech artist Ales Janak portrayed a lonely clown in *The Finger*, the Igdyz company presented *Tanec Zivota* (*Lively Dance*), and the Slovak Stoka actors staged their dadaist, award-winning *Impasse*.

A third festival celebrating the bicentenary of Deburau's birth took place in September 1996. Opening the program, Milan Sladek—the renowned mime, teacher, and theatre director from Bratislava—presented traditional Pierrot works entitled *The Raincoat*, *Jealous Pierrot*, *The Charity Donor*, and *Pierrot Becomes a Tailor*. Sladek's students Olga and Björn utilized masks and grotesque elements in *Girl Meets Boy*. Among the mimes from the Czech Republic were the Cvoci Crazy Mimes, who staged a farcical *Crazy Carmen* in the style of the early silent movies. Ondrej Lipovsky, a student of mime master Ctibor Turba, presented a solo entitled *The Bread and Butter Paper-Wrap*. From the 1Q Free Society, two Czech mimes, Jana Kacerová and Jana Klicková, who performed in *The Sad Café* at the 1994 Kolin Festival, and Swiss clown Bernard Stockli created a new work based on the quality of "stick zipper" material. A former member of Ladislav Fialka's Theatre on the Balustrade in Prague, Rudolf Papezik demonstrated Marcel Marceau's and clown Leonid Jengibarov's styles in an original interpretation of classical mime and black humor. In *Caprichos*, the Czech Jamu Brno group offered a nonverbal portrayal of Francisco de Goya's etching, created while he was experiencing a hearing defect. The work grew out of an Educational Drama of the Deaf student project.

France's Théâtre du Mouvement, founded by Claire Heggen and Yves Marc, created a retrospective of its creations from 1975 to 1995. In *Amore Captus*, French acrobat–clowns known as Agathe and Antoine played a girl and boy who meet on a tightrope. French mime Laurent Decol interacted with his audience in his poetic and comic *Timoleon Mangus*.

The three-member modern dance Second Hand Dance Company from the United States staged a collective work expressing joy, trust, and unison. Theatre Espace from Holland—with Marcus Schmid and Judith Nab, who perform on beaches, in meadows, and in other unusual places—staged comedy sketches in Mestsky Park. In *Figurazione*, which won the itinerant award at the 1990 Périgueux Mimos Festival, the Italian Silence Teatro presented sculptural figures of ancient village life throughout the city.

The festival culminated in Czech clown Boleslav Polivka's *The Jester and the Queen* with Polivka as the clown and Chantal Poullain as the queen, who symbolizes a power figure whom the clown is obliged to entertain.

The 1996 Kolin Festival also included seminars on various artists and schools of mime.

Mime Centers, Schools, and Other Festivals in Europe

Mime Centers

Mime's growth and diversity in the second half of the twentieth century brought about the need to establish European mime centers. The Netherlands Mime Centrum, founded at the Amsterdam Theatre School in 1969 by the Dutch mime Jan Bronk, began as a documentation center and an institution that encouraged mime as a form of artistic education and, later, promoted it as an art form. From 1985 on, under Ide Van Heiningen's direction, it has published surveys of the activities and creations of Holland's mime companies and artists and in 1986 began awarding an annual mime prize to the best mime company or artist. It also has published a manual based on Étienne Decroux's mime grammar; developed a mime video and photo library; collected documentation on artists, schools, and teachers; and organized colloquia and courses in mime marketing and management. One of its major accomplishments was the 1989 founding of the European Mime Federation to create an international network promoting mime's visibility on a broader level. This has encompassed the development of mime centers in European countries; the exchange of artists, teachers, teaching methods, and documentation; and the encouragement of artistic quality, professionalism, and innovative creativity in the field. To this end, the Netherlands Mime Centrum, which has merged with other performing arts institutes to develop Holland's theatre arts and presently is called the Theater Instituut Nederland, also has been collaborating with European mime centers, such as the Mime Action Group in London, the Mime Centrum in Berlin, the International Centre for Stage Movement in Moscow, De Beweeging in Antwerp, the Théâtre du Mouvement in Paris, and the École du Mime Corporel Dramatique in London (see appendix for addresses). Its activities include drama, dance, mime, puppetry, object and image theatre, opera and operetta, musicals, cabaret, circus, and all phases of theatre production. It collects information on contemporary theatre arts in Holland; organizes conferences, debates, workshops, and exhibits; promotes research and the publication of books and periodicals; stimulates international collaboration; and furthers the appearance of Dutch theatre and dance abroad.

London's Mime Action Group was founded in 1984 with the voluntary administrative support of Helen Lannaghan to raise the public and professional profiles of mime, physical theatre, and related arts. The organization, which over the years has received increased funding, represents performers, directors, teachers, administrators, and all persons and groups working in mime and related arts. It develops training, educational, marketing, and funding opportunities for mime; provides information; maintains a mime mailing list; produces publications and research; and publishes the quarterly magazine *Total Theatre*.

The Mime Centrum in Berlin, founded in 1990 to stimulate and develop theatre that is movement-oriented, serves as a public information area, with a specialized library, photo and video archives, and documentation on European mime. It supports the experimental and innovative projects of mimes, actors, directors, dramatists, and movement teachers; distributes videos; and makes contacts for productions, tours, and international mime theatre festivals.

The Maison du Mime in Périgueux is part of the city's Cultural Center, harbored in the ancient Convent of the Visitation. It contains offices, a rehearsal space, and indoor and outdoor performance theatres to host the yearly International Mimos Festival and workshops. It publishes an international mime newspaper entitled *Gestes* and holds photo exhibits of mime artists and companies. It aims to develop a collection of written and video documentation on French and European mime. Among the publications it has sponsored is Jean-Marc Lachaud and Martine Maleval's book, *Mimos, Eclats du Théâtre Gestuel*, about the Périgueux International Mimos Festival.

The Theatre Union in Russia researches the art of theatre movement, including the actor's skills and techniques, for all forms of plays. The center offers seminar–laboratories for Russian teachers, teacher methods, and training; periodic competitions for student work; and practical studies for actors. An experimental movement laboratory researches expressive movement and new training systems for verbal, movement, and clown theatre.

The Internationale Mime Associatie, begun in 1987 in Antwerp, Belgium, which later became the Vlaamse Mime Federatie (Flemish Mime Federation), has organized mime workshops and published information on mime performances, events, and training in Flanders and abroad, and has hosted mime festivals.

For additional information and mime center addresses, see Appendix A.

Mime Schools

Aside from the aforementioned companies and artists, many of whom teach and have their own schools, a number of established European mime schools represent Decroux, Lecoq, and other physical training styles and methods. Marcel Marceau's École Internationale de Mimodrame de Paris offers a program based on Decroux and Marceau techniques, including the creation of mimodramas and other physical training classes. The École de Mime Corporel Dramatique in London has a three-year program based on the Decroux technique. The Desmond Jones School of Mime and Physical Theatre in London includes in its shorter and longer course programs the Decroux mime, along with other movement techniques. The Amsterdam School for the Arts Mime School offers mimes and mime teachers training and an opportunity to create works in various traditions and techniques, including Decroux's grammar, which has a central position there. The students, also trained in acting, modern dance, acrobatics, tai chi, voice, anatomy, mime history, art history, drama theory, lighting, scenography, and video, are prepared for professional work in the theatre and in educational fields.

The Ecole Jacques Lecoq in Paris offers a two-year certification program and periodic summer workshops in mime, pantomime, *commedia*, mask, clown, and other movement theatre techniques. The Arts Academy in Utrecht, Holland, begun in 1990 under the direction of Luc Desmets, founder of the Little Academy in Brussels, is based on the Lecoq method and also encompasses the study of commedia dell'arte, Greek tragedy, and masks.

Besides the individual artists already mentioned, many of whom have taught Decroux's corporeal mime in their respective countries, other renowned, Decroux-trained mime teachers are Anja Dashwood, who taught in a private school in England, and American Anne Dennis, who trained movement theatre students in Yugoslavia, in San Francisco, and at Rose Bruford College in England. Decroux's corporeal mime and other styles also have been included in the curricula of a number of English drama schools.

For additional information and addresses of European mime schools and teachers, see the appendix.

Mime Festivals

Since the 1970s, the number of European festivals dedicated to mime theatre or that have included it in their programming has multiplied. Other than the aforementioned

London International Mime Festival, first held in 1977; Périgueux Mimos Festival, inaugurated in 1983; and Gaspard's Kolin Memorial Festival, which began in 1992, a number of other festivals periodically presented gestural theatre (even though they did not all continue to exist for financial or other reasons). Among these were the International Pantomime Festival Gaukler in Cologne, which relocated to Bratislava, Slovakia, in the fall of 1996; the Mime Festival in Strasbourg; the Pantomimenzirkus Festival in Marburg, Germany; the International Festival of Clowns and Pantomime in Hamburg; the Pinok and Matho International Festival of Mime at the St-Maur Theatre in the Paris suburbs; the Kendal Northern Festival of Mime, Dance, and Visual Theatre and the Brighton International Festival in England; the British Festival of Visual Theatre in London; the International Festival of Mime in Sueca, Spain; the International Creative Workshop of Mimes in Wroclaw, Poland; and many others in various European cities.

A number of international street theatre festivals have incorporated mime, clown, dance, and other theatre forms, such as the Festival of Aurillac and the Chalon dans la Rue festival of Chalon-sur-Saône in France; Holland's Limburg International Street Festival, which first took place in 1983; Russia's Arkhangelsk International Street Festival, which has existed since 1990; the twenty-year-old Winchester Hat Fair in England; and the annual Tarrega Theatre Street Festival in Catalonia, Spain. There are also theatre, dance, and music festivals that have presented some mime, such as the Holland Festival and the Festival of Fools in Amsterdam, the Edinburgh International Festival and the Edinburgh Fringe Festival in Scotland, the Avignon Festival in France, the Biennale Teatro in Venice, Italy, and the Idéklic Family Festival for children and adults in Moirans-en-Montagne, France.

For additional information on European festivals see Appendix B.

Why Festivals?

London International Mime Festival directors Joseph Seelig and Helen Lannaghan express the need for mime festivals in the following statement:

> Who needs mime festivals? For the organizers of long established festivals such as the London International Mime Festival, established in 1977, and the Mimos Festival, which began in 1983, the answer is as clear as ever. Such festivals are vital for the art form itself, for performers and for the public.
>
> For any performance form, but especially for one as fragile, special and as magical as mime and visual theatre, the regular opportunity of a well promoted and prestigious performance season ensures an important profile and a sustained focus on, and for, this special area of theatre work.
>
> For performers, a festival brings a chance to meet other artists, to learn, to establish contacts, to develop new work under sympathetic conditions and to reaffirm their artistic identity.
>
> Little of the above means much without an audience. Festivals which succeed in attracting audiences beyond a coterie of devotees bring mime to the attention of those who would otherwise ignore it. By their scale and professionalism, they make an important statement about the art form they promote. Certainly festivals are necessary, but neither the art form nor its exponents can afford to let the public down in terms of quality.[5]

Peter Bu

Peter Bu, a leading organizer since the 1970s of European mime festivals that offer a wide range of movement theatre, was also the first to originate the term "gestural theatre" for any performance in which mime remains the unique or predominating means of expression, without systematically excluding dance, clown art, or speaking theatre. If several of these arts have the same importance in a performance, Bu prefers to call this form polyphonic or "pluridisciplinary" theatre.

Born in 1940 in Bratislava, in the former Czechoslovakia, Bu studied at that city's Theatre Academy from 1957 to 1962. After the Communist regime took over his country and banned pantomime as a decadent art, he wrote about mime as well as theatre, film, and books. Upon completing a doctorate on Constantin Stanislavsky's actor-training method, its effects on modern theatre, and the reasons the Stalinist regime utilized Stanislavsky's method as a means of political propaganda, Bu obtained a University of Paris scholarship to research the Soviet Russian policy. In 1971, he arranged mime artist Milan Sladek's first tour and, in 1976, organized the first Festival of Mime in Cologne with fifteen mime soloists and companies. In 1977, he presented ten mime companies at the Avignon Theatre Festival and, in 1978, was in charge of the foreign mime and theatre artists' section at the Cockpit Theatre's London International Mime Festival. After collaborating with the City Theatre of Utrecht, Holland, to organize an international theatre and mime festival in the spring of 1978, that same year he participated in two festivals at tourist resorts in Tabarka, Tunisia, and Asilah, Morocco. He next initiated a festival, entitled Mimes and Clowns, in Strasbourg, and, in 1979, organized clown festivals in Dijon, Lyon, and Paris. In 1981 and 1982, he directed a mime festival in Paris, Barcelona, and Modena, Italy, entitled Other Theatre. Since 1982, Bu has organized outdoor and indoor festivals and tours for theatre, dance, music, mime, and plastic arts artists. In 1987, he undertook artistic direction of the annual Périgueux Mimos Festival, begun in 1983 by theatre animators Ginette and Paul Tellier. From 1990 to 1993, Bu was artistic director of the yearly Idéklic Family Festival in France's Jura mountains.

In the following interview, Bu describes twentieth-century mime's development and how festivals, including broader forms of physical theatre, can free mime from limited movement expressions.

Why have you originated the term "théâtre gestuel" or, to coin a term in English, "gestural theatre," to describe mime theatre today?

Bu: I proposed this term to include all theatre in which actors express uniquely or principally with their bodies, with the exception of dance–theatre. Gestural theatre can exist in a pure state, with no other means of expression other than gestures and attitudes, as in the art of Decroux or Marceau. But there are also other kinds of theatre based on gestures and attitudes that are aesthetically very different from the work of these masters. There are also other spectacles in which the body remains the predominant element but not the only means of expression. Why should they be excluded from corporeal theatre? Does verbal theatre not continue to be considered as such even if at times the actors dance and sing? There should be no barriers between gestural theatre in a pure state and those forms in which the mimes speak, dance, sing, do clown acts, and acrobatics. The latter still represent gestural theatre if mime, gestures, and attitudes remain the predominant language. Because pantomime in the ancient Greek sense refers to theatre of imitation without words, and because we are accustomed to calling the Deburau mimes of the nineteenth century pantomimes and to identifying mime with the teachings and work of Decroux, to describe theatre that incorporates other kinds of nonverbal theatre forms, I chose the term gestural theatre.

Could you give examples of artists engaged in gestural theatre or mime in its broader sense?

B: The academic period of gestural theatre seems to be terminated, and this art is now rich and diversified. The research in mime during the second part of the twentieth century has produced a multitude of original languages. To mention only a few, the work of Daniel Stein, Cary Rick, Karine Saporta, and Shusaku and Dormu Dance Theatre emphasize corporeal mastery and dance; clowning and the use of text, along with comical effects, are found in the work of Hector Malamud and Boleslav Polivka; committed and philsophical theatre are combined with mime in the pieces of Benito Gutmacher and the Chwilowa Theatre from Poland. All of these artists and companies participated in the International Festival, which I organized in the spring of 1981 and 1982 in Paris.

Does gestural theatre have qualities not found in other forms of theatre?

B: Gestural theatre has kept a freshness, a naiveté, and a communicative warmth that one does not find often in other kinds of theatre today. This is because of its marginal situation in relation to official theatre, from which it differs because it is not as yet familiar with hardened structures or the theatrical machine, which allow it to hide its weaknesses behind exterior effects. Because mimes make a greater effort to dialogue with their audience, they are inventive and sensitive to audience reaction.

Why do you think that mime is rediscovered in periods of synthesis?

B: The greatest epochs of mime theatre were during periods of synthesis, as in the last five centuries before Christ in Greece and Rome, during the Renaissance, and in the nineteeth and twentieth centuries. By a period of synthesis, I mean the eradication of frontiers and barriers to free communication and exchange, the barriers between past and future, between social classes, between continents, and between head and heart. The most diverse ideas confront one another, and there is a search for new concepts that encompass all available knowledge. This search encompasses the rediscovery of a direct, nonverbal representation of reality. We need the confrontation of scientific, philosophic, and artistic concepts with reality, and the new techniques—films, TV, photo offset printing, etc.—permit us to represent things in a visual manner not reduced to linguistic symbols. Such universally accessible representation is especially important in an epoch when man's interdependence has reached a planetary level.

As a period of synthesis—beginning with the great silent film artists to the renaissance of the visual aspects of the stage in the Soviet avant-garde theatre of the twenties and the research of Etienne Decroux, Harald Kreutzberg, Martha Graham, and Edward Gordon Craig—our century is especially rich. All of these have influenced the dance of the sixties and seventies and beyond. It is a period when time and space are less limiting and communication is quick and direct. Thus, depending upon the period in which he lives, the mime can be analytical or tend toward synthesis.

Accustomed to living on the edge of society, during periods of synthesis he is able to move closer to the vital center.

What is the role of the body in verbal theatre and in contemporary theatre today?

B: First of all, since the early part of the twentieth century, the theatre in general ceased being dominated by literature and actors found a balance between vocal and corporeal expression. Although traditional theatre interpreted the text through the utilization of beautiful declamation accompanied by insignificant gestures, this was no longer the case with the stagings of Edward Gordon Craig, Adolphe Appia, Vsevolod Meyerhold, Eugene Vakhtangov, Jacques Copeau, Leopold Jessner, Max Reinhardt, Peter Brook, Giorgio Strehler, the Living Theatre, the Odin Teatret, Bread and Puppet, Meredith Monk, Bob Wilson, Peter Stein, and Luca Ronconi, among others.

Second, a number of theatre companies and soloists staged spectacles based solely on attitudes and gestures. Since the seventies, there has been an afflux of rich and diversified forms, such as Tadeusz Kantor's *The Dead Class*, Circus Alfred, Boleslav Polivka's Theatre on a String, Bob Wilson's *Deafman Glance*, Serapion's Theater of Piplits, Shusaku and Dormu Dance Theatre, Theatre Beyond Words, the United Mime Workers, Tom Leabhart's Corporeal Mime, Richmond Shepard's Mime Company, Dog Troep, Pilobolus Dance Theatre, among many others. Before the seventies, besides Etienne Decroux, Jean-Louis Barrault, and Marcel Marceau, there were Henryk Tomaszewski, Kazuo Ohno, Rolf Scharre, Samy Molcho, Ladislav Fialka, Milan Sladek, etc. Today there are also street clowns and performers who utilize the body more than the voice or other means. All of these examples manifest the special attention merited by mime theatre and the evolution of the theatre in general.

What are the differences between dance theatre and gestural theatre?

B: Dance and mime have been both sisters and enemies. Research in both arts in the sixties and seventies has brought them together more closely. Mime now has no more in common with the paralanguage of classical pantomime, where the body speaks through signs, nor with narrative stylization. Today it is oriented toward a dynamics of gesture expression, evoking an entire universe of the unconscious, just as the modern dance of Martha Graham sought to return to the sources of movement and to redefine the relationship of the dancer with space.

What do mimes and clowns who have appeared together at your festivals have in common? Could you describe a clown today?

B: There are many reasons why mimes and clowns have appeared together. Both have been on the border of recognized art and have retained the capacity to marvel over things in life that appear too simple or banal for the blasé public. Both have not lost the capacity to dialogue with the public, and both often deal with the comical in life.

Because the clown performs most of the time in the circus, where the acoustics are not very good, he utilizes mime, gestures, and attitudes, along with his voice. Some clowns do not speak and can be called clown–mimes, like Dimitri, Boleslav Polivka, Don Rieder, and Boris Hybner. But clowns do not only have mimes as first cousins. In the clown family, there are also clowns who speak. One of the best today is Franz Josef Bogner. There are clowns who dance, like Katie

Duck and the Pilobolus Dance Theatre; clowns who utilize music and song, like John Duykers and Clovis; clowns who perform with marionettes, like Mister Punch and Guignol; as well as clown–magicians. Today the clown is basically an actor who interprets a character, usually the same one all of his life, but nothing can prevent him from playing another character. He might perform in the street or on stage in full-length pieces that revolve around a single theme during an entire evening, as in the Circus Alfred and the Clown Company. Yet the clown is a special type of actor. Even when he changes his means of expression to incorporate music, dance, or another language, his attitude toward the public, toward his art and life, remains the same. Besides his fresh and naive allure, he has an irresistible desire to dialogue with his partners, as well as with his public. He is a clever virtuoso who is able to dominate his means of perception and expression, even if he seems totally incapable of doing so. Besides, he is able to perform anywhere—in the circus, the theatre, the street, the movies, on TV, and in advertising media—even though the mass media only show a very traditional and limited image of him. Like today's mimes, the new wave of clowns has arrived very much on time.

Is there a relationship between gestural theatre and other artistic forms?

B: The theatre in general can only gain by collaborating with writers, painters, sculptors, composers, musicians, dancers, and architects. Gestural theatre should not be an exception and content itself with stagings that have no setting, music, nor scenario. Gestural theatre combines these elements with movement and corporeal expression. Rather than contribute to the development of aesthetic categories or so-called "pure" single styles, gestural theatre synthesizes them today in a rich performance art. As a reaction against the spoken word, which because of the language of the mass media and of ideologues, often becomes meaningless, gestural theatre, centered on new corporeal languages, possesses much diversity. Not only new forms of expression but also new themes have been discovered, and the content of gestural theatre is as rich as other theatre forms. To mention a few recent examples, there is the depiction of violence in Benito Gutmacher's *The Cry of the Body,* or in *Auto-da-fé* by the Théâtre du Huitième Jour. The totalitarian system, which forces the public to express its attitude in relation to this type of indestructible social organization, is seen in Chwilowa Theatre's *Scenario*. The mythologies of American cinema appear in Hector Malamud's *People Love Me*. In gestural theatre we find all forms—committed theatre, the theatre of the absurd, ritual theatre—also new corporeal techniques, along with the use of theatrical elements like silent movies, acrobatics, dance, masks of the Occident or the Orient, etc. At the crossroads of all techniques of expression, it is open in a limitless way to creative invention. This theatre, in which the principal expression is the human body, expressive movement, gestures, and attitudes, has brought a more innovative impetus to all other kinds of theatre.

What do you think mime festivals have brought to the development of gestural theatre?

B: Since 1960, many festivals have been held in all parts of the world without leaving a durable trace. Since the middle of the seventies, the number of festivals has multiplied considerably and, still more important, some have taken place regularly for the past eight to thirteen years in cities like Cologne, Utrecht, London, Strasbourg, Brussels, Berlin, and Périgueux. Although we do not know the aesthetic implications of the various forms of physical theatre that appear at these festivals, they have helped to establish this theatre. It is absurd that spoken and musical theatre have permanent theatres, while mimes and dancers do not. It seems unjust that an entire theatrical domain has fewer rights and possibilities than other kinds of theatre. I tried to remedy this by popularizing mime. Because I also do not like frontiers, I am happy to have organized not only mime festivals but street performances and speaking theatre festivals, too. My activities and the work of others are no guarantee that gestural theatre will be able to escape from its ghetto soon. It will escape, eventually, under its own power. All that festivals can do is help accelerate the process.[6]

Notes

1. Letter to author, January 1986.
2. Letter to author, March 1974.
3. Interview with author, August 1974.
4. Interview with author, June 1985.
5. Letter to author, August 1994.
6. Letter to author, September 1991. Excerpts from "New Mime in Europe," *Mime Journal* (1983), 9–49.

13

Mime and Movement
Theatre in North America

Mime in North America owes much to French, English, and Italian mimes who performed on American stages. At the end of the eighteenth century, harlequinades from the English stages and pantomimes from the French music halls and fairgrounds, where mimes had been prohibited from playing, already had appeared on American Colonial stages. Although pantomime was familiar to American audiences in popular entertainments, the art of European mimes, clowns, and dancers would enrich the nineteenth-century American music hall and influence the silent films of the early twentieth century.

Toward the middle of the twentieth century, Paris was still the place for mimes to be. There, American mimes studied with Étienne Decroux, Marcel Marceau, Jacques Lecoq, and their disciples. However, in 1957, Paris came to New York, where Decroux trained mimes in corporeal movement. Jean-Louis Barrault had already brought his company to New York, where American audiences applauded him as Baptiste in the film *Children of Paradise*. Meanwhile, Marceau toured the United States, inviting a number of American mimes to study with him. As the styles and schools of these French masters became familiar to the American theatre, mime as a single stage art recaptured the American public's interest.

The direct and indirect influences and offshoots of Barrault, Decroux, Marceau, and Lecoq sparked American mimes to expand upon the styles and techniques of these masters and create their own schools and companies. Mime became a vital adjunct for clowns, jugglers, New Vaudevillians, and dancers, who blended it into their art. American folklore, culture, and social and political issues were integrated into physical theatre. Women mimes began voicing feminist opinions in their pieces. Stage directors and theatre companies incorporated expressive movement into spoken text. Mime was introduced to the blind, the hearing impaired, and the physically challenged, for whom it served artistic as well as therapeutic purposes. Clowning and dance–mime workshops were included in church ministry programs. Mime in twentieth-century America not only became an art appreciated for itself on stage and screen, but also merged with other stage arts and benefited therapy and religion.

This chapter traces the path of mime in North America from its role in the theatre during the eighteenth and nineteenth centuries, through its contribution to silent films, to its twentieth-century rebirth under the tutelage of French masters Étienne Decroux, Marcel Marceau, and Jacques Lecoq and their trainees, as well as other teachers and schools. Mime companies and artists who combine their art with such styles and content as the commedia dell'arte, clowning, New Vaudeville, political comment, street theatre, and the Theatre of the Deaf are placed under these headings. Others are characterized by their incorporation of puppets, masks, dance, therapy, ministry, and a mixture of elements and styles particular to postmodernism. And because of the significant influence of the French masters on the growth of this art in Canada, a separate section has been devoted to Canadian mime. In describing the contributions of individual performers and companies, no particular importance or rank has been assigned. In this panorama of artists and companies, they have been identified under the headings of the basic forms and genres they represent, revealing the kind of mime each has developed, along with examples of their major works whenever that information has been available. For reasons of space and availability of documentation, some descriptions are briefer, and some artists and companies have not been included because of lack of information.

Early Pantomime

Little is known about mime in America until the end of the eighteenth century, when clowns and dancers, inspired by artists from abroad, began to incorporate it into their art. In Philadelphia and New York, one of the first American clowns, John Durang, performed with his son, Charles, and other family members in such pantomimes as *The Wapping Landlady* (1790). Anna Gardie from Santo Domingo made her American debut in the pantomime *La Forêt Noire* in 1794 and that same year danced in the ballet–pantomime *Sophia of Brabant.* French tightrope walker and mime–dancer Alexandre Placide arrived in America in 1793 to stage patriotic masques, such as *Americania and Elutheria* (1798). Jean-Baptiste Francisquy, a member of Placide's company, created pageants, such as *The Grand Historic and Military Pantomime* and *The American Heroine* (1796), in which Gardie danced the title role.

During the nineteenth century, American pantomime continued to develop under the influence of European clowns and mime–dancers. English harlequin James Byrne toured the United States from 1796 to 1800 with *The Death of Captain Cook* and *Oscar and Malvina.* George L. Fox (1825–1877), who played Humpty Dumpty to full houses for many years, learned pantomime from the Ravels, a French ballet–pantomime company. Clown–mime Tony Denier, of French origin, the Marinettis, the Zanfrettis, and the Ravels were all headliners at the Hippodrome in New York. James S. Maffitt combined traits of the French Pierrot with the humor and costume of the English clown Grimaldi. By the turn of the century, vaudevillians Ernest Hogan and Bert Williams were among the first black pantomimists. Williams, who appeared on Broadway with his partner George Walker in *Dahomey* (1902), *Bandanna Land* (1908), and the Ziegfield Follies of 1910, was applauded not only for his graceful dancing but for his miming of, for example, the intricate details of a poker game. But with the disappearance of these mime–clowns, pantomime was no longer on New York Hippodrome's bill or those of the Philadelphia stages. Relegated to the circus and to vaudeville, pantomime soon took on a grotesque and trivial character.

Mime Clowns on Screen

What seemed to be a dying art in early twentieth-century America was infused with new life in the silent movies. Fatty Arbuckle, Chester Conklin, W. C. Fields, and Ben Turpin perpetuated the mime–clown's art on screen. Buster Keaton's technically perfected art as a passive character was applauded in *Navigator* (1924), as were Harold Lloyd's perilous and humorous stunts in *Girl Shy*. The elegant French actor Max Linder, inspired by vaudeville and the circus, displayed his acrobatic prowess as the comic lead in *Too Much Mustard* and *Max the Toreador*. The last of the silent-film comedians was the irresistible, baby-faced, and innocent Harry Langdon, who appeared in *The Big Kick* (1930) and *Hallelulia, I'm a Bum* (1933). With the advent of sound, Laurel and Hardy, Abbott and Costello, the Three Stooges, and the Marx Brothers combined physical extravagence and slapstick with verbal gags. In the movies and on TV, grimaces and physical comedy won popularity for former vaudeville comic Bert Lahr, as well as for Jimmy Durante, Joe E. Brown, Danny Kaye, Ernie Kovacs, Jerry Lewis, and Red Skelton. Even when they spoke, Rich Little, Frank Gorshin, imitator David Frye, and comic singers, dancers, and actors Sid Caesar, Dick Van Dyke, Jackie Gleason, and Lucille Ball were all good movement artists. And while circus clowns Emmett Kelly, Otto Griebling, Paul Jung, and Lou Jacobs mimed in their clown acts and Richard Cardini, the great magician, enhanced his magic with mystifying gestures, these and others would become known to movie and TV audiences for an expressive tic or twitch, a comical smirk or facial distortion. All of these artists perpetuated the mime–clowning that belonged to the golden age of the cinema.

Evolving both as an independent art and as an extension of the theatre, the cinema borrowed actors from the stage and lent them back again. This exchange continued in other respects. The close-up and other technical devices that D. W. Griffith and his cinematographers developed to capture movement in turn inspired the use of less formal facial expressions and gestures on stage. Transferred directly to the screen, stage movements and broader gestures seemed theatrical and exaggerated. Yet, if this art of the moving image, which derived its name from the Greek *kinema*, meaning "motion," had remained silent, the mime technique it used might have developed into a stylized form of its own. With the advent of the talkies, this silent art was soon eclipsed, except in the films of such actors as Charlie Chaplin, who began as a music hall pantomime artist and whose miming on screen, even when he spoke, was at the core of his comical genius.

Charlie Chaplin

Born in 1889, the son of music hall performers, Charlie Chaplin grew up on the London stage. It was to his mother, Hannah Chaplin, that he attributed his gift for miming:

> Without my mother I wonder if I would have succeeded in pantomime. She remained at the window for hours looking into the street and reproducing with her hands, her eyes and the expression of her face all that passed below, and this never stopped. And it is in observing her that I not only learned to translate emotions with my hands and my face, but also to study man. She had something prodigious in her way of observing. (Chaplin 1919, 4)

At the age of six, Chaplin appeared on stage singing "Jack Jones" and, in 1897, danced a jig with the Eight Lancashire Lads. In 1902, he made his London debut as Sammy the newspaper boy in *Jim* and then played Billy in *Sherlock Holmes.* In October 1912, during Chaplin's second American tour with Fred Karno's company, in which he played a drunk in *In a London Music Hall,* Mack Sennett of Keystone Studios in Los Angeles offered him a movie contract. Chaplin created an innocent little cockney out of "a tired bowler hat, a little fitted jacket, a pair of old pants and worn shoes from which he abolished the heels; the flexible cane and the moustache familiar to us all completed his garb. Soon was born, during the action of *Between Showers,* the character of Charlie Chaplin, now known to the world" (Henry 1931, 7–9).

Chaplin's first film, *Making a Living* (1914), was not successful, but in *Kid's Auto Races at Venice* (1914) and *Between Showers* (1914), he combined the buffoonery and slapstick that popular taste demanded. Many of his pantomime scenes remain unforgettable. In *The Gold Rush* (1925), he imitates a chicken and performs a ballet with his fingers and bread rolls. Aided by the camera, he accelerates the rhythm of his movements until he is frenetically hopping about on the screen. In the same film, with frenzied prowess, he tries to keep the cabin from falling off the cliff. In these and other scenes, slapstick contrasts with the inherent dignity of the Little Tramp, who, even after he is kicked, always picks up his cane and straightens his tie just as his trousers are falling. Chaplin's Little Tramp triumphs over every defeat, every kick in the backside.

While his contemporaries relied on sight gags and stock comical types to provoke laughter, Chaplin's physical comedy derived from the exploits of a browbeaten character at odds with the world around him. Added to his talents as a mime were those of a magician, juggler, and dancer. Even after he incorporated sound into his films, his sense of gravity and rhythm, his precise choreography, and his natural use of movement continued to enhance the content of his films.

For thirteen years after the first talkies appeared, Chaplin remained convinced that the voice destroys comic illusion. In *Modern Times* (1936), mime, dance, and song, along with an imaginary language, serve to satirize the machine age. In *City Lights* (1931), Chaplin mocks spoken language by delivering a speech full of pompous clichés and unintelligible words. Not until 1940 did he consent to make a talkie, *The Great Dictator*, but he still resorted to silent movement to delineate character, as in the celebrated scene in which the dictator dances with a world globe to symbolize his desire to possess the world.

Of his belief in silence, Chaplin said:

> Silence, that universal grace, how many of us know how to profit of it, perhaps because we cannot buy it. The rich buy noise. The soul feasts in the heart of natural silence, that silence which never refuses whoever searches it. (Leprohon 1946, 207)

Influence of American Film Comedians in Europe

During and after the First World War, the American cinema triumphed at home and abroad with a flourishing number of film comedians. The presence and success of Hollywood films in Europe had repercussions on such French film directors as Louis Delluc and René Clair, as well as on such film comedians as Jacques Tati.

Born in 1918 in Lepecq, France, Tati played in a broader, yet refined, physical comedy style than did Chaplin, who, in turn, had something of French film actor Max Linder's elegance and restrained physicality. Like Chaplin, Tati began by playing pantomimes based on old music hall gags. He incorporated his early parodies of rugby matches and other sports into his films. One of his finest parodies, in *Mr. Hulot's Holiday,* is of a tennis game.

Tati's characters, like Chaplin's, are highly theatrical. Hulot is a caricature of both an eccentric architect and a good-natured sergeant whom Tati knew. His face inanimate, he takes long, exaggerated strides, his body bouncing forward with a determined gait. But unlike Charlie Chaplin or Buster Keaton, he engages in little slapstick and his physical comedy is never a display of prowess. Rather, he trips down a village street like a graceful toe-dancer; in *Playtime,* he has whole crowds moving like ballet dancers. Like Max Linder's characters, Hulot deals with the world around him in a gentlemanly manner.

Like Chaplin's Little Tramp, Hulot is an innocent victim of society. He is apologetic for his clumsiness, his indecisiveness, his eccentric short coat and trousers, and even for his pipe, which makes his speech incomprehensible. Contrary to Harold Lloyd and Buster Keaton, he is never the center of a catastrophe but always the cause; he is to be pitied rather than blamed. In *Mr. Hulot's Holiday,* the hero's clumsiness, which provokes an uproar among the guests at a seaside inn, serves as a vehicle to ridicule the snobbish behavior of waiters and English guests toward the innocent Hulot.

Tati's spontaneous animation of inanimate objects, such as his car, boat, and umbrella, and his comic gags based on objects and persons mistaken for other things play a more central satirical role than the inclusion of such props employed for subordinate comic means in the films of Chaplin and other silent clowns. In one scene of *Mr. Hulot's Holiday,* a tire from Hulot's car rolls into a mud puddle, is covered with leaves, and ends up being mistaken for a wreath by a mourner in a funeral procession. Mistaken identity also serves to satirize the pomposity of the funeral procession. Tati's mime art consists of discovering humor in ordinary people and events, making us aware of the absurdity of modern life and nostalgic for old-world values.

Twentieth-Century Stage Mimes

While twentieth-century comic film actors carried on the mime–clowning traditions of Max Linder, Charlie Chaplin, Buster Keaton, Harry Langdon, Jacques Tati, and other film comedians, several female pioneers of American mime, such as Ruth Draper, Angna Enters, and Lotte Goslar were developing mime on stage. Their important contributions, along with those of women mimes performing after the midtwentieth century—such as Mamako Yoneyama, Marguerite Mathews, Dulcinea Langfelder, and others working in mime, clown, physical theatre, and dance–mime— are examined in chapter 14, "Women's Voices in Mime." By the middle of the twentieth century, because of the influence of the French masters, a number of American stage mimes renewed this ancient art. Their interest also was inspired by Marcel Marceau's tours of America after 1955, and their art was given a solid foundation through the workshops that Etienne Decroux taught and the troupes that he created in New York from 1957 to 1962. Among the first to train in France were Richmond Shepard, Paul Curtis, and Alvin Epstein, who integrated mime with acting techniques.

Richmond Shepard

Richmond Shepard (born in 1929 and also known as Lionel Shepard) began his acting and dance career in New York at Adelphi University. He studied acting and mime
with Jean-Louis Barrault's student Philip Schrager, and mime with Alvin Epstein. In
1952, Shepard's Mime Theatre, one of America's first twentieth-century mime companies, performed at the Circle in the Square Theatre in Greenwich Village. After
studying with Etienne Decroux and Marcel Marceau, in 1956 Shepard and a group
of mimes played in cabarets and coffeehouses in Los Angeles and San Francisco. In
1971, his book *Mime: The Technique of Silence* was acclaimed as a "how-to" introduction to mime. The following year, he founded the Mime Guild, a union for
mimes.

Inspired by Gaspard Deburau's classical mime and twentieth-century mime
masters, Shepard's ensemble movement theatre remained closer to silent acting. It
contained plot and character, music, lighting, and narration of themes based on a
cyclical history of mankind, war and peace, love, and conformity. *The Man Who Said
No* portrays a nonconformist. *Pierrot*, based on Deburau's life, includes Deburau pantomimes. *The Family of Harlequin* (1973) revives *commedia* characters and situations. *The Big Top* (1974) explores absurdist abstraction in a circus ambience. *Dreams*
(1975) depicts a frustrated individual's desire for wealth and power. *Movies Movies*
(1976) is a mimed history of the cinema. *Pastorale* and *The Giant*, based on a fairy
tale and legend; a mime version of Lewis Carroll's *Jabberwocky*; *Genesis*, adapted
from James Thurber's story; and *The Stripper*, a witty caricature, were all performed
at the 1984 International Mime and Clown Festival at Davis and Elkins College.

As a mime director, teacher, and performer, Shepard has revived this art on the
American stage, in films, and on TV. He gives his views on the importance of mime
in acting and in dance and how this art has expanded:

> I believe that mime is very important in speaking theatre and in films. It is true that
> while the mime concentrates on externals such as how to climb a ladder or how to ar-
> ticulate inclinations, rotations and translations of the body, the actor works on the inner
> mechanisms in order to communicate emotions of the character he is portraying. And
> although in acting one does not utilize the exaggerated gestures or movements as in
> mime (especially in films), mime still gives you a subtle means of communication
> which helps you project. All actors need an innate or developed physical sense.
> Lawrence Olivier is a wonderful mime. Every character he portrays has a physicality.
>
> Mime is less important for a ballet dancer who is concerned with conveying,
> demonstrating and displaying form. The dancer's body goes beyond itself in great
> leaps, twirls, beautiful movements and the body moving so superbly that we are up-
> lifted by it. And the plot generally is only a vehicle to display beautiful form. In mime
> we want to tell a story with characters and the form is only a means to communicate a
> story. Great ballet dancers do not need expressivity. Baryshnikov, who is one of the
> greatest dancers today, is more or less unexpressive emotionally but his display of form
> is superb. Nijinsky also had emotion but it is not vital for a superb dancer. However,
> modern dance is different. Charles Weidman's dancers, who studied mime with me, did
> theatre dance. They leapt in the air and twirled like dancers but they also mimed open-
> ing a door or picking up a telephone. I believe that a mime also should study dance be-
> cause strength, muscularity and flexibility are needed in mime.
>
> By the middle of the 1970s mime was growing by leaps and bounds in America.
> When I wrote my book in 1969 I was the only mime making a living in the Los Ange-
> les area. By the 1980s there were a number of professional mimes in that area. Though

there are better mimes now, it is unfortunate that a lot of the public's experience is in encountering amateur mime performers who are bad. When the public sees a dull show it does not want to see another one. The appearances of Marcel Marceau and Robert Shields on TV have done more than anything to make the art known.[1]

The American Mime Theatre

Paul Curtis first trained in acting with Erwin Piscator. After studying mime and theatre in Europe for five years, he returned to New York with a new concept of mime theatre that, at a rehearsal of Curtis's first mime show, Jean-Louis Barrault spontaneously called "American Mime." With the 1952 founding of the American Mime Theatre, Curtis became a pioneer of twentieth-century mime in America.

The American Mime Theatre unites movement and acting with symbolic themes. In *The Pinball Machine* (1953), a pinball is knocked about. *Dreams I and II* (1958, 1962) reveal a rigid man's alter ego moving in an illogical dream world. *Scarecrow* (1962) is a storybook romance in which a young prince must choose between a scarecrow he created and the girl he loves. *Lovers* (1963) symbolizes the eternal male-female love cycle. *Birds* (1965) is about a strange bird born from a huge egg. In *Hurlyburly* (1969), three men perched on a tiny stool struggle to protect their privacy, which conflicts with their need to relate to each other. *Evolution* (1973) is a darkly toned poem depicting the force of evolution. *Sludge* (1974) becomes a madcap farce when a group's collective goal conflicts with myopic personal views. *Unitaur* (1982) develops the birth, hunt, capture, and escape of a mythical beast and how his courtier captors do not understand his significance. Through a series of blackouts, *Peepshow* (1988) explores the sexual and psychological development of an introverted male. *Music Box* (1991) reveals the romance of two figures on top of a mechanical toy. In *Six* (1975), the characters conduct themselves like inmates in an asylum. The mimes in these works perform on a bare, cycloramic stage (a stage with a concave backdrop), wearing black tights and regular make-up rather than whiteface or masks, to vocal sounds or electronic scores.

A school created to train company members was extended to teachers, directors, designers, playwrights, actors, dancers, children, and performers in general. The school and company have functioned since 1952, developing a syllabus and a teaching methodology published in a textbook. In Paris in 1994, Curtis established an American Mime course in cooperation with the Ministry of Culture.

For Curtis, American Mime is primarily an acting medium, a new performing art created by a unique balance of acting, moving, pantomime, design, and playwriting in which the performer communicates the character's desires and feelings through movement that is both theatrical and beautiful:

We call it American Mime to delineate it from other kinds of mime such as French pantomime. This delineation has nothing to do with the nationality of the people who practice it. Many Americans who call themselves mimes are really practicing a variant of the French school of mime just as there are Frenchmen practicing American Mime.

Concerning the American public's understanding of mime, I don't think it has ever been at issue historically. It has been the theatre businessmen such as producers and agents who have looked at mime as being too "special" for general audience consumption. Mime in the United States, and in the world as well, will soon be accepted as a performing art on an equal basis with other performing arts.[2]

In 1973, Curtis founded the International Mimes and Pantomimists Association, which publishes a directory of mimes and newsletters about their activities.

Alvin Epstein

Considered the first American Decroux student, Alvin Epstein studied and performed leading mime roles in the Etienne Decroux Mime Theatre between 1947 and 1951. The theatre played in Paris, throughout the European continent, and in Israel.

In 1951, Epstein moved to Israel, where he performed with the Habimah company and taught mime at the Chamber Theatre Drama School. As Marceau's partner, he made his New York City premiere in 1955, a theatrical event that revealed mime to the American audience. He then received a Ford Foundation grant to develop the relationship between mime and theatre. Creating numerous roles on the American stage, he was singled out for characterizations with unique physical and vocal requirements, such as Lucky in *Waiting for Godot* and Clov in *Endgame.*

Epstein joined the Yale School of Drama faculty in 1966 and in 1972 he became director of the Yale Repertory Theatre. In 1978, he left Yale to become artistic director of the Guthrie Theatre in Minneapolis for a short period.

Like Barrault and a number of Decroux students, as mime, actor, teacher, stage director, and artistic director, Epstein lent his talent and training to a more total vision of the theatre.

The Mime Theatre of Etienne Decroux in New York

Etienne Decroux was brought to New York City in 1957 by the Actor's Studio and the Dramatic Workshop to give a short lecture series and workshops. However, with the aid of an American student, Sondra Pearlman, he remained to open an American school, which he directed for five years. Out of this school, he created two performing troupes, one following the other, that staged his earlier works and those created in New York.

The first troupe included Decroux, Sterling Jensen, Leslie Snow, Jewel Walker, Nell Taylor, Michael Coerver, and Sunja Svendsen. The American premiere of the Mime Theatre of Etienne Decroux took place on November 22, 1959, at the Kauffman Concert Hall and opened on December 23 at the Cricket Theatre for a limited run.

The second troupe was composed of Decroux, Jensen, John M. Casey, Abbey Imber, Lucy R. Becque, Vivian Schindler, Jerry Pantzer, and Solomon and Mina Yakim. Under the sponsorship of the cultural section of the French Embassy, the Mime Theatre of Etienne Decroux performed on November 7, 9, and 11, 1961, at Carnegie Hall.

Before Decroux arrived in New York, Jensen had studied mime with Alvin Epstein and performed with Paul Curtis's American Mime Theatre. Appearing in many of the works of Decroux's two troupes in New York, Jensen is most remembered for his solo piece *Envelopment*, which he performed under a large white cloth.

Jensen was the only student from this period in Decroux's life who remained with his school and theatre. When he departed, Decroux officially left New York's Mime Theatre of Etienne Decroux in Jensen's directorial hands. The school remained open for some time.

Later, Jensen co-founded the Roundabout Theatre, which staged productions of classical plays. Among the many roles he performed in this company, he was praised especially for his portrayal of King Lear. In the mid-1980s, Jensen received acclaim for his work with the Roundabout.

Jewel Walker

A Decroux student and a member of his first New York troupe, Jewel Walker received special critical attention for his 1959 performance in *The Evil Spirit*. He later performed with Lionel (Richmond) Shepard in *A Show with Mime and Jazz* and as Tony Montanaro's first partner in 1963. Besides playing solo mime on stage, he appeared as Mime Walker from 1965 to 1975 on the *Mr. Rogers' Neighborhood* TV program and as Harlequin in *Oefoti the Troll,* for which he won a 1965 Peabody Award. Walker also created several mime pieces, among them *Noah and the Ark* (1965), *The Mime Circus* (1974), and *Tuesday* (1975), about the humdrum of characters passing in the street.

Both before and after his work with Decroux, Walker studied theatrical movement under several masters. In 1964, he joined the faculty of Carnegie Tech (later Carnegie Mellon University) in Pittsburgh as one of the America university system's first movement teachers for actors. In 1977, he helped to establish the professional actor training program at the University of Wisconsin–Milwaukee and later brought that program to the University of Delaware in 1989. His essay entitled "Stage Movement" appeared in *Master Teachers of Theatre* (1986) and in 1998, Walker received an American Association Award for Outstanding Teacher in Higher Education. A pioneer in teaching stage movement to actors, Walker has contributed to making it an academic discipline presently acknowledged as essential to the actor's formation.

Mime Expands

A number of mimes who worked in the 1960s and early 1970s are important to the continuation and growth of mime in America. Some performed on stage and also toured. These and others taught the young movement artists who would become the next generation of mimes.

Claude Kipnis trained with Marcel Marceau and founded a mime school in Tel Aviv. After his first mime show, *Men and Dreams*, performed in Israel in 1962, Kipnis staged several productions at the Boston Opera Company in 1966 and 1967, such as *The Miraculous Mandarin*. His Mime Theatre company appeared on American TV, and his piece *Au Clair de la Lune*, a space trip set to music; his mime sketch *Point of View*; and his pantomimic versions of Igor Stravinsky's *Renard* and *l'Histoire du Soldat* joined mime to music. Kipnis published *The Mime Book* (1974), an introduction to mime theory and practice.

Tony Montanaro, a former Marcel Marceau and Etienne Decroux student in the 1950s, began the Montanaro Mime Theatre School in South Paris, Maine, in 1972, which produced several national touring companies. He also founded the Celebration Theatre Ensemble, acquired by his associates Carolyn Brett and Leland Faulkner in 1988, which stages experimental works by new playwrights and composers. At the Celebration Barn Theatre, Montanaro taught workshops in mime, storytelling, voice, fight performance, clowning, masks, *commedia*, and other forms to develop creativity in the performing artist. A pantomimist, storyteller, and improvisational actor, he first gained national attention in the 1960s with his show *A Mime's Eyeview*, which included folk tales, fantasies, and selections from literature using voice, music, narrative, and movement. During this time, he wrote, hosted, and performed in *Pretendo*, an award-winning improvisational mime show for CBS-TV in Philadelphia. His popular stage piece, *Mime Spoken Here,* presents a guided tour of theatre, mime, storytelling, and improvisation. In 1985, Montanaro played Zoug the storyteller in the film *Clan of the Cave Bear*. He then performed with his wife, Karen Hurll, in their Montanaro-Hurll Theatre.

After studying with Israeli mime Shai K. Ophir, a former Marceau student who performed in the master's style, Schlomo Bachar toured the United States with Ophir in 1959 and appeared in New York in 1960 in the pantomimes *Flamenco Dancer* and *Cigarettes*.

Juki Arkin came to New York from Israel to perform in the comedy sketches *American Tourist in Israel* and *Dancing the Hora*. In 1963, Arkin and his company staged *The Laughing Man* and *The Pioneer from Brooklyn City,* depicting a Brooklyn boy's first experience in a kibbutz.

Moni Yakim trained with Decroux and, after joining his New York school, performed in his newly founded mime company. After Decroux left New York, Yakim opened his own school and mime company, and by 1975 he was director of the Pantomime Theatre of New York. In 1967, Yakim also established the movement section of New York's Juilliard Drama Division, where he has since taught. Besides utilizing the Decroux technique to teach actors movement, he incorporated it into his own system of physical acting, contained in his book *Creating a Character: A Physical Approach to Acting.* Yakim directed the original production of *Jacques Brel Is Alive and Well and Living in Paris* and was movement director of the movie *Robocop* and two sequels.

Decroux Corporeal Mimes beyond the 1960s

Thomas Leabhart

Until the 1980s, Thomas Leabhart was among the purists of Etienne Decroux's corporeal mime. After studying and teaching at Decroux's Paris school from 1968 to 1972, Leabhart returned to America to found his Corporeal Mime Theatre company and teach at several American universities, including Pomona College in California. Meanwhile, he performed with his company and in solo pieces, as well as conducted workshops throughout America, Canada, and Mexico. In 1974, he founded the first mime magazine in America, *Mime Journal*, and also edited *Mime News* and *Mime, Mask and Marionette*. In 1989, he published his book *Modern and Post-Modern Mime*. He was a founding member and president of the National Mime Association, established in 1986.

Among the first pieces Leabhart performed was Decroux's *Washerwoman,* which evokes both universal and concrete images of the female worker, and *Carpenter,* a study of the artisan dedicated to his craft. Both works reflect corporeal mime as the champion of manual workers. They also portray the muscular drama of man's struggle against gravity, the source of his tragic destiny.

In *Table, Chair, Glass Suite*, created and arranged by Leabhart and his company, two mimes play with a table, a chair, and a glass, moving from serious passages to comedy, from legato to staccato rhythms, from light, frenetic movements to solemn, statuary attitudes. Facial expressions, seldom seen in corporeal mime, heighten the piece's spontaneity and comic aspects. Throughout, there is a minimum of text, music, costumes, and lighting effects.

Sudden Arrivals, Brusque Departures marks a transition from the exclusive use of corporeal mime to the inclusion of a text. In this satire of modern life, which blends poetry with ironic reality, body attitudes punctuate the rhythmic patterns of words that Leabhart wrote. At one point, the protagonist, lying on his back like a Greek warrior at rest, relates that an airplane transports a lady passenger while she busily chews on Life Savers and does crossword puzzles. If the plane thus symbolizes a poem that transports the passenger to new worlds, the question arises as to whether the artist's work might similarly transport the spectator.

In *How I Was Perplexed and What I Did About It* and *We Can Outrun a Train, or The Rose Colored Valley We Knew,* which includes slides and music, Leabhart integrates mime with storytelling. Through corporeal mime and narration, he satirizes his own evolution as a mime artist and examines the current image of mime. In *Like, Is There a Difference between Abstract and Bizarre?* the spectator is offered a guided tour of Southern California's shopping malls by means of slides and abstract movement sequences with comments on the ecological state of our world, in which animals are sacrificed for lab testing and forests for grazing cattle. Asymmetrical and abrupt movements illustrate humorous content combined with Decroux technique. *A Simple Thing* (1996), based on a text by Gertrude Stein and with music by Erik Satie and Virgil Thomson, juxtaposes movement, consisting of sudden shifts of weight, emphasis, and imbalance, upon Stein's repetitive words on memory, resemblance, confusion, and loss. Leabhart's pieces, like Daniel Stein's works, derive from cubist-inspired techniques.

Leabhart's tightly constructed and synchronized style is based on an articulate physical language in which the body is used like a keyboard. As gestures dissolve into attitudes to create a statuary effect, each flawlessly composed and thoroughly distilled attitude flows into another. Here, the mime does not imitate life in the ancient Greek sense of the term. His is an aesthetic representation of life, a statue come to life. Nonrealistic in form, Leabhart's art is nonetheless concrete in that the mime's body remains the prime reality.

This balance of movement and content in a continuous process of perfection evokes the classic ideal. Théophile Gautier's poem *Art,* in which he tells the poet to continuously "carve, polish, and chisel his floating dream until it is sealed in the hard block,"[3] comes to mind. Transparent movement and content, also fundamental to classicism, recall José Ortega y Gasset's ideal that art be full clarity, high noon of the intellect. Such clarity is never light or frivolous. Leabhart's work is an *art difficile* that arrives at clear expression through labor and effort, endowing it with a noble and philosophical spirit. And like all corporeal mime expressing universal concepts, his art negates feeling to allow the spectator to create his own emotions.

Leabhart describes his art as the simplification and amplification of everyday movement. His mime–actor aspires to become the instrument of his own movements, which carve space and color time. His juxtapositions of lines and dynamic qualities surprise and show weight, resistance, and the hesitation inherent in drama. Through collective or solo improvisation, unanticipated movement that evokes sudden concepts springs from one sequence to a previously arranged one, altering itself *ad infinitum,* forever sparking new images. In true Decroux spirit, Leabhart continues the quest for a poetic vocabulary and an articulate corporeal grammar to achieve a keenly defined and well-grounded lyricism.

Concerning his years of devotion to mime, Leabhart says:

> Everyone has to do something. Some people collect stamps. Others play golf. I do mime. I like to perform it, teach it, write about it, talk about it and see it as often as possible, in all its varied theatrical and non-theatrical manifestations, in the theatre or in the street. As Decroux often joked, one has to do something between breakfast and lunch, and something between lunch and dinner!
>
> It's really not a bad way to spend one's time. It does not pollute, it keeps the imagination and the body supple (more or less) and usually gives pleasure to the performer if not always to the spectator. It may not be the universal language, as some claim, but it's probably not as detrimental to mental health as watching television. So there may be some advantage in keeping it around, at least for a few more years![4]

Leonard Pitt

Born in 1941 in Detroit, Michigan, Pitt abandoned a successful career in commercial art to do whiteface pantomime—against his friend Stan Laurel's advice. After studying corporeal mime and teaching it for four years at Decroux's school, he performed in children's theatre in France and conducted workshops there and in Switzerland. In Denmark, he worked with Decroux-trained Yves Lebreton at his Studio II. In 1970, he opened the Leonard Pitt Mime School in Berkeley, California, where he performed and gave lecture–demonstrations. He went to Bali in 1973 to study Topeng mask theatre with I Nyoman Kakul and perform in village and temple festivals. From 1975 on, he toured, appearing in his own works and in two George Coates Performance Art pieces. In 1986, he became artistic director of Life on the Water, an experimental theatre venue in San Francisco. In 1991, he produced a program entitled *Eco-Rap*, a Bay Area rap contest based on ecological themes. Besides teaching mime at his own Mime, Mask, and Theatre School, he has taught at San Francisco State University and lectured on mime and mask theatre throughout America.

Although Pitt began as one of the foremost exponents of Decroux mime, he soon moved away from exclusively practicing abstract corporeal mime to explore other kinds of physical theatre. For Pitt, Balinese mask theatre was—as it had been for Antonin Artaud—a revelation, changing the direction of his teaching, his mime style, and that of his company. He discovered elements in common between Decroux mime and Balinese dance, such as the use of isolated movements, punctuated rhythms, and geometric spatial arrangements. To these Decroux elements he added Balinese and other types of masks, dialogue, costumes, props, percussion music, and lighting effects. He adapted his Decroux grammar to a vocabulary of technical and improvisational skills that could be used in conventional, experimental, or any type of theatre.

His solo pieces *Doppo, Clown of Yesteryear* (1975), awarded a Bay Area Theatre Critics Award in 1980, and *2019 Blake Street* (1977) integrate the masks and movement of Balinese Theatre with commedia dell'arte, vaudeville, and corporeal mime. Choreographed by George Coates, *2019 Blake Street* depicts mature mischievousness through Decroux-style mime unleashed, masks, surrealist dreams, vocal sounds, happenings, and mime–clowning. *Doppo, Clown of Yesteryear* is a modern version of Pantalone in which *lazzi* and dialogue integrate to develop a caricature of an old, French ham entertainer with a Marseilles accent.

In the George Coates Performance Art pieces *The Way of How* (1981) and *Are Are* (1983), Pitt interacts with a composer and two opera singers in a blending of polished physical theatre and abstract performance art with visual and aural effects. As in postmodern art, when unconventionally juxtaposed, dissimilar visual and aural elements collide, forming an ambiguous ensemble that cannot be categorized or identified by a single style and that remains open to multiple interpretations. Pitt's *Meantime* (1984) is an autobiographical work with masks, movement, clown art, vaudeville, and projection visuals. Its underlying theme is the artist's struggle to safeguard his individuality against the onslaught of media information continually programming his way of thinking. *Not For Real* (1987), created and directed with Rinde Eckert, continues some of the themes of *Meantime* concerning the control of technology over modern man, his alienation from other humans, and his mind–body split, which is reintegrated by becoming one with Mother Earth. Here, movement is allied with words in a highly imaginative and absurdist physical theatre. *Spleenex*, recreated in 1988, is a collection of humorous movement and verbal sketches. Playwright David Barth's *Ned* (1991), in which a talkative mobster copes with his girlfriend's suicide, was Pitt's first attempt to physicalize a character in a script. *Seduction* (1997), a physical theatre piece directed by Rinde Eckert and performed with mime–dancer Ruth Zaporah, explores the relationship between a man and a woman.

Pitt's art moved from modern, Decroux-style mime as an autonomous movement form to a postmodern synthesis of movement, masks, props, costumes, and dialogue. Based on a total command of the body as instrument, the art of the mime–actor, not dependent upon a text, here created a new and unconventional *commedia* form. Blending Decroux technique and codified movement with poetic content, Pitt sought a natural movement expression free of any aesthetic. Of this natural movement, he writes:

> Watch a candle's flame. Every movement that we perceive on the outside is a direct expression of something taking place inside. It never betrays itself, not for a moment. All the different aspects of the phenomenon flow together; the heat, energy, light, color, movement. There is no antagonism of forces. The only tension which exists is the tension necessary for its own natural functioning. It is natural tension, organic tension, like the natural tension and relaxation of a plant. Any tension in the organism that is unnecessary for its natural functioning will inhibit the flow of energy outward.
>
> Natural movement is like a plant. It does not obey an aesthetic. A plant does not try to express anything. It merely functions and in its function is its being. Its only expression is its life. Natural movement is very soft but also very solid and powerful. The energy exudes from the center encompassing the whole body with all its parts flowing together in the movement. In order to feel the movement you have to find your source lower in the body so you are guided by something else other than the ego.[5]

Daniel Stein

From his Decroux training, corporeal mime Daniel Stein extracted and developed one of the purest, most poetic of movement expressions. After studying acting with former Decroux student Jewel Walker at Carnegie Mellon University in Pittsburgh and ballet with Suzanne Oussov, Stein trained with Decroux in France from 1973 to

1976. In 1978, *Timepiece*, premiered at the Milwaukee Mime Festival, was the first of Stein's creations to reveal the intensity and nobility of corporeal mime. Since 1976, he has also acted in and directed such plays as *The Oedipus Project*, staged at the Milwaukee Repertory Theatre, founded a Corporeal Mime School based both in Paris and Studio City, California, and performed and taught throughout Europe and the United States.

In *Timepiece*, based on the passage of time in the life of a man, Stein, clothed in a full-length knit suit, moves from one sculptured attitude to another, his body resembling that of a statue of a Greek athlete. With majestic and sensual movements, he interacts with chairs, ropes, discs, and a swinging plumb line to evoke intricate movements of a clock and the passing of time. Animating these objects like a puppeteer, at one point he has two chairs seemingly swaying and interacting on their own.

In *Scenes Apparent*, first performed with David Shoemaker in New York in 1981, while reading a book entitled *The Nude*, Stein falls asleep and his dreams spring to life. From gray foam blocks, he creates triangles, squares, pyramids, a bird, a boat, and a woman, with whom he becomes obsessed. Stein and Shoemaker continue to shape the blocks, creating a wellspring of images and emotions, and then don masks of a fussy rooster and a cat. Here, mime and masks fuse allegory with stark realism. His autobiographical piece *Windowspeak* (1989) contrasts American, French, and Japanese culture through corporeal mime, acting techniques, and animation of objects.

Stein creates architectural rhythms that dictate how the piece develops. Yet, his technique is transparent, leaving the audience with clear, powerful images—ones that, like a well-struck chord, resonate across space and inside each individual. His work depicts tragic conflicts between man and his destiny. In *Timepiece*, for example, the objects on stage play dreamlike roles, becoming virtual characters that evolve in time's ceaseless flow as Stein explores it, donning masks of young and old, future, and present.

Although his art is often categorized as abstract, Stein believes that, because it deals with clear and comprehensible themes, it is concrete. Because it is concerned with principle and form rather than with a mimetic interpretation of reality, he prefers to describe his aesthetic as cubist. Like the cubist painters, Stein's polished images are broken down into sharp, blocklike, geometrical fragments in which his clean-cut, juxtaposed lines convey emotions and thoughts. Even the props he animates continue the articulate flow of his body attitudes. And, again, his sculptured forms always transcend technique to embody philosophical concepts that challenge the barriers of time and place. Angular and arduous movement suggests that our destiny is to cope with malaise. And, rather than impart this silent message overtly, Stein's use of ambiguities allows his audience to "overhear" ideas rather than be bombarded with doctrine.

Despite its metaphysical content, Stein's work does not lack humor. In *Timepiece*, his casual play with a plumb line provokes laughter because the object is set in an unconventional orbit. He also upsets expectations by abandoning an object, such as a chair, which then seemingly twirls all by itself behind his back. For Stein, the meaning is deeper when delivered comically.

The arm, hand, or facial movements of Stein's antinarrative creations never contain, in Decroux's words, any "idle talk." Rather, his entire body becomes an instrument from which he extracts magic and poetry. Stein plays on the strings of his body as on a cello. From the shapes, tones, and rhythms of his body movements, he extracts the most solemn of metaphors. In his own words, "Our future lies with metaphor and poetry—even if our choice is concrete or comic."[6] Even props turn into metaphors, such as the plumb line in *Timepiece,* which represents truth and clarity, while the chairs symbolize strength. In Stein's physicalized poems, in which he orchestrates sculptural forms with the utmost simplicity, the body and real objects interact in tense, concentrated, and dynamically geometric patterns. Meanwhile, an inner, chronometric rhythm lends unity and harmonious flow to his highly structured movement compositions.

Stein shares his views on what movement theatre means to him:

> I see movement theatre like an opera, where the soul is massaged by the tide of overwhelming emotions that caress and mold our humanity. I love opera because the instrument is the message. I don't go to see *La Boheme* countless times hoping that the story will change and Mimi won't die. I go back time and time again to be moved by that human voice that is the quintessential human condition. Whether that voice is the cry of anguish or that of delight, it is the bare sound of what we all share, our humanity. In so many ways, movement theatre is exactly that same thing. But, alas, the general public has yet to see it in this way, for what I think are two basic reasons. First, they may believe that dance fills this role. I suppose I see dance less like an opera and more like a symphony, where the spirit is moved by the ebb and flow of the dynamic energy. I enjoy a symphony, but I love opera. The second reason I think the general public doesn't know what they are missing in movement theatre is due to the confusion created by whiteface pantomime, which has had such broad exposure thanks to Marcel Marceau and via the television.[7,8]

Margolis Brown Adaptors

Kari Margolis and Tony Brown first met in the mid-1970s at Étienne Decroux's school of corporeal mime in Paris. After training with Decroux, they toured internationally for seven years, including four years with the Montreal-based movement theatre company Omnibus. In 1982, they established their school in New York and by 1983 had formed their ensemble company, Margolis Brown Adaptors. Because their content satirized aspects of American culture, they named their company Adaptors, a term derived from the technological function of devices that fit parts together.

In their first movement piece, *Aeroglyphics,* created for video in 1983, Margolis and Brown introduced toy jet bombers and destroyer robots to symbolize humanity's naive relationship with technology, a theme that later became the tenet of their major stage work, *Autobahn* (1984). As with all their pieces, Margolis and Brown choreographed and directed *Autobahn.* It is composed of a series of twelve scenes that parody—through dramatic ensemble movement, video, props, multilayered and digitally processed soundtracks, singing, and text—the America of Nixon's era, the first landings on the moon, women's liberation, the armament frenzy, sexual liberation, the threat of nuclear war, pop culture, consumerism, and other aspects of the American Dream in reverse. As though moving full-speed on a freeway with fast-changing landscapes, the spectator is bombarded with one image after another that lampoons these modern dilemmas. To spoof the social conformity of the 1930s, 1940s, and 1950s, movement artists with life-sized cardboard dolls portray such American fetishes as the ironing board (the idol of women of the period); here, the hair dryer is transformed into an erotic object to which a female protagonist succumbs. In this highly visual and kinetic piece, every theatrical device is used to portray our fast-moving, chaotic twentieth-century society, in which technology as the ultimate end never equals fulfillment.

Decodanz (1986) further extends the limits of the multimedia aesthetic found in *Autobahn*. It ranges from a caricature of the gold-chain machismo set, to self-parodying TV game-show images, to the more serious ironies of the blood-sucking crassness of American culture. It depicts love, marriage, and death made into media events. Margolis and Brown play a vampirish couple whose brief, unsatisfying interludes weave through the production like TV commercials, satirizing the superficiality of Hollywood and its influence on American romance, marriage, dress, and hair styles. The piece literalizes the gap between myth and reality.

In *The Bed Experiment One* (1987), a great white bed serves as the central prop on and around which four men and women, equalized by white body makeup and black wigs, wrestle with the rituals of being awake and alive. Billed as a bizarre nature documentary, the piece features the players, silent except for an occasional grunt or animal-like scream, who aggressively move through a series of emotional movement tableaux, like a mime–ballet, portraying the insanity of being Homo sapiens—from birth's innocence, through desire and love, to disease, death, and rebirth. With graphic and disturbing realism, the movement exposes scenes around the bed, which undergo a series of metamorphoses. One moment it is a hospital bed, the next a love nest. It later becomes a wrestling mat and a hell in which two gangs war. For the community of men who inhabit the great white bed, it is a lifeboat for human civilization or, as Margolis and Brown call it, the last "icon of the past." The piece has a provocative soundtrack. The audience hears facts about the animal kingdom and observations on the beginning of the universe, sounds of rain, a chorus of angelic voices, a Frédéric Chopin ballad, and a tolling bell. In a society where rituals are no longer rites but have become rote and the electronic media dictate our thoughts and reactions, dreams are the last untouched frontier. The piece was awarded a Bessie New York Dance and Performance Award in 1987.

Suite Sixteen (1987) surrounds the audience with peaceful, juvenile images and choreography designed to disarm. Masked players identically outfitted in knickers and suspenders and skirts and blouses interact with large red rubber balls, a skipping rope, or tiny chairs to act out their experiences, conveying an eerie sense of disquietude. These prototypical children move through sixteen choreographed vignettes, each of which highlights a point in childhood, such as parental roles, early lessons, and the discovery of sex. The piece obliges the spectator to reexamine his own amusing and disturbing childhood experiences.

Koppelvision and Other Digital Deities (1992) poignantly and humorously comments on the power of specific media-generated images and personalities to create belief and fact from mere superstition. By overlapping modern and medieval images within the choreography, costumes, video projections, even in the sets themselves—as in the scene where modern-looking couples have simultaneous phone conversations about love, business, and gossip while standing, kneeling, or leaning on ancient church pews—Margolis and Brown make the technodeity a kind of false prophet. From actors undergoing a dance of self-inflicted suffering, to the humming of electric razors with which they shave off every inch of body hair, to overwrought churchgoers looking to a lunar orb for meaning and finding reassurance in the face of Ted Koppel—depicted as a nighttime news anchorman with a deceptively calm and reassuring voice—Margolis and Brown mix media to create a surrealistic tableau in which illusions mingle with reality and ancient superstitions with modern myths.

Café Paradise (1992) is a multimedia extravaganza in which the audience sits at cabaret tables sipping exotic refreshments and watching movement theatre, performed to live music. *Vidpires* (1998) portrays through dance, mime, theatre, and multimedia two vampires obsessed with eternal youth who, like Hollywood stars, refuse to age.

The art of Kari Margolis and Tony Brown, based on a codified grammar of movement, Decroux technique, and original choreography, allies powerful ensemble movement imagery with satirical content. Beneath perfected bodily expression is a biting pastiche about the deceptions of modern materialism, harmonizing, as in classical art, well-worked form with challenging content. Beyond this, their work is a well-proportioned blend of multimedia and rich forms, from light satire to tragedy, from vaudeville to abstract corporeal movement theatre, and from musical comedy and cabaret to video and image theatre. Through a variety of styles and artistic expressions, a juxtaposition of provocative metaphors, and a barrage of theatrical effects and technological elements depicting the disarray of our times, Kari Margolis, Tony Brown, and their ensemble company represent postmodernism at its very best.

Bert Houle and Veera Wibaux Mime Theatre

Two mimes who have continued to work with both corporeal mime and traditional pantomime are Bert Houle and Veera Wibaux, who met at Decroux's school in 1968. Joining careers, they staged mime pieces, taught residencies in the United States and abroad, and in 1982 opened a school, where they also trained mimes for their own company. While many of their pieces contain universal themes and Decroux-style mime, they also include conventional mime. *The Seeker,* which depicts the hero's mystical quest for spiritual fulfillment, incorporates traditional mime. Through nonfigurative movement by the entire body as well as pantomiming by specific parts of the body to concretize such arts as dance, music, and poetry, *The Muse* depicts a dove that gives birth to art. In *Homage to Sculpture,* which portrays javelin- and discus-throwing, one statuelike pose dissolves into another through arrested movement, establishing a parallel between mime and sculpture. In *Love Dance,* the dancer's repeated and explicit elevations before his imaginary beloved enhance the work's lyrical quality. In *Lover's Suicide*, conventional pantomime conveys specific images of the rejected lover who tries to commit suicide by tickling himself to death.

The soul-searching and spiritually challenging content of Houle and Wibaux's work achieves a classical unity and beauty of form while remaining true to both Decroux-style and traditional mime. In their full-length ensemble pieces, *Pilgrimage* (1987) and *Arcana* (1989), mime, pantomime, grandiose masks, symbolic costumes, lighting effects, Byzantine chants, Indian ragas, Bach fugues, and Paul Dresher's original compositions are all part of a journey into the inner self to explore various states of mind and emotions. Because of the highly mystical elements of these creations, the uninitiated would be impervious to this visual symphony of mobile sculpture. Yet, the sheer beauty of the movement and the dramatized inner spiritual search of this mime theatre offer an aesthetically and spiritually engaging experience.

Robert Fleshman and Mime Therapy

Robert Fleshman became interested in movement theatre through his readings on the movement theories of Edward Gordon Craig and Isadora Duncan. From 1957 to 1959, he studied corporeal mime with Etienne Decroux in New York and worked under Drid Williams in neuromuscular reeducation and later in human movement anthropology. He also trained in psychodrama under J. L. Moreno. In 1968, he began teaching mime and drama therapy at Loyola University (New Orleans) in one of the few United States undergraduate programs of this kind.

Fleshman's works marked by Decroux-style mime are *The Beach Comber, Prayer, Mime Combat, Psalm of David, The Sea as Metaphor, Chinese Jugglers, Flower Children, Creation of Eve, Temptation of Eve, Masking, The Courtesans,* and *St. Sebastian.* Some of these pieces were created out of group improvisation and incorporate masks and ritualistic movement.

In 1975, Fleshman began a mime conservatory, which offered mime classes, a film documentation center, mime articles and books, a performance ensemble, and performances and workshops by guest-artists. Mime and videotapes stored at the conservatory were shown at mime festivals in 1973 and 1976.

Fleshman's mime and movement therapy research includes the publication of *The Arts in Therapy* with Jerry Fryrear (1981) and the editing of a multicultural movement study, *Theatrical Movement: A Bibliographical Anthology* (1986).

On mime as an integral part of the human being, Fleshman said in the 1980s:

> I interpret teaching to mean to make sense out of life or to give shape and form to life, which also includes the artistic form. Healing seems to mean "to make whole again," which also carries the concept of form. The hidden part of the Commandment to "go forth" and teach and heal is perhaps the most difficult; to struggle forward in spite of handicaps, or even in some cases talents, and move in a consistent direction. The human being is one complete organism, with silver-like threads (the nervous system) connecting the body and the mind. Along these strings flow images in a special code which the human mind and body can decipher, either consciously or unconsciously.[9]

In the 1990s, he added:

> Reflecting on the state of the art of mime, it has become more difficult to think in terms of a linear line forward. The world has always revolved around the sun, but the cultural circles have grown quite wide and wild in their whirling. The mime as a part of the cultural circles touches upon and sometimes clashes into other forms, creating spin offs with circles and vibrations of their own. What seems to be needed is to find a way to struggle back in an inward direction centripetally, with a stringent mime technique and a kind of internal mime, in search of a new sense of center. The simultaneous encircling, outward and inward, may act somewhat like a gyroscope to help us stand upright and avoid falling into a very deep black hole.[10]

E. Reid Gilbert

A number of Decroux students have adopted, along with their performance skills, careers as mime administrators and teachers. In 1978, E. Reid Gilbert, founder and director of the Valley Studio and the Wisconsin Mime Theatre, organized the Festival of American Mime in Milwaukee, which presented mime artists, panels, and workshops from America as well as abroad. From 1975 to 1979, he was administrator of the International Mimes and Pantomimists. Gilbert, who also studied modern dance with Charles Weidman, conducted workshops in mime, illusion pantomime, and mask work. After retiring from Ohio State University in 1994, he reincorporated the Valley Studio into his Valley Ridge Studio in West Virginia and developed his regional storytelling with *Tucker Tales.*

Gilbert's performance work has ranged from Appalachian storyteller, to playwright, to stage director of Asian scripts. Aside from creating pantomime sketches such as *The Bird,* his solo work-in-progress *Oedipus at Home* (1993) offers a humorous Appalachian version of the Greek hero. Through storytelling and mime, the piece unravels in a balloon vendor's small apartment, with balloons representing Agamemnon, Clytemnestra, and the people of Athens while a TV set with a recording of Gilbert's prophesying voice represents the Oracle of Delphi.

Gilbert has contributed to establishing mime not as an exclusive art but as a solid foundation for all theatre performance, as well as for multicultural understanding. His teaching has corroborated Stanislavsky's contention that acting starts with movement choices.

Kuperberg Morris Movement Theater

Rich Kuperberg, founder and artistic director of the Kuperberg Morris Movement Theater, later renamed Ko-Motion, trained with Decroux and with corporeal artists Steven and Corinne Wasson, Jean Asselin, Denise Boulanger, and George Molnar. To his corporeal mime style he added dance and clowning techniques that he learned with the José Limón company, Sophie Maslow, Bond Street Theatre Coalition, and Avner the Eccentric. Ann Morris, who studied modern dance with the José Limón company and Twyla Tharp and corporeal mime with Decroux and Steven and Corinne Wasson, joined the company in 1981. Their New York company toured art centers, colleges, and schools with a dance–mime style that mixes serious content with light comedy and modern dance choreography. It has also created pieces combining laser art, pantomotion, and movement theatre and collaborated with other artists including musicians, a sculpture artist, and a painter. *Vectors* (1981) makes use of elastic straps connected to the arms and legs to symbolize the relationship between two people battling gravity and supporting each other while dealing with their own emotional baggage. Among the company's other major works are *Endangered Species* (1984), *Night Exhibit* (1989), and *Gold* (1991). *Night Exhibit* takes place in a museum after the public has gone home and inflatable sculptures come alive to compete with other media such as TV for attention. *Gold,* the company's first work with scripted verbal content, reflects social and psychological effects of a family in a cultureless, materialistic society, too busy to communicate with one another. *Chocolate* (1997) is an arts and technology collaboration with inventor Michael Carlito, featuring programmed infrared sensors that are released by movement. The desire for the sweet taste of chocolate symbolizes our dreams as we work to survive, constantly "whipping that lazy horse," as Decroux would always remind us to do.

William Fisher

Among other Decroux-trained mimes, William Fisher, head of the undergraduate acting program at Ohio University School of Theatre, studied with Decroux for five years and was his assistant. With Fanny de Sousa, he co-founded the Zeta Collective, an artist-run consortium dedicated to contemporary theatre performance and exploration. His performance and directing credits include early Zeta Collective productions of Franz Kafka's *A Report to an Academy*, the *Half Life* solos series, and *Crowd Work* by Paul N. Jones, performed by de Sousa. *Mime Flesh, Mime Bone, Flute Fabrics* (1989), one of the *Half Life* solos, is based on Ellen Schimmel's structured improvisation for solo flute. Fisher's ensemble pieces are the Zeta Collective's *Myths of Freedom* trilogy—I *Freedom of Information*; II *Ready? Begin!*; and III *Uncivil Liberties*—and *Hype: PerFORMance*, staged at the Los Angeles Contemporary Exhibitions. As in Fisher's other corporeal mime–based works, *Freedom of Information* (1989) unites corporeal mime with verbal theatre, poetry, music, and performance art. The work was created through solo and collective improvisation, with precise, geometric movement to depict the effects of the media on the individual. In 1995, the Zeta Collective created *Human Rites,* an international performance project based on travel to Slovakia, South Africa, and Great Britain, and a piece with co-director de Sousa and poet John Lane entitled *Virtual Memory.*

A Tribute to Decroux

In the summer of 1993, under the auspices of Movement Theatre International (MIT) in Philadelphia, in tribute to Decroux after his death in 1991, a festival of performances, master classes, panels, lectures, films, a photographic exhibit, and a showcase with awards for new mime talent revealed Decroux's influence on the theatre artists and students of his time and the expansion of that influence into postmodern movement theatre. The Théâtre de l'Ange Fou from France reconstructed Decroux's creations in *The Man Who Preferred to Stand,* first presented at an MIT pilot program in Philadelphia in the spring of 1992. This reconstruction of works that had not been viewed since Decroux performed at Carnegie Hall in 1960 included *La Méditation*, *L'Usine*, *Le Combat Antique*, *Duo Amoureux II*, *Le Menuisier*, *La Femme Oiseau*, *L'Esprit Malin*, *La Lavandière*, *Duo Amoureux dans le Parc*, *Le Fauteil de l'Absent*, *Le Prophète*, and *Les Arbres.* Two of Decroux's ex-students, Dulcinea Langfelder in *Vicious Circle* and Daniel Stein in *Timepiece*, were hailed as exponents of pure corporeal mime. The Decroux-trained Margolis Brown Adaptors performed *Koppelvision and Other Digital Deities,* which satirizes the bizarre universe of the media. Frits Vogel of the Decroux movement-based Griftheater from Amsterdam staged *Sa Griffe,* composed of sensual plastic images inspired by the dadaist, surrealist painter–photographer Man Ray's *Objects of My Affection* and performed in various areas of an old church gymnasium. Eugenio Barba's mime fantasy *The Castle of Holstebro*, a mystical wedding between Shakespeare's Ophelia and Yorick, featured Julia Varley. The event was a tribute to Decroux as the father of modern corporeal mime.

Mimes Unlimited

Since the mid-twentieth century, mimes and companies have developed mime styles that evolve from their training with various mime masters and have utilized their art for diverse purposes.

   The mimes and companies mentioned in this section are only a handful of those who perform and teach primarily in America. There are many others who have studied with the French masters or their trainees or have derived styles from other sources.

Born in Holland, Francisco Reynders studied in Paris with Decroux before coming to the United States in 1956 to be a scenic artist in New York and tour as a solo mime. In 1967, he accepted a teaching position at Lewis and Clark College in Portland, Oregon. Then, in 1974, with two of his mime students—Elizabeth Page and Burl Ross—he founded the Oregon Mime Theatre, which toured the United States and Europe, performing for both adult and student audiences.

Japanese-born Yass Hakoshima, who studied mime with Decroux and modern dance with Erick Hawkins, began performing in New York in 1967 and, after opening his Yass Hakoshima Theatre in 1976, appeared throughout the United States and abroad. To the Western techniques of Decroux mime, pantomime, and modern dance, Hakoshima added the fatalism and intensity of Japanese theatre. *Eagle* (1964) depicts a wounded eagle that rises again; *Puppet* (1972) offers political comment as a wooden marionette frees itself from bondage; *Spell* (1977) is based on Japanese allegory; *Insane Shogun* (1987) portrays a powerful ruler who fights invisible enemies; and *Cocoon* (1989) is a symbolic work about an insect emerging from its cocoon. Hakoshima's later works include ceramic sculptures by Toshiko Takaezu and live music by traditional Japanese drummers.

Samuel Avital, who studied mime with Étienne Decroux, Jean-Louis Barrault, and Marcel Marceau, toured Europe in the 1960s with Maximilien Decroux's company and performed in solo mime. In 1971, he founded a mime school entitled Le Centre du Silence in Boulder, Colorado, and from 1972 to 1982, established and directed the Boulder Mime Theatre, which toured locally and nationally. His Avital Integrated Method, later called Body Speak and based on principles of Decroux mime, integrates body and mind to achieve personal harmony.

Former director of the Actor's Mime Theatre in Wichita, Kansas, Ron Wilson taught mime and acting and directed movement and theatre productions throughout the United States.

Louis H. Campbell, who wrote a doctoral dissertation on selected mime philosophies and techniques ranging from 1954 to 1974 (see bibliography), has performed and taught mime, pantomime, *commedia*, mask, acting, and stage movement and has directed. Campbell, who has worked in seventeen countries, has published articles on mime and movement for actors and was director of the First International Mime Institute and Festival in Lacrosse, Wisconsin, in 1974.

Polish-born Stefan Niedzialkowski's dance–dramas *Facets of Life* and *Beret* are influenced by Henryk Tomaszewski's Polish Mime Theatre, with which he performed for twelve years before opening his American School of Polish Mime in New York. In *Facets of Life,* Niedzialkowski weaves mime, dance, drama, and eroticism into a grandiose work. In *Beret,* he satirizes misused political power and abuse of the common man by manipulating his hands with different-colored gloves, like a puppeteer.

In Leningrad in 1961, Edward Rozinsky—pantomimist, actor and stage director—organized one of the first pantomime ensembles in the Soviet Union, which toured Europe. He also began a professional pantomime school at the Leningrad Theatrical Institute. He taught stage movement, pantomime, and acting in New York and directed the movement in several off-off-Broadway productions. After teaching movement and acting at the University of Miami, he founded a children's theatre company in that city. His *Public Telephone* (1978) is a cleverly constructed illusion-type pantomime about a man locked in a telephone booth. Traditional pantomime, clowning, and Russian folklore characterize *The Stubborn Donkey* and *Oh*, in which the protagonist dances with a puppet composed of a female mask, a coat hanger, and a dress.

Dan Kamin, author of *Charlie Chaplin's One-Man Show* (1991), performed magic at age twelve and, after seeing Chaplin's films, has toured in whiteface pantomime since 1970. His *Confessions of an Illusionist* (1990), which exposes the performer's tricks and the grim life of touring, was the hit of the 1990 London International Mime Festival. *The Corpozoid Man*, also performed at the 1990 festival, reveals the secrets of a prestidigitator's sleight of hand. Kamin choreographed movement, created comedy sequences for the film, and trained actor Robert Downey, Jr., in *Chaplin* (1992) and actress Lisa Marie in *Mars Attacks!* (1996), appearing in *Chaplin* as a Keystone cop and as the wooden Indian in *Creepshow 2*.

Born and raised in Chicago, T. Daniel began training in mime with Marceau and Decroux in 1969. After he premiered *A World of Mime* in 1971, he performed at colleges and in communities throughout the United States and created visual interpretations of symphonic works for such orchestras as the Chicago Symphony. He has taught mime at his Studio of Mime in Chicago since 1972.

A former student of Tony Montanaro, Maryland native Thomas Casciero performed with the Towson State Mime Troupe in 1975 before playing in solo mime. In *Fool's Gold* (1985) and *My Sad Face* (1986), he revealed his eclectic talents for mime, acting, and European-style clowning. A certified movement analyst in Laban Theory and Practice, he has taught mime and body awareness to the learning disabled, the blind, and persons with emotional problems, as well as mime, improvisation, and movement to actors at Towson State University in Maryland.

After training in mime with Richmond Shepard in 1975, Gregg Goldston established the Rocky Mountain Mime Alliance in Salt Lake City, Utah, which grew into the Goldston Mime Foundation and the Goldston and Johnson School for Mimes after it moved to Gambier, Ohio, in 1980. The foundation and school aim to preserve and develop the art, artists, and audience of mime. Their Invisible People Mime Theatre, founded in 1987, has performed group, solo, and guest-artist works in Ohio and on tour. Their work in contemporary classical mime stems from the styles of Decroux, Marceau, and artists such as Stefan Niedzialkowski, Moni Yakim, Claude Kipnis, Gregg Goldston, and C. Nicholas Johnson. In their repertory of both whiteface and nonwhiteface pieces are *Writers Block* (1985); *Angels Rising* (1987), which depicts man's competitive nature throughout history; *Act Two* (1990), a classical mime duet with Goldston and Pamela Chermansky ranging from the comic to the poetic; *One Mime Show* (1978); and other sketches by Goldston entitled *The Umbrella*, *The Derby*, and *The End All,* a piece on the horrors of war. Company member Rick Wamer has toured his humorous one-man show *Contra Diction* (1984) and *Geometrics* (1984). The Goldston and Johnson School for Mimes at Kenyon College in Ohio has offered intensive summer programs on all levels, with such guest mime masters as Marceau, who became artistic advisor of the Goldston Mime Foundation.

The founding members of Touch—Sheila Kerrigan, Laurie Wolf, and Jef—met while studying mime with C. W. Metcalf in 1975. They began their company in 1976 in North Carolina and together studied with Tony Montanaro in 1978. They staged works that foster progressive social change and performed with symphonies, at rock concerts, in prisons, hospitals, malls, and at the zoo, for conventional as well as for nonconventional audiences. Although some company members studied corporeal mime and briefly underwent Lecoq training, their style was based on a simplified mime technique they called "American body language." They drew elements from acrobatics, mime, dance, acting improvisation, puppetry, storytelling, mask, music, lighting design, juggling, and clowning. These elements, along with props, masks, and dialogue, comprise *Just One of Those Days* (1989), which reveals a woman's encounters with global dilemmas on a personal level, including a toxic waste spill, a terrorist attack, overpopulation, and love in the age of AIDS. Touch's final piece, *In the Outfield* (1991), combined storytelling, mime, bunraku puppetry, magic, slides, music, sound effects, and baseball to relate the story of a lesbian coming of age in a state that elected Jesse Helms. During the company's 1993 season, *Carnival of Animals* was rewritten and performed to the music of Camille Saint-Saëns played by the North Carolina Symphony. *We Askew This,* a collection of vignettes, as well as improvisations based on audience suggestions, toured the United States. Touch also staged children's shows, such as *The Heart of the Ladder, The Wizard Who Couldn't Smile,* and *UFO.* Touch disbanded in 1993.

Michael Thomas began studying mime in 1970 while enrolled in the theatre department of Chicago's Northwestern University. He later became the assistant director of and a performer in the Northwestern University Mime Company. He made the films *Homage to Rodin* (1975) with the Northwestern University Mime Company and *From My Heart* (1975), based on teaching and performing mime. In 1975, he appeared in his first one-man show in Chicago and directed the Loyola University Mime Company. From 1975 to 1977, he studied with Decroux in Paris, played in one-man shows, and taught in Israel, Great Britain, and Northern California.

Working more directly with the public, Imagimime, a nationally established duet company that Carol and David Geyer founded in 1976 in Maryland, performed in educational institutions, malls, and festivals and for advertising campaigns and corporations. Trained in theatre, dance, and education, the couple mimed and clowned in whiteface on stage and in public areas, improvising with their spectators as mechanical robots. They appeared on TV and taught workshops. In 1989, they began the Mid-Atlantic Movement Theatre Festival at Western Maryland College in Westminster, Maryland, which continued at other universities with performances by national and local artists, workshops, and conferences.

After observing close to a hundred of Marceau's performances in the early 1970s and working on Diana Ross's world tours in 1976, 1977, and 1978, Stewart Fischer taught acrobatics at Marceau's Paris school. In 1980, Jean-Louis Barrault invited him to perform his piece *Jonathan Livingston Seagull* at his theatre, where it was appreciated as an aerial ballet with extraordinary gymnastic images. He then toured Europe, receiving a gold medal and a grand prize in international pantomime competitions.

In 1977, Genevieve Aichele and Dennis McLaughlin founded Kitchensink Theatre in Portsmouth, New Hampshire. Both had trained in acting, modern dance, ballet, mime, and movement theatre with Tony Montanaro, Claude Kipnis, Don Reider, Valerie Dean, Marguerite Mathews, and Carlo Mazzone Clementi. Kitchensink's major original productions include *Dreams on a Sleeve* (1984), a classical illusion pantomime piece; *Heart on a String* (1986), a *commedia* piece with puppetry, dance, and juggling; *A Fool's Journey* (1988), a clown theatre work; *Womenswerk* (1991), which unites poetry, song, storytelling, clowning, and dance; and *Beyond Myth* (1992), composed of mask, dance, chamber theatre, and stage combat, with philosophical and social issues found in ancient myths and stories. Kitchensink is an example of postmodern pluralism, which blends abstract and illusion pantomime, *commedia*, story theatre, dance, acting, stage combat, clowning, and masks.

In 1977, Richard Davidson, Elizabeth Roth, Bruce Wylie, and Pat Tyler began the Seattle Mime Theatre. Roth and Davidson had studied with Tony Montanaro and Jacques Lecoq, and Wylie had trained with Leonard Pitt. The company performed throughout the United States and abroad for both adults and children. One of its major works, *Eye of the Wolf* (1987), was a collaboration between the Seattle Mime Theatre and the Seattle Improv Company that depicted a group of actors who interpret a medieval German folktale in a surrealistic manner. Since 1991, the Seattle Mime Theatre has used literary works as the basis for its physical performances in such pieces as James Thurber's *The Secret Life of Walter Mitty* (1992) and Walter Steig's *Sylvester and the Magic Pebble* (1994).

Lesley Bannatyne and John Bay founded the Studebaker Movement Theater of Somerville, Massachusetts, in 1978. Bannatyne studied with Decroux, Tony Montanaro, and Marceau trainees, and Bay had worked in San Francisco as an actor. From 1978 on, the company has performed, taught, and created works at the Performance Place in Somerville and toured the United States, Canada, and Europe. Since its beginnings, it has moved from mime and dancelike pieces that rely on the performers' movement ideas to physical theatre works that involve social satire, psychological relationships, and traditional dialogue, sets, costumes, lighting, and sound design. Text and imagery harmonize in *Monopolis* (1984), parodying the world of money, real estate, and industry; *Pulcinella* (1985) develops *commedia* to Stravinsky's score; *Saltimbanques* (1988) is based on Picasso's paintings and sketches; *Shadow of a Doubt* (1990) offers a Kafkaesque collage of movement, text, shadow, music, and giant machines, using the chaos theory to explore the issue of predestination; and *Elvis in Exile* (1991) depicts Elvis as a migrant laborer who examines migrant labor capitalism. *The Man Himself* (1993), by British playwright Alan Drury, is a one-man show that John Bay played and Lesley Bannatyne directed about an ordinary man's insidious seduction by fanatics of the political right. Outdoor installation–performance *Invisible Cities* (1994) mixes local history with performance art and a love story; *Ghost Factory* (1995) evokes memories on a neighborhood tour; *Dream Home* (1996) develops what a home means through an interactive art exhibit; and *Watching the Detectives* (1997) explores a neighborhood mystery through a city performance tour.

Midsummer Mime Theatre, which Martin and Victoria Kappel began in Indianapolis in 1978 and continued through 1986, developed a variety of mime, mask, and clown styles. These styles ranged from mimodrama, portraying comical exploits at a town fair in *Fardry's Adventure at P. T. Nickel's Fair,* to *commedia*, involving the disputes of two captains in *The Braggart's Battle,* to a spoof of teaching mime in *The Academy,* presented at the Midwest Mime and Clown Festival which the Kappels hosted in 1985. Martin Kappel's clown–mime show *My Turn*, first staged in 1986 and with subsequently close to five hundred performances for adult and children's audiences, features a gentleman clown called Fardry Barlafumble who finally gets his act together. Teachers who have influenced Kappel's solo creations and mimodramas and his stage direction of mime productions, which foster a positive image, are C. W. Metcalf, Jacques Lecoq, E. Reid Gilbert, Avner Eisenberg, Sigfrido Aguilar, and Shozo Sato.

Mark Jaster, a former Decroux and Marceau student and teaching assistant to Marceau in Ann Arbor, Michigan, was mime director at the Round House Theater in Silver Spring, Maryland, in the late 1970s and early 1980s. Here, he constructed the full-length mime plays *Abelard and Heloise* (1979) and *Tristan and Isolt* (1983), as well as duets and solos that toured the Washington, D.C., area. Since 1985, Jaster has taught and performed for adults and children in corporeal movement theatre, *commedia*, performance art, and clown theatre. In 1990, he created *Cirque d'Automne* to the music of Erik Satie and Darius Milhaud, and, in 1992, performed *Foolspells* at the Mid-Atlantic Movement Theatre Festival.

Performance artist Dan Hurlin, artistic director since 1978 of the New Hampshire children's theatre Andy's Summer Playhouse, is renowned for his Obie Award–winning two-man show, *Hunchback of Notre Dame*, performed since the early 1990s. Hurlin wrote, narrated, and performed the characters in *Archaeology*, which through storytelling and mime moves from earlier periods into the future. His moving *The Day the Ketchup Turned Blue*, performed at Boston's Beau Jest Moving Theatre in 1996 and based on a short story by playwright and AIDS victim John Russell, is a short, theatre-in-miniature production featuring a unique toy theatre that Hurlin built.

After Seus Edwards studied with Tom Pierce and his partner C. W. Metcalf in Florida, she and her husband founded their Dr. Tom and Seus Mime Theatre in Atlanta in 1979. They expanded their mime, clowning, juggling, and puppetry through training with Ronlin Foreman, Avner Eisenberg, Tom Leabhart, and Jacques Lecoq. Their repertory included *William Tell*, *Creation*, *The Froggie Prince*, *Wash Day Blues,* and *Bus Stop*, which spanned from classical pantomime to corporeal mime sketches, and from serious themes and crafty movement to broad, physical comedy with live music and dialogue.

David Barker's eclectic background includes training with Jacques Lecoq, Richmond Shepard, Robert Morse, Tom Leabhart, and Daniel Stein. After he toured with the Claude Kipnis Mime Theatre from 1980 to 1981, this company's use of pantomime, clowning, and masks greatly influenced him. In 1984, he founded the Aurora Mime Theatre and served as its artistic director for five years. An associate professor of theatre from 1989 on, he has directed the acting program at Arizona State University, where he has taught acting and movement and directed theatre productions. His satirical solo *Out of My Mime* (1977) combines visual and aural elements with classical and contemporary music, sound effects, costumes, and props. *Menace* (1981), performed to Béla Bartók's String Quartet Number 4, responds through mime and mask to the rape, murder, and child abuse incidents that saturate the evening news. *Mimania* (1982), a mime concert presented at University of California–Santa Barbara and at Arizona State University in 1984, *For Men Only* (1987), *I Am an Art Machine* (1989), and *The Gas Heart* (1991) interweave illusion pantomime, figurative mime, corporeal technique, slapstick, mask, puppet theater, modern dance, and surrealist theater.

Touchstone Theatre in Bethlehem, Pennsylvania, was founded in 1981 by Bill George, his wife Bridget, and creative partner Lorraine Zeller to create original ensemble works in which the physicality and emotional dynamics of image and space are as important as the text. The company performed at Lincoln Center in New York, the White House in Washington, D.C., and in Mexico, London, and Scotland, where it received the Edinburgh Fringe First Award for outstanding new work. Among the company pieces are a *Candide* adaptation by William Pope and the ensemble; *We All Fall Down, or A Seesaw Named Desire*, by ensemble members Eric Beatty and Susan Chase; and *Daedalus in the Belly of the Beast,* a bilingual drama by Marco Antonio de la Parra featured at the Theatre of Nations Festival in Santiago in 1993. Bill George's solo creation, *The Kingfisher's Wing* (1992), is based on the true story of the matyrdom of a rebellious seventeen-year-old Persian—Aqa Buzurg, known as Badi the Wonderful—who, after a pilgrimage, converted to a persecuted faith and suffered torture and death. Performed by George, this mystical work, conveyed through visual elements and a spoken text, unfolds with the dramatic passion of a classical tragedy, along with a contemporary use of movement, storytelling, puppetry, mask, and shadows.

In March 1994, Touchstone Theatre and Lehigh University organized a festival, entitled Theatre of Creation, that celebrated the work of Jacques Lecoq and his International School of Theatre. Besides a public lesson–demonstration by Lecoq and panels about his work and related topics, there were performances and workshops by Touchstone Theatre (*Don't Drop Grandma*), Avner the Eccentric, Jim Calder (*Nervous Tissue*), Robert Astle (*Heart of a Dog*), Theater Grottesco (*Grottesco Shorts*), Theatre Spirale (*Beginnings*), and Erick Bouvron, Mercedes Chanquia-Aguirre, and Anatol Wechtl (*The Cabin on Chicken Legs*). The Touchstone company, several members of which are Lecoq trainees, has offered teaching residencies in movement, mask, theatrical styles, and the actor as creator.

Solo mime performer Gary Shore, founder of the Gary Shore Mime Theatre, is also founder and co-director of the New England Shoda Movement Theatre and a faculty member in dance at Roger Williams University in Barrington, Rhode Island. His piece *Canned Trash* (1981)—which incorporates plastic garbage bags, gas masks, and toilet plungers, along with comedy, acrobatics, and a Samuel Beckett atmosphere—develops an interaction between a janitor and a woman he finds in a trash can. *The Waiter and the Waitress* (1992), performed with Heather Ahern, co-artistic director of the Groundwerx Dance Theatre, is built around a waitress and her impatient client, with surrealist metaphors concerning birth, death, relationships, and the relative nature of time. Through dialogue, dance, mime, and shadow play, *Backyard* (1994) reveals a suburban character's fears about the cosmos after reading the *New York Times* and feeling the solace of Wagner's music. In his work, Shore draws upon corporeal mime, dance, pantomime, gymnastics, and karate.

The Texas Mime Theatre was founded in 1981 by producing director Casey Coale and associate directors Mick Corley and Alicia Church, former trainees of mime teacher Claude Caux at the University of Houston. The company offers workshops and performs mimes and pantomimes, such as *Aesop's Fables* for children and *Frankenstein, Better Left Unsaid,* and *Opus Mime* for adults.

Under the sponsorship of the University Musical Society of the University of Michigan in Ann Arbor, the Marcel Marceau Summer Sessions began in 1983 and were held until 1988. Students were selected for five weeks of summer training in mime performance techniques and concepts. Led by four Marceau assistants, the workshop served as an introduction for beginners or as a refresher course for advanced students. The students then participated in an advanced, two-week seminar, directed by Marceau, in mime technique and improvisation, with individualized attention and lectures on the history and art of mime. The Marcel Marceau World Centre for Mime, scheduled to open in the autumn of 1988 to host year-round mime performances, conferences, and lectures and sponsor Marceau's touring company, did not materialize.

John Flax and Didier Maucort, graduates of the Ecole Jacques Lecoq and former members of the Théâtre de la Jeune Lune, began Theater Grottesco in Paris; they were later joined by Lecoq graduate Elizabeth Wiseman. Based in Detroit from 1987 to 1996, when it relocated to northern New Mexico, the company, which has toured nationally and internationally, has created full-length and shorter pieces, such as *The Insomniacs* (1984), played with half-masks and invented gibberish; *Fortune* (1987), an expressionistic melodrama depicting the rise and fall of a cookie factory; *The Richest Dead Man Alive* (1988), a modern farce; and *The Angel's Cradle* (1993), a melodramatic tale of buffoon outcasts living beneath our cities. *This Is Life As We Know It . . . Or Something* (1996) mirrors today's reality through advertising and the media. Inspired by German dance–theatre director Pina Bausch and Polish director Tadeusz Kantor, the piece integrates movement, dance, magic, illusion, and story-telling. During their 1998–99 tour the company performed *The Angel's Cradle* and *Fortune: The Rise and Fall of a Small Cookie Factory* in North American universi-ties and theatres. The company's visual creations blend elements of the ridiculous with the grave, *commedia*, clowning, buffoonery, farce, and mask work to offer a fresh perspective on contemporary culture.

Davis Robinson formed the Boston-based Beau Jest Moving Theatre, com-posed of five actors, in 1984. A director, actor, and drama and mime teacher at Emer-son College (Boston), Robinson had studied with Tony Montanaro and Jacques Lecoq. Beau Jest's collaborative productions, which have toured North America and Europe, are a surrealistic blend of movement, clowning, acting, satire, and music. *Ubu Roi* (1987) is a burlesque adaptation of Alfred Jarry's satire of Shakespearean tragedy played with Rabelaisian characters, masks, puppets, giant figures, and music. The serio-comic piece *Motion Sickness* (1989), revived in 1999, examines five characters' individual attempts to avoid stress, ranging from job pressures to separation, isolation, and the need for freedom. *A Mall and Some Visitors* (1990) is a satire of the depressive aspects of holiday rituals, gift-buying, and how people in the 1990s combat the onslaught of winter. *Cardiff Giant* (1992), later called *The Naked Giant*, is a nineteenth-century tale about fraud applied to the search for the truth in the TV game-show scandals, the Anita Hill–Clarence Thomas hearings, and the Gulf War. *Krazy Kat* (1994), which is based on George Herriman's comic strip and blends dance, music, and physical comedy, won the company the 1995 Boston Theater Award for Best Show by a Small Resident Company. *War of the Worlds* (1998) develops the tale by H. G. Wells of the invasion from Mars through dance, physical comedy, and music. In 1999, the company premiered a collaborative work in which sex, death, and taxes interact in a secluded resort.

Eliot Fintushel, former artistic director of the Mime Workshop in Rochester, New York, which developed new mask drama, mime, and theatrical clowning works, was a resident instructor of mask and mime at the Dell'Arte International School of Physical Theatre in Blue Lake, California, and founder of the Mime Workshop in mask, mime, and meditative inquiry in Santa Rosa, California. In *Heart Mask,* Fin-tushel creates poetic images through mask and movement while playing on a recorder. *Einstein's Hitler* is an exorcism of the destructive effects of war on hu-manity. In *Babymama, a Mirror for Parents* (1986), Fintushel portrays family vio-lence through epic theatre, *commedia*, French funambulists, circus, puppetry, music, and narration.

Miming along with puppets and masks, New York–based Eric Bass's theatre consists of moving the wrists, fingers, heads, and other body parts of his handmade puppets. Silent attitudes and gestures interweave in a narrative in which Bass some-times intervenes as a masked character (*Darius*), integrating puppet and puppeteer. In *Autumn Portraits,* a puppet master of ceremonies invites spectators on stage to play toy instruments while he mocks their incompetencies. In *Maya,* an old woman storyteller punctuates an ancient African tale with facial and head movements, and in *Zedyl* an old shoemaker begs for time from the angel of death, making each shoe in his shop sing and dance a lullaby of the old man's youth.

A. Opshinsky has been director of Déjà Vu in New York since 1988. The company succeeded Mutuus Mime Theater, founded by Mary Grace Stewart in 1982, where Opshinsky was artistic director and writer. Trained by Richard Hayes Marshall, Jacques Lecoq, Tom Leabhart, Daniel Stein, and Bert Houle, Opshinsky also acted, danced, and performed with the Theatre Mask Ensemble for two years. His creations include mimed vignettes entitled *Refractions* (1984); *Peter and the Wolf* (1984), staged in 1986 to the music of Sergei Prokofiev as played by the Buffalo Philharmonic; *Pierrot Coiffeur* (1986); *Dancing to the End of the World* (1987), a clown and buffoon show; and *A Musical Map of the World* (1988), performed with the Buffalo Philharmonic.

Opshinsky's wife, Jackie Wildau, a 1972 graduate of Lecoq's school, has since 1985 directed Pastiche, a movement theatre company in which the actors appear as statues that suddenly come to life. Wildau has written and performed for *Merci Bernard* (on French national TV) and created and performed in *Prisoners of Love* (1992), a two-person comedy show.

Mime and movement teacher Robert Rivest, who studied with Marcel Marceau, Stefan Niedzialkowski, and Maximilien Decroux, began his Mime Theatre in Springfield, Massachusetts. Two of his pieces that mix movement, silent acting, and dance are *The Bird Watcher* and *Slave Ship*.

Bob Bellamy, a former student of Paul Curtis, dancer with the Doug Elkins Dance Company, and performer with Touchstone Theatre in Bethlehem, Pennsylvania, founded the Azzizz Company. Among the pieces he created on video at the March 1996 New York Sunday Salon were *Flywheel*, evoking the story of Sisyphus, and *Silent Partners*, a psychological study of individuals trapped in a room together. These were followed by *Heaven and Hell* (1995); *The Shaft* (1996), about three people stuck in an elevator; *Sexual Healing* (1997); and *Four Play* (1998), in which the heroine searches for love in the ad pages.

Marc Bauman—actor, stage director, and physical theatre specialist—received a diploma from Marcel Marceau's Ecole Internationale de Mimodrame and taught at Marceau's School for Mime in Ann Arbor, Michigan. In 1987, he developed *Eternal Thought* with Maximilien Decroux, which he later performed with Chuck Hudson in Paris, Ann Arbor, and Detroit. In 1988, with Axel Jodorowski, he created and played in a multidisciplinary physical theatre piece entitled *Freud's Children* at Marceau's Paris school, later performed with Dennis Schaller and Mark Jaster in America. In 1991, he created a nineteenth-century pantomime and interpreted Monsieur Jules in *Cabaret Chat Noir* in Hollywood and San Francisco. Bauman has taught acting and movement throughout the United States and Europe, including at Solano College, California, and at the Dell'Arte International School of Physical Theatre in California. In 1993, he co-directed and choreographed Peter Shaffer's award-winning *Equus*.

Lorin Eric Salm, trained in both Decroux and Marceau techniques, has performed in solo shows and with Marceau in Paris and the United States. He has taught mime to high school and university acting students as well as to animation artists. Among his solo pantomimes, performed without stage or hand props and with music, is his collection of sketches entitled *C'est à Dire* (That Is to Say); *Elevator Ups and Downs* (1988); *Seasons*, a lyrical portrayal of the ages of man; *The Balloon*

(1989), in which the real protagonist is the balloon; and *Imprisoned* (1994), on captivity and freedom. Salm created the World of Mime Website in 1996, diffusing world-wide information on the history, definition, companies, artists, and current events in mime theatre. (See appendix for website address.)

Ron and Ludvika Popenhagen of Theatre Oblique, based in Wadena, Iowa, studied and became assistants to Jacques Lecoq. They later toured with their pantomimes and *commedia* pieces with masks throughout Europe, Canada, and the United States. Their comic sketch *Going Places* portrays naive tourists on a twenty-seven-minute tour of Europe.

Countless other mimes and movement artists have taken their art into new artistic realms that offer a spectrum of forms within many areas. Charles Metcalf, a former actor who trained with Japanese Noh actor and mime Yass Hakoshima, performed solo mime, introduced it into healing programs for the physically challenged and the developmentally disabled, and later became a corporate advisor for health and humor. The Great American Mime Experiment, active since 1977 under Sandra Hughes and Michael Hickey's artistic direction, in 1986 staged *Uktena*, a tale of a giant, destructive serpent and a shaman–magician who delivers the Cherokee people from this evil force, and in 1987 presented a piece on Antonin Artaud's madness, *Artaud at Rodez*. The New England touring company La Mer Mime and Mask company developed a repertory of varied mime styles and clowning. Mime Act from Dallas, Texas, integrated mime, theatre, dance, and acrobatics in such productions as *Snow White* and *Pinocchio*. Street mime Matt Mitler, a former member of the Lecoq-influenced Archaesus Mime Troupe in Washington, D.C., and his partner Leonora Logan performed throughout America and Europe.

A founder of the New Mime Troupe with his wife dancer–choreographer Linda Yoder-Krohn, in Columbus, Ohio, in 1972, David Jon Krohn developed folksy solo works (*The Bell Ringer and the Bee* and *The Cremation of Sam McGee*), which he performed at the 1985 American Midwest Mime Festival. Krohn then toured Eastern Europe with his mime, clown, dance, and theatre works.

Also based in Columbus, performance artist Robert Post, who has appeared as a solo performer since 1981 throughout the United States and abroad, as well as on TV, integrates movement with storytelling and social and philosophical satire in *Robert Post in Performance* (1994). With inventive content and rapid character and set changes, Post plays six roles in *Beyond the Wall*, communicating the action of a murder mystery with a minimum of movement and gestures. *Another Head* is a comical version of the seven ages of life portrayed solely with his head and facial expressions, along with some text.

Michael Hennessy, who trained with Marceau, founded the Michael Hennessy Mime and Music Theatre in 1974, performing in versatile works that extended from a modern dance and mime mix, such as *Haiku Set,* to clown–mime shows, such as *Out of the Can and into the Ring*, presented at the 1985 American Midwest Mime Festival. Andrew Glenn, a former Hennessy student, combined mime with song, dance, and vaudeville in his *Mime Song*. Harris John Botwinik from Yoncalla, Oregon, who studied with Marceau in Ann Arbor, performed and taught mime in Oregon. Todd Larsen, who trained with Daniel Stein, Tom Leabhart, Tony Montanaro, and Stefan Niedzialkowski, taught on the East and West Coasts. His *Silent Reminiscence,* a postmodern solo work dealing with memories and the need to hold on to one's past, was presented at the 1989 Philadelphia Movement Theatre International Festival. Kiko the Mime, a former student of Jewel Walker and Dan Kamin, began performing and teaching in the 1970s, and in 1982 founded the Gold Coast Mime company with Jude Parry.

Since the 1970s, Illusion Theatre of Minneapolis has created works that reveal today's myths and realities and how theatre can bring about personal and social change. For its 1995 season, it staged *Rez Road Follies*, based on Jim Northup's book *Walking the Rez Road,* which won the Minnesota Book Award in 1993.

The Moving Dock company was founded in Chicago by actress–director–teacher Dawn Arnold to create collaborative, improvisational movement pieces. The company presented *Galway Bay*, inspired by Morgan Llywelyn's novella and with Celtic music, at the 1998 Association of Movement Educators and Laban/Bartenieff Symposium sponsored by the University of Iowa Theatre Arts Department. It also organizes workshops to explore creativity and develop movement, voice, and acting skills.

A former mime with the Margolis Brown company, Christopher Eaves created *Class,* an exploration of American social structures, and *Birthmarks*, an adopted boy's search for his biological roots, which develops a narrative with mime, dance, song, and video; the two works inaugurated the new movement theatre program at Towson State University in 1991. His piece *The Well-Hung Man and the Hung-Up Lady* (1993), by Theresa Francomaro, continued the Towson State University series. Eaves's play *The Conservator, Act I* (1995), on the conservation of Michelangelo's *Last Judgment,* incorporates movement, sound, and dialogue, along with current issues. *Slip* (1995) focuses on the work of AIDS activist, writer, photographer, and visual artist David Wojnarowicz.

In California, which has provided a diverse group of mimes, Jack Lang captivated audiences with his silent-movie style. Anne Dennis Jancovic, who studied with Decroux and Marceau, founded the Mime Project, taught and directed corporeal movement at Epic West Theatre in Berkeley, and published a physical training book for actors entitled *The Articulate Body*. In 1974, Decroux-trained Jan Munroe, along with Colleen Larkin, founded the Rags and Patches Theatre of the Après Garde in Berkeley, California, mixing Decroux mime with Balinese dance and miming with accessories. Among Munroe's major solo and group pieces, which contain mime, dance, music, video, and text, is his autobiographical *Alligator Tales and Other Appendages.*

Clown–mime Hintin, formerly with Tony Montanaro's company, and Black mime Fred Jackson, who began the Jackson Mime and Puppet company, appeared in the San Francisco Bay Area streets and parks. Hayward Coleman, who trained with Decroux and Marceau, blended Harlem blues, yoga, and spiritual meditation with movement. Jack Cook, who studied with Angna Enters and Jacques Lecoq, staged mime and clown shows at San Francisco State University.

Dennis Schaller, who studied with Richmond Shepard, Marcel Marceau, Stefan Niedzialkowski, Tom Leabhart, and Marc Bauman, taught and performed in Southern California. Among his creations — which range from clowning, pantomime, and mask work to abstract and Decroux-style mime — are *Black Elk's Prayer,* about the Native American medicine man's struggle to survive, and *The Marionette,* a traditional pantomime in which the puppet's attempts to take control represent the human quest for freedom. Southern California mime Jay Miller performed his solo pantomimes *Baseball Metamorphosis* and *The Samurai and the Zen Master*, which he also narrated, at the 1988 Philadelphia Movement Theatre International Festival.

Among the dancers who have incorporated mime into their works are Steve Krieckhaus and Helmut Gottschild, both dance teachers at Temple University in Philadelphia who performed at the 1988 Movement Theatre International Festival.

Krieckhaus's *The Book* fuses dramatic themes with dance in a contrapuntal dialogue in which his interaction with a book evokes baseball, being a dog, sex, and other subjects. Trained by Mary Wigman, Gottschild's *Songs of the Humpback Male* depicts the protagonist threatened by the division of man from nature, woman, and himself. Terry Beck, a former student of the Mary Wigman technique under Gottschild and founder of the Terry Beck Troupe in 1984, also performed at the 1988 Movement Theatre International Festival in *Waiters.*

Martin Frick, who studied with Henryk Tomaszewski of the Polish Mime Theatre, trained mime students at the Toronto Actor's Studio in Canada before moving to California in the 1970s, where he taught choral music and occasionally blended mime with music, for example, in his interpretation of various roles in Stravinsky's *Histoire du Soldat.* Lecoq-trained Gordon Keller, founder of the Berkeley Mime Troupe, along with Ed Holmes experimented with nontraditional mime forms that included props and sound. Joan Merwyn, Cyd Nepon, and Terry du Soleil worked in children's mime in San Francisco.

A number of mimes, such as Adam Darius, Richmond Shepard, Alvin Epstein, and Phil Burns have appeared on Broadway. Still others, such as Rich Little, who uses mimicry along with his voice; Frank Gorshin, a master of face mimicry; and David Frye, the clever imitator of celebrities, are known to TV viewers.

Street Theatre

Although street theatre can be traced back to the female performers who played in the marketplaces and on the streets of ancient Greece and Rome, it became particularly popular in America in the 1970s. The number of street performers in the United States is inexhaustible, and they are difficult to trace because some have moved to performing in New Vaudeville or on the stage. One of the first to popularize this form in America was Robert Shields, whose success as a mime in San Francisco's Union Square led to a stage and TV career.

Robert Shields

Born in 1951, Robert Shields began playing as a party clown at the age of fourteen. He then performed his act "Robbie the Mechanical Man" with the Royal American Circus and in a sidewalk show for the Hollywood Wax Museum. After engaging in whiteface pantomime at California Renaissance Faires, he went to France in 1970 to train briefly with Marceau. The following year, he became one of America's first street mimes. At Union Square in downtown San Francisco—wheeling, spinning, and flipping about, climbing invisible ladders, descending imaginary stairs, and tugging at make-believe ropes—he mimicked passers-by. While he triumphed over police citations for directing traffic and hopping buses, he still landed in jail on occasion; he also was battered by park drunks and hobos for his bold imitations of them. Shields relates how he began street miming in San Francisco:

> My father was an optician and when I was a child I liked to play with his collection of glass eyes. I began perfecting my mannequin movements by jabbing a fork into my hand until I bled. From practicing this I soon was able to do one controlled mannequin movement after another. I did my mannequin movements at side shows, traveling circuses and at bar mizvahs. I was also hired to do them in front of the Hollywood Wax

Museum to attract people there. One day I went to San Francisco and made forty dollars doing my act in Union Square. I became so popular imitating people and involving them in what I did that I soon had many imitators in the streets.[11]

Shields brought his keen observations of street people into his stage pieces. Among them were the arrogant *Biker,* the self-assured *High Diver,* and the complacent *Cowboy. The Robot* is a masterpiece in technical precision and corporeal virtuosity of a mechanical, computer-age creature with glazed eyes and a bobbing head, jerking about with ultraprecise movements. Shields's animal sketches intensified the range of his art; in *Gorilla,* after bending the bars of his cage, the crouching animal looks out at the gaping crowd and decides to remain in his cage. In *The Box*, Shields mimes a trapped fellow feeling the walls of a box, which grows smaller and smaller; his struggle ends with a humorous gesture of blasphemy toward the heavens. In *The Skin Diver*, dives, handsprings, and tumbling enhance the dramatic content. In *The Princess and the Frog*, fantasy is allied with caricature. Poetry alternates with parody in *Bubble Gum Machine, The Puppet, Evolution,* and *Late Breakfast.* His trilogy *Broken Heart, Last Laugh,* and *The Kiss* was mimed with dancer Lorene Yarnell. *Rebirth* develops the birth and reincarnation of a soul throughout three lives, and *Balloon* depicts the attainment of inner peace. In the late 1970s, Shields and Yarnell, who were married in a mime ceremony in Union Square, appeared on TV in their *Shields and Yarnell Show,* which earned them a special Emmy Award in 1977. Shields wrote and starred in the TV special *Toys on the Town*, for which he received an Emmy Award, and performed at the 1989 Philadelphia Movement Theatre International Festival.

Inspired by mechanical toys in his skits, Shields has collected more than six thousand antique and rare toys. He has also created ceramic castles, animals, and court jesters, as well as painted storybook landscapes.

A spontaneous and adept street artist, Shields slips with ease from fantasy to automatism, slapstick, caricature, and animalism. Few street mimes have possessed his joie de vivre and ingenuity.

The Bond Street Theatre Coalition

Founded in 1976 by Patrick Sciarratta, the Bond Street Theatre Coalition became one of America's foremost political and folk street theatres. Besides performing in New York City, the company has played throughout the United States, Europe, Brazil, Israel, Japan, Indonesia, and Canada. It has also developed a school and an apprentice program in physical theatre studies that include mime, music, dance, circus arts, clowning, mask work, commedia dell'arte, storytelling, ritual and gesture, and the physical performance arts of many traditions. Under the artistic direction of Sciarratta and Joanna Sherman, the Bond Street Theatre Coalition ensemble is composed of actors, musicians, and designers with many skills. Sciarratta trained with Polish mime Henryk Tomaszewski and Polish theatre director Jerzy Grotowski. Sherman worked with vaudevillian Joe Price and Decroux-trained Swedish director Ingemar Lindh. Both Sciarratta and Sherman studied with the Colombaioni clown family in Italy and with *commedia* specialist Carlo Mazzone Clementi.

Through new combinations of such classic structures as myth, folklore, and *commedia*, the company's works reveal truths about topical events and current lifestyles. In *The Myth of Erysichthon* (1976), Greek myth and *commedia* serve to

Some thoughts on mime from Robert Shields.

expose political sellouts and local politicians' destruction of Mother Nature to build a superhighway. *A Tale of Vision* (1978) satirizes the dehumanizing effects of television as a young girl is lured into a TV station operated by robot mimes who attempt to turn her into a robot. In *Capidome, the Malling of America* (1978), merchants transform the country into a huge shopping center. *Powerplay* (1979–84) comments on nuclear armament. Musical and imagistic parades in *Roadworks* (directed by Danish director Torben Bjelke in 1982) develop the global danger of nuclear arms. Movement and text fuse in such classics as Molière's *The Flying Doctor*, Franz Kafka's *The Hunger Artist*, Charles Dickens's *A Christmas Carol,* and *Shakespeare Party*, which blends Shakespeare's finest poetry and prose with unusual physical and musical interpretations. Through the true story of a female medicine-show huckster and an eccentric heiress, *Of Sand and Thunder* (directed by Carey Perloff in 1987) illustrates the myth of the American Dream in the late 1800s. Joanna Sherman's solo piece, *Dancing the Fire* (1991), satirizes a pressurized and materialistic American lifestyle through a blend of storytelling, slapstick, music, dance, and film. *Nightmare on Wall Street* (1990) addresses greed and ethics in big business and politics. Dario Fo's *Accidental Death of an Anarchist* (1993) featured Patrick Sciarratta as the anarchist. *Werk*, premiered at the International Theatre and Dance Festival in Brazil in August 1996, is a nonverbal piece directed by Joanna Sherman that, through movement, masks, dance, and physical comedy, explores work as daily sustenance and survival for a working mother and her small child.

No longer limiting itself to street theatre, the company evolved into an experimental ensemble that continued to make theatre socially and politically relevant. It synthesized age-old performance techniques within a modern folk theatre to better reach its audiences. An international theatre appealing to all ages and social classes, it attempted to communicate—in nontraditional spaces and by means of eclectic physical, vocal, and musical techniques—with the largest body of people. In the 1970s Sciarratta wrote:

> Our present objectives are to find a clear Western codification of theatrical styles and structures in order to make theatre useful as a tool for social change and life, as it had been for hundreds of years in the Orient. Today most American theatre is useless. It is confused with dating and dining and has no cultural reference point. It is often an imitation of television and the movies. Theatre should be an understandable social tool. It should be as necessary as the need for chopped meat. Our theatre is a social folk theatre which attempts to help people progress in their own lives and encourage them to think for themselves rather than by means of TV and other mass media. And no matter where we perform we carry a feeling of the streets along with us. Yet, we do not belong only on the street. We can perform in many different areas, in a church, a park, anywhere, bringing street theatre into social gatherings of all sorts.[12]

Concerning the more global orientation of their company, Sherman wrote in the 1990s:

> Our current objective is to create relevant work which exemplifies theatre's ability to illuminate the social, environmental and artistic concerns which affect us all, both here in our own country and globally. To create a physical theatrical vocabulary which can cross any cultural border, we have studied the rituals, symbolism, gestures, game structures and performance forms from many cultures and from this created a rich language of imagery and action. Beyond performance, we have found some of our most effective and fulfilling theatre work in collaborating with our audiences, sharing the ways in which we play, entertain, and communicate with each other. This openness and versatility has allowed us to work with homeless children on the streets of Brazil, create pageant plays with Arabs and Jews in Jerusalem, and teach street theatre techniques to young political refugees in Montreal.[13]

Commedia dell'Arte, Folklore, and Political Mime

The San Francisco Mime Troupe

One of the most vocal political theatres in America today began as a silent mime company and then developed *commedia,* broad physical comedy, and musical works with controversial themes. The founder of the San Francisco Mime Troupe, Ronnie Davis, trained with Martha Graham, José Limón, and Doris Humphrey in dance and with Maximilien Decroux in mime. After joining Paul Curtis's American Mime Theatre, he left to found the San Francisco Mime Troupe in 1959. That same year, Davis brought his first mime piece, *Mime and Words,* to the San Francisco Art Institute and in 1961 staged Samuel Beckett's *Act without Words II.* Inspired by the total theatre of Jean-Louis Barrault, Davis adjoined movement to speaking theatre and staged minstrel shows, vaudeville, circus acts, and traditional commedia dell'arte. Among the plays he directed in the *commedia* style are *The Dowry* (1962), based on Molière's *Scapin,* and Carlo Goldoni's *The Servant of Two Masters.* In his book *The San Francisco Mime Troupe: The First Ten Years,* Davis describes how the troupe began by performing indoor theatre and presenting poetry readings, lectures, and films to later become the first company to play in San Francisco's parks and squares. Upon adapting current issues to *commedia lazzi* and characters, the troupe was accused of indulging in obscenity; in 1965, the San Francisco Park Commission arrested Davis and revoked the group's permit to perform. After a number of other arrests, the company was back performing in the parks for decades. Davis left the San Francisco Mime Troupe in 1970 and in 1975 founded his Epic West Theatre, in which he joined movement to Brechtian epic theatre.

After staging Bertolt Brecht's *The Exception and the Rule* (1965), the San Francisco Mime Troupe grew into a political protest theatre. To attract attention to local, national, and international issues and to project the action of outdoor performances in a spacious area and on a bare stage with few props, the troupe developed an exaggerated physical comedy style. Its plays depicted social, political, and economic injustice; racism; minority groups; war; city life; housing; and sexual politics. Beginning with bawdy *commedia* and combined with original music, song, and dance, the pieces moved from American melodrama to westerns, mysteries, science-fiction thrillers, cartoon comedy, and slapstick. From the 1960s on, the company members shared the roles of actor, musician, director, writer, and stagehand. In collective productions, the actors as well as the public contributed to a socially relevant scenario. A live band with an original score became an important part of each staging.

Since the 1960s, the San Francisco Mime Troupe has staged a variety of topical theme plays in San Francisco and abroad. In its repertory are the antiwar play *The Minstrel Show, or Civil Rights in a Cracker Barrel* (1967); *L'Amante Militaire* (1967), an Obie Award–winning satire of the Vietnam War; an adaptation of Brecht's *Congress of the Whitewashers* (1969); *The Dragon Lady's Revenge* (1971); Brecht's *The Mother* (1973); *Frijoles* (1975); *False Promises* (1976); and *Hotel Universe* (1977), which depicts unfair housing practices in San Francisco. In 1979, the troupe staged Dario Fo's social farce about food-price inflation, *We Can't Pay: We Won't Pay,* and *Squash,* which focuses on food prices and shortages in Southern California. *Americans, or Last Tango in Huahuatenango* (1981) unmasks minority and Third World issues, and *Secrets in the Sand* (1983) reveals the consequences of radioactive fallout and atomic-weapons testing in the Utah desert. *Steeltown* (1984), which develops the American labor movement from the 1930s on, was followed by *Factwino, The Opera* (1985) and *Spain 36* (1986), a musical based on the Spanish Civil War and international politics. *The Mozamgola Caper* (1986) depicts American foreign policy, and *Ripped Van Winkle* (1988) is a satire on the social and political changes in San Francisco since the 1960s hippie period. *Seeing Double* (1989), an Obie Award–winning mistaken-identity musical farce performed in Israel in 1990 for Israeli and Palestinian audiences, offers a simplistic "share the territory" solution to the Israel–Palestine conflict. Performed in outdoor, physical comedy style, the piece is enhanced by pop and rock songs. *Rats* (1990), a fantasy nightmare, satirizes the era of George Bush, Donald Trump, and Jesse Helms. *Back to Normal* (1991), directed in broad farce style by Ed Holmes, spoofs an American war hero's enthusiasm for waging war against Iraq. *I Ain't Yo Uncle* (1991), a revival of the 1990 production *Uncle Tom's Cabin*, updates Harriet Beecher Stowe's antislavery theme with today's racism. To celebrate thirty years in the nation's parks, in 1992 the San Francisco Mime Troupe staged *Social Work, an Election Year Fantasy,* which satirizes the Bush administration's neglect of the impoverished. Its musical comedy *Off Shore* (1993), which incorporates Kabuki and Chinese opera, develops a trade dispute over California microchips and Japanese rice and its effects on the world economy and global integration. *Soul Suckers From Outer Space* (1996) parodies outer-space intervention and greedy, profit-making motives when seismologist Franklin Brown returns to his home town after an earthquake to find that an alien-introduced, fast-food hamburger has made the townspeople money-hungry. With the aid of scientist Celeste, with whom he falls in love, and the intercession of Mother Nature, a second earthquake restores the town to normal. The troupe's 1996 repertory also included *13 Dias/13 Days*, a full-length show with music and video about the Zapatista uprising in Chiapas, Mexico, and *Gotta Getta Life,* dealing with today's youth problems, which toured high schools. *Killing Time* (1997) satirized the U.S. government's accomplishments in the 1990s. In 1979, 1981, and 1984, the troupe won the Bay Area Critics Circle Award, and in 1987, it received the Tony Award for outstanding regional theatre.

Although the San Francisco Mime Troupe has gradually moved from the use of mime and silent theatre to verbal protest comedy that draws upon current topical issues and in which the actor is a speaking comedian, dancer, singer, and musician, it remains a physical comedy company with roots in ancient mime. Like Doric mime farces and commedia dell'arte, the troupe presents modern stock characters in real life, confronting current issues through improvised dialogue. A harmonious balance between mime and verbal comedy has rendered the San Francisco Mime Troupe one of America's foremost political and physical theatre companies.

Bread and Puppet Theatre

German sculptor Peter Schumann, a civil rights and antiwar activist, founded the Bread and Puppet Theatre in a loft in New York's Lower East Side. For Schumann and his company, theatre is not commercial entertainment but is as essential as bread; it should make spectators aware of social and political issues in a spirit of communion. Their productions have included sharing bread with the spectators to convey a "return to the earth" philosophy of living.

The company first presented *Dance of the Dead* at the Judson Memorial Church in 1961. It went on to stage *Fire, The Cry of the People for Meat, The Stations of the Cross, Hunger Cantata*, and other works in the streets, peace marches, parades, pageants, and many other locales, as well as in conventional theatres in America and abroad. *Life and Death of a Fireman* (1987) is a symbolic work in ten tableaux concerning the life and death of a fireman played by actors and giant puppets representing good and evil forces. *Columbus, the New World Order* (1991) conveys—through singing and moving ensembles in an outdoor space, elemental voice and prop sounds, and narration—the evils of colonialism and imperialism. The piece also explores good and evil in our society.

The company, based on Glover Farm in Vermont, each summer has invited volunteers to make puppets and help stage the yearly production of *Our Domestic Resurrection Circus,* a two-day outdoor festival that celebrates the beauties and sorrows of existence through a creative process involving puppets, masks, music, dance, acting, and miming.

A political, ritualistic, and expressionist theatre, Bread and Puppet has adopted many traditional and artistic resources, such as the animation of giant puppets along with live actors, masks, pantomime, storytelling, dance, painting, sculpture, and lighting effects. Its works are a rich blend of primitive and symbolic ritual, ancient folklore traditions, Punch and Judy shows, Sicilian and Balinese puppetry, masks, Japanese bunraku, and medieval morality plays.

Besides arousing the spectator's conscience regarding contemporary social and political issues, this company's productions offer a full aesthetic experience through the juxtaposition of diverse art forms and artistic traditions along with ancient folk art and legends. This experience is transmitted through the presence of awesomely large, primitive puppets and masks that move slowly and silently to create a visually dramatic impact.

Dell'Arte Players Company

The Dell'Arte Players company has staged original plays in traditional *commedia* style, as well as modern verbal and movement theatre grounded in *commedia* techniques. The group began as a training program with Italian mime Carlo Mazzone Clementi and his wife, Jane Hill, in Berkeley, California, in 1971. After moving to Blue Lake, California, in 1974, in 1977 the Dell'Arte Players company played locally and toured nationally and internationally, performing in theatres and at universities and festivals. A number of the productions in this grass-roots company's repertory would focus on themes relating to its community. The founding members and artistic directors—actor–director Michael Fields and actress Joan Schirle, who were later joined by actor–artistic director Donald Forrest and stage director Jael Weisman—were also responsible for developing a unique, full-time training program that gradually expanded to include such physical acting methods as the Alexander Technique and Clown Theatre and the improvisational techniques and stock characters of the commedia dell'arte.

The company's first productions, *The Loon's Rage* (1977) and *Whiteman Meets Bigfoot* (1980), depict Native American legends based on the *commedia* format. *Malpractice, or Love's the Best Doctor* (1984), an adaptation of Molière's satire of charlatan doctors, is played in period comedy with the use of masks and melodrama. *Intrigue at Ah-Pah* (1980), published in the eighth volume of *West Coast Plays*, and *The Road Not Taken* (1986) are mystery plays revolving around the female detective Scar Tissue. Incorporating physical comedy, slapstick, and clowning, the first play deals with California water politics and the second with the environmental issue of the Gasquet–Orleans road project to destroy a pre–Ice Age forest in the Klamath Mountains. With *The Bacchae* (1987), the Dell'Arte Players company departed from modern-day *commedia* to offer a stylized production of the ancient

Greek play, with a chorus in original Greek. The group received three Hollywood Drama Logue Critics Awards and Bay Area Theatre Critics Circle Awards for ensemble performance for its productions of *The Bacchae, Malpractice,* and *The Road Not Taken. Performance Anxiety,* an earlier production revived in 1988, explores with *commedia lazzi* and stock characters the safe-sex question. Peter Barnes's *Red Noses* (1988), which depicts the Black Plague in medieval France during which strolling players provoke laughter among the dying, received Best Production and Best Musical Score Awards from the San Diego Circle in 1988. *Slapstick* (1989), about violence among vacationing family members, toured California.

Beautiful Swimmers (1990) by Lynne Abels depicts a paraplegic woman and a Vietnam veteran who ward off their past to fight for virgin redwoods. *Journey of the Ten Moons* (1990), which interweaves the discovery of Humboldt Bay with the Native American tale of Coyote's defeat of the Winter Moons, was revived to tour nationally in 1995 and 1996. *Fear of Falling* (1991), the third Scar Tissue mystery, contrasts the lifestyle of the homeless with those of San Francisco Pacific Heights high society and computer-obsessed motel clerks in a fast-moving missing persons play. *Punch* (1992) by Joan Schirle, played in traditional commedia dell'arte, blends medieval religious and social institutions with the present-day struggle for free expression, hampered by church and state. *Korbel: A Humboldt County Soap Opera* (1993) and *Korbel II: The Wedding* (1995), among the group series about regional history and themes, reveals the secrets of a tiny mill town a few miles from the Dell'Arte Players company in Blue Lake. *Shadow Catchers* (1993) focuses on Humboldt County photographers Emma Belle Freeman and Ruth Roberts, who photographed and documented the lives of Yurok women and dedicated themselves to Native American rights. At the Dell'Arte Mad River Festival in 1996, Joan Schirle premiered her one-woman show *Up All Night With Joan*, a mythological, humorous, and lyrical piece about a kidnapped child's account of the conflicting desires of her mother, uncle, sister, and herself, performed with mime, masks, and music. During the 1996 holiday season, the company toured California with its comedies *Out of the Frying Pan*, a clown show in which four zany chefs look at regional history by cooking up a menu that demonstrates how successive waves of immigrants transform and obliterate the previous inhabitants' cuisine, and *Further Frying*, a sequel performed to gather food donations for hungry families.

The Dell'Arte Players company has perpetuated *commedia*'s improvisational spirit in a lively and outrageously comical theatre composed of mime, text, masks, clowning, martial arts, and thought-provoking content.

Carlo Mazzone Clementi

The founder of the Dell'Arte training program, Carlo Mazzone Clementi, an internationally recognized commedia dell'arte expert and master of improvisational comedy, mime, juggling, and acrobatics, taught many theatre clowns, mimes, and physical comedy teachers. A former partner of Marcel Marceau, Clementi worked with Jacques Copeau for three years as a student assistant and performer and played in such European companies as the Piccolo Teatro in Milan and Vittorio Gassman's National Theatre in Italy. In 1957, he toured the United States, performing with Sartori masks in his one-man show, *Six Characters in Search of Commedia.* He taught movement styles, mime, and *commedia* at New York University, Carnegie Institute of Technology, University of California at Berkeley and Davis, and the American

Conservatory Theatre in San Francisco. After founding a training program in 1971 with his wife, Jane Hill, in Berkeley, California, in 1974, he taught at their Dell'Arte School of Mime and Comedy in Blue Lake, California, and organized summer seminars in mime, clown, and mask. He staged student productions of Shakespeare and musical comedy and, in 1976, began to direct original plays with Native American subjects and an Italian format, such as *The Loon's Rage* (1977). In 1983, Clementi founded the Commedia School of Copenhagen with Ole Brekke. *American Village*, a film he co-produced, won an Italian award for best documentary in 1958.

In the following passage, Clementi relates *commedia* to twentieth-century mime and clowning and emphasizes the human value and sense of creative discovery of both mime and *commedia* in the computer age:

> Because it is based on *lazzo*, which means to catch an action, *commedia* contains mime, which is the source of all comedy. For example, in the following *lazzo* the *commedia* character Pulcinella enters in the dark and bumps against a tree center stage and then moves back and forth and around the tree, bumping into it over and over, finally screaming, "Mama, Help! Help! I'm lost in the forest!" The mime is an explorer, and so is the *commedia* actor wearing a mask who suddenly somersaults or sings. What is important here is the sense of discovery, the "improviso" which eventually brings about the spoken word. Commedia dell'arte consists in creative discovery. The comical or ironical element in a *commedia* situation is not first found in sound but in silence. Everything comes from silence. The dynamic aspect of my body, from the feet to the pelvis, begins with walking. From the kind of walking I do, I develop a character and his expression. In this process, mime helps you find yourself, for which the computer is useless because it only teaches you what you already know.
>
> Today mime is expanding and being combined with speaking theatre. Man has to be represented fully in the theatre, not just by words and literature, which have been saturating the theatre. The need for action in the theatre is important. Mime is the intelligence of action. Self-discovery is part of the nature of the human being, and mime is still part of this. In America, *commedia* is keeping up with the pace of circus and mime. But *commedia* is found in many forms of theatre in the world, as in the Kabuki theatre of Japan and the Topeng in Bali. It is wherever professional acting is performed as though it is the first time and is never performed in exactly the same way but always inventively. *Commedia* is wherever mimes are creative performers.[14]

The United Mime Workers

In the early 1970s, the United Mime Workers, a collective of composer–performers, set out to explore our society's social and political ideologies. After meeting at the University of Illinois, Bob Feldman, Deborah Langerman, Jeff Glassman, and Candace Walworth began studying mime with Claude Kipnis, Kabuki with Shozo Sato, and musical composition with Herbert Brun. From 1971 on, the group toured and taught in the United States and abroad, staging shows for adults and children that explored various forms of visual language and incorporated musical scores, props, projections, sound effects, and words. Its early pieces—*What Do You Say?, Psychiatrist, Is the Price Right?*, and *Chaos*—examine the social, economic, and political conventions and contradictions in our lives. *A Visual Performance of Compositions* extracts visual images from musical scores and explores communication forms such as gestures, words, projections, and sounds. *Mime Is No Object* comments on our economic system and the value placed on the money-making process. *Shadows Beyond the*

Benefit of a Doubt (1982) revolves around a typical American household no longer functioning on its own. The piece experiments with actors, texts, and objects placed on compositionally independent tracks to break down basic, ideological assumptions in our society that need change. The group utilized a film technique for cutting scenes called "pivoting," which establishes time spans not limited by conventional means and depicts action through short, dense glimpses of the characters' lives. This vocal, manual, and gestural "pivoting" was conveyed as much through a set of techniques as through classical pantomime or mime. The United Mime Workers' performance and experimental composition projects have established a creative process for a theatre that does not rely upon conventions of time and space illusion. Although the company disbanded in 1986, its members continue to work in theatre.

Friends Mime Theatre

Founded in 1973 by Michael Moynihan and Barbara Leigh, the Friends Mime Theatre of Milwaukee has developed into a community-based physical theatre company that presents works of social concern at such unconventional sites as prisons, parking lots, churches, and barns. Like the *commedia* players, the company has explored the meaning of present-day issues through the use of mime, clowning, masks, music, and verbal text. From its first production, *A Myth of Changes*, to such later ones as *Earthworks* (1982), it has related modern-day myths to ancient myths and how they influence the community. The company aims to activate social change for its own members, as well as for spectators.

Comediantes Pantomima-Teatro

Sigfrido Aguilar began his Comediantes Pantomima-Teatro in Guanajuato, Mexico, in 1979 to stage works that use techniques and methods developed at his Estudio Busqueda mime school, a nucleus for contemporary mime in Latin America that he founded in 1972. Along with his school and company, Aguilar organized a National Encounter and International Festival of Contemporary Mime, which invites international companies to perform and tour in Mexico each year. His company of multinational mimes, which has performed in Mexico and North America, incorporates both natural and abstract movement into comical and serious pieces. *La Loteria* (1979), based on a game that resembles bingo, manifests the Mexican love of fun and fiestas while it depicts the customs, humor, gestures, and local music of Mexicans dressed in native costumes. *El Juguete Popular* (1981) conveys a personal vision of Mexico's social life through a portrayal of country women who travel to the city to sell their wares and folk-art toys in markets and on sidewalks. *Lo Mexicano en la Calaca* (1982) depicts popular Mexican symbols that evoke death. *Ocumicho,* presented at the Second International Festival of Contemporary Mime in 1985, is a collective creation, with Mexican themes concerning death and politico-social issues such as exploitation of the poor by big business and the military. This ethnic theatre evokes rare images of Mexican folklore and life, both realistic and surrealistic, in a poetic ensemble of movement, music, and narration.

Aguilar has trained many American mimes at his Estudio Busqueda mime school in Mexico, as well as in workshops in the United States. Among the mime artists and companies he has influenced is the Chicago-based Partners in Mime.

El Teatro Campesino

El Teatro Campesino was founded by Luis Valdez as a farmworkers' theatre that satirizes working issues with farm owners. Influenced by the San Francisco Mime
Troupe, the Teatro Campesino style is comprised of exaggerated slapstick and verbal humor. The company has also staged puppet shows and one-act folk musicals. It
took on broader political clowning with *Vietnam Campesino* (1970), which derided
the Pentagon's policy of buying nonunion farmers' lettuce and drafting Mexican-
Americans to fight in Vietnam. Their musical *Zoot Suit* (1978), based on a 1940s Los
Angeles trial in which seventeen Mexican-Americans were unjustly tried for murder, was performed on Broadway and made into a film.

Clowns and New Vaudevillians

Through the influence of Jacques Lecoq's training methods and the expansion of a
new wave of clowning that combined acting and mime with circus techniques,
clowns often called New Vaudevillians, became an important part of movement theatre in America.

New Vaudeville was born in the 1980s, when clown–mimes began to perform
in shows in which they integrated their eclectic skills with acting and miming. Their
full-length acts consisted of clowning, music hall entertainment, song and dance,
whiteface pantomime, slapstick, *cabotinage* (ham acting), and silent-film acting. Its
roots in street entertainment, this new-wave, performance-oriented clowning thrived
greatly on audience participation. Continuing the spirit of the 1960s experimental
theatre, it developed nontraditional entertainment that fused movement with multiple theatre and clown skills in a spontaneous and anarchistic manner.

In some respects, New Vaudeville did not differ from Old Vaudeville. In
nineteenth-century France and in the beginnings of American theatre, "Vaudeville"
was a term employed to give a sense of unity to entertainment in which a short dramatic sketch or pantomime was interspersed with songs and dances, acrobatic feats,
and other unrelated diversions that different artists performed. Today, "New Vaudeville" is a term used to give a sense of unity to the disparate forms and skills of a
group of performers difficult to categorize. This variety can also be found within
each performer's act. Thus, the New Vaudevillian might be simultaneously a juggler,
clown, mime, actor, magician, dancer, or other kind of performer.

To the presence of multiple forms and skills is added the element of physical
virtuosity common to both Old and New Vaudeville. However, in New Vaudeville
this physical virtuosity is combined with character development and dramatic situations. The New Vaudeville clown's skills are thus rarely separate from the actor's.
Juggling and clowning devices might also be introduced in a production based on a
dramatic text, as in the Flying Karamazov Brothers' version of Shakespeare's *Comedy of Errors*. Yet, contrary to Old Vaudeville, New Vaudeville does not content itself solely with entertainment value. It can make bold political statements and criti-
cize modern social institutions.

Late twentieth-century clowning and New Vaudeville are good examples of
the postmodern trend to experiment with outrageously novel combinations. Moreover, through the development of New Vaudeville and clown theatre, a number of
clowns and jugglers have brought clowning back to the stage, enhancing their own

skills with mime and acting, just as many mimes have enriched their art with clowning skills.

John Towsen

John Towsen—clown, teacher, festival director, and theatre historian—is among those who have fostered new directions in clowning and brought the circus clown into the theatre. Born in New York in 1948, at age six he appeared as a TV actor with Red Skelton and Jackie Gleason. After receiving a Ph.D. in theatre from New York University, Towsen studied juggling with Hovey Burgess, theatre clowning with Lecoq-trained Cheryl McFadden, *commedia* at the Dell'Arte School of Mime and Comedy, circus techniques at the Ringling Bros. and Barnum and Bailey Clown College, and comedy with Carlo Mazzone Clementi. Towsen produced New York's first clown festival in 1983. At this event, he and Fred Yockers performed in Towsen's *A Beautiful Friendship*; Towsen also staged *Conflict, No Resolution* with Jan Greenfield and Peter Von Berg. In 1985, Towsen organized a second clown theatre festival for which he directed an ensemble show entitled *All Fall Down*. In 1986, he and eight actors formed a repertory company to perform plays and clown theatre.

The author of *Clowns: A Panoramic History*, consulting editor of Hovey Burgess's *Circus Techniques*, and assistant editor of the *Drama Review* and *Mask, Mime and Marionette*, Towsen has written numerous articles and reviews on physical comedy. He has also taught at New York University, Ohio University, Greenfield College, Juilliard School of Drama, and universities and movement festivals nationwide.

The main thrust of Towsen's physical theatre has been to employ clowning to enrich social, political, and all theatre. In *A Beautiful Friendship*, he adeptly unifies movement and verbal expression, clown humor and drama, through the failures, trials, and illusions of two veteran showmen lugging their tattered trunks, stage, and sets in search of El Dorado, show-business heaven. In *Conflict, No Resolution*, Towsen develops a Faustian theme in which two clown characters sell their souls to director Sandor Diablo to become serious artists. Their clowning is only secondary to their plight of being bound to their art and audience. Here, classical clowning evolves into a dramatic piece with substance. Both pieces exemplify Towsen's belief that virtuosity should be removed from physical theatre through ensemble work, in which the performer can lose himself in the art as a whole. For Towsen, twentieth-century clown art is a fast-changing one:

> To me, clowning is more of a character-oriented form of theatre than a branch of movement theatre. The clown is a universal type of character with millions of variations, but, despite the different clown styles, there are some striking similarities between all clowns. Every clown is a sort of archetype, an innocent character, an actor who performs not a role but something of his own personality, of his alter ego. He is different from a stand-up comic in that he is always the butt of the joke. Although movement is important in order for a clown to express himself, I don't see clowning necessarily as a movement art because I feel the technique is secondary. You can be a great clown without being a mime. You can be a good juggler and not be a clown. Some of the greatest clowns did not depend that much on technique. What makes a good clown is experience in front of an audience, vulnerability, acting talent and some technique, above all, a certain way of thinking—that is, with a certain clown logic—which goes beyond everyday realism.
>
> A hundred years ago, the clown was more in the circus and on the fairgrounds. He was part of a theatre family tradition. If his parents were performers, he performed.

Today it's different. In our clown theatre festivals, the performers come from a mime or theatre tradition and have been drawn to clowning. Their parents are stock-brokers or dentists or garbage collectors. Clowns are more educated and familiar with modern theatre. They have acted in rep companies. They have more serious theatre background. But something in the clown grabbed them and never let them go. The virtuoso aspect of clowning as one saw it in great clowns like Grock is magnificent, but many clowns are taking clowning to new places now. They feel the clown is a character or a theatrical being.

In the future, I think we are going to see a lot more of the solo virtuoso clown and the clown concert. But we are also beginning to see a reexploration of the clown partner. We are going to see clowns getting into theatre and conceptual pieces. Some clowns—as Stanley Allen Sherman, for example—do performance art in their clown shows. Bill Irwin is also somewhat in that area. He is not so much into narrative and dramatic framework. He toys with the postmodern mentality and satirizes it, but he also uses it in his pieces.

I feel I did some ground-breaking work in the field of physical comedy. I have gathered and organized material from many sources, such as circus clowning, Chinese acrobatics, silent films, *commedia*, Lecoq training, and mime, and synthesized it and applied it to dramatic material. I have tried to give content to physical theatre and to vitalize regular theatre with greater physicality.[15]

Pickle Family and Big Apple Circuses

Some of the best New Vaudeville performers have emerged from the Pickle Family Circus, begun in San Francisco in 1974 by two former San Francisco Mime Troupe members, clown–juggler Larry Pisoni and designer–juggler Penny Snider. Under the artistic direction of juggler Judy Finelli, who also directed the Pickle Family School, this favorite West Coast, one-ring family circus with eighteen performers and a five-piece jazz band offered traditional clown acts, juggling and trapeze artists, dance, and mime. It later moved into the realm of fairy tales and magic with a lighter form of clowning. In the early 1990s, it became the New Pickle Circus, adding such New Circus multidisciplinary elements as dance, costumes, and high-tech visuals to its productions and no longer performing outdoors. In 1992, modern dancer Tandy Beal choreographed *Tossing and Turning,* which was performed at the 1995 Mid-Atlantic Movement Theatre Festival. In 1994, Beal wrote, choreographed, and directed *Jump Cuts! The Circus Goes to the Movies.* And in 1997, she created and directed *The Big Bang and Other Rude Noises,* in which a couple snatched by an alien is shown striking visuals of the creation of the universe. The Pickle Family Circus has harbored improvisational comedians and clowns with acting backgrounds, such as Diane Wasnak, Jeff Raz, and Joan Mankin, lead clown for four years. Mankin went on to found the Miracle Theatre in 1983 with Paoli Lacy and Mark Kennedy, collaborating with Wasnak, visual and stage artists, composers, and playwrights.

It was at the Pickle Family Circus that three talented American vaudevillians—Bill Irwin, Geoff Hoyle, and Bob Berky—began as clowns. Irwin, Hoyle, Berky, and Larry Pisoni were also among those who participated in San Francisco's first New Vaudeville Festival in the summer of 1986.

An ex-member of the San Francisco Mime Troupe, Paul Binder left to found the one-ring Big Apple Circus with his juggling partner, Michael Christensen, in 1977. Former French circus historian and clown Dominique Jando, who helped establish the French National Circus, that country's first professional circus school, undertook the artistic direction. Performing at Lincoln Center, the Big Apple Circus has harbored a number of talented vaudevillians, such as juggler–dancer–illusionist–physicist Michael Moschen.

Bill Irwin

One of the most avant-garde of the New Vaudevillians, Bill Irwin studied acting at the University of California in Los Angeles, worked in theatre with Herbert Blau in Oberlin, Ohio, and trained at the Ringling Bros. and Barnum and Bailey Clown College before entering the Pickle Family Circus and performing in the Oberlin Dance Collective. In 1981, Irwin left for New York to stage his Obie Award–winning show, *The Regard of Flight*. In 1984, he played in the Broadway production of Dario Fo's *Accidental Death of an Anarchist*; in the summer of 1985, he appeared in Brecht's *A Man's a Man* and in Chekhov's *The Seagull* at the La Jolla Playhouse. In 1989, Irwin's *Largely New York* became a Broadway hit. Collaborating with David Shiner and the Red Clay Ramblers, Irwin performed in the zany clown show *Fool Moon* (1993).

Irwin has skillfully fused the art of the actor with that of the clown and the slapstick, silent-film comedian, along with vaudevillian and music hall elements, to create a dynamic, postmodern clown art. Postmodern in its revealing glimpses inside the performer's art, *Largely New York* portrays the clown–mime's mishaps with technological stage trappings and with the invasion of new skilled performers who jeopardize his own art. In his clown acts, Irwin introduces the simplest devices to provoke laughter. His flexible body, which he contorts and distorts, moves in frenzied circles and spasmodically jitter bugs. In one of his funniest bits—that of a waiter serving spaghetti—he wears a Groucho Marx wig and nose and struggles with a long strand of spaghetti, which unwinds across the stage and behind the backdrops to reappear on the other side. Irwin's clown is always the grotesque butt of unforeseen hazards. Although he seems in control as he operates a remote-control device, the device never fails to act up. One of Irwin's magical moments is his illusion pantomime of descending several flights of stairs while inside a trunk, creating a poetic, dreamlike image that lingers long after the performance.

Bob Berky

Theatre clown Bob Berky claims that his early trumpet and French horn lessons influenced his future clowning. After training and touring with mime Tony Montanaro, he won the Obie Award for *Foolsfire,* created with clown–jugglers Michael Moschen and Fred Garbo in 1983, and wrote and performed with Moschen in the off-Broadway success *The Alchemedians*. Besides touring extensively with *An Evening with Bob Berky*, he has appeared in original works with symphony orchestras and in planetariums.

In his versatile clown sketches, Berky plays, among other characters, a bird-watcher, a man showering with a wee piece of soap, and a character who chooses a card from a deck entitled "Destruction of the World" and hurls an imaginary globe to the ground. In *An Evening with Bob Berky,* after playing a nostalgic accordion tune in semidarkness, he removes from a big trunk two toilet plungers that become earphones, a telescope, and deer antlers. Summoning two spectators onto the stage with his kazoo, he has one pound on a small bell and the other blow on a whistle while he dances about in a tutu. Another rides an imaginary motorcycle and then chooses between a smaller unicycle or a six-footer, to which Berky carefully tapes his victim before he takes off. In *The Alchemedians,* Berky and Moschen juggle and clown throughout an ancient ritual of transforming bowls, balls, and rods into gold.

Berky is at his best playing with his audience. His gentle authority sparks his intimidated volunteers into actively taking part, while he offers choices to his timid participants. His energetic zaniness soon has them jumping at the toot of his kazoo. This irresistible and loving clown's need to involve his spectators stems from his desire to share his character's problems, failures, and moments of delight. Much of the success of Berky's clown lies in his talent for animating his audience members as performers.

Berky describes the art of clowning and how clowning and miming are linked with acting:

> The basic elements of clowning are honesty, vulnerability, incisiveness and a need to expose the characteristics of the human animal without being hurtful, without forcing the audience to withdraw from the truth because of its obvious connection with their own lives. And any and all skills can be used as a foundation for clowning. Victor Borge uses the piano and music. Grock used acrobatics and music, along with an incredible understanding of human nature.
>
> Certainly the best actors move well, each movement filled with the intention of the character. The best mimes also do not become mired in technique but express character and emotion through gesture. Clowns are certainly actors and movement is important to their perception of the world.[16]

Geoff Hoyle

Before studying mime with Etienne Decroux in Paris, Geoff Hoyle trained in English and drama at Birmingham University in England. After working with a London community art group called Inter-Action, he joined San Francisco's Pickle Family Circus in 1975, where he played the long-nosed clown Mr. Sniff for six years. His one-man shows, *Boomer* (1986) and *The Fool Show* (1988), were followed by *Geoff Hoyle Meets Slap Happy,* for which he and comedian–percussion musician Keith Terry won the Bay Area Critics Award in 1982. *Boomer* is an autobiographical piece about family values, and *The Convict's Return* (1992) revolves around the great vaudeville comics of the past and survival in show business. *Geni(us)* (1995), created by Hoyle and Tony Taccone and performed by Hoyle and Sharon Lockwood, examines death and old age; through mime, clowning, vaudeville, and audience interaction it also satirizes superstar entertainment, depression victims, psychiatrists, the media, and current politicians. In *The First 100 Years* (1999), Hoyle creates an aging and forgotten existential clown through modern *commedia*, mime, clowning, magic, and a Punch and Judy show. Hoyle also played the leads in Dario Fo's *Ubu Unchained* (1982) and *Accidental Death of an Anarchist* (1984) and appeared with clown Bill Irwin in Bertolt Bercht's *A Man's a Man* (1985) and in Fo's *Archangels Don't Play Pinball* (1987). As Volpone's servant Mosca in *Volpone* (1993), he mixed physical comedy with villiany. He performed at the Davis and Elkins Movement Theatre International Festival, the Winnipeg International Mime Festival, and the Lincoln Center "Serious Fun" Festival. His film, radio, and TV credits include playing in Robert Altman's film *Popeye* (1980), in a clown segment on the BBC's *Paul Daniels Show* (1984), and in Showtime TV's *Faerie Tale Theatre* (1984).

Hoyle's talents range from ribald slapstick and stand-up comedy to boisterous, English-style clowning, pantomime, corporeal mime, mimicry, puppetry, tap dance, commedia dell'arte, and absurdist comedy. While his mime–clowning has grown more verbal, with French, Italian, and British accents enhancing his characterizations, his physical comedy skills have enlivened his roles in speaking theatre.

Hoyle deploys his physical comedy skills in a classical manner. Rather than combining them all in New Vaudeville style, he utilizes a single skill to develop the comic elements of a particular sketch. This permits him to more fully explore his range of talents. In his *Fool Show*, for example, he employs one of his many talents in each of his sketches. In *Cartoon,* he resorts to dance–mime to move like a pinball in a cartoon film. His comic character *Mr. Sniff*, a long-nosed, sniffing clown who judges objects and people according to their good and bad odors, engages in traditional pratfalling and tumbling, knocking down scenery and falling through the stage floor. He engages his physical virtuosity to deal with tyrannical inanimate objects such as a chair to which his hand is stuck and has to be sawed off to liberate it, or a music stand that is either too tall or too small. Jumping on a wavering chair mounted on a trunk, he then climbs over a terrified audience. *Two Waiters* calls for stylized, whiteface illusion pantomime as the protagonists pursue one another and disappear and reappear from behind a screen. Hoyle turns puppeteer in *Court Jester,* in which he interacts with his twin alter ego: a puppet head on a stick with a cap and mask, large spectacles, and a big nose and moustache. In the same skit, he transforms himself into a nobleman by mimicking a rooster. Hoyle's gift for playing type characters is seen in *Commedia,* in which he plays Pantalone, wearing a mask to portray the miserly, impotent pedant who rattles off in Italian while he fingers his crotch and his moneybag and flirts with a female spectator. He makes use of outrageously bold clowning, sneezing all over the stage, passing gas, and swearing at Arlecchino. At one point, he dons the Arlecchino mask to play the servant, who is so hungry he eats a fly. In his sketch *The Fundraiser,* Hoyle carefully delineates a slow-speaking, stuffy Englishman with an uncontrollable twitch who tells a joke with serious memory lapses. In *Spare,* he creates a deadpan-faced character wearing a baggy trenchcoat who has three legs and waltzes about, his third leg dragging behind. Hoyle's expressionless face and three waltzing legs augment the absurdist elements of his comedy. He explores other kinds of comic absurdism as Ubu in *Ubu Unchained*, the fool in *Accidental Death of an Anarchist,* the pope in *The Pope and the Witch,* the convict in *The Convict's Return,* and Clov in *Endgame.*

With his clowning and miming Hoyle combines his acting skills and talent for creating eccentric type characters. He extracts the best from the English music hall and circus, artfully blending his physical skills with his corporeal movement training to achieve a wide range of clown comedy.

Avner the Eccentric

Avner the Eccentric's clown–juggler–mime skills and his early experience as a street entertainer render him one of New Vaudeville's avant-gardists. Born Avner Eisenburg in Atlanta, Georgia, in 1948, at age twelve he learned to juggle with Hovey Burgess. After studying chemistry and biology, he received his B.A. in drama. It was

MACCUS Acteur comique des Attellanes des Latins. duquel on a tiré le nom et l'habit du Polichinel moderne.

Maccus, Stock Peasant in Atellan Farce. Courtesy of Bibliothèque Nationale, Paris.

GAVTIER GARGVILLE.

1

Gautier, dont tu vois la posture.   Sa mine n'eust point de Seconde:
Sceut ioindre L'Art à la Nature.   Et L'on le pleure Iustement,
Pour railler agreablement: Puis qu'il fit rire tout le monde.

Harve Inuentor Rossolet fecit   *Mariette exch Auec priuilege du Roy*

Gaultier-Garguille, Seventeenth-Century French Comic Type. Courtesy of
Bibliothèque Nationale, Paris.

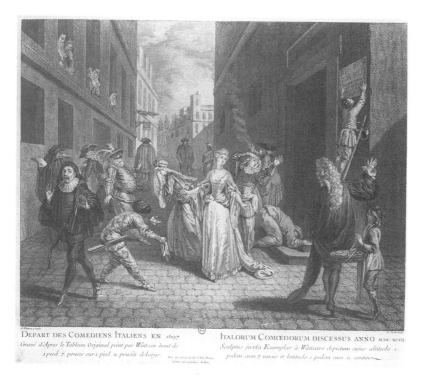

Departure of the Italian Comedians, 1697. Courtesy of Bibliothèque Nationale, Paris.

Pantalon, Harlequin, Francisquina, 16th century. Courtesy of Bibliothèque Nationale, Paris.

JEAN-BAPTISTE DÉBURAU

Jean-Baptiste Déburau. Courtesy of Bibliothèque Nationale, Paris.

Angelo Musco, Sicilian Mime-Actor.

Etienne Decroux in *Sport*, 1948. Photo by Etienne Bertrand Weill.

Eliane Guyon in Decroux's *La Statue*, 1948. Photo by Etienne Bertrand Weill.

Decroux's company in *L'Usine* (The Factory), 1948. Photo by Etienne Bertrand Weill.

Etienne and Maximilien Decroux in *Combat Antique*, 1948. Photo by Etienne Bertrand Weill.

J.-L. Barrault fait une magistrale composition du rôle de Debureau, le célèbre mime

Jean-Louis Barrault as Debureau in the film *Les Enfants du Paradis*. Courtesy of Bibliothèque Nationale, Paris.

Marcel Marceau in *Bip As A Street Musician.*

Marcel Marceau in *The Public Garden*.

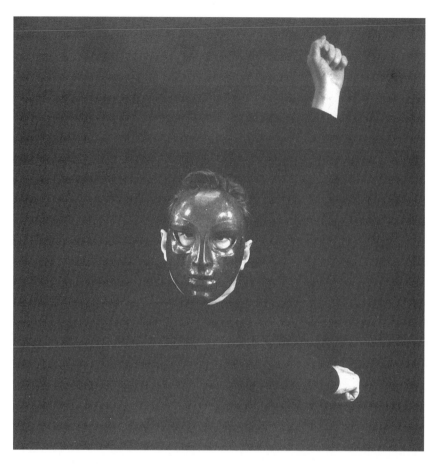

Jacques Lecoq with the Neutral Mask by Amelto Sartori. Photo by P. Lecoq.

Tomaszewski Polish Mime Theatre in *Faust*, 1975. Photo by Tadeusz Drankowski.

Mime-clown Leonard Pitt in *Dopo the Clown*. Photo by Dave Patrick.

Daniel Stein in *Inclined to Agree*.

Karen Hoyer in *Apparent Appearances*.

San Francisco Mime Troupe in *I Ain't Yo Uncle*. Photo by Cristina Tacone.

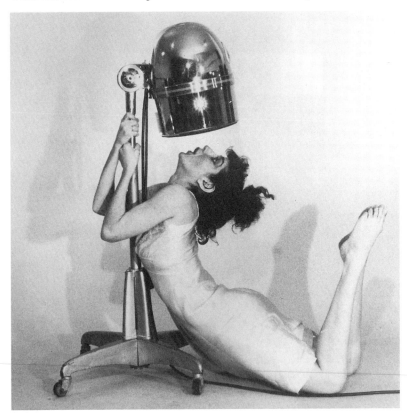

Kari Margolis of the Margolis Brown Company in *Autobahn*. Photo by Daniel Collins.

Bob Berky and Michael Moschen in *The Alchemedians*. Photo by Dan Wagner.

American Mime Theatre in *Peepshow*. Photo by Jim Moore.

Bread and Puppet Theatre.

Fred Curchack in *Stuff As Dreams Are Made On*.

Thomas Leabhart in *How I Was Perplexed and What I Did About It*.

The Cabanas Pink Inc. Art in Motion. Photo by Linda Marraccini.

Bond Street Theatre in *Cozmic Jazz*. Photo by Joanna Sherman.

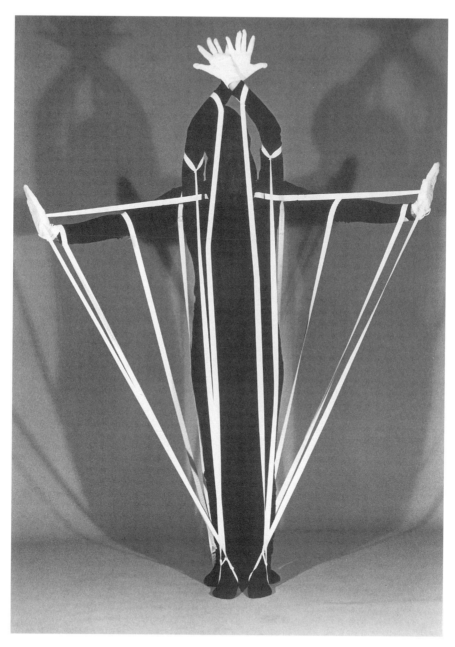

Ko-Motion Movement Theater in *Vectors* with Ann Morris and Rich Kuperberg.

Hors Strate Company in *Groudeck* at the Mimos Festival 1993. Photo by Pascal Couillaud.

New Pickle Circus, Diane Wasnak and Jeff Raz in *Tossing and Turning*. Photo by Chris Wahlberg.

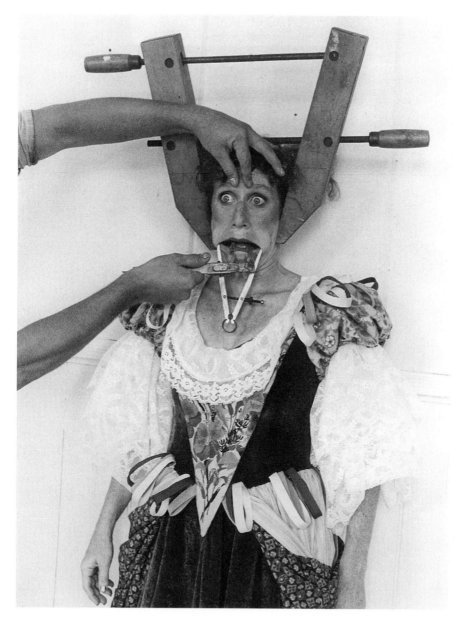

Joan Mankin in Dell' Arte Players' *Malpractice*.

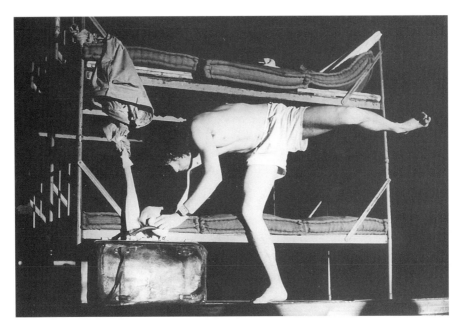

Czech clown Bolek Polivka in *The Survivor*. Photo by Josef Kratochvil.

Gest Polish Mime Theatre in *The Dogs*. Photo by Andrzej Leparski.

National Theatre of the Deaf in *Ophelia*. Photo by A. Vincent Scarano.

Axis Mime Company and Touchstone Theatre in *The Number 14*. Photo by David Cooper.

Valerie Dean and Don Rieder in Klauniada Company's *Bivo Road Show*. Photo by Rex Rystedt.

Vancouver Moving Theatre in *Samarambi*. Photo by David Cooper.

Theatre Beyond Words in *The Boy Who Could Sing Pictures*.

Odin Teatret Company in *Talabot* by Eugenio Barba. Photo by Tony D'Urso.

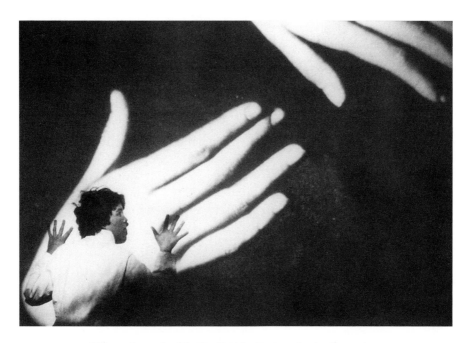

Mime-clown Letitia Bartlett in *Ecstasy in the Everyday*.

Balinese Clown I Nyoman Wenten in *The Old Man Dance*.

Vol Ras Company in *Strip Tease*. Photo by Andrzej Leparski.

Pulcinella, Commedia Stock Type, 1618.

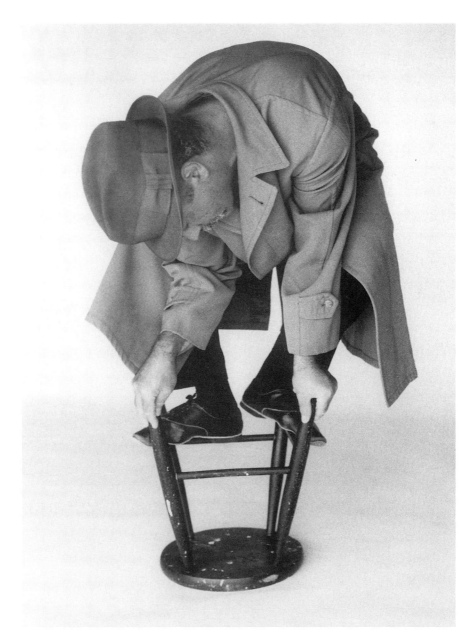

Giuseppe Condello of 40 Below Mime in *D.P.*

DonDoro Theatre in *Beauty and the Monk* at the Mimos Festival 1995. Photos by Takaharu Karaki.

at Jacques Lecoq's school in Paris, from 1971 to 1974, that he discovered his clown character. He later trained and taught with Carlo Mazzone Clementi at the Dell'Arte School of Mime and Comedy in Blue Lake, California. He began juggling, performed magic and puppet shows, and mimed in the streets, at fairs, and in theatres across America and in Europe, Israel, Asia, South America, and North Africa. He has conducted workshops in movement theatre, *commedia*, and circus skills at universities, colleges, medical conferences, and festivals nationwide and in Europe and Mexico. He also taught mime therapy at the Institute of Expressive Therapies at the University of Louisville. Among the plays he has directed are Molière's *The Doctor in Spite of Himself* and Stanley Harrison's *Machiavelli and the Mandrake* at the University of Louisville. He co-starred in the Goodman Theatre's vaudeville version of *The Comedy of Errors*, played Estragon in Beckett's *Waiting for Godot* at the Pittsburgh Public Theatre, and appeared in the movie *Jewel of the Nile*.

Avner the Eccentric has been called Avner the Charming, Avner the Whimsical, Avner the Ingenious, and Avner the Entertaining. Because of his flair for targeting responsive spectators to perform with him, he could also be called Avner the Psychologist. His clown art, though highly improvisational, is tightly constructed, each comic bit building to a climax. Looking like a bearded rabbi wearing a round, red nose mask, he appears on stage hugging several baseball bats. After dropping one bat, he bends to pick it up with an appologetic air, only to drop a second one, then bends to pick up both bats, only to end up losing his derby hat in the pile of fallen objects. His antics consist of awkwardly balancing a ten-foot ladder, a newspaper, or a handkerchief on his nose or bearded chin; swallowing paper napkins, which he pulls out of his mouth in an endless chain of daisies that become a colorful bouquet of flowers; and conducting his audience in a lively symphony of clapping, whistling, and cheering. Mime serves Avner's portrayal of a naive, old-world clown who confidently approaches each stunt and belligerent object, only to end with a feeling of stunned inadequacy when things go awry. Yet, Avner's virtuosity and skills as a clown–juggler–magician are secondary to his clown's psychological and physical reactions to a world that never ceases to menace his peaceful lifestyle.

Avner describes the meaning and origins of New Vaudeville as well as his own clown art:

> New Vaudeville is a journalistic term that describes a group of performers who were growing prominent, like Bob Berky, Michael Moschen, Fred Garbo, the Karamazov Brothers, and Tom Noddy, the Bubble Guy. Although I was included in that group, we did not fit any of the stereotypes of their definitions, especially because some of us later broke the barriers of playing on and off Broadway. Mel Gussov, the critic, was one of the first to use the term New Wave Vaudeville to describe a group of performers who were doing shows together. When asked, I would reply that it's a kind of one-man vaudeville show in which I do several skills simultaneously, almost everything except singing and dancing.
>
> Among the elements of New Vaudeville is that it is nonviolent and nonracist, and it is a reaction to the kinds of theatre we don't like. Another element is that the performer doesn't need many expensive props. The Karamazov Brothers have a stage set made of cardboard boxes. Everything in my show is junk found in anyone's household. We also do not need fancy lighting or equipment to create good theatre. It is a theatre of kindness and love and of cooperation with the audience.
>
> It has nothing to do with Old Vaudeville, which, as I understand, was basically a variety show. It was a bill of eight different acts. One of them might have been a novelty

act, a juggler, or a musician. It was mostly images, dramatic sketches, monologues, and stand-up comedians, and each performer never did more than fifteen minutes utilizing one skill at a time. On the contrary, most of the performers in New Vaudeville do full-evening theatre shows combining several skills simultaneously.

New Vaudeville did not grow out of Old Vaudeville. We reinvented theatre for ourselves. We reacted against TV and Hollywood movies. We didn't react against Old Vaudeville because we didn't know it that well. We created a theatre that grew out of the streets and out of the political sense of the sixties. I happened to be a juggler. Others were doing magic or comedy. We performed at fairs, festivals, and clubs and then in theatres. There was a definite progression from the streets to Broadway.

As for my own clowning, I've always considered the audience as my partners. I try to discover what makes them laugh. Good clowns make you laugh, but great clowns can make you cry, too. Some day I will also find pathos. I create expectations and then violate them because the basis for comedy is to create the unexpected. My show is about a character who arrives on stage and begins dropping things. He is trapped there and embarrassed. He becomes a performer only when he succeeds in diving over three little kids. What is interesting is not how well he can do things, but that he cannot, for example, walk a tightrope. The clown who can dance on a rope is beautiful, but there is no drama in his act.[17]

In his work with children with communication problems, Avner has found clowning to be an effective therapy:

One of my finest experiences was working with therapists at the University of Louisville in an art-therapy graduate program called Expressive Therapy for Children with Communication Problems. The results of my workshops there were staggering. They invited me back and offered me an assistant professorship. I find the therapy tie in my work one of the most interesting aspects. The healthiest thing you can do for someone is to make them laugh. Laughter dissolves tension and is like "internal jogging." I discovered very slowly how to make people laugh, and I am now proud and happy that often when I just appear on stage people laugh.[18]

Ronlin Foreman

Ronlin Foreman, a forerunner of the clown theatre movement in America, has brought to the theatre a clowning form that is more traditional and independent from the New Vaudeville trend. Born in Alabama, Foreman received a B.F.A. in acting and directing from the University of Southern Mississippi. He then studied movement at the Valley Studio in Spring Green, Wisconsin, and with Jacques Lecoq in Paris. He has performed in lyrical, clown solo, and ensemble work, as well as in children's theatre. He has also taught children's theatre and clowning for the hearing impaired, the Ringling Bros. and Barnum and Bailey Clown College, the Dell'Arte School of Mime and Comedy, and the International School of Movement Theatre. His solo works include an adaptation of a German fairy tale, *The Golden Bird* (1976–79), and the clown pieces *A Happy Fellow* (1983) and *Pigeon Show* (1988).

Foreman innovatively integrates acting, miming, juggling, and clowning. His *A Happy Fellow* revolves around a child clown, "Ba," who attempts to engage in tightrope-walking and other clown skills. Ba portrays a child's fantasies and joys in a make-believe world in which, for example, a wooden spoon and a loaf of bread become the protagonists of a puppet show. In Ba we also see the child's first struggles with reality and suffering. Ba plays havoc with his audience, hurling cookies at them and making two spectators hold up his tightrope, only to reprimand them for their awkwardness. His wide-eyed naiveté disconcerts his spectators, who become as vulnerable as he, allowing themselves to be lured into having bananas pulled out of their ears or to be subjected to other antics. Foreman conquers his audience by creating an intimate child's world that is both comical and moving. Stemming more from a stage characterization than from circus techniques and clowning, Ba's high-pitched utterings and facial distortions, his spontaneous climbing over spectators and hiding behind the backdrop, offer a poetic rendition of the child we all have within us.

Foreman's *Pigeon Show*, subtitled *A Play of Fools,* is a metaphysical clown show that stirs both the heart and the mind. The action is centered around a doorway through which a giggling clown enters and exits, playing many characters. As in Beckett's use of props, the opening and shutting of a door marks the passage of time. Man passes through the door from one stage to another, helplessly playing the fool who must senselessly perform. In this philosophical clown piece without a central theme, a multitude of rich images that evoke anguish, fear, shame, and rapture confronts us. The despair or joy of our lot is dramatized in an intricate tapestry layered with many threads of meaning.

Foreman relates mime to his clown work and develops the relationship between movement and speaking theatre:

> My clown work has evolved out of my interest in mime. I believe that acting is an important basis for both. A lot of mimes who are not actors do not feel that it is necessary. For them, mime is associated with a particular type of technique and tricks. They feel that there is the actor, the mime, the dancer, and the clown. I don't believe these are separate.
>
> For me, mime is physical or gestural theatre. It is a theatre based on the language of the body and not on verbal language. In the theatre, there are times when the spoken word is more important, as in tragedy, where the voice plays a bigger role. In less literary works, the body takes over. In silent parts, it also plays a more important role. In theatre there are times when the dramatic expression rests totally on the body and others when it rests on the voice. And at other times they are joined, which is when the theatre is at its greatest height.[19]

Fred Curchak

As original and as divergent as Fred Curchak's art is from that of other clowns and New Vaudevillians, it has elements in common with postmodern theatre clowning, such as the intertwining of multiple forms and the honest exposure of the illusions comprising the performer's art. After receiving his B.A. and M.A. in theatre arts from Queen's College in New York, Curchak taught at Sonoma State University and at the University of Texas. Besides his innovative adaptations of *The Birds*, *Lysistrata*, *Hamlet,* and William Blake's *The Mental Traveler*, Curchak created several solo works. In *Stuff As Dreams Are Made On* (1984), based on Shakespeare's *The Tempest*, Curchak interpreted several roles through mime, clowning, masks, shadow puppetry, and audience interaction, as well as elements of Noh theatre, Balinese Topeng, Kathakali, African dance, and Grotowski's acting methods. In *Inquest for Freddy Chicken* (1988), a solo mystery play in which Curchak incorporates many of these same elements, a movie actor reveals the behind-the-scenes magic of showmanship and the witchcraft of stage visuals. *Sexual Mythology* (1989) is a postmodern opera containing clowning, music hall, mime, dance, and classical jazz and rock music that utilizes ancient legend to satirize present-day disenchantment with romantic love, sex, and marriage. It fuses magical stage effects with commentary on prejudiced social beliefs and the control of society over the individual's life. As in the eclectic antitraditionalism that characterizes postmodern art, Curchak has adapted divergent stage forms and incorporated multicultural influences, along with the *nouveau vaudeville* spirit of poking fun at oneself.

Clowns, Clowns, and More Clowns

Many other New Vaudevillians and clowns belong to the ranks of those performers who, by integrating acting and miming with the clown's physical skills, have brought clowning to the stage.

Among these are the Flying Karamazov Brothers, who have juggled to varied musical rhythms everything from bowling balls, umbrellas, cleavers, raw livers, eggs, flaming torches, cameras, and cats. In their version of Shakespeare's *Comedy of Errors,* aided by juggling, belly dancing, slack-wire walking, unicycling, and trapeze stunts, they perform an anarchistic butchering of the text. Visual poetry created from novel uses of their clowning skills enriches the acting and the characters' dramatic emotions.

Featured performers in the Flying Karamazov Brothers' New York production of the *Comedy of Errors* were the San Francisco–based Vaudeville Nouveau performers Jeff Raz, lead clown with the New Pickle Circus and member of the Pino and Raz clown team, along with Daniel Mankin and Mark Sackett, jugglers, acrobats, and variety artists who engage in theatre, clowning, and vaudeville.

A second San Francisco–based company of New Vaudevillians, who began performing at the University of Iowa in the late 1970s, is the Duck's Breath Mystery Theatre, which engages in stand-up comedy, slapstick, rock and folk singing, female and animal impersonations, and the spoofing of everything imaginable in a patchwork of New Vaudeville humor. The Duck's Breath Mystery Theatre has appeared live and on National Public Radio with its popular show, *Ask Dr. Science.*

An Obie Award recipient for *The House of Horror*, Paul Zaloom, a storyteller, political satirist, puppeteer, and former member of the Bread and Puppet Theatre, blends performance art with social and political commentary. In *My Civilization*, he humorously evokes man's beginnings up to the present and spoofs current figures and issues by manipulating everyday objects, which he enlarges on a screen. At the 1991 Philadelphia Clown-Theatre Congress, a spoof of the NEA censorship and Jesse Helms followed his comic lecture, *Phood.*

In his signature piece, *Every Dog Has Its Day,* performed at the Festival of Clown Theatre in 1963, magician–mime–clown Ezekial L. Peterhoff (known as Peterhoff), who trained at the Ringling Bros. and Barnum and Bailey Clown College and at the Valley Studio, interweaves vaudeville jokes, magic, and juggling to heighten truculent content drawing upon Native American and Egyptian mythology and metaphysics. Peterhoff has performed in Aspen, Colorado, cabarets and in American and Western European streets. From 1978 to 1980 he taught and directed mime productions at the Adelphi University of the Performing Arts. Besides contributing to the development of theatre clowning, he has explored the clown as divinity.

A former member of the San Francisco Pickle Family Circus, Derique McGee, who juggles, clowns, performs acrobatics, and dances, creates eccentric New Vaudeville characters for his audiences.

New Vaudeville clown–juggler Fred Garbo and bubble-blower Tom Noddy have performed in national mime–clown festivals.

James Donlon—pantomimist, movement teacher for actors, director of the movement theatre program at the University of California–Santa Barbara's Department of Dramatic Art and former head of mime training at the Ringling Bros. and Barnum and Bailey Clown College—founded the Menagerie Mime Theatre in 1970. Donlon's *Truck Dog*, performed at the 1991 Philadelphia International Clown-Theatre Congress, revealed the American West through the eyes of a truck dog; *Purge* (1994) satirized the thwarted condition of women; and *Wrench* (1994) depicted two brothers running their auto shop haunted by a Chicano muse. James Donlon and company's repertory mixes text, movement, song, circus, and performance arts.

A verbal and visual comedian and a teacher of mime and circus arts, Randy Judkins has appeared on TV programs such as *Good Morning America* and *The Today Show.*

The San Francisco Bay Area's Fratelli Bologna is an intimate nouveau-slapstick quartet whose members, along with clown–actor Ed Holmes of the San Francisco Mime Troupe, initiated the Saint Stupid's Day Parade, held each April 1 in San Francisco.

Silent clown Kenny Raskin's antics include animating and conversing with a coat sleeve and blowing on a flute with his nostrils.

A former Lecoq student, performance artist Jim Calder develops his sociopolitical buffoonery with subtle humor, dramatic flair, and a flexible body in *Thup, Thup, Thup,* performed at the 1988 Philadelphia Movement Theatre International Festival, in which he unveils his troubled youth and Army experiences. Among his other works are *Luftkugle Lecture*, *Locomotives*, and *Nervous Tissue*, a spoof of the academic world and politics presented at the 1993 Mid-Atlantic Movement Theatre Festival. He has been a director and instructor at the New York Tisch School of the Arts.

A graduate of the Ecole Jacques Lecoq, performance art clown, and leather maskmaker, Stanley Allan Sherman exhibits sharp political commentary in his *AeroShow,* presented at the 1992 Mid-Atlantic Movement Theatre Festival, offering playfully derisive clowning, such as sending paper airplanes and red, white, and blue toilet-paper streamers into the audience while everyone sings *The Star Spangled Banner.*

New Vaudeville jugglers who have incorporated mime–clowning and other performance skills into their acts include Hovey Burgess, author of *Circus Techniques* and a teacher of circus skills at New York University who has trained many theatre clowns and New Vaudeville artists, and San Francisco street juggler Ray Jason, who interacts with his audience in clever repartee. In *On the Edge,* Frank Olivier recites Shakespeare while juggling and performing ballet on a unicycle. Michael Davis plays an eccentric, telling jokes as he juggles globs of butter and slices of raw liver. New York illusionist–entertainer Jeff McBride joins mime to juggling, magic, and martial arts in his visually brilliant *Mask, Myth and Magic*, which opened the 1992 London International Mime Festival.

Among the musicians who have added clowning to their repertories is the San Francisco Brass Band, clown–musicians dressed in flea-market uniforms who play more with their audience than on their instruments, fusing brass-band music with corny slapstick and gags. The seven-piece Kamikaze Ground Crew band mixes circus, rock and roll, cartoon jazz, and Turkish music in a clownish manner. Musign, a musical theatre company for hearing-impaired performers, joins jazz, be-bop, rock, and Broadway tunes to sign language, mime, and dance.

A number of performers have remained closer to more traditional clowning, even when they ally it with other skills. Circus clown Steve Smith, director of the Ringling Bros. and Barnum and Bailey Clown College, integrates whiteface pantomime with clowning in *Slapstick and Sawdust.* Former Lecoq student Tim Carryer and Babs Bailey of Circus Ridiculous, who founded their Theatre Club Funambules in New York and a Lecoq-style movement school in 1988, engage in old-time and absurdist clowning. Theatre Plexus, with Jyl Hewston, Robert Morse, and Robert Mori, fuses traditional clowning with dramatic intrigue in *Kurlytov Family Cirkus,* in which a mediocre, one-ring Russian circus makes its first tour to America. (For more on Jyl Hewston, see chapter 14.)

Make-A-Circus, based in San Francisco, plays throughout California parks and recreation areas with traditional clown, acrobat, juggling, and trapeze acts. Since 1974, the company has provided clown therapy programs for persons with emotional, physical, and developmental disabilities throughout the San Francisco Bay Area. Among its tour shows, *The Mouth That Roared* (1990) featured acrobat–contortionist Patricia Howard, Vaudeville Nouveau artists Dan Mankin and Mark Sackett, acrobat Jay Laverdure, clown–tumbler Warren Sata, and clown Maria Calderone in lively tumbling, clowning, juggling, trapeze work, and stilt-walking.

Rob List, founder of Kite Tails Mime company with Letitia Bartlett in 1973, performed in both mime and dance. From 1985 to 1991, he was artistic director of the Dutch National School of Mime. Since 1990, he has been co-director of the Institute of New Dramaturgy in Amsterdam.

Don Jordan, who studied at the Ecole Jacques Lecoq in Paris and became co-director of Roy Bosier's Teatro Studio in Rome and Florence, developed a personal approach to clowning that he brought to his performing and teaching. After touring the United States and Europe as a solo artist and appearing with the Mummenschanz company on Broadway, in 1991 he was invited to direct the New Pickle Circus, where he weaved new forms into traditional circus acts.

Calling themselves the Magic Makers, popular clown–mime Naomi Caspe and her partner, Doug Kipping, have performed in the San Francisco Bay Area in living history pieces about nineteenth-century California heroines and in clown shows. The duo also has organized children's workshops that include puppetry, magic, storytelling, and face-painting.

Mime, comedian, and dancer Wayne Doba, who has performed in plays, movies, and solo theatrical works in the San Francisco Bay Area and is known as Crazy Crab, the mascot of the Giants baseball team, incorporates tap-dancing, singing, and trap drums into his acts. For the 1993–94 season of San Francisco's Cultural Odyssey, Doba and musician–tap-dancer–comedian Idris Ackamoor played in *Shoehorn,* in which a white performer and a black performer attempt to survive as a duo in a racially prejudiced society.

The Wright Brothers, clown–acrobats from Greenfield, Maine, became popular with such sketches as *The Race*, a slow-motion satire in which five runners frantically compete until the winner loses his pants, disclosing his butt, which has "The End" printed on it.

Humorous acrobatics and dance are found in New York's Second Hand Dance company, begun in 1987 by Greg O'Brien and Andy Horowitz, who have performed in street and other festivals in Europe.

Other clown and vaudeville performers are Tom Dougherty, a former member of the Ringling Bros. and Barnum and Bailey Circus who also writes and directs clown theatre; Brian McNelis, a professional clown and vaudeville performer who teaches; Larry Malkus, who founded the Flying Tongues, a comedy–improv group; and solo performer Rob Peck, artistic director of the children's theatre company Foolsproof Productions. In Arizona and California, specialist in teaching circuit skills to juveniles Doyle Ott mixes circus skills, traditional mime, masks, multimedia, folk tales, and zen in such solo pieces as *Parable*.

One of the foremost clown instructors in America, Yury Belov, the former director of clowning at the Moscow School of Circus and Variety Arts and a teacher of Leonid Yengibarov, taught at the North Carolina School of the Arts. Belov has performed with and directed his wife—clown–actress, director, and teacher Tanya Belov—in clown routines that stem from Russian circus traditions, such as *The Two Stooges from Russia, My Heart Is in Your Shoes,* and *Laughing Gas.* In 1982, he staged *The Clown Conspiracy* with Tanya Belov and Joe Killian at New York's Theatre for the New City and at the Movement Theatre International Festival at Davis and Elkins College. Belov has trained a number of American and European clowns and taught clown workshops throughout the United States.

An ethnic clown–dance form appreciated in America is Balinese Topeng. A number of Balinese and Javanese dancers, some of whom have taught in the United States, stage performances of Topeng masked dance theatre. Originating in religious ritual, Topeng mixes history, myth, religion, morals, and current issues, which the clown here incorporates into his comical improvisations. The Balinese clown is also looked upon as a spiritual guide who maintains peace and harmony. A favorite Topeng work is *King Bungkut,* which develops the exploits and downfall of a cruel and lustful king–magician. Topeng performers and teachers in the United States, Canada, Europe, and Asia include I Nyoman Wenten, who has taught music and dance in the United States and Canada; I Nyoman Catra of the Dance Academy in Denpesar, Bali; John Emigh, a theatre professor at Brown University who studied Balinese Topeng with I Nyoman Wenten and Bapak Kakul; and I Nyoman Sedana, who teaches music and dance at Brown University.

These various kinds of late twentieth-century clowning have served other purposes than entertainment. Clown therapy has also developed considerably since the 1980s. Scientific findings on the importance of humor and laughter for both physical and mental health and for easing tension and pain have led to the use of humor by some doctors and hospital care units. Dr. Patch Adams, founder and director of the Gesundheit Institute in 1971, is a clown and performer of fun shows, as well as a lecturer and author on humor. Adams hopes to construct a hospital based on using laughter and play to care for the sick. Dr. Michael Christensen, a former San Francisco Mime Troupe performer and a co-founder of New York's Big Apple Circus, where he also performed, left the ring in 1986 to become the founder–director of the Clown Care Unit, which provides clown visits to children's wards at eight New York hospitals. Dr. Meyer Rohtbart, a humor consultant, co-directed a therapeutic clowning project at the University of Pennsylvania's hospital. Some hospitals, such as Duke University's, have made use of humor by welding humor carts with humorous books, videos, juggling equipment, games, and toys.

Theatre for the Hearing Impaired and the Disabled

The National Theatre of the Deaf

The National Theatre of the Deaf has developed a professional physical theatre that provides the deaf community with an opportunity for vocational and artistic expression. The company originated in 1961 during rehearsals for the Broadway production of *The Miracle Worker,* when actress Anne Bancroft contacted the Lexington School of the Deaf and psychologist for the deaf, Dr. Edna Levine, to learn sign language for her role as Helen Keller's teacher. This production led to the creation of a theatre with both deaf and speaking actors for deaf and hearing audiences. In 1966, after Gallaudet College of the Deaf's performance of *Iphygenia in Aulis,* deaf actors were recruited along with speaking actors. Among the company members were Bernard Bragg, who trained with Marceau, comic actresses June Russi and Mary Beth Miller, Richard Kendall, Dorothy Miles, mime Joe Velez, and hearing actor Lou Fant. The company has performed in commercial theatres, high schools, and universities, on TV, in documentary film, and in a feature film of Federico García Lorca's *The Love of Don Perlimplin and Belisa in the Garden.* Among its stage productions are the Kabuki play *The Tale of Kasane* (1967); Puccini's opera *Gianni Schicchi* (1967); Chekhov's monologue *On the Harmfulness of Tobacco* (1968), directed by Decroux-trained mime Alvin Epstein; Richard Sheridan's *The Critic* (1968); Molière's *Sganarelle* (1969); Stephan Zweig's *Volpone* (1978); an adaptation of Carson McCullers's novel *The Heart Is a Lonely Hunter* (1986), based on the deafness and isolation of John Singer; an adaptation of Shakespeare's *Hamlet* entitled *Ophelia,* portraying a more determined heroine (1992); and stagings of Ibsen's *Peer Gynt,* which toured in 1998 and 1999, and of Romulus Linney's *The Unwritten Song*, comprised of heartfelt stories, songs, and poems, which toured in 2000. In 1968, five company members began the Little Theatre of the Deaf for children, touring America and abroad with Dylan Thomas's *A Child's Christmas in Wales* (1983) and programs of poetry, fairy tales, and dramatized short stories.

What role does mime play in the National Theatre of the Deaf? The body's movements and facial expressions provide the dramatic elements for a sign language based on twenty-six hand shapes that correspond to the letters of our alphabet and on signs that represent both objects and concepts. Because the deaf person makes use of body expression to communicate his ideas in sign language, he has developed a physical aptitude and a readiness to expand his movements into mime images. According to founding artistic director David Hays, because there are not as many signs in his language as there are words in spoken language, the deaf person has a natural tendency to accompany his sign language with body movement. Mime is woven into a stage sign language called "sign-mime," rendering the deaf actor's art unique.

The National Theatre of the Deaf Professional Theatre School, established by Hays in 1967, has offered courses each summer—for deaf and nondeaf actors, and on introductory and advanced levels—in acting, directing, improvisation, play-writing, dance, creative movement, storytelling, and the history of sign language and its use on stage. Gordon Davidson, managing director for the Mark Taper Forum, has found that after speaking actors learn sign language and return to using their voices, they have a keener awareness of their bodies and feel the text more deeply (Hays 1969, 9).

Flying Words Project and the Visual Theatre of the Deaf

Two deaf theatre companies, one from the United States and the other from Quebec, began collaborating in 1989. The first company, the Flying Words Project, was founded in 1986 by Peter Cook, a deaf actor and poet, and Kenny Lerner, a choreographer and narrator, to promote American sign language literature and present creations by deaf actors. Joining American sign language to mime, dance, and cinema techniques, the company performed in theatres throughout the United States and on TV.

In 1989, Cook and Lerner invited the members of Quebec's International Visual Theatre of the Deaf to show their visual research. This company was founded in 1968 by Serge Brière and a group of young deaf actors exclusively for deaf audiences. In 1980, after Brière returned from working with the Vancouver Canadian Theatre of the Deaf, company members began to perform for nondeaf audiences. They were joined by deaf actress Johanne Boulanger, who received her degree in Dramatic Art at the University of Quebec and taught sign language there.

In the summer of 1992, the two companies presented a collection of skits entitled *Silence, We Move* at the Lucernaire Center for Art and Experimentation in Paris. In these skits, the performers take signs further than a text's literal translation, developing them into a mime language that communicates poetic, tragic, and humorous action. In the poetic and tragic skit *Only Thirteen Years Old*, a deaf man and his daughter are incarcerated in a concentration camp. In the humorous *Televised News*, when the TV news announcer's microphone no longer functions, he resorts to gestures to communicate the number of deaths and survivors, as well as other details, from a plane accident. Their belief in their identity as deaf artists who can play for hearing audiences has given both companies the opportunity to perform.

Theatre Unlimited

San Francisco's Theatre Unlimited is an ensemble theatre company founded in 1977 composed of actors with developmental or physical disabilities and of nondisabled performers. Modeled after the National Theatre of the Deaf, Theatre Unlimited fosters original pieces from the life experiences and creativity of its members through collective improvisations that develop visual and corporeal images revealing both pain and exhilaration. Its first piece, *The Initiation,* presented in 1978 at San Francisco's Fort Mason Center, grew out of the physical and verbal improvisations of two groups of strangers exchanging rituals. *Sidewalk* (1979) integrates American sign language, song, and poetry with movement. *Unsheltered* (1980) explores the personal lives of the company members and *Willard Joins the Army* (1990) is based on the U.S. government's experiments with drafting the developmentally disabled into the armed services. *Beauty and the Beast* (1993) is a verbal and movement version of the children's story.

The roots of this company lie in developmental theatre, which builds on the actor's rather than the director's ability, aiming primarily—as in the ensemble efforts of the Open Theatre and the Polish Lab Theatre of the 1960s and 1970s—to expand the actor's potential for personal and creative improvement. In short, the audience comes not to see a public performance but a process that develops a poetics of the disabled. The company's experiments have proven that the nonverbal talents of the developmentally disabled can foster a creative theatre form.

Besides being brought into nursing homes and hospitals as forms of therapy, mime and clowning have become important adjuncts in the church, where they are utilized to spread the gospel of Christ. These amateur mime ministry companies play in many places other than churches and schools, including prisons, nursing homes, and senior citizen homes. Among those who integrate clowning and mime performances and workshops with ministering are Eileen Kuhn of the Mesmerize Clown and Mime Troupe, working out of St. Richard's Catholic Church in Richfield, Minnesota; Susie Toomey, director of the Rainbow Connection Mime Ministry Troupe and author of *Mime Ministry*; and Mark McMasters of North Carolina. Bill Pindar, minister of New York's Central Presbyterian Church, has used clowning in his ministry and health care for more than thirty years. A number of other performers combine their art with their work in religious ministry, such as mime artist Susan Pudelek (see chapter 14) and dancers Cynthia Winton-Henry and Phil Porter, who integrate physical, spiritual, and psychological activity in their dance–movement performance–workshops at the Pacific School of Religion in Oakland, California. Carla De Sola, founding director of the Omega Liturgical Dance company in New York, director of the Omega West company in Berkeley, California, and a teacher at the Pacific School of Religion and the Dominican School of Philosophy and Theology, is a liturgical dance pioneer whose performances and workshops have taken her throughout America and abroad. Many dance artists working nationally and internationally in ministry are members of the Sacred Dance Guild, which holds an annual festival.

Mime, which increasingly is incorporated into dance and verbal theatre, has also become a vital adjunct to dramatic art, dance, and movement education programs in the United States. A growing interest in nonverbal communication has encouraged actors as well as mimes to train in other movement methods. Among these are the Alexander Technique, a system that corrects injury and improves posture and movement; the Feldenkrais Method, which remedies incorrect movement developed through nervous habits; yoga for relaxation and body awareness; martial arts such as judo, aikido, karate, and tai chi to develop strength and precision of movement; and circus skills for physical liveliness and flexibility. Many of these methods have been included in acting and mime school programs. Beyond this, movement research has expanded into areas such as psychology, anthropology, and biology. The studies in these fields explore body language to aid the actor and the mime in the use of stage movement, as well as in the creation of physical characterization.

In the United States, the aforementioned mimes and mime teachers, as well as many others, have given this art an impetus on the stage, on the screen, and in the streets, as well as in educational institutions and workshops, where they are developing their own styles and mime schools.

Mime in Canada

A number of companies and solo artists in Canada have studied mime with Etienne Decroux, Jacques Lecoq, Marcel Marceau, or their trainees, which has not only given birth to that country's renewed interest in the art of mime, but also revitalized its theatre and reestablished the actor's art as a total one. The disciples of these masters have founded their own companies and schools and expanded upon Decroux's teachings, rendering Canada's physical theatre one of the most fecund.

Omnibus

Jean Asselin and Denise Boulanger, co-founders of Omnibus in 1970 and the Ecole de Mime Corporel de Montreal in 1977, studied, worked, and taught with Etienne Decroux in Paris for five years. After returning to Montreal, they developed a movement style that includes verbal theatre. Their first piece, *Zizi et la Lettre,* created in 1978, is a *commedia* sketch with comical *lazzi*, type characters, and multilingual dialogue. That same year, the company performed three Decroux corporeal mime pieces, each entitled *Duo Amoureux,* and created a philosophical piece, *D'où Venons Nous,* inspired by a Gauguin painting. In 1982, *L'Eau,* based on Decroux's statuary movement, was followed by two full-length mimodramas with some dialogue, *Beau Monde* and *Alice,* inspired by Lewis Carroll's *Alice in Wonderland.* A speaking actress narrates the action in an adaptation of Sébastien Japrisot's detective novel *La Dame dans l'Auto avec des Lunettes et un Fusil* (1985). In 1986, the company staged Adam de la Halle's thirteenth-century minstrel farce *Li Jus de Robin et Marion,* with music performed by a medieval music ensemble. Written by Robert Claing and stage director Asselin, *Le Temps Est au Noir*, derives from the actors' improvisations and fuses corporeal imagery with the spoken word. A musical tragicomedy caricaturing bourgeois stereotypes, *Le Festin Chez la Comtesse Fritouille* was presented in 1987, and, in 1988, a Shakesperean cycle, *Le Cycle des Rois,* based on *Richard II*, *Henry IV,* and *Henry V*, integrated text and movement. *Alberto d'Arrigo*, with a Claing script derived from the actors' improvisations, reverted to a more movement-oriented form in 1989. In 1990, *La Mort des Rois* combined mime, monologues, and music from the Middle Ages, and *Célestine là-bas près des Tanneries* captured the fifteenth-century Spanish ambience of romance and witchcraft. In 1991, Asselin's corporeal mime–based company staged four musical theatre pieces, including a Bernard Bonnier opera entitled *Eurydice*, directed by Dutch mime Jan Ruts; a work based on a man's love for a star, featuring a flutist, a mime–actress and a chorus of seven musicians, entitled *Oh Combien et Pour Toujours;* a piece revolving around a harpsichord, *Ni Terrible Ni Simple;* and *La Flèche et le Coeur*, drawing upon music from and life in the Middle Ages. *Le Précepteur* (*The Tutor*, 1995), as much an oral as a visual rendition, is a stylized version of Michael Mackenzie's Jamesian play *Geometry in Venice,* which offers physical counterparts to the characters' thoughts. Besides touring and training mimes, Omnibus has made films and videos and participated in international festivals. In March 1999, it hosted a week-long celebration of Etienne Decroux's centennial (1898–1998), entitled *Les Voies du Mime* (*The Tracks of Mime*), featuring performances, lectures, workshops, and an Homage to Decroux evening with Decroux mimes, pedagogues, and mime–dancers. Among the participants were Canadian mime–dancers and dance companies Omnibus, solo performer Dulcinée Langfelder, the Other Theatre, Sophie Wilhelm, Diluvine Dance, Joycelyne Montpetit Danse, Tenon Mortaise Dance, choreographer Aline Gélinas, and Decroux-trained Ivan Bartolini and Isabelle Thivierge; American mime and teacher Thomas Leabhart; and London company Le Théâtre de l'Ange Fou.

Because of its company's strong belief in the body's endless capacity to develop a whole scale of expressions, Omnibus has explored multiple forms of movement theatre. We are reminded of Decroux's belief that "the mime has many moods; playful gracefulness, buffoonery, comedy à la Daumier, tragedy and that he may even attain the dream state." And so the company has achieved these many moods, moving from playful gracefulness in *Duo Amoureux,* to buffoonery in *Zizi et la Let-tre,* to comedy à la Daumier with underlying tragedy in *Beau Monde,* to *L'Eau* and *Alice*, all of which achieve this "dream state."

While outright bawdiness, exaggerated type characters, and an inventive lan-guage mixing French, English, Voual, and Italian comprise the *commedia* buffoon-ery of *Zizi et la Lettre*, delicate movement punctuated by sculptural attitudes char-acterize *Duo Amoureux*. In these duets, the partners poorly time their love for one another: as one shows his love, the other remains indifferent, or vice versa. In *L'Eau,* hermetic fantasy in the form of a dreamlike atmosphere serves metaphorical content. While unceasing tides evoke life's struggles and the dispersal of the family nucleus in perpetual migration, the seaweed and marine life are mirrors reflecting all of human nature. The mimes in their blue-green leotards are the puppeteers of a large satin cloth, which they animate to take on many shapes, such as a giant creature that is at once water, marine life, seaweed, or some liberated element of nature. *L'Eau* is Omnibus's first piece to evolve into a freer, more surrealistic form.

Beau Monde, inspired by the *Reader's Digest* articles of the 1950s, caricatures the period's bourgeois dress, coiffures, and stylized gestures through mime, dance, audience interaction, and the company's first use of dialogue. Mixing sex and violence with surrealistic images and black humor, the work portrays trapped, self-destructive members of society who are victims of the idealized illusion that divorce, old age, death, and so on, don't exist. The content explores the tragic futility of war, the dis-tortion of sex, the fragility of marriage, and family and social alienation.

La Dame, a murder mystery involving a nearsighted blonde secretary, exem-plifies the postmodern juxtaposition of multiple elements. Movement, props, and a speaking actress serve to relate the action. In postmodern manner, the piece pokes fun at its own corporeal mime style, simultaneously plays video scenes with live act-ing, and replaces one action with another to destroy the theatrical illusion.

By the time Omnibus staged *Le Cycle des Rois* (1988), it was fully engaged in verbal theatre. In this six-hour staging based on Shakespeare's *Richard II*, *Henry IV,* and *Henry V*, which received an award for best production of the 1987–88 season, mimes interact with speaking actors. The visual components of mime, costumes, and sets revitalize Shakespeare's literary text and enhance the work's dramatic quality. Costumes found in flea markets not only offer an inventive use of secondhand cloth-ing representing no particular period, but also challenge the spectator's imagination and allow freedom of movement. For example, to caricature their power status, a bird's cage serves as the King of France's crown and a soup pot as Falstaff's head-gear. Simply constructed sets allow for a maximum of movement on several levels. While movement evoking a circus ambience enhances this cycle's satirical aspect, these visual means reveal the deeper meanings in Shakespeare's text, as well as bring life to it.

Although Omnibus is among the most faithful interpreters of Decroux's mime style, it has moved away from idealizing the concept of the statuary and the ideal of universal beauty toward a visual language related to theatrical mimodrama and to social and psychological satire. As the company has evolved from corporeal mime to speaking theatre, thanks to their solid foundation in movement, its members have come to possess, in Asselin's words, "astonishing powers." In its quest to develop and expand corporeal expression, Omnibus is fulfilling Decroux's belief that "dra-matic art, until it is a real art, cannot become a better one" (Decroux 1963, 46).

Asselin gives his views on postmodernism, the relationship between mime and theatre, and the future role of mime:

> One might say of *La Dame,* in which there was a plurality of elements but with no synthesis of the latter, that it was postmodern—what I understand by the word postmodern. Our work is mostly pure. We have achieved a harmony with our mime–actors' integration of the Decroux technique, reconciling body and mind. The mind working from the interior gives the élan to the body on the exterior. As Decroux said, "The muscles and bones are the gloves of thought."
>
> Decroux loved the theatre. I believe he was looking for a new race of actors. I think the theatre will change because movement has entered into it. Mime ought to play a role in modern theatre. I only hope that people will become more open to this art.[20]

Three of the long-standing members of Omnibus left in 1984 to create their own mime company, entitled Productions Le Pool. After training at Jean Asselin's corporeal mime school in Montreal, Suzanne Lantagne, Roger Proteau, and Danielle Trépanier began a movement theatre in which text and voice are the natural prolongations of movement. Because, for some critics, this company's work resembles a theatrical form of modern dance, it has also been associated with Pina Bausch's style. In 1985, Productions Le Pool staged *La Grandeur du Geste et des Passions*, a caricature of love's various forms and its resemblance to animal life. *It Must Be Sunday* (1986) depicts the humorous confrontation and love affair between a nun and a football player. In 1987, the company collaborated with Omnibus in staging the burlesque comedy *Le Festin Chez la Comtesse Fritouille*, based on Vitold Gombrowicz's story of decadent aristocrats preparing to feast on a young boy's flesh. In this baroque satire, words and music adjoin to movement. Productions Le Pool, which includes theatre elements and dialogue in its corporeal mime–based productions, has helped bring mime to the fore on the Quebec stage.

Carbone 14

Gilles Maheu, at first an actor, pantomimist, and street performer in Montreal, studied mime with Étienne Decroux and also trained in corporeal mime with Yves Lebreton at Eugenio Barba's Odin Teatret. After staging corporeal mime pieces such as *Possession* in 1972, Maheu founded his Les Enfants du Paradis mime company in 1975. In 1979, he was among three founders of an experimental theatre space called L'Espace Libre, in a renovated Montreal firehouse. After renaming his company Carbone 14 in 1982, Maheu staged works on contemporary social issues, such as *Vies Privées*, surrealist cabaret sketches of bourgeois lifestyles; *Pain Blanc* (1981), a caricature of modern man falsely secure at work and play; and *L'Homme Rouge* (1982), based on a protagonist's childlike inability to cope with the superficial norms of society.

Although Maheu's company performed principally mime, dance, and acrobatics, it gradually has incorporated spoken dialogue and silent acting into themes involving social issues. *Le Rail* (1983) depicts a heroine confronted with surrealist images of war and the Holocaust in silent scenes of physical and moral violence. The text of *Marat/Sade* (1984) remains secondary to the explosive images of the French revolution, created through physical movement, video, and a postmodern use of multiple visuals. In Heiner Muller's *Hamlet Machine* (1987), Maheu introduces video, dance, mime, acrobatics, puppets, song, and dialogue in several languages to interpret the death of Shakespeare's hero as a symbol of the Western world's ruination. *Opium* (1987), a collective creation, portrays through dance and theatre the clash between the ideals in one's subconscious and the struggle for financial success. In *Le Dortoir* (1988), Maheu communicates—through poetic mime, dance, acrobatic movement, and very little text—playful and despairing students in a dormitory during Quebec's 1960s political and religious revolution. Here, innocent childhood memories and dreams coupled with violence and rebellion are dramatically evoked through the body. Like Antonin Artaud, Maheu believes that the theatre must free itself from the text's domination; expand beyond words into a novel use of space, vocal sounds, and intonations; and develop a lyric and visual language of movement and gestures that appeals to the senses. As with Artaud, in Maheu's nonverbal theatre, silence reveals the inner truths of the unconscious.

40 Below Mime

Giuseppe Condello came to Winnipeg, Canada, from Bovalino, Italy, in the early 1950s while still a boy. After studying at the Manitoba Theatre Center School and at the National Theatre School of Canada in Montreal, he performed at the Stratford Festival Theatre, the Young People's Theatre, and the Manitoba Theatre Center, earning two Tyronne Guthrie acting awards. In 1974, following several years of training with Etienne Decroux, Condello and his wife, Kathryn, opened a school and organized the 40 Below Mime company, which moved from Stratford to Winnipeg in 1975. In their repertory, they developed both corporeal-style and commedia dell'arte works that focus on the antics of Pulcinella, Capitano, and Pantalone. *La Terra* depicts the cycle of life, from the planting of seed to the milling of grain. *The Attic* is a solo piece in which the protagonist retrieves a lost top hat. *Future Shokk* is an abstract work centering on the psychological and social change of the technological revolution. *D. P.* (1989), which grew out of the memories and feelings of Canada's immigrants, is built on the truth of collective experience. In this narrative punctuated by corporeal movement, Condello's stylized mobile statuary meshes with his talent for acting and storytelling. In 1983, he hosted the world's first International Corporeal Mime Festival, which he dedicated to his mentor, Étienne Decroux. Through the 1980s it was an annual event and the only one of its kind in Canada.

Larry Swanson

A member of the 40 Below Mime company, Larry Swanson, mime–actor and teacher, created and performed *At the Point* at the 1989 Winnipeg International Mime Festival. The piece develops the myth of Daedalus to symbolize modern man's communicative alienation and emotional deprivation. Dialogue and sound effects are woven into Decroux's corporeal mime to depict man as a victim of excessive programmed information and industrialization, which deprive him of myths and poetry.

Vincent Marcotte

Corporeal mime Vincent Marcotte, who was born in Quebec, studied modern dance and then entered the National Mime Theatre of Quebec to tour Canada. After performing *Un Geste à l'Autre* in Paris in 1976, Marcotte trained with Decroux, Pinok and Matho, and Annie Fratellini at the Ecole Nationale du Cirque in Paris. He toured France in 1978 and in 1980 was mimographer for an adaptation of *Capitaine Fracasse,* performed at the Paris Sud-Est Theatre and in Tempelhof, Germany.

Corporeal Mime Teachers

A number of renowned mime teachers have taught corporeal mime in Canada. Hungarian-born George Molnar, a Decroux assistant in Paris from 1970 to 1975 who had a company in Canada for fifteen years, became one of the truest exponents of Decroux mime, which he displayed in such creations as *L'Effort* (1978). André Fortin trained students in corporeal mime at Montreal's Omnibus company. David Alberts, the director of the Toronto Mime Ensemble and School of Mime who performed throughout Canada and the United States, is the author of a book based on the mime fundamentals of Decroux, Barrault, and Marceau, entitled *Pantomime: Elements and Exercises.*

Among other corporeal mime teachers and performers in Canada, Dean Fogal—who trained with Decroux and Marceau for a three-year period and with Thomas Leabhart and the Arkansas Mime Theatre for another three years—opened a private corporeal mime studio in 1978. In 1986, he founded the Corporeal Mime Society. In 1995, he established the TooBa Physical Theatre Center, with classes in corporeal mime, acting, voice, and the healing arts, in Vancouver, British Columbia. Among the corporeal mime pieces he has created are *The Prisoner* (1987), *Chairing* (1988), and *Labyrinths* (1991). In 1990, Fogal received a Canada Council grant to create a work fusing corporeal mime with live orchestral music. His original research, entitled *Assimilation Work,* prepares the participant emotionally, psychologically, and physically for the subtle and geometric articulations of corporeal mime technique. Works that followed were *Oasis* (1994), on facing failed water resources; *Everyone Has One* (1994), a mime duo using ropes, which appeared in a British Columbia TV film; *Media Madness* (1995); and *Shadow Evolving* (1995). In the summers of 1991 and 1992, Fogal taught workshops in Copenhagen. Since 1991, he has been artistic coordinator of the Beaux Gestes Society in British Columbia.

Moebius

Closer to the classical whiteface pantomime style, the Toronto–based Moebius, formerly the Paul Gaulin company, was founded in 1972. Gaulin, who studied with Decroux and Marceau in Paris and with Henryk Tomaszewski–trained Martin Frick in Canada, incorporates these masters' styles and techniques in his creations. Among his illusion pantomimes are *Neighbors,* a slapstick piece about neighbors trying to dine who are interrupted by dripping faucets in their respective apartments, and *The Burden of Guilt,* which centers around a guilt-ridden individual's attempt to rid himself of his chains. Besides whiteface pantomime, Gaulin incorporates masks in *Heads*, a comic love duet between two giraffelike figures, and in *The Sleeper*, a surrealistic comic piece in which a female interacts with a giant hand while a huge fly sucks on a dead chicken. Gaulin introduces Kabuki techniques in *Forger of Swords,* acrobatic dance in *Fog,* and the play of props in *Space Worms*, which derives poetic effects through a clever use of Mummenschanz-like objects.

Théâtre National de Mime du Québec

Elie Oren, who first studied in France in 1949 with disciples of Decroux and Marceau and with Willy Spoor, went to Quebec in 1965. There, he founded the Théâtre National de Mime du Québec, a company and school, in 1972.

Axis Mime Theatre

A Vancouver company that has undergone the influence of Lecoq's mime–clown theatre is Axis Mime Theatre, co-founded by Lecoq-trained Wayne Specht in 1975. Although Axis Mime Theatre began by performing semitraditional mime vignettes, it soon moved to the use of dialogue and verbal theatre elements. By the 1980s, it staged full-length plays—with mime and a text for both adults and children—that ranged from mime musicals (*Hotsy Totsy*), to multimedia (*Impact*), to clowning (*Synthetic Energy*), to commedia dell'arte (*The Number 14*). In 1980, the company staged a highly successful thriller entitled *Rude Awakening*, and, in 1986, presented *Synthetic Energy* at the Vancouver Beaux Gestes International Festival of Mime, Clown, and Movement Theatre, which Specht directed. *Synthetic Energy* blends outrageous clowning, acrobatics, slapstick, improvisation, and illusion mime to examine the tyrannical reign of sound in a technological society. Written by Kim Selody, the play revolves around two vaudeville players and their ineffective manager, whose sound system wreaks havoc during their performance. Sound is physicalized as the tyrannical system drowns out the performers' words, rendering only their movements communicable. *Fools' Angel* (1982), also written by Selody, is a poetic allegory revolving around two fools marooned on a desert island that combines slapstick and clowning with a Beckett-like atmosphere. *The Number 14* (1992), which received four Jessie Awards in 1993, is a collective creation by Axis Mime Theatre and Touchstone Theatre of Canada composed of *commedia*-style vignettes, with masks, clowning, mime, and sixty bus riders of all ages and walks of urban life. *Rhythm in Theatre: The Dramatic Beat*, co-conceived and co-directed with the Vancouver Moving Theatre, was performed for secondary school students during the company's 1995–96 season (see below, "Vancouver Moving Theatre"). *Disposing of the Dead* (1996), by Katherine Schlemmer, based on the 1924 murder of Scottish nursemaid Janet Smith, is a text-based, multimedia thriller touching on racism and power abuse that Axis Mime Theatre and Pink Ink Theatre Productions staged collaboratively. Axis Mime Theatre's program for young audiences, which toured schools and communities, includes *Trolldom: As If by Magic* (1996) and *For Art's Sake* (1997), both productions incorporating masks, puppetry, and text.

Not bound by the traditions of any mime school or style, Axis Mime Theatre has adopted Lecoq's aim to bridge the gap between mime and dramatic art to achieve a total theatre expression not limited by the exclusive use of words or movement. By experimenting with numerous movement styles and content to create meaningful and entertaining works, Axis Mime Theatre, which changed its name to Axis Theatre company in 1997, has become one of Canada's most innovative alternative theatre companies.

Clown–mime Gordon White was Axis Mime company's principal performer and writer for six years and performed and toured in his own solo shows. In one of his *Gord Show* sketches, White portrays the mishaps of a fellow who starts his car, only to be overcome by a series of mechanical hang-ups. Through comic movement and sound effects, he depicts a key being forced into the car door, a stubborn seat belt's screeching, and tires deflating one by one. In another sketch, in which a lonely man gives himself a birthday party, White reveals the isolated hero's pathos through clowning, mime, sound effects, and music.

Collaborating with Axis Mime Theatre in *The Number 14* (1992), Touchstone Theatre of Canada, established in 1976, has produced both physical and verbal collective creations and premiered innovative contemporary plays, such as *Sex Tips for Modern Girls* (1985) and *Springboard* (1989). Also joining in the *Number 14* production, Gina Bastone, lead clown with the Cirque du Soleil and founder of Vancouver's Basta company, gained popularity by touring in *Basta Does Basta* (see chapter 14.)

Founded by Sandhano Schultze in 1985, Vancouver's Pink Ink Theatre Productions produces translated French-Canadian scripts and new Canadian plays. With Touchstone Theatre of Canada, the company co-produced the Quebecois play *Lilies*, which won six Jessie Awards; *The Fall of the House of Usher*, which garnered three Jessie Awards; and Robert Lepage's *Polygraph*. In 1996, Pink Ink Theatre Productions collaborated with Axis Mime Theatre on *Disposing of the Dead*, committing itself to future productions with Axis.

Theatre beyond Words

Founded in 1977 by Harro Maskow and Canadian Mime Theatre members as a theatre collective, Theatre beyond Words, based in Niagara-on-the-Lake, Ontario, is a Lecoq-style movement theatre company in which pantomime, masks, puppets, props, sound effects, music, and scenery are part of stage concepts pushed beyond their imaginative limits in nonverbal and verbal works. With the Lecoq-trained Maskow and Robin Patterson-Judd as its artistic directors, this company has performed in Canada and toured Europe and the Pacific Rim countries with a unique, visual fantasy style.

Theatre beyond Words's *Five Good Reasons To Laugh* (1977) is a collection of humorous sketches about characters from various walks of life. *Tourists* (1983) depicts passengers of a tour-bus conductor, who has them obeying his every command. In *Dummies* (1977), a puppet bride and groom come to life. *Pear* (1977) offers poetic content coupled with skillful technique as an innocent pear falls from its tree into the real world. *Night Train to Foggy Bottom* (1990) is a surreal fantasy staged in collaboration with Coad Canada Puppets that includes mime, modern dance, slides, and text; its theme is about a voyage through the artist's subconscious with erotic experiences, which then transpire in his work. *The Boy Who Could Sing Pictures* (1991), based on Seymour Leichman's children's story, is performed by puppets and actors, with singing, dancing, live music, masks, and elaborate medieval costumes. In this *commedia* satire, dialogue also serves to depict the story of Ben's magical voice, which soothes the misery of the poor and serves as a lesson to a warmonger country's king. The company's Young People and Potato Family shows offer episodes with cartoonlike characters wearing expressionless, larva masks, based on the Basel Fastnacht masks, as in *Nothin' but Trouble* (1991). *School Daze*, from 1994 to 1997, continues Nancy Potato's adventures at school, and *Potato People in Space* (2000) depicts the latter in the new millennium. In its productions, staged with clearly designed and precise movement, Theatre Beyond Words extracts humor and poetry from the most banal situations.

Théâtre à l'Oblique

Montreal's Théâtre à l'Oblique, established in 1981 by Decroux-trained George Molnar, has developed a corporeal language using the cube as a medium of expression. In *Attraction*, presented at the 1983 Festival International de Mime Montréal, each actor uses a cube as a means to express emotions and characters and to depict a power emanating from the earth, which affects and fuses with matter and human beings.

Bouffon de Bullion

Bouffon de Bullion, a Montreal-based theatre company founded in 1983 by former Lecoq students Grant Heisler and Bob Pot, developed the Lecoq buffoon style and tradition committed to the support of folly. *Qui Rit* (1985), based on Victor Hugo's *The Man Who Laughs,* satirizes societal injustices through the story of a traveling caravan of buffoons and distorted outcasts who adopt an abandoned boy. *Celui-ci N'Est Pas Mon Fils* (1986), written and directed by Philippe Gaulier, a teacher of the Lecoq buffoon style, and played by three female buffoons, satirizes Catholic myths in the mode of the ancient court jester and the Shakesperean fool. With irreverent malice, the work derides the abuse of religious traditions and power over the credulous, portraying Christ as the crackpot son of a raped virgin. The striking visual impact of the repertory of this company, which disbanded in the early 1990s, recalls the grotesque and scurrilous figures in the tableaux of Hieronymus Bosch and Pieter Bruegel.

Snake-in-the-Grass Moving Theatre

Snake-in-the-Grass Moving Theatre, founded by Paul Gibbons and Tsuneko Kokubo, began in 1978 with clown shows that examined academic anthropology issues concerning our contemporary culture. Although the company has incorporated a range of artistic styles, it was predominantly concerned with environmental issues. Besides clown shows, these issues were mirrored through traditional mythology, science-fiction, giant masked creatures, shadow plays, theatrical versions of developments in physics and biology, and satires of contemporary sociocultural phenomena. *Through the Black Hole* and *In the Photon Zone*, developed by Gibbons from 1984 to 1986, are science-fiction works connecting ancient metaphysical systems with recent scientific discoveries to reveal the ecological balance between all living organisms. *Ghosts in the Machine* (1988) is an installation performance of sounds and images that explores the relationship between nature and technology. In June 1990, Snake-in-the-Grass Moving Theatre received the United Nations Global 500 award for its environmental work in the performing arts.

Klauniada

With a clown style influenced by Eastern European clowning traditions, as well as Lecoq and Decroux mime, Don Reider and Valerie Dean's works are both comical and poetic. Klauniada ("clown-play" in Czech) was founded in 1980 by Reider, who trained at the Prague Circus Alfred and Lecoq's Paris school, and Dean, who studied corporeal mime and was a founding member of Thomas Leabhart's Corporeal Mime Theatre in the United States. Both Reider and Dean taught at the National Theatre School of Canada and the Ecole Nationale de Cirque in Montreal, as well as choreographed and directed for Canadian theatre companies and the Cirque du Soleil. Klauniada's clown–mime style blends Eastern and Western European clowning, including elements of surrealism, black humor, silent film, and corporeal mime technique. Its dream play *Gag* (1984) engages traditional circus and puppetry to portray a Beckett-like character confined to a basement who emerges from a coal pile to encounter invisible elements and relive his memories. Reider and Dean have also staged Beckett's *Krapp's Last Tape* and *Act Without Words II* (1984); *Weight,* akin to a Buster Keaton film; and *Am and Em* (1987), a clown–mime parable of Adam and Eve portraying the loss of innocence, directed by Boleslav Polivka. *Scraps II* (1990), which humorously depicts man's depraved universe after its demolition, blends science-fiction, absurdist theatre, puppetry, and clowning. *Opal* (1991) is based on the diaries of Opal Whitely, and *Dr. Sax* (1992), a one-man clown show, interprets the Jack Kerouac novel. Succeeding clown sketches combine clowning with puppets and shadow play. Klauniada's clowning style is composed of fantasy, black humor, and themes of deprivation and solitude that recall the theatre of the absurd.

Vancouver Moving Theatre

Among the interdisciplinary theatre companies in Canada that engage in dance, music, mime, and theatre and that draw upon transcultural sources and ethnic and indigenous community celebrations is the Vancouver Moving Theatre, founded in 1983 by Savannah Walling and Terry Hunter as the Special Delivery Moving Theatre. After obtaining her B.A. in anthropology, artistic director Walling trained in dance at several studios, including the Nikolais Dance Theatre Lab, performed as a dancer, and studied theatre in workshops with Richard Schechner, Jerzy Bogajewicz, and Eugenio Barba at his International School of Theatre Anthropology in Denmark. Associate director Hunter also trained in dance and then in theatre with André Gregory and Bogajewicz. After studying mime with Harro Maskow and performing in the Simon Fraser Mime Troupe in 1971, Walling and Hunter co-founded their own company, touring Canada and abroad.

Influenced by North America's rapidly expanding multicultural heritage, Vancouver Moving Theatre's artistic expression is informed by training practices, theatrical principles, and archetypal themes recurring in the dance, drama, rituals, and legends of Asia, Europe, Africa, and North America. These elements form a foundation from which an original repertory is generated. Through its exploration of ancient dance–drama, the company has developed a total theatre expression in which vocal sounds, music, and percussion are joined to dance, ritualistic movement, legend, masks, costumes, simple lighting, and sets. Like ancient dance–drama, it synthesizes movement, dance, dramatic content, and music in a visual totality.

Trained in music since childhood, Walling and Hunter have explored the creation of drum dances since the 1980s. From the company's formation, it has specialized in creating original and music-driven masked dance–dramas that feature interactions between larger-than-life archetypal characters or between these characters and the audience. Its repertory has been enhanced by drum dancing, a unique feature of most of its productions. Drum dancing is integrated with physical theatre, music, and dance and requires the coordination of these disciplines within a single performer.

Vancouver Moving Theatre's first major creation, *Samarambi, Pounding of the Heart*, staged in 1986, portrays the struggle between primal forces to restore balance in a world where technology and environment are in dangerous disharmony. The action revolves around four masked figures that move rhythmically to drums and gongs. Upho, a guardian drum master in a white costume who pulls a wagon of instruments, is joined by Drum Mother, whirling and playing on a drum mysteriously imbedded in her large skirt; then by Chamelea, a figure in glittering gold on stilts; and lastly by Kronis, a warrior angel with claws and a masked helmet, also on stilts. The piece develops Kronis's tormented state after he has exchanged his heart for power and lost his soul. Upho, Drum Mother, and Chamelea, assisted by a trickster named HeHeHe, aid their lost friend in transforming and healing, eventually finding harmony through a new balance with nature. In this mythical dance–drama composed of ritualistic movement, ornamental costumes, masks, accessories, and incantatory music, the characters interact in scenes of battle, peace-making, and rebirth during which cosmic forces make materialistic values threaten spiritual ones.

Some of the sources of *Samarambi* are more than two thousand years old. One of the earliest is that of the ritual ceremonies conducted by the shaman priests of paleolithic cultures, which were reproduced in the Lascaux caves in France. It also draws from the Doric mime that developed in Megara after 581 B.C., in which everyday characters interact with gods and devils in legends depicted in a burlesque manner. Like the ancient mimes, the piece discovers source material through improvisation and comments upon the existing social system. Besides drawing from the ancient dance–dramas of Asia, Africa, Europe, and North America, *Samarambi* is inspired by the carnival costumes and headdresses of medieval street pageantry. The masks in this work recall the devil-like ones of the mystery and miracle cycles and the grotesque, masked characters of the commedia dell'arte. More immediate ethnic predecessors are Vancouver's Chinese Festivals and Parades, Hispanic folk plays, Pueblo ceremonials in the southwestern United States, and the rituals of British Columbia's Coastal Indians, enacted with oversize masks to represent spirits.

House of Memory (1989) is an interdisciplinary masked dance–drama in which five company members interpret large animals and archetypal characters with masks, puppets, stilts, ornate costumes, props, musical instruments, and food shared with the public. It incorporates thirty to fifty community members of all ages to participate as dancers, musicians, clowns, actors, storytellers, and backstage help. A nonlinear, mythological piece, it houses a collection of dance–dramas that enact different journeys of the human spirit through life, amid the sound of drums, animals, and song accompanying dance. Its dramatic sources include the traditional healing dramas, which incorporate shared archetypal memories and questions, as well as current concerns such as community disintegration and the loss of shared values between humans and their natural environment. Beyond this, *House of Memory*, like *Samarambi*, breaks down the barriers between music and movement, audience and performer, to reintegrate the performance and the audience with the natural environment.

After the company's performance ensemble dissolved in 1992 to generate a solo and duet repertory and a series of co-productions, *Ab Audire: Gifts of the Heart* was created between 1993 and 1996 as a nonverbal solo allegory portraying two characters from the *Samarambi* cycle: Drum Mother and HeHeHe. Terry Hunter performs both characters in a drama of bonding among Drum Mother, her trickster son, and the spectators. This performance–audience work, with its spectacular costumes, percussion, drum dancing, and clowning, is a contemporary descendent of ancient mask and clown performance forms found in theatre around the world, including that of indigenous groups of British Columbia. This piece is the company's personal response to twentieth-century ethical dilemmas and a polarized age preoccupied with acquisition, consumption, and self-gratification.

Wak (1994), performed by soloist Hunter, is composed of stylized movement, symbolic costumes and props, drum dancing, clowning, audience interaction, and an original musical score played with scrap metals by ethno-jazz composer Joseph Danza. Wak's efforts to recover his voice, identity, and ability to communicate awaken forces that help him rediscover his relationship with society, the earth, and himself.

Rhythm in Theatre: The Dramatic Beat, co-conceived and co-directed with Wayne Specht and Axis Mime Theatre during its 1995–96 seasons for secondary school drama students, features a cross-section of the company's repertory to investigate the power and potential of rhythm for shaping theatrical performance and how rhythm can be used to create original theatre, based on principles and techniques developed during three thousand years of theatrical history.

Luigi's Kitchen, which Hunter co-created with David Chantler of Calgary's Trickster Theatre and composer Danza, toured Calgary schools in November 1996 and was performed at Alberta festivals in May 1997. The fifty-minute duet features drumming, physical theatre, drum dancing, clowning, and cooking.

Blood Music, premiered in April 1997, is a forty-minute visual and sonic ecosystem of life rhythms work that is inspired by the personal, biological, and cosmic rhythms of life around us, which is performed by four drum dancers.

The Ramayana, created and performed in October 1977 as a joint collaboration with Seattle's Carter Family Marionettes and the Northwest Puppet Center and in consultation with Vancouver's and Seattle's East Indian communities, combines mask and puppet theatre, actors, drum dancing, and live music.

Among the contemporary influences on Vancouver Moving Theatre's work are Jacques Lecoq's mime–mask theories and analysis of physical gestures, the dance–drama of Alwin Nikolais, the physical theatre of Eugenio Barba, the masked figures of the Odin Teatret parades, the Grotowski acting methods, Richard Schechner's performance experiments, the community-based outdoor image theatre of John Fox, the sonic explorations of Murray Schafer and Elizabeth Swados, and the theatrical taiko drum concerts of Kodo and Ondeko-Za.

In returning to the most ancient sources, Vancouver Moving Theatre has achieved, through evocative visual and auditory sensations, a rebirth of dance–drama. By fusing elements of ancient and modern dance–drama with heterogeneous cultural sources, it is likewise a postmodern movement theatre. As it draws all of these components into a harmonious ensemble, it becomes a model of what dance–drama was and can still be. This integration of diverse artistic elements goes beyond offering a revitalized theatre of myth. As in the theatre's original function—the fulfillment of social, spiritual, and cultural needs—it infers truths, such as society's need to find a balance with natural forces before nature and society destroy themselves. Years of research into past forms that are combined with present-day dance, mime, and acting methods, along with the continuous development of a personal artistic expression, have endowed Vancouver Moving Theatre with one of the most original and meaningful movement theatres in North America today.

Codco

Among the popular Canadian collective improvisational theatre groups in the 1970s and 1980s—such as Toronto's Théâtre Passe Muraille and Newfoundland's Mummers Troupe, which were not predominantly mime companies but utilized miming and clowning along with a text—CODCO became one of the most prominent. It was born in 1973, when six Newfoundland actors, ages sixteen to twenty-five, created a series of sketches entitled *Cod on a Stick*, humorously mocking Newfoundlanders as awkward foreigners tolerated in Canada. Utilizing improvisational clowning, mime, dance, songs, and language satire and based on local subject matter and political and social abuse, CODCO's success continued with *Sickness, Death and Beyond the Grave* (1974), *Das Capital* (1975), *Would You Like to Smell My Pocket Crumbs?* (1975), about the deterioration of family life, *The Tale Ends* (1976), *Who Said Anything About Tea?* (1977), and *CODCO Revived, CODCO Is Back* (1986), which toured Canada. Since 1988, CODCO's sketches have appeared regularly on TV. Through bold and outspoken modern *commedia*, the company has succeeded in portraying Newfoundlanders' search for cultural identity as a universal theme, in which the victims of the power-hungry confront the modern evils of commercial growth and monetary values.

Clowns, Vaudeville, and Special Audiences

In Canada, numerous other mimes and companies have innovated movement styles by blending movement with additional elements or simply by perfecting corporeal or traditional mime expression. This stylistic variation was manifest at the 1983 Festival International de Mime Montréal in the creations of a number of companies. The Toronto Mime Company Unlimited fused movement, verbal sounds, masks, music, marionettes, and slides in *George Orwell: The Crystal Spirit*. The Mime Ensemble of Alberta, a performance unit of the Academy of Corporal Mime, founded in 1978 as a research and training center, performed poetic mime sketches entitled *Music of Mime*. Theatre Corporeus from Vancouver presented a Decroux-style piece entitled *Companions.* Quebec solo mime Pierre Bernier told stories through movement, and Claude Saint Denis, also from Quebec, performed humorous sketches based on daily situations.

A clown director and teacher who has left a mark on the development of miming and clowning in Canada is Richard Pochinko. Leaving home when he was fourteen to enter the theatre, he later studied with Jacques Lecoq in Paris and Jerzy Grotowski in Denmark. After working with Native American clown teacher Jonsmith in Seattle, Washington, Pochinko began the Theatre Resource Center in Ottawa, along with voice teacher Annie Skinner and dance instructor Linda Rabin, and later organized a clown company featuring some of Canada's finest clowns.

One of the clowns in Canada who worked with Pochinko was Cheryl Cashman, whose *Turning Thirty* explores female humor. Her piece *What Do Clowns Do in a War?* is a full-length clown musical on the theme of nuclear war.

Another Pochinko trainee, Nion (Ian Wallace), developed a style of clown theatre based on North American and European shamanistic mask and clown art, puppetry, and German cabaret. His one-man show *Nion*, later called *Birth of a Clown* and *Commedia Bizarro*, revolves around an outer-space figure in a dazzling costume who plays a series of characters, ranging from a squealing baby to a female stripper, motorcyclist, and rock star.

Toronto-based clowns Mump (Michael Kennard) and Smoot (John Turner)— who trained in clowning with Pochinko, buffoon style with Philippe Gaulier, and physical comedy with John Towsen—have performed as a duo since 1988 under the stage direction of Karen Hines, who also studied with Pochinko and Gaulier. In *Something* (1989), they speak gibberish in a chic restaurant, attend the funeral of a dead clown, and play surgeon and patient. In *Caged* (1990) and *Ferno* (1992), this Canadian Laurel and Hardy mix slapstick, horror elements, and grotesque clowning.

Several members of the Small Change Theatre, founded in Edmonton in 1982, also trained with Pochinko, as well as with Lecoq. In the company's lively clown and mask show *Hazard and Darlene in Love*, a couple about to retire moves through a gamut of emotions and exhausting physical feats. *One Beautiful Evening*, with Robert Astle, Jan Henderson, Jan Miller, and Franck C. Turner, relates the love story of two senior citizens who meet at a bingo game. In 1990, Astle returned to Europe to create his solo show *Heart of a Dog,* based on Russian author Mikhail Bulgakov's novel about a scientist who performs a transplant on a scroungy, starving dog, transforming it into a human who has vulgar, proletarian ways that exasperate the good doctor.

Calgary's Areté Physical Comedy Troupe was founded in 1976 by three graduates—Randy Birch, Kevin McKendrick, and Don Spino—of the Canadian Mime School, where they worked with Lecoq's physical theatre methods. Playing to both adults and children, the company combined words, sounds, music, and masks with their dynamic pantomime, vaudeville, and physical comedy style in vignettes that portray everyday events (*Physical Symphonies*, 1983; *Gallery*, 1986) and in such full-length pieces as *Musketeers* (1986), which evokes the era of silent films.

The Lecoq-trained Dean Gilmour and Michelle Smith toured Europe and Canada with *No Escape*, a comedy about the last two survivors on earth. *O Canayen*, based on Canadian history, and a clown–opera entitled *Carmen* blend Lecoq-style clowning with slapstick. The couple performed *The Cry Is Not So*, from a story by Argentinean author Julio Cortazar, at the 1993 London International Mime Festival. This surrealistic piece depicts, among other improbable events, a bride who watches her groom slowly sink into the ground beside her.

Rick Skene founded Winnipeg's Mimeworks in 1983 to present illusion pantomime and story theatre to both children and adults. *Dirty Laundry* (1987) is a mime revue with satirical skits based on current topics, such as *Safe Sex I* and *II, The Weightlifter*, *Women's Lib, Sports Bits*, *No Smoking,* and others. In Mimeworks' repertory of children's pieces are *The Emperor's New Clothes*, *Jack and the Beanstalk,* and *The Thief of Baghdad.* These pieces captivate audiences through accessible and zany improvisational miming and storytelling.

Jest in Time of Halifax, Nova Scotia, founded in 1983 by Sherry Lee Hunter, mixes satire with contemporary mime, puppets, masks, and music in verbal and nonverbal pieces. This four-member company, which performs solos, duos, and ensemble pieces, has been influenced by mime master Tony Montanaro, Charlie Chaplin, Buster Keaton, and Jacques Tati. *Sleep Tracks* explores dreams, memories, and unconscious desires. *Handmade* (1990) comments on the automation of modern man. *Jest in Time Meets Beckett* (1992) develops Beckett's shorter works.

Kaleidoscope is a young people's theatre company that has strived to develop the imagination and emotional needs of young audiences. This Victoria, British Columbia, group, originally begun as an adult theatre in the late 1960s by Elizabeth and Colin Gorrie under the name Total Theater, joins mime, dance, mask, music, and text. In its repertory are *About Free Lands* (1979), which depicts the European settlement of western Canada, and the musical *My Country* (1985). Its story theatre program includes acted-out myths and fables from such works as *Aesop's Fables* (1984–85).

The Théâtre de la Marmaille, a creative, nonverbal children's theatre founded in 1973, has produced historical and legendary works. *L'Umiak* (1982) depicts the Inuit hunter Luckas in search of a seal to feed his hungry family. In the movement fresco *Promised Land* (1989), which takes place in prehistoric times, a gray rock animated by mimes is the main protagonist, with sound effects depicting humankind throughout the ages.

Quebec playwright Serge Marois's visual fantasy pieces appeal to both adults and children. *Glass Heart* (1983) is a poetic movement work with music and text revolving around the four seasons and time's rapid passing. *The Boxes* (1983), a play of images that takes place in a storehouse in which a male protagonist continually moves boxes to wipe up dripping water, harmonizes mime, narrated prose and poetry, and slides to represent the stages of the world's creation. *Night Train, or The First Love of Roy Rogers* (1986) describes a young man's imaginary voyage on a night train, where he relives his first love affair in a surrealistic ambience.

Quebec's Théâtre de l'Aubergine with Josette Dechene and Paul Vachon, performed sketches with music, mime, and clowning for family audiences, such as *Double Trouble*, which revolves around the encounters of Belle and Barbouillette, who meet on a train station platform.

The Electric Mimes, Patrice Arbour and Bernard Carez, who depict animals, objects, and characters through movement and vocal sounds, performed at the 1975 Avignon Festival.

A number of Canada's New Vaudeville clowns engage in miming, juggling, acrobatics, magic, and other theatre arts. Paul Wildbaum—magician, stand-up comedian, and mime, though not a clown per se—frequently has performed at mime and clown festivals. In his *Human Piano,* Wildbaum has his spectators performing outrageous feats on stage, such as ringing bells in concert as he taps them on the head with a rubber hammer when they miss a beat. His *Atom in the 21st Century* and *Mime Mask Cabaret* include mime, mask, clowning, and audience participation in vignettes about hitchhiking, riding a bus, a sperm racing to an egg, a good guy–bad guy western, and many others.

Former Ringling Bros. and Barnum & Bailey clown Pepper Kaminoff, based in Vancouver, creates original clown theatre in *Silent Structures,* in which he struggles to build a twelve-foot replica of the Eiffel Tower on a precarious scaffold of planks with his audience's help. Kaminoff's street entertainer experience and clown training enrich his wordless acts of body contortions, daring pratfalls, and breathtaking physical stunts, which can have him stuck in a barrel, legs over head, or poised on a fragile limb.

Quebec mime–clown Omer Veilleux is an eloquent, whiteface silent clown who appeals to both young and old audiences in such pieces as *The Old Soldier Opens the Envelope* (1986).

A number of Canadian circus companies have brought theatre to the circus arts, joining juggling, acrobatics, and clowning to miming and acting. Among these is Cirque du Soleil, an outgrowth of the Club des Talons Hauts street performers created in 1981. After playing in Quebec City streets from 1982 to 1984, they founded

Cirque du Soleil and toured throughout Canada and abroad. Most of the company's members trained at the Montreal National Circus School, while others are well-known international artists. Actor Franco Dragone, who came to the Ecole Nationale du Cirque de Montréal in 1982 to teach commedia dell'arte and became stage director of Cirque du Soleil in 1985, has brought a theatrical style to the company. Three of the its most popular shows are *Saltimbanco* (1992); *Alegria* (1994), an intimate and traditional European-style circus entertainment with Russian clowns, acrobats, Chinese tightrope artists, and Mongolian contortionists; and *Mystère*, an extravaganza with a story line, baroque costumes, and a surrealist ambience.

La Troupe Circus is a touring company begun in 1981 that explores the relationship between clown techniques and theatre. Its *Creation 858*, performed at the Vancouver Beaux Gestes Mime, Clown, and Movement Festival, is composed of twelve clowning, acrobatics, and juggling vignettes.

In 1988 in Montreal, Dr. George Mager and Dr. Bernie Warren of Concordia University's drama in education program launched a theatre to integrate the disabled with the community. In their company, entitled 50:50, disabled and nondisabled performers work together. In 1989, they staged *Another Day*, a nonverbal piece that Mager and Warren created, followed by Seneca's *Oedipus*, with a cast of twenty performers, in 1990.

Festivals and Mime Organizations in North America

As early as 1974, Bari Rolfe, author and mime, mask, and *commedia* teacher, and Dr. Louis H. Campbell, stage movement professor at Ohio State University, organized a major mime festival of American and international performers in La Crosse, Wisconsin. In 1978, E. Reid Gilbert, founder and director of the Valley Mime Studio in Wisconsin, initiated another major festival, the Festival of American Mime, in Milwaukee. Since 1979, mime–clown festivals have been held in Syracuse, New York, and, in 1985, John Towsen and Fred Yockers began a mime–clown festival in New York City. Stage director, teacher, and theatre department administrator Michael Pedretti took the initiative to continue such festivals. In 1979, Pedretti began his Movement Theatre International as a summer training program at Davis and Elkins College in Elkins, West Virginia, organizing yearly mime festivals there from 1982 on. After relocating to Philadelphia in 1985, Pedretti continued to organize international mime and clown festivals, including movement theatre conferences and a summer training program in movement and clowning. Many festival performances took place in an old church sanctuary that Pedretti had converted into a 350-seat, fully equipped theatre, which also became a center for Philadelphia's performing arts community. Aided by managing director Nancy Hill, also a dancer, choreographer, and former associate artistic director of the Terry Beck Troupe, the Movement Theatre International summer institute, festival, and conference have made Philadelphia a major American, as well as a world, center for movement theatre.

In an interview on his role as festival organizer, Pedretti reveals how movement festivals contribute to the mime field in America:

> In America, the mime field has no infrastructure. There are no national research centers, no important venues for performers, no institutes comparable to Jacques Lecoq's school. There are no institutions devoted to supporting artists and their art. Yet the performers are independent soloists in most cases and therefore most in need of organizational support.

Actors and dancers belong to institutions which have the wealth to support them as they create their art. They also have multiple educational, research, and service organizations which buttress their work. Mimes, on the contrary, have nothing except the festival.

The festival serves as a platform for our field to be presented to the press, the public, the government representatives, etc. It is the only national platform for the field. Festivals are a service to the field, bringing artists together to renew their commitments and to explore alternatives for their work. They provide a national forum to gain attention and respectability. Movement Theatre International is committed to providing the infrastructure which will render the presentation, support, and recognition of this art form healthy, which, I believe, was the most vital art in America in the 1980s.

Concerning the changing nature of movement festivals and the influence of mime on verbal theatre, I believe that movement festivals play a role in broadening the definition of movement theatre. When the public thinks of the clown or the mime, they still see sexist and prejudiced red noses at the circus or a romantic whiteface walking in place. A principal task of the festival is to broaden the definition and to introduce the newest forms and styles.

The most exciting work in the fourth quarter of the twentieth century has been movement theatre. It has influenced the very fabric of verbal theatre. Directors and actors are more aware of movement. But more important, playwrights and producers have moved toward movement theatre as a vehicle.[21]

Regional movement theatre festivals have also grown in America. The Atlanta Mime Festival, which began in 1978 and continued annually more than seven years, held performances and workshops with nationally known mime artists. Touch Mime company hosted the Southeast Regional Mime Festival in 1984. Karen Hoyer, Carol DeLong, and Susan Pudelek produced the 1984 and 1985 Evanston Mime Festival in Illinois. In June 1985, the Midwest Mime and Clown Festival in Indianapolis, hosted by Martin and Victoria Kappel of the local Midsummer Mime Theatre, featured mime artists from several states. The New Hampshire Movement Theatre Festival, begun in 1986 by the Kitchensink Mime Theatre, presented American performers and teachers and continued in 1988, 1989, and 1990. The Mid-Atlantic Movement Theatre Festival, first organized by David and Carol Geyer in 1989 in Westminster, Maryland, and subsequently at Towson State University in Towson, Maryland, included the participation of nationally known artists. The Dell'Arte Players company held its sixth Mad River Festival of movement theatre, clown art, storytelling, and vaudeville in the summer of 1996. Such festivals, which often occur yearly, have promoted awareness of movement arts through performances by major artists and companies, workshops by master teachers, panel discussions, showcases, and open cabarets giving young artists and companies an opportunity to present their work.

In Canada, mime festivals, in which both international mimes and Canadian mimes have participated, received government funding from 1970 to 1990. The first festival took place in Ontario in 1978, followed by Vancouver in 1980 and 1986, and Montreal in 1983 and 1986. Among festival organizers who have helped to increase the mime's visibility through these festivals are Wayne Specht in Vancouver and Robert Dion in Montreal.

The Winnipeg International Mime Festival, created by Giuseppe Condello, artistic director of the 40 Below Mime company, occurred annually from 1983 to 1990, with artists and companies from Europe, the United States, and Canada. The first festival was dedicated to Etienne Decroux, with Decroux-trained mimes performing. Decroux's son Maximilien conducted a workshop. An exhibit of Etienne

Bertrand Weill's photos of the work of Decroux, Marcel Marceau, and Jean-Louis Barrault was displayed in the Gas Station Theatre's lobby, and films of Decroux's creations were shown. In the following years, the Winnipeg festivals continued to feature Decroux-trained mimes, as well as those of other schools and styles.

Since 1979 in Guanajuato, Mexico, Sigfrido Aguilar has organized annual international mime festivals and encounters for mime artists, entitled Encuentros Nationales y Festivales Internacionales, during which the participants were invited to tour their pieces throughout Mexico. (See the appendix for additional information on festivals in America.)

Among American mime organizations, the Mime Guild, a mime association and union, was founded by Richmond Shepard in 1972 and existed until 1978. The International Mimes and Pantomimists, organized by Paul Curtis in 1973 and lasting through 1979, intended to promote mime and pantomime throughout the world. Begun in 1984, the National Mime Association, which was renamed the National Movement Theatre Association in 1990, has provided a matrix for interaction and communication within the movement theatre field—as well as information about movement theatre artists and companies, festivals, and training centers—and promoted movement theatre to presenters, audiences, and agencies funding mime.

The National Movement Theatre Association has published *Movement Theatre Quarterly,* formerly called *Mime News,* since 1984. It includes articles on movement theatre, as well as reviews of performances. *The Mime Journal,* edited by Thomas Leabhart at Pomona College in Claremont, California, contains articles and photographs of mimes and mime companies. *Mimenet,* published by Jef of North Carolina's Touch Mime Theatre from 1986 to 1994, was a news network that reached out to mimes throughout America, providing international as well as national information on movement artists and events. Bari Rolfe and Thomas Leabhart are among the journalists who specialize in mime and publish articles in these publications, as well as in others.[22] Canadian mime, theatre, and dance critic Aline Gélinas has published numerous articles on mime in Montreal. (See the appendix for additional information on periodicals.)

Mimes Dean Fogal and Philip Maxwell formed the Corporeal Mime Society in Vancouver in 1986 to cultivate an awareness of mime and to encourage a community of mime artists using corporeal techniques in British Columbia. The society provided financial support for a mime training program, advanced study abroad, and theatre equipment and props for performance. It worked with the Beaux Gestes Society to build the only British Columbia venue for mime–physical theatre. It supported the development of a series of mime training manuals, gathered a large collection of international mime and movement theatre videos for its Mime Observatory, and aimed to develop a new collaborative facility for experimental theatre and mime training.

Following in the footsteps of its predecessor, the Canadian Association of Mime, the Beaux Gestes Festival and Symposium Society began in Vancouver in 1988. The society, which represents British Columbia's mimes, physical theatre artists, and interdisciplinary artists, created *Spontaneous Combustion*, the only British Columbia performance series designed specifically for mime and physical theatre. It has published a quarterly newsletter, *Press and Release*, and hosted guest artists' workshops. In 1992, it hosted workshops and lectures by Frits Vogel from Griftheater in Holland and Ide Van Heiningen of the European Mime Federation. (See the appendix for additional information on mime associations and training centers in North America.)

In North America, as in Europe, whenever existing mime festivals and organizations disappeared, new festival directors and organizations took up the torch in an effort to perpetuate the art of mime and foster the continuation of physical theatre.

Notes

1. Letter to author, April 1979.
2. Letter to author, December 1972, reapproved by Curtis, January 1994.
3. Gautier, Théophile, "L'Art," in *Les Grands Ecrivains Français*, edited by J. D. Gautier and L. A. M. Sumberg (New York: Holt, Rinehart, and Winston, 1964): 558.
4. Letter to author, September 1983.
5. Letter to author, August 1970.
6. Interview with author, July 1985.
7. Interview with author, July 1985.
8. Letter to author for corrections, December 1996.
9. Letter to author, June 1980.
10. Letter to author, March 1994.
11. Letter to author, January 1971.
12. Letter to author, July 1975.
13. Letter to author, February 1993.
14. Interview with author, August 1988.
15. Interview with author, June 1985.
16. Letter to author, November 1988.
17. Interview with author, June 1989.
18. Ibid.
19. Interview with author, June 1988.
20. Ibid.
21. Letter to author, July 1991.
22. Annette Lust is also an international theatre journalist who has published numerous articles on mime and movement theatre.

14

Women's Voices in Mime

Similar to the chapters on European and North American mime, this chapter is an overview of women mimes with a variety of movement styles. Although women mimes working with male mimes have been mentioned previously, this chapter has been devoted to those who have been working independently, though not exclusively, as females in the field and who have utilized content in some of their works that touch upon women's issues. Many of these women have undergone training and influences similar to those of the artists and companies in the aforementioned chapters. Because some female artists are unfamiliar to the author or information about them has been difficult to obtain, there are women mimes who have not been included in the following pages.

From Ancient Rome to Mid-Twentieth Century

A brief look at the role women have played in mime throughout history shows that, though they have not performed frequently in solo works or created their own pantomimes and mime pieces, they have played in mime companies and made use of expressive movement in speaking theatre, dance, music hall, and, more recently, in the cinema and on TV.

In ancient Rome, many famous women mimes, such as Cytheris, Denisa, Valeria Cloppia, Dionysia, Thymele, Arbuscula, Eucharia, Pelagia, Lucilia, Hermione, Lucia, Antiodemis (a mime–singer), and Julia Bassilla, were highly appreciated for their art. A number of seductive and talented women mimes of Asia Minor and Egypt became the courtesans of the rich and even achieved high social rank. An example given in a previous chapter was that of Theodora, a libertine mime who became the wife of Emperor Justinian of Byzantium in A.D. 527.

During the Renaissance and up to the eighteenth century, actresses in commedia dell'arte companies were required to have a talent for miming in a lively theatre form in which movement was essential. The famed Isabella Andreini, for example, was applauded not only for her beauty, but also for her measured gestures and harmonious movements. While touring throughout France and performing in their native tongue, Zanetta Rosa Benozzi (Sylvia), Catherine Biancolelli (Colombine), Helena

Balletti (Flamania), and other *commedia* actresses depended on the use of gestures and movements. In his book on the commedia dell'arte in France, after describing how movement in the Italian theatre had inspired such authors as Molière and enriched the quality of his theatre (1950, 145), Gustave Attinger adds that the presence of women on the Italian stage heightened the comic element. In fact, comedy could neither flourish nor raise itself above a commonplace level without women (1950, 327).

During the nineteenth century, in France's Théâtre des Funambules in France, a number of Pierrots succeeded Gaspard Deburau, and women mimes performed opposite them. In 1890, Jane May played Pierrot in the classic *L'Enfant Prodigue* in London, while Francesca Zanfretta interpreted Phrynetta in the same pantomime. That same year, Felicia Mallet played Pierrot in the Paris production of *L'Enfant Prodigue*.

In France at the turn of the twentieth century, the mime Georges Wague engaged La Belle Ortero and Colette, the future novelist, to perform in his Pierrot pantomimes. Colette and Wague had the main roles in *Rêves d'Egypte* in 1906 and *La Chair* in 1908. Colette describes her life as a music hall mime and her love for the art in *La Vagabonde*: "There is only one thing that is real—dancing, lights, liberty, music. What is real is to place rhythm into one's thoughts, to translate them into beautiful gestures" (1910, 60).

Other women mimes who performed in Wague's pantomimes were Christine Kerf; Christiane Mendelys; Angèle Heraud, a singer who, after losing her voice, became a mime and also played men's roles; and Charlotte Wiehe, a Danish mime–actress.

In England, Irene Mawer made her 1916 debut as Harlequin in *Et Puis Bonsoir*, in which the author, Ruby Ginner, played Pierrot. Mawer also performed in a 1928 revival of *L'Enfant Prodigue* and published *The Art of Mime* in 1932.

German dancer and actress Valeska Gert (1900–1978) became renowned throughout Europe, in German cabarets, and in her Beggar Bar in New York (1943–45) for her highly exaggerated and stylized mime–dance. In her dance interpretations and satirical and grotesque character portrayals, she improvised her observations of traffic, boxing, fencing, ice skating, the circus, a streetwalker, a fortune-teller, a procuress, and many others.

Born in Switzerland, Trudi Schoop went to Berlin in 1929 to perform as a mime–dancer in cabarets and to organize a company, which won first prize at the 1932 International Dance Congress in Paris. In both Europe and North America, she was appreciated for her pantomimic qualities and was called the female Charlie Chaplin. In 1932, she created and performed the main role in *Fridolin*, a dance–mime about a naive young man coping with a materialistic world, followed by *Want Ads*; *Blonde Marie,* in which a maid turns into a star; and *Barbara*, about a dancing clown. Schoop developed dance therapy classes for persons with mental illnesses and trained dance therapists in Europe and America.

In the United States, several women mimes developed their styles prior to the influences of the French masters. Ruth Draper (1884–1956) was one of the first to perform in solo shows, which combined expressive movement with spoken monologue. In the 1920s, mime–dancer, playwright, painter, and novelist Angna Enters toured North America and Europe, staging one-woman character pantomimes such as *Pagan Greece* (1938), in which she interpreted fourteen roles. Among her creations are *Boy Cardinal*, *Auto da Fé, Pavana*, and *Artist's Life*. While Etienne Decroux still was evolving his mime grammar in Paris, Enters was among the first to express the need to codify mime, like dance, to make it a recognized art. In her book *On Mime* (1965), she relates her experiences as a mime teacher and her belief that mime that is not merely imitative can be the most universal of the arts and one that best expresses human behavior's nuances. She compares the painter, the poet, and the composer, who create color, form, word, and sound images, to the mime artist, who creates movement images.

Many women dancers have introduced expressive or dramatic movement into their art. In nineteenth-century Europe, French poet and critic Théophile Gautier praised the ballerinas Carlotta Grisi, wife of the circus pantomimist Jules Perrot, and Fanny Elssler for their talent as pantomimists. In early twentieth-century Austria, Mary Wigman encouraged individual expressivity in her dance students, among whom were Hanya Holm, Vera Skoronel, Harald Kreutzberg, Lotte Goslar, and Kurt Joos, who founded the modern dance–drama. In her creations, Isadora Duncan revealed inner feelings and the soul's emotions. Expressive movement enhanced the dramatic and lyrical quality in the dance of this American "Goddess of Gestures." Martha Graham understood the importance of expressive gestures to reveal human emotions in her dance–dramas. Doris Humphrey incorporated pantomime and even recitation into her choreographies. Charlotte Weidman's kinetic pantomimes united abstract mime with dance.

One of the first female clown–mime–dancers to appear on the American stage, Lotte Goslar, who ends this first period and begins that of the mid-twentieth century, combined mime with comic dance and circus techniques, which were largely self-taught, to create her female clown. Born in Dresden, Germany, she trained and performed with expressionist modern dancers Mary Wigman and Gret Palucca. After touring Europe in Erika Mann's anti-Hitler show, *The Peppermill,* which appeared in New York in 1938, and playing in solo mime, she joined the Turnabout Theatre in Hollywood in 1943, and in 1947 choreographed the carnival scene for Brecht's *Galileo.* Goslar founded her Pantomime Circus company in 1951, touring the United States and Europe with *For Humans Only* (1954) and *All Is Fun* (1963). She staged *Clowns and Other Fools* at the 1966 Central Park Dance Festival, choreographed dances for stage companies and films, and taught mime at the University of California in Los Angeles and the Pasadena Playhouse.

As a dancer, Goslar reveals the body's need to express emotions:

> I believe that the total being is involved in emotional expression. If something tragic happens to you in life your entire body feels it. And on stage total stillness is also movement, even if it is not visible movement.[1]

After the Mid-Twentieth Century

During the second half of the twentieth century, the woman's voice in all of the arts grew louder and more articulate. Despite the rarity of female role models in mime, a number of women mimes created their own pieces and performed in solo and group works comparable with those of male artists. Several developed content that protested a male-dominated world, while others asserted their feminism through more subtle channels. As the social climate grew more favorable for female artistic creation, women, conscious of their feminine sensitivity and potential, invented new artistic values. Through the art of mime, women acquired another voice, even though it was a silent one.

Mamako Yoneyama

Mamako Yoneyama's artistic contribution lent a strong voice to the modern Japanese woman's social plight. Born in 1935 in Minobu Town, Japan, she first studied dance with her father. In 1953, she entered Tokyo Educational University to do dance research while she trained in modern dance at the Eguchi Dance Studio. Upon seeing Marcel Marceau perform in Tokyo in 1955, Mamako began to develop her mime skills. After playing Puck on Japanese TV, in 1961 she renounced stardom to come to the United States. She first performed in nightclubs and taught mime at the American Conservatory Theatre in San Francisco and at the California Institute of the Arts in Southern California. In 1971, she studied with Etienne Decroux and Jacques Lecoq in Paris. Mamako returned to Japan in 1972 to teach mime and bring her mimodrama *Ten Bulls*, premiered in 1970 at the American Conservatory Theatre, to Japanese audiences. In 1981, she and her Japanese company toured the United States with her musical comedy *Pierrette*. Having integrated Kabuki dance movement with her training in the French schools of mime, Mamako was the first to introduce Western-style mime into her country.

Zen Buddhism comprises the basis of Mamako's earlier works, in which the protagonists submit to their destinies. In *The Pond,* the fisherman is transformed into a bird, a monkey, a rock, a snake, and the fish that he catches. In *Ocean*, the boatman casts a net into the ocean and becomes the net, a fish, crabs on a rock, and finally the boatman rowing away. In *Ten Bulls,* based on a Buddhist parable, an oxherder's search for a lost bull, symbolizing misplaced values and destructive emotions, culminates in a quest for enlightenment. Dance, poetry, and spectacular choreography enhance this mimodrama.

Satire is integrated with mime, spoken narrative, song, and dance in *Pierrette*, Mamako's first piece on the tragic predicament of women. Performed as a musical comedy, it portrays women's changing roles in Japanese society. Although the satire is poignant, the lyricism of Mamako's art is never forsaken. Pierrette is the symbol of the wounded dove fleeing the earth in search of a purer existence.

In *Pierrot's Jewel*, a poetic and philosophical mimodrama depicting human selfishness and alienation, Pierrot creates a jewel made of his tears, which shatters as others try to take it from him. With his tears, Pierrot creates another jewel, which he throws to the audience to share with others. Mamako's illusion pantomime images bring concrete, as well as lyric, meaning to this philosophical piece.

In her art, which blends pantomime and silent acting with dance, Mamako does not rely on anecdotal pantomime or dramatic development. Although spiritual symbolism is basic to a number of her pieces, they never lack dramatic interest. In her lighter sketches, such as *Pollution* and *Laundromat*, conventional pantomime is used solely for purposes of satire and social comment. Grounded in traditional Oriental and modern dance, as well as on Occidental mime, Mamako's technique, largely self-taught, is composed of assertive, and sometimes violent, Kabuki-style attitudes that alternate with soft, rounded movement. Yet, her use of traditional Oriental and modern dance never jeopardizes the purity of her mime expression.

Beyond elevating mime to spiritual heights to depict the self's metaphysical struggle with the chaos of reality and disillusion, this poetic Japanese Pierrette portrays the irony of woman's tragic struggle. To the female plight, drawn from observations of Japanese and American life, Mamako has brought an original mime style containing stylized, Eastern dance movement and Western mime techniques.

For Mamako, mime is a means of voicing the female's quest for quiet self-realization. In the following poem, she compares it to the purity achieved in creating a poem that culminates in Zen's silent void:

Mime and Zen

As a Japanese
I can't think of Mime without
thinking about Zen.

The essence of Zen is to teach
yourself how to experience the
joy of Void as it was experienced
by Buddha.

Mime resembles the Void
in that it is the world of silence.

For instance a Haiku poem is one of
the art forms which is born from Zen
This creative process seeks the
same state of being as Mime does.

Haiku is a poem composed of three lines,
Five syllables for the first line,
seven for the second, five for the third.
In this brief statement all of
life's phenomena is expressed
as inspirationally, as existentially,
as economically as possible.

These few words are dropped
into the pond of silence,
they ripple for a moment and
then silence returns.

The mutual communication of words
and silence—this is Haiku
and this is Mime.
Yes, Mime is Haiku in movement.
As movement becomes simpler
and simpler it gradually enters
into the world of Zen.

What a Yugen [mysteriously profound]
art Mime is!

The world is growing more polluted
with noise and plastic

I love Mime as I love a clear
river, a quiet forest, and a deep pond.

The soul of Mime is this calm nature
and it must not be polluted.[2]

Pinok and Matho

From 1960 to the early 1980s, French mimes Pinok and Matho were the only professional women mimes in Europe. After studying with Étienne and Maximilien Decroux, dancer Karin Waehner in Paris, and Pearl Lang and Yuriko Doi of the Martha Graham School, they staged mime shows in cabarets and café theatres and taught and performed mime throughout Europe, Canada, Africa, Asia, and Japan. In 1964, Pinok and Matho founded their Théâtre École Mouvement and Pensée (Temp). In the early 1970s, they began the Théâtre des Deux Portes, where they presented many of their own works and invited other movement theatre artists to perform. Besides initiating and participating in a number of mime events and festivals, they directed the International Mime Festival of Saint Maur from 1990 to 1993. In 1994, they created and directed the Tremplin Théâtre, designed to present new works by unpublished authors and unknown artists. They also made films of their creations, choreographed movement for stage productions and TV, performed in plays, and published adult and children's mimes and essays and books on corporeal mime.

In Pinok and Matho's repertory of early serious and comical pieces are *Le Crépuscule de l'Orchidée* (*The Twilight of the Orchid*, 1972), an ironic and surrealistic piece on the vanity of all things; *Où Sont Tous Mes Amants?* (*Where Are All My Lovers?* 1976), a melodramatic reminiscence of such famous artists as Isadora Duncan and Sarah Bernhardt; *Le Rendez-Vous* (1976), in which a character in black and a mysterious visitor waltz their way into hell; *Romeo and Juliette* (a section of *Drôle de Mime*, 1965), a parody in Swiss village costumes; *Le Cycle de l'Azote* (*The Nitrogen Cycle*, 1970), a parable about the eternal cycle of life and death; *Le Temps Distille* (*Time Distills*, 1970), in which female insect divinities spin, unwind, and cut the threads of men's lives; *Totem* (1970), about ancient gods who awaken and speak on a stormy night; *Les Comères* (*The Gossips*, 1970), *Abracadabracula* (1983), a modern absurdist fantasy; *Tango avec la Mort* (*Tango with Death*, 1981), an opera-reverie with variations on Hamlet's famous "To be or not to be" soliloquy; and *Cries, Nuit, Lune, Nuages et Quelques Gaudrioles* (*Cries, Night, Moon, Clouds and Jesting*, 1976), which combines humor with existential unease. In their 1996–97 season at the Tremplin Théâtre, Pinok and Matho presented *L'Extravagant Voyage de Monsieur P. K.*, based on an Henri Michaux text in which the hero, who begins as an awkward traveler, ends up discovering the poetry of the universe, and *Mimes et Ritourelles* (*Mimes and Jingles*), a children's program consisting of several pieces, including *Cadeau de Noël pour Anna* (*Christmas gift for Anna*), in which a nasty little girl mistreats a precious gift.

Through total mastery of their bodies and keen senses of gesture and rhythm, Pinok and Matho explore facets of both dance and mime, from the graceful to the mechanical and from fast-moving rhythms to statuary attitudes. With masklike faces, they move from one sex to the other and from animals to inanimate objects and abstract images. Their movement expression is simultaneously rich and inventive, precise and calculated. Their art offers a wide range of spiritual and sensual sentiments and ideas. It combines metaphysical and poetic content far-removed from object illusions and pantomime charades. Not limited to Étienne Decroux's mime, it encompasses other movement styles and acting and includes props, costumes, and vocal sounds. Through bitter satire, burlesque humor, noble stylization, tender lyricism, and surrealistic parody, Pinok and Matho's art comments on time, love, death, and our absurd world. Here, the fantastic turns into the unexpected and the absurd, evoking a quasimagical atmosphere, along with clownish and baroque elements.

Ella Jaroszewicz

Born in Poland, Ella Jaroszewicz was at first a choreographer at the Opera of Wroclaw and then a member of Wroclaw's Theatre of Pantomime, where for eight years she played main roles in the company's mimodramas, which received two gold medals at the 1962 Moscow Pantomime Festival. She then opened a mime school in Paris and was invited to teach the first mime course at the Paris Opera dance school, with the support of such dancers as Roland Petit, who believed in training dancers in mime. In 1973, Jaroszewicz began her mime company, Magenia (alluding to "dream" in Polish), in which she created mimodramas with costumes and music based on abstract as well as classical mime. The company's first creation, *La Forêt,* combined the Wroclaw mime style with contemporary dance and mime. Performing in Paris and abroad, in 1977 her company received second prize for choreography at the International Concours de Bagnolet for *La Lune*; in 1979, her company received the Fondation de la Danse's humor prize for *The Adventures of the Ants.* In 1981, Jaroszewicz choreographed *Mélancolie*, a melodrama in which the moon cures a little boy's melancholy. This piece was followed by *L'Aube Lunaire*, a visual poem based on the dissention that divided her native Poland, which, through its subtle symbolism, escaped censorship in that country.

The members of Jaroszewicz's company trained at her school in mime, stage movement, and gestures. The program, also open to nonmembers, consisted of courses in technique, improvisation, and construction of mime pieces. Workshops in classical pantomime, mask work, mime, and stage acting have been offered periodically.

Jaroszewicz's Polish- and French-style mimodramas represent neither mime, dance, nor theatre, but a poetic fusion of all three arts.

Nola Rae

Nola Rae is one of those rare mime artists who preserved the arts of illusion pantomime and traditional clowning well into the postmodern era. Born in Sydney, Australia, she began studying ballet when she was eight years old and then went to London in 1963 to train at the Royal Ballet School. She began her career as a ballet dancer at the Malmö Stadsteater in Sweden and also played at the Tivoli Pantomime Theatre in Copenhagen. After seeing Marcel Marceau perform in London in 1969, Rae abandoned ballet to study with him in Paris. She performed in the French physical theatre company La Troupe Kiss in 1970 and 1971, returning to England in 1972 to co-found the clown company Friends Roadshow with American clown Jango Edwards. In 1975, she began her London Mime Theatre, touring with it and as a solo mime in Europe, the Middle East, Latin America, Africa, India, Australia, and New

Zealand. She also performed at the Festival of Fools in Amsterdam and at the International Festival of Mime and Theatre in Nancy, Avignon, Cologne, London, Florence, Berlin, and Hong Kong, as well as numerous other festivals in Europe, Canada, Latin America, and New Zealand. A documentary about her work was made for the BBC in 1977.

Rae's art, based on illusion pantomime and traditional clowning in her earlier works, incorporates ballet, silent-movie comedy, fables, puppetry, and cartoon and object animation. These elements are found in *Mime and Clown* (1976); *Some Great Fools from History* (1977); *Future Fool* (1979); *Prime Cuts* (1980); *Double Up* (1981); *Upper Cuts* (1983); *The Urge* (1985); *Shakespeare, the Works* (1986); *Bottom of the Garden and other Twisted Tales* (1988); *Elizabeth's Last Stand* (1990); *And the Ship Sailed On,* in which two women emigrants sail into the unknown, performed with dancer Sally Owen at the 1994 London International Mime Festival; and Rae's clown show *Mozart Preposteroso*, which opened in London in February 1998.

In all of Rae's works, minimal sets and costumes and no technical or scenic effects are used to ridicule universal type characters. *Some Great Fools from History* depicts man's foolishness from cave-dweller to astronaut, beginning with a look at the first fools, Adam and Eve; then passing through Greece, Rome, the Dark Ages, the Renaissance, commedia dell'arte, and puppetry traditions; and ending with a portrayal of today and tomorrow's fools. *Future Fool*, in nine tableaux, centers on the traditional fool attempting to unravel secrets of the hereafter and reincarnation. *Upper Cuts* offers a spectrum of characters, among whom are a surgeon obsessed with washing his hands; a magician whose trick of putting swords through the body fails; an orchestra conductor who is tormented by visions of cows, chickens, and pigs as he directs Beethoven's "Pastoral" Symphony and is knocked over by imaginary galloping horses during the *William Tell* Overture; a gambler addicted to slot machines who ends up in the electric chair, pulling the lever on himself; and a ballet dancer who contorts her body into grotesque positions. Rae's pieces evoke the surrealistic and the illogical, the macabre and the enchanting, the hilarious and the poetic.

Rae's androgynous mime–clown sharply derides either sex. Her clown is earthy, naive, and timid, at once grotesque and dignified, and has a whimsical sense of humor that sometimes turns to black humor. While engaging in nonsensical humor, Rae introduces the fantasy of a Walt Disney cartoon. Employing whiteface with exaggerated clown make-up or portraying a character in an extravagant costume, she creates a comical figure whose eccentricities are clearly drawn and exposed in the manner of classic art. In her picaresque storytelling, she gives as much importance to content as to a traditional use of pantomime, communicating a comic incident's essence through a cartoon's economy of means.

On her art as a silent mime and a clown, Rae says:

> I must be the only English mime today who doesn't speak. I feel I can say much more without speaking and that it is more interesting to solve problems without words. However, I also feel my work going much more toward the clown than toward pure mime. I like to say I am a clown who uses mime (and anything else I think appropriate). I believe mime to be the most difficult of the physical arts and also the most satisfying. It is also the most international when mixed with clowning and when one steers clear of cultural barriers and sticks to concepts experienced by all. I also firmly believe that in its pure and rigid sense mime is not sufficient. It is preferable to think of the word pantomime as a word which comes from the Greek "to play all." These days I like to de-

scribe my characters as fools. I set out to make my audience laugh and think, feel sympathy, but most of all to come out of the show having had a memorable evening.[3]

Rae adds that her art also includes audience interaction:

Pantomime for me is not only the white-faced, white-costumed, lonely figure in a black void. It is one of the few arts which demands the participation of its audience. It reaches all peoples of every background and speaks directly to their inner feelings. It is entirely personal and because of that, dangerous and excruciating when performed by people of little or no talent, whose only aim is to do their own thing without thought of their audience. It is most important that there be a partnership with one's audience. It is ninety percent of the performance.[4]

Rae's dynamism as a clown lies in her ability to interpret male roles. Regarding male roles and women as clown–mimes, she says:

I do not play many women, preferring to take the piss out of men who are better material for a joke. Not that my men are very manly, more like neutral human beings, struggling with their foolishness. But since women move more softly than men and their movements are less articulate, they often lack the confidence to become mimes. However, since I come from a ballet background, it has never occurred to me to feel intimidated or inferior to male performers. After all, the ballerina is often more important than the male dancer. I have never found difficulty in performing as a woman. It is not important to my work and I have really got to where I am by persevering and working a lot, without the distractions of being married and having children. Early in my career I threw off all vestiges of glamour and performed the ridiculous and sometimes even the grotesque. Until women do this they will not achieve a clown of any great depth or universality.[5]

A well-balanced combination of pantomime, dance, cartoon humor, silent-movie comedy, and traditional comic values, which have resisted the appeal of current visual novelties, has made Nola Rae's silent art unique.

Marguerite Mathews

Marguerite Mathews began her Pontine Movement Theatre as an all-female company, with creations perceived as being female. After receiving an Asian theatre degree from Michigan State University in 1972, Mathews gathered all of her savings—which she earned as a waitress in Portsmouth, New Hampshire—to study mime with Etienne Decroux in Paris. Commuting between Paris and Portsmouth, she also trained with corporeal mime Thomas Leabhart, director of the Corporeal Mime Theater in California. In 1977, while Mathews was performing at the Prescott Park Arts Festival in Portsmouth, Anne Suavé, a teacher of German, inspired by Mathews's solo works, became her student. In 1979, another student, Ellen Brown, joined them and Mathews began to choreograph pieces for the group. The company's creations gradually moved from abstract–corporeal mime to theatre-oriented works with a narrative line. In Mathews's words:

In my work with Pontine Movement Theatre since 1977, we have created pieces of a highly abstract nature exploring the dynamics of design in space. We have produced pieces with a strong narrative line and fully developed characters. We have labored to discover humor in our work and to weave lines of thought with intricate detail, breath and rhythm.[6]

After touring New England as the New Hampshire Mime Company, the company's name changed to Pontine Movement Theatre, referring to the electrical process that connects the intuitive and ritualistic brain with the logical neocortex during sleep to enable dreaming. In 1983, after Brown left the company, student Tony Staffier joined Mathews and Suavé. With his presence, the female group's abstract, androgynous style and work content changed. By 1990, the artistic staff included Mathews and co-director Gregory Gathers, who began in 1980 as a costume designer and later designed sets, performed, and became co-artistic director of Pontine.

Pontine Theater company's repertory ranged from corporeal mime, *commedia*, and nineteenth-century pantomime to light corporeal sketches and full-length theatre pieces, to puppet performances, lectures, and poetry readings. From Étienne Decroux–style solo pieces entitled *The Baker* and *Work,* it moved to lengthier works with stock *commedia* characters and classical pantomime, such as *Pierrot and Harlequin* (1979), based on the Gaspard Deburau pantomimes. *Trio* (1980) is an abstract composition consisting of formal gestures, meticulously designed choreography, and three mimes' clever use of the geometric patterns of sticks. *Wordworks* (1982) explores relationships between words and movement, including a humorous sketch called *A. B. C. Hungry* (1982), in which names relate food to movement forms. *The Way Forward* (1981), based on Shakespeare's *The Tempest*, offers visual imagery depicting universal themes of human struggles through the use of narrator and rhythmic instruments. *The Tale of William Mariner* (1983), created in collaboration with composer John Appleton, blends electronic music and corporeal movement to relate the seventeenth-century's seaman's adventures. *Café* (1985) is composed of monologues, vaudeville, slapstick, farce, and social commentary. *A Dream Away* (1985), based on the writings of Maine author Sarah Orne Jewett, depicts nineteenth-century characters through narration and movement. *Face the Music* (1986) ridicules two 1930s couples who flirt with one another and swap partners in a swank rooftop restaurant in Manhattan. *City Shadows* (1986) consists of tableaux with mixed media and corporeal mime. The two-act mimodrama *Bitter Bliss* (1987) conveys a couple's day-to-day, love–hate relationship. *A Child's Eye* (1988) is a movement and vocal rendition of childhood memories as they affect the present. *Familiar Fields* (1989, 1994), based on another Jewett work, reveals nineteenth-century life in New England fishing villages through mime, dance, puppets, stories, and projected images. *Paradise* (1990) dramatizes the Adam and Eve theme through poetic movement imagery, vocal sounds, Buddhist drums and bells, and Javanese percussion. *Still Life in a House of Dust* (1991) portrays through verbal drama, dance, mime, puppetry, poetry, charades, and home movies a couple's struggle with domestic boredom in an aimless life. The piece reflects the theme of decay and rebirth that occurs throughout many of Pontine Movement Theater's works. *The Heloise and Abelard Project* (1992) draws upon the medieval lovers' correspondence, revealing the schism between body and mind in their tempestuous love. Blending narrative with rich imagery, the work is staged with live actors, marionettes, Bunraku puppets, movement, text, and music. *Correspondence of Desires* (1993) further develops Heloise and Abelard's passionate love through corporeal-based movement, life-size puppets, angelic marionettes, liturgical candles, original guitar music, and Gregorian chants, with a dialogue based on a translation of the lovers' letters written in Latin. *Voices from the Spirit Land* (1996) integrates a toy theatre lecture on the history of spiritualism, a Henry James ghost story acted out by Bunraku-style puppets, and excerpts from Walt Whitman's *Leaves of Grass. Pontine Premiere* (1998) is a dramatic and lyrical collage that explores the personal and professional life of Maxfield Parrish, who played a part in developing the artists' colony of sculptor Augustus St. Gaudens in the early part of the century.

Without abandoning its corporeal mime base, Pontine Movement Theater has evolved into a physical theatre in which the performers create their own rhythms as they work with dance, music, costumes, sets, props, slides, a script, and vocal expression. Yet, the use of these components is secondary to the creation of visual images that serve function more than form. The company's incorporation of multiple elements is akin to the postmodern pluralism in dance and mime. Yet, the group has retained corporeal mime's discipline and purity, achieving the hard-earned classicism of a modern mime form enriched by other means of theatrical expression.

Mathews, who has served as president of the National Mime Association and editor of *Movement Theatre Quarterly*, chaired a panel on "Women in Mime" at the Philadelphia Movement Theatre International Festival in the summer of 1987. In the following passage, she describes her feelings about working as a woman in mime:

> Because I am a woman raised in the United States, because my background is in Asian theatre forms and because of my particular life experiences, what I choose to say and how I structure my message is, quite naturally, particular to me as a woman. This inevitable blend of the personal and the universal makes a technique live.
>
> I think of my experiences as being human ones and of my work as portraying human problems. The really important issues are beyond male and female — death, isolation, goodness, evil. I am made aware of the female quality of my work only by the reactions of others. Like a spider spinning a web, we all express our essence subconsciously. There are many layers to any work.
>
> I am not displeased that my work is perceived as female. I like the work of other women. My favorite writer is Sarah Orne Jewett. Her work could not have been written by a man raised in our culture. But what makes her work female is an overall quality, an indefinable essence, a particular sensibility. I trust that it is for these sorts of reasons that my work is perceived as female.[7]

Dulcinea Langfelder

Etienne Decroux–trained Dulcinea Langfelder has contributed to female achievement in mime through her hard-earned success as a solo mime. Born in New York, she first studied modern dance with Merce Cunningham and Paul Sanasardo. After apprenticing at London's Oval House Theatre Club in 1974, Langfelder trained at Decroux's Paris school from 1975 to 1978 and at the National Circus School of Paris from 1975 to 1976. In 1978, she joined Montreal's Omnibus company, where she stayed until 1982. After training with Decroux and doing theatre research with Eugenio Barba and Yoshi Oida, Langfelder began to develop her own solo movement theatre. She has choreographed movement for actors in more than twenty stage and TV productions and taught both mime and dance.

Langfelder's first solo piece, *Vicious Circle*, about a little girl who couldn't stop running and who evolved into a woman searching for meaning in her life, began as a corporeal mime piece in which the protagonist interacts with a plastic hoop in a bittersweet relationship. At first she is a fetal ball in the hoop's center; then she moves through stages of self-discovery, in which the hoop takes on a life of its own. Culminating in a dance to the air of a Spanish guitar, the work concludes that inevitably it is only ourselves that we find in the vast sea. Through the years, what began as a short, corporeal movement piece grew into a fifty-five-minute work with music and songs by Kurt Weill, film, poetic monologues, dance, and movement.

Langfelder's tragicomedy *The Neighbor*, developed in the late 1980s, revolves around an old spinster, who begins by spitting at the audience and saying, "I don't like you!" As she sits before her TV, she falls asleep and dreams of dancing like a young girl with her handsome neighbor. Upon awakening, she is again alone before her TV, an embittered old maid.

In *Portrait of a Woman with a Valise*, performed at the March 1999 Montreal Voies du Mime tribute to Decroux, Langfelder mimes a woman bound to her valise, with which she converses and disputes, and in which she finds her soul.

Langfelder's style, which remains corporeal mime-based, incorporates dance and movement techniques with an engaging sensuality.

Jyl Hewston

Jyl Hewston's contribution as a mime, clown, and teacher is an example of women's changing roles in miming and clowning. After training with James Donlon at his San Francisco mime school in 1972, she taught, organized mime companies, and performed as a mime, clown, and juggler. While directing and teaching stage movement, mime, and acting at Humboldt State University, Hewston tap-danced in a street company in Arcata, California, and co-founded Proteus Mime Theatre, based at Humboldt State University. In 1979, she began Theatre Plexus near Washington, D.C., with clown–mime Robert Morse, who trained with James Donlon and Leonard Pitt in corporeal mime and with mime, juggler, musician, and writer Joe Mori. Hewston and Morse toured nationally and abroad, playing at the 1985 London International Mime Festival. They also conducted workshops in mime, circus arts, and mask work. In 1986, Hewston was a resident writer, director, and teacher at Gallaudet College's Model School for the Deaf in Washington, D.C., where she directed a mime show with deaf students, that was performed at the Beaux Gestes International Mime Festival in Vancouver, British Columbia. A proponent of women playing a more prominent role in movement theatre, she has participated in conferences and on panels, such as "Women in Mime" at the 1978 Festival of American Mime in Milwaukee.

Theatre Plexus combined *commedia* with mime, masks, acrobatics, music, and varied theatrical styles in a lively mime–clown theatre. *Grumps* (1979) is a chronometric interplay among three angry performers, which provokes laughter within a tightly woven set of visual images. *The Kurlytov Family Cirkus* (1979) parodies Russian circus clowning, along with pseudo Russian dialogue. Unable to open their prop trunk, the clowns do other tricks to distract the audience, such as juggling with a rubber chicken called Nancy, a frying pan, and whatever they can find. One scene alludes to the liberation of female clowns, as Hewston drags a male spectator on stage to make him a victim of the club-throwing to which she has just subjected her two male partners.

After Theatre Plexus moved west in the fall of 1987, Hewston organized a mime festival at Humboldt State University and, with Morse, staged the world premiere of *Ghost Dance*, created collaboratively with professionals and university students. The action occurs in the great desert of the Southwest, where two computer programmers encounter a juggling waitress, a singing cactus, and two manic coyotes. Original masks, puppets, mime, dance, and a voice disclose the Native American prophecy that the coyotes' ancestors will return, along with the buffalo herds, in a ghost dance, symbolizing the need for revitalization in an imprisoning, materialistic world.

Gardi Hutter

One of Switzerland's most talented clown–mimes, Gardi Hutter is the recipient of the 1990 Best Actor of the Year prize in her country. Born in 1953 and trained at the Actor's Academy in Zurich, she is one of the few female clowns who have succeeded in creating clown characters that achieve levels of comedy and professionalism equal to those of her male counterparts. In *Joan of Arppo* (1981)—directed by Ferruccio Cainero of Milan's Teatro Ingenu, who directs and co-writes Hutter's pieces—her down-to-earth clowning is based on a tousled washerwoman's dream of becoming Joan of Arc. With exacting clown techniques and a keen sense of selectivity, Hutter incorporates feminist undertones as she contrasts the clumsy washerwoman facing her dreary chores with the enlightened dreamer who escapes from banal reality to read avidly Joan of Arc's story and become the heroine. Here, as in all of her work, Hutter renounces the female reticence to play an ugly washerwoman and pokes fun at the predicament of the washerwoman who dreams of being a heroine. These elements strengthen her clown character and deepen the irony of her content, enabling her to achieve the sublime in her art.

Since 1981, Hutter has toured throughout Europe, performed in the United States, and appeared on European TV. *Abra Catastrophe, a Witch Comedy* (1984) draws upon two witches who have survived the Inquisition through their stupidity and malice. *Cheese* (1988) depicts a poor mouse who finally disengages the cheese from the mousetrap only to find himself bored with it.

As a successful female clown, Hutter shares her views on the obstacles she faces:

> In spite of the many preparatory training roles, it is very difficult to find examples of comical women or female comedians. This disadvantage is also an advantage. Novelty in this craft is a gamble and allows more freedom in the discovery. Similar presentations are more difficult to achieve, making imitation impossible. If a female clown finds a new clown figure she has an advantage because a lack of competition makes the product easier to sell.
>
> There are few female comedians because womanly virtues like beauty, tenderness, and maternal qualities are the opposite of comical characteristics such as frivolity, lust, hate, and contempt for morality and authority. The moral pressure on women is stronger, thereby limiting her freedom and creativity. Comedy deals with spiritual freedom and mirrors reality.
>
> Female as well as male clowns are not only performers but also authors, dramatists, and inventors who take their roles seriously. We are able to develop and grow through repetition. More important than new stories and gags for the clown, is the authenticity of his feelings and his evolving maturity. This takes time, just as it does to make good cognac.[8]

Erika Batdorf

After relocating from Nova Scotia, Canada, to the United States, Erika Batdorf studied with Etienne Decroux and Daniel Stein in Paris and Omnibus in Montreal. In

1988, she directed her movement piece *The Seven Mysteries of Life* for Touchstone Theatre. While teaching movement theatre at Brandeis University, Emerson College, the Massachusetts College of Art, Boston Conservatory, and the University of Alaska–Anchorage, she developed her own solo pieces, which integrate elements of dance, movement theatre, and performance art. *I Have Something for You*, performed at the 1988 Movement Theatre International Festival in Philadelphia, depicts childhood, symbolized by innocence; youth, represented by violent separation; and adulthood, associated with confidence and masking. *The Watcher and the Watched* (1990) candidly looks at stereotypical masculine and feminine roles and incorporates audience reaction in the portrayal of the traditional male–female relationships. *Waiting for the Dawn* (1991) is an autobiographical, storytelling-movement monologue that relates the anger, frustration, and depression of Mr. Vain Imagination and Miss Idle Fancy. *Je T'Attends; Facing East* (1993) is a ritualistic dance–theatre piece on death and prayer, a tribute in movement, words, and song to three of Batdorf's mentors. *Mr. Raisin Head and Other Delights*, performed in Cambridge, Massachusetts, in 1996, is Batdorf's Americanized version of a European-type clown. In it she plays — through mime, singing, and improvisation — a computer whiz with a Brooklyn accent who engages in soul-searching; she also performs short pieces, including a movement version of a David Mamet monologue.

Batdorf describes the intent of her movement theatre work:

> I am not interested in a theatre that is merely design, style or idea motivated or constructed. I believe in form manipulated by real personal subtext. I am constantly searching for movement that is emotionally connected, that has the theatrical "want" we strive for in speaking theatre, and the form determined by that "want." I direct that movement to the audience as a continuation of spoken monologue in the style that Decroux described as physical oration. I watch my audience, asking them questions or speaking directly about our relationship with movement. It is storytelling, autobiographical monologue, stand-up comedy and movement. Technically I work with a corporeal mime base, but with a freer, more relaxed use of weight. I strive to bring together naturalism and stylization.[9]

A Variety of Female Mimes and Clowns

As the century progressed, a variety of miming and clowning forms appeared. While the following section divides these performers' styles and forms into several groupings according to their art's predominating characteristics, in reality many of these artists engage in forms that overlap and blend. And as their art evolved and enriched itself, a growing number of women mimes and clowns in Europe and North America became recognized. The following are only a handful of those who succeeded.

From Mime to Physical Theatre

Mime and physical theatre styles tend to overlap in the work of many performers. Several of the following female artists have evolved toward physical theatre styles that no longer represent the mime styles in which they originally trained. The term "physical theatre" which refers to a broader mime form that often includes stage acting and other theatre elements, is not restricted to a single expression, and emphasizes neither corporeal mime nor classical pantomime.

Formerly with Partners in Mime, Elizabeth Tabler of Kaleidoscope Mime became interested in mime while still in high school, when she studied with Tony Montanaro. At sixteen, she left her native Oklahoma to study mime in the San Francisco Bay Area with Leonard Pitt, Bert Houle, and Sophie Wibaux. Since 1979, she has played in solo performances as a red-nosed clown, in traditional whiteface pantomime, in abstract mime pieces, and with masks she created from leather and fabric. Her *Foibles of Our Time* is composed of vignettes about the revolt against technology, such as those of a scientist who confronts her own inventions and a washing machine that functions on its own. *A Cast of Thousands* portrays characters living in a tiny suitcase.

Marj Bly, a former San Francisco mime who toured the Orient in the 1980s, performs with the precision and control of Étienne Decroux's corporeal mime, to which she has added elements of classical pantomime. While some of her pieces revolve around Bipette, the female counterpart of Marcel Marceau's Bip, others—such as *Streetwalker*, which portrays a woman who sells her body to survive, and *Waiting*, about a violent relationship between a female and a male—deal with women's liberation from society's trappings with humor and sentiment.

Street mimes Carol Sue Thomas (Suggs the Mime) and Joan Merwyn, former students of Leonard Pitt, performed in the San Francisco Bay Area. Merwyn went on to do extravagant clown–mime abroad and then joined New York's Margolis Brown Adaptors movement theatre company in 1986, later creating her own Sound-Image Theatre company.

Solo performer Laura Shepard received her theatre training at Boston University from 1969 to 1973 and studied mime with E. Reid Gilbert. After joining the Wisconsin Mime company in 1970, she served as Gestural Theatre company's artistic director from 1976 to 1988 and developed *Still Life with Stein*, a full-length solo mime show with three musicians that toured New England for five years. From 1979 to 1981, Shepard produced the Boston Mime Festival. Her company, Living Art International, begun in 1988, specialized in tableaux vivants of famous works of art and historical periods. In *Still Life with Stein* (1985), based on Gertrude Stein's *Tender Buttons*, she performs in a cubist acting style, breaking up the stage action and the structure of the work, which revolves around formal dining conventions. Shepard's zany social satire incorporates mime, comic characters, dance, and conversation in a foreign language with passages from Stein's text, which spoofs language in an extravagantly ironic style.

Native American folklore, culture, and social and political issues became part of the physical theatre of such companies as the Spiderwoman Theatre, the oldest women's native theatre group in North America, founded by Muriel Miguel in the 1970s. Composed of three Kuna-Rappahannock sisters—Lisa Mayo, Gloria Miguel, and Muriel Miguel—the company is named after the Hopi goddess Spiderwoman, who taught the people to weave. The sisters' weaving intertwines stories with movement, comedy, ritual, impersonation, and satire to foster social change. *Women in Violence*, *The Lysistrata Numbah!*, and *An Evening of Disgusting Songs and Pukey Images* were performed in North America and at festivals in Nancy, France, Amsterdam, and Edinburgh from 1977 to 1979.

A member of the Loyola University Mime company in 1975 and of the Northwestern Mime company one year later, Karen Sheridan began performing whiteface pantomime in *The Venus Flytrap* (1975), based on a girl's relationship with her pet plant. After studying with Etienne Decroux from 1978 to 1980 and with Thomas Leabhart's Corporeal Mime Theatre from 1980 to 1981, she created *The Nap* (1984), which depicts—through movement, voice, costumes, and props—a little girl trying to take a nap. While earning an M.F.A. at the Goodman School of Drama, Sheridan and Susan Pudelek developed a pantomime, clown, and corporeal mime show, *Two Women*; a movement study entitled *Sonnet*; and a piece based on a search for content and form called *The Sculptors*, performed at the 1985 Midwest Mime and Clown Festival in Indianapolis. In the fall of 1985, Sheridan abandoned whiteface to bring a new solo show to the Atlanta Mime Festival. In 1989, she created *Home Video*, a nonverbal clown piece with costumes, props, and music for two people, which is resonant in its feminism through its rejection of the female ideal of the macho male image. In 1990, she directed the movement theatre piece *Apparent Appearances,* performed by Karen Hoyer. In 1992, Sheridan collaborated with Rick Carver in *But, How Many Can Fit in a Volkswagen?* which communicates clown humor through mime, voice tone, magic, music, and dance. An associate professor in Oakland University's Department of Music, Theatre and Dance in Rochester, Michigan, since 1991 Sheridan has taught mime, comedy, acting styles, and character movement. She has also directed student productions that necessitate her clown–mime skills, such as *That Scoundrel Scapin* (1992), a vaudeville and clown show with jugglers, tap dancers, singers, contortionists, slapstick, and a one-man band. She collaborated with Laurie Eisenhower on a movement piece about success entitled *Not Even a Postcard* (1992), which the Eisenhower Dance Ensemble performed. Sheridan's direction of feminist Caryl Churchill's *Cloud Nine*, which explores sexual and gender roles through broad styles and cross-gender casting, was one of six U.S. productions chosen to perform at the Kennedy Center for the Performing Arts in Washington, D.C., for the 1993 American College Theatre Festival. Sheridan taught at the Ringling Bros. & Barnum and Bailey Clown College for six years and continues to teach, act, and direct professionally.

Born in San Francisco, Gaetana, who studied with corporeal movement artists Maximilien Decroux, Leonard Pitt, and Ron Leeson and trained in modern dance and Butoh sword work, first created whiteface comedy pantomimes. In 1979, she staged *Dinner for Two*, *Bus Stop*, and *Just Another Day*, which portray women as sex objects attempting to survive in everyday situations. She choreographed and performed abstract dance–mime with narration in *A Man by the Name of Zeigler* (1981), based on Herman Hesse's short story. Mime, masque, and music characterize *Pierrot Lunaire* (1980), from Arnold Schonberg's work by the same title; *Alienation of the Soul* (1984), with music by Toru Takemitsu; *White Dance* (1985), with Japanese Shakuhatchi music; *Coral Island* (1988), a poetic narrative; and *City of Ashes—City of Dust* (1990), a memorial performance for the bombing of Hiroshima, played to bamboo flute music. In *The Celestial Millennium Beat: A Rant* (1997), Gaetana satirizes sociological and astronomical theories, statistics, and facts, and in *The Sign* (1998), a Born Again devotee undergoes the devil's influence. Gaetana also taught mime in the adult education program at Dominican College in San Rafael, California.

In 1981, Claire Griffin and Cheryl Couch, who performed duo mime shows throughout the Midwest, founded the Intuition Mime company in Cincinnati, Ohio. Bet Hopkins, a solo mime–clown from Dayton, Ohio, later joined them. Among the company members' mime and clown teachers were John Towsen, Yuri Belov, Leonard Pitt, E. Reid Gilbert, Sigfrido Aguilar, and Ron Wilson. In 1983, the three women collaborated on *Faces of the Moon*, a movement piece that explores female spirituality through the ancient myths of three moon goddesses, which they performed at the 1985 Midwest Mime and Clown Festival in Indianapolis. Expanding its repertory to integrate corporeal and whiteface pantomime with dance, theatre, clowning, *commedia*, music, and lyrics, the group created *The Lemon Sisters Cabaret Show*, a vaudeville-style farce; *Electronic Fix,* a piece exposing our society's chemical and electronic addictions; and *Raggedy Ann and Andy and the Magic Elf*, a family show with Italian folk tales, original songs, acrobatics, and magic. Working from the heart rather than the intellect, Intuition Mime company was one of the first women's groups with a movement theatre basis to synthesize varied stage forms.

Karin Abromaitis began training at a Claude Kipnis workshop in 1972 and then studied with Wolfram Mehring in Germany from 1973 to 1974. After working as a whiteface street pantomimist, in 1984 she joined Axolotl, a mask–movement company in Washington, D.C., under Jack Guidone's direction. She then became a member of Theatre Plexus. Living and working in the Washington, D.C., area as a solo performer, actress, teacher, choreographer, and director, Abromaitis's pieces, which deal with sociological problems and healing, are better characterized by the broader term "movement theatre." Among her major solo works are *White Noise/2* (1985) and *White Noise/3* (1989), which are about child sexual abuse and received the Best of Showcase Awards at the Mid-Atlantic Movement Theatre Festival and the 1989 Movement Theatre International Festival, and *Domestic Snakes* (1989), which revolves around Alzheimer's disease, incest, child abuse, and female empowerment.

Elsa Kvamme from Norway—who studied at the Odin Teatret Laboratory in Norway from 1973 to 1975 and at the Kathakali Theatre School and worked in mask dance in Bali—performed in solo pieces based on feminist concerns, such as *The Right To Be Ugly* and *Lady Out of Work.* Her clown–theatre piece, *The Man Who Gave Birth to a Woman*, and *Handbook for Tourists* were presented at European and North American mime and clown festivals. In *The Man Who Gave Birth to a Woman*, which includes song, cabaret theatre, and clownish characters bordering on the grotesque, Kvamme interprets Adam as a cheerful alcoholic who copes with a rebellious Eve. In other scenes, a waitress daydreams about her liberation and a child falls in love with her father. Kvamme's stirring creation of *Medea*, based on Heiner Muller's *Medeamaterial* (1982) and performed at the 1990 Festival of International Experimental Theatre in Oslo, mixes tragedy with grotesque farce. In all of her works, Kvamme's powerful, masculine vibrations give her art another dimension.

Agnés Limbos studied with Jacques Lecoq and in 1984 began her Compagnie Gare Centrale in Brussels, which brought her international acclaim. Her object theatre productions of *Petrouchka* and *Petit Pois* have been performed in Europe, Hong Kong, the United States, and Canada. Limbos directed the Edmonton-based, Lecoq-trained, actor–mime–director Robert Astle in *Heart of a Dog,* performed as a Lecoq tribute at Lehigh University's 1994 Theatre of Creation Festival in Bethlehem, Pennsylvania.

The Partners in Mime Company began in Chicago in 1984 with the performance of a classical mime piece entitled *Partners in Mime,* which explores the theme of working together. Artistic director Karen Hoyer's four solo pieces, inspired by her training with Mexican mime Sigfrido Aguilar and entitled *Apparent Appearances* (1986), merge mime, mask, puppetry, clown theatre, and abstract theatre movement. In an excerpt from this work, which Karen Sheridan directed and which depicts the conflicts between the artist as a creator and as a female, there is an original use of vertical movement on a bed, which is placed upright on stage and on which the protagonist tosses and turns in her sleep. In 1991, under Aguilar's direction, the company created *Caprichos*, based on Francisco de Goya's work, which makes use of a variety of physical theatre arts. In 1992 and 1993, Hoyer presented original movement pieces entitled *Flights of Fancy* and *The Angel Project*, the latter work incorporating aerial acrobatics into the theme of women and their guardian angels.

Susan Pudelek, a former Northwestern Mime company member, taught and performed extensively in the Chicago area in original works, such as *Einsteins*, *Clowncave*, and *Penta/Benta*. After studying mime with Etienne Decroux in Paris in 1979 and 1980, she co-produced the Evanston Mime Festival with Partners in Mime in 1984 and 1985, also appearing as a guest artist. Pudelek studied dance and liturgy with Carla De Sola and movement improvisation with Cynthia Winton-Henry and Phil Porter. In 1982, she created *The Wait*, an emotional and spiritual journey of waiting in Decroux-style mime, which was performed at New York's Maryknoll School of Theology in December 1994. The performance was part of a lecture-workshop entitled "Wisdom of the Body: Movement and the Spiritual Journey." Pursuing a master of divinity degree, Pudelek has combined movement theatre with religious ministry and interfaith and cross-cultural dialogue.

After studying with Tony Montanaro in 1977, Laura Bertin has performed as a mime from 1979 on. She toured throughout the United States with her husband in their "Micah and Laura Mime Theatre." In 1987, she founded the "Mimely Yours, Laura and Leigh" high school outreach program with Leigh Bohannon, one of the few women to tour with the Ringling Bros. and Barnum & Bailey Circus after graduating from Clown College with a Master of Fun Arts degree.

Linda Kerr Scott began as an actress in the English company Théâtre de Complicité in 1986. In her one-woman show, *Ave Maria* (1992), presented at the 1991 Edinburgh Fringe Festival and the 1992 London International Mime Festival, she plays a spinster in curlers and a dressing gown having fantasies about the crimes she would like to commit as she undergoes fits of anger, pity, violence, and fright.

Debra Roth, artistic director of Pink Inc. in New York, is both a movement theatre artist and a sculptor who combines corporeal mime with the visual and performing arts. Since 1979, the company has toured the United States and abroad with sculptural performances that fuse illusion, color, movement, sound, puppetry, and comedy. In *Nuts and Bolts*, premiered in New York in 1992, Roth depicts the biological differences between the male and the female through awesome and humorous moving sculptures and images. Here, the male and female sex organs are transformed into a fantasy world through Roth's striking designs and movable, artist-propelled sculptures. In 1992, the company initiated a biannual program called Visual Visceral, which hosts the creations of artists who utilize the body for dramatic expression through dance, physical theatre, and corporeal movement. In the spring of 1993, this program sponsored "An Evening of Movement Theatre by Women," which began with Louise Heit's *Data Day,* a modern dance and corporeal movement piece that contrasts the chaos of the city with the peace of nature. Joan Evans's *The Floor Keeps Turning* portrayed female desire's twofold nature. Marcus Dance Theatre's *Tangos Build Strong Bodies* combined tango dancing, acting, and corporeal movement to depict youth and old age. *Minus One Man* by Beyondance Inc. satirized mating through dance and theatre. Sabina Peck's Performance company's *Tomorrow at Seven* conveyed through movement and voice three women driven by their busy schedules. In the fall of 1993, Visual Visceral organized an evening of male artists' works and staged *Tale of the Dog*, an Art-In-Motion piece for adults and children that featured a softsculpture called TurtleDog. Pink Inc.'s fifth Visual Visceral, entitled "An Evening of Movement Theatre," took place in June 1994. It included Liquid Theater's *Noa*, an allegorical journey between object and action; Rajeckas and Intraub in *Brotherly Love,* about a bond between two men; Ruth Tamir in *Drought*, about a couple's absurdist thirst for one another; Amy Rose's *Curses Foiled Again*, a comic view of a woman and her ukulele; Liz Korabek in the seductive, voyeuristic *How Much Is the Lady in the Window?*; and Pink Inc. dancing and miming to Motown tunes in *Royal Purple and the Fortunettes*. The 1994 fall festival featured Ellen Cornfield's dance–mime *Tangle*; Katya Mormon's autobiographical modern dance piece, *Notes to a Missing Person*, about a missing father; clown–mime Fred Curchak's *What Fools These Mortals Be* and *Stuff as Dreams Are Made On*; and the Pink Inc. trio in *Chains, Boots and Sleigh Rides*. Visual Visceral's 1995 fall festival offered a variety of movement theatre pieces. Victoria Labalme's *Overtime* portrayed a late-night secretary dancing with a garbage can, a stapler, and her pantyhose, and her piece *Marcel Marceau: Making the Invisible Visible* satirized the great mime master. Anahi Galante performed Dolores Zorreguieta's *Nostalgia,* on the theme of homesickness, while dancing in a glass box, nude except for high heels, to the tango song *Nostalgias*. Christopher Eaves and Nicolas Bruce collaborated in a sensitive portrayal of AIDS activist David Wojnarowicz's life and art. Mary Clark and Andy Braum from Théâtre du Jour interpreted vaudevillesque French chefs in a chaotic kitchen in *Hors d'Oeuvres*. Joan Merwyn's Sound-Image Theatre performed *Money Matters*, and the Chalasa Performance company presented *Chalasa*. In ornamental costumes and Christmas decorations, Pink Inc. clowned and sang Christmas carols in *Royal Purple and the Fortunettes*. In the summer of 1996 Pink Inc. performed at international theatre festivals in England, Canada, and Spain and in the Jacob's Pillow and Wolf Trap festivals in the United States. Pink Inc.'s tenth Visual Visceral in the fall of 1996 included the G. Gibbons Dance company's dance–theatre, Christopher Eaves's performance art, Amy Champ's video cabaret–travelogue, and clown–artist Liz Korabek's *A Woman with Too Much to Hold*. The festival's eleventh edition in the spring of 1997 included works by Joan Merwyn's Sound-Image Theatre with solos by Merwyn and ensemble pieces by Lauren Farber, Dale Fuller, and Christi Minarovich. Shelley Brenner mixed movement and visuals with folklore and music. Estelle Eichenberger of Azahar performed a solo from *Carried by the Wind*, dedicated to ski-racing champion Ulrike Maier, with Mongolian chants and video. Catherine Sand's poetry evoked tenderness and pity, and Pink Inc.'s Fortunettes appeared in towering caps and bright costumes.

Linda Mancini, a New York–based Canadian performance artist, trained with Lecoq-style clown teacher Richard Pochinko. Her solo work *Good As It Gets*, which toured during the 1993 and 1994 season, includes movement, dance, clowning, voice, sound, and visual elements. Among her bold caricatures of women on the verge of hysteria, her piece *Not Entirely Appropriate*, performed for Pontine Movement Theatre's 1993 and 1994 season, reveals oneself in private and public situations.

New York solo artist Laura Segal's *Remembrance of Things Past* develops the reasons why Marcel Proust became a writer, with Segal playing several roles through aesthetically intriguing facial expressions, gestures, and costume changes.

Mime Judith Jackson's *The N-gg-er Café,* performed with a fifteen-member cast, is a multimedia satire of African Americans' roles on TV and in film.

Tokyo-born Yuriko Doi, founder and artistic director of San Francisco's Theatre of Yugen, has trained, directed, and performed in stylized Kyogen and Noh theatre.

Although male performers traditionally play Kyogen theatre, Doi has used females for women's roles in her Kyogen productions. She also has chosen a number of plays that depict the liberation of women, such as Carol Sorgenfrei's Noh-style adaptation of *Medea* (1983), depicting Medea's own female choices. Aside from directing traditional Kyogen and Noh works, Doi directed and performed in modern works, such as Shogo Ohta's *Komachi Fuden* (1986), which relates the story of silent, old Komako, who lives in modern-day Tokyo and dreams she is a legendary medieval poetess. Doi also has staged classical Western plays, such as Molière's *Tartuffe* as *The Imposter* (1992), which incorporates Kyogen and commedia dell'arte to depict current Japanese American relations. As a Japanese female, Doi has renewed classical Japanese, European, and American theatre by breaking through traditional barriers to find parallels between Eastern and Western theatre and by integrating Japanese, European, and American acting styles.

The women's troupe of Britain's Black Mime Theatre, which presents works on contemporary social issues, performed *Mothers* at the 1991 London International Mime Festival to celebrate the influence of women in shaping our lives. *Drowning*, performed at the 1992 London International Mime Festival, dramatizes alcohol abuse in the lives of three women who attempt to begin anew.

Moniek Merkx, director at Holland's Suver Nuver Theatre, staged *Plaster Rage, or Anger at Covering Up Pain* in 1992 with disabled performers to reveal the disabled's anger and confusion.

Ris Widdicombe, who trained with Desmond Jones and taught at his School of Mime and Physical Theatre, founded the Anglo–Brazilian mime company Mimus Mundanus in 1992.

Ruth Ben-Tovim, founder and artistic director of Louder Than Words Productions, has been a freelance director interested in new writers and works. In April 1995, she directed *The Counting of Years*, written by Pete Brooks of Insomniac Productions.

Among other European women mimes, Lecoq-trained Jane Sutcliffe performed solo works based on social issues such as women and their eating disorders. Elsbetia Pastecka, a Henryk Tomeszewski–trained mime, created works that combine psychological insight with perfected technique. Mirna Zager of the Croatian Institute of Movement and Dance has brought movement workshops and lectures from Western Europe to develop mime and dance in Croatia.

Clown–Mime

Clown–mime Tanya Belov-Sabofyeva, who trained at the Moscow State Academy of Circus and Variety Arts, has toured throughout Russia and abroad and taught clowning in the United States. In *The Clown Conspiracy,* staged by her husband Yuri Belov and performed at the 1982 Davis and Elkins International Mime and Movement Festival, she plays a lazy female clown who prefers to flirt with the male audience members rather than perform. In *Confessions of a Russian Woman,* presented at the 1988 Philadelphia Movement Theatre International Festival, Belov-Sabofyeva, playing a Russian immigrant in oversize shoes and wearing a dotted tunic over knickerbockers, naively encounters American life. Plate-breaking and sitting on the laps of male spectators to compare their heartbeats to different types of music typify her clown, who exudes feminine innocence.

Vancouver clown–comedian Gina Bastone studied with Leonard Pitt in Berke-ley, California, with Moni Yakim in New York, and at what was later known as the Dell'Arte International School of Physical Theatre in Blue Lake, California. Writ-ing, performing, teaching, and directing comedy since 1974, she toured as the lead clown with Cirque du Soleil and in 1984 founded her own comedy theatre company, Basta Productions. Her play *Millions Die* captivated audiences at Vancouver's Com-edy and Fringe Festivals and at the Toronto Theatre Festival. From 1992 to 1994, she performed in the award-winning *Number 14* with Axis Mime Theatre and Touch-stone Theatre of Vancouver.

Clown Karen McCormick's *Ciao Frivola*, staged at the 1983 New York Clown Theatre Festival, is an autobiographical work about the artist's struggle for fame in Hollywood that features McCormick's youthful clowning, tap-dancing, and doing acrobatics. McCormick formerly played with tap-dancer–clown Noel Parenti in *El Floppo* (1978–1981), a comedy about Frivola and Freduccio, two Italian immigrants living the American dream in oversize tail coats and derby hats.

Among the female mimes whose work manifests a feminist element is Julie Goell whose mime–clowning career began in Boston in the early 1970s when she founded the Pocket Mime Theatre, one of America's first professional mime troupes, while studying drama at Boston University. In 1974, Goell joined the Swiss Mum-menschanz company to perform and assist in making masks. In 1975, she became known as the Clown of Piazza Navona in Rome. After co-founding La Compagnia I Gesti with Swiss clown Roy Bosier and Don Jordon in the early 1980s, her first show, *The Story of a Woman in Pajamas,* toured from 1981 to 1983. Besides being a singer, mime, and clown in European bands and on TV and radio, she wrote com-edy sketches for Italian TV and taught *commedia* and Molière's theatre at Boston University, as well as directed a number of productions, such as *Tartuffe* at the Uni-versity of Southern Maine and *Venetian Twins*, chosen to represent New England at the American College Festival. In *Woman in a Suitcase,* which was performed at the 1988 Philadelphia Movement Theatre International Festival and toured internation-ally, Goell mimes, clowns, and employs her vaudeville skills to portray a Russian immigrant who lives in a suitcase until she encounters Mr. Big Time, who makes her a Las Vegas star. Disillusioned by the glittering falsehood of nightclub life, where she is a female idol, she is soon on her way back to her country, bailing out of a plane and floating on her valise at sea. In a poetic ending, she discovers a pearl, symbolic of her pain and love, and offers it to the audience. Through movement, story telling, and singing, Goell unfolds the tale of an immigrant who faces the female plight of being an object of adulation.

Dollee Mallare's clown career began in 1978 in San Francisco where she per-formed at City Hall and created clown skits on Pier 39 while selling helium-filled silver balloons. In Boston in 1983, she co-founded "Dollee and Debbie," a clown–mime team for schoolchildren. After studying clowning with Hovey Burgess, Avner the Eccentric, Bill Irwin, Yuri Belov, Lenny Zarconi, Carlo Mazzoni Clementi, and Sigfrido Aguilar and mime with Leonard Pitt and E. Reid Gilbert, she developed a style based on corporeal mime technique, classical pantomime, *com-media*, dance, costumes, masks, props, puppets and storytelling. Her repertory com-prises *Tales from Mother Earth*; *Mime Music*, a children's show with inanimate ob-jects that come to life; and *First Aid*, in which she and her partner teach the basics of emergency treatment for choking, bleeding, and poisoning through mime, dance, clowning, and puppetry.

California mime Antoinette Attel (Toad the Mime), a former trainee of Jean-Louis Barrault and of Japanese mime Mamako, integrated slapstick and music hall in her pantomimes, which she performed for the physically challenged and the blind.

The artistic director of Make-A-Circus from 1983 to 1990, Letitia Bartlett studied mime with Leonard Pitt; performed in her own clown and variety shows, such as *Julietta and Jeremy*, and in a spiritual comedy piece entitled *Ecstasy in the Everyday* (1994); and has been teaching movement at the American Conservatory Theatre in San Francisco.

Maria Cassi, from Florence, Italy, trained at Bologna's Theatre School and in 1986 formed a comic, musical duo with instrumentalist Leonardo Brizzi that toured throughout Europe. In *A Saintrotwist,* in which a musician accompanies a prima donna whose antics grow increasingly outrageous, Cassi reveals her exhuberant sense of fantasy and her talent for exaggerated facial expressions.

In her creation of a clown character in *Veni, Vidi, Vici,* New York clown Debra Kaufmann integrates traditional clowning with masks, buffoonery, and a satire of human nature.

In *The Magnificent Monsieur Henri Le Fou*, Seattle, Washington, artist Victoria Millard created a magical female clown with a sense of wonder who interacts with a tiny balloon and other miniature objects.

In *The Gift*, performed at the 1994 London International Mime Festival, Brazilian clown–mime Angela de Castro interprets an enamored woman playing tricks and doing magic as she anxiously waits for her date.

Dance–Mime

During the second half of the twentieth century, a number of women dancers have integrated mime, acting, and clowning to their art

In the early 1970s, Katie Duck, who began as a ballet dancer and learned the modern dance techniques of Martha Graham, Merce Cunningham, and Alwin Nikolais, was one of the founders of the Salt Lake City Mime Troupe, which blended dance, mime, theatre, and music. After 1978, Duck worked in solo dance–mime, collaborating with mime artist Carlos Trafic and clown George Peugot and performing and teaching dance–mime throughout Italy, Germany, Holland, and Japan. Her *Duck Play* (1976) is a dance–mime on the destiny of four personal clowns. *Love Story* (1976), with the Argentinean Trafic, focuses on a tragicomic wife–husband relationship. *Mathilda's Suicide* (1977) reveals self-destructive impulses, and *Mad Women* (1979) portrays a woman's need to give birth. *Don Quixote* (1980), with Hector Malamud, Carlos Trafic, and Mia Stalle, brings Don Quixote into the modern world. After 1981, Duck and cellist, singer, and improvisational actor Tristan Honsinger staged such pieces as *Three Girlfriends* (1982), utilizing the cello, recitation, and dance. Duck does not see herself as a mime, clown, dancer, or actress, but as a creator of an improvisational and personal physical theatre form.

Born in Paris, Karine Saporta studied classical ballet and flamenco dance in Spain and, from 1971 to 1973, trained in the United States with Merce Cunningham and Erick Hawkins. In 1974, she founded her dance research school in Paris and two years later, with members of her school, created her company, Corps Graphique. In 1978, she and five other choreographers organized the experimental dance group Indépendanse. In Saporta's theatrical, nonanecdotal dance–mime, psychophysical states connect the body with deep unconscious desires. Semitorpor is explored in *Camille* (1976), animal nature in *Judith*, eroticism in *L'Amoureuse*, and infantile sexuality in *Pour un Retour*. In *Nonchalance Déchirée* (*Broken Nonchalance*, 1981), to the music of a double bass and plaintive vocal sounds, two sleeping women in deck chairs lethargically reach out for one another, flee, and finally consume each other. Saporta's compositions of feminine desire and passion fuse mime with modern dance in a highly personalized, sensual, and sculptural manner.

After studying dance at Martha Graham's London school and mime with Etienne Decroux in Paris, Annie Stainer joined the Lindsay Kemp Mime Troupe in London. In the early 1970s, she began her career as a solo mime artist with *The Legend of Lilith*, a dance–drama staged in the Cathedral of Saint John the Divine in Manhattan. *Moon*, which first was performed at the 1975 Edinburgh Fringe Festival and received a Scotsman Fringe First Award, blends clowning, mime, and expressive dance as it parallels a woman's life-cycle with the four seasons.

As artistic director and chief choreographer of TNR/Moebius, a performing arts company founded in 1972 to promote original work that fuses art forms with different cultures, explores our past heritage, and experiments with new visual technologies, Yen Lu Wong's pieces range from intimate solo performances to epic works in natural and architectural settings. Her creations have been influenced by her Chinese and American heritage; Rudolf Laban, Mary Wigman, Martha Graham, Kurt Joos, and the German Expressionists; her collaboration with Irmgard Bartenieff, a Laban disciple; and her studies with masters in China, Bali, and Japan. Among Wong's works are *The Gathering, the Journey* (1975), a large-cast ceremonial piece depicting the history of the Chinese revolution, performed on the University of California campus in San Diego. *Golden Mountain* (1977), an epic work based on the experiences of Chinese-Americans, weaves movement into spoken and sung texts.

Swiss-based mime–dancer Erika Ackermann, born in Bucharest in 1943, trained in expressionistic dance at the Swiss Sigurd Leeder School of Dance and with Samy Molcho and Roy Bosier. She first performed as a solo mime in 1973 and then toured with Swiss circus clowns Pic and Pello in 1975. Her pieces convey surrealistic images of the soul's aspirations. *Shadock* (1979) caricatures feelings of oppression while in a car, and *I Shout and Everything Remains Quiet* (1981) depicts loneliness in a materialistic world. Her search for a new expression in clown–dance–pantomime has inspired female clowns of her generation.

San Francisco Bay Area dancer Margaret Fisher, founder of the Ma Fish Dance company with composer Roger Hughes, has created interdisciplinary performance works based on a gestural movement methodology entitled Cellular Movement Technique. *To Be Seen In and Out of the Light, Even*, performed for the 1994 Bay Area Dancers Series, intertwines dance and movement theatre to portray Marcel Duchamp's dadaist painting on glass, *The Bride Stripped Bare By Her Bachelors, Even*.

Rhodessa Jones of San Francisco's Cultural Odyssey company, founded by Jones and Idris Acakamoor in 1981 to produce original, contemporary dance–theatre, has toured with solo works such as *Big-Butt Girls, Hard-Headed Women* (1990), a series of monologues that grew out of Jones's work with San Francisco City Jail inmates. The piece's movement, acting, and songs reveal the traumas of female jail inmates awaiting liberation.

Marti Cate—San Francisco Bay Area mime, dancer, actress, teacher, and founder of Unexpected Company—combines Asian dance theatre with ballet, modern dance, Decroux's corporeal mime technique, and illusion mime. *Dancing in My Mother's Room* (1985) is a biographical solo utilizing mime, dance, and text. Her New Vaudeville piece *Flip Side* (1988–89) includes mime, dance and a monologue, and *Night Garden* (1995) is a yoga–mime solo.

A New York mime–dancer known as Rebecca, who trained with Marcel Marceau, developed women's themes in her creations and employed dance and mime in her therapy workshops.

Dancer Beth White has taught modern dance, choreography, and improvisation and played in physical theatre and street stilt-walking shows with Challee Erb.

Philadelphia dancer and teacher Audrey Bookspan incorporated mime and circus arts into her modern, ballet, tap, African, and flamenco dance choreographies. Among her solo works are *Strange Fruit*, a protest against lynching; *John Henry*, a glorification of strength and determination; and *Dreams and Nightmares*, an introspective journey.

Tina Kronis studied ballet, modern and jazz dance, and mime in Florida; joined Mummenschanz; toured and taught abroad; and began her own theatre–mime–dance company in Florence, Italy. In the summer of 1996, she performed her movement and dance theatre, clown, and mask works-in-progress with actor–playwright Richard Alger at the New York Sunday Salon.

Many other women mimes who have been trained by the French masters Etienne Decroux, Marcel Marceau, Jacques Lecoq, and their trainees or by teachers and artists of other mime, dance, acting, and clowning styles perform and teach mime and movement theatre. Rather than vying with male counterparts serving as models, these women have become conscious of their female potential and sensitivity. Their talent and training and women's growing emancipation in all domains have favored the artistic creativity, contribution, and voice of women in mime, as well as all arts.

Notes

1. Letter to author, August 1967.
2. Letter to author, May 1971. Mamako's translation.
3. Letter to author, January 1990.
4. Ibid.
5. Ibid.
6. Letter to author, November 1987.
7. Ibid.
8. Letter to author, August 1990.
9. Letter to author, December 1991.

15

Movement and Silence in Modern and Postmodern Verbal Theatre

Language is the threshold of silence.

Brice Parain

The role of mime in verbal theatre has not always been fully recognized or visible. Yet, whenever theatre ceded exclusively to words, it was deprived of one of its most vital elements.

By mid-twentieth century, when silence began to play a more important role in several forms of modern art, power of the spoken word was challenged. Works of the visual arts were no longer illustrations of their verbal counterparts. This resistance to the spoken word manifested itself in paintings with titles that did not always correspond to their content. Silence pervaded in the music of poet–composers. It crept into the antinovel, the antitheatre and the new cinema, which gave less importance to plot, character development, or a given meaning. Adaptations of classical playwrights' works ranged from musical comedy to productions with dance and mime in which the text was secondary. Silence heightened the dramatic content of classical and literary works. Throughout his book *Silence in Shakespeare,* Harvey Rovine points out the many ways in which silence has contributed to the meanings of and characterizations in Shakespeare's and other playwright's plays. The age of screen and video images was also a defiance to the pontifical authority of the written and spoken word. In place of verbal literacy, there developed a new visual literacy.

Playwright Eugene Ionesco is among those twentieth-century authors who reacted to the impotence of words. "The word prevents silence from speaking; it deafens and wears out thinking. Instead of being action, the word consoles for not acting. The guarantee of the word must be silence" (1967, 104). In short, words were no longer appreciated for themselves but, rather, for their power to evoke images and emotions within silence.

Early Twentieth-Century Theatre: An Explosion of New Approaches

The late nineteenth and early twentieth centuries were affluent with many new theatre forms and styles. The new theatre was imbued, on the one hand, with realism and naturalism, on the other hand, with radical, nonrealistic production methods.

This dichotomy continues to exist. In both forms, movement and silence have become important elements.

Early in the twentieth century, as the stage director's role grew more important in European theatre, a number of pioneers already had introduced innovations in play-writing, stage direction, scenic design, costumes, and lighting. Among these innovations were the use of silence and movement.

Because it would be impossible to include here each of the early twentieth century's many new approaches, much less follow the numerous threads related to movement and silence, it might be rewarding for the reader to review this period through the appropriate chapters of, for example, Mordecai Gorelik's *New Theatres for Old* (1975), or another history of the theatre. Among the many creators of these innovations, the following represent that development's flow.

Edward Gordon Craig and Adolphe Appia opened up the theatre to a new visual and spatial performance potential. Craig, a theatre visionary, wrote about a new stage art form centered in the actor (*übermarionette*) and performed in silence, with all the production elements unified by and expressing one artistic force: the director. Appia expanded upon the nature of the performance area, transforming it into a new, three-dimensional space—and with it introduced another potential for the performer's expression and meaning. His use of lighting and sets enhanced the actor's movements and attitudes, giving his physical expressivity new meaning and rendering his artistic presence central to the production.

One of the first playwrights to integrate silence and movement into his dialogues was Anton Chekhov. Staged by Konstantin Stanislavsky at the Moscow Art Theatre, Chekhov's plays contained dialogue with nonverbal subtexts that challenged the spectators' imaginations. In France, the theatre of silence was represented by Maurice Maeterlinck's *Pelléas et Mélisande* (1892); founder of the futurist movement author F. T. Marinetti's pantomimes, *The Tactile Quartet* and *Indecision*, written in the 1920s; and Jean-Jacques Bernard's *L'Invitation au Voyage* (1924).

As we saw in chapter 6, stage directors such as Max Reinhardt also revolted against the predominance of the playwright's text. In his 1912 staging of the poet Karl Gustav Vollmoeller's pantomime *The Miracle,* Reinhardt filled the stage with pageantry, transforming it into a cathedral in which religious liturgy enhanced the wordless play. Vsevolod Meyerhold, breaking from Stanislavsky's realism, worked in the theatrical and constructivist styles. The actor used his detailed movement system, Biomechanics, in training and performance. Irwin Piscator converted the stage space into a political platform, using a multimedia approach. His epic theatre, later developed by Bertolt Brecht, introduced innovations in space, actor–audience relationship and acting styles, along with the use of marionettes and other stage devices to enhance the political message.

Meanwhile, the stage director's growing importance continued to diminish the playwright's autocracy. In France, Jacques Copeau's productions integrated silence, gestures, and movement with the text. For Copeau, the dramatic atmosphere began and ended with silence, and the outcome was achieved through action rather than words.

In his theatre productions and writings, Antonin Artaud attempted to capture the kind of visual poetry that ancient rites evoked among worshippers. Movement and gestures played an incantatory role in Artaud's theatre of myth and magic, particularly in such productions as his 1927 version of August Strindberg's *A Dream Play* (1902) and his 1935 staging of Percy Bysshe Shelley's *The Cenci* (1818).

By 1938, Artaud already had warned of the danger of literature's role if the theatre were to be a creative art. He placed the value of movement, visual effects, and music above that of spoken dialogue, claiming that the latter often paralyzes true theatre language because scenery, staging, and acting have their own physical language, which fulfills the senses and provides a more dynamic theatrical expression. For Artaud, because the stage is, above all, a space to fill and a place where something happens, the language of signs is superior (1938, 114).

Toward the 1950s, Jacques Copeau's dream of giving birth to a theatre in which the actor plays a more creative role began to be realized. His training methods to revitalize the actor's art through corporeal expressivity not only inspired his student Etienne Decroux to provide a springboard for a modern mime revival, but they also enriched the actor's body expression. As mentioned in an earlier chapter, Decroux believed that the theatre of his time had to undergo a thirty-year period of separation from speaking theatre and that the actor should depict thoughts and emotions solely through movement and gestures until he was in total possession of his body's expressivity. Only then could a text be integrated into his performance. Thus, besides establishing a movement grammar, Decroux's findings developed into a system of corporeal aesthetics that would influence the use of movement and silence in speaking theatre several decades later.

A number of other early twentieth-century stage directors and playwrights relegated to the spoken text no more than its equal importance with other production elements. As a result, their works' content and form grew more closely allied, achieving a better balance between dialogue and movement.

Mid- to Late Twentieth-Century Theatre: Innovations in the Scripted Drama

Just as the exclusive use of movement and silence were no longer criteria for mime theatre, words, too, now played a less prominent role in verbal theatre. While mime artists started to introduce words and literary texts into their pieces, movement and silence began to be incorporated into dramatic productions. Inherent in the dramatist's text, or introduced into the production by the actor or stage director, movement and silence manifested themselves in several ways. Gestures, facial expressions, and attitudes enhanced the text's emotional value. They served to create dramatic visual images in a totally nonverbal scene, to portray characters who remain mute for purposes of dramatic action and characterization and could likewise arrest the words of a dialogue to emphasize suppressed thoughts and emotions. Movement could accompany a dialogue in which the characters use banal or repetitive words or speak excessively to hide deeper thoughts and emotions. The playwright also might maintain silence concerning the workings of his characters' minds as well as the reasons for his choice of a particular dramatic action. In all of these uses, nonverbal elements, cradled within silence, offered physical avenues of expression that transcended the literal meaning of words.

In chapter 10, we saw how Jean-Louis Barrault made use of Etienne Decroux's corporeal mime in his total theatre. Barrault, who began his career in mime, went on to enhance his speaking theatre productions with movement. The world will never forget his incarnation of the mime Baptiste in the film *Children of Paradise* (1945).

He returned to performing pantomime in his last staging, entitled *The Language of the Body*, a 1985 pantomime–monologue.

Earlier in the century, stage directors such as Bertolt Brecht had already introduced visual elements into their productions. Although his episodic theatre has been performed since the 1920s, it only began to be a model for stage directors during the 1960s. By the 1970s, Brecht was appreciated as much for his avant-garde stage direction as for his playwriting. Today, his works have been adopted to the postmodern aesthetic of textual fragmentation and include the use of improvisation and multiple artistic devices, such as singing, dancing, and clowning, to distance the spectator. Seen as a precursor of postmodernism, Brecht induced the viewer to participate in experimentation with varied theatrical means and encouraged him to be aware of and even question the validity of the elements incorporated in a dramatic staging. His use of these varied theatrical means also might make him, along with Piscator, a precursor of multimedia performance art. As in multimedia performance art, in Brecht's plays mixed genres such as dance, pantomime, film, slides, and clown acts are juxtaposed to disrupt the work's continuity. He also incorporated elements of Japanese Noh to distance the dramatic action and impart a didactic lesson. As in Noh drama, the formal, ritualistic acting and movement in a number of his productions alternated with speech and song. Brecht's introduction of these means to disclose the theatrical illusion may have anticipated the theatre which broke away from a conventional or set dramatic form and from a resolved action and psychological development.

Brecht's use of what he called the *gestus* to demonstrate the play's social significance was reinforced by the characters' physical appearances, movements, and facial expressions, including the tones of voice. In the Performance Group's 1975 production of *Mother Courage*, directed by Richard Schechner, the performers began with movement improvisations that consisted of pulling one another's bodies, trunks, ropes, and other objects to develop the basic *gestus* of pulling a wagon, symbolic of Mother Courage's struggle to survive. The gestures of such characters as Mother Courage's mute daughter, Kattrin, who communicates through gestures and signs, served to depict still other hardships in the mother's struggle. The company also developed gestures to represent money-bargaining and other traits of bourgeois society.

The acting throughout Brecht's plays ranged from pantomime and broad farce to dance and Oriental theatre, which served to dramatize visually current issues and themes of social and political import. In 1973, the San Francisco Mime Troupe staged Brecht's *The Mother*, based on Maxim Gorky's novel. Incorporating clowning and juggling, company members made a parallel between the exploitation of the illiterate elderly in nineteenth-century Russia and in twentieth-century America. They also employed exaggerated gestures to identify the exploiters' character traits. And in his 1987 production of Brecht's *Good Woman of Setzuan* at the American Repertory Theatre in Cambridge, Massachusetts, André Serban combined dance, acting, Peking Opera–style movement, and singing to depict the good-hearted woman's struggle in a capitalist society.

The use of silence and antiverbal elements became an integral part of Absurdist theatre, particularly in that of Samuel Beckett and Eugene Ionesco, which reflects a skepticism of words and ideas. Overcome by alienation and solitude, their protagonists, living in the void of a disintegrating universe, experience a state of incomprehensible anguish in which their voices often are silenced. Whenever the protagonists do speak, their conversation is difficult or sparse and often dies. Some absurdist playwrights reduced the number of their characters to only a few, who, to dissimulate their feelings, speak in repetitive and conventional language or meaningless gibberish. In this theatre, where silence and antiverbal expression reign in one form or another and which appeals more to the senses than to the intellect, lighting, sound effects, movement, audiovisual means, and other scenic effects often replace the spoken word.

The most blatant example of a playwright who incorporates silence into his writing is Samuel Beckett, who believed that each word he wrote was a "stain on silence." He chose to write in French, which, because of language's nature and because it was not his native tongue, obliged him to be concise. In her biography on Beckett, Deidre Bair reveals how he quizzed composer Igor Stravinsky about devising notations for the tempo and the silent pauses in the performances of his plays. Although Stravinsky liked the idea, he felt that the circumstances of dramatic production were too variable to make such notations enforceable (Bair 1978, 547–48). Beckett described his one-minute play in five acts, *Breath* (1970), as portraying a life cycle. Here the action, or nonaction, consists of light projected on a mound of white sand—symbolizing a human diaphragm—in which silence alternates with the amplified sound of breathing. Besides his pantomimes *Act I* and *Act II*, silence is essential in all of Beckett's plays. In *Happy Days*, Winnie, to fill a dreaded, empty silence, ceaselessly speaks to Willie, who, for the most part, remains mute and immobile. The play culminates in unbearable silence. Silence often accompanies the use of circus and music hall elements in Beckett's plays. Pitiful specimens of the human race, his characters, like circus and music hall clowns, employ *lazzi* or silent, comical stage business based on physical movement. In *Waiting for Godot*, to pass time the characters play with their shoes, juggle with their hats, lose their pants, kick one another, and mime carrying baggage and playing like little children. Their pointless movements manifest the emptiness of their human condition. Jean Anouilh describes Beckett's plays as sketches of Blaise Pascal's *Pensées* played by the famous European clowns, the Fratellini Brothers (Surer 1969, 359).

Eugene Ionesco's anti-verbal theatre incorporates guignol, mime, farce, music hall, and circus. On the role of words in the theatre, he says:

> Theatre is not only words. The theatre is as visual as it is auditory. It is not a series of images, as in the cinema, but a construction, a moving architecture of stage images. (1962, 15)

The Baldheaded Soprano (1950) is a tragedy of language that assaults words' mechanical character. In *The Chairs* (1952), in which the characters are the pivots of moving objects, Ionesco indicates that the old couple carrying chairs on stage move as if in a ballet. He adds that, in this play, "many gestures, almost pantomime, are needed," along with objects that move and doors that open and close, to render a sense of emptiness and absence (1962, 167–69).

Like the absurdists, American playwright Edward Albee interspersed dialogue with pauses, fragmented language, one-word responses, and repetitions to depict the desperation and the void in his characters' lives. At the end of *Tiny Alice* (1964), for example, the dying Brother Julian depicts his physical pain and disillusion about a meaningless world by speaking in broken sentences. In *A Delicate Balance* (1968), the two middle-age couples manifest the senseless emptiness and automatism in their lives by responding with few words or repeating the latter.

In Harold Pinter's plays, dramatic emotion is so overcharged that words inadequately communicate feelings. Brief sentences and phrases depict the insecurity of Pinter's characters. The predicament of the destitute Davies, thrown out at the end of *The Caretaker* (1959), is expressed through fragmented sentences, his last, unfinished line ending in a long, desperate silence. When Jerry and Emma meet for the last time in *Betrayal* (1978), their silences reveal the trauma of their breakup. As she tries to remove the key from her key ring to return it to Jerry, Emma's faltering movements offer a dramatic subtext. The scene ends with Emma leaving Jerry standing speechless. In his plays, Pinter, who was also an actor and stage director, indicates precise gestures and movement. His silences, filled with movement and static attitudes, intensify his characters' desolate isolation.

Silence is the key to Marguerite Duras's work, in which much is left unsaid. In her film *Hiroshima Mon Amour* (1959), there are many pauses between the lovers' lines, which are spoken and acted out in slow tempo. The characters wait incessantly for nothing to happen. In her play, *Eden Cinema* (1977), the mother and her children passively endure the monotony of colonial life in the torpor of Cambodia's climate. In *Moderato Cantabile* (1958), which Peter Brook adapted for the screen in 1960, each pause allows the male protagonist to imagine still another way to seduce Anne Desbaresdes and thus prolong his anticipation. According to Gaeton Picon, what happens in this play is not said or perhaps nothing ever happens (Vircondelet 1972, 132). The hero and heroine's drawn-out encounters consist of dialogues punctuated with empty pauses. In the 1969 staging of *Suzanna Andler* at The Mathurins Theatre in Paris, stage director Tania Balachova asked Catherine Sellars to prolong her silences, which the director felt were more important than her words. Here, the silences more effectively portray Suzanna and Michel's gnawing relationship, in which words fail to communicate feelings.

The insufficiency of words plays an important role in Nathalie Sarraute's *Silence* (1967), adapted for the stage at Petit Odéon in Paris in 1976. The protagonist Jean-Pierre, to whom the other characters continually refer, remains silent, asking only two questions at the play's end. In her vignettes *Childhood* and *For No Good Reason*, adapted and directed by Simone Benmussa at New York's Samuel Beckett Theatre in 1985, Sarraute conveys how words are unable to express the truth. In Benmussa's staging, the hidden hostility between two friends is not communicated by words, which would mask their feelings, but by movements.

Words have their roots in spectacle, plastic art, legend, and atmosphere in Flemish playwright Michel de Ghelderode's theatre. Gest Pantomime Theatre in Wroclaw, Poland, successfully adapted his *Escurial* and *School for Buffoons* in a 1975 pantomime entitled *The Dogs*. In *Christopher Columbus,* dance, music, and acrobatics enhance the dreamlike quality of this fairy-tale play, which revolves around Columbus's dream of discovering a new world devoid of corruption. In *Mademoiselle Jaire*, staged as an ancient mystery play, witches with masks dance and jump about to revive the dead heroine. The play ends in a visual incantation scene in which the young heroine, granted her wish to return to death, is struck by lightning and then cradled in old Antiqua Mankabena's arms while masked figures dance about the heroine.

Spanish playwright Fernando Arrabal's tragic and sadistic farces evoke a visual ceremony containing ritual, guignol, poetry, and happenings in a nightmarish atmosphere. In the silent opening scene of *The Architect and the Emperor of Assyria*, played at New York's La Mama in 1986, the stage directions indicate that after an explosion on the island, the Architect, a savage in an animal skin, buries his head in the ground as the Emperor, the sole survivor of a plane accident, enters, causing the Architect to flee on all fours. In the second tableau, the two mime a crucifixion and a bombing and engage in frenetic dances. Throughout, the protagonists imitate a judge and the accused, a blind man and his dog, a confessor and his penitent.

Influenced by absurdist theatre's metaphysical anguish, Quebec playwright Robert Claing created a theatre in which silence expresses the human solitude and alienation of our times. In *La Femme d'Intérieur* (*The Housewife*, 1986), silent action reinforces the void in the life of a female protagonist abandoned by her husband. After she relates her inner thoughts to her neighbor Nicole, who quietly listens, the house-wife appears in silent scenes. In the "shower curtain" scene, for example, she sits on a stool in her bathroom, shoving objects around with her feet, removing a letter from her pocket, pocketing it again without opening it, and then taking up tweezers to pull hair from her legs. The housewife's mute attempts to fill her empty life with in-significant activities are more gripping than her verbal account to her neighbor.

A Quebec playwright whose alienated characters live in metaphysical anxiety, Marie Laberge effectively uses silence by opposing speaking characters with mute ones. *Avec l'Hiver Qui S'en Vient* (*With the Coming of Winter*, 1988) depicts a cou-ple that no longer can communicate. As the husband falls into mute prostration, his wife revolts against his silence. *L'Homme Gris* (*The Tipsy Man*, 1986) revolves around the voyage home of an alcoholic father and his introverted daughter, who spend a night in a motel. As he drinks and speaks to himself, his daughter's mute-ness renders him increasingly violent. In *Oublier* (*To Forget,* 1987), Laberge depicts the failure of the mother–daughter relationship as the mother, reduced to infantile dependency through Alzheimer's disease, is abandoned by three of her daughters, leaving the eldest, a silent, submissive martyr, to care for her. Through silence, Laberge depicts characters unfulfilled in their desires to communicate with and love one another.

The theatre of these playwrights and directors, which extends into the late twentieth century, does not appeal to the ear alone. It has overthrown traditional hi-erarchies to give value not only to the text, but to acting, movement, stage space, set-ting, and directing. It is one in which silence and movement are essential to evoking moods and images. In these playwrights' and directors' works, the spoken word, having exhausted its ability to stimulate feelings and thoughts, yields to the visual image's evocative power, born of silence and movement.

Mid- to Late Twentieth-Century Theatre: Beyond the Script

To give free vent to movement, silence, and stage images, twentieth-century stage directors searched for still other means to challenge the spoken word's hegemony. Indeed, the text became a pretext for more visual realizations by directors and per-formers who were their own playwrights. Because their productions appealed pri-marily to the spectator's perceptions, they had to be seen rather than read.

One way to intensify dramatic emotion through creating visual means, as well as to discover the organic pulse behind the printed page and release material from the subconscious, was to use improvisation (Harrop 1992, 62). This way was achieved through collective creations in which actors, stage directors, and play-wrights worked together to improvise action. Rather than function as separate enti-ties, playwrights, and stage directors, without using a given text or scenario, created dialogue from the actors' improvised movements, based on themes that the stage director suggested. And even when words were born of these collective creations, they did not take precedence over other stage elements. To incorporate visual images into their productions, some collective playwright–directors staged free interpretations of Shakespearean and classical plays. This process recalls Antonin Artaud's replacement of the playwright's text with the actor and stage director's own stage creation of the latter to revitalize the theatrical expression.

In the United States, the Living Theatre, founded by Julian Beck and Judith Malina in 1951, and the Open Theatre, established by former Living Theatre member Joe Chaikin in 1963, developed scenarios from the actors' movement and voice improvisations. The Living Theatre's politically bent production *Frankenstein* (1965) and Kenneth H. Brown's *The Brig* (1963), about life in a military prison, utilized gestures, sounds, and text to depict oppression, while Jack Gelber's *The Connection* (1959) portrayed in free, physical style the drugged beatniks of the 1950s. Chaikin, who believed silence to be one of the highest forms of communication, made extensive use of the subtexts that the actors' movements and gestures expressed. He worked closely with playwrights to develop a theatrical language which went beyond the conventional use of words. With productions such as Megan Terry's *Viet Rock* (1965–66) and Jean-Claude van Itallie's *America Hurrah* (1966), the Open Theatre became one of the most experimental avant-garde theatre companies in the United States.

In the productions of his New York Performance Group, founded in 1967, Richard Schechner, a self-declared Antonin Artaud and Jerzy Grotowski disciple, attempted to recapture elements of the primitive ceremony; the audience represented the community, witnessing and even participating in these productions. Rather than interpret a text conventionally, Schechner aimed to create a work in which the dramatic action, the set design, and the actor's vocal and physical expression were all-essential. His actors added their personal experiences to a given text or collectively invented one. For example, in his 1969 staging of *Makbeth*, parts of Shakespeare's text were combined with the actors' own findings and audience members participated, such as in the banquet scene when they were invited to sit at the table. Vocal and movement improvisations were basic to developing Schechner's stagings. After he withdrew in 1970, a section of the collective, led by Spalding Gray and Elizabeth LeCompte, continued to explore alternative theatre forms and became the Wooster Group in 1975. Under LeCompte's artistic direction, the pioneer theatre company introduced our technological age's modern concepts into classic texts and created radical assemblages of live performances through deconstructing classic texts and using discovered materials, films and videos, dance and movement, multitrack scoring, and an architectonic approach to stage design. The Wooster Group's form of expression, which utilizes a comical physical language, has appealed to European as well as American audiences. Among its multimedia pieces created since the mid-1970s are *Three Places in Rhode Island* (1977); *Route 1 & 9*; *Rumstick Road* (1980); *LSD (Just the High Points)* (1984); Frank Dell's *The Temptation of Saint Anthony*; *Brace Up!*, based on Anton Chekhov's *Three Sisters*; *Fish Story*, inspired by a documentary on a traveling Japanese theatre company and the fourth act of Chekhov's *Three Sisters*; and adaptations of Eugene O'Neill's *The Emperor Jones* and *The Hairy Ape*.

Among the stage productions of Italy's postwar period in which body expressivity was primary were those of Giorgio Strehler, who, with Paolo Grassi founded Milan's Piccolo Teatro in 1947. His stagings of the works of Carlo Goldoni, Shakespeare, Bertolt Brecht, and Luigi Pirandello were renowned for their harmonious blend of movement and text. His actor-training program included Etienne Decroux's mime, dance, and fencing.

Meanwhile, in London, inspired by Antonin Artaud's theories, Peter Brook explored nonverbal and gestural language and incorporated silent passages in plays ranging from *Measure for Measure* (1950), *The Tempest* (1957), and *King Lear* (1962) to *Marat/Sade* (1964); *U.S.* (1966), an anti–Vietnam War musical drama; and *Mahabharata* (1985), based on the Indian epic. In his total theatre plays, Brook made use of *commedia*, Noh drama, circus, and music hall, often creating the texts from the actors' intensive physical improvisations.

In the 1960s, 1970s and beyond, a number of avant-garde directors developed theatre that gave more importance to gestures, movement, and sounds than to language and text. They also revived the ritualistic element found in ancient theatre. To give more breadth to their visually oriented plays, some abandoned the conventional stage to present works in unconventional areas. A stage director who early on renounced rigid adherence to a given text and renewed the actor's art through body training and expression was Jerzy Grotowski. With the 1965 founding of his Polish Laboratory Theatre, his rigorous training methods formed the basis of productions composed of movement and sounds without words. Although Grotowski did not use mime techniques per se, he believed that training the actor's body could activate his creative powers and serve as a basis for his spiritual evolution. His plea for a so-called poor theatre to enrich theatre as an art recalls Etienne Decroux's rejection of theatre that subordinates the actor's contribution to sets, costumes, music, and text. For Grotowski, the actor had to go beyond literature to create a language of human impulses and reactions. By creating his own gestures and sounds, the actor could be his own poet and perform his own magic.

The productions that developed from Grotowski's Polish Laboratory Theatre represent a work model in which research on the actor's art could be put into practice. Among his major productions, based on classical works freely interpreted to represent modern times, are Christopher Marlowe's *Doctor Faustus*, performed in the early 1960s; Pedro Calderon's *The Constant Prince*, played in Paris in 1966; and Stanislaw Wyspianski's *Akropolis*, performed in Paris in 1968.

In Ingmar Bergman's stage productions, the visual took precedence over all other elements. His 1986 staging of *Hamlet* at Stockholm's Royal Dramatic Theatre culminated in a deconstruction of the original text, which the director's own interpretation replaced.

Among the painters who have brought their visual talents to the stage is Polish director Tadeusz Kantor, whose Cricot 2 Theatre, founded in 1955, would become one of Poland's foremost avant-garde theatres. For Kantor, the text was only a departure point for creating haunting dramatic moods through movement and static attitudes. What makes his *Dead Class* (1975) so powerful is his use of grotesque dummies, as well as actors who move like dummies, to symbolize the children whom we have killed within ourselves. This use of dummies recalls Edward Gordon Craig's supermarionette as a model for the actor to rediscover the elements of creation and ritual that the theatre had lost. Other works, such as *Let the Artist Die*, which was performed at New York's La Mama in 1985 and depicts Kantor's life as an artist, provoke stark stage images through movement and sound. For Kantor, the stage direction and acting are independent from the text: "The author of the text is not the author of the performance of a play. The semantic value of the text should not be a primary source either of the stage action or the acting. The latter is fully autonomous and should be derived from and shaped by the actor's creativity" (1986, 155). Kantor is reiterating what Jacques Copeau, Antonin Artaud, Edward Gordon Craig, Jerzy Grotowski, and the Polish stage director's European predecessors have decried regarding theatre, which does not give full reign to the actor's creative contribution, much of which includes his use of physical expression.

Eugenio Barba, who studied with Jerzy Grotowski, founded his Odin Teatret in Oslo, Norway, in 1964 and his International School of Theatre Anthropology in 1979 in Holstebro, Denmark. Aside from the influences of Vsevolod Meyerhold, Konstantin Stanislavsky, Jacques Copeau, Oriental theatre, Kathakali, and Peking Opera, that of Grotowski is the most important for Barba's nonrealistic style, which emphasizes the body's expressivity. Most of Barba's productions are based on improvisational work developed in rehearsals and contain little or no dialogue. Three of his major street productions—*The Book of Dances, Anabasis*, and *The Million* (also performed indoors), staged between 1974 and 1988—are examples of collective rehearsal improvisations with comedy, pantomime, song, and dance. *The Million*, performed at New York's La Mama in April 1984, consisted of a swiftly run sequence of images that illustrate a series of associated ideas through Kathakali, Kabuki, Balinese dance and masks, circus techniques, stilt-walking, and Western-style dance. His mime fantasy *The Castle of Holstebro*, presented at the 1993 Philadelphia Movement Theatre International Festival, developed the theme of a mystical wedding between Shakespeare's characters Ophelia and Yorick.

Movement training is an essential part of Barba's school and Odin Teatret productions. Grotowski and Kathakali physical exercises are used for developing the actor's bodily control and for personal training and research. This prepares the actor for improvisational explorations, which provide the material for a production. Odin Teatret's focus on physical training thus aids the actor in discovering his personal qualities and inventing dramatic action. Rather than interpret a text or a director's vision, this emphasis on the actor's individual creativity has rendered the Odin Teatret's collective creations highly original.

Since 1980, Barba has held nine open sessions of his International School of Anthropology, with the participation of actors, dancers, directors, choreographers, scholars, and critics in performances and panels.

Ariane Mnouchkine, who studied mime, clowning, and acting with Jacques Lecoq and who believed that acting takes precedence over the text, incorporated these skills into the Théâtre du Soleil's collaborative stagings. Among these were a piece on circus clowning, *Les Clowns* (1969), and two historical caricatures, *1789* (1970) followed by *1793*. The two latter plays evoked the 1968 uprisings in France, along with the era of the French Revolution with fairground scenes, acrobats, puppets, and jugglers. In *L'Age d'Or* (*The Golden Age*, 1975), *commedia* type characters, improvisations without a text, and the miming of imaginary objects depicted the twentieth-century, sociopolitical struggle of the masses. So that the text would not limit the actor's creative process, Mnouchkine approached characterization largely through movement and gestures, as seen in her lively staging of *Twelfth Night* and in her use of Asian acting styles to express emotion through body movement in such pieces as *L'Indiade ou L'Inde de Leurs Rêves* (1987). While her adaptations of Shakespeare's *Richard II* (1982) and *Henry IV* (1984) incorporate more traditional movement techniques, along with masks and costumes, the ensemble of Mnouchkine's productions innovatively use mime, mask, and clowning.

A number of American stage directors are engaged in image theatre, which communicates visual imagery by scenery, costumes, props, masks, video, film, puppetry, lighting, music, and other means. Based also on the visual imagery that the mimes' and actors' bodies create, image theatre emphasizes performance rather than literary values. One of the most prominent image theatre exponents is Robert Wilson. A stutterer until the age of seventeen, he began to work as a therapist for the mute after dancer Byrd Hoffman corrected his speech impediment through the use of slow, rhythmic movement patterns (Arens 1991, 25). Influenced by this experience, Wilson believes that, while words remain conventional and limited, silence can evoke new forms of visual theatre. In his musical theatre, in which he introduces very slow movement to sharpen the spectator's perceptions, text and images interact. For Wilson, "movement is line, music is light, a gesture is a sound, objects are performers" (Curiger, Bice, and Burckardt 1988, 117). Because of movement's importance in their stagings, his productions have been called *chansons de geste* or songs of gesture. *Deafman Glance,* staged in 1971, which reveals a deaf man's view of the world, was performed entirely in silence. In *A Letter for Queen Victoria* (1974), in which Christopher Knowles, a seventeen-year-old autistic boy, played the protagonist, nontraditional movement and objects replace language. *Einstein on the Beach*, a Philip Glass opera in four acts, nine scenes, and five knee plays (segments or interludes connected by a musical structure), staged in 1976 and revived in 1984, and the multimedia opera *The Civil Wars*, with music by Glass (intended for but not performed at the Olympics in 1984), are composed of visual imagery, music, dance, theatre, architecture, and movement. Wilson's creations also represent the postmodern, antitraditional aesthetic of—in his words—separating sound and image to give individual lives to both (Arens 1991, 24).

Two stage directors and playwrights whose productions stem from a nonliterary and nonverbal approach—words, when present, remain independent from any meaning or connection with the action—are Richard Foreman, the producer–director of the New York Ontological-Hysteric Theater company, founded in 1968, and Lee Breuer of Mabou Mimes, which he began in 1970. In Foreman's *Pandering to the Masses: A Misrepresentation* (1975), depersonalized language accompanies performers, who move in precise patterns, like living statues evolving within complex and unrelated scenic images. In his fragmented, surrealist stagings, such as *The Particle Theory* (1973), influenced by modern physics, the performers remain as motionless as mannequins or move in slow motion to sharpen the spectator's perceptive faculties and incite him to find unconventional meanings. In Breuer's *Red Horse Animation*, staged at the Guggenheim Museum on November 30, 1970, with music by Philip Glass, the actors' sculptural movements, inspired by modern dance and painting, are primordial. *Peter and Wendy*, which made its world premiere in 1996 at the Spoleto Festival and won two Obie Awards in 1997, is based on J. M. Barrie's novel and integrates puppetry with movement, narration. music and lyrics. Breuer won three Obie Awards for his stagings of Samuel Beckett's works, which enhanced the text with visual images. Both Foreman and Breuer, in whose creations the text, when present, is subordinate to the visual effects, have contributed significantly to a vital image theatre.

On the West Coast, Alan Finneran's Soon 3, begun in 1972, developed performance landscapes based on image associations, which fuse live performance with movement, cinema sculpture, video, original music, and text. Formerly a sculptor and a painter, his early works consisted of elaborate moving sculptures. He later created what he described as task-activated performance landscapes, as seen in *Black Water Echo* (1977), in which the performers' activities are reduced to mechanical tasks. Finneran also unified sculpture, projections, and performers to convey a social theme. *Voodoo Automatic* (1983) deals with the relationship of film and video to our culture, and *Magi* (1986) depicts nuclear holocaust. *Plasma Lagoon* (1989) evokes dream states, with geometric designs and props concisely manipulated to develop political, social, and philosophical themes. In *Veer* (1989), three protagonists climb a wall, veering from one direction to another in dynamic movement patterns. Soon 3's first outdoor work, *Asylum Red*, played in May 1992 in San Francisco parks and provoked varied reactions from spectators viewing this performance–architecture piece, in which a man, woman, and child dressed like ancient desert-dwellers are enclosed in a high, red, steel cage.

Anne Bogart, who has directed more than fifty productions since 1976, developed a method called Viewpoints, which aims to reveal inner meanings through movement. Based on this system, Bogart co-founded the International Theatre Institute with Tadashi Suzuki, producing works in both Japan and Saratoga Springs, New York. Bogart's productions, which combine movement, gestures, song, and spoken word, locate a work's meaning through repetitive gestures, tableaux vivants, speech patterns, and visual images. Her direction of *Baltimore Waltz* won her an Obie Award in 1991. In 1992, she directed Claire Booth Luce's *The Women*, utilizing a highly stylized expressionist form to create layers of meaning concerning the author's biting satire on women.

Théâtre de la Jeune Lune grew out of a five-year collaboration between Minneapolis native Barbra Berlovitz Desbois and Parisian Dominique Serrand, who trained at Jacques Lecoq's school. Founding their company in 1978 with Lecoq-trained Vincent Gracieux, they were later joined by another Lecoq student, Robert Rosen, and permanently established themselves in Minneapolis in 1992. Actors in and creators, designers, and directors of their own plays, they developed a style based on a wide range of American and European theatrical techniques and traditions, such as commedia dell'arte, mime, clowning, American musical theatre, vaudeville, classical farce, and psychological theatre. Théâtre de la Jeune Lune's repertory includes *August, August, August* (1985), Pavel Kahout's circus play about the struggle between the imagination and bureaucratic power; *Circus* (1986), performed in the spirit of the one-ring European circus; a highly physical staging of *Romeo and Juliet* (1986) depicting the couple as middle-aged; Edmond Rostand's *Cyrano* (1989); *Children of Paradise: Shooting a Dream* (1992), a fictional documentary on the making of the film and the artist's place in society; and *Don Juan Giovanni* (1994), in which a blend of Mozart's opera and Molière's play fuses postmodernism with *commedia*.

Antenna Theatre, based in the San Francisco Bay Area and founded in 1980 by Chris Hardman—a designer, actor and technician for Bread and Puppet Theatre from 1969 to 1971—explores a variety of visual means and new technologies to confront social issues such as homelessness, idolatry of the automobile, and the media's influence on our lives. After beginning San Francisco's Snake Theatre with Laura Farabough in 1977, in which performers wearing large masks played in site-specific works (*Somewhere in the Pacific*, 1978), and on indoor stages, Hardman founded the Antenna Theatre, based on the concept of receiving, transforming, and transmitting information to the populace. Although not primarily a movement theatre, it devised visual works with live actors wearing giant puppet masks, along with the animation of objects and cardboard sculptures. These were combined with the use of Walkmen, infrared-transmitted sound, three-dimensional slides, radio programming, and active audience participation. Examples of visual works that weave social concerns into their content are *Russia* (1985), which deals with superpower paranoia in the 1980s, and *Caveat Emptor, Buyer Beware* (1991), which conveys man's compulsion for security through the ages. In the latter piece, the use of animated plywood cutouts, live actors inside balloons, screen images, and miniature shadow projections is akin to a postmodern puppet show in which the puppets take on technological shapes and characteristics. *Etiquette of the Undercaste*, performed at the Experimental Gallery of the Smithsonian Institution in 1992, is one of Antenna Theatre's installations that have expanded visual and auditory theatre's frontiers to interpret social issues in parks, historical sites, and museums. In this piece, as he listens to live interviews with social workers and indigents by means of a tape player and a headset, the audient spectator is plunged into a homeless environment. *The Appearance of Civilization* (1992) was performed on the shores of the Pacific Ocean in San Francisco by actors resembling puppets with giant-size mask heads, much in the style of the Bread and Puppet Theatre. Transmitted through Walkmen, the narration relates the written testimonies by Dominican missionary Bartolomé de Las Casas about European oppression of Native Americans, interspersed with interviews with Korean War and Vietnam War veterans living in homeless encampments, Holocaust survivors, and the director of a post-traumatic stress disorder center. Aided by auditory technology, Antenna Theatre's visual tableaux decry all forms of invasion and war.

Some performance art companies have blended music with their visual art. George Coates's performance work trilogy, *The Way of How* (1981), based on the preparation for flight and discovery; *Are Are* (1982), depicting ascendance; and *Seehear* (1984), which culminates in fusion, integrated scenic effects, movement, song, and music. Through the collaborative improvisations of Coates, the singers, the composer, and mime artists, such as Leonard Pitt and Hitomi Ikuma, the movement, singing, and action recall a modern-day *commedia* that incorporates both technology and metaphysics. *Right Mind* (1989), depicting the life and works of Charles L. Dodgson—also known as Lewis Carroll, author of *Alice's Adventures in Wonderland*—and *Invisible Site* (1992) fuse live performers with computer images and multimedia to depict a new reality. Through theatre, film, music, and other new media, *Box Conspiracy* (1993) offers a humorous musical about TV's role in our lives. Coates's creations of postmodern visual and aural pluralism have established connections among music, technology, acting, and miming.

The San Francisco–based Modus Ensemble was formed in 1993 as a multidisciplinary performing arts group, with a mission to push the boundaries of theatre, dance, and music in exploring humanistic concerns in the information age. Through original works and fresh interpretations of the classics, a highly visual and stylized aesthetic enhances a meaningful text. This aesthetic is akin to the expressionist movement, which renounced realistic representation to express the artist's subjective and inner impressions. The Modus Ensemble's creative process involves rigorous physical training methods, such as the Tadashi Suzuki physical discipline for actors to develop the total body's theatrical expressivity. The group also incorporates Anne Bogart's Viewpoints training method, which grew out of postmodern dance movement improvisation.

Modus Ensemble's productions include the West Coast premiere of director Anne Bogart and the Saratoga Theatre Institute's *The Medium,* which was performed in 1995 and depicts Marshall McLuhan's findings about the electronic media's influences on the human mind. *Esperance* (1996) develops the struggle among political, religious, and social forces and the individual's inner will to achieve his destiny. It includes expressionist elements such as exaggerated vocal effects and movement and decors with scaffolding, stairways, balconies, runways, and intricate lighting. Through the use of these elements, as well as an international cultural exchange to introduce new theatre styles, Modus Ensemble offers an alternative to realism's overuse in the American theatre and a revitalization of theatre in the United States.

Rough and Tumble, begun in 1994 in the San Francisco Bay area by Cliff Mayotte, a Ringling Bros. and Barnum & Bailey Clown College graduate, aims to present good comedy—from Aristophanes to George Bernard Shaw, Shakespeare, Molière, Anton Chekhov, and contemporary playwrights—with grace, precision, and verve. Exemplary of Rough and Tumble's total theatre form, in which the spectator is challenged physically, emotionally, and mentally, is its production of *Tom Jones* (1996), a dynamic, movement-oriented production utilizing minimal sets, space, and props. In 1996, the production won two Drama-Logue Awards, one for Mayotte's outstanding stage direction and the other for Michael Carroll's rendering of the scheming Blifil. Company actors train regularly in *commedia*, the Suzuki method, the Viewpoints method, and the Théâtre de la Jeune Lune's movement training, influenced by Jacques Lecoq's mime–clown theatre.

For a growing number of Canada's stage directors, written poetry has ceded its place to the poetry of movement, which includes the use of dance, plastic art, architecture, music, and text. In Quebec, Jean-Pierre Ronfard's productions have been likened to a baroque celebration. His *Vie et Mort du Roi Boiteux* (*Life and Death of a Limping King*), staged at the Nouveau Théâtre Experimental in 1981 and 1982, is a grandiose fifteen-hour fresco consisting of six plays about two rival families' quests for power and love surrounding King Richard III's life. While the production preserved the spirit of Shakespeare's work, Ronfard's carnival ambience, grotesque choreography, grandiose stage sets, and extravagant costumes enriched the presentation.

Quebec stage director Robert Lepage engages in collaborative improvisation to reinforce the perceptivity of his visual stage images. In 1981, he joined Quebec's Théâtre Repère, founded by Jacques Lessard in 1978, which derives its name from the French *repère*, meaning "landmark." Based on a method that architect Lawrence Halprin originated in California in the early 1970s for the dance works of his wife Anne Halprin, Théâtre Repère's creations developed from collective improvisations around a concrete resource or specific object. Lepage's initial resource in *Trilogie des Dragons* (1985–87) is a crystal ball a Chinese parking-lot attendant found on the site of the former Chinatown. This discovery serves as the beginning of an archeological exploration of the parking lot. Other objects, such as shoes and sheets, are departure points for the creation of symbolic visuals. The dramatic action moves from Quebec City from 1910 to 1935, to Toronto until 1960, and then to Vancouver from 1960 to 1986, juxtaposing ancient China with twentieth-century Canada and contrasting Oriental and Occidental cultures. To communicate parts of the dramatic action, Lepage uses pantomime. For example, one of the characters simulates a plane flying from Vancouver to Tokyo by lying face-down on an upright valise and miming the flight with his arms and legs. Movement was also inspired by tai chi techniques. And, to turn the spectator's attention from hearing words to seeing visual images, Lepage mixes Chinese, French, and English cultures and languages. In

Polygraph (1991), a metaphysical murder mystery filled with physical imagery, he makes use of improvisation and image association.

Because she believes that physical expression is necessary for the theatre's survival, Vancouver stage director Kate Weiss began each of her productions with physical images, to which the character's psychological and verbal lives were later added. For her staging of *Knitequest* (1984–85), by her playwright husband Peter Eliot Weiss, she cast dancers rather than actors. In Eugene Ionesco's *Rhinoceros* (1986), she used animal images and movements to develop the characters. Weiss also believes that a physical and metaphoric approach is important in staging Shakespearean and classical theatre because a realistic or naturalistic acting style does not reveal the text's scope. A script-oriented text that primarily communicates what is happening on the stage does not appeal as extensively to the imagination. Movement serves to release material from the subconscious to create images and to make the spectator feel the production's live quality. Weiss's husband, author of *Sex Tips for Modern Girls* (1984–85) and *Going Down for the Count* (1984–85), wrote the scenarios for these plays by observing the actors' physical improvisations, which for him bring more surprise, excitement, and freshness to a script (Thompson 1986, 133).

In their creations for verbal theatre productions, twentieth-century scenic and costume designers have likewise been sensitive to stage movement's importance. One example is that of scenic and costume designer Louis Bercut (1949–1994), considered the most talented set designer of his generation in France. He began designing innovative sets and costumes for the Comédie Française in 1985, later signing his name, among other productions, to Pierre Corneille's *Polyeucte* (1987); Richard Wagner's *Tetralogie* (1988), staged at the Nice and Paris operas; Shakespeare's *Titus Andronicus* (1989); Thomas Bernhardt's *Heldenplatz* (1990), for which he received the 1991 Molière Prize for best scenic design; Molière's *Ridiculous Ladies* (1993); and Victor Hugo's *Lucretia Borgia* (1994). In his designs, Bercut created space in relation to the characters' movement and the dramatic action. His closed, circular set, for example, in *Polyeucte* provoked a concentric acting style in which the actors turned and whirled, trapped in their passions, crushed by the constraints of power and unable to escape their destinies. He conceived costumes for *Polyeucte* in the form of large Oriental robes in silk voile to amplify the protagonists' circular movements. Such set and costume designs manifest the role that movement and visual, conceptional unity had for one of Europe's finest scenic and costume designers.

To explore new aesthetic arrangements, these playwrights, stage directors, and scenic designers had to break through the boundaries that limited them. As in postmodern dance, in the theatre, the ears, eyes, and muscles shared novel combinations of auditory, visual, and kinesthetic elements. One art form evoked another, intensifying the spectator's perception of new harmonies. We are reminded of Charles Baudelaire's poem "Correspondences," in which the synaesthetic experience of transferred sensations causes color to evoke sound and touch to recall color: "Vast as the night and as the light, perfumes, colors, and sounds respond to one another" (1962, 43).

The theatre that incorporates silence and movement rather than rely on the spoken word grew as a reaction to a society that had become highly verbal, a society in which movement had separated itself from words to give birth to mime as an autonomous art. As dramatic action in verbal theatre became more and more buried in words, the latter began to lose its vitality. The theater soon needed to discover other means to revitalize its dramatic expressivity. Stage directors and playwrights thus explored the use of movement and silence, along with lighting and other scenic elements. No longer mere illustrations of the spoken word, which was now only one means of dramatic expression, movement and silence actually could give words more dramatic impact and meaning. This rebirth of a more complete theatre not only allowed the actor to challenge his own creative resources, but it also communicated to the spectator as a total being, giving him a better reflection of himself. Just as the earliest theatre drew the participant into a full sensory experience, this form, too, was a return to theatre as spectacle. In this theatrical rebirth, a new scenic language was discovered. Today, this language goes hand in hand with the postmodern theatre of images, composed of heterogenous visual—as well as nonverbal, auditory—sources. It is one that appeals to the senses and in which the mime–actor creates images with his body to devise a new physicality.

By exploring other domains of expressivity, the stage director and playwright rekindled dramatic lyricism in the theatre. This lyricism, in which the imagination soars beyond verbal poetry's limitations to incorporate multiple kinds of expression, mirrors the highly visual age in which we live. This all-encompassing means of creation challenges the spectator's sensitivity concerning life's very sources. In short, it offers a broader theatre expression that revitalizes one's vision of life. Physical expression's reintegration into the theatre, as in the first forms of the dramatic spectacle, also renders back to the theatre much of its primordial force, of which it has long been deprived.

In their search for a new theatre language, mimes, actors, stage directors, and playwrights of the twentieth century's second half attempted to integrate movement and text, as well as body and voice, and to fuse mind and body, as in the ancient Greek ideal of theatre. Because words alone can be as limiting or excessive as empty silences, exchanges developed between verbal and mime theatre. These exchanges brought about a greater span of dramatic interpretation and renewed the expressivity of both verbal and mime theatre, providing a new harmony of words, movement and silence. Silence and movement in verbal theatre and words in mime theatre, combined with other means of expression such as clowning, dance, and film, challenged those frontiers that alienated verbal theatre from mime and other kinds of stage entertainment, giving free rein to the development of a new and fertile total theatre.

16

Whither Mime?

From an art so well integrated with verbal drama in the Greek theatre that the play was impoverished without this harmony of words and movement; to the glorious heights of the specialized and popular Roman pantomime; to the beauty of the religious medieval tableaux and the spirited commedia dell'arte of the Renaissance, which in turn, inspired the masterpieces of Molière; to the silent expression of the ingenious Gaspard Deburau, the stoic, mobile statuary of Etienne Decroux, the poetic genius of Marcel Marceau, and the innovative, postmodern pluralism of Jacques Lecoq–trained mimes, the art of mime never has died but only has undergone a frequently changing role. The most yielding of all the arts, through the centuries it has moved from one end of the dramatic spectrum to the other, from being a silent and self-contained expression to becoming so well integrated with other stage arts and with spoken theatre that its dramatic power often remained concealed.

Mother to all stage arts, mime thus has had to take on many visages. In the Greek drama, the art of gestures played as important a role as vocal expression. It endowed the commedia dell'arte with a comic élan and was at the heart of Molière's physical comedies. At times, this art alone portrayed serious mythological themes, as in the Roman pantomimes; expressed tragic and universal emotions, as in Jean-Louis Barrault's tragic mime pieces; or depicted a world of fantasy, as in Pierrot's escapades, and one of poetry, as in Bip's comical adventures. As a subtle adjunct to another theatre form or as an independent art, mime as a dramatic expression never has lost its power; it only has changed its visage to continue endowing the theatre with lyricism and life.

Having opened its doors to many kinds of expression in a highly visual world, at the end of the twentieth century, mime and movement theatre attempted to bring meaning and coherence to this plurality of elements. The presence of these multiple elements in postmodern mime and movement theatre arose from an impetus to go beyond established norms and discover new ones. Just as all postmodern artists sought to create new ways of envisioning reality, mimes, too, abandoned conventional gestures and codified movement to reinterpret reality through new means. The spirit of research in itself became more vital than establishing set forms, which, if they did exist, were buried in a profusion—even in a cacophony—of novel combinations. And so, amid these new combinations, the age-old art of mime once again was reinvented.

Among these postmodern combinations were exchanges between mime and dance. Just as twentieth-century dance enriched mime, mime, in turn, became part of dance theatre. Mime enhanced the theatrical quality of the ballet and modern dance choreographies of, among others, Maurice Béjart, Jerome Robbins, Pina Bausch, and the Pilobolus Dance Theatre. Meanwhile, mime shows included dance sequences and such elements as repetitive and style-free rhythmic steps. Postmodern dance and mime also developed common elements. As postmodern dance grew into antidance and satirized classical and modern dance, mime, too, began to poke fun at whiteface pantomime and abstract–corporeal mime. And as dance began to combine diverse styles and forms—such as ballet, modern, social, jazz, and tap dance, along with pantomime, clowning, juggling, voice, improvisation, film, and video—so mime, too, encompassed varied mime styles, along with dance, clowning, puppetry, and other forms, in a heterogenous stage art. And because the interruption of one form and style by another, with no logical sequence, often challenged the spectator's expectations, he was left to seek his own interpretations. Yet, what postmodern dance and mime did reveal to the spectator was how their respective aesthetic processes evolved during a work's creation. Many of these tendencies, some of which were found in the newer movement pieces of such Decroux-trained mimes as Carbone 14, Omnibus, Margolis Brown Adaptors, and Daniel Stein, also characterized the dance creations of, for example, Merce Cunningham, Twyla Tharp, Grand Union, Meredith Monk, and Trisha Brown.

There were still more exchanges between mime and other theatre forms. No longer an art apart, mime as expressive stage movement had become an essential element of speaking theatre. Body expression's growing importance in speaking theatre manifested in the publication of numerous books and articles on stage movement. Movement-training programs for actors included the study of costumes and movement in period plays, ranging from the ancient Greek and Roman times through the Victorian and Edwardian eras. Actors trained in stage combat and martial arts to undertake fencing and the use of weapons in Elizabethan and classical plays and fight scenes in modern plays.

Just as dance, acting, and circus skills penetrated mime and regular theatre, mime and acting techniques were incorporated into clowning. New Vaudeville clowns developed acting skills and utilized mime to enhance their art. Circus companies, such as Cirque du Soleil, engaged stage directors trained in theatre. And just as many mimes today learn mime, acting, and circus skills at movement theatre schools, such as that of Jacques Lecoq, students in clown colleges, such as that of Ringling Bros. and Barnum & Bailey, continue to train in mime and acting.

Literature, too, experimented with that silence familiar to mime. Reflecting the meaningless context of words and our century's metaphysical void, American author Henry Miller wrote, "Our words are made of nothing but the current of our habitual emptiness of heart, mind, and soul" (Hassan 1968, 20). Postmodern authors, such as Marguerite Duras, no longer believed in the power of words per se as the novel's core. Through their revolt against the need for plot and character and their refusal to render content meaningful or give literary shape to form, these authors developed a literature in which the reader discovered images and meaning beyond explicit verbal concepts. Paradoxically, to broaden its dimensions, the word returned to the silence of its origins.

These artistic exchanges occurred because of a growing disdain for the inadequacy of fixed formulas and the limitations of artistic traditions to which the artist no longer felt bound. Similar to the antinovel—which embraced history, poetry, essay, monologue, drama, and other forms until now not found in the novel—and to the antitheatre—which paid no heed to dramatic structure and psychological development—mime broke away from the rigid purity and wholeness of mid-twentieth-century, modern expression. Postmodern mime, and even pantomime, were also no longer exclusively silent expressions founded upon a codified movement grammar or upon a limited pantomime vocabulary. Like antitheatre, mime and pantomime performers changed their identities. Mime and pantomime performers spoke a new language, which included elements of both verbal and movement theatre. Because of their refusal to comply with the aesthetic limitations implied in the meanings of the words "mime" and "pantomime," they were forced to modify or abandon these terms. Their art also grew into a kind of antimime. Purposely impure and intentionally incomplete, mime and pantomime underwent a deconstruction of aesthetic wholes. Like other postmodern artists, mimes explored contradictory layers of reality in new styles and forms that reflected twentieth-century society's heterogeneity and multicultural, global aspects.

To revive mime, viewed as a dying solo art, masters such as Lecoq broadened it and gave it the impetus of its postmodern form. Lecoq believed that, for 1980s mime, the best means of survival was through a kind of artistic internationalism. Mime thus abandoned rigid codes and conventional content and experimented with seemingly unprecedented forms and elements. It began to integrate those arts from which it long had been separated, such as the circus, vaudeville, dance, puppetry, cinema, text, and song. Yet, the forms that mime embraced and the elements it incorporated did not always imply crossbreeding as much as a juxtaposition of unrelated components. Words were not necessarily related to gestures, and clown acts did not always pertain to miming. And while the content encompassed issues of concern, such as drug abuse, ecology, and feminism, these did not necessarily harmonize with each mime piece's theatrical form.

This juxtaposing of diverse forms and elements gave birth to broader kinds of physical theatre, which had little in common with the mime and pantomime of the earlier part of the century or with those of the nineteenth century. On the other hand, mime's reincorporation into spoken theatre restored the latter to the ritualistic, visual nature of its most ancient origins, where the spoken word was born of silent movement and never separated from it. Among the Greeks and Romans, this ancient art was a broad and total theatre form. If we recall the original meaning of the word "mime" (as seen in chapter 1), from the Greek *mimos* and the Latin *mimus*, it signified "imitator" and referred to a short comedy written in prose that portrayed life and included expressive gestures and dance. Twentieth-century mime has been no less expansive than the ancient *pantomimus*, which included acting and dancing and depicted noble and serious themes. Today, there are dancers who mime, evoking the ancient *saltator*, the mime-dancer whose dance movements were dramatically expressive and rhythmical. Presently, mime–jugglers, mime–magicians, and puppeteers are, in a broad sense, like the *joculators*, prestidigitators, and puppeteers of the Middle Ages, imitators of life. Our multitalented performers, much like the Renaissance *commedia* players, also mime, sing, and perform acrobatics. Their art, which is rapidly evolving, perhaps might develop into a modern *commedia* in which mime; clowning; dance; verbal theatre; political, social, and philosophical content;

and all other elements are so well harmonized that there will no longer be a need to label each element as such.

The nineteenth century might have known exactly what to do with each artist and art form, but with twentieth-century mime styles appearing more rapidly than descriptions or categories can be invented, we will need to find ways to describe the fast-changing nature of mime and pantomime. Already, the findings of Etienne Decroux, Jean-Louis Barrault, Marcel Marceau, and Jacques Lecoq have taken seed, spurring mimes, actors, dancers, and clowns on to unearth new movement expressions. And in the realms of theatre and dance, the research of such theatre theoreticians as Alexander Tairoff, Vsevolod Meyerhold, Jacques Copeau, Edward Gordon Craig, Antonin Artaud, Bertolt Brecht, Jerzy Grotowski, and Eugenio Barba and of such dancers as Mary Wigman and Martha Graham has reaffirmed expressive movement's essential role in both arts and the importance of reinventing visual poetry in all stage art.

If the twentieth century has not developed the means to describe these new styles, and if the different definitions of mime create ambiguity, we nevertheless have begun to reevaluate mime as one of the most experimental and avant-garde theatre forms because of its natural propensity to incorporate other kinds of art into its silent expression. Likewise, we also have begun to recognize mime's vital role in enabling the actor, dancer, clown, puppeteer, juggler, and acrobat to give full expression to his art. Thus, in its postmodern phase, mime has not only expanded its frontiers, but it also has enriched the art of the actor, dancer, puppeteer, and clown.

There are, no doubt, more differences between the mime of the nineteenth century, which knew how to categorize each classical mime artist's specialized form, and the mime of the twentieth century, which became the harbinger of broader forms evolving so quickly that they have not yet found their own identities. In reality, there might be fewer real differences between today's mime in the Western Hemisphere and mime in the ancient Greek theatre, where miming, dancing, singing, text, acting, and all stage elements were rarely separate from one another.

As in the theatre, where the actor ideally communicates with a harmony of voice and body, in everyday life an integration of the physical, emotional, and mental is beneficial. Among the ancient Greeks, each citizen strived to harmonize body and mind; the philosopher exercised his body to develop his perceptive faculties; and the soldier learned to coordinate the mental with the physical. However, with the machine age's advent each citizen might have bettered his physical existence, realizing the need for physical exercise and the practice of sports, but he has not always integrated it with his emotional and mental life. In *A Psychology of Gesture*, Charlotte Wolff demonstrates how the use of gestures helps balance the human personality:

> It is no exaggeration to say that a gesture language would develop a better centralization of personality. Expressive movements being the natural discharge of nervous tension, gesticulation therefore eases the mind by keeping it supple and mobile, as gymnastics do for the muscles and the circulation. In helping to develop the flexibility of the mind, gesture language encourages the flow of associations and images, increasing the power of both and also of the emotions. Emotions are freed by unrestricted movements. They become inhibited and atrophied by the suppression of gesture.
>
> Man without movement is dead and the vital concern of each individual is to find adequate expression for his inner dynamism. (1945, 2–3)

Movement, the very essence of life, reflects human thoughts and acts. The need for movement to express human life fully is described in the following anecdote, in which Michelangelo, after completing his statue of Moses, wanted to break it because it would not move:

> In his cry of dissatisfaction in looking at his Moses, he expressed the desire for movement. He did not want to hear the voice of Moses; he wanted to see the statue alive and breathing, the beard palpitating, and a movement on the lips. He sought one thing, life, that is movement. Michelangelo would not have been astonished to hear a voice come out of the statue; the miracle would have been to see movement. (Bragaglia 1930, 256–57)

To conclude, silence and movement are essential to all the theatre arts. A dramatic work that portrays action only through the spoken word and in which action is little more than auditory and cerebral is faint-hearted and lifeless. In our first form of communicative expression, gestures accompanied voice sounds and continue to do so, words not always sufficing. Whenever moved to express our most intrinsic feelings, to this language we must return by nature. As in the ancient Chinese proverb:

> In joy man pronounces words.
> His words not sufficing,
> He prolongs them.
> The prolonged words not sufficing,
> He modulates them.
> The modulated words not sufficing,
> His hands make gestures
> And his feet begin to move.

Appendix A

Schools and Centers for Movement Training

The following is a list of schools and centers for movement training in North America and Europe. A list of American schools and centers can also be obtained from Joan Schirle, P.O. Box 305, Blue Lake, CA 95525, tel. (707) 668–5663. Information about European schools and centers for movement training can be procured from the European Mime Federation, Herengracht 168, 1016 BP Amsterdam, The Netherlands. *Total Theatre* magazine publishes a list of workshops and training centers in Europe. (See Mime Action Group address in Appendix B for contact information).

Sigfrido Aguilar Estudio Busqueda de
  Pantomima-Teatro
Apdo Postal #51
Guanajuato, Gto. 36000, Mexico
New York (914) 359–3733
    Training in physical acting, movement, clowning, and the creation of theatre pieces.

The American Mime Theatre
Paul Curtis, director
61 Fourth Street
New York, NY 10003
(212) 777–1710
    Ongoing classes in American mime that combine acting, playwriting, pantomime, and the use of theatrical equipment.

Antwerp Mime Studio
Cobdenstraat 7, 2018 Antwerpen, Belgium
or Arendstraat 52, 2018 Antwerpen, Belgium
    Professional day and evening courses on all aspects of mime, including Lecoq and Decroux techniques and new trends in mime. Dance, drama, voice, modern movement, acrobatics, and clowning.

Letitia Bartlett
American Conservatory Theater
30 Grant Avenue
San Francisco, CA 94108–5800
(415) 439–2350
    Dynamic movement, body communication, physical acting, mask characterization, commedia dell'arte, clowning, and contemporary archetypes.

Batdorf School for Movement Theatre
327 A Street, 4th Floor
Boston, MA 02210
(617) 338–7288
    Classes in emotional–physical connection, corporeal mime, and muscular dynamics for actors, dancers, performance artists, and students interested in body awareness.

Marc Bauman
American Conservatory Theater
30 Grant Avenue
San Francisco, CA 94108–5800
(415) 439–2444
    Physical acting, Decroux and Marceau
techniques, mask, and improvisation. Private
coaching in acting and movement.

Bond Street Theatre
2 Bond Street
New York, NY 10012
(212) 254–4614
    Workshops in physical comedy and related
techniques for the actor.

Marti Cate
364 Cascade
Fairfax, CA 94930
(415) 459–0140
    Mime–clowning, improvisation, make-up,
and mask for adults and children.

Celebration Barn Theater
190 Stock Farm Road
South Paris, ME 04281
(207) 743–8452
    Spring and summer workshops in mime,
improvisation, stage combat, clowning, juggling,
masks, commedia, storytelling, and voice.

Le Centre du Silence Mime School
P.O. Box 1015 (NMT)
Boulder, CO 80306–1015
(303) 661–9271
    Annual summer classes in the Samuel Avital
Integrated Method, including movement, mask,
and creative improvisations.

Centre Sélavy
John Rudlin
Grosbout
16240 La Forêt de Tessé, France
    One- to two-week workshops from April to
December by specialized teachers on various
themes, such as the 1996 course offerings on
Commedia dell'Arte and the Modern Actor,
African Dance, Balinese Mask, the European
Fool, and the Natural Actor.

Dell'Arte International School of Physical
  Theatre
P.O. Box 816 T
Blue Lake, CA 95525–0816
(707) 668–5663
    Six-month to yearly programs in commedia
dell'arte, mime, clowning, melodrama, voice,
improvisation, mask, yoga, and the Alexander
Technique. Summer workshops for children and
adults.

Desmond Jones School of Mime and Physical
  Theatre
20 Thornton Avenue
London W4 1QG, England
    A three-month, intensive foundation course
and a four-term course in mime technique,
mime-acting, masks, storytelling, verbal and
physical improvisation, *commedia*, acrobatics,
and stage and body dynamics. Also two-day
workshops.

Dominican College Certificate-in-Storytelling
  Program
Ruth Stotter, director
Bonnie Sullivan, coordinator
50 Acacia Avenue
San Rafael, CA 94901
(415) 435–3568 or (415) 485–3255
    Classes in storytelling performance, including
the use of movement, props, puppets, and masks
to enhance storytelling skills. Certificate upon
completion of eight units.

Ecole de Mime Corporel Dramatique
Corinne Soum and Steve Wasson
Islington Arts Factory
2 Parkhurst Road
London N7 0SF, England
    Professional training in Decroux-style
dramatic corporeal mime.

L'Ecole de Mime Omnibus
3673 Rue Saint-Dominique
Montreal, Quebec, Canada H2X 2X8
(514) 843–3009
    Beginning to advanced training in corporeal
mime technique and nonverbal dramaturgy.
Movement for the actor and stage performer and
the relationship of movement to the text and
other stage elements.

Ecole Internationale de Mimodrame de Paris
 Marcel Marceau
17 Rue René-Boulanger
75010 Paris, France
   Movement training based on the Decroux and
Marceau techniques, including the creation of
mimodramas and supplementary disciplines such
as acrobatics, fencing, and dance.

Ecole Internationale Lassaad
Lassaad Saidi
Place Saint-Gilles 18
1060 Bruxelles, Belgium
02–538–32–85
   An international school of gestural theatre,
circus, and clowning founded in 1983 by Lecoq
trainee Lassaad Saidi.

Ecole Internationale Magenia
16 Rue Saint-Marc
75002 Paris, France
   Classes in mime, movement, gestures, and
stage expression and periodic workshops in
classical pantomime, masks, and mime for
actors, under the direction of Ella Jaroszewicz,
former member of Tomaszewski's Polish Mime
Theatre and professor at the Paris Opera's École
de Danse.

Ecole Jacques Lecoq
57 Rue du Faubourg Saint-Denis
75010 Paris, France
   Two-year certificate program offering theatre
training in mime, pantomime, *commedia*, masks,
clown and buffoon work, juggling, acrobatics,
tragedy and chorus, movement and music,
movement and writing, and concrete dance.
Summer workshops every four years.

Ecole Phillipe Gaulier
Paul Milican
P.O. Box 1815
London N5 1BG, England
   Yearly workshops in clown work, melodrama,
Shakespeare, writing, directing, and other topics.

Goldston Mime Foundation
P.O. Box 02189
Columbus, OH 43202–0189
(614) 291–0011
   Intensive summer training begun with Marcel
Marceau designed to instill artistic excellence.

Humboldt State University Theatre Arts
 Department
Jyl Hewston
Humboldt State University
Arcata, CA 95521
(707) 826–5492
   Physical Theatre I: an introduction to
movement for the actor and the use of mime,
mask technique, juggling, and clown work.
Physical Theatre II: advanced development of
these performance skills and work in *commedia*,
clown theatre, and abstract movement forms.
Creation of performance works for the stage.
Classes in stage combat and in the dance
curriculum.

International School of Theatre Anthropology
Eugenio Barba
Nordisk Theaterlaboratorium
P.O. Box 1283
7500 Holstebro, Denmark
   Research in the principles of the performer's
acting technique and public sessions for
international participants.

Dan Kamin
366 Avon Drive
Pittsburgh, PA 15228
(412) 563–0468
   Private classes in physical alignment,
structural awareness, and comedy choreography.

De Kleine Academie
Lou Iockens
Rue de L'Ecuyer 43
1000 Bruxelles, Belgium
   A private school in gestural theatre, circus,
and clowning founded by Lecoq trainee Luc De
Smet. Up to three years of training.

K0-Motion Movement Theatre
7 View Avenue
West Sand Lake, NY 12196
(518) 674–8715
   Training in corporeal mime and performance
presentation.

Yves Lebreton
L'Albero Corporeal Theatre
  Workshops–Laboratories
Via Casciani 3
50025 Montespertoli (FI), Italy
    Workshops on body and voice techniques and
research on the relationships between the actor's
art and all theatre components from play-writing
to set design to creative activity. Open to
dancers, actors, and all persons interested in
corporeal and vocal language.

Ron Leeson
224 Hugo Street
San Francisco, CA 49122
(415) 566–4631
    Decroux corporeal mime.

London School of Mime and Movement
Anja Dashwood
47 Groveway
London SW9 0AH, England
    One-year foundation course and a second-
year performing course based primarily on
Decroux technique, with an appreciation and
understanding of other influences.

Margolis Brown Physical Theatre Laboratory
616 East 15th Street
Minneapolis, MN 55404
(612) 339–4709
    Ongoing, eight-week sessions on the study of
dramatic movement as the basis for theatrical
expression with exercises incorporating the
Decroux technique and philosophy. Intensive,
four-day workshops each year.

Mid-Atlantic Movement Theatre Festival
  Workshops
David Geyer
72 Liberty Street
Westminster, MD 21157
(410) 876–6640
    Workshops in mime, movement, stage
combat, dance, clowning, improvisation, and
other skills during the festival period.

Mime Centrum Berlin
Schönhauser Allee 73
D10437 Berlin, Germany
    Summer and autumn physical theatre
workshops.

Mime Course in the Theatre School Amsterdam
Hortusplantsoen 2
1018 TZ Amsterdam, The Netherlands
    Four-year course for mime performers and
teachers. Student creations of varied forms and
techniques. Interpretation of the Decroux
vocabulary and classes in acting, modern dance,
acrobatics, tai chi, voice training, mime and art
history, drama theory, lighting techniques, and
scenography.

Mime Studio Amsterdam
Postbus 4537
1009 AM Amsterdam, The Netherlands
    An open studio for professionals and semi-
professionals, with training in basic mime
techniques, improvisation, composition, and
theatre techniques.

Mime Theatre International
Giuseppe Condello, Ph.D., director
103–1070 Kings Road
Victoria, BC, Canada V8T 1X1
(250) 360–9014
    Private or group training in corporeal mime,
acting, mask, and improvisation. Theatre/festival
management, performances, lecture/
demonstrations, and stage movement/directing
services and consultation.

Mimos Festival Workshops
Centre Culturel de la Visitation
Rue Littré, F
24000 Périgueux, France
or Peter Bu
14 Avenue Pascal
78600 Maisons Laffitte, France
    Master workshops by internationally reputed
movement artists during the August Mimos
Festival.

Oakland University
Department of Music, Theatre, and Dance
Karen Sheridan
Rochester, MI 48309–4401
(248) 370–2045
    Mime, acting, styles, comedy, and character
movement.

Ohio University School of Theatre
William Fisher
208 Kantner Hall
Athens, OH 45701
(614) 593–9194
    Corporeal movement taught by former
Decroux assistant William Fisher. Also a B.F.A.
program in acting, production design, and
technology.

Enrique Pardo
Pantheatre
20 Rue Saint-Nicolas
75012 Paris, France
    Voice and physical theatre based on
mythological figures and stories.

Leonard Pitt
1542 Grant Street
Berkeley, CA 94073
(510) 841–0686
    Physical theatre workshop focusing on
movement technique, improvisation, and masks.

Pomona College Theatre Department
Thomas Leabhart
300 East Bonita
Claremont, CA 91711
(714) 621–8186
    Corporeal mime, movement for actors, and
mask study.

Pontine Movement Theatre
Marguerite Mathews and Gregory Gathers
135 McDonough Street
Portsmouth, NH 03801
(603) 436–6660
    Ongoing classes based on Decroux corporeal
mime, movement for actors, and body language
workshops.

Ringling Bros. and Barnum & Bailey Clown
  College
Steve Smith, director
P.O. Box 1528
Venice, FL 34284–1528
(800) 755–9637, extension 129
    Circus clowning, pantomime, juggling,
unicycling, stilt-walking, and performing arts
related to clowning.

Bari Rolfe
434 66th Street
Oakland, CA 94609
(510) 658–2482
    Workshops in physical theatre, mask,
commedia, story theatre, period movement, and
puppetry.

Sabattini Mime Academie
Solange Coppens
Burgstraat 24
9000 Gand, Belgium
    Founded by Marceau trainee M. A. J. Hoste
in 1952. Training up to three years in modern
and classical mime and gestural theatre.

Daniel Stein
Dell'Arte School of Physical Theatre
P.O. Box 816
Blue Lake, CA 95525–0816
(707) 668–5663
    Decroux technique, acting, directing,
improvisation, and creating pieces.

Studio Bob Fleshman
1000 Joliet Street
New Orleans, LA 70118
(504) 865–1522
    Private classes in movement theatre, body
orientation, and movement therapy and
professional training in psychodrama and drama
therapy. Physical training based on Decroux
technique and improvisational mime.

Teatro a l'Avogaria
Carla Poli
Castello 6450
30122 Venezia, Italy
    Year-long courses in movement, voice,
improvisation, acting and make-up. Summer
workshop in commedia dell'arte.

Théatre du Mouvement
Bénédicte Simon–Yasmina Adem
21 Rue du Grand Prieuré
75011 Paris, France
    Periodic workshops in France and abroad in
movement and voice, with Claire Heggen and
Yves Marc of the Théâtre du Mouvement and
other theatre specialists.

TooBa Physical Theatre Centre
Dean Fogal
2182 West 12th Avenue, Room 50
Vancouver, BC, Canada V6K 2N4
(604) 738–1057
   A two-year, integrated program in corporeal
mime, acting, voice, and the healing arts.

Trielle
Jacques Lours
15800 Thiezac, France
   Center organized by Claire Heggen and Yves
Marc of the Théâtre du Mouvement, offering
five- to fourteen-day workshops by renowned
artists and teachers from June to October on
various themes relating to the expression of the
body in mime, theatre, circus, music, and dance.

Valley Ridge Studio
E. Reid Gilbert
Thomas, WV 26292
(304) 469–4490
   Workshops in pantomime, corporeal mime,
mime for actors, mime with masks, and
storytelling.

Webster Movement Institute
Theresa Mitchell
c/o Webster University
Department of Theatre and Dance
470 East Lockwood
St. Louis, MO 63119–3194
(314) 963–9078
   Summer program with specialized teachers in
movement theatre, such as Laban Movement
Analysis, Bartenieff Fundamentals, Williamson
Technique, and Masks and Movement for Actors.
Webster University offers a B.F.A in regional and
musical theatre, which includes a four-year
sequence of movement courses incorporating the
study of the Alexander Technique, Laban
Movement, circus skills, period movement,
martial arts, stage combat, and tai chi.

Appendix B

Archives, Resource Centers, and Artist Directories; Periodicals and Publications; Library and Museum Collections; Pantomime and Mime Scripts and Bookshop Collections; Festivals

Archives, Resource Centers, and Artist Directories

Documentation on national and international physical theatre and movement training; books, journals, and periodicals such as *Movement Theatre Quarterly* and *Gestes;* and background material on artists and companies that perform and organizations that support mime in America and abroad are stored at the Margolis Brown Movement Theatre Center, 616 East 15th Street, Minneapolis, MN 55404, tel. (612) 339–4709. The International Mimes and Pantomimists published a *Mime Directory* Volume 1 in 1974–75 and Volume 2 in 1977–78. Volume 1 is listings of members and nonmembers of the International Mimes and Pantomimists; Volume 2 contains an annotated bibliography of books, articles, periodicals, and reference works and annotated titles of mime films and scripts. Inquiries for the directory can be made at public libraries, such as the New York Public Library for the Performing Arts, Dance Collection, 40 Lincoln Center Plaza, New York, NY 10023–7498, tel. (212) 870–1659; at the Billy Rose Theatre Collection at the same address, tel. (212) 870–1639; and at the Margolis Brown Movement Theatre Center (see address and phone number above). The Association of Theatre Movement Educators has published a bibliography on the Alexander Technique; body language; clowning and circus, *commedia*; dance and choreography, Feldenkrais; improvisation

and theatre games; Laban/Bartenieff; mask, mime, and movement for the actor; dance movement therapy; and stage fighting. For information, write Mandy Rees, Fine Arts Dept., California State University, 9001 Stockdale Highway, Bakersfield, CA 93311–1099.

The Marcel Marceau Foundation for the Advancement of the Art of Mime, Inc., established in 1996, fosters the art of mime and mimodrama and the work of Marcel Marceau in the United States and abroad and promotes theatrical productions and public exhibitions featuring the art of mime. The foundation aims to produce master level workshops by Marceau and videotapes to document his teaching in an educational mime video for school distribution and broadcasting. The foundation is located at 253 West 73rd Street, Suite 8G, New York, NY 10023, tel. (212) 874–2030. Information on Marcel Marceau and his foundation is available on the Internet at www.marceau.org.

The World of Mime Theatre website, created in 1996, promotes mime as a serious theatrical art and provides worldwide information on mime training, schools, workshops, books, publications, films, videos, mime artists, companies, festivals, performances, organizations, and other websites. It also has an international mime theatre calendar for current events in the field. It is available on the Internet at www.geocities.com/Broadway/5222/.

Information on European mime can be obtained at the European Mime Federation, Heren-

gracht 168, 1016 BP Amsterdam, The Netherlands, tel. 31–20–623–5104, and at the Mime Action Group, Information, Research, and Publications Center, at The Circus Space, Coronet Street,
London N1 6NU, England, tel. 0171–729–7944.
The European Mime Federation also collaborates
with mime centers and companies in Europe that
have documentation on their own work and some
information on other European mime. Among
these centers are Mime Centrum Berlin, Documentation and Training Center, Schönhauser
Allee 73, D 10437 Berlin, Germany; Théâtre du
Mouvement (coordinator for the European network of the Transversales which supports movement theatre in Europe), 21 Rue du Grand Prieuré,
75011 Paris, France; Centre du Mime, 15 Rue
Ernst Lacoste, 75012 Paris, France; International
Centre for Stage Movement, B. Tsherkizowskova
22–2–19, 107553 Moskva, Russia; De Beweeging, Gasstraat 88–90, B 2060 Antwerpen, Belgium; the Vlaamse Mime Federatie VZW (Flemish Mime Federation), Sergeyselsstraat 6, 2140
Borgerhout, Belgium; Scottish Mime Forum,
Stepping Stones, 112 West Bow, Edinburgh EH1
2HH, Scotland, UK; Austrian Mime Federation,
Gold Egg Studio, Goldeggasse 29–A2–1, 1040
Wien, Austria; Studio Caple, Zámecké Schody 6,
11800 Praha 1, Czech Republic; Ukrainian Mime
Center, Irpenskaya 2–86, Kiev 142, Ukraine;
Croatian Institute for Movement and Dance,
Biankinijeva 5, 41000 Zagreb, Croatia; and Con-
temporary Dance Theatre Association, Körösy u.
17, 1117 Budapest, Hungary. La Maison du
Mime, Centre Culturel de la Visitation, 24000
Périgueux, France, has also begun to collect infor-
mation on European mime.

The Belgian Center of the International Theatre Institute (UNESCO) Flemish Community
collected information worldwide on Etienne Decroux's work for his 1998 centennial, declaring
November 13, 1998, an international day dedicated to mime: Jetty Roels/Herman Verbeeck,
Flemish Center of ITI, Place Berouw 55, 9000
Gent, Belgium. The Center for Performance Research at the University of Wales hosted a Past-
master Symposium and workshops on Etienne
Decroux in November 1997. For information
about future conferences, write Judie Christie, ex-
ecutive director, Centre for Performance Research, University of Wales, 8 Science Park,
Aberystwyth SY23 3AH, Wales, UK. The Prague
Theatre Institute, under the Department of Czech

Theatre Studies, began preparing a *Dictionary of
Ballet, Pantomime and Dance,* edited by Jana
Holenová and Vladimir Vasut according to
themes and genres in 1997 (Celetná 17, 110 00
Praha 1, Czech Republic).

Other resource centers that could provide some
information on the movement arts are the
Dance/Theatre Workshop/National Performance
Network, 219 West 19th Street, New York, NY
10011, tel. (212) 691–6500; the National Association of Schools of Theatre and the National Association of Schools of Dance, 11250 Roger
Bacon Drive, Suite 21, Reston, VA 22090, tel.
(703) 437–0700; the National Dance Association,
1900 Association Drive, Reston, VA 20191, tel.
(703) 476–3436; the American Alliance for Theatre and Education, Department of Theatre, Arizona State University, P.O. Box 87287–2002,
Tempe, AZ 85287, tel. (602) 965–6064; the National Association of Dance and Affiliated Artists,
Inc., P.O. Box 8, San Bruno, CA 94066, tel. (650)
330–6998; the Society of Movement Specialists,
147 Chestnut Street, Apartment E–22, Ithaca, NY
14850, tel. (607) 273–2661; and the Association
for Theatre Movement Educators, Millikin University, Department of Theatre and Dance, 1184
West Main Street, Decatur, IL 62522–2084, tel.
(312) 341–3719. The Laban-Bartenieff Institute
of Movement Studies, which has a library and
archives of Laban-Bartenieff fundamentals and
related materials, is located at 39 West 14th
Street, Room 307, New York, NY 10011, tel.
(212) 477–4299. Information on mime in Canada
and North America can be obtained from the Corporeal Mime Society, 1912 Blenheim Street,
Vancouver, BC, Canada V6K 4H9, tel. (604)
738–1057.

A *Membership Directory* of American mime
artists and teachers belonging to the National
Movement Theatre Association can be obtained
from the National Movement Theatre Association, c/o Margolis Brown Movement Theatre
Center, 616 East 15th Street, Minneapolis, MN
55404, tel. (612) 339–4709. To inquire about a
list of the members of the Association of Theatre Movement Educators, write to Dawn
Arnold, 2970 North Sheridan Road, Apt. 1021,
Chicago, IL 60657. Information on mime artists,
presenters, and festivals in Europe can be procured from the European Mime Federation,
Herengracht 168, 1016 BP Amsterdam, The
Netherlands.

Mime and Movement Theatre Periodicals and Publications

Periodicals specializing in mime and movement theatre in the United States are *The Mime Journal* (Pomona College Theatre Department, 300 East Bonita Avenue, Claremont, CA 91711–6349, tel. (909) 626–2171) and *Movement Theatre Quarterly* (originally c/o Pontine Movement Theatre, P.O. Box 1437, Portsmouth, NH 03802–6660, tel. (603) 436–6660; since 1996, c/o Kari Margolis, 115 Washington Avenue North, Minneapolis, MN 55401, tel. (612) 339–4709. In 1995, a newsletter on national mime activities entitled *Sunday Salon News* was begun by Janet Carafa and Lavinia Plonka and disseminated by New York Entertainment Connection, 1173 Second Avenue, #289, New York, NY 10021, tel. (212) 260–6100. The Association of Theatre Movement Educators publishes a newsletter biannually on movement theatre conferences, workshops, festivals, etc. (Association of Theatre Movement Educators, Millikin University, Department of Theatre and Dance, 1184 West Main Street, Decatur, IL 62522–2084, tel. (217) 424–6211). In Great Britain, *Total Theatre* publishes short articles on mime, physical theatre, and visual performance and on current activities in the field in Europe (see Mime Action Group address under Resource Centers above). In France, *Gestes* prints articles on movement theatre (see La Maison du Mime address under Resource Centers above). The Vlaamse Mime Federatie publishes a newsletter on European mime, with some articles in English and French (Sergeyselsstraat 6, 2140 Borgerhout, Belgium). The European Mime Federation publishes *State of Mime*.

Other magazines and journals that, though they do not specialize in mime or movement theatre, have published articles on these subjects are *Dance Magazine,* 33 West 60th Street, New York, NY 10023; *Ballett International*, Verlags-GmbH Richard Wagner Street 33, P.O. Box 270443, D 5000 Cologne 1, Germany; *Calliope*, Clowns of America, 1052 Foxwood Lane, Baltimore, MD, 21221; *Impulse Magazine* (ended publication in October 1996), Human Kinetics Publishers, P.O. Box 5076, Champaign, IL 61825–5067; *Werner's Magazine* (articles on movement and vocal expression), New York, 1879 to 1902; *The Mime Review,* vols. 1–3, July 1935 to April 1939 in West Dulwich, England; *Theatre Movement Journal* (an American Theatre Association Stage Movement Project publication), 1973 to 1974; *Dance Scope*, New York, winter 1965 to fall 1981; *Movement News* (a Laban-Bartenieff Institute of Movement Studies biannual newsletter), 39 West 14th Street, Room 307, New York, NY 10011, tel. (212) 477–4299. For information on publications no longer published such as *Mime, Mask and Marionette*, *Mime Times*, and *Source Monthly*, see Works Consulted and Cited. For information on or to consult copies of other publications no longer published, inquire at public, state, or university libraries.

Library and Museum Mime and Theatre Collections

The Bibliothèque de l'Arsenal, a section of the Bibliothèque Nationale de France, 1–3 Rue De Sully, 75004 Paris, France, has in its Collection Rondel of the Département des Arts du Spectacle an extensive collection of books, biographies, newspaper articles, photographs, drawings, portraits, programs, and correspondence from different periods of mime and related theatre arts. In this collection can be found drawings of commedia dell'arte and other period productions. Much of this collection has been donated by such mime artists as Marcel Marceau. There is also documentation on international mime festivals, such as the annual Mimos Festival in Périgueux, donated by festival director Peter Bu.

The Museo Theatrale Alla Scala, Via Filodrammatici 2, 20121 Milano, Italy, possesses a collection of engravings, printed matter, posters, sculptures, costumes, and marionettes of all periods and particularly of the commedia dell'arte. There is also a section containing photos on ancient theatre of archeological interest.

The London Theatre Museum has—in addition to costumes, props, designs, programs, photographs, and other research materials on the circus, magic, opera, ballet, music hall, and rock and pop music—articles and books on mime, mime festivals, mime training, and biographies of well-known mimes.

The nineteenth-century Jonathan King Collection at the Museum of London, 150 London Wall, London EC2Y 5HN, England contains portraits, theatre scenes, and figurines on miniature stages in silk and velvet costumes and wearing jewels. The collection belonged to Jonathan King (1836–1912), a Christmas card and theatre reproductions salesman.

In the American Avant-Garde and Radical Theatre Collection at the University of California–Davis, the archives on the San Francisco Mime Troupe consist of company scripts, promptbooks, musical scores, photographs, correspondence, business files, and visual material. Also in this theatre collection is San Francisco Mime Troupe founder Ronald G. Davis's collection of videotapes, scrapbooks, and early business correspondence. For information, contact the Department of Special Collections, University of California, Davis, CA 95616, tel. (916) 752–9869.

The Universal Movement Theatre Repertory Archives has a large collection of videotapes, audiocassettes, photographs, correspondence, publicity releases, and posters of experimental and radical theatre from 1967 on. Companies such as the Bread and Puppet Theatre are on videotape, and directors such as Judith Malina, Julian Beck, and Joseph Chaikin are interviewed on audiotape. For information, contact the Department of Special Collections, General Library, University of California, Davis, CA 95616, tel. (916) 752–9869.

The New York Public Libary for the Performing Arts, Billy Rose Theatre Collection, at 40 Lincoln Center Plaza, New York, NY 10023–7498 (tel. (212) 870–1641) has programs and newspaper articles and a small collection of books on mime and pantomime.

Pantomime and Mime Scripts and Bookshop Collections on Mime and Mime-Related Arts

Pantomime and mime scripts can be found in the *Mime Directory Bibliography,* vol. 2, edited by Bari Rolfe and published by the International Mimes and Pantomimists in Spring Green, WI, in 1978. Although the directory no longer is available at that address, public libraries and the National Movement Theatre Association Archives might have information about it. (See "Archives, Resource Centers, and Mime Artist Directories" above.) The New York Public Library for the Performing Arts at 40 Lincoln Center Plaza, New York, NY 10023–7498, has a number of pantomime and mime scripts.

Robert Storey's book *Pierrots on the Stage of Desire: Nineteenth-Century French Literary Artists and the Comic Pantomime* contains an extensive list of nineteenth-century pantomime scenarios and libraries where they can be found.

The Librairie Garnier Arnoul, 5 Rue Montfaucon, 75006 Paris, France has a considerable collection of pantomimes and works in French and other languages on the circus, mime, pantomime, dance, ballet, marionettes, guignol, puppets, theatre, and other performing arts. In the past, the library listed a set of booklet–programs of nineteenth-century pantomimes (no. 2117), a second set of booklet–programs interpreted at the Théâtre des Funambules between 1844 and 1952 (no. 2118), and Toole Stott's *Circus and Allied Arts,* a world bibliography (1500–1957) of circus, pantomime, mime, and related arts and literature, including plays, in the British Library, the Library of Congress, the Bibliothèque Nationale, and his private collection.

The Librairie Bonaparte, 31 Rue Bonaparte, 75006 Paris, France, has numerous titles on mime, theatre, the circus, dance, marionettes and other theatre arts.

Nineteenth-century and other French pantomimes may be consulted at the Bibliothèque Historique de la Ville de Paris, at the Bibliothèque de l'Opéra and at The Archives Nationales. For information about these collections, inquire at the Archives Nationales Centre de Paris, 60 Rue des Francs Bourgeois, 75141 Paris, Cedex 3, France, or at the Bibliothèque de l'Arsenal, 1–3 Rue de Sully, 75004 Paris, France.

Mime and Theatre Festivals

A number of other festivals besides those mentioned in chapters 13 and 14 host mime performances. The following are short descriptions of some of the existing movement theatre, dance, theatre, and performing arts festivals, which include addresses and phone numbers that might be subject to change.

Names and addresses of some festivals mentioned in the chapters on European and American mime follow. The contact address of the Edinburgh Fringe Festival—which began in 1947, takes place in August and early September, encompasses every type of performing art, and is open to anyone who wishes to perform—is 180

High Street, Edinburgh EH1 1QS, Scotland, U.K. The address of the Edinburgh Theatre Festival is 13/29 Nicolson Street, Edinburgh EH8 9FT, Scotland, U.K. The London International Mime Festival, held annually since 1979, is under the artistic direction of Joseph Seelig and Helen Lannaghan, 35 Little Russell Street, London WC1A 2HH, England. The address of the Mimos Festival in Périgueux, France, held annually since 1983 under the direction of Peter Bu, is Rue Littré, F, 24000 Périgueux, France, or Peter Bu, 14 Avenue Pascal, 78600 Maisons Laffitte. The annual British Festival of Visual Theatre is located at BAC, Lavender Hill, Battersea, London SW11 5TF, England. The Northern Festival of Mime, Dance and Visual Theatre, held annually since 1984 in April and May, is at The Brewery, 122A Highgate, Kendal LA8 4HE, Cumbria, England. The Marburg Pantomimenzircus or Balance-Bewegungstheater International, held biennially since 1979, is organized by Michael Kustermann and Armin Klein Kulturamt, Markt 7, D 35037 Marburg, Germany. The Hamburg Festival of Clowns and Pantomime has taken place in Hamburg, Germany, since 1992 under the direction of Elie Levy. Information on the International Festival of Mime in Sueca, Spain, begun in 1990, can be obtained from Abel Guarinos, Lluna Plena Teatre, Cantarana 43, E 46410 Sueca, Spain or from the Agencia Valenciana del Turismo, Caballeros 2, 46071 Valencia, Spain. Information on the International Mime and Theatre of Gestural Festival COS 98, begun in November 1998 to continue biannually, may be obtained from Lluis Graells, COS 78, Casa Rull, Sant Joan 27, 43201 Reus, Tarragoha Spain. The Gaukler Festival, revived in Bratislava in the autumn of 1996, presents contemporary European mime and other forms of movement theatre (Theatre Arena, Viedenska 10, SK 851 01 Bratislava, Slovakia). The biennial Gaspard's Kolin Memorial Festival, which began in 1992, is under the direction of David Dvorak and Jiri Turek, Mestské divadlo v Koline, Smetanova 557, 280 00 Kolin IV, Czech Republic. The annual Chalon dans la Rue street festival, which includes some mime and clown artists, was founded in 1987 by Pierre Layac and Jacques Quentin, 5 Place de l'Obélisque, 71100 Chalon-sur-Saône, France. In the United States, Movement Theatre International, which has held international mime and clown festivals since 1982, was organized by Michael Pedretti. The

Mid-Atlantic Theatre Festival, begun in 1989 by Carole Roberts and David Geyer, featured movement theatre artists and workshops each January (138½ Liberty Street, Westminster, MD 21157, tel. (410) 840–8128).

The July center for the Avignon-Public-Off Festival, which includes movement theatre works, is at the Conservatoire de Musique, Place du Palais, 84000 Avignon, France, or during the year at Avignon-Public-Off, BP 5, 75521 Paris Cedex 11, France. The Grenoble Festival de Théâtre Européen in June and July incorporates world movement theatre (Compagnie Renata Scant, 8 Rue Pierre Duclot, 38000 Grenoble, France). The International Festival of Pantomime in Saarbrucken, Germany, held for the fifth time in September and October of 1995 and for the sixth time in October 1997, included a number of international European and Latin American solo mime artists (Büro Jomi, Postfach 3008, D 66791 Saarwellingen, Germany). De Beweeging in Antwerp is a biennial festival of Belgian dance and gestural theatre (Gasstraat 90, B 2060 Antwerpen, Belgium). The Brussels Festival de l'Humour, first organized in May and June 1991, presents national and international classical mime and traveling theatre (Rue Grates 3, B 1170 Bruxelles, Belgium). The Moving Parts Festival in Birmingham, England, held its fifth dance and movement theatre event February 15–March 30, 1996 (MAC Cannon Hill Park, Birmington B12 9QH, England). The International Workshop Festival, founded in 1988 and occurring for two months in London and other cities such as Glasgow, Edinburgh, Newcastle, Derry, and Nottingham each September and October, features theatre, mime, and puppetry for artists and teachers exploring experimental and avant-garde theatre (52 Tottenham Street, London W1P 9PG, England). The Brighton International Festival is held in April and May (Old Steine 54, Brighton BN1 1EQ, England). Visions 96 is the United Kingdom's biennial festival of animated theatre promoted by the University of Brighton (Methras House, Lewes Road, Brighton BN2 4AT, England and held in October and November 1996). The International Festival of Alternative Theatre in Kracców, Poland, also includes movement theatre (K. Lipski, UJ "Rotunda," Rue Oleandry 1, 30060 Kraków, Poland). Le Festival de Théâtre Masqué in Avrillé, France (presently extinct), presented artists working in masked performing arts each March (Allée G. Brassens,

F 49240 Avrillé, France). The Festival de Welkenraedt in Belgium, which has occurred each September since 1971, offers a varied program of dance, theatre, and mime (Rue Belle Vue 1, B 4840 Welkenraedt, Belgium). The Festival Dimitria in October and November in Greece is an international theatre, visual arts, and music festival that follows the world fair and international film festival (VO Municipality of Thessaloniki, Cultural Off Karbola 8, GR 54631 Thessaloniki, Greece). The biennial Festival Latinoamericano de Teatro Cordoba includes mime, puppetry, dance, theatre and children's and youth theatre (Chacabuco 1300, RA 5000 Cordoba, Argentina). The Freiburger International Theater Festival of theatre, dance, and mime has taken place from June to September since 1977 (Freiburger Theater Bertoldstrasse 46, D 79098 Freiburg, Germany). The Jenaer Pantomimetage International Movement Theatre Festival has occurred biennially in November since 1979 (Schillergasschen 1, D 07745 Jena, Germany). The Linzer Kleinkunst Festival, held each autumn since 1984, features cabaret and mime (Posthofstrasse 43, A 4020 Linz, Austria). The Inter Festival of Young Theatre, taking place annually in May since 1985, features experimental forms of theatre, dance, and mime (Horbaczewskiego 15/12, PL 54–130 Wroclaw, Poland). The fourth Festival of Mime in Viterbo, Italy, in 1996 included Marcel Marceau and Mummenschanz and was organized by Francesca Pietropaolo (Via Volturno 80, Fiori 252, 20047 Brugherio, Milano, Italy). The Vlaamse Mime Federatie held its first International Mime Festival in 1997 and continues to host one annually in October (Sergeyselsstraat 6, 21401 Borgerhout, Belgium). The International Festival of Deaf-Mutes hosted fifteen companies at its thirteenth festival in 1995 (Divaldo B. Polivka, Jakubské n. 8, Brno, Czech Republic).

Other festivals contain several performance genres. Mime, puppetry, and street theatre are performed at the Taff Art Festival in Malta, Poland, held every June and July since 1991 in the country's largest open-air theatre (27 Grudnia 3, PL 61–737 Poznan, Poland). The Euro-Scene-Leipzig Festival has presented mime, contemporary dance, and theatre each November since 1991 in several Leipzig theatres (Gottschedstrasse 16, D 04109 Leipzig, Germany). All genres comprise Belgium's Festival D'Art de Huy in August (Ave Delchambre 7, B 4500 Huy, Belgium). The International Comedy Arts Festival in Moers, Germany, which has occurred each July and August since 1976, fosters circus and *commedia* traditions (P.O. Box 10221, D 47412 Moers, Germany). The Rencontres Internationales de Théâtre Contemporain has been held each October since 1958 for both children and adults (Esplanade de l'Europe 2, B 4020 Liege, Belgium). The Ruhrfestspiele Recklinghausen, taking place annually from May to July since 1946, features a large variety of theatre forms (Otto-Burrmeisterallee 1, D 45657 Recklinghausen, Germany). Micro Macro is a national and international visual theatre festival occurring in July (Parco Ducale 1, 4311 Parma, Italy). Oriente Occidente invites dance and dance–theatre companies from Asia, Africa, Europe, and elsewhere to perform in September (Via Dante 63 CP 80, 38068 Rovereto, Italy). Italy's Amandola Festival on the Adriatic Sea has produced an International Theatre festival since 1984 with mime, clown, and circus elements [Brigitte Christensen and Marco Di Stefano, Via G. Marconi, 63021 Amandola (AP), Italy]. The Festival Internacional de Teatro, hosted by Granada University, features avant-garde international theatre and dance in May and June (Oficios 14, E 18001 Granada, Spain). The annual, multiple arts, international Festival of Perth in Australia since 1953 has presented each February and March spectacular outdoor performances and innovative art (University of Western Australia, Nedlands 6009, Western Australia). The Divadelna Nitra Theatre Festival includes all theatre genres, along with children's and youth theatre (Svatoplukovo Nam. 4, SK 95053 Nitra, Slovakia. The Ukrainian company Gestes created a festival in May 1996 in Uzgorod). The International Meeting of Moving Theatre in Budapest has been organized biennially by Pal Regos since 1979 (Muegyertem RKP 3, H 1111 Budapest, Hungary). The Festival of Images in Arnhem, the Netherlands, consecrated mostly to gestural theatre, takes place at the Municipal Theatre in the Museum of Modern Art (Arnhemsestraatueg 358 6881 NK Velp, Postbus 82, NL 6800 AB Arnhem, The Netherlands). England's Beyond Words 1998 Festival of Mime, Physical, and Visual Theatre offered a seminar, movement theatre, and dance performances. The New Zealand International Festival of Arts, held biennially under the direction of Joseph Seelig, includes some international mime performances (P.O. Box 10–113, Wellington, New Zealand. The

Hong Kong Arts Festival has since 1973 offered from January to March dance, theatre, music theatre, mime, and children's and youth theatre (13/F Hong Kong Arts Centre, 2 Harbour Road, Wanchai, Hong Kong).

In the United States, a number of theatre companies, theatres, and theatre festivals organize events and festivals that feature or include the works of movement theatre artists. In the spring of 1992, the Pink Inc. company in New York began its biannual Visual Visceral Festival of physical theatre, corporeal movement, and dance theatre presentations (Pink Inc., 152 East 23rd Street, New York, NY 10010, tel. (212) 253–6666). The Dell'Arte Players in Blue Lake, California, periodically host performances and workshops by movement theatre artists. From June 18 to July 19, 1998, it held its eighth Mad River Festival of movement theatre, vaudeville, storytelling, *commedia*, and clown art performances by national and international artists, along with its annual summer workshops (Dell'Arte, P.O. Box 816, Blue Lake, CA 95525–0816. tel. (707) 668–5666). In March 1994, Touchstone Theatre and Lehigh University organized a Theatre of Creation Festival, with performances and workshops celebrating the work of Jacques Lecoq. (Touchstone Theatre, 321 East Fourth Street, Bethlehem, PA 18015, tel. (215) 867–1689). The Climate Theatre in San Francisco held its fifth Fantochio Festival in 1994, featuring international puppetry, robotic, and animation artists and some mime, and by 1997, had sponsored eight annual Solo Mio Festivals with mime and solo mime performers (285 Ninth Street, San Francisco, CA 94103, tel. (415) 626–6422). The International Theatre Festival of Chicago, which since 1986 has taken place biennially from May to July, has hosted foreign troupes performing visual and movement theatre (215 West Ohio Street, Chicago, IL 60610–4118, tel. (312) 664–3370). The Asolo Theatre Festival in Florida, held annually from October to June, also programs street theatre and mime shows (5555 North Tamiami Trail, Sarasota, FL 34243, tel. (941) 351–9010). The International Theatre Festival at the State University of New York each June and July hosts movement theatre companies (Attention: International Theatre Festival, State University of New York, Level 2, Room 27, Stony Brook, NY 11794–8276, tel. (516) 632–7235).

Most fringe festivals accept movement theatre performances, clown shows, and new-wave vaudevillians. Among these are the Chicago Fringe Festival in June (Organic Theatre, 3319 North Clark Street, Chicago, IL 60657, tel. (312) 327–8947); the San Francisco Fringe Festival in September (Exit Theatre, 156 Eddy Street, San Francisco, CA 94102, tel. (415) 031–1094); and the Minnesota Fringe Festival in January (P.O. Box 580648, Minneapolis, MN 55458–0648, tel. (612) 770–9746).

Many arts festivals in the United States incorporate mime into their programs. Among them, the annual Kennedy Center Open House Arts Festival includes mime, puppet, and street theatre (John F. Kennedy Center for the Performing Arts, Washington, DC 20565, tel. (202) 416–8033). The Celebrate Brooklyn Festival–Performing Arts in Brooklyn Park each summer hosts mime and puppet shows, along with music and dance performances (30 Flatbush Avenue, Suite 427, Brooklyn, NY 11217, tel. (718) 855–7882). The annual Cleveland Performance Art Festival also includes mime, puppet, and street theatre (1365 Webb Road, Cleveland, OH 44107, tel. (216) 221–6017). The California State University–Long Beach Summer Arts Festival, held annually in July, presents mime and puppetry, along with music, theatre, and modern dance performances (California State University Chancellor's Office, 400 Golden Shore, Suite 108, Long Beach, CA 90802, tel. (310) 985–2064). In September of each year, the Arts Festival of Atlanta hosts performances of all art forms, including mime and street theatre (140 First Union Plaza, 999 Peachtree Street Northeast, Atlanta, GA 30309–3964, tel. (404) 885–1125). The Firefly Festival for the Performing Arts, which takes place from June to August, has puppet and mime shows (202 South Michigan, Suite 845, South Bend, IN 46601–2012, tel. (219) 288–3472). Artscape–Baltimore's Festival of the Arts, Inc., held anually in July, includes mime and street theatre in its programs (21 South Eutaw Street, Baltimore, MD 21201, tel. (410) 396–4575).

Most children's festivals contain mime, as well as clowning, puppetry, dance, music theatre, and magic. Among the children's festivals that include mime, dance, puppetry, and music theatre is the Vetrina Europa, which has taken place annually in June since 1992 [Teatro Della Briciole, Parco Ducale 1, I 43100 Parma (PR), Italy]. The Bruxelles Babel 2000 is a multidisciplinary festival by and for youngsters between twelve and twenty (166 Avenue Louise, B 1050 Bruxelles, Belgium). Since 1982, Noël au Théâtre offers annual dance, mime, and theatre performances for young audiences (Avenue de la Couronne 321, B 1050 Ixelles, Belgium). The annual Idéklic International Children's Festival, which began in 1989, has five days of workshops for children and dance, mime, theatre, and storytelling performances for the whole family (Christian Piron, and Office du Tourisme, 39260 Moirans-en-Montagne, France). Leading mime, clowning, dance, and puppetry companies and artists are hosted by the Vancouver International Children's Festival, which takes place from the end of May to June (302–601 Cambie Street, BC, Vancouver, Canada V6 2P1, tel. (604) 280–4445); the Calgary International Children's Festival in May (Calgary Center for the Performing Arts, 205 Eighth Ave. SE, Calgary, AB, Canada T2G OK9, tel. (403) 298–8888); and the Seattle International Children's Festival, which has taken place annually in May since 1984 (305 Harrison Street, Seattle, WA 98109–4645, tel. (206) 684–7338). The International Children's Theatre Festival in Pennsylvania features mime, puppetry, folk music, and dance (P.O. Box 486, Wilkes-Barre, PA 18703, tel. (717) 823–4599). The Pittsburgh Children's Festival in May includes mime, along with theatre, puppetry, street theatre, and music (134 Allegheny Center Mall, Pittsburgh, PA 15212–5334, tel. (412) 321–5520). The Philadelphia International Festival for Children each May hosts mime companies from around the world (Attention: Annenberg Center, University of Pennsylvania, 1 College Hall, Philadelphia, PA 19104–6376, tel. (215) 898–6791).

The International School of Theatre Anthropology, under the direction of Eugenio Barba, held its tenth international session in Copenhagen in May 1996, which consisted of a symposium on theatre and dance with demonstrations and performances by actors and dancers from different genres and traditions (Box 1283, DK 7500 Holstebro, Denmark).

Information on mime encounters and festivals organized by mime artist and teacher Sigfrido Aguilar from 1978 on in Guanajuato, Mexico, can be found in a bilingual journal entitled *Revista de Los Encuentros Nationales y Festivales Internacionales de Pantomima* (*En y Fip*), founded in 1994 under the direction of J. L. Rodriguez Avalos and Sigfrido Aguilar. The journal also contains current mime developments in Mexico, national and international mime news, and essays on the art of mime. For information about the journal, mime artists, mime schools, and mime festivals in Mexico, write to: Ap Postal 359, CP 58000 Morelia, Michoacán, Mexico.

Cuba's Theatre National de Pantomime organized a mime festival in July 1993.

Addresses of other European mime festivals and symposiums can be obtained from the Theater Instituut Nederland, P.O. Box 19304, NL 1000 GH Amsterdam, The Netherlands; the European Network of Information Centers, VTI, Anspachlaan 141–143, 1000 Bruxelles, Belgium; the Mime Action Group, at The Circus Space, Coronet Street, London N1 6NU, England, and the International Festivals and Events Association Europe, c/o Stockholm Water Festival, Tullvaktsvagen 11, Stockholm S–115 76, Sweden. A number of festivals have been announced in *Gestes*, published by the Centre Culturel de la Visitation, 24000 Périgueux, France.

Information on all United States arts festivals, some of which include mime and have been listed above, can be obtained from the International Theatre Institute of the United States, 47 Great Jones Street, New York, NY 10012, tel. (212) 254–4141. Some mime festival listings can be obtained at the Margolis Brown Movement Theatre Center, 616 East 15th Street, Minneapolis, MN 55404, tel. (612) 339–4709. A comprehensive listing of U.S. festivals can be found in the 1996 edition of the *Music, Opera, Dance and Drama in Asia, the Pacific and North America* (*MOD*) directory, and a listing of festivals worldwide can be found in the 1996 edition of the *Performing Arts Yearbook for Europe* (*PAYE*). Both are published by Arts Publishing International Ltd., 4 Assam Street, London E1 7QS, England.

Appendix C

Filmography

UNESCO (Place de Fontenoy, Paris 7, France) has published a catalogue entitled *Films on the Theatre and Art of Mime* (1965), edited by André Veinstein, that contains titles of mime, pantomime, commedia dell'arte, Oriental theatre, and dance films, with information on each film's subject matter, artist, date, size, length, and distributor. Some of the following films are listed in the UNESCO catalogue.

The information available about the film titles that have been selected for this filmography did not always provide the date, length, or whether the film is in black and white (b & w) or in color. This information may in some cases be obtained by writing to the addresses provided with the film titles. Also, if the releasing company's or distributor's name was not accessible, that of the producer, when given, could help locate the film or video. Owing to changes in distributors, it has been difficult to keep this list accurate and up-to-date. Some films that are no longer available have been listed for research purposes.

The author would like to acknowledge the contributions to this filmography of the centers, libraries, organizations, and companies in the United States and abroad, the names and addresses of which are mentioned in the following film and video listings. The key for film formats is ½ and ¼ = inches; U = U-matic cassette.

Decroux Films

The following are titles of films that Etienne De-croux made. Although inquiries about the mimodramas created and performed by Decroux and his students have been made at the Ecole Etienne Decroux, they may no longer be obtainable at that address. Other sources for a limited number of films and video reconstructions of his works are listed.

L'Abecedaire Corporel. circa 1968–69. b & w, 16 mm. Ecole Etienne Decroux, 85 Avenue Edouard Vaillant, 92100 Boulogne-Billancourt, Seine, France.

Les Arbres. 1960. b & w, 9 min., 16 mm. See address above; also, and Centre National de la Cinématographie, 7 bis Rue Alexandre Turpault, 78395 Bois d'Arcy, Cedex, France.

La Boite à Violin. 1962. b & w, 6 min., 16 mm. See Decroux address.

Combat. 1962. b & w, 5 min., 16 mm. See Decroux address.

La Conférence. 1962. b & w, 6½ min., 16 mm. See Decroux address.

Le Duo Amoureux. Jean Asselin and Denise Boulanger in Decroux's creation at the Winnipeg Mime Festival. 1983. color, 10 min., VHS. Giuseppe Condello, 103–1070 Kings Road, Victoria, BC, Canada V8T 1X1.

Le Duo Amoureux I. (Matin). 1960. b & w, 6 min., 16 mm. See Decroux address.

Le Duo Amoureux II. 1962. b & w, 6 min., 16 mm. See Decroux address.

Le Duo Amoureux III. 1960. b & w, 5 min., 16 mm. See Decroux address.

L'Esprit Malin. 1962. b & w, 5 min., 16 mm. See Decroux address and Centre National de la

Cinématographie address.

Le Passage des Hommes sur la Terre. 1962. b & w, 16 min., 16 mm. See Decroux address.

Les Petits Soldats. b & w, 35 min., 16 mm. See Decroux address.

Protectorat. 1962. b & w, 3 min., 16 mm. See Decroux address.

Le Salut Final. 1962. b & w, 3 min., 16 mm. See Decroux address.

Scènes du Parc. 1962. b & w, 4 min., 16 mm. See Decroux address.

La Statue à Bougé. 1962. b & w, 6 min., 16 mm. See Decroux address and Centre National de la Cinématographie address.

Table d'Hote. 1962. b & w, 5 min., 16 mm. See Decroux address.

L'Usine. 1962. b & w, 3 min., 16 mm. See Decroux address.

The Mime of Etienne Decroux. Decroux demonstration of basic techniques of Decroux mime. 1957. b & w, 30 min., 16 mm. Theatre Department, Baylor University, Waco, TX 76798–7056.

The Mime of Etienne Decroux. Decroux and his students in *Duo Amoureux, L'Usine, L'Espirit Malin,* and *Les Arbres.* Also Decroux demonstrating mime. 1957. b & w, 50 min., VHS. Annette Lust, 1274 Filbert Street, San Francisco, CA 94109.

The Theatre of Etienne Decroux. Etienne Decroux and his students in *Les Arbres, L'Usine, L'Esprit Malin,* and *La Statue.* 1961. b & w, 23 min., 16 mm. Radim Films.

The Washing and *The Carpenter.* Decroux pieces directed by Decroux and performed by Thomas Leabhart. 1971. b & w, 14 min., VHS. Thomas Leabhart, Department of Theatre, Pomona College, 300 East Bonita Avenue, Claremont, CA 91711–4307.

A video reconstruction by the Théâtre de l'Ange Fou in color (1992) of Decroux's *La Méditation, L'Usine, Le Combat Antique, Duo Amoureux II, Le Menuisier, La Femme Oiseau, L'Esprit Malin, La Lavandière, Duo Amoureux dans le Parc St. Cloud, Le Fauteuil de l'Absent, Le Prophète,* and *Les Arbres* can be purchased from Michael Pedretti (formerly at Movement Theatre International, 3700 Chestnut Street, Philadelphia, PA 19104) or from Ecole de Mime Corporel Dramatique, Théâtre de l'Ange Fou, Islington Arts Factory, 2 Parkhurst Road, London N7 0SF, England.

The Film Study Center of the Museum of Modern Art (11 West 53rd Street, New York, NY 10019, tel. 212–708–9480), has the following films with Etienne Decroux, which can be seen at the center upon request.

Children of Paradise. Featuring Jean-Louis Barrault in the role of Gaspard Deburau and Decroux as his father. 1945. b & w, 189 min., 16 mm.

The Raven. 1943. b & w, 90 min., 35 mm.

Marcel Marceau Pantomimes

Gros Plan: Marcel Marceau. Marceau defines mime and interprets *Bip Chases the Butterfly; Youth, Maturity, Old Age, Death;* and *The Mask Maker.* 1962. b & w, 45 min., 16 mm. L'INA-Archives Audiovisuelles, 4 Avenue de L'Europe, 94366 Bry sur Marne, Cedex, France.

Day at Night. Cassette no. 2, pt. 2. Interview with Marceau on his art. 1974. color, 28 min., ¾ U. New York Public Library for the Performing Arts, Dance Collection, 40 Lincoln Center Plaza, New York, NY 10023–7498.

A Fable. Marceau and a cast representing ten countries, about a hero who builds a wall around his paradise, which becomes his prison. 1973. color, 17 min., 16 mm. University Film and Video, University of Minnesota, 1313 Fifth Street Southeast, Suite 108, Minneapolis, MN 55414–1524. In video format at Guidance Associates, P.O. Box 1000, Mount Kisco, NY 10549–0010.

The Hands. Marceau's hands portray the struggle of good and evil. 1975. color, 7 min., 16 mm. See University of Minnesota address; also, Britannica Films, 310 South Michigan, Chicago, IL 60604.

Un Jardin Public. Marceau plays characters in a public garden. 1955. b & w, 17 min., 16 mm. See New York Public Library for the Performing Arts address.

Marcel Marceau, or The Art of Mime. In French and English. 1961. b & w, 17 min, 16 mm, ½ VHS. Facsea, 972 Fifth Avenue, New York, NY 10021.

Marcel Marceau. Performance by Marceau and Terry Goldmann of *First Class,* depicting characters on an ocean liner. 1984. color, 30 min., ½ VHS. See New York Public Library for the Performing Arts address.

Marcel Marceau. Lecture–Demonstration by Marceau on mime. 1970 to 1975. color, 120 min.,

¼ U. See New York Public Library for the Performing Arts address.

Meet Marcel Marceau. Marceau skits and Bip pantomimes. 1965 and circa 1981. b & w, 52 min., ½ Beta. See New York Public Library for the Performing Arts.

Le Mime Marcel Marceau. In English. Marceau plays Bip and other pantomimes. color, 30 min., ½ VHS. See Facsea address.

The Mime of Marcel Marceau. Documentary of Marceau at work on stage and behind the scenes. 1972. color, 23 min., 16 mm. Budget Films, 4590 Santa Monica Boulevard, Los Angeles, CA 90029.

Pantomimes. Marceau's Bip and Style Pantomimes. 1954. color, 20 min., 16 mm and 35 mm. Centre National de la Cinématographie, Archives du Film, 7 bis Rue Alexandre Turpault, 78395 Bois d'Arcy, Cedex, France. Also 16 mm. or ½ VHS. See Facsea address.

Pantomimes. Marceau in some of his most famous routines. circa the 1960s. color, 10 min., 16 mm. See Budget Films address.

Les Sept Pechés Capitaux. Marceau performing the seven deadly sins. 1980. color, 41 min., ½ Beta. See New York Public Library for the Performing Arts address.

Vibrations. Marceau speaks about mime. Sketches on and photos of history and technique of mime. Excerpts from Peking Opera. 1972 and 1957. color, 60 min., ¼ U. See New York Public Library for the Performing Arts address.

The following Marceau films—16 mm, in color, and made in 1975—can be obtained at Indiana University, Center for Media and Teaching Resources, Bloomington, IN 47405–5901.

Bip as a Skater. 8 min.
Bip as a Soldier. 18 min.
Bip at a Society Party. 14 min.
Bip Hunts Butterflies. 10 min.
The Cage. 9 min.
The Creation of the World. 11 min.
The Dream. 9 min.
The Mask Maker. 9 min.
The Painter. 8 min.
Pantomime: The Language of the Heart. 9 min.
Sideshow. 8 min.
Youth, Maturity, Old Age, Death. 7 min.

Mime, Pantomime, and Acting

Films, Filmstrips, and Videos

Any Empty Space. Creation of a student mime company organized by Bud Beyer at Northwestern University. 1980. b & w, 35 min. Northwestern University Theatre Department, P.O. Box 3060, 1801 Hinman Ave. Evanston, IL 60604.

Angna Enters: Drawn from Life. Enters in three funny skits. 1959. b & w, 28 min., VHS and other formats. Creative Arts TV Archive, P.O. Box 739, Kent, CT 06757.

The Art of Mime. Dr. E. Reid Gilbert explains and demonstrates illusion pantomime, corporeal mime, and mime with masks. 1991. color, 30 min., VHS. Contemporary Drama Service, P. O. Box 7710–U, Colorado Springs, CO 80933.

Baggage. Mamako Yoneyama in an allegory on the burden of conscience. 1969. b & w, 22 min., 16 mm. University Film and Video, University of Minnesota, 1313 Fifth Street Southeast, Suite 108, Minneapolis, MN 55414–1524.

Jean-Louis Barrault and Madeleine Renaud. Barrault and Renaud recite poetry in French and perform a scene from Molière's *Le Misanthrope*. Barrault performs his circus horse pantomime and discusses theatre today. 1969. color, 28 min., VHS and other formats. See Creative Arts TV Archive address.

Baxter Earns His Wings. Slapstick humor by the Mimes Electriques about Baxter, who leaves his farm for the big city. 1981. color, 15 min., 16 mm and 35 mm, VHS. National Film Board of Canada, 1251 Avenue of the Americas, 16th Floor, New York, NY 10020–1173.

Benny and Joon. A romantic comedy about an eccentric clown and a young woman. 1993. color, 98 min., VHS. Obtainable in video stores.

Bewegung, Sprache von Körpern (Le Mouvement, Langage du Corps). Film by Günter Hess on rhythmic dance and pantomime. 1959. b & w, 13 min., 16 mm and 35 mm. Deutsches Institut für Filmkunde, Kreuzberger Ring 56, D 65205 Wiesbaden, Germany.

Bitter Bliss. A corporeal mime–based piece by Pontine Movement Theatre that conveys the love–hate relationship of a couple. 1993. color, 60 min., ¾ VHS, Super-Beta, PAL, or SEACAM. Pontine, P.O. Box 1437, Portsmouth, NH 03802.

Bounds/Le Cadre. A Chaplinesque mime moves through the routine of his workday. 1984. color, 7 min., 31 mm, 16 mm, 35 mm, and VHS. See National Film Board of Canada address.

The Box. A condensed odyssey of twentieth-century life performed in mime with music. 1979. color, 16 min., 16 mm and VHS. Mass Media Ministries, 2116 North Charles Street, Baltimore, MD 21218.

Children of Paradise. The life of the nineteenth-century mime Gaspard Deburau, played by Jean-Louis Barrault. 1945. b & w, 100 min., VHS. Films Inc., 5547 North Ravenswood Avenue, Chicago, IL 60640.

The Christmas Tree. Julian Chagrin mimes a fir tree that is cut, purchased, and decorated as a Christmas tree. 1975. color, 12 min., 16 mm and VHS. Pyramid Films, P.O. Box 1048, Santa Monica, CA 90406.

Cirque du Soleil: We Reinvent the Circus. The renowned Quebec circus of human performances without animals. 1989. color, 55 min., VHS. Les Productions Telemagik, Canadian Film Distribution Center, SUNY Plattsburgh, Plattsburgh, NY 12901.

Cirque du Soleil: Nouvelle Experience. Acrobats, contortionists, jugglers, and clowns in a modern circus show. 1992. color, 73 min., VHS. Les Productions Telemagik. See Canadian Film Distribution address.

A Clown Is Born. Clown ministry. mid-1970s. color, 15 min., 16 mm. and VHS. See Mass Media Ministries address.

Clown White. A drama about a deaf boy who is introduced to the magic of mime. 1980. color, 51 min., 16 mm. Coronet Instructional Media, Ltd., 1870 Birchmount Road, Scarborough, ON, Canada M1P 2J7.

The Clown Within: Jacques Lecoq. Documentary on Lecoq's workshops and lecture–performances and an interview with Lecoq. 1977. 26 min. Ron Bozman–Billy Colville (address unknown).

Come Dance With Me. Documentary on eighty-eight-year-old dancer–movement therapist Trudi Schoop's work with psychiatric patients in Switzerland. English subtitles. 1992. color, 66 min., VHS. University of California Extension for Media and Independent Learning, 2000 Center Street, Fourth Floor, Berkeley, CA 94704.

The Concert. Julian Chagrin mimes a London musician who turns a street crossing into a giant piano keyboard in a comical mime fantasy. 1976. color, 12 min., 16 mm and VHS. See Pyramid Films address.

The Conquest of Emptiness. Interviews with dancer Trudi Schoop and documentaries on her dancing and dance therapy. In German and English. 1993. color, 45 min., VHS. See University of California Extension for Media and Independent Learning address.

The Construction and Use of the Personal Neutral Mask. Documentary on the construction of the mask by Louis H. Campbell. 1976–81. 45 min., VHS. Fine Arts Division, Paris Junior College, Paris, TX 75460.

Edward Gordon Craig. Art of the comedian, scenography, stage direction, and architecture. 1963. b & w, 20 min., 16 mm. Bibliothèque de l'Arsenal, 1 Rue de Sully, 75004 Paris, France.

The Dance. Dance history and different forms of dance. Mime section with Marcel Marceau. 1960. b & w, 74 min., VHS or Beta. Cinema Guild, 1697 Broadway, Suite 506, New York, NY 10019.

Dance Masks: The World of Margaret Severn. The mask dances of the international dancer, portraying a character or emotion. 1983. color, 33 min., VHS ¾ U. See University of California Extension Center for Media and Independent Learning address.

Dance Therapy: The Power of Movement. Actor Christopher Reeve narrates an exploration of dance and movement therapy. 1983. color, 30 min., VHS ¾ U. See University of California Center for Media and Independent Learning address.

A Dog and His Boy. Silent film about how a boy creates heroes with a dog. 1993. color, 16 min., VHS. See Pyramid Films address.

Eagle, Tiger, Fly. Juki Arkin performs to semi-electronic music, with poetry recitation between scenes. 1959. b & w, 28 min., VHS and other formats. See Creative Arts TV Archive address.

Ersatz Erratum. Members of the Celebration Mime Ensemble. 1979? color, 10 min., 16 mm. Films by Huey, 103 Montrose Avenue, Portland, ME 04103.

Etoiles de Demain. Drama courses by Charles Dullin, René Simon, Jean-Paul Sartre, and Jean-Louis Barrault, with stars who became famous. 1942. b & w, 31 min., 16 mm. Centre National de la Cinématographie, Archives du Film, 7 bis Rue Alexandre Turpault, 78395 Bois d'Arcy, Cedex, France.

Exeunt. Celebration Mime Ensemble and Tony Montanaro performing in several pieces. 1977. color, 28 min., 16 mm. Mica, Box 201, Belgrade Lakes, ME 04918.

Football. Pantomime by Gilles Segal performed at the Théâtre de France. 1962. color, 10 min., 16 mm. Jean-Jacques Languepin, 1 Rue de Pontoise, Paris 5, Cinecim, France. Also see Centre National de la Cinématographie address.

From Fish to Fools. Shai K. Ophir performs seven mimes, four with Karla Most. 1960. b & w, 28 min., VHS and other formats. See Creative Arts TV Archive address.

Gifts to Share. Clown ministry and pantomime skits of Christian giving. 1988. color, 22 min., VHS. Ecu Film, 810 Twelfth Avenue South, Nashville, TN 37203.

Gordon Craig à Quatre-Vingt-Ans. Art of the comedian, marionettes, scenography, and stage direction. 1962. b & w, 7 min., 16 mm. ORTF, Avenue du Président Kennedy, Paris 16, France.

The Human Face: Emotions, Identities, and Masks. The face as a channel for nonverbal communication. 1995. color, 38 min., VHS. See University of California Extension Center for Media and Independent Learning address.

The Human Language Evolves with and without Words. Explores gestures and facial expressions that form human language. 1995. color, 55 min., VHS. See University of Minnesota address.

I'm Wonderful. O. J. Anderson shows ways to build self-esteem through pantomime and dance. A film for young children. 1988. color, 30 min., VHS. Hart Studios, WGTE-TV Home Video, 804 Phoenix Drive, Ann Arbor, MI 48108.

An Introduction to Mime. Dr. E. Reid Gilbert explains the basics of mime and its relation to the performing arts. 1979. color, 13 min., 106-frame filmstrip with cassette soundtrack and script. See Contemporary Drama Service address.

Jan's Pantomime. Swiss mime Jan Kessler in *The Last Day of Our Scissors Grinder* and *The Mosquito.* 1965. b & w, 28 min., VHS and other formats. See Creative Arts TV Archive address.

Jesus Stories. Three videotapes entitled *Jesus Teaches, Jesus Cares,* and *Jesus Heals.* Mime and Mask Ministry with Doug Berky. 1993. color, 47 min., VHS. See Ecu Film address.

The Last Butterfly. Holocaust theme in a ghetto city of former Czechoslovakia, in which a mime performs *Hansel and Gretel* to symbolize Nazi treatment. 1992. color, 106 min., VHS. New Line Home Video, 116 North Robertson Boulevard, Los Angeles, CA 90048.

Light in the Darkness. Mime Ministry with Doug Berky in the Easter story. 1994. color, 15 min., VHS. See Ecu Film address.

The Listener. A story in mime that teaches the importance of listening to music. 1987. color, 29 min., VHS and Beta. SIRS Mandarin, Inc., P.O. Box 2348, Boca Raton, FL 33427–2348.

Bob Stromberg, Live on Purpose. Storyteller and mime Bob Stromberg. 1982. color, 41 min., VHS. Covenant Video, 3200 Foster Avenue, Chicago, IL 60625.

Le Marionettiste. Pantomime by Gilles Segal with Sabine Lods. 1962. color, 10 min., 16 mm. See Jean-Jacques Languepin address.

The Mark of the Clown. Clown ministry. mid-1970s. color, 15 min., 16 mm and VHS. See Mass Media Ministries address.

Martha Clarke: Light and Dark. The creation of four theatrical dance pieces. 1981. color, 54 min., 16 mm and VHS. Phoenix BFA Films and Video, 2349 Chaffee Drive, St. Louis, MO 63146.

The Mastery of Mimodrame. An in-depth study of mime technique with Todd and Marilyn Farley. 1993. color, 55 min., VHS. See Contemporary Drama Service address.

The Mechanisms and Techniques of Mime. Dr. E. Reid Gilbert demonstrates and explains the basics for mimes and actors. 1980. color, 15 min., 129-frame filmstrip with cassette soundtrack. Out of print. See Contemporary Drama Service address for more information.

Mime. Educational film on the use of mime. 1987. 13 min., VHS. See Access Network Program Services address.

The Mime. Mime artist Tony Montanaro's views on mime training and a preparation for mime performance. 1966. b & w, 29 min. *Sketches* includes four vignettes performed by Tony Montanaro. 16 min. *Illusions* has eight vignettes performed by Tony Montanaro. 15 min., 16 mm. Audio-Visual Services, Pennsylvania State University, Special Services Building, University Park, PA 16802.

Mime over Matter. Exploring ideas with mime Ladislav Fialka. 1970. color, 15 min., 16 mm. RMI Media Productions, 1365 North Winchester, Olathe, KS 66061.

Mime Spoken Here. Tony Montanaro's instructional video book on the art and skill of mime. Vol. 1, 1991. color, 120 min. Vol. 2, 1992. color, 109 min. Tony Montanaro Mime Spoken Here, P.O. Box 1054, Portland, ME 04104.

Mime Technique: Part I. An ape becomes a man and uses mime to communicate with mime Paul Gaulin. 1977, color. 27 min., VHS ¾ U and 16 mm. Phoenix/BFA Films and Video, 2349

Chaffee Drive,. St. Louis, MO 63146.

The Morning Spider. Julian Chagrin and his troupe create a vividly colored fantasy about a spider and his insect friends. 1976. color, 22 min., 16 mm. and VHS. See Pyramid Films address.

Movement and Gesture: Action for Illusion. The contribution of mime and gesture to theatre. 1955. b & w, 29 min., 16 mm. Indiana University, Center For Media and Teaching Resources, Bloomington, IN 47405–5901.

Mr. Bean: The Amazing Adventures of Mr. Bean. Rowan Atkinson in seven short segments of silent comedy. 1989. color, 61 min., video cassette. Polygram Video, 825 Eighth Avenue, New York, NY 10019.

Mr. Bean: Merry Mishaps of Mr. Bean. Rowan Atkinson as Mr. Bean visiting a hotel during the holidays. 1998. color, 52 min., video cassette. See Polygram Video address.

The Pantomime Dame. A favorite female impersonator in a British holiday celebration. 1984. color, 50 min., VHS. A.G.C. Educational Media, 1560 Sherman Avenue, Suite 100, Evanston, IL 60201.

Pas un Mot. Guy Glover performs a bank robbery dramatically, comically, and in pantomime. 1957. b & w, 29½ min., 16 mm. See National Film Board of Canada address.

The Parable. A mime in a circus sideshow enacts an allegory of Christ. 1965. color, 22 min., 16 mm. and VHS. See Ecu Film address.

Pierrot in Montreal. Guy Hoffman plays Pierrot losing his love Colombine to Harlequin. 1957. b & w, 30 min., 16 mm. See Film Board of Canada address.

Positive Motion. Award-winning documentary on movement therapy in workshops led by Anna Halprin. 1992. color, 37 min., VHS ¾ U. See University of California Extension Center for Media and Independent Learning address.

Saltimbanco. Third in the series of the Cirque du Soleil's performance videos featuring comedians, clowns, acrobats, and music. 1994. color, 78 min., VHS. Les Productions Telemagik. See Canadian Film Distribution address.

The Shape of Time. Performance by Elisabeth Burke and Pierre Thibeaudeau, based on Decroux mime. 1980. color, 50 min., PAL and ¼ U. New York Public Library for the Performing Arts, Dance Collection, 40 Lincoln Center Plaza, New York, NY 10023–7498.

Silent Lotus. A deaf girl communicates through dance. 1993. color, 30 min., VHS. Great Plains National, P.O. Box 80669, Lincoln, NE 68501–0669.

Silent Movie. Tribute to old, silent movies. Marcel Marceau, Sid Caesar, and others. 1976. color, 88 min., VHS, Beta, and LV. CBS Fox, 1330 Avenue of the Americas, Fifth Floor, New York, NY 10019. Also available at video stores.

The Silent Outcry: The Life and Times of Samuel Avital. The spiritual and physical journey of Avital and three of his pantomimes: *The Insect, Pierrot Visits New York,* and *Black and White.* 1992. color, 55 min., VHS. Le Centre du Silence, P.O. Box 1015 (TSO), Boulder, CO 80302–1015.

The Steadfast Tin Soldier. Robert Shields and Lorene Yarnell mime. 1955. color, 60 min., VHS. Video Treasures, 500 Kirts Boulevard, Troy, MI 48084.

Step by Step. Canadian mime artist Paul Gaulin and his group in mime routines. 1977. color, 14 min., 16 mm. Canadian Filmmakers Distribution Centre, 67A Portland Street, Toronto, ON, Canada M5V 2M9.

The Streetwalker and the Gentleman (K. F. Cohen). Erotic mime portrays both title roles. 1975. color, 6 min., 16 mm. Kit Parker Films, 1245 Tenth Street, Monterey, CA 93940–3692.

That's Life. Clown ministry. mid-1970s. color, 16 mm and VHS. See Mass Media Ministries address.

Tony Silent Spots. Series of pieces with Tony Montanaro. 1978. color, 15 min., 16 mm. See Films by Huey address.

Videocrafts for Kids: Will You Be Mine? A how-to film about face painting, pantomime, and acting for ages three to eight. 1991. color, 30 min., VHS. Krafty Kids, Inc., 11358 Aurora Avenue, Des Moines, IA 50322.

A World of Gestures. Gestures from many cultures and their meaning, function, origin, and significance. 1991. color, 28 min., 16 mm and VHS. See University of California Extension Center for Media and Independent Learning address.

Yass Hakoshima: Art of the Mime. Hakoshima performs several pieces and gives a mime demonstration on the influence of Japanese culture on his mime style. 1971. color, 28 min., VHS and other formats. See Creative Arts TV Archive address.

Yass Hakoshima: Aspects of Pantomime. Includes segments of Hakoshima's *Labyrinth* and *Eagle,* utilizing Noh and Kabuki traditions. 1966. b & w, 28 min., VHS and other formats. See Creative Arts TV Archive address.

The Yoshi Show. Yoshi performs with actors from Peter Brook's experimental theatre company, Iranian and African villagers, and students from the National School of the Deaf. 1974. color, 28 min., VHS and other formats. See Creative Arts TV Archive address.

Commedia dell'Arte Films

And a Time to Dance. Commedia and the Perry Mansfield School. 1954. color, 13 min., 16 mm. Portia Mansfield Motion Pictures, P.O. Box 61, La Porte, CO 80535.

Arlequin à la Guerre. Commedia dell'arte. Theatre Foscari of Venice. 1962. color, 13 min., 16 mm. and 35 mm. Compagnie Française du Film, 5 Boulevard Poissonière, Paris 2, France.

Arlequin, Messager de l'Amour. Commedia, mime, and masks. 1962. color, 13 min., 16 mm. and 35 mm. See Compagnie Française du Film address.

La Comédie Populaire avant Molière. Commedia, Molière scenes, and the *Pédant Joué* by Cyrano de Bergerac. 1946. b & w, 19 min., 16 mm. and 35 mm. I.N.A., 4 Avenue de l'Europe, 94366 Bry sur Marne, France, and Centre National de la Cinématographie, Archives du Film, 7 bis Rue Alexandre Turpault, 78395 Bois d'Arcy, Cedex, France.

Commedia dell'Arte. color, 15 min., 16 mm. Michigan State University. Instructional. Media Center, East Lansing, MI 48826–0710.

La Dent d'Arlequin. Commedia and mime by the Theatre Foscari of Venice. 1962. color, 13 min., 16 mm. and 35 mm. See Compagnie Française du Film address and Centre National de la Cinématographie address.

Harlekin Commedia and masks. 1957. b & w, 12 min., 35 mm. Kulturfilm Institut, GmbH, Berlin, Germany (current address unknown).

Harlequin. Story of an anonymous Casanova. 1930–31. b & w, 16 min., 24 mm. Cecile Starr, 50 West 96th Street, New York, NY 10025.

Intermezzo alla Scala Il Museo Theatrale. Galleries of famous La Scala actors. Latin comedy, masks, and *commedia.* color, 14 min., 35 mm. Distributed by M. Nascimbene.

The Mask of Comedy: The Story of Commedia dell'Arte. 1960. color, 17 min., 16 mm. Film and Video Section, University of Michigan, 400 Fourth Street, Ann Arbor, MI 48103–4816.

Molière aux Sources. Commedia dell'arte and French theatre. 1959. b & w, 40 min., 16 mm. Institut Pédagogique Nationale, 25 Rue d'Ulm, 75005 Paris, France.

Odin Teatret Videos

The following are examples of some of the videotapes about or relevant to the pedagogy and performances of Eugenio Barba. They can be purchased in VHS or PAL form at the Odin Teatret, Box 1283, DK 7500 Holstebro, Denmark. A list of other titles may be obtained from the same address.

Abstract Mime. In this section of the film *Corporal Mime,* Yves Lebreton develops Decroux's corporeal mime into abstract mime. 1971. color, 20 min. Produced by Odin Teatret Film.

Ascent to the Sea. The use of urban environment as a theatrical space. 1982. color. 36 min. Produced by Odin Teatret Film.

The Castle of Holstebro. Performance based on scenes created from Shakespeare's *Hamlet.* In English. 1994. color, 55 min. Co-produced by Peter Sykes and Odin Teatret Film.

Corporal Mime 1 and 2. Yves Lebreton demonstrates Decroux's training and performs short, abstract mime pieces. In English. 1971. color, 90 min. Produced by Odin Teatret Film.

The Dead Brother. A demonstration of the stages of a creation at the Odin Teatret. 1993. color, 68 min. Video produced by Claudio Coloberti for Odin Teatret.

Dressed in White. A film symbolizing the solitude of the actor's journey. 1974 to 1976. b & w, 45 min. Produced by Odin Teatret Film.

The Million. Performance of Odin Teatret's meetings with other landscapes and cities throughout the world. 1979. color, 60 min. Produced by Odin Teatret Film.

Physical Training at Odin Teatret. Odin Teatret's physical training program, from collectively learned skills to the personalization of exercises. 1972. color, 50 min. Produced by Odin Teatret.

In Search of Theatre. Bartered performances between Odin Teatret and the villagers of the Carpignano area in southern Italy. 1974. color, 60 min. Produced by director L. Ripa di Meana.

Theatre Meets Ritual. Fragments from the *Book of Dances* and *Come! And The Day Will Be Ours* by Odin Teatret, along with barters in

Venezuela with the Yanomami and their tribal dances. 1976. color, 25 min. Produced by Kurare Film Company.

Traces in the Snow. The technique of the actress is the protagonist as she reveals the secrets of building a character and creating a performance. 1994. color, 99 min. Co-produced by Document Films, Athens, and Odin Teatret Film.

Films on Oriental Theatre and Dance and Aboriginal Dance

The Butterfly Dream. Mr. and Mrs. Hu from Hong Kong in a classical Chinese play translated by A. C. Scott. Mr. Hu mimes and dances the Monkey King. 1961. b & w, 28 min., VHS and other formats. Creative Arts TV Archive, P.O. Box 739, Kent, CT 06757.

Circles-Cycles Kathak Dance. The classical dance of northern India, demonstrated by native performers. 1989. color, 28 min., 16 mm. and VHS. University of California Extension for Media and Independent Learning, 2000 Center Street, Fourth Floor, Berkeley, CA 94704.

Dance of the Buffalo Hunt. Australian aboriginal corroboree dance enacting the hunt and killing of a buffalo. 1963. b & w, 5 min. Australian Information Service, 632 Fifth Avenue, New York, NY 10020.

Destroying the Giant Serpent. Japanese pantomime. 1972. color, 21 min., 16 mm. Indiana University Instructional Support Services, Franklin Hall 0009, 601 East Kirkwood Avenue, Bloomington, IN 47405–1223.

Edo Dance and Pantomime. Dance from the Tokyo of the Tokugawa period in Japan (1600–1867). 1972. color, 50 min., 16 mm. Museum at Large, 20 West 22nd Street, New York, NY 10010.

Excerpts from Chinese Opera. color, 15 min. Chinese Information Service, Republic of China, 1230 Avenue of the Americas, New York, NY 10020; or Chinese Taipei Film Archive, 4F, No. 7 Ching-Tao East Road, Taipei, Taiwan.

The Fable of the Peacock. Mudras and stylized gestures relate the other animals curing the peacock of his vanity. 1950. color, 14 min., 16 mm. Audio Brandon, formerly of New York, NY.

Folk Dance "Kams-g-Sum." Tibetan folk dances with pantomime. 1967. color, 4 min., 16 mm. Audiovisual Services, Pennsylvania State University, Special Services Building, University Park, PA 16802.

Kabuki: Classic Theatre of Japan. Excerpts from four Kabuki plays, with highly stylized gestures and speech and elaborate costumes. 1964. color, 30 min., 16 mm. See University of California Extension Media and Independent Learning address.

Kabuki Techniques. Onoe Baiko VII and Shoroki II demonstrate this stylized Japanese drama. 1969. color, 30 min., VHS. Insight Media, 2162 Broadway, New York, NY, 10024.

Kathakali: Dramatic Dance of India. 1959. color, 33 min., 16 mm and 35 mm. Film Division, Ministry of Information and Broadcasting, Government of India, Film Bhawan, 24 DR, Gopalrao, Deshmuth Marg, Bombay 40026, India.

Kathakali: Dances of India. 1949. b & w, 10 min., 16 mm. Budget Films, 4590 Santa Monica Boulevard, Los Angeles, CA 90029.

Lord Siva Dancing. Dances by Ram Gopal on traditional themes. b & w, 20 min., 16 mm. Cultural Service of the Embassy of India, 15 Rue Alfred Dehodency, Paris 16, France; or India Information Service, 2107 Massachusetts Avenue, NW, Washington, DC 20008.

Momiji gari. Kabuki and Noh drama. Parts made in 1899. 10 min., 35 mm. Shochiku Company, Ltd., Togeki Building, 1–1 Tsukiji 4-Chome, Chuo-Ku, Tokyo 104–8422, Japan.

Traditional Dances of Indonesia. A twelve-film series of the traditional dances of Bali, Central Java, and West Sumatra. 1975 to1976. color, 11 min. to 40 min., 16 mm and VHS. See University of California Extension Center for Media and Independent Learning address.

Early Comedies with Mime and Silent Era Classics

Chaplin. Biography of Charlie Chaplin, played by actor Robert Downey, Jr. Movement choreographed and coached by mime Dan Kamin. 1993. color, 135 min., VHS. Obtainable from video stores.

Chaplin: A Character Is Born. The evolution of Charlie Chaplin's "Little Tramp" in his early comedies. 1987. color, 40 min., 16 mm. and VHS. Phoenix Learning Group, 2349 Chaffee Drive, St. Louis, MO 63146.

Clown Princes. The comic techniques of Charlie Chaplin, Harold Lloyd, Laurel and Hardy, Ben

Turpin, Charles Chase, Larry Semon, and Billy West. 1960. b & w, 27 min., 16 mm. Audiovisual Services, Pennsylvania State University, Special Services Building, University Park, PA 16802.

Keaton: The Great Stone Face. Documentary with examples of Buster Keaton's growth as a film comic. 1987. color, 50 min., 16 mm. and VHS. See Phoenix Learning Group address.

The Sad Clowns. A study of the comedy art of Charlie Chaplin, Buster Keaton, and Harry Langdon. 1960. b & w, 26 min., 16 mm. See Pennsylvania State University address.

Slapstick. The era of silent comedy and the clowns who made it great. 1960. b & w, 27 min., 16 mm. See Pensylvania State University address.

Unknown Chaplin: Three Hidden Treasures. Sequences from *City Lights, Modern Times,* and *The Gold Rush.* 1983. b & w, 52 min., VHS. See Pennsylvania State University address.

The following titles, most of which are listed under Charlie Chaplin, W. C. Fields, Buster Keaton, Harry Langdon, Laurel and Hardy, Harold Lloyd, the Marx Brothers, Our Gang, and Jacques Tati, are mostly shorter versions of other films available in this category. If not otherwise specified, the following are 16-mm films in black and white and can be obtained from a number of companies, such as Kit Parker Films, 1245 Tenth Street, Monterey, CA 93940–3692.

Charlie Chaplin Films

The Adventurer. 1917.
The Bank. 1915.
Between Showers. 1914. 5 min. to 10 min.
Caught in a Cabaret. 1914.
The Champion. 1915.
The Cure. 1917. Biograph Entertainment, 2 Depot Plaza, Suite 202 B, Bedford Hills, NY 10507.
Easy Street. 1917.
His New Job. 1915.
The Immigrant. 1917.
Kid Auto Races at Venice. 1914. 5 min. to 10 min.
Laughing Gas. 1914. 5 min. to 10 min.
Making a Living. 1914. 5 min. to 10 min.
A Night Out. 1915.
One A.M. 1916.
The Pawnshop. 1916.
The Tramp. 1915.
A Woman. 1915.

Charlie Chaplin Extra-Length Silents

A Burlesque on Carmen. 1915.
The Gold Rush. 1925. 83 min. Biograph Entertainment, 2 Depot Plaza, Suite 202 B, Bedford Hills, NY 10507.
Tillie's Punctured Romance. 1914.

W. C. Fields Films

The Barbershop. 1933.
The Dentist. 1932.
The Fatal Glass of Beer. 1933.
The Golf Specialist. 1930.

Buster Keaton Films

Balloonatics. 1923.
The Blacksmith. 1920.
The Boat. 1921.
Buster Keaton Rides Again. 1965. b & w, 55 min., 16 mm and 35 mm. National Film Board of Canada, 1251 Avenue of the Americas, Sixteenth Floor, New York, NY 10020–1173.
Coney Island. 1917.
Cops. 1922.
The Garage. 1917.
The General. 1926. b & w, 79 min., 16 mm and LD. Biograph Entertainment, 2 Depot Plaza, Suite 202 B, Bedford Hills, NY 10507.
One Week. 1920.
The Railroader. 1965. color, 21 min., 16 mm and 35 mm. See National Film Board of Canada address.
Silent Partner. With Joe E. Brown, Zazu Pitts, and Bob Hope. 1955.

Harry Langdon Films

All Night Long. 1924.
Feet of Mud. 1924.
Fiddlesticks. 1926.
Remember When? 1925.
Smile, Please. 1924.

Laurel and Hardy Films

Big Business. 1929.
The Call of the Cuckoo. 1927.
Double Whoopee. 1929.

Habeas Corpus. 1929.
Liberty. 1929
Putting Pants on Philip. 1927.
Should Married Men Go Home? 1928.

Harold Lloyd Films

All Aboard. 1917.
Backstage. 1917.
The Chef. 1919.
Chop Suey and Co. 1919.
Don't Shove. 1919.
Girl Shy. 1924. b & w, 63 min. Biograph Entertainment, 2 Depot Plaza, Suite 202 B, Bedford Hills, NY 10507.
Going, Going, Gone. 1916.
Spring Fever. 1919.

Marx Brothers Films

Monkey Business. 1931.
The Stowaways. 1932.
This Is War? 1933.

Our Gang Films

Barnum and Bailey, Inc. 1929.
Dog Heaven. 1929.
Sundown Limited. 1924.

Jacques Tati Films

Jour de Fête. 1948. b & w, 95 min., VHS. Films Incorporated, 5547 North Ravenswood Avenue, Chicago, IL 60640.
Mr. Hulot's Holiday (Les Vacances de M. Hulot.) Dubbed in English. 1953. b & w, 85 min., 16 mm. Budget Films, 4590 Santa Monica Boulevard, Los Angeles, CA 90029.
Mon Oncle. 1958. color, 110 min., 16 mm. See Budget Films address.
Parade. 1973. A Tati-written and-directed film of vignettes in a circus. color, 85 min., VHS. See Films Incorporated address.
Playtime. 1996. color, 108 min., 16 mm. and 35 mm. See Budget Films address.
Sylvia and the Phantom. Tati in a comedy about a lonely girl befriended by a phantom. 1945. b & w, 98 min., 16 mm and VHS. See Films In-

corporated address.
Traffic. 1971. color, 89 min., VHS. See Films Incorporated address.

National Theatre of the Deaf

Deaf Mosaic #912. The National Theatre of the Deaf in Chester, CT, and on tour with Dylan Thomas's *Under the Milkwood.* 1994. color, 30 min., VHS. Gallaudet University, Department of TV, Photography, and Educational Technology, Kendall Green, 800 Florida Avenue, NE, Washington, DC 20002–3695.
The Mike Douglas Show. Interview by Mike Douglas with Theatre of the Deaf actors. Hamlet's soliloquy. 1968. b & w, 20 min. National Theatre of the Deaf, P.O. Box 659, Chester, CT 06412.
Shakespeare Unmasked. Scenes and poetry of William Shakespeare for young audiences. 1995. color, 55 min., VHS. See National Theatre of the Deaf address.
The Starting Line. National Theatre of the Deaf students. 1967. b & w, 11 min. See National Theatre of the Deaf address.
Theatre of the Deaf. Company discussions and scenes. 55 min. See National Theatre of the Deaf address.
Wild, Wild Wits. Adaptations of Carl Sandburg's *Rootabaga Stories* for young audiences. 1995. color, 32 min., VHS. See National Theatre of the Deaf address.

Video Collections Available for Viewing

A video collection of the entertainment arts was created in 1980 at the Maison Jean Vilar/Avignon, 8 Rue de Mons, 84000 Avignon, France, where videos may be viewed free of charge. The following videos belong to the collection. To view them at the Maison Jean Vilar, write to the above address or call 90–86–59–64.
Bienvenue au Silence: Marcel Marceau. 1971. b & w, 48 min., ¾ SECAM. I.N.A., 4 Avenue de l'Europe, 94366 Bry sur Marne, France.
Le Grand Départ. Peter Wyssbrod. Art video diffusion. 1977.
Un Jardin Public. Marcel Marceau pantomimes. 1955. b & w and color, 40 min., ¾

SECAM. RBF, Boulevard A. Reyers 52, 1040 Bruxelles, Belgium; and Centre National de la Cinématographie, Archives du Film, 7 bis Rue Alexandre Turpault, 78395 Bois d'Arcy, Cedex, France.

Le Manteau: Pantomime. Performed by Marcel Marceau, Roger Desmare, and Gilles Segal. 1951. color, 30 min., ¾ PAL. Films Bip.

Marcel Marceau. Marceau speaks about his art and performs. 1974. b & w, 40 min., ¾ SECAM. I.N.A., Tour Gamma A, 193–197 Rue de Bercy, 75582 Paris, France.

Marcel Marceau. Marceau demonstrates mime and performs in *The Mask Maker.* b & w, 45 min., ¾ SECAM. See preceding address.

Theatre Beyond Words. Presentation of the Canadian Theatre Beyond Words. 1979. color, 20 min., ¾ NTSC. Haber Artists, 553 Queen Street West, Suite 400, Toronto, ON, Canada M5V 2B6.

Théâtre du Mouvement: Carte de Visite. The diverse expression of the Théâtre du Mouvement company. 1985. color, 25 min., ¾ PAL.

The Vidéothèque de Paris has a film collection of Gaspard Deburau, Etienne Decroux, Jean-Louis Barrault, Marcel Marceau, Jerome Deschamps, Paul Paviot, and Max Linder, among others.

The New York Public Library for the Performing Arts has a collection in the Theatre on Film and Tape Archive in the Billy Rose Theatre Collection, which includes mime videotapes that may be viewed by theatre professionals, students, and researchers at the library, located at 40 Lincoln Center Plaza, New York, NY 10023–7498, tel. (212) 870–1641. The following videotapes are listed in the library catalogue.

American Mime Theatre. Paul Curtis. Mime demonstration and Gene Shalit interview with Paul Curtis on the *Today* show. 1975. b & w, 20 min., ½.

Comediants. Excerpts from the Italian Bobina Comediants company. 1986. color, 15 min., VHS.

The Courtroom. Created and directed by Bill Irwin. 1985. color, 53 min., ¾ U.

Dialogue with Claude Kipnis and Dore Schary. Reflections on mime as an art form and vital component of the performing arts. 1972. b & w, 23 min., ¾ U.

Factwino Meets the Moral Majority. San Francisco Mime Troupe. 1982. color, 120 min., VHS.

Fool Moon. Bill Irwin and David Shiner. 1993. color, 107 min. ¾ U.

The Hearing Test. Willy Conley's one-act play produced by the New York Deaf Theatre. 1994. color, 34 min., VHS.

Images: The American Mime Theatre. Brief clips of the American Mime Theatre's repertory. 1989. color, 10 min., VHS.

Imagings. Claude Kipnis performing. 1971. b & w, 97 min., ¾ U.

Largely New York. Bill Irwin performing. 1989. color. 66 min., ¾ U.

Marcel Marceau. Marceau at Belasco Theatre. 1983. color, 22 min., ¾.

Marcel Marceau in "Creation." b & w, 7 min., ¾ U.

Mime Forum. Lectures and slides by Will Spoor, Christina Petrovska, Jacqueline Rouard, and Jim Moore. 1977. b & w, 90 min., ¾ U.

Promenade. National Theatre of the Deaf's excerpts of *Promenade* by David Hays. 1972. color, 30 min., ¾.

Question of Balance. Touch Mime Theatre. 1985. color, 80 min., VHS.

Regard of Flight. Bill Irwin performing. 1982. color, 70 min., ¾ U.

A Rose in Winter. Dallas's Callier Theater of the Deaf's piece adapted from Leprince de Beaumont's fable. 1985. color, 77 min., ¾.

Solos—Michael Moschen. Solo performances by Moschen. 1986. color, 16 min., VHS.

Steeltown. San Francisco Mime Troupe. 1985. color, 120 min., VHS.

Street Theatre Performances. Mime Jim Moore, magician Jeff Sheridan, chamber ensemble Tequila Mockingbird, and unicycle juggler Steve Mills. 1977. b & w, 8 min., ¾ U.

Talley and Son. An excerpt of Lanford Wilson's play, with some stage movement, presented by the Theatre of the Blind. 1991. color, 3 min., VHS.

25 Cents. Aaron B. Weir's one-act play produced by the New York Deaf Theatre. 1993. color, 34 min., VHS.

The New York Public Library Donnell Media Center — located at 20 West 53rd Street, New York, NY 10019–6185 — has a collection of videos and 16-mm. films on mime and pantomime. The following titles can be found there.

The Art of Silence: Pantomimes with Marcel Marceau. 1975. color, four videos, 30 min. each,

VHS. John Barnes, Encyclopedia Britannica, Chicago.

Dolly, Lotte, and Maria. 1988. color, 60 min., 16 mm. First Run/Icarus Films, New York.

Exchange Place. Sketches by Don Jordan. 1975. color, 10 min., 16 mm. Marc De Rossi, Gary Gasgarth Texture Films, New York.

Insomnia. Classical mime with Paul Claudon and Pierre Etaix. 1972. color, 17 min., 16 mm. International Film Bureau, Chicago.

Mime Over Matter. (See under Mime, Pantomime, and Acting Films, Filmstrips, and Videos.)

The Morning Spider. (See under Mime, Pantomime, and Acting Films, Filmstrips, and Videos.)

The Pantomime Dame. 1982. color, 50 min., 16 mm. Elizabeth Wood. Wombat Productions, New York.

Rabbit's Moon. 1950. color, 8 min., 16 mm. American Federation of Arts, New York.

Step by Step. (See under Mime, Pantomime, and Acting Films, Filmstrips, and Videos.)

The Corporeal Mime Society in Vancouver, British Columbia, has a collection of mime and dance videos, including ones of Decroux and his company (*The Factory, Les Arbres*) and mime creations and instructional videos by European and North American companies and artists, such as Théâtre du Mouvement, Griftheater, Yves Lebreton, Axis Mime Theatre, Vancouver Moving Theatre, Dean Fogal, Thomas Leabhart, and others. To inquire about titles and viewing, write to Dean Fogal, 3353 West Fourth Avenue, Vancouver, BC, Canada V6R IN6, or Room #50, 2182 West 12th Avenue, Vancouver, BC, Canada V6K 2N4, tel. (604) 738–1057.

Author and mime teacher Bob Fleshman has a private film and videotape collection of the performances and lecture–demonstrations of Etienne Decroux, Marcel Marceau, and Jacques Lecoq and of various mime artists of the 1970s. For information, write Bob Fleshman, 1000 Joliet Street, New Orleans, LA 70118, tel. (504) 865–1522.

Pontine Movement Theatre has a collection of VHS, one-camera shoots of forty pieces of the company's repertory. For viewing information, contact Marguerite Mathews, Pontine, P.O. Box 1437, Portsmouth, NH 03802, tel. (603) 436–6660.

The Maison du Mime in Périgueux, France, has a video collection of all Mimos Festival performances since 1989, which may be viewed at the Visitation, Rue Littré, 24000 Périgueux, France.

As mentioned in Appendix B, a list of mime films may be found in the International Mimes and Pantomimes *Mime Directory*, Vol. 2, *Bibliography,* edited by Bari Rolfe.

A number of theatre companies and artists mentioned in this book have films and videos of their works. For example, the Théâtre du Mouvement has videos of its creations and films on artistic exchanges in Africa and Asia. (For company addresses, see Schools and Centers for Movement Training in Appendix A.) As mentioned in the section on mime artists directories, a list of names and addresses of mimes and companies belonging to the National Movement Theatre Association in North America can be obtained from the National Movement Theatre Association. c/o Margolis Brown Movement Theatre Center, 616 East 15th Street, Minneapolis, MN 55404, tel. (612) 339–4709, and in Europe from the European Mime Federation, Herengracht 168, 1016 BP Amsterdam, The Netherlands. To the author's regret, the date, length, precise location or other film and video information was in some cases unavailable and certain films and videos may no longer be obtainable.

Works Consulted and Cited

Abraham, Pierre. *Le Physique du Théâtre*. Paris: Coutan-Lambert, 1933. In French. Physical expression in theatre.

Adams, Joseph Quincy. *Chief Pre-Shakespearean Dramas*. Boston: Houghton Mifflin, 1924. English drama to 1500, mystery and miracle plays, early modern and Elizabethan drama, 1500–1600.

Alain. *Vingt Leçons sur les Beaux Arts*. Paris: Gallimard, 1931. In French. Twenty lessons about the beaux arts.

Albert, M. *Les Théâtres de la Foire*. Paris: Hachette, 1900. In French. Theatre of the fairs, 1660–1780.

Alberts, David. *Pantomime: Elements and Exercises.* Lawrence: University of Kansas Press, 1971. Textbook of corporeal mime exercises.

——. *Talking about Mime: An Illustrated Guide*. Portsmouth, NH: Heinemann, 1994. Photography by J. J. McClintock.

Allain, Paul. "Interview with David Glass." *Movement Theatre Quarterly* (Winter 1996): 3–4. Art and rehearsal process of the British movement theatre artist.

Ambrière, Francis. *La Galerie Dramatique.* Paris: Correa, 1949. In French. Theatre in France after the liberation, 1945–48.

Anderson, Tim. "Mummenschanz Interview." *Movement Theatre Quarterly* (Fall 1993): 6–10. Interview with Jacques Lecoq–trained Floriana Frassetto on the Mummenschanz company's beginnings and growth.

Angiolini, Gasparo. *Dissertation sur les Ballets Pantomimes des Anciens*. Vienna: Jean Thomas de Trattnern, 1765. In French. Ballet–pantomimes of the ancients and the tragic pantomime *Semiramis*.

Apollinaire, Guillaume. *Le Théâtre Italien*. Paris: Michaud, 1910. In French. On the Italian theatre.

Appel, Libby. *Mask Characterization: An Acting Process.* Carbondale: Southern Illinois University Press, 1982. Mask exercises for acting, clowing, and mask work.

Arens, Katherine. "Robert Wilson: Is Postmodern Performance Possible?" *Theatre Journal* 43, no. 1 (March 1991): 14–40. Criteria for postmodernism and Wilson's scenography.

Arlaud, R. M. *Cinéma Bouffe*. Paris: J. Melot, 1945. In French. Comic cinema.

Arnaud, Lucien. *Charles Dullin*. Paris: L'Arche, 1952. In French. Biography of the actor–stage director who trained Etienne Decroux, Jean-Louis Barrault, and Antonin Artaud.

Arnold, Paul. *L'Avenir du Théâtre*. Paris: Savol, 1947. In French. The future of theatre.

Arnoux, Alexandre. *Du Muet au Parlant*. Paris: La Nouvelle Edition, 1946. In French. From mute to speaking theatre.

Aronson, Arnold. "Postmodern Design." *Theatre Journal* 43, no. 1 (March 1991): 1–13.

Characteristics and comparisons of modern and postmodern stage design.

Artaud, Antonin. *The Theatre and Its Double.* Translated by Mary Caroline Richards. New York: Grove Press, 1958. Artaud's theatre of cruelty and physical language.

———. *Le Théâtre et Son Double.* Paris: Gallimard, 1938. In French. See description above.

Aslan, Odette. *L'Art du Théâtre.* Paris: Seghers, 1963. In French. The art of the theatre.

———, ed. *Le Corps en Jeu.* Paris: CNRS Editions, 1993. In French. Essays by Aslan and movement specialists on the role of the actor's body.

Attinger, Gustave. *L'Esprit de la Commedia dell'Arte dans le Théâtre Français.* Paris: Librairie Théâtrale, 1950. In French. *Commedia* in the French theatre.

Aubert, Charles. *L'Art Mimique.* Paris: E. Meuriot, 1901. In French. Textbook on pantomime with illustrations of movement and facial expression.

———. *The Art of Pantomime.* New York: Henry Holt & Co., 1927, and Benjamin Blom Inc., 1970. See description above.

———. *Pantomimes Modernes.* Paris: E. Meuriot, n.d. but circa 1900. In French. Twenty pantomimes with illustrations.

Auriac, Eugène de. *Le Théâtre de la Foire.* Paris: Garnier Frères, 1878. In French. Plays at the Saint-Germain and Saint-Laurent Fairs.

Avital, Samuel. *Le Centre de Silence Workbook.* Boulder, Colo.: Aleph-Beith Publishers, 1975; distributed by Brillig Works Bookstore, Boulder, Colo. Exercises, essays, and interviews with Avital.

———. "The Unique Art of Pantomime." *The Rosicrucian Digest* (December 1973): 21–23. Pantomime as a spiritual movement art.

Bair, Deidre. *Samuel Beckett: A Biography.* New York: Harcourt Brace Jovanovitch, 1978. Beckett's life, work, and use of silence.

Baker, H. Barton. *History of the London Stage and Its Players.* London: G. Routledge, 1904.

Ballerini, Luigi, and Giuseppe Risso. "Dario Fo Explains." *The Drama Review* 22, no. 1 (March 1978): 33–48. Interview with Fo on his popular improvisational and political theatre influenced by storytelling, puppetry, and commedia.

Balsimelli, Rossano, and Livio Negri, eds. *Guida al Mimo e al Clown.* Milan: Rizzoli, 1982. In Italian. A guide to mimes and clowns of contemporary genres.

Barba, Eugenio. *Beyond the Floating Islands.* New York: PAJ Publications, 1986. Essays on theatre anthropology, Western and Eastern acting techniques, and the origin of the Odin Teatret.

———. "Le Corps Dilaté." *Jeu 35 Cahiers de Theatre* (1985.2): 41–59. In French. Relationship between the physical and the mental in the actor's art.

———. "Eftermaele: 'That which will be said afterwards.'" *TDR The Drama Review* 36, no. 2 (Summer 1992): 77–80. Philosophical essay on the actor's legacy to the spectator.

———. *The Paper Canoe: A Guide to Theatre Anthropology.* Translated by Richard Fowler. London: Routledge, 1991. Barba's account of his thirty years with the Odin Teatret performing in different environments and in European, Asian, and American theatrical traditions.

———. "Steps on the River Bank." *TDR The Drama Review* 38, no. 4 (Winter 1994): 107–19. Barba's discovery of Kathakali in India in 1963 and its influence on the Odin Teatret.

———. *Le Théâtre Qui Danse.* Paris: Bouffonneries, 1989. In French. Report on the 1987 ISTA session in Salento, Italy.

———. "Words or Presence." *TDR The Drama Review* 16, no. 1 (March 1972): 47–54. Physical training and creativity.

Barba, Eugenio, and Nicola Savarese. *A Dictionary of Theatre Anthropology: The Secret of the Performer.* New York: Routledge, Chapman and Inc., 1991. Explanations from research at Barba's ISTA concerning body techniques, training, dramaturgy, and design. Photos and illustrations.

Barjavel, R. *Cinéma Total.* Paris: Denoël, 1944. In French. Total cinema.

Barlanghy, Istvan. *Mime: Training and Exercises.* Translated by Hugo Kerey. Edited by Cyril Beaumont. London: Imperial Society of Teachers of Dancing, 1967; New Rochelle, N.Y.: Sportshelf, 1967. Dance-influenced mime exercises and character study.

Barrault, Jean-Louis. *A Propos de Shakespeare et du Théâtre.* Paris: Editions La Parade, 1949. In French. Shakespeare and the theatre.

———. "Le Corps Magnétique." *Cahiers Renaud Barrault* 99 (1979): 71–135. In French. Mesmerizing quality of the human body.

———. "De l'Art du Geste." *Cahiers Renaud Barrault* 20 (1957): 85–103. In French. On the art of gesture.

———. "Dramatic Art and the Mime." In *Opera Ballet Music-Hall in the World, 35–40.* Paris: International Theatre Institute III, 1953.

———. *Memories for Tomorrow: The Memoirs of Jean-Louis Barrault.* Translated by Jonathon Griffin. London: Thames and Hudson, 1974.

———. *Mise-en-Scène et Commentaire sur Phèdre.* Paris: Editions du Seuil, 1946. In French. Barrault's notes for his staging of *Phèdre.*

———. *Nouvelles Réflexions sur le Théâtre.* Paris: Flammarion, 1959. In French. Essays on mime, pantomime, and dance.

———. "Le Problème du Geste." *Cahiers Renaud Barrault* 7 (1954): 85–92. In French. The problem of gestures.

———. "Propos sur la Pantomime." *Formes et Couleurs*, no. 5 (1947). In French. The role of gestures in theatre and dance.

———. *Reflections on the Theatre.* Translated by Barbara Wall. London: Rockliff, 1951. Translation of *Réflexions sur le Théâtre* first published by Jacques Vautrain, Paris, 1949.

———. *Réflexions sur le Théâtre.* Chap. 3. Paris: Editions du Levant, 1996. In French. Barrault's beginnings in theatre, his company and productions, and Decroux mime.

———. *The Theatre of Jean-Louis Barrault.* Translated by Joseph Chiari. New York: Hill and Wang, 1961. Translation of *Nouvelles Réflexions sur le Théâtre.* Continued reflections on theatre and mime.

Bartlett, Letitia, and Marc Bauman. "Interview with Bari Rolfe." *Movement Theatre Quarterly* (Spring 1996): 2–4. Rolfe's contribution to mime as author, teacher, and performer.

Bates, Alfred, ed. *The Drama: Its History, Literature, and Influence on Civilization.* Vol. 1. London: The Athenian Society, 1903.

Baudelaire, Charles. "Correspondences." In *French Poetry from Baudelaire to the Present*, edited by Elaine Marks. New York: Dell, 1962, 43. In French. Baudelaire's poem speculating on the relationship between one art and another.

Bayer, Raymond. *Essais sur la Méthode en Esthétique.* Paris: Flammarion, 1953. In French. Essays on method in aesthetics.

———. *L'Esthétique de la Grace.* Vol. 1. Paris: Alcan, 1933. In French. The aesthetics of grace.

———. *L'Esthétique Mondiale du XXième Siècle.* Paris: Presses Universitaires de France, 1961a. In French. World aesthetics in the twentieth century.

———. *Histoire de l'Esthétique.* Paris: Armand Colin, 1961b. In French. History of aesthetics.

Beacham, Richard C. *The Roman Theatre and Its Audience.* Chap. 5. Cambridge, Mass.: Harvard University Press, 1992. The origin of Roman theatre, Roman playwrights, and Roman mime and pantomime.

Beauchamp, Hélène, and Thierry Hentsch. "The Generous Word of René-Daniel Dubois." Translated by Albert Jordan. *Canadian Theatre Review* 50 (Spring 1987): 29–36. Canadian playwright Dubois's collaboration with Omnibus company.

Beaumont, C. W. *The History of Harlequin.* London: C. W. Beaumont, 1926; New York: Benjamin Blom and 1967. Harlequin from 1760 on in France and England and history of the commedia dell'arte.

Beaumont, C. W., comp. *A Bibliography of Dancing.* New York: Benjamin Blom, 1963. Dance bibliography in the British Museum Library.

Beaumont, Guy de. *Etudes Psychomorphologiques de Visages.* Paris: Calliope, 1947. In French. Study of psychomorphology in faces.

Beerbohm, Sir Max. "The Sound of Pantomime." *Newsweek* 65 (4 January 1965): 52–53. Description of the unique art of pantomime.

Bennetts, Leslie. "The New Vaudevillians Stir Up Some Serious Fun." *The New York Times* (12 May 1985): B27–30. Advent of such New Vaudevillians as Bill Irwin, Geoff Hoyle, and Avner the Eccentric and their influences on today's theatre.

Bentley, Eric. "Marcel Marceau." In *What Is Theatre?* New York: Atheneum, 1968, 342–45. Review of Marceau's art.

———. "Poet in New York." *New Republic* 127 (1 December 1952): 23. Review of Barrault's *Baptiste.*

———. "The Purism of Etienne Decroux." In *In Search of Theatre.* New York: Vintage Books,

1959, and Applause Theatre Books, 1992. Decroux's pure and rigorous corporeal mime aesthetics.

———. *L'Evolution Créatrice.* Paris: Alcan, 1934. In French. Creative evolution.

Bergson, Henri. *Laughter.* New York: Macmillan, 1911.

Bernard, Jean Jacques. "La Théorie du Silence." *La Revue Théâtrale,* no. 6 (June, July, August 1947): 278–81. In French. The theory of silence.

Bernhardt, Sarah. *The Art of the Theater.* Translated by H. J. Stenning. London: G. Bles, 1924.

———. *Memories of My Life.* New York: D. Appleton & Co., 1907.

Berson, Misha. "The Dell'Arte Players of Blue Lake, California." *Drama Review* 27, no. 2 (1983): 61–72. The beginnings and early years of the Dell'Arte Players and their use of *commedia* and environmental issues.

Bertheroy, Jean. *Le Mime Bathylle.* Paris: Armand Wein & Co., 1894, and Libraire L. Borel, 1902. In French. Description of the Roman mime.

Bertrand, Monique. "L'Expression Corporelle." *L'Ufoléa* , no. 103 (December 1956). In French. Physical expression.

———. "Le Geste, Musique et Magie." *Education Physique et Sport,* no. 30 (April 1956): 19–21. In French. Gestures, music, and magic.

———. "Le Mime, Art Inconnu." *Education Physique et Sport,* no. 35 (May 1957): 10–12. In French. Mime, the unknown art.

Bestland, Sandra J. "Margolis: Using the Body as a Dramatic Tool." *Movement Theatre Quarterly* (Fall 1993): 11–12. Kari Margolis's training method.

Bevington, David. *Action Is Eloquence: Shakespeare's Language of Gesture.* Cambridge, Mass.: Harvard University Press, 1984. Movement, props, costumes, space, and ceremony in Shakespeare.

Bieber, Margarete. *The History of the Greek and Roman Theatre.* Princeton, N.J.: Princeton University Press, 1961. History of ancient theatre, with sections on mime and pantomime.

Bildlexikon der Mimen. Florian Noetzel Verlag, 1990. In German. A picture lexicon of mime.

Billington, Sandra. *A Social History of the Fool.* New York: St. Martin's Press, 1984.

Development of the fool figure in the past 600 years.

Birringer, Johannes. *Theatre, Theory, Postmodernism.* Drama and Performance Series. Bloomington: Indiana University Press, 1991. The corporeal in postmodern theatre and criticism.

Blake, William H. *Preliminary Study of the Interpretation of Bodily Expression.* New York: Columbia University, 1933.

Blanchart, Paul. *Gaston Baty.* Paris: Editions de la Nouvelle Revue Critique, 1939. In French. Art of stage director Gaston Baty.

Blau, Herbert. "The Surpassing Body." *TDR The Drama Review* 35, no. 2 (Summer 1991): 74–98. The aesthetics and changing attitude toward the body, from Antonin Artaud and Jerzy Grotowski in the 1960s to postmodernism.

Boal, Augusto. *Games for Actors and Non-Actors.* Translated by Adrian Jackson. New York: Routledge, 1992. Use of movement to the extreme.

Boll, André. *Le Cinéma et Son Histoire.* Paris: Sequans, 1941. In French. History of the cinema.

———. *Théâtre, Spectacles, et Fêtes Populaires dans l'Histoire.* Paris: Sablon, 1945. In French. Theatre, spectacles, and popular holidays throughout history.

Borch, Michel Jean, Comte de. *Lettres sur la Sicile et sur l'Ile de Malthe.* Vol. 2. Letter 20. Turin: Frères Reycends, 1782. In French. Letters on Sicily and the island of Malta. Section on gestures.

Boulanger de Rivery, CI-Fr. F. *Recherches historiques et critiques sur quelques anciens spectacles, et particulièrement sur les mimes et les pantomimes.* Paris: Mérigot, 1752. In French. Historical essay on ancient spectacles, particularly on mime and pantomime.

Bowers, Faubion. *Broadway, USSR.* New York: Thomas Nelson, 1959a. Twentieth-century ballet, theatre, and entertainment in the Soviet Union.

———. *Japanese Theatre.* New York: Hill & Wang, 1959b. Sections on mime in the Japanese theatre.

Bowman, Walter Parker, and Robert Hamilton Ball. *Theatre Language Dictionary.* New York: Theatre Arts Books, 1961. Includes definitions of mime and pantomime.

Bowra, C. M. *From Virgil to Milton*. London: Macmillan, 1945. Poetry from Virgil to Milton.

Brachart, Adolphe. *L'Art de se Grimer*. Brussels: Librairie Théâtrale E. Lelong, 1920. In French. The actor's art of make-up.

Bragaglia, Anton Giulio. *Evolutione del Mimo*. Milan: Ceschina, 1930. In Italian. Evolution of mime, from the Greeks to twentieth-century cinema.

——. *Maschere Romane*. Rome: Colombo, 1947. In Italian. Roman masks.

Brandes, Janet. "Pantomime, an Old English Custom." *Opera and Concert* 13, no. 12 (San Francisco) (December 1948): 14–15, 30–31.

Brecht, Bertolt. *Bertolt Brecht*. New York: Routledge, 1995. Journals from 1934 to 1955.

Brecht, Stefan. *The Bread and Puppet Theatre*. 2 vols. London: Methuen and Routledge, 1988. History of the Bread and Puppet Theatre and biography of founder Peter Schumann.

Bremmer, Jan, and Herman Roodenburg, eds. *A Cultural History of Gesture*. Ithaca, N.Y.: Cornell University Press, 1992. Papers read at the 1989 Utrecht Conference by philology, anthropology, folklore, and history scholars on the cultural meanings and social relationships of human movement.

Broadbent, R. J. *A History of Pantomime*. London: Simpkin, Marshall, Kent & Co., 1901; New York: Citadel Press, 1965. From ancient Greece to eighteenth-century English pantomime.

Brown, Frederick. *Theatre and Revolution: The Culture of the French Stage*. New York: Viking Press, 1980. From the theatre of the fairs to the present. Chapters on actor–stage directors Charles Dullin and Jean-Louis Barrault and mime Etienne Decroux.

Brown, Moses True. *The Synthetic Philosophy of Expression as Applied to the Arts of Reading, Oratory, and Personation*. Boston: Houghton Mifflin, 1886.

Bruford, Rose. *Teaching Mime*. London: Methuen, 1958, 1964. Exercises, solo mimes, and mime plays.

Bu, Peter. "Consensus?" Translated by Annette Lust. *Movement Theatre Quarterly* (Fall 1994): 14–15. Mime festival director's views on the renewal, broadening, and diversification of twentieth-century mime.

——. "Mimes, Clowns, and the Twentieth Century?" *Mime Journal* (1983): 9–58.

Renaissance and multiple forms of contemporary mime.

Buhrer, Michel. *Mummenschanz*. Translated by Mavis Guinard. New York: Rizzoli International Publications, 1986. Photo essay, biography, and creative processes.

Buraud, Georges. *Les Masques*. Paris: Editions du Seuil, 1948. In French. Masks of all forms, times, races, and cultures, instinctive and symbolic.

Burdett, Osbert. *Critical Essays*. New York: Holt, 1925. Includes an essay on Charlie Chaplin's art.

Burgess, Hovey. *Circus Techniques*. New York: Drama Book Specialists, 1976. Elementary to advanced circus techniques.

Burian, Jarka M. "K. H. Hilar and the Early Twentieth-Century Czech Theatre." *Theatre Journal* 34, no. 1 (March 1982): 55–76. Hilar's influence on the avant-garde Czech theatre.

Calandra, Denis. "Experimental Performance at the Edinburgh Festival." *The Drama Review* 17, no. 4 (December 1973): 53–68. Origin of the Edinburgh Fringe Festival and such experimental performances as Tadeusz Kantor's Cricot Theatre.

Cambridge Guide to the Theatre. Edited by Martin Banham. New York: Cambridge University Press, 1995.

Camerlain, Lorraine. "Art de la Comédie, Comédie de l'Art: Entretien avec Carlo Boso." *Jeu* 35, 2 *Cahiers de Théâtre* (1985): 60–73. In French. Interview with Italian *commedia* specialist.

Campbell, Louis H. "An Analysis of Selected Contemporary Mime Philosophies and Techniques." Doctoral dissertation, University of Minnesota, 1976. Available from UMI, 300 North Road, P.O. Box 1346, Ann Arbor, MI 48106–1346. Mime philosophies and techniques ranging from 1954 to 1974.

Capp, A. "The Comedy of Charlie Chaplin." *Atlantic Monthly* 185 (February 1950): 25–29.

Carlson, Marvin. Review of *Medea*, by Heiner Müller. *Theatre Journal* 43, no. 1 (March 1991): 118–19. Norwegian artist Elsa Kvamme's interpretation of *Medea* at the 1990 Oslo Festival of Experimental Theatre.

Carr and Siquot (Mmes). *36 Danses Chantées et Mimées pour les Petits*. Paris: Librairie Classique Fernand Nathan, circa 1920. In

French. Ancient children's dances to sing and mime.

Carrington, Walter. *Thinking Aloud.* Berkeley, Calif.: North Atlantic Books, 1995. Talks on teaching the fundamentals of the Alexander Technique.

Cashman, Cheryl. "Canada's Clowns." *Canadian Theatre Review* 47 (Summer 1986): 63–72. 1980s clowns, New Vaudeville, and street performers in Canada.

——. *La Pantomime de l'Avocat.* Librairie Centrale, 1866. In French. The pantomime of the lawyer.

Champfleury, J. H. F. *Pantomimes de Gaspard et Charles Deburau.* Paris: E. Dentu, 1889a. In French. Pantomimes of Gaspard and Charles Deburau.

——. *Le Peintre Ordinaire de Gaspard Deburau.* Paris: Imprimerie de l'Art, 1889b. In French. The painter of Gaspard Deburau.

——. *Souvenirs des Funambules.* Paris: Michel Levy Frères, 1859; Geneva: Slatkine Reprints, 1971. In French. Deburau and pantomimes at the Théâtre des Funambules.

Champfleury, Gautier, Nodier, and Anonymes. *Pantomimes.* Edited by Isabelle Baugé. Paris: Cicéro, 1995. In French. Collection of pantomimes performed by Deburau and nineteenth-century mimes at the Funambules Theatre.

Chancerel, L. *Jean-Louis Barrault, ou L'Ange Noir du Théâtre.* Paris: Presses Universitaires de France, 1953. In French. On Jean-Louis Barrault, the black angel of theatre.

Chaplin, Charles. "L'Art de Faire Rire." *Ciné Pour Tous,* no. 5 (15 August 1919): 4–6. In French. The art of making one laugh.

——. "Contre le Film Parlant." *Ciné* no. 137 (15 July 1929). In French. An apology for silent films and Chaplin "against talkies."

——. *My Autobiography.* New York: Random House, 1960.

——. "Pourquoi Je Reste Fidèle au Muet." *Cinéma,* no. 13 (March 1931): 6. In French. Why Chaplin remained faithful to silent films.

Chappel, W. *Popular Music of the Older Time.* 2 vols. New York: Dover Publications, 1965.

Charrié, Guy. *Mimages.* Périgueux, France: Imprimerie Moderne, 1995. Superb photographs of artists at the annual Périgueux Mimos Festival in France.

Chase, Michael. "Tools for Transformation." *Total Theatre* (London) 7 (Fall 1995): 7. The transformative power of the mask, a tool for heightening body awareness.

Chekhov, Michael. *Etre Acteur: Technique du Comédien.* Translated by Elisabeth Janvier and Paul Savatier. Paris: Pygmalion/Gérard Watelet, 1980. In French. Techniques and exercises to coordinate the actor's physical and psychological expressions.

——. *To the Actor: On the Technique of Acting.* New York: Harper, 1953. See description above.

Cheney, Sheldon. *The Theatre (3000 Years of Drama).* New York: D. McKay Co., 1929, 1952. History of theatre.

Chisman, Isabel, and Gladys Wiles. *Mimes and Miming.* London: Thomas Nelson & Sons, 1934. Mime training and mime plays.

Christoffersen, Erik. *The Actor's Way.* New York: Routledge, 1993. Four Odin Teatret actors relate their development and training techniques and the relationship of mental and physical action on stage.

Le Cirque Knie. Lausanne, Switzerland: Librairie Marguerat, 1975. In French. Articles by Charles-Ferdinand Ramuz and other authors on the famous Swiss circus, with illustrations.

Clark, Barrett H. "Last of the Pierrots." *Drama* 13 (August–September 1923): 351–55. Interview with French mime Séverin on the evolution of mime.

Cluzel, M. *Mimes et Poètes Antiques.* Paris: Scorpion, 1957. In French. Mimes, theatre, and poets of antiquity.

Cohen, Gustave. *Histoire de la Mise-en-Scène dans le Théâtre Religieux Français au Moyen Age.* Paris: Librairie Champion, 1926. In French. History of stage direction in the French religious theatre of the Middle Ages.

——. *Le Livre de Conduite du Régisseur et le Compte des Dépenses pour le Mystère de la Passion.* Paris: Librairie Champion, 1925. In French. The stage manager's book and expenses for the *Mystery of the Passion.*

——. "Le Symbole dans le Théâtre du Moyen Age." *Masques* (15 March 1947): 61–66. In French. Symbols in the theatre of the Middle Ages.

——. *Le Théâtre en France au Moyen Age.* Paris: Presses Universitaires de France, 1948. In French. The French theatre in the Middle Ages.

Colette. "Music Hall." *Akademos* (15 June 1909): 47–51. In French. Description of Colette's life in the music hall.

———. *La Vagabonde*. Paris: Librairie Paul Ollendorff, 1910. In French. Colette's life as a mime artist.

Colpi, Henri. *Le Cinéma et Ses Hommes*. Montpellier, France: Causse, Graille et Castelnau, 1947. In French. The cinema and its people.

Cooper, Barbara T. "Exploitation of the Body in Vigny's *Chatterton:* The Economy of Drama and the Drama of Economics." *Theatre Journal* 34, no. 1 (March 1982): 20–26. Alfred de Vigny's dramatic use of gestures and pantomime in *Chatterton.*

Copeau, Jacques. *Texts on Theatre*. Edited and translated by John Rudlin and Norman H. Paul. London: Routledge, 1990.

———. *Le Théâtre Populaire*. Paris: Presses Universitaires de France, 1942. In French. Popular theatre.

Coquelin, Constant. *The Actor and His Art*. Translated by Abby Langdon Alger. Boston: Roberts Bros., 1881. Famous French actor's ideas on the art of acting.

Courthope, William John. *A History of English Poetry*. London: Macmillan, 1919. Section on the minstrels of the Middle Ages and the art of mime.

Cowan, Suzanne. "The Throw-Away Theatre of Dario Fo." *The Drama Review* 19, no. 2 (June 1975): 102–13. Dario Fo's radical, improvisational theatre in the 1970s.

Craig, Edward Gordon. "Enfin un Créateur au Théâtre." *Empreintes* (4 January 1980): 55–56. In French. The creative contribution of Decroux to theatre.

———. *On The Art of the Theatre*. London: Heinemann, 1924. Craig's ideas on theatre.

———. *De l'Art du Théâtre*. Paris: Odette Lieutier, 1943. In French. See description above.

———. "The Characters of the Commedia dell'Arte." *The Mask* 4 (1911–12): 199–202.

Critchley, Macdonald. *The Language of Gesture*. London: Longmans, 1939.

———. *Silent Language*. London: Butterworth, 1975. Gestures in the theatre, dance, everyday life, and various professions.

Curiger, Bice, and Jacqueline Burckardt. "The Weight of a Grain of Dust." *Parkett* 16 (1988): 111–19. The aesthetics of Robert Wilson.

Curtis, Paul J. "Exploring Silent Acting." *Dramatics* 44 (May 1973): 22. Author's approach to mime.

Cuvelier, Eugène-Henri. *Le Mime, le Jeu Dramatique et l'Enfant*. Paris: Fernand Nathan, 1981. In French. Exercises and pantomimes to initiate children into mime.

Daly, Ann. "Movement Analysis: Piecing Together the Puzzle." *TDR The Drama Review* 32, no. 4 (Winter 1988): 40–52. Introductory article for *TDR* movement-analysis issue, on movement-analysis as an interdisciplinary study.

Darley, Christian. "Move into Theatre." *Total Theatre* (London) 7 (Fall 1995): 14–15. Movement training in classical acting courses.

Darwin, Charles. *The Expression of the Emotions in Man and Animals*. Chicago: University of Chicago Press, 1974. Analogy of emotional and physical expression in man and animals.

Davis, Martha, and Dianne Dulicai. "Hitler's Movement Signature." *TDR The Drama Review* 36, no. 2 (Summer 1992): 152–72. Analysis of Hitler's body language as a speaker, with illustrations by Ildiko Viczian. Hitler portrayed by Charlie Chaplin and Alec Guinness.

Davis, R. G. "Method in Mime." *TDR The Drama Review* 6, no. 4 (June 1962): 61–65. Founder of the San Francisco Mime Troupe on different forms of mime.

———. *The San Francisco Mime Troupe*: *The First Ten Years*. Palo Alto, Calif.: Ramparts Press, 1975. The political theatre company's growth, 1962–72.

Deák, Frantisek. "Antonin Artaud and Charles Dullin: Artaud's Apprenticeship in Theatre." *Educational Theatre Journal* 29, no. 3 (October 1977): 345–53. Influence of Dullin's actor training on Artaud. Dullin's use of improvisation and masks.

———. *Symbolist Theatre*. Baltimore: Johns Hopkins University Press, 1993. Historical and theoretical examination of the avant-garde and experimental nature of the symbolist theatre that influenced Craig, Meyerhold, Artaud, and other modern movement theatre precursors.

———. Review of "Mimos in Périgueux." *Theatre Forum,* no. 1 (Spring 1992): 81–84. Description of performances at the 1991 Périgueux Mimos Festival.

Decroux, Etienne. *Paroles sur le Mime*. Paris: Gallimard, 1963. In French. Decroux's technique and philosophy of mime and theatre. Origins of mime, comparisons

with dance, and the use of movement for
actors.
———. *Words on Mime*. Translated by Mark
Piper. *Mime Journal* (1985). Translation of
Paroles sur le Mime.
———. [For interviews with and essays on and
by Decroux see Decroux titles under Thomas
Leabhart.]
Delarue, Maurice. "Jean-Louis Barrault, Mime
Retrouvé." *Signes,* no. 4 (Winter 1946–47):
68–72. In French. Barrault's talent as an actor
who has rediscovered mime.
Delluc, Louis. *Charlie Chaplin*. Translated by H.
Miles. London: John Lane, 1922.
De Marinis, Marco. *Mimo e Mimi.* Florence: La
Casa Usher, 1980. In Italian. Mime and
mimes.
———. *Mimo e Teatro nel Novecento*. Florence:
La Casa Usher, 1993. In Italian. Twentieth-
century mime and mimes from 1898 to 1992.
Copeau, Decroux, Barrault, Marceau and
Lecoq. Interviews and photographs.
Demetz, Peter. *Brecht*. Englewood Cliffs, N.J.:
Prentice Hall, 1962.
Dennis, Anne. *The Articulate Body: The Physical
Training of the Actor.* New York: Drama
Book Publishers, 1995. The actor's need for
an articulate body. Exercises, technique, and
mask work.
Deshoulières, Christophe. *Le Théâtre au XXe
Siècle.* Paris: Bordas, 1989. In French.
Evolution of twentieth-century theatre in
France.
Despot, Adriane. "Jean-Gaspard Deburau and the
Pantomime at the Théâtre des Funambules."
Educational Theatre Journal 27, no. 3
(October 1975): 364–76.
Destaville, Abbé. *Le Secret du Célèbre Roscius,
Acteur Romain Dévoilé.* Paris: Bureau de
l'Oeuvre du Commissaire du Clergé, 1886. In
French. The secret of the famous Roman
actor Roscius revealed.
    *A Dictionary of Greek and Roman
Antiquities*. Edited by Sir William Smith.
New York: Harper & Bros., 1857, Boston:
Longwood Press, 1977. Definitions of mime
and pantomime.
Diderot, Denis. *Paradoxe sur le Comédien*. Paris:
Plon, 1929. In French. Dialogue on the art of
acting and the actor's emotional spontaneity
and intellectual control.
Dimitri. *Dimitri Album.* Bern: Bental Verlag, 1973.
In French, Italian, and German. The Swiss
clown's autobiography, with numerous photos.

Disher, Maurice Willson. *Clowns and
Pantomimes*. London: Constable, 1925; New
York: Benjamin Blom, 1968.
———. *Fairs, Circuses, and Music Halls.*
London: William Collins, 1942.
Doat, Jan. *Entrée du Public*. Paris: Editions de
Flore, 1947. In French. Collective psychology
and mental contagion in theatre.
———. *L'Expression Corporelle du Comédien*.
Paris: Bordas, 1944. In French. Exercises and
training for the actor.
Dobbels, Daniel. "Jean-Louis Barrault:
Entretien." *Empreintes* 4 (1980): 48–54. In
French. Interview with Barrault.
Donval, Raoul. *Pantomimes du Vieux Cirque*.
Saint Valéry-en-Caux: Eugène Dangu, 1896.
In French. Old circus pantomimes.
Dorcy, Jean. *The Mime*. Translated by R. Speller
Jr. and Pierre de Fontnouvelle. New York:
Speller and Sons, 1961. Essays by Decroux,
Barrault, and Marceau.
Doucet, Jérome. *Notre Ami Pierrot*. Paris: Paul
Ollendorff, 1900. In French. On Pierrot, with
pantomimes and aquarelles by L. Morin.
Drack, Maurice. *Le Théâtre de la Foire, la
Comédie Italienne, et l'Opéra Comique.*
Paris: Firmin-Didot, 1889. In French. The
theatre of the fairs, the Italian comedy, and
the opéra comique.
Duchartre, Pierre Louis. *The Italian Comedy*.
Translated by Randolph T. Weaver. New
York: John Day Co., 1929; New York: Dover,
1965. Important work on the history of the
Italian comedy. Illustrations, characters, and
scenes. Extensive bibliography.
Duckworth, George E. *The Nature of Roman
Comedy*. Princeton, N. J.: Princeton
University Press, 1952. History of Roman
comedy.
Dullin, Charles. *Souvenirs et Notes de Travail
d'un Acteur*. Paris: Odette Lieutier, 1946. In
French. French stage director–actor's
souvenirs and notes.
Dumas, Georges. *Nouveau Traité de Psychologie*.
Vol. 3. Paris: Alcan, 1933. In French. Treatise
on psychology.
Duncan, Edmondstoune. *The Story of Minstrelsy*.
London: Scribner's, 1907. Includes accounts of
mime entertainment during the Middle Ages.
Duncan, Irma. *Duncan Dancer, An
Autobiography*. Middletown, Conn.:
Wesleyan University Press, 1966.
Duncan, Isadora. *My Life*. New York: Horace
Liveright, 1927.

Durant, John, and Alice Durant. *Pictorial History of the American Circus*. New York: Barnes, 1964. An important work on the history of the American circus, with more than five hundred illustrations.

Eastman, Gilbert C. *From Mime to Sign*. Silver Spring, Md.: T. J. Publishers, 1989. Sign language, gestures, mime, and visual communication.

Eldredge, S. A., and H. W. Huston. "Actor Training in the Neutral Mask." *The Drama Review* 22, no. 4 (1978): 19–28. The Lecoq neutral mask for actor training.

Emigh, John, with Ulrike Emigh. "Hajari Bhand of Rajasthan: A Joker in the Deck." *TDR The Drama Review* 30, no. 1 (Spring 1986a): 101–30. History of the wandering professional Hindu mimics and comics and of Hajari Bhand, who performed from 1937 on.

———. Review of *The Kathakali Complex: Actor, Performance and Structure*, by Phillip Zarrilli. *TDR The Drama Review* 30, no. 2 (Summer 1986b): 172–75. Review of study on Kathakali training, expressive technique, and types of performances, with photographic illustrations and diagrams.

Emnpreintes 4, January 1980. Jean-Luc Poivret, director of the publication, 14 Rue de Saussure, 75017, Paris, France. In French. Articles by Decroux, Barrault, Craig, and other mime specialists.

Engel, Johann Jacob. *Idées sur le Geste et l'Action Théâtrale*. 2 vols. Geneva: Slatkine Reprints, 1979. In French. The meaning of gestures in theatre.

Enters, Angna. *The Dance Has Many Faces*. Edited by Walter Sorell. New York: Columbia University Press, 1966. Includes Enters's ideas on the union of mime and dance.

———. "The Dance and Pantomime: Mimesis and Image." In *The Dance Has Many Faces*. Edited by Walter Sorrell. Cleveland, Ohio: World Publishing Co., 1951. See Enters, *The Dance Has Many Faces*.

———. *On Mime*. Middletown, Conn.: Wesleyan University Press, 1965. The author's ideas on mime and her activity in the art.

Epstein, Alvin. "The Mime Theatre of Etienne Decroux." *Chrysalis* 11, nos. 1–2 (1958): 3–13. A former Decroux student's account of Decroux's mime theatre.

Erichsen, Svend. "Pantomime in Denmark: The Commedia dell'Arte Is Still Alive in Danish Pantomime." In *Opera Ballet Music-Hall in the World*, vols. 45–50. Paris: International Theatre Institute III, 1953. *Commedia* pantomime at the Theatre of the Tivoli Gardens in Copenhagen.

Esslin, Martin. *Brecht*. New York: Doubleday 1960. Brecht and his work.

———. *The Field of Drama: How the Signs of Drama Create Meaning on Stage and Screen*. London: Methuen, 1987. Survey of dramatic structural principles. Section on gestures as a sign system.

Evreinoff, Nicolas. *Histoire du Théâtre Russe*. Paris: Editions du Chêne, 1947. In French. History of the Russian theatre.

———. *The Theatre in Life*. Edited and translated by A. Nazaroff. New York: Brentano's, 1927. The author's ideas on theatre and antinaturalism. Reprint, New York: B. Blom, 1970.

Eynat-Confino, Irène. *Beyond the Mask: Gordon Craig, Movement, and the Actor*. Carbondale: Southern Illinois University Press, 1987. The actor's need to control his physical expression and use a symbolic acting style.

Faherty, Teresa J. "*Othello dell'Arte*: The Presence of Commedia in Shakespeare's Tragedy." *Theatre Journal* 43, no. 21 (May 1991): 179–94. *Commedia* elements in the content, form, and characters of *Othello*.

Falk, Florence. "Physics and the Theatre: Richard Foreman's *Particle Theory*." *Educational Theatre Journal* 29, no. 3 (October 1977): 395–404. The concept of reality in Foreman's Ontological-Hysteric Theatre and physics as a metaphor in *The Particle Theory*.

———. *Les Jongleurs en France au Moyen Age*. Paris: Librairie Champion, 1910. In French. Jongleurs of the Middle Ages in France.

Faral, Edmond. *Mimes Français du XIII Siècle: Contributions à l'Histoire Comique au Moyen Age*. Paris: Champion, 1890. In French. Contributions of medieval mimes to the comical history of the Middle Ages.

Farnell, Brenda, ed. *Human Action Signs in Cultural Context: The Visible and Invisible in Movement and Dance*. Metuchen, N.J., London: Scarecrow Press, 1995. Ethnographic essays by dance and movement anthropology specialists and commentaries by scholars on philosophical issues.

Feder, Happy Jack. *Mime Time: Forty-Five Complete Routines for Everyone*. Colorado

Springs, Colo.: Meriwether Publisher, 1992. Illustrations by Marc Vargas.

Feldenkrais, Moshe. *Awareness through Movement*. New York: Harper and Row, 1972. Feldenkrais method.

Feldman, Peter. "Action to Image." *Canadian Theatre Review* 50 (Spring 1987): 4–9. The use of images in today's avant-garde theatre and in actor training.

Felner, Myra. *Apostles of Silence: The Modern French Mimes*. Cranbury, N.J.: Associated University Presses, 1985. Essays on Copeau, Decroux, Barrault, Marceau, and Lecoq.

———. "Circus and the Actor." *The Drama Review* 16, no. 1 (March 1972): 39–46. Interview with juggler Hovey Burgess on circus techniques for the actor.

Fifield, William. *In Search of Genius*. New York: William Morrow and Co., 1982. Conversations with Pablo Picasso, Jean Cocteau, Jean Giono, Joan Miro, Robert Graves, Roberto Rossellini, Salvador Dali, Marc Chagall, Jean Lurçat, and Marcel Marceau. Interview with Marceau on his training as a mime and life during the Second World War.

Fink, Joel. Review of *The Alchemedians*. *Theatre Journal* 38, no. 4 (December 1986): 485–87. New Vaudevillians Bob Berky and Michael Moschen clown, juggle, mime, and do magic.

Fleshman, Bob. "Sterling Jensen, Heartbeat of the Mime Theatre of Etienne Decroux in New York." *Movement Theatre Quarterly* (Summer 1994): 1–5. Mime, actor, and director Jensen's contribution to Decroux's company from 1959 to 1966 and Jensen's later New York productions.

Fleshman, Bob, ed. *Theatrical Movement: A Bibliographical Anthology*. Metuchen, N.J.: Scarecrow Press, 1986. Bibliographical anthology of essays on movement and performance in Western and other cultures by specialists in theatre, dance, psychology, history, anthropology, and other disciplines.

Fo, Dario. *The Tricks of the Trade*. London: Methuen, 1991. Fo's experience with *commedia* and improvisational theatre.

Foster, Hal. "Re: Post." In *Art after Modernism: Rethinking Representation*, edited by Brian Wallis, 189–201. New York: New Museum of Contemporary Art, 1988. Critical essay on the meaning and complexity of postmodernism.

Foster, Hal, ed. *The Anti-Aesthetic: Essays on Postmodern Culture*. Port Townsend, Wash.: Bay Press, 1986. Essays on various postmodern arts.

Fougère, Valentine. "Masques, Mimes, et Marionettes dans le Spectacle Contemporain." *Tendances*, no. 34 (April 1965): 5–24. In French. Article on masks, mimes, and marionettes in France.

Fournel, Paul. *Guignol, Les Mourguet*. Paris: Editions du Seuil, 1995a. In French. Illustrated study of the French Guignol theatre.

———. *Les Marionettes*. Paris: Bordas, 1995b. In French. Illustrated study of marionettes.

Fowlie, Wallace. *Pantomime: A Journal of Rehearsals*. Chicago: Henry Regnery Co., 1951. The use of mime and pantomime in theatre and dance productions.

Freedley, George. *History of the Theatre*. New York: Crown Publishers, 1968. Section on Greek and Latin mime and pantomime.

Garfein, Herschel, and Mel Gordon. "The Adriani Lazzi of the Commedia Dell'Arte." *TDR The Drama Review* 22, no. 1 (March 1978): 3–12. Illustrated article describing thirty-nine *lazzi* of a small Italian troupe in the early 1700s, translated by the authors.

Gassner, John. *The Theater in Our Times*. New York: Crown Publishers, 1954. Survey of modern theatre movements and people in the theatre.

Gautier, Théophile. "Carnaval." In *Emaux et Camées: XIXe Siècle*. Edited by André Lagarde and Laurent Michard. Paris: Bordas, 1969, 268. In French. Gautier's poem referring to Pierrot and other *commedia* characters.

Gelabert, Raoul. "Etienne Decroux Has Much to Teach Us." *Dance Magazine* 33 (September 1959): 66–67. The contribution of mime master Decroux.

Gélinas, Aline. "Le Pool: Speaking the Body." Translated by Roger E. Gannon. *Canadian Theatre Review* 50 (Spring 1987): 26–28. The physical theatre of the Decroux-trained Le Pool company.

Gherardi. *Recueil Général du Théâtre Italien de Gherardi*. Paris: Cusson et Witte, 1700. In French. General collection of Gherardi's theatre.

Gielgud, John. *Stage Directions*. New York: Theatre Arts, Routledge, 1987. Actors, correspondence, and souvenirs.

Glass, David. "Jean-Louis Barrault." *Total Theatre* (London) 6 (Spring 1994): 7. The life and contribution of Barrault.

Goby, Emile, ed. *Pantomimes de Gaspard et Charles Deburau.* Paris: E. Dentu, 1889. In French. Original Gaspard Deburau pantomimes.

Godard, Colette. *Jerome Savary, l'Enfant de la Fête.* Paris: Editions du Rocher, 1996. In French. Written testimonies about the life and art of actor, clown, stage director, and father of the Grand Magic Circus.

Gonsalez, Arturo, and Maureen Gonsalez. "He Is Mime." *American Way* (19 March–1 April 1985): 101–3. Marceau talks about his life and art.

Gordon, Mel. *Lazzi: The Comic Routines of the Commedia dell'Arte.* New York: Performing Arts Journal Publications, 1983.

———. "The S.F. Mime Troupe's *The Mother.*" *TDR The Drama Review* 19, no. 2 (June 1975): 94–100. Detailed description of the San Francisco Mime Troupe's staging of Brecht's *The Mother.*

Gorelik, Mordecai. *New Theatres for Old.* New York: Octagon Books, 1975. Overview of theatre movements and styles, stage setting, and scenery.

Gouhier, Henri. *L'Essence du Théatre.* Paris: Plon, 1943. In French. Philosophical essays on theatre. Chapter on Georges Pitoëff, Charles Dullin, Louis Jouvet, and Gaston Baty.

Gourdon, Anne-Marie, comp. "La Formation du Comédien." In *Les Voies de la Création Théâtrale* 9. Paris: Editions du Centre National de la Recherche Scientifique, 1981. In French. Essays by Eugenio Barba and international theatre specialists on the actor's training. Section on Jacques Lecoq's school by Catherine Skansberg, 81–94.

Gourfinkel, Nina. *Théâtre Russe Contemporain.* Paris: Renaissance du Livre, 1931. In French. Contemporary Russian theatre.

Gousseff, James W. *Street Mime.* Woodstock, Ill.: Dramatic Publishers, 1993.

Grace-Warrick, Christa. "Vancouver: Getting Physical." *Canadian Theatre Review* 47 (Summer 1986): 125–30. Movement theatre in Vancouver.

Gratiolet, Pierre. *De la Physionomie et des Mouvements d'Expression.* Paris: Hetzel, 1865. In French. On physionomy and expressive movements.

Graves, Russel. "The Nature of Mime." *Educational Theatre Journal* 10, no. 2 (May 1958): 101–4. Mime and speech.

Green, Martin Vurgess, and John Swan. *The Triumph of Pierrot: The Commedia dell'Arte and the Modern Imagination.* University Park: Pennsylvania State University Press, 1993. The Pierrot figure in the works of Picasso, Stravinsky, and other modernist artists.

Green, Stanley. *The Great Clowns of Broadway.* New York: Oxford University Press, 1984. Revival of clowning and famous twentieth-century clowns.

Grotowski, Jerzy. *Towards a Poor Theatre.* New York: Simon and Schuster, 1968. Grotowski's Theatre Laboratory, a theatre stripped of the unessential. Voice and physical exercises.

———. "Towards the Poor Theatre." *Tulane Drama Review* 11, no. 3 (Spring 1967): 60–65. Condensed article on Jerzy Grotowski's ideas on theatre.

Gueriot, Patrick. "Notions of Movement: Contributions of Scenic and Costume Designer Louis Bercut." Translated by Annette Lust. *Movement Theatre Quarterly* (Fall 1995): 3–4. The visual and conceptual unity in the sets and costumes of French scenic designer Louis Bercut.

Guest, Ivor. *The Dancer's Heritage.* Baltimore: Penguin Books, 1960. A short history of ballet.

Gunderson, Phil. "Reflections on the State of Mime." *Total Theatre* (London) 6 (Summer 1994): 16. Short article on the current state of mime, its evolution, and its future needs.

Hacks, Charles. *Le Geste.* Paris: Marpon & Flammarion, 1892? In French. Important work on gestures in daily life, pantomime, and theatre.

Hall, Edward T. *The Silent Language.* New York: Doubleday, 1990. Intercultural communication.

Hamblin, Kay. *Mime: A Playbook of Silent Fantasy.* New York: Doubleday, Dolphin Books, 1978. Introductory mime games and exercises, with photographic illustrations.

Hanly, Beverly. "Low Art in Blue Lake." *Theatre Forum,* no. 7 (Summer/Fall 1995): 4–11. Description of the development, originality, style, school, and activities of the Dell'Arte Players in Blue Lake, California.

Hardison Jr., O. B. *Christian Rite and Christian Drama in the Middle Ages.* Baltimore: Johns Hopkins University Press, 1965. Essays on the origin and early history of modern drama, based on Christian liturgy.

Harrop, John. *Acting.* New York: Routledge, 1992. Section on the use of improvisation and movement to release creativity and discover meaning.

Harwood, Eliza. *How We Train the Body.* Boston: Walter H. Baker, 1933.

Hassan, Ibab. *The Literature of Silence: Henry Miller and Samuel Beckett.* New York: Alfred A. Knopf, 1968. Modern revolt against verbal discourse and the vision of silence in Miller and Beckett.

Hausbrandt, Andrzej. *Tomaszewski's Mime Theatre.* Warsaw: Interpress, 1975; New York: De Capo Press, 1977. Photo description of Henryk Tomaszewski's mime theatre.

Hays, David. "We've Come of Age." *Theatre Crafts* 3, no. 1 (January–February 1969): 6–14. The Theatre of the Deaf.

Hazard, Paul. "Un Nouvel Acteur Sicilien: Angelo Musco." *Revue des Deux Mondes* Sixième Période 40 (15 July 1917): 378–86. In French. Sicilian mime–actor Angelo Musco.

Heggen, Claire, and Yves Marc. *Si la Joconde Avait des Jambes.* N.p., 1996. In French. Lecture–performance with the Théâtre du Mouvement on the theme of walking.

Henry, Pierre. "La Carrière de Charlie Chaplin." *Cinea,* no. 13 (March 1931): 7–9. In French. Description of Chaplin's early films.

Hernando, Victor. *Mimografias: Un Recorrido por la Historia, la Teoría y Técnica del Mimo y la Pantomima.* Buenos Aires: Ediciones Vuelo Horizantal, 1996. In Spanish. History, theory, and technique of mime and pantomime.

Hinde, R. A., ed. *Non-Verbal Communication.* Cambridge: Cambridge University Press, 1972.

Histoire des Spectacles. Publication directed by Guy Dumur. Paris: Gallimard, 1965. In French. Comprehensive history of all forms of theatre spectacles, including radio, T V, and cinema. Section on mime.

Hobbs, William. *Fight Direction for Stage and Screen.* Portsmouth, N.H.: Heinemannn Educational Books, 1995. Guidelines for fight scenes on stage and screen. Fight notation and brief history of swords.

———. *Stage Combat.* New York: St. Martin's Press, 1981. See description above.

Hort, Jean. *Les Théâtres du Cartel.* Geneva: Skira, 1944. In French. Contributions of French stage directors Charles Dullin, Gaston Baty, Georges Pitoëff, and Louis Jouvet.

Houghton, Norris. *Moscow Rehearsals.* New York: Grove Press, 1962. Theatre, stage, and scenery in Moscow and the Soviet Union.

Houseman, J. "Charlie's Chaplin." *Nation* 199 (12 October 1964): 222–25.

Hoyer, Karen. "Collisions without Cause: An Observation of Streb/Ringsides *Popaction.*" *Movement Theatre Quarterly* (Winter 1996): 4–5. A review of acrobatics in Streb's Ringside company's *Popaction.*

———. "Mime That Speaks." *Movement Theatre Quarterly* (Fall 1995): 9. Use of movement in current Chicago speaking-theatre productions.

Huff, Theodore. *Charlie Chaplin.* New York: Henry Schuman, 1951.

Hughes, John P. *The Science of Language: An Introduction to Linguistics.* New York: Random House, 1962.

Hugounet, Paul. *Mimes et Pierrots.* Paris: Fischbacher, 1889. In French. History of mimes and Pierrots.

———. *La Musique et la Pantomime.* Paris: Ernest Kolb, 1892. In French. The use of music by nineteenth-century French mimes.

Hugounet, Paul, and Felix Larcher. *Les Soirées Funambulesques.* Paris: N.p., N.d. In French. Nineteenth-century pantomime in France.

Hunningher, Benjamin. *The Origin of the Theatre.* New York: Hill and Wang, 1961. Important history of the origins of theatre.

Hunt, Douglas, and Kari Hunt. *Pantomime: The Silent Theatre.* New York: Atheneum, 1964. Short history of pantomime.

Huston, Hollis. Review of *The Actor and His Body,* by Litz Pisk. *Educational Theatre Journal* 29, no. 3 (October 1977): 438–39. See Litz Pisk.

———. *The Actor's Instrument: Body, Theory, Stage.* Ann Arbor: University of Michigan Press, 1992. The actor's use of his body and its relation to thought and the playing space.

———. "Dimensions of Mime Space." *Educational Theatre Journal* 30, no. 1 (March 1978): 63–72. Italian actors in France, influence on Molière, and the Gherardi repertory.

——. "The Zen Mime of Mamako."
Educational Theatre Journal 28, no. 3
(October 1976): 355–62. Japanese mime
Mamako combines Eastern spirituality with
Western mime techniques in *Ten Bulls* and
other works.

Ihering, Herbert. *Marcel Marceau und die
Welkunst der Pantomime, Ein Gesprach.*
Berlin: Henschel, 1956. In German. Marcel
Marceau and pantomime.

Ionesco, Eugene. *Journal en Miettes.* Paris:
Gallimard, 1967. In French. Ionesco's journal,
with sections on the importance of silence in
theatre.

——. *Notes et Contre-Notes.* Paris: Gallimard,
1962. In French. Section on the use of
movement and pantomime in Ionesco's plays.

Jacquart, Emmanuel. *Le Théâtre de Dérision.*
Paris: Gallimard, 1974. In French. The theatre
of rebellion of Samuel Beckett, Eugene
Ionesco, and Arthur Adamov.

Jacques Copeau et le Vieux Colombier. Paris:
Bibliothèque Nationale, 1963. In French.
Jacques Copeau and the Vieux Colombier
theatre.

Janin, Jules. *Deburau, Histoire du Théâtre à
Quatre Sous.* Paris: Charles Gosselin, 1832;
Paris: Librairie des Bibliophiles, 1881; Paris:
Gosselin Editions d'Aujourd'hui, "Les
Introuvables," 1981; New York: McBride,
1928. In French. Translated into English by
Winifred Katein. Gaspard Deburau's theatre.

Jaques-Dalcroze, Emile. *Eurhythmics, Art, and
Education.* Translated by Frederick Rothwell.
New York: Barnes, 1930, and Benjamin
Blom, 1972. Rhythmic movement in the arts
and education.

Jenkins, Ron. "Acrobats of the Soul." *American
Theatre* 1, no. 11 (March 1985): 4–10. New
Vaudeville artists and comic anarchy.

——. "Dario Fo: The Roar of the Clown." *TDR
The Drama Review* 30, no. 1 (Spring 1986):
171–79. Fo's celebration of popular culture,
his blend of politics and art, and his
pantomimic, comedic talent.

Jones, Desmond. "Deburau." *Total Theatre* 5, no.
4 (Winter 1993): 8–9. Life and work of
Gaspard Deburau.

Jones, Edward Trostle. *Following Directions: A
Study of Peter Brook.* New York: Peter
Lang, 1985. Examination of Brook's
productions and his exploration of nonverbal
language.

Jousse, Marcel. *L'Anthropologie du Geste*: *Le
Parlant, la Parole, et le Souffle.* Paris:
Gallimard, 1974. In French. Important study
of linguistic psychology, the anthropology of
gestures, and gestures as the origin of all the
arts.

Jouvet, Louis. *Réflexions du Comédien.* Paris:
Librairie Théâtrale, 1952. In French. Jouvet's
reflections on theatre.

Kamin, Dan. *Charlie Chaplin's One-Man Show.*
Metuchen, N.J.: Scarecrow Press, 1984·
Carbondale: Southern Illinois Univer·
Press, 1991 (reprint). Chaplin's co·
to the cinema, his use of mime, ·
from his films. Introduction by
Marceau.

——. "Is Mime an Endangered Species.
Movement Theatre Quarterly (Fall 1990).
3–5. Review of *Modern and Post-Modern
Mime* by Thomas Leabhart.

Kane, Leslie. *The Language of Silence.* Cranbury
N.J.: Associated University Presses, 1984.
Silence in the theatre of Maurice Maeterlinck,
Anton Chekhov, Tristan Bernard, Samuel
Beckett, Harold Pinter, and Edward Albee.

Kantor, Tadeusz. *A Journey through Other
Spaces: Essays and Manifestos, 1944–1990.*
Edited and translated by Michael Kobialka.
Berkeley: University of California Press,
1993. Essays and director's notes by Kantor,
founder of Cricot 2 in Poland, followed by a
critical study of Kantor's theatre.

——. *Le Théâtre de la Mort.* Lausanne,
Switzerland: Editions l'Age de l'Homme,
1977. In French. Collection of writings by
Kantor on his experimental Cricot Theatre of
Death. Sections on the nonliterary structure of
his plays.

Keaton, Buster, with Charles Samuels. *My
Wonderful World of Slapstick.* New York:
Doubleday, 1960. Autobiography.

Kellein, T. *Pierrot, Mélancholie und Maske.*
Munich: Prestel, 1995. Catalogue of the
exposition at the Hans der Kunst in Munich,
September 15, 1995, with color illustrations
of Pierrot by artists since the seventeenth
century.

Keller, M., and Mme. Keller. *Poses et Tableaux
Mimiques et Plastiques.* Lyon: Chanoine,
1849. In French. Mime tableaux created by
the Kellers.

Kemp, Robert. "Le Procès de Kafka au Théâtre
Marigny." *Le Monde* (Paris) (12–13 October

1947): 6. In French. Review of Franz Kafka's *The Trial* at the Marigny Theatre in Paris.

Kesell, Pat. *Mime Themes and Motifs*. Boston: Plays Inc., 1980. Study and teaching of mime.

Key, Mary Ritchie. *Non-Verbal Communication: A Research Guide and Bibliography*. Metuchen, N.J.: Scarecrow Press, 1977. Information and titles on nonverbal communication in life, the arts, animals, etc.

Kiernander, Adrian. *Ariane Mnouchkine and the Théâtre du Soleil*. Directors in Perspective. Cambridge: Cambridge University Press, 1993. Influence of Mnouchkine on twentieth-century theatre, her methodology, and the collective spirit of her company.

Kipnis, Claude. *The Mime Book*. New York: Harper & Row, 1974. Mime technique, with photographic illustrations.

Kirstein, Lincoln. *Dance*. New York: G. P. Putnam's Sons, 1935. History of dance. Section on ancient mime.

Kirby, E. T. "The Delsartre Method: Three Frontiers of Actor Training." *The Drama Review* 16, no. 1 (March 1972): 55–69. Influence of François Delsartre's actor training. Illustrated gestures and exercises.

Kirkland, Christopher D. "The Golden Age, First Draft." *The Drama Review* 19, no. 2 (June 1975): 53–60. Ariane Mnouchkine's socio-political theatre based on commedia dell'arte, ancient Chinese theatre, and circus.

Klauniada. "A Conversation with Yves Lebreton." *Movement Theatre Quarterly* (Winter 1995): 2–10. Interview by Valerie Dean and Don Rieder with mime Yves Lebreton about four of his works at his Teatro dell'Albero in Italy.

Klugman, Natasha. "Body Language." *Total Theatre* (London) 8 (Summer 1996): 15. Movement specialist Lorna Marshall's method of freeing emotion and imagination in the actor.

Knapp, Bettina L. *Antonin Artaud, Man of Vision*. New York: D. Lewis, 1969. Contribution of Artaud and his theatre of cruelty.

——. "The Reign of the Theatrical Director: Antoine and Lugné-Poe." *French Review* 61, no. 6 (May 1988): 866–77. Experimental productions of André Antoine and Aurélien-Marie Lugné-Poe and the use of movement in Lugné-Poe's *La Gardienne*.

Kobialka, Michael. "Writings of Tadeusz Kantor: The Work of Art and the Process, 1976." *TDR*

The Drama Review 30, no. 3 (Fall 1986): 114–76. The creativity of the actor separate from that of the playwright.

——. "Putting Some Meat on the Bones." *Movement Theatre Quarterly* (Fall 1995): 2–3. The fusion of dramatic structure and movement in Anne Bogart's experimental productions, such as *The Medium*.

Korabek, Liz. Review of *At Work with Grotowski on Physical Actions*, by Thomas Richards. *Movement Theatre Quarterly* (Winter 1996): 6. Jerzy Grotowski assistant Thomas Richards's research on Konstantin Stanislavsky's method of physical actions.

Kourilsky, Françoise. "Dada and Circus: Bread and Puppet Theatre." *The Drama Review* 18, no. 1 (March 1974): 104–9. Peter Schumann's Bread and Puppet Theatre's affinities with the circus.

Kreigsman, Alan M. "This Thing Called Mime." *The Washington Post* (8 July 1984): H1 and H8. Resurgence of mime and the new mime of Decroux and his adepts.

Kumiega, Jennifer. *The Theatre of Grotowski*. London: Methuen, 1985. Jerzy Grotowski's experimental Polish theatre.

Laban, Rudolf. *The Mastery of Movement*. Boston: Plays Inc., 1971. The Laban system. Section on the stage arts developing from mime.

Lachaud, Jean Marc. "Mélange Des Arts/Arts du Mélange." *Crises,* no. 3 (June 1995): 205–12. In French. Mixture of the arts and arts of mixture. Section on postmodern dance and theatre.

Lachaud, Jean Marc, ed. "Mélange des Arts au XXe Siècle." *Skene,* no. 1 (1996). In French. Essays by scholars at a University of Michel de Montaigne conference in Bordeaux, France, including one by Martine Maleval on the other arts in mime.

——. *La Mise-en-Scène du Geste*. Bordeaux: Publications du Service Culturel de l'Université Michel de Montaigne, 1994. In French. Essays by scholars and artists from a conference at the University of Michel de Montaigne, Bordeaux.

Lachaud, Jean Marc, and Martine Maleval. *Mimos, Eclats du Théâtre Gestuel*. Périgueux, France: Ecrits dans la Marge, 1992. In French. The international Mimos Festival in Périgueux, France, from 1983 to 1993, with photographic illustrations.

Lane, Lupino. "The Art of Pantomime." *World Review,* no. 10 (London) (December 1949): 19–21. What pantomime brings to children.

Lawson, Joan. *Mime: The Theory and Practice of Expressive Gesture.* London: Sir Isaac Pitman & Sons, 1957 and 1966. A short history of mime and technique of expressive gesture for dancers and actors, with ballet illustrations.

Leabhart, Thomas, ed. *California Performance.* 2 vols. *Mime Journal* (1989–90). Interviews and essays on theatrical performance in the San Francisco Bay Area, vol. 1, and Southern California, vol. 2.

——. ed. *Canadian Post-Modern Performance.* *Mime Journal* (1986). Articles on the Cirque du Soleil, Special Delivery Moving Theatre, Winnipeg Mime Festival, Omnibus, and Diana McIntosh.

——. ed. *Etienne Decroux 80th Birthday Issue.* *Mime Journal,* nos. 7 and 8 (1978). Photos and interviews with Decroux on the origin of corporeal mime, the mask, marionettes, Victor Hugo, and Charles Baudelaire, as well as a corporeal mime design lecture.

——. "Etienne Decroux on Masks." *Mime Journal,* no. 2 (1975): 54–62.

——. "Homme de Sport: Sport, Statuary, and the Recovery of the Pre-Cartesian Body in Etienne Decroux's Corporeal Mime." *Mime Journal* (1996a): 31–65. Relationship between Decroux's corporeal mime and sports and the influence of nineteenth-century sculptors François Delsartre and Paul Bellugue on Decroux, as well as his recovery of the pre-Cartesian body.

——. ed. *Incorporated Knowledge. Mime Journal* (1995). Eight essays by theatre anthropologists, theoreticians, and specialists on mime, mask, and mime-related subjects. Illustrations of performances and masks.

——. ed. *In/sights: Moore Photographs. Mime Journal* (1987–88). Photos of mime artists by mime–photographer Jim Moore from 1972 to 1988. Essays by Michael Smith, Paul Zaloom, Michael Pedretti, and John Towsen.

——. "An Interview with Decroux." *Mime Journal* no. 1 (1974): 26–37.

——. ed. *Jacques Copeau's Theatre School. Mime Journal* nos. 9 and 10 (1979).

——. ed. *Mask Theatre. Mime Journal,* no. 2 (1975).

——. ed. *Mime in Czechoslovakia. Mime Journal,* nos. 3 and 4 (1976). Six essays on twentieth-century artists and companies in former Czechoslovakia.

——. "Mime: Speaking Out." *Arts Review* (Summer 1984a): 13–15. Growth of mime and the new mimes of the 1980s.

——. *Modern and Post-Modern Mime.* New York: St. Martin's Press, 1989. Contributions of Jacques Copeau, Etienne Decroux, Jean-Louis Barrault, Marcel Marceau, Jacques Lecoq, and late twentieth-century mime artists to modern and postmodern mime.

——. ed. *New Mime in Europe. Mime Journal* (1983). Articles by Peter Bu and European mime artists, with photos.

——. ed. *New Mime in North America. Mime Journal* (1980–82). Articles about and photos of new mime companies and artists in North America.

——. ed. *No/Kyogen Masks and Performance. Mime Journal* (1984b).

——. "Reflections on a Production." *Movement Theatre Quarterly* (Winter 1994): 11–12. Description of Molière's *Scapin,* staged at Pomona College, October 1992.

——. ed. *Theatre and Sport. Mime Journal* (1996b). Essays by Thomas Leabhart, Franco Ruffini, John Rudlin, and Janne Risum on the relationship between theatre and sports.

——. ed. *Words on Decroux. Mime Journal* (1993). Essays in memory of Etienne Decroux by twenty-four former Decroux students and teachers.

——. *Words on Decroux 2. Mime Journal* (1997). Essays on Etienne Decroux's corporeal mime by Eugenio Barba, Thomas Leabhart, Marco de Marinis, Deidre Sklar, Corinne Soum, and Kathryn Wylie, and by Decroux on Antonin Artaud and on dance.

Le Barillier, Berthe. *Le Mime Bathylle.* Paris: Colin, 1894. In French. The art of the Roman mime Bathyllus.

Lecoq, Jacques. "Art of the Actor." In *Les Voies de la Création Théâtrale 9.* Paris: Editions du Centre National de la Recherche Scientifique, 1981. Texts assembled by Anne Marie Gourdon. In French. Lecoq's ideas on the actor's art.

——. *Le Corps Poétique.* Arles, France: Actes Sud-Papiers Anrat, 1997. In French. A historical, technical, and artistic account of Lecoq's school and language of gestures.

——. "Mime, Movement, Theatre." Translated by Kat Foley and Julia Devlin. *Yale Theatre* 4

(Winter 1973): 117–20. Lecoq's method and school.

Lecoq, Jacques, ed. *Le Théâtre du Geste: Mimes et Acteurs*. Paris: Bordas, 1987. In French. Historical and aesthetic essays by Lecoq and mime and theatre specialists.

Lee, Alison. *A Handbook of Creative Dance and Drama*. Portsmouth, N.H.: Heinemann Educational Books, 1991. A "how to" book with an excellent section on masks for various educational aims, especially for elementary and middle school levels.

Leeper, Janet. *Edward Gordon Craig*. London: Penguin Books, 1948.

Legge, Valerie. "Resistance and Celebration." *Tickle Ace: A Journal of Literary and Visual Art*, no. 25 (Spring–Summer 1993): 220–25. Review of *The Plays of Codco*, edited by Helen Peters, a popular collective company that represents the Newfoundlander's search for identity.

Leprohon, Pierre. *Charles Chaplin*. Paris: Jacques Melot, 1946. In French. Art of Chaplin.

Lesage et d'Orneval. *Le Théâtre de la Foire*. Paris: Ganeau, 1721–37. In French. The French theatre of the fairs.

Lessac, Arthur. *Body Wisdom: The Use and Training of the Human Body*. New York: Drama Book Specialists, 1981.

Lévesque, Solange. "Opéra Fête: The Power of Image." Translated by Rosalind Gill. *Canadian Theatre Review* 50 (Spring 1987): 20–25. Visual language of Canadian stage director Pierre A. Larocque versus verbal theatre.

Lewis, Charlton T., and Charles Short. *A Latin Dictionary*. Oxford: Clarenden Press, 1933. Definitions and descriptions of ancient mime and pantomime.

Lifar, Serge. "The Mime and the Dancer." In *Opera Ballet Music-Hall in the World,* vols. 41–44. Paris: International Theatre Institute III, 1953.

Littlewood, Samuel Robinson. *The Story of Pierrot*. London: Herbert and Daniel, 1911. History of Pierrot.

Loeschke, Maravene. *All About Mime: Understanding and Performing the Expressive Silence*. Englewood Cliffs N.J.: Prentice-Hall, 1982. Illustrated introduction to mime, performance techniques, and creating mime.

Logie, Lea. "Theatrical Movement and the Mind–Body Question." *Theatre Research International* 20. no. 3 (Fall 1995): 255–65. The need for physical expression in the second half of the twentieth century. Body–mind unity of Konstantin Stanislavsky, Emile-Jaques Dalcroze, Rudolf Laban, Jerzy Grotowski, and Eugenio Barba.

Longman, Stanley Vincent. "The Modern *Maschere* of Ettore Petrolini." *Educational Theatre Journal* 27, no. 3 (October 1975): 377–86. Modern use of *commedia* and *lazzi* by the Italian actor, director, and playwright Petrolini.

Lorelle, Yves. "Corps Théâtral Corps Coupable." *La Revue du Théâtre* 15 (Winter 1997a): 31–44. In French. Historical censuring of the actor's use of his body.

——. *L'Expression Corporelle: Du Mime Sacré au Mime de Théâtre*. Paris: La Renaissance du Livre, 1974. In French. From religious mime to mime in the theatre. Section on French mimes, from Decroux to Marceau.

——. "Rituel et Théâtre." *La Revue du Théâtre* 18 (Fall 1997b). In French. Ritual and body expression in the theatre.

Louys, Pierre. *Mimes des Courtisanes de Lucien*. Paris: Ambroise Vollard, 1935 (reprint). In French. Mimes of the courtesans of Lucian.

Lucian. "Of Pantomime." *The Works of Lucian of Samosata*. Vol. 2. Translated by H. W. Fowler and F. G. Fowler. Oxford: Clarendon Press, 1905. The relationship between ancient dance and pantomime.

Lumley, Frederick. *Trends in Twentieth Century Drama*. New York: Oxford University Press, 1972. Twentieth-century drama, from Ibsen to Shaw.

Lust, Annette. Review of *Apostles of Silence*, by Mira Felner. *Theatre Journal* 38, no. 1 (March 1986a): 128–30. Study of the new French mime masters. See Mira Felner.

——. Review of *Are Are*. *Theatre Journal* 35, no. 4 (December 1983a): 543–44. George Coates's Performance Work.

——. Review of *The Articulate Body: The Physical Training of the Actor*, by Anne Dennis. *Movement Theatre Quarterly* (Fall 1995a): 14. See Anne Dennis.

——. Review of *Bert Houle Mime Theatre*. *Theatre Journal* 36, no. 4 (December 1984): 531–32. Solo pieces of Decroux trainee Bert Houle.

———. Review of *Carousel*. *Educational Theatre Journal* 30, no. 2 (May 1978): 265. Gest Student Pantomime Theatre's mimodrama at the 1977 International Pantomime Workshop in Wroclaw, Poland.

———. Review of *Charlie Chaplin's One-Man Show*, by Dan Kamin. *Theatre Journal* 37, no. 4 (December 1985a): 526–27. See Dan Kamin.

———. "Clowning Around." *Dance Magazine* 57 (October 1983b): 7, 10. Review of 1983 Clown–Theatre Festival in New York.

———. Review of "The Dogs." *Educational Theatre Journal* 28, no. 3 (October 1976): 414. *The Dogs*, based on Michel de Ghelderode's *Escurial* and *School for Buffoons*, performed by the International Mime Workshop in Wroclaw, Poland.

———. "Du Mime et de la Danse." *Théâtre Public* 118–119 (July–October 1994d): 82–83. In French. The fusion and separation of mime and dance from the Greeks to the present.

———. Review of "The Eighth Annual Mimos 90 International Festival of Mime." *Theatre Journal* 43, no. 21 (May 1991a): 259–61. Performances at the annual Mimos Festival in Périgueux, France.

———. Review of "The Eleventh Annual Mimos 93 International Festival of Mime." *Theatre Journal* 46, no. 2 (May 1994a): 278–81. Performances at the annual Mimos Festival in Périgueux, France.

———. "Etienne Decroux and the French School of Mime." *Quarterly Journal of Speech* 57, no. 3 (October 1971): 291–97. Decroux's contribution to French Mime.

———. "Etienne Decroux: Father of Modern Mime." *Mime Journal* 1 (1974): 14–25 Decroux's contribution to modern mime and theatre.

———. "From Pierrot to Bip and Beyond." *Mime Journal* (1980–82): 9–15. Evolution of nineteenth-century pantomime to twentieth-century mime.

———. Review of "George Coates's Performance Works Trilogy." *The Drama Review* 29, no. 1 (Spring 1985b): 140–46. Use of mime in George Coates's works.

———. Review of *Gestures of Genius: Women, Dance, and the Body,* by Rachel Viguier. *The American Review of Canadian Studies* 24, no. 3 (Fall 1994b): 422–25. See Rachel Viguier.

———. "In Memoriam Etienne Decroux (1898–1991)." *Movement Theatre Quarterly* (Summer 1991b): 2–3. Tribute to Decroux's contribution to mime and theatre.

———. Review of "International Festival Fantochio." *Movement Theatre Quarterly* (Fall 1994c): 20–21. The fifth international festival of contemporary mime, puppetry, robotics, and animation at the Magic Theatre in San Francisco.

———. Review of "International Movement Theatre Festival in Winnipeg." *Movement Theatre Quarterly* (Spring 1990a): 4–5. Performances at the Winnipeg Mime Festival.

———. "Interview with Samuel Avital." In *Le Centre du Silence Workbook*, by Samuel Avital, 131–35. Boulder, Colo.: Aleph-Beith Publishers, 1975; distributed by Brillig Works Bookstore, Boulder, Colo. Mime in the life and works of Avital.

———. Review of "Midwest Mime and Clown Festival." *Theatre Journal* 38, no. 1 (March 1986c): 111–14. Performances at the Midwest Mime and Clown Festival.

———. Review of *Mimages*, by Guy Charrié. *Impulse* 4, no. 2 (April 1996a): 177–79. See Guy Charrié.

———. "Mime in North America." *Total Theatre* (London) 6 (Spring 1994e): 14–15. Twentieth-century mime forms and artists in Canada and the United States.

———. Review of "Mimos International Mime Festival 97." *Association of Theatre Movement Educators* 6, no. 1 (January 1998): 8–9. Fifteenth annual Mimos Festival in Périgueux, France, under the theme of "Women and Others."

———. Review of *La Mise-en-Scène du Geste*, edited by Jean-Marc Lachaud. *Impulse* 3, no. 4 (October 1995b): 330–31. See Jean-Marc Lachaud.

———. Review of "Movement Theatre International Clown Congress." *Movement Theatre Quarterly* (Fall 1991c): 1–4. Performances, panels, and workshops at the tenth Philadelphia Movement Theatre International Festival.

———. Review of "Movement Theatre International Tribute to Mime Master Etienne Decroux." *Movement Theatre Quarterly* (Summer 1992): 1–3. Decroux mime artists and companies at the 1992 Philadelphia Movement Theatre International Festival.

———. "On the Meaning of Mime and Pantomime." *Theatrical Movement: A Bibliograhical Anthology*, edited by Bob Fleshman, 66–78. Metuchen, N.J.: Scarecrow Press, 1986b. Meanings of mime and pantomime throughout the centuries and today.

———. Review of "Ottawa International Mime Fest and Mask Symposium." *Movement Theatre Quarterly* (Spring 1991d): 8–10. Performances of international artists and panels at the Ottawa Fest.

———. Review of "Pantomimenzirkus Festival." *Theatre Journal* 42, no. 2 (May 1990b): 255–58. Performances at the International Mime–Clown Festival in Marburg, Germany.

———. Review of "Périgueux, Center of European Mime." *Movement Theatre Quarterly* (Winter 1991f): 1–4. Annual Mimos Festival performances in Périgueux, France.

———. Review of "Périgueux Mimos 90 Festival." *Movement Theatre Quarterly* (Winter 1991e): 1–3. Annual Mimos Festival performances in Périgueux, France.

———. Review of "Périgueux Mimos Festival 1992." *Movement Theatre Quarterly* (Winter 1993a): 2–6. Annual Mimos Festival performances in Périgueux, France.

———. Review of "Périgueux Mimos Festival 1993." *Movement Theatre Quarterly* (Winter 1994f): 5–8, and in *Total Theatre* 5, no. 4 (Winter 1993): 19. Annual Mimos Festival performances in Périgueux, France.

———. Review of "Périgueux Mimos 94." *Movement Theatre Quarterly* (Winter 1995c): 14–17. Annual Mimos Festival performances in Périgueux, France.

———. Review of "Périgueux Mimos 94 International Movement Theatre Festival." *Impulse* 3, no. 1 (January 1995d): 52–58. Annual Mimos Festival performances in Périgueux, France.

———. Review of "Périgueux Mimos '95 International Movement Theatre Festival." *Impulse* 4, no. 1 (January 1996b): 73–78. Annual Mimos Festival performances in Périgueux, France.

———. Review of *Pierrette. Theatre Journal* 34, no. 3 (October 1982a): 409. Japanese mime–dancer Mamako and her company's performance in San Francisco.

———. "Reviews by Annette Lust." *Movement Theatre Quarterly* (Spring 1993b): 7–10.

Reviews of Mark Wing-Davey's *Mad Forest*, San Francisco Mime Troupe's *Social Work*, Franca Rame's *The Pope and the Witch*, and the National Theatre of the Deaf's *Ophelia*.

———. Review of *Samarambi, Pounding of the Heart. Theatre Journal* 40, no. 3 (October 1988): 406–8. Vancouver Special Delivery Moving Theatre at the Winnipeg Mime Festival.

———. "Sets in Constant Motion: Another Form of Movement Theatre." *Movement Theatre Quarterly* (Spring 1995e): 9–10. Review of *Angels in America* at the American Conservatory Theatre.

———. Review of *Le Théâtre de Geste*: *Mimes et Acteurs*, edited by Jacques Lecoq. *Theatre Journal* 42, no. 2 (May 1990c): 283–85. See Jacques Lecoq.

———. Review of *Le Théâtre Repère: Du Ludique au Poétique dans le Théâtre de Recherche*, by Irène Roy. *American Review of Canadian Studies* 25, no. 1 (Spring 1995f): 151–53. See Irène Roy.

———. Review of *Thinking Aloud,* by Walter Carrington. *Impulse* 4, no. 1 (January 1996c): 81–82. See Walter Carrington.

———. "Voix de la Femme dans le Mime." *Gestes* no. 8 (April 1997): 2. In French. Women's role in mime through the ages.

———. Review of *The Way of How. Theatre Journal* 34, no. 2 (May 1982b): 256. George Coates's performance piece.

———. Review of *Words on Mime*, by Etienne Decroux. *Theatre Journal* 39, no. 4 (December 1987): 534–35. Mark Piper's translation of Decroux's *Paroles sur le Mime* on the technique and philosophy of mime and theatre.

Lyonnet, Henry. *Pulcinella & Co*. Paris: Paul Ollendorff, 1901. In French. Story of Pulcinella.

———. *Le Théâtre en Italie*. Paris: Paul Ollendorff, 1900. In French. Nineteenth-century theatre in Italy.

MacDougall, Jill. Review of *Polygraph* and *Le Dortoir. Theatre Journal* 43, no. 21 (May 1991): 252–55. The expressive body in the performances of the Quebec Théâtre Repère and Carbone 14 at the 1990 BAM Next Wave/Next Door Festival.

Magnin, Charles. *Les Origines du Théâtre Moderne*. Paris: Librairie de l'Université Royale de France, 1838. In French. Mime in Greek and Roman entertainment.

Magriel, Paul David. *A Bibliography of Dancing*. New York: H. W. Wilson Co., 1936. Dance and dance-related titles.

Makeieff, Macha. *Deschamps Deschiens: Le Théâtre de Jérôme Deschamps*. Paris: Librairie Séguier Archimbaud, 1989. In French. The comedies of playwright, stage director, and actor Jerome Deschamps.

Maletic, Vera. *Body, Space, Expression: The Development of R. Laban's Movement and Dance Concepts*. Berlin: Mouton de Gruyter, 1987.

Mallarmé, Stephane. "Mimique: Notes sur le Théâtre." *Revue Indépendante* 3ème série (November 1886): 42–43. In French. The author's attempt to understand Paul Margueritte's art of pantomime in *Pierrot Assassin de Sa Femme*.

Mandel, Dorothy. *Uncommon Eloquence: A Biography of Angna Enters: Writer, Dance–Mime, Artist*. Denver: Arden Press, 1986.

Mander, Raymond, and Joe Mitchenson. *Pantomime*. London, 1973. A story in pictures, with 249 illustrations.

Mantinband, James H. *The Dictionary of Latin Literature*. New York: Philosophical Library, 1956. Definitions of ancient mime and pantomime.

Marash, Jessie. *Mime in Class and Theatre*. London: Harrap, 1950.

Marceau, Marcel. "The Art of Mime." In *Opera Ballet Music-Hall in the World*, 19–34. Paris: International Theatre Institute III, 1953.

——. *La Ballade Autour de Paris et du Monde*. Paris: Elmayan, 1968. In French. Bip in Paris and throughout the world, with lithographs.

——. *L'Histoire de Bip*. Paris: L'Ecole des Loisirs, 1976. In French. The story of Marceau's character, Bip.

——. "Language of the Heart." *Theatre Arts* 42 (March 1958): 58–59. Marceau explains why he became a mime.

——. *Le Mime Marcel Marceau: Entretiens et Regards, avec Valérie Bochenek*. Paris: Edition d'Art Somogy, 1997. In French. Marceau interviews with Valérie Bochenek, homages from other artists, and iconography in black and white and color.

——. "Who Am I?" *Dance Magazine* 39 (November 1965): 49–51. Marceau on his life and art during his October–February 1965 tour of the United States.

Martin, Ben. *Marcel Marceau: Master of Mime*. Ottawa: Optimum Publishing Co., 1978; New York: Paddington Press, 1978. Brief history of mime. Photos of Marceau on and off stage.

Martin, Jacqueline. *Voice in Modern Theatre*. New York: Routledge, 1991. Reevaluation of the spoken word and the visual and physical elements in twentieth-century directorial vision.

Martinez, J. D. *Combat Mime: A Non-Violent Approach to Stage Violence*. Chicago: Nelson-Hall, c. 1982.

Mason, Jeffrey D. Review of *Rarearea, George Coates's Performance Works*. *Theatre Journal* 38, no. 1 (March 1986): 104–5. Evolution of Coates's Performance Works.

Matho (Mathilde Dumont). "Decroux, le Sculpteur: Les Elèves Sa Glaise." In "Paroles Pour un Mime." *Telex-Danse* 38 (1991): 9. In French. The mime Decroux as a sculptor, his students as his clay.

Mawer, Irene. *The Art of Mime*. London: Methuen & Co., 1949. Short history and technique of mime.

Mazur, Kathe, and Danny Sandford. "Anne Bogart's *Women and Men: A Big Dance*." Review of *Women and Men: A Big Dance*, by Anne Bogart. *The Drama Review* 27, no. 2 (Summer 1983): 77–83. Bogart's mime–dance piece about the interaction between women and men in a 1940s atmosphere.

Mazzone-Clementi, Carlo. "Commedia and the Actor." *The Drama Review* 18, no. 1 (March 1974): 59–64. Teaching *commedia* acting in the twentieth century.

McGill, Kathleen. "Women and Performance: The Development of Improvisation by the Sixteenth-Century Commedia dell'Arte." *Theatre Journal* 43, no. 1 (March 1991): 59–69. How improvisation developed with the appearance of women performers in the commedia dell'arte.

Mehl, Dieter. *The Elizabethan Dumb Show*. Cambridge, Mass.: Harvard University Press, 1966. The role of pantomime in Elizabethan theatre.

Mei Lan-Fang. *My Life on the Stage*. Italy: Tipo-Graf, 1986. Autobiography, essays, and articles about the actor's work.

Mic, Constant. *La Commedia dell'Arte*. Paris: La Pléiade, 1927. In French. Important study of *commedia*.

Michaut, Gustave. *Sur les Trétaux Latins*. Paris: Fontemoing, 1912. In French. Roman Theatre.

Mignone, Mario. *Eduardo De Filippo*. Boston: Twayne Publishers, 1984. Contribution of the Neapolitan mime, actor, and playwright.

"Mime et Danse." *Théâtre Public* 118–119 (July–October 1994): 80–96. In French. Texts about mime and dance.

Mime, Mask, and Marionette. Edited by Thomas Leabhart. Marcel Dekker, Inc., Box 11305, Church St. Station, New York, NY 10249. Journal with articles about mime and mime-related subjects, published 1978–80.

Mime News. Edited by Diane Babel. International Mimes and Pantomimists. The Valley Studio, Route 3, Spring Green, WI 53588. Bimonthly newsletter, published March 1976–June 1979.

Mime Times. Edited by Tony Montanaro. RFD 1, Box 236, South Paris, ME 04281. Quarterly newsletter, published 1976–82.

Mitchell, Theresa. *Movement from Person to Actor to Character*. Lanham, Md.: Scarecrow Press, 1998. A guide for actors, stage directors, teachers, and students to utilize movement in creating a character. Includes exercises and projects.

Montanaro, Tony. *Mime Spoken Here: The Performer's Portable Workshop*. Gardiner, Maine: Montanaro and Montanaro, Tilbury House Publishers, 1995. A guide for the performer to develop performance skills.

Moy, James S. "Entertainments at John B. Ricketts's Circus, 1793–1800." *Educational Theatre Journal* 30, no. 2 (May 1978): 187–202. Equestrian pantomimes of the eighteenth-century circus manager.

Mroczka, Paul. "The Dramaturg and Movement Theater Artist: Finding the Balance Between Literature and Physical Action." *Movement Theatre Quarterly* (Fall 1993): 2–5. Combining the dramaturg's text and movement in Pontine Movement Theatre's *Correspondence of Desires* (1993).

Mufson, Daniel. "Cool Medium: Anne Bogart and the Choreography of Fear." *Theater* 25, no. 3 (1995): 55–63. Bogart on her Viewpoints method and her Essay Theatre concerning the theatrical expansion of theories.

Muller, Max. *Three Lectures on the Science of Language and Its Place in General Education*. Chicago: Open House Publishing Co., 1890. Essays on thought and language.

Mullin, Michael. Review of *Everyday Life After the Revolution, Part Two*, by the Akademia Ruchu, and *Dérives*, by the Compagnie Philippe Genty. *Theatre Journal* 45, no. 1 (March 1993): 99–100. Movement-oriented political theatre of the Polish Akademia Ruchu and Genty's imaginative theatre of mimes, puppets, and floating silk pieces at the International Theatre Festival of Chicago, May 27–June 21, 1992.

Najac, Raoul de. *Souvenirs d'un Mime*. Paris: Emile Paul, 1909. In French. Autobiography of a mime.

Navarre, Octave. *Le Théâtre Grec*. In French. Paris: Payot, 1925. Greek theatre.

Nicoll, Allardyce. *The Development of Theatre*. New York: Harcourt Brace, 1946. Development of theatre, with a section on mime.

——. *Masks, Mimes, and Miracles*. New York: Cooper Square, 1963a. Critical study of mime from the Greeks and Romans through the commedia dell'arte. Abundant illustrations.

——. *The World of Harlequin*. Cambridge: Cambridge University Press, 1963b. Critical study of Harlequin and the commedia dell'arte.

Niklaus, Thelma. *Harlequin, or The Rise and Fall of a Bergamask Rogue*. New York: George Braziller, 1956. History of Harlequin.

Noverre, Jean G. *Letters on Dancing and Ballets*. (Original French edition, 1803.) Translated by C. W. Beaumont, 1930. New York: Dance Horizons, 1968. Mime in ballet.

Ogilvy, Jack David Angus. "Mimi Scurrae Histriones: Entertainers of the Early Middle Ages." *Speculum* 38 (October 1963): 603–19. Information about mimes as entertainers in the Middle Ages.

Ohno, Kazuo. "Selections From the Prose of Kazuo Ohno." Translated by Noriko Maehata. *TDR The Drama Review* 30, no. 2 (Summer 1986): 156–62. Ohno's thoughts on theatre and dance.

"On Pantomime." *La Plume*, no. 82 (15 September 1892). In French. Essays about Gaspard Deburau, Pierrot, Harlequin, and other related subjects.

O'Regan, James. "Making Image Theatre." *Canadian Theatre Review* 50 (spring 1987): 10–13. New conventions for image theatre in Canadian productions.

Palmer, Winthrop. *Theatrical Dancing in America*. New York: B. Ackerman, 1945. Expressive movement in dance.

Palmquist, Chris. "Street Performers at the Pompidou Center." *The Drama Review* 28, no. 1 (Spring 1984): 97–102. Performances and endurance of mimes at the Pompidou Center.

Paseková, Dana. "Modern Mime and Its Evolution." *Ballett International* 9/9, no. 1 (January 1986): 14–19. Development of mime from the ancients to the present; differences among mime, theatre, and dance.

Pasolini, Pier Paolo. "Manifeste pour un Theatre Nouveau." *Du Théâtre*, no. 16 (Spring, 1997): 49–57. In French. The ritual element in theatre.

Passman, Arnie. "Stop, Look, and Listen." *San Francisco Sunday Examiner and Chronicle*, California Living section, 30 September 1973: 40, 43, 48, 50, 52. Ronnie Davis's definition of mime and pantomime.

Paterson, Doug. "Two Productions by Copeau: *The Tricks of Scapin* and *Twelfth Night*." *TDR The Drama Review* 28, no. 1 (Spring 1984): 37–51. Stage direction, acting, and type of stage in Jacques Copeau's two productions.

Pavis, Patrice, and Rodrigue Villeneuve. "Gestualités." *Protée* 21, no. 3 (Fall 1993). In French. Issue consecrated to research on the art of gesture, with illustrations.

——. *Theatre at the Crossroads of Culture*. Translated by Loren Kruger. London: Routledge, 1992. Essays on theatre semiotics and the intercultural theatre of Peter Brook, Ariane Mnouchkine, and Eugenio Barba.

Pawlikowski-Cholewa, Harald von. *Le Mime Marcel Marceau*. Hamburg: J. M. Hoeppner, 1955. Photographic descriptions of three Marceau pieces.

——. *Le Mime Marcel Marceau*. West Germany: Overseas Publishers Vaduz, 1963. Photographic description of five Marceau pieces.

Pegnato, Lisa J. "Breathing in a Different Zone: Joseph Chaikin." *TDR The Drama Review* 25, no. 3 (Fall 1981): 7–18. Chaikin's contribution to theatre. Section on Chaikin's use of language.

Pepler, Hilary. *Mimes Sacred and Profound*. London: Samuel French, 1932. Mime in ancient religious theatre.

Péricaud, Louis. *Le Théâtre des Funambules*. Paris: Léon Sapin, 1897. In French. The history of mimes and actors of the Théâtre des Funambules.

Petit de Julleville. *Histoire du Théâtre en France: Les Comédiens en France au Moyen Age*. Paris: L. Cerf, 1885. In French. French actors in the Middle Ages.

——. *Histoire du Théâtre en France: Les Mystères*. 2 vols. Paris: Hachette, 1880. In French. The history of French theatre: the mysteries.

Petrolini, Ettore. *Nerone Romani di Roma*. Rome: Biblioteca Romana Italia, 1945. In Italian. Petrolini's and the Roman mime–actor–playwright's use of the text as a pretext.

Picon-Vallin, Béatrice. "L'Entrainement de l'Acteur Chez Meyerhold." *Bouffonneries* 18/19 (1989): 212–19. In French. Vsevolod Meyerhold's actor training.

Piderit, Theodor. *La Mimique et la Physiognomie*. Translated by A. Girot. Paris: Alcan, 1888. In French. Mimic art and physiognomy.

Pinok and Matho. *Dynamique de la Création, le Mot, et l'Expression Corporelle*. Paris: J. Vrin, 1976. In French. Creativity in scenes, words, and movement.

——. *Expression Corporelle à l'Ecole*. Paris: J. Vrin, 1973. In French. Movement in education.

——. *Expression Corporelle, Mouvement et Pensée*. Paris: T.E.M.P., 1994. In French. The relationship between movement and thought.

——. *Le Fabuleux Voyage aux Pays de Tout en Tout*. Paris: J. Vrin, 1979. In French. Ideas for children's and adult performances.

Pinok, Matho, and Maximilien Decroux. *Ecrits sur Panomime, Mime, Expression Corporelle: Origine et Principaux Moments d'Evolution*. Paris: T.E.M.P., 1975. In French. Short history of mime from the Greeks to the present.

Pinter, Harold. *Complete Works*. Vol. 4. New York: Grove Press, 1981. Pinter's use of silence and pauses.

Pisk, Litz. *An Actor and His Body*. New York: Theatre Arts, Routledge, 1987. An actor–training program with principles and exercises related to all parts of the body.

Prévost, Jean. *Polymnie, ou Les Arts Mimiques*. Paris: Emile Hazan, 1929. The mimic arts in the cinema and art.

Pujade-Renaud, Claude. *Expression Corporelle: Langage du Silence*. Paris: Editions E. S. F., 1976. In French. Corporeal expression and the language of silence.

Que Dit le Corps? Transcribed by Marc Aubaret. Actes de la Table Ronde, Le Cratère Théâtre d'Ales (25 March 1995). In French. Papers

presented at the Actes de la Table Ronde
meeting about how dance and the body were
regarded from the fifteenth to the twentieth
centuries.

Racine, Jean. *Phèdre: Collections Mises-en-
Scène*. Paris: Editions du Seuil, 1945. In
French. Jean-Louis Barrault's fusion of
speech and movement in his staging of
Phèdre.

The Random House Dictionary. New York:
Random House, 1967. Definition of
pantomime.

Redgrave, Michael. *Actors' Ways and Means*.
New York: Theatre Arts, Routledge, 1995.
The actor's art and his surroundings.

Reich, Hermann. *Der Mimus*. Berlin: Weidmann,
1903. In German. Important work on the
history and literary aspect of mime.

Reinelt, Janelle. Review of "The Los Angeles
Theatre Festival." *Theatre Journal* 43, no. 1
(March 1991): 107–14. Description of
companies such as Chile's El Gran Circo
Teatro, the United States's Wooster Group,
and Canada's Théâtre Repère and works such
as Robert Lepage's *Dragon Trilogy* and the
opera *Nixon in China*.

Rémy, Tristan. *Clown Scenes*. Translated by
Bernard Sahlins. Chicago: Ivan R. Dee, 1997.
Classic clown routines for class or
performance.

———. *Jean-Gaspard Deburau*. Paris: L'Arche,
1954.

Remy, Tristan, and Nicole Wild *Catalogue de la
Bibliothèque de l'Opéra: Le Cirque,
Iconographie*. Paris: Bibliothèque Nationale,
1969. In French. Catalogue of the Opera
Library and iconography of circus and
pantomime performers.

———. *Les Clowns*. Paris: B. Grasset, 1945. In
French. History of clowns.

———. *Georges Wague, Mime de la Belle
Epoque*. Paris: Georges Girard, 1964. In
French. Belle Epoque mime Georges Wague
and mimes of the period.

———. *Jean-Baptiste Gaspard Deburau*. Paris:
L'Arche, 1954. In French. Nineteenth-century
mime Deburau's life and work.

Restif de la Bretonne. *La Mimographie*. Geneva:
1980. In French. Reprint of the original 1770
edition.

Riccoboni, Luigi. *Histoire du Théâtre Italien
depuis la Décadence de la Comédie Latine*.
Paris: Delormel, 1728. In French. History of

the Italian theatre from the decadence of
Latin comedy on.

———. *Le Nouveau Théâtre Italien*. 8 vols. Paris:
Briasson, 1733. In French. The new Italian
theatre.

Richards, Thomas. *At Work with Grotowski: On
Physical Actions*. London: Routledge, 1995.
Jerzy Grotowski's assistant since 1985, on
Grotowski as Konstantin Stanislavsky's
disciple and on Stanislavsky as a teacher.
General description of exercises.

Richy, Pierre, and J. C. Mauriage. *Initiation au
Mime*. Paris: L'Amicale, 1960, 1982. In
French. An introductory mime textbook.

Rieder, Don. "A Conversation with Jean Asselin
and Michael Mackenzie." *Movement Theatre
Quarterly* (Spring 1995): 2–10. Interview with
the artistic director of Montreal's Omnibus,
Jean Asselin, and Montreal playwright
Michael Mackenzie on the movement and
aesthetics in *Geometry in Venice*.

———. "Robert Lepage's *Elseneur*." *Movement
Theatre Quarterly* (Winter 1996): 2–3.
Review of Lepage's exploration of stage
space in his solo based on Shakespeare's
Hamlet.

Robinson, Alan Young. "Physicalizing *The Little
Prince* by Saint-Exupéry." *Movement Theatre
Quarterly* (Summer 1994): 12–13. Interview
with Annette Lust on the use of movement in
staging Antoine de Saint-Exupéry's *Little
Prince*.

Rodowicz, Jadwiga. "Rethinking Zeami: Talking
to Kanze Tetsunojo." *TDR The Drama Review*
36, no. 2 (Summer 1992): 97–105. Interview
with Tetsunojo about Zeami's medieval treatise
on Noh theatre and movement for the actor.

Rolfe, Bari. *Actions Speak Louder Than Words*.
Berkeley, Calif.: Personabooks, 1992.
Introductory workshop with movement
exercises and improvisations.

———. Review of *The Actor's Image: Movement
Training for Stage and Screen*, by Jean
Sabatine. *Theatre Journal* 37, no. 4
(December 1985a): 525–26. Sabatine's all-
inclusive movement training, which
coordinates movement, acting, and voice.

———. *Behind the Mask*. Oakland, Calif.:
Personabooks, 1977a. Introduction and
exercises to mask work, with photographic
illustrations.

———. "Commedia dell'Arte and Mime." In
Theatrical Movement: A Bibliographical

Anthology, edited by Bob Fleshman, 46–65. Metuchen, N.J., London: Scarecrow Press, 1986a. Essays and extensive bibliographies on commedia dell'arte and mime.

——. *Commedia dell'Arte: A Scene Study Book.* San Francisco: Personabooks, 1977b. Scenes and *lazzi* for the classroom and other purposes.

——. *Farces, Italian Style.* Oakland, Calif.: Personabooks, 1981. Short plays for the classroom and performance.

——. "Mime in America: A Survey." *Mime Journal* 1 (1974): 2–12. History of American mime.

——. "The Mime of Jacques Lecoq." *The Drama Review* 16, no. 1 (March 1972): 34–38. Lecoq mime training.

——. Review of *Modern and Post-modern Mime*, by Thomas Leabhart. *Theatre Journal* 43, no. 21 (May 1991): 267–68. See Thomas Leabhart.

——. Review of *Movement and Meaning*, by Anya Peterson Royce. *Theatre Journal* 38, no. 2 (May 1986): 250–52. Review of an anthropologist's viewpoint on mime and ballet.

——. *Movement for Period Plays.* Oakland, Calif.: Personabooks, 1985.

Rolfe, Bari, ed. *Mime Directory/Bibliography.* Vol. 2. Spring Green, Wisc.: International Mimes and Pantomimists, 1978a. Books, articles, scripts, films, and reference works on mime.

——. ed. *Mimes on Miming.* Los Angeles: Panjandrum Books, 1978. Interviews and contributions of famous mimes.

Roose-Evans, James. *Experimental Theatre.* New York: Universe Books, 1973. Experimental theatre and dance from Stanislavsky to Peter Brook, and Martha Graham to Alwin Nickolais.

Rose, Mark V. *The Actor and His Double: Mime and Movement for the Theatre of Cruelty.* Chicago: Actor Training Research Institute Press, 1986. Antonin Artaud's use of mime and movement.

Rosenblatt, Mark. "Toward a Theatre of Gesture: Gesture and Non-Verbal Elements in Late Nineteenth- and Twentieth-Century European Theatre." Doctoral thesis, University of California–Berkeley, Dunbar Ogden, 1981.

Rovine, Harvey. *Silence in Shakespeare.* Ann Arbor, Mich.: UMI Research Press, 1987. How silence contributes to content and characterization in the work of Shakespeare and other playwrights.

Roy, Claude. *L'Opéra de Pékin.* Paris: Editions Cercle d'Art, 1955. In French. Illustrations and chronicle of the Peking Opera.

Roy, Irene. *Le Théâtre Repère: Du Ludique au Poétique dans le Théâtre de Recherche.* Quebec: Nuit Blanche, 1993. In French. Contribution and creative process of Robert Lepage, founder of Canada's Théâtre Repère.

Royce, Anya Peterson. *Movement and Meaning: Creativity and Interpretation in Ballet and Mime.* Bloomington: Indiana University Press, 1984. An anthropologist's analysis of mime and ballet and the nature of performance.

Rudlin, John. *Commedia dell'Arte: An Actor's Handbook.* London: Routledge, 1994. Origin of the *commedia* and guide to *commedia* techniques in performance.

——. *Jacques Copeau.* Cambridge: Cambridge University Press, 1986. Directorial career and influence of Jacques Copeau. His *commedia* and mask work.

——. "The Masked Apprentice." *Total Theatre* (London) 7 (Fall 1995): 4–5. Rudlin's mask work at the Centre Sélavy, France, to develop the natural actor.

Rykner, Arnaud. *L'Envers du Théâtre: Dramaturgie du Silence de l'Age Classique à Maeterlinck.* Paris: Librairie José Corti, 1996. In French. Silence in French theatre, from Jean Racine, to Maurice Maeterlinck and Denis Diderot, to Emile Zola, passing through Pierre de Marivaux.

Sabatine, Jean. *Movement Training for the Stage and Screen: The Organic Connection Between Mind, Spirit, and Body.* New York: Back Stage Books, Watson-Guptill Publications, 1995. Movement program that integrates the physical, mental, and emotional.

Salacrou, Armand. "Portrait de Jean-Louis Barrault." *Formes et Couleurs*, no. 5 (1947). In French. The art of Barrault.

Salovey, Todd. "Violently Awake: Anne Bogart Directing *The Women*." *Theatre Forum*, no. 2 (Fall 1992): 68–71. Interview with Bogart about her physical theatre interpretation of Claire Booth Luce's *The Women*.

Sand, Maurice. *The History of the Harlequinade.* 2 vols. Philadelphia: Lippencott, 1915.

Reprint of the 1862 original. *Commedia* characters, with illustrations.

———. *Masques et Bouffons.* 2 vols. Paris: Lévy Fils, 1862. In French. See description above.

San Francisco Mime Troupe. *By Popular Demand: Plays and Other Works.* San Francisco: The Troupe, 1980.

Santini, Pierre. Review of *Le Corps Poétique*, by Jacques Lecoq. *Action Theatre*, no. 8 (Winter 1998). Lecoq's contribution as an educator and teacher.

Saxon, A. H. "The Circus as Theatre: Astley's and Its Actors in the Age of Romanticism." *Educational Theatre Journal* 27, no. 3 (October 1975): 299–312. Development of theatre elements in the circus. Section on mimetic scenes in the circus.

Scarpetta, Guy. *L'Impureté.* Paris: Bernard Grasset, 1985. In French. Impurity of postmodernism and the arts at the end of the twentieth century.

Schechner, Richard. *Durov's Pig: Clowns, Politics and Theatre.* New York: Theatre Communications Group, 1985. Political clowning and satiric theatre from Brecht, Grock, and Fo to Irwin and the San Francisco Mime Troupe.

———. *The Future of Ritual: Writings on Culture and Performance.* New York: Routledge, 1993. Ritual in culture and theatre. Avant-garde theatre forms.

———. "Kazuo Ohno Doesn't Commute." *TDR The Drama Review* 30, no. 2 (Summer 1986a): 163–69. Interview with Kazuo Ohno about how he began in dance.

Schechner, Richard, Mathilde La Bardonnie, Joel Jouanneau, and Georges Banu. "Talking with Peter Brook." *TDR Drama Review* 30, no. 1 (Spring 1986b): 54–71. Interview with Brook about his collective staging of the *Mahabharata.* Section about the importance of the actor's eyes and gestures over scenery.

Scheier, Helmut. "Jugglers '76–'85 Gaukler '76–'85: 10th International Pantomime Festival, Cologne, 1985." *Ballet International* 9/9, no. 1 (January 1986): 20–23. Review of the tenth International Pantomime Festival in Cologne in 1985.

Schmidman, Jo Ann, Sora Kimberlain, and Megan Terry, eds. *Right Brain Vacation Photos.* Omaha, Neb.: The Magic Theatre Foundation and Megan Terry, 1992. Photo chronicle of the Omaha Magic Theatre's visual performance art.

Schmitt, Jean-Claude. *La Raison des Gestes dans l'Occident Médiéval.* Paris: Gallimard, 1990. In French. The reason for gestures in the medieval Occident.

Schoop, Trudi, with Peggy Mitchell. *Won't You Join the Dance?* Palo Alto, Calif.: National Press Books, 1974. Schoop as a dance–mime and dance–movement therapist.

Schoora, Yurgen. "Naming the Man with His Horse." *Total Theatre* (London) 6 (Summer 1994): 17. Short article about the need to respect mime as an art in itself, relevant to today's society.

Schwartz, I. A. *The Commedia dell'Arte and Its Influence on French Comedy in the Seventeenth Century.* Paris: Librairie H. Samuel, 1933.

Scott, Virginia. "The Infancy of English Pantomime, 1716–1723." *Educational Theatre Journal* 24 (May 1972): 125–38.

Séverin. *L'Homme Blanc, Souvenirs d'un Pierrot.* Paris: Plon, 1929. In French. Autobiography of the early twentieth-century French pantomimist.

Shakespeare, William. *As You Like It.* In *The Annotated Shakespeare.* Vol. 1, act 2, scene 7, 360. L. 139–66. New York: Clarkson N. Potter, Inc., 1978. Reference to Pantaloon.

Shank, Theodore. "Political Theatre as Popular Entertainment: The San Francisco Mime Troupe." *TDR The Drama Review* 18, no. 1 (March 1974): 110–17. Use of *commedia*, circus, puppetry, music hall, mime, vaudeville, and other popular forms to convey a political message.

———. Review of "The San Francisco Mime Troupe's *Americans,* or *Last Tango in Huahuatenango.*" *The Drama Review* 25, no. 3 (Fall 1981): 81–83.

Shawn, Ted. *Every Little Movement: A Book about Delsartre.* New York: Dance Horizons, 1963. Movement and François Delsartre's method.

Sheets-Johnstone, ed. *Giving the Body Its Due.* Albany: State University of New York Press, 1992. Essays by psychologists and therapists about the importance of body knowledge and by dancer Sally Ann Ness about the body's intelligence.

Shepard, Richmond. *Mime: The Technique of Silence.* New York: Drama Book Specialists, 1971. Textbook of mime, with line drawings.

Shields, Robert. *Mime in Our Time.* San Francisco: Get the Hook Productions, 1972.

Photographic description of Shields's street mime.

Siegel, Fred. "Clown-Politics: Report on the International Clown Theatre Congress." *TDR The Drama Review* 36, no. 2 (Summer 1992): 182–86. Review of artists and panels at the Movement Theatre International Clown Congress.

Simon, Erika. *The Ancient Theatre.* Translated by C. E. Vafopoulou-Richardson. London: Methuen, 1982. Brief history of Greek and Roman theatrical performance, with illustrations.

Simpson, Mona. *Mime: The Art of Silence.* The Committee for Arts and Lectures Program. Berkeley: University of California–Berkeley, Arts and Leisure Publications, May 1980. Short article on the history of mime and Jean-Louis Barrault's art, preceding his performance at Zellerbach Hall on the University of California–Berkeley campus.

Skeel, Rina, ed. *The Tradition of ISTA.* Translated by Judy Barba and Leo Sykes. Holstebro, Denmark: International School of Theatre Anthropology, 1994. Record of eight ISTA sessions, masters, and performing traditions.

Sklar, Deidre. "Decroux and Prometheus: Applying the Dance Ethnology Model to a Contemporary Artist." Master's thesis, University of California–Los Angeles, 1983. Study based on classes and writings by Etienne Decroux and other mime specialists on corporeal mime as a movement symbol that parallels the Promethean myth.

———. "Etienne Decroux's Promethean Mime." *TDR The Drama Review* 29, no. 4 (Winter 1985): 64–75. The ritualistic element of Decroux's art.

Slater, Emi. "Mime Is Back in Town." *Total Theatre* 9, no. 4 (Winter 1997–98): 4–5. Interview with the London International Mime Festival directors about mime and their festival.

Slonim, Marc. *The Origins of Russian Theatre.* Cleveland, Ohio: World Publishing Co., 1961. History of early Russian theatre.

"Something to See: Marcel Marceau." *Time* Atlantic edition, New York 66 (3 October 1955): 3–12. Marceau performance.

Source Monthly. Edited by Louise S. Jenkins. Mimesource, Inc. 125 Sherman Street, Brooklyn, New York, NY 11218. Monthly information for mimes, jugglers, puppeteers, and clowns. Published from 1982 to 1983.

Souriau, Paul. *The Aesthetics of Movement.* Translated and edited by Manon Souriau. Amherst: University of Massachusetts, 1983. Objective analysis of movement in humans and animals and of principles of visual and aural perception.

Spolin, Viola. *Improvisation for the Theater.* Evanston, Ill.: Northwestern University Press, 1990. Improvisational exercises and games. Steps in preparing a production.

———. *An Actor Prepares.* New York: Theatre Arts, Routledge, 1989b. The Stanislavsky method.

Stanislavsky, Konstantin. *The Actor's Handbook.* New York: Theatre Arts, Routledge, 1989a. An alphabetically ordered handbook about acting.

Stebbins, Genevieve. *Delsartre System of Dramatic Expression.* New York: E. S. Werner, 1886. François Delsartre's system of exercises and analysis of expressive movement.

Stefanesco, Lucien. "La Formation de l'Acteur au XXe Siècle, L'École J. Lecoq." Thèse de doctorat de 3e cycle, Université de la Sorbonne, Paris III, 1972. In French. Actor training in the twentieth century and Lecoq's school.

Steiner, George. *Language and Silence: Essays on Language, Literature, and the Inhuman.* New York: Atheneum, 1967. Relationship between language and silence.

Steinman, Louise. *The Knowing Body.* Berkeley, Calif.: North Atlantic Books. 1995. Understanding the body through dance and performance art. Interviews with Meredith Monk, Whoopi Goldberg, Spalding Grey, Trisha Brown, and Ping Chong.

Stevensen, R. "Silence of Mr. Chaplin." *Nation* (London) (19 July 1930). The role of silence in Chaplin's art.

Sticca, Sandro. *The Latin Passion Play: Its Origin and Development.* New York: Albany State University Press, 1970. Section on the contribution of mime and jongleurs to theatre.

Stodder, Joseph H. Review of *The Mahabharata,* by Jean-Claude Carrière. Translated by Peter Brook. *Theatre Journal* 40, no. 3 (October 1988): 398–400. The influence of Bertolt Brecht, Vsevolod Meyerhold, Jerzy Grotowski, and Antonin Artaud in Brooks's cross-cultural production at the 1987 Los Angeles Festival.

Stolzenberg, Mark. *Exploring Mime*. New York: Sterling Publishing Co., 1979. Illustrated exercises, short mime pieces, and make-up for mime.

Storey, Robert. *Pierrots on the Stage of Desire: Nineteenth-Century French Literary Artists and the Comic Pantomime*. Princeton, N.J.: Princeton University Press, 1985. Nineteenth-century Pierrots in Paris. A history of Pierrot, his role in the theatre, and literature of the romantic and modern periods. An extensive list of nineteenth-century pantomime scenarios and libraries in Paris where they can be found.

Straub, Cindie, and Matthew Straub. *Mime: Basics for Beginners*. Boston: Plays Inc., 1984.

Surer, Paul. *Cinquante Ans de Théâtre*. Paris: Société d'Enseignement Supérieur, 1969. In French. Modern stage directors' views of the playwright's role.

Taladoire, Barthélemy. *Commentaires sur la Mimique et l'Expression Corporelle du Comédien Romain*. Montpellier: 1951. In French. Expressive movement of the Roman actor.

Taussig, Michael. *Mimesis and Alterity: A Particular History of the Senses*. London: Routledge, 1993. History of the mimetic faculty, from the primitives to the present.

Tempkine, Raymonde. "Antigone." *Gestes*, no. 7 (April 1996): 2. In French. Review and background of the International Visual Theatre of the deaf's production of *Antigone*, performed in France.

Ten Cate, Ritsaert. "Festivals, Who Needs 'em" *Theatre Forum*, no. 1 (Spring 1992): 85–87. Essay about the need to create festivals motivated by the heart, mind, and soul.

Thétard, Henry. "L'Evolution du Clown." *Formes et Couleurs*, no. 5 (1947) In French. Evolution of the modern circus and clown.

Thompson, Peggy. "Who Is Peter Eliot Weiss?" *Canadian Theatre Review* 47 (Summer 1986): 131–39. Interview with Weiss about his plays based on actors' improvisations.

Toole Stott, Raymond. *Circus and Allied Arts*. 4 vols. Derby, England: Harpur, 1958–70. A world bibliography (1500–1957) about the circus, pantomime, mime, and related arts based on circus literature in the British Museum Library, the Library of Congress, the Bibliothèque Nationale, and the author's own collection.

Toomey, Susie Kelly. *Mime Ministry*. Colorado Springs, Colo.: Meriweather Publishing, 1986. How to organize a mime company for Christian ministry. Exercises and sketches.

Towsen, John. *Clowns: A Panoramic History*. New York: Hawthorn Books, 1976. History of clowns in North America and Europe. *Commedia* and mime.

Turner, Craig. "Contemporary Approaches to Movement Training for Actors in the U.S." In *Theatrical Movement: A Bibliographical Anthology*, edited by Bob Fleshman, 29–45. Metuchen, N.J.: Scarecrow Press, 1986. Description and annotated bibliographies of contemporary movement systems.

———. Review of *Mimes on Miming*, by Bari Rolfe. *Theatre Journal* 33, no. 2 (May 1981): 278–79. Appreciation of Rolfe's book, which traces the development of mime through the written contributions of recognized mimes.

Udine, Jean d'. *L'Art et le Geste*. Paris: Alcan, 1910. In French. Essays about gesture and art.

Vallillo, Federico. La Scuola Teatrale di Jacques Lecoq. Testi di Laurea (thesis), Università di Bologna, 1990. In Italian. Jacques Lecoq's school.

Verlaine, Paul. "Pierrot." In "Jadis et Naguère" section of *Choix de Poésies de Paul Verlaine*, 190. Paris: Bibliothèque Charpentier, 1939. In French. One of Verlaine's Pierrot poems.

Verriest-Lefert, Guy, and Jeanne Verriest-Lefert. *Marcel Marceau, ou L'Aventure du Silence*. Paris: Desclée De Brouwer, 1974. In French. Interview with Marceau. Photos and works of Marceau.

Vigeant, Louise. "Jean-Pierre Ronfard: Impure Theatre." Translated by Roger E. Gannon. *Canadian Theatre Review* 50 (Spring 1987): 14–19. The impure theatre of celebration of the Canadian stage director, actor, and playwright.

Viguier, Rachel. *Gestures of Genius: Women, Dance, and the Body*. Stratford, Ontario: Mercury Press, 1994. Female freedom of expression and mental and emotional liberation through dance and body movement.

Villiers, André. *L'Art du Comédien*. Paris: Presses Universitaires de France, 1953. In French. The art of the actor. Short section about miming and symbolism.

Vircondelet, Alain. *Marguerite Duras*. Paris: Editions Seghers, 1972. Silence in Duras's plays.

Visé, Donneau de. Introduction to *Les Précieuses Ridicules*, by Molière. Paris: Bordas, 1963. Description of Molière's physical expression as an actor.

Waddell, Helen. *Poetry in the Dark Ages*. London: Constable, 1948. Medieval and modern Latin poetry. European history from 392 to 814.

———. *The Wandering Scholars*. Ann Arbor: University of Michigan Press, 1990. Medieval and modern Latin poetry, translated by Helen Waddell.

Wague, Georges. "De l'Expression." *Comoedia*, no. 3740 (14 March 1923): 1, col. 6. In French. On expression in modern pantomime.

———. "La Pantomime au Conservatoire." Paris: *Les Spectacles* (12 June 1916). In French. Pantomime at the conservatory in Paris.

———. "La Pantomime Moderne." Paris: Éditions de l'Université Populaire, 1913. In French. Published lecture on early twentieth-century pantomime, January 19, 1913.

———. "Sur le Geste et l'Expression." *Bulletin de l'Univers de l'Artiste*, no. 27 (January–February 1930). In French. On gesture and expression in modern pantomime.

Walker, Katherine Sorley. *Eyes on Mime*. New York: John Day Co., 1969. History and technique of mime in the ballet, theatre, and cinema.

Walton, J. Michael. *Craig on Theatre*. New York, London: Methuen, 1983. Selections of Edward Gordon Craig's writings about theatre from 1907 to 1957.

Warton, Thomas. *The History of English Poetry*. Vol. 1. London: T. Tegg, 1824. Section about the performances of mimes and minstrels in the Middle Ages.

Watson, Ian. *Towards A Third Theatre*. New York: Routledge, 1993. Eugenio Barba's training, dramaturgical methods, major productions, and research at the International School of Theatre Anthropology.

Weaver, John. *The History of Mimes and Pantomimes*. London: J. Roberts, 1728. Ancient mime and English pantomime.

Wehle, Philippa. Review of "The Twentieth Nancy World Theatre Festival." *Theatre Journal* 34, no. 2 (May 1982): 269–70. Performances of Bill Irwin and other American artists at the Nancy Festival.

Weiss, William. "Le Mime au Québec." *Jeu 6 Cahiers de Théâtre* 15 (Summer–Fall 1977): 16–37. In French. Mime and mimes in Quebec.

Wiles, David. *The Masks of Menander: Sign and Meaning in Greek and Roman Performance*. Cambridge: Cambridge University Press, 1991. Masks in Greek and Roman theatre, Noh, and *commedia*. The relationships among mask, movement, costume, language, and voice.

Willett, John. *Theater of Bertolt Brecht*. London: Methuen & Co., 1959.

Williams, Clifford. "Mime in Great Britain." *Opera Ballet Music-Hall in the World*, 51–54. Paris: International Theatre Institute III, 1953. The different forms of mime in Great Britain.

Williams, Drid, ed. *Anthropology and Human Movement: The Study of Dances*. Lanham, Md.: Scarecrow Press, 1997. Introductory textbook with essays by anthropology of human movement specialists about dance forms.

Wilson, Albert E. *King Panto*. New York: Dutton, 1935. The history of pantomime.

———. *The Story of Pantomime*. London: Home & Van Thal, 1949. Pantomime from the eighteenth to the twentieth centuries.

Wilson, Edwin. *The Theater Experience*. New York: McGraw-Hill, 1985. An introductory, nonhistorical text about the elements of theatre of various periods and styles, with illustrations.

Wilson, James D. "Sidewalk Vaudevillians." *Newsweek* 104, no. 13 (24 September 1984): 83. Growing national popularity of street performers, from the 1960s on.

Wilson, Robert. *The Theatre of Images*. New York: Harper and Row, 1984. Essays by John Rockwell, Robert Steams, Calvin Tomkins, and Laurence Shyer about the Byrd Hoffman Foundation, which influenced Wilson. Details about *The Civil Wars* and photographs of Wilson's work.

Winter, Marion Hannah. "That Magnificent Mute." *Opera Ballet Music-Hall in the World*, 9–17. Paris: International Theatre Institute III, 1953. The development of mime in France.

———. *The Theatre of Marvels*. Translated by Charles Meldon. New York: Benjamin Blom, 1964. Mime and theatre of spectacle, with illustrations.

Wolff, Charlotte. *A Psychology of Gesture*. London: Methuen & Co., 1945. The psychological need for gesture.

Wolford, Lisa. "Remembering Home and Heritage: The New World Performance Laboratory." *TDR The Drama Review* 38, no. 3 (Fall 1994): 128–50. The Jerzy Grotowski–inspired group's long-term training and stagings, which integrated University of Akron students with Cleveland Public Theatre actors.

Wylie, Laurence. "A l'Ecole Lecoq J'ai Découvert Mon Propre Clown." *Psychologie* 43 (1973): 17–27. In French. Sociologist Wylie discovers his own clown at Jacques Lecoq's school.

Wysick, Max M. "Language and Silence in the Stage Plays of Samuel Beckett and Harold Pinter." Doctoral dissertation, University of Colorado, 1972.

Xenophon. *Anabasis.* Bks. 4–7. New York: G. P. Putnam's Sons, 1922. Includes a description of Greek mime performances.

Yakim, Moni, with Muriel Broadman. *Creating a Character: A Physical Approach to Acting.* New York: Back Stage Books, 1990; New York: Applause, 1993.

Zaporah, Ruth. *Action Theatre: The Improvisation of Presence.* Berkeley, Calif.: North Atlantic Books, 1995. An improvisational, twenty-day workshop program of exercises, solo pieces, and group scenes, with philosophic and aesthetic descriptions.

Zorn, J. W., ed. *The Essential Delsartre.* New York: Scarecrow Press, 1968 (reprint). François Delsartre method.

Index

About the Author

Annette Lust, Professor Emerita at Dominican College in San Rafael, California, holds a Doctorat de l' Université from the University of Paris. In addition to teaching theatre production and French, she directs plays and produces an annual Bay Area Original One-Act Play and Solo Festival at Dominican College. An accomplished teacher and author, she received the Palmes Académiques from the French Government in 1973 for her teaching of the French language and literature, her activity in French theatre and culture, and her publications on French mime and theatre. She is also a member of the Bay Area Theatre Critics Circle for the selection of Theatre Awards and has served on the jury of the International Mimos Festival in Périgueux, France since 1990 for the Critics Award for best performing group.

A board member and former vice-president and secretary of the National Association of Movement Theatre, Annette Lust is active in national and international organizations that promote the art of mime. She is an international freelance mime journalist, having published extensively on mime in America and Europe. She is considered one of the major mime critics in America.